DEAR BESS

Give 'Em Hell Harry Series

Editor, Robert H. Ferrell

GIVE 'EM HELL HARRY

Harry S. Truman, the "man from Missouri" who served as the thirty-third president of the United States, has been the subject of many books. Historians, political figures, friends, foes, and family members—all have sought to characterize, understand, and interpret this figure who continues to live in the minds and imaginations of a broad reading public. The Give 'Em Hell Harry Series is designed to keep available in reasonably priced paperback editions the best books that have been written about this remarkable man.

DEAR BESS

THE LETTERS FROM HARRY
TO BESS TRUMAN, 1910-1959

❀ ❀ ❀

Edited by ROBERT H. FERRELL

UNIVERSITY OF MISSOURI PRESS
Columbia and London

Copyright © 1983 by Robert H. Ferrell
Originally published by W. W. Norton and Company
First University of Missouri Press paperback printing 1998
University of Missouri Press, Columbia, Missouri 65201
Printed and bound in the United States of America
5 4 3 2 1   02 01 00 99 98

Frontispiece: Photograph by Bradley Smith.

Library of Congress Cataloging-in-Publication Data
    Truman, Harry S., 1884 -1972
    Dear Bess : the letters from Harry to Bess Truman, 1910–1959
/ edited by Robert H. Ferrell.
    Includes index.
    ISBN 0–8262-1203–4 (alk. paper)
    1. Truman, Harry S., 1884–1972. 2. Truman, Bess Wallace. 2.
Presidents—United States—Correspondence. I. Truman, Bess Wallace.
II. Ferrell, Robert H. III. Title.
E814.A4   1983
973.918'092'2
[B]   83–8006
                                                              CIP

♾™ This paper meets the requirements of the
American National Standard for Permanence of Paper
for Printed Library Materials, Z39.48, 1984.

CONTENTS

PREFACE

OR MANY YEARS historians assumed that former President Truman gave all of his correspondence, official and private, to the Harry S. Truman Library. This federal depository lies a few blocks to the north of the rambling Victorian house at 219 North Delaware Street, Independence, Missouri, where the Trumans spent most of their married life. Students of the Truman era—the tumultuous period after April 12, 1945, that marked the end of World War II, reconstruction of Western Europe under the Marshall Plan, and the Korean War—gained access to some of the private papers in the mid-seventies. By the end of 1980 the Library had opened all of that material to the public. But the dozen steel filing cases full of letters and documents contained nothing Truman wrote before the presidency. Seemingly, no papers from his earlier years existed, and his daughter's reminiscences in *Souvenir* explained why. At Christmastime 1955, her father came into the living room of the Delaware Street house and saw her mother making a small fire on the hearth out of what appeared to be letters or documents. Flames were licking up the handwriting. "What are you doing, Bess?" asked the President.

"I'm burning your letters to me," said Mrs. Truman.

"Bess!" he said. "You oughtn't to do that."

"Why not?" she replied. "I've read them several times."

"But think of history!" said the President.

"I *have*," answered Bess.

This was a good story, and surely it happened as Margaret related, but it is now evident that Harry Truman sent so many letters to the woman he loved that no small fire could have consumed them. The newly opened letters from Harry to Bess span the years 1910 to 1959 and number over twelve hundred. Xeroxed and filed vertically in storage boxes in the Truman Library, they extend for three feet.

Apparently as Bess received the letters, she casually secreted them in her bedroom, perhaps, or carted them (once the mass reached inconvenient proportions) to some storage room. Her filing system was haphazard, but she evidently threw very little away. The sequence of letters that remains suggests that all of those written during the early years have survived. Later years show occasional gaps, and the letters thin out after 1947. Perhaps Bess's fire of 1955 was fueled by most of the subsequent letters.

That any of the letters survived can be attributed to Bess having lived in the same house for most of her life. In 1904 with her three younger brothers and her mother she moved to 219 North Delaware Street—the house built by her grandfather George P. Gates shortly after the Civil War. Her grandparents were still living but did not need the whole seventeen-room house. Bess's father had died the preceding year, and her mother naturally took the Wallace brood to two-nineteen. When Harry Truman married Bess after World War I, he joined them. Bess stayed in that house for seventy-eight years.

After Bess's death, in 1982, Margaret Truman as her mother's executor gave the letters to the people of the United States. The collection was opened in March 1983 at the Truman Library. In this massive cache is found what amounts to an American saga—the setting out by an astonishing letter writer the manner in which his life moved forward. The first letter shows Truman running a farm near the little Missouri village of Grandview, twenty miles from Independence. By the last, we have heard his reflections on being president of the United States from 1945 to 1953. Love letters in the sense that they express the enduring, mutual love of two human beings, they would have little historical importance if that were their only message. They would pass into the limbo reserved for presidential letters of affection—one thinks of the love letters of Truman's predecessor, President Woodrow Wilson, published in two books during the past generation and instantly forgotten, if they were ever noticed. Wilson's daughter edited the letters of her father to his first wife, Ellen Axson Wilson; very recently his letters to his second wife, Edith Bolling Wilson, whom he married in 1915, have appeared. The Wilson epistles are filled with affection and occasional references to public policy, but they are principally love letters in the usual sense —at first stiltedly careful, then fond, then passionate. The Truman letters show something that is far more interesting, namely, how their author worked from morning to night trying to make the most of whatever project was at hand: managing the farm, making the lead and zinc mine work, trying the oil business, leading an artillery battery in World War I, and running Jackson County's business in the twenties and early thirties. The letters continue through his two terms in the Senate, his brief vice presidency, and his years as President. It is a simply extraordinary account of what a man can do if he puts his mind and will to it. His writing shows an incessant and deep concern for other people, not just the principals of the correspondence. He often wrote about his friends and acquaintances—their successes, their failures, their often droll behavior. In this wider sense the letters, taken together, draw unerringly a half-century of an American landscape that is gone forever.

A special quality of these letters deserves mention. Bess and Harry Truman seem to have considered themselves equals, and Harry wrote Bess without any effort to simplify or qualify. They were, of course, adults when they married; Harry was thirty-five, Bess a year younger. When their daughter was born, in

1924, Harry was forty; Bess, thirty-nine. The maturity of the relationship, from the outset, must have contributed to their mutual respect. But more than that, they so liked each other that any sense of inferiority, one to the other, was impossible. Certainly Harry liked to tell Bess that ever since he had known her he had "put her on a pedestal." By that he meant that there was no ceasing of his affection and love—not that he would shield her from any truths. Here was a no-nonsense relationship. Once in a while Bess seems to have lashed out at him, telling him off. She apparently had the self-respect to do that, and served thus as his balance wheel.

Harry Truman liked to write letters. As Margaret has related, he was a "demon letter writer." In the selection that follows, all but the one written during the hectic negotiations at Potsdam in 1945 were handwritten. When away from Bess he usually wrote daily, and they were frequently separated. Bess bore the responsibility of caring for Mother Wallace, who suffered fragile health until her death in 1952. Bess had to spend months at a time in Independence. Moreover, she disliked Washington life, the White House not the least, and one senses that her long absences from Washington were frequently contrived. Whatever the cause, separation brought more letters, for which present-day readers will be grateful.

EDITORIAL NOTE

H OW TO CHOOSE AMONG the delightful letters that Harry S. Truman wrote to Bess Wallace (after June 28, 1919, Bess W. Truman)—letters that reflect nearly five decades of United States history! The present book offers only about half of the complete selection, but readers can see which letters were cut in entirety by consulting the List of Letters, herein. Deletions within letters are marked by ellipses. I made the deletions with no effort to force an opinion on the reader, not censoring the former President's expressions of prejudice. In his early years Truman made fun of immigrants; he made reference also to the "bohunks" encountered at "Standardoilville," the huge refinery being built at Sugar Creek, near Independence. Typical of Missouri farm boys in the early twentieth century, for Truman black people were niggers and coons; Jews were Hebrews or kikes. Often unconscious, such name calling showed unawareness of the ultimate ties that in many ways bind humans one to another.

Truman, however, unloaded his prejudices in advance of most of his contemporaries in the United States who learned only through the object lesson of Adolf Hitler. Well before World War II the young Truman came to understand that the workers at Sugar Creek labored with their hands in every bit as dignified a fashion as he had on the farm outside Grandview. And once he read about the history of the United States he recognized the error of his perception of negroes. He had grown up in a family of negro haters. But while his mother believed to her dying day in the rightness of Lincoln's assassination, Truman became a fierce champion of black rights, sure that Lincoln had been right and the South wrong. Similarly his Jewish slurs diminished once he discovered Jewish friends, such as Edward (Eddie) Jacobson, with whom he ran a haberdashery from 1919 to 1922.

And so the letters, after selection and excision, appear here with their warts, their occasional embarrassments. As for the technical side of editing, I have corrected misspelling, which would only have slowed the reader. Truman never mastered the old rhyme about 'i' before 'e.' Double consonants bothered him; 'professor' became 'proffessor.' (One time my good friend Louis L. Gerson, professor of political science at the University of Connecticut, asked Truman to autograph a copy of his memoirs. The President spelled 'professor' his usual way.

"But Mr. President," Lou pointed out, "that's a misspelling." "Oh, never mind," grinned the President. "It'll make the book more valuable.") Truman usually kept a pocket dictionary at hand, but it did not list geographical names. Family names often proved impossible; he never got Dean Acheson's last name right, despite many opportunities to do so, confusing it with the railroad and somehow choosing the compromise "Atcheson."

Where Truman did not date his letters I have added in brackets estimated dates taken from either the postmark or the content. Occasionally the day, the month, or both were impossible to determine. In a few instances Truman's bold hand is unreadable; such passages appear with a bracketed "illegible." Once in a while he dropped obvious words—articles, prepositions—and they have been added without brackets, in the belief that bracketing would only be pedantic. His frequent abbreviations and ampersands have been, for the most part, spelled out. The style for times of day, dollar amounts, and units of measure stands according to the *Chicago Manual of Style*. Finally, where postscripts have been excised, no ellipses appear—again in the belief that such would amount to pedantry.

For assistance with the present book I am indebted to many individuals, especially the director of the Harry S. Truman Library at Independence, Benedict K. Zobrist; the assistant director, George Curtis; and the library's staff— Vicky Alexander, Dennis E. Bilger, Lenore Bradley, Patty Bressman, Carol Briley, Robin Burgess, Mildred L. Carol, Donna Clark, Harry Clark, Mary Jo Colle, John Curry, Diane Farris, Nell Flanagan, J. R. Fuchs, Sara Greb, Pat Kerr, Philip D. Lagerquist, Erwin J. Mueller, Warren Ohrvall, Tanya Paskowski, Doris Pesek, and Joy Woodhull. Pauline Testerman and Niel M. Johnson helped with the photographs. Elizabeth Safly, librarian, made the library search room the most attractive place I have ever worked in.

My thanks also to W. W. Norton & Company—Donald S. Lamm, president, George Brockway, chairman, James L. Mairs, vice president. Without Jim Mairs this book could not have appeared. Sue J. Lowe, my manuscript editor at Norton, contributed immeasurably to the project. Marjorie J. Flock was the talented designer.

John M. Hollingsworth was the able cartographer.

And a special thanks to my wife, Lila, and daughter, Carolyn.

I

ON THE FARM

❀ ❀ ❀

O NE DAY IN 1890 the minister of the Presbyterian Church in Independence, Missouri, was walking along a quiet, shady street at the edge of town when he noticed some children he did not know. Dr. Addison Madeira asked for their names and invited the little Trumans to visit his Sunday school if their mother would permit them to come. Mrs. Martha Ellen Truman approved, the children enrolled, and Harry Truman soon glimpsed a little girl with golden curls named Elizabeth Virginia (Bess) Wallace. He fell in love, he afterward said, and never really liked another girl. Harry was six years old; Bess, five.

The town was a typical turn-of-the-century Middle Western county seat. It boasted the usual courthouse, an empire-style building with a fine tower. Around the square clustered the saloons, drugstores, and notion stores, a department store, and several banks. Farmers in buggies came every Saturday night with their families. Otherwise they drove farm wagons into town, doing business with the mills, especially the largest: the Waggoner-Gates, co-owned by Bess Wallace's grandfather George P. Gates and producer of Queen of the Pantry flour, the "finest biscuit and cake flour in the world."

Harry Truman's parents, John Anderson Truman and Martha Ellen Young Truman, arrived in Independence after having lived on a succession of farms since their marriage in 1881. Harry was born on May 8, 1884, in the village of Lamar, 120 miles south of Independence. The next year the family moved to a farm, then to another in 1886, and in 1887 to one near Grandview (about 20 miles from Independence) owned by Mrs. Truman's parents and farmed by Martha Ellen's brother, Uncle Harrison, after whom the youngster had been given the diminutive "Harry." The future President's middle initial (people still quarrel about whether to follow the initial "S" with a period) stood for the names of his maternal and paternal grandfathers, Solomon Young and Anderson Shipp Truman. Harry Truman did not much care if there was a period after the "S", although when he thought about it he used it.

The John Truman family's first house in Independence was on Crysler Street. Surrounded by several acres, it was a good location for Harry's father to conduct his horse and mule business, as he had in Lamar. In 1896 they moved —John Truman was an inveterate trader—to a house with a rambling porch at the corner of West Waldo and River Boulevard, a Victorian frame house typical of the nineties. The Waldo house also had enough land for the elder Truman to run his business. Often he was seen driving a buckboard wagon about town, sometimes with an animal or two roped and following behind. Occasionally he rode horseback, carrying a calf with the mother cow trailing along until both animals reached the enclosure behind the Truman house.

The Wallace family, the head of which was David Willock Wallace, a handsome man with sideburns, lived down the street and around the corner, at 608 North Delaware—probably the most prestigious street (in those days one

Vivian and Harry Truman, c. 1888, ages two and four. *Harry S. Truman Library*

Elizabeth Virginia (Bess) Wallace, August 1889, aged four. *Harry S. Truman Library*

would have said "illustrious") in Independence. Grandfather Gates lived at 219, a block or two south. The Wallaces had built their house in the early nineties, adding a cupola and the expanse of porch so fashionable at the time. Screened by stringed ivy in summers, it offered the occupants a refuge on hot evenings. David Wallace was a rising politician and worked for a while in the courthouse on the square, where he had charge of marriage licenses. He offered two or three varieties, one of which was stunningly embellished with garlands of flowers and scrolls and cupids. A prominent town father who often led parades, he could be seen seated handsomely on a horse and perhaps wearing a sash to display the fact that he was the parade's marshal.

Madge Gates, daughter of the flour magnate, was considered the prettiest of his three daughters (Madge, Myra, and Maude) and had eloped with David Wallace. Grandfather Gates seems not to have considered this course extraordinary, and in a show of affection arranged for her likeness to appear on Waggoner-Gates flour sacks—a girl in a bustle, bearing a fan and standing in front of a beaded curtain. She was the proud mother of Bess and, by the turn of the century, Bess's three younger brothers.

One might have thought Bess and Harry would expand on their chance encounter at Sunday school—skipping down the street and around the corner to see each other. Such proved not to be the case. In school, Harry wrote, Bess "sat behind me in the sixth, seventh, and high-school grades, and I thought she was

First Presbyterian Church, Independence, Missouri. *Copyright unknown*

A view of Independence, Missouri, c. 1900. *Harry S. Truman Library*

the most beautiful and the sweetest person on earth." That, however, was largely the extent of their association until some years after both had graduated from high school. Once in a while their paths crossed, as during Latin tutorials with Harry's cousin Nellie Noland, who lived farther along Delaware Street; two evenings a week for one or two years the three of them worked through translations. For the rest of it, their schooldays and after-school hours were marked by little camaraderie.

One reason Bess and Harry saw little of each other socially during the nineties was Harry's job at the drugstore—dusting bottles, sweeping and scrubbing the floor. Mary Paxton, Bess's nextdoor neighbor and closest girlhood chum (now ninety-five and in a Columbia, Missouri, nursing home) vaguely recalls Bess saying to her that she wished Harry did not have to work so much. Harry also spent time on his music lessons and seemed headed toward a career in that direction until he gave up the piano at around age fifteen. Someone apparently complained to him that it was a "sissy" occupation. In addition, Harry received a pair of glasses when he was six years old to correct his farsightedness, known in those days as "flat eyeballs." Wearing glasses kept him from many childhood games, further separating him from children like Bess, who was very much a tomboy; she was the only girl in Independence who could whistle through her teeth. With rough-and-tumble pastimes ruled out, Harry began to patronize the local public library, which consisted of a room or two in the high school and contained about two thousand books. Later he often said he had read them all, including the encyclopedias.

Also coming between Harry and Bess were the social distinctions of the little town. The Trumans were country people, and John Truman proved it, if such were necessary, by running a farm within the town boundaries. The Wallaces, however, as relatives of the Gates family, were fairly high up the social ladder.

In determining who played with whom or went to which parties, the church's influence was considerable. Mary Paxton remembers the town's clannishness as based on church membership. The Presbyterians stood at the top, but Harry's mother had not thought of that when she sent him to Presbyterian Sunday school. Rather, she was annoyed with the beliefs at one of the country Baptist churches, from which she recently had escaped; she was willing to try anything else, even Presbyterianism. But the latter did not take, and the Truman children must have returned to the Baptists. According to Mary, the Baptists were considerably down the social ladder, which was organized as follows: the Presbyterians; the Campbellites, later known as the Christian Church, or Disciples; the Methodists, North and South; the Baptists; the Lutherans; the Catholics, most of whom came into Independence each Sunday from the country; the Reorganized Church of Latter Day Saints (RLDS). The blacks had their own small church, for a few of them lingered from antebellum years, still working for town families.

The RLDS amounted to little more than one thousand of the town's population of six thousand in 1890. Their presence, however, accounts for a large measure of Independence's historical distinction. During the days of RLDS prophet Joseph Smith (the 1830s), Independence was the last settlement from whence ran the great western trails: to Santa Fe and the Southwest, to Salt Lake and the Far West and California. Harry Truman's grandfather Solomon Young left his wife, Harriet Louisa, on countless occasions during the forties, fifties, and sixties to drive wagon teams westward. One time he arrived in Salt Lake unable to sell his goods for enough money to get him back home. He consulted the Mormon leader Brigham Young, who arranged a lot where he might show the wares brought from Missouri. The return trip was always a gamble.

Such were the backgrounds of Harry Truman and Bess Wallace. Their town was not far removed from frontier America—but a generation or two, which in the minds of youngsters is all that counts. They grew up during the placid nineties, oblivious of how quickly Independence had changed from its frontier origins, yet somehow sensing the newness of everything. A postcard view of the town at the turn of the century displays street after wide street of houses framed with trees that had grown to size after the Civil War. The war had divided the town, mostly in favor of the South, but the enmities had been almost forgotten. In 1898 a new war brought everyone together. Harry and a few friends even drilled in a field, thinking that the nation might need them; it was great fun for them to prepare.

Politics touched the children of the nineties hardly at all, perhaps because

Bess, February 11, 1898. *Harry S. Truman Library*

On the porch of Bess's house at 608 North Delaware. L. to r., unidentified girl, George, Fred, Bess, Frank. *Harry S. Truman Library*

almost everyone in Independence belonged to the Democratic party, even the children. There were, however, a few Republicans, as Harry discovered in 1892 when he began the first grade at the time of a presidential election. He wore a white hat to school bearing the names of Grover Cleveland for President and Adlai Stevenson (grandfather of a later Democratic presidential nominee) for Vice President. As he later told the story, some older Republican boys snatched the hat and tore it up.

High school in those days was less straitened than it was to become, so Harry and Bess found themselves in the same classes each fall, even though Harry was a year older. He started school at the age of eight and, after nearly dying from a bout with diphtheria two years later (for months his mother had to push him around in a baby carriage), skipped a grade, catching up with Bess again; he graduated with the Independence High School class of 1901. A photograph of the class's forty-one students—eleven young men, thirty young women—showed the future President standing in the back row, fourth from left, in a carefully brushed suit and knotted tie, his glasses catching the light of the occasion. Bess sat in the second row, at the extreme right, smiling into the camera. The photographer framed the group in the large Romanesque doorway of the school;

Senior class, Independence High School, 1901. Charles G. Ross, valedictorian, front row, far left; Bess Wallace, second row, far right; Harry Truman, top row, fourth from left. *Harry S. Truman Library*

above them was a stained-glass decoration bearing the legend *Juventus Spes Mundi* ("Youth the Hope of the World").

After graduation the idyl of Independence came to an end, and for a while Harry and Bess—as is the case with most members of graduating classes—went their separate ways. Harry's parents remained in Independence until 1902, but in the year of their elder son's graduation John Truman had speculated in grain futures in Kansas City, losing everything the family possessed—the fruits of their work over the years. The Waldo house went, a farm that Martha Ellen owned, and their savings. Any hope that Harry might have had about college died with this financial collapse, and he had to go to work so John Vivian and his sister, Mary Jane, could remain in school. He started as a timekeeper for a construction company. Then he spent time "wrapping singles" in the offices of the Kansas City *Star*. For a few weeks he even attended Spalding Business College, studying the rudiments of accounting, with some attention to typewriting. A half-sheet of typescript composed by the young business student on July 1, 1901, to Grandmother Young, Uncle Harrison, and Harrison's sister Laura Jane Young Everhart, all on the farm near Grandview, is his first and only extant example of typing. Afterward he seems to have abandoned the machine in favor of the bold hand that marked his letters, diaries, and other records, personal and public.

After the year of odd jobs Harry went into banking in an elementary way, working in the "cage" at first the National Bank of Commerce and then the Union National, from 1902 until 1906. He later declared that knowing the fundamentals of banking was one of the three prerequisites for anyone in high public office (along with farming and the U.S. Army). In addition to working as a clerk with tellers in the cage he received and sent checks from small banks throughout the Middle West (before the Federal Reserve System, large city banks often acted as clearing houses for country banks). Harry lived part of the time with his parents, who moved to Kansas City in 1902, where John Truman took a job in a grain elevator. In 1905 when his parents and sister moved to Clinton, near which the elder Truman again farmed, this time eighty acres, Harry lived in a rooming house. His brother, John Vivian, also worked in a Kansas City bank cage during these years.

Harry Truman seems to have enjoyed Kansas City, not so much its banks —although he did all right, boosting his monthly salary from thirty-five dollars to a hundred dollars—but its cultural activities. He ushered at the Grand Theater on Saturday afternoons and thereby saw the vaudeville shows for free. He paid his way to the Auditorium and watched Shakespeare. He thrilled to the music of the metropolis. In those days the Metropolitan Opera traveled, and the world's best pianists, including Ignace Jan Paderewski and Josef Lhévinne, came to Kansas City. Paderewski, he liked to say in after years, "taught" him to play the "Minuet in G." From Lhévinne he learned an appreciation of Chopin.

The high-school friendship of Harry and Bess could not have developed during the bank years. The two young people saw little, maybe nothing, of each other. Bess remained in Independence, and while the distance was hardly insuperable, ten miles from Delaware Street to downtown Kansas City, there seemed other reasons not to look up Harry Truman.

After high school Bess had several beaux, and years later Harry enumerated them in a chatty letter to his cousin Ethel Noland. "Suppose," he wrote, "Miss Lizzie" (his epistolary name for Bess) had "gone off with Mr. Young, Julian Harvey, or Harris. What would have been the result? For Harry, I mean." Fortunately she did not.

Also confining Bess to the circle within which she moved as a young woman was the stark tragedy that beset her family in the summer of 1903. Mary Paxton knew more about what happened than anyone save Bess and her mother and perhaps Mary's father, the lawyer John Paxton. Mary recalls how, late in the spring of 1903, her own mother had died, apparently of tuberculosis, which in those days was a fatal illness. Her mother had faced the grave with stoicism, based upon her Christian faith, and with the restraint common to the time did not tell her children what was about to happen. Instead she asked them to carry on if by chance she might be forced to go away. She talked in this sad manner to young Mary, and then one day she quietly died. During the funeral at the house David Wallace came over and helped in every way; Mary later remembered how he arranged the chairs. Three weeks later, at 5:00 A.M., her father woke her up and said, "Go over right away and see Bess. Mr. Wallace has killed himself."

David Wallace had sat in the bathtub and shot himself with a pistol, for a reason or reasons that no one then or later divined. His young life had gone along in what appeared to be a series of successes, with everyone in Independence impressed by his promise. Then, according to a newspaper obituary, unfathomable instability caused him in a moment of weakness to take his life.

Mary found Bess outside at the rear of the house, pacing up and down with clenched fists, saying nothing. She did not know what to do, and so paced up and down with her. She has no memory of what followed, including the funeral, but remembers vividly that Madge Wallace took Bess and the three young brothers, to Colorado Springs for a year; they returned to move in with Grandfather and Grandmother Gates at 219 North Delaware.

Bess's mother talked a bit to Mary about what had happened but said little

The Gates's house on North Delaware, cf. p. 533. *Harry S. Truman Library*

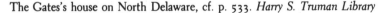

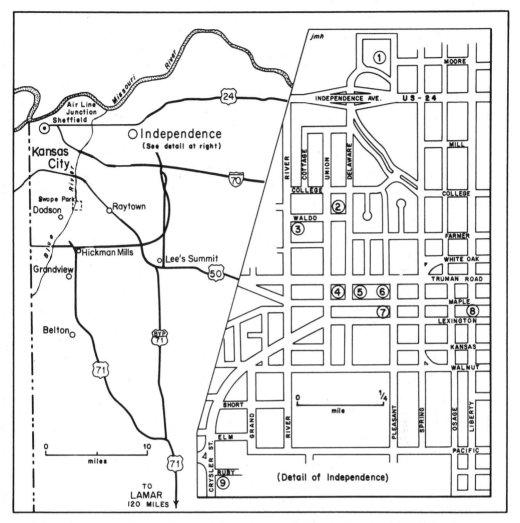

Present-day map of Kansas City and Independence including the locations of Air Line Junction, Sheffield, and Dodson, all now incorporated in greater Kansas City. Key to the detail of Independence:

1. The Harry S. Truman Library

2. Wallace house, c. 1895–1903, 608 North Delaware

3. Truman house, 1896–1902, Waldo and River Boulevard

4. Noland house, 1900–1971, 216 North Delaware

5. Truman House, 1919–1982, 219 North Delaware

6. Independence High School

7. First Presbyterian Church

8. Independence courthouse

9. Truman house, Crysler Street, 1890–1896

other than how ashamed she had been of her husband's suicide. She certainly needed Bess's companionship, which she had for the next several years. For two years Bess commuted daily by streetcar to Kansas City to attend the Barstow School, a finishing school. Then she remained with her mother.

Meanwhile, Harry worked in Kansas City until 1906 when he received word from his parents, who had returned to Grandmother Young's farm near Grandview (where they had lived from 1887 to 1890), that he should quit the bank and help them run the farm. John and Martha Truman, as their luck had it, lost an entire crop of corn on the Clinton farm during a spring flood in 1906. They had retreated to the Young farm because Uncle Harrison, who was thinking of retiring to town, proposed that they should take it over. Harry and John Vivian (usually known as Vivian, once or twice as Pete) went back to help out.

Until 1917 when United States entry into World War I brought Harry to the army (he had already served two terms as a reservist) he stayed on the farm. Life was hard there, and he worked from morning to night, winters in preparation, spring and summer and autumn in tilling and taking crops. Gradually the "firm" J. A. Truman & Son (Vivian left to get married and take over his own farm) brought order to its near-full section of land—600 acres, almost a square mile—and sometimes worked rented land totaling as much as three full sections, nearly 2,000 acres, at one time. Truman teams had to be out in the fields at sun up, planting, growing, and harvesting. They remained out until it dipped over the flatland at day's end. Planting the usual crops—corn, wheat, oats—young Harry rotated grain with hay every third year in order to rest the land. He and his father did all they could themselves and hired hands for fifteen or twenty cents per hour plus meals to run the extra teams. All the while they kept Black Angus cattle and Hampshire hogs. Accidents cut into farming time, as when a 300-pound calf broke Harry's leg. He had to spend a long time in bed and then on crutches. In such manner the months and years passed.

For a short time, beginning in 1916, Harry Truman commuted between the farm and a lead and zinc mine in Commerce, Oklahoma, where he hoped to make enough money to pay his farm debts. He also tried his hand at drilling for oil. The farm, however, remained the foundation of Harry's livelihood.

At the outset of his work on the farm he seldom got to Independence. After he became somewhat more accustomed to the work, however, he made time to visit his cousins, Ethel and Nellie Noland, daughters of his father's sister, Aunt Ella. It was not easy to get to Independence. He could walk the short distance, less than a mile, into Grandview and take a train (which unfortunately did not run often), and after that a streetcar; or he could drive a buggy for several miles to Dodson, take the streetcar to Kansas City, and catch another streetcar to Independence. During some of these trips he spent the night on the couch in Aunt Ella's parlor.

Aunt Ella, let it be added, had moved from the house where Nellie had helped Harry and Bess translate Latin and lived at 216 North Delaware—a little Victorian frame house with ivy strings on the porch that faced right across the street, at 219. Harry was visiting in the year 1910, perhaps a Saturday or Sunday,

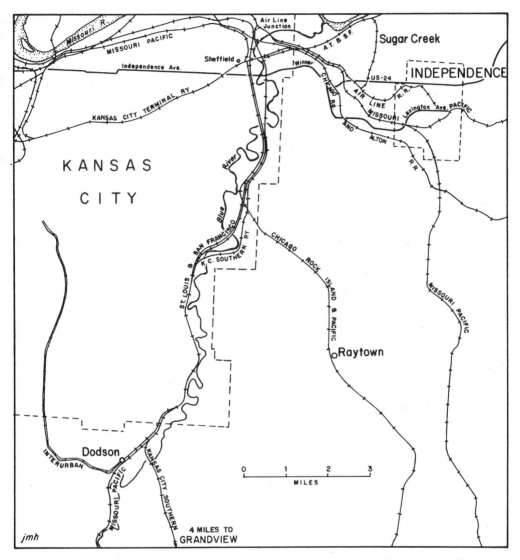

Railroad lines between Grandview and Independence, c. 1910. From Dodson, a small town not on present-day maps, an interurban (streetcar) ran north to central Kansas City; another, the precise route of which is uncertain, ran east from central K.C. to Independence. The city boundaries shown here are approximate. Kansas City now extends to Independence and Grandview.

and came into the Noland kitchen to hear his aunt talking about a cake that Mrs. Wallace had sent over. The cake plate needed to be returned.

What happened next became one of the Truman family's favorite stories about Harry. According to Margaret Truman's biography of her father, he seized the cake plate "with something approaching the speed of light" and announced that he, himself, at once, would return it. He walked across the street and rang the bell; Bess answered the door. Thus began their courtship, marriage, and shared fascination with the world around them reflected in the letters that follow.

ONE

HEAD OVER HEELS

Harry Truman, a young farmer near Grandview, was immensely proud of his vocation; he considered the tilling of land a thoroughly honorable enterprise in the Jeffersonian sense. The founder of the Democratic party had written over a century before that "Those who labor in the earth are the chosen people of God, if ever He had a chosen people. . . ." Truman would have agreed. The Grandview farmer made no apologies. Without embarrassment he explained to Bess the tasks, large and small, that marked his days. Nothing was too laborious, too dirty, too common for him. He was never too proud to help his mother—Mamma, he always called her—with kitchen tasks. The only aspect of farm life he disliked, even detested, was the daily rising before dawn; he seems to have believed that his father, who enjoyed getting up early, imposed this torture quite unnecessarily. To be sure, once the son began spending late evening hours with Bess in Independence—his return trips thwarted by endless failures in streetcar and train schedules—the early hours became especially difficult.

Withal, Truman was no stick-in-the-mud, confined to the fields he farmed, his horizons reaching no farther than the square miles or portions thereof that belonged to J. A. Truman & Son. He managed to travel not only to nearby Grandview or Dodson, a few miles away, but to Kansas City, to St. Louis, and after 1911 occasionally to faraway Texas and Montana. Railroad travel was speedier than later automobile travel, the trains frequent and fairly comfortable. If necessary, Truman took a Pullman, a luxury that Americans today can hardly appreciate. This, then, was no farmer with geographical blinders.

Despite the daily tasks that demanded far more energy than did the city worker's schedule, Truman the farmer was also a reader. His favorite magazines, which arrived regularly at the post office in Grandview, were journals long since defunct. He and Bess admired Everybody's, which printed illustrated short stories and serials, gay and sad. He also liked the blood and thunder of Adventure, none too adventurous by later standards, but full of enough derring-do to keep tired readers awake. Beyond these journalistic entertainments the two correspondents read novels of the time, the sort that presently fill shelves of secondhand bookstores, stories of love and remorse and death—happiness and bliss alongside *ineffable tragedy, assisted by tipped-in illustrations of young men in elegant suits and willowy young ladies in long, lacy dresses. Their tastes, however, differed a bit. Harry admired Mark Twain, the celebrated humorist who died in 1910; his droll stories, gusto, and admiration of American virtues appealed to the young farmer immensely. Bess took pleasure in Dickens and Stevenson and tried vainly to get Harry to read their longer novels. Harry's letters indicate that Mamma Truman advocated eighteenth-century writers, pressing her son to read them. It may surprise us today that the tastes of some farm families in the American Middle West were at this time so wide ranging.*

Grandview, Mo.

My Dear Bessie: December 31, 1910

I am very glad you liked the book. I liked it so well myself I nearly kept it. I saw it advertised in *Life* and remembered that you were fond of Scott when we went to school.

Nothing would please me better than to come to see you during the holidays or any other time for the matter of that, but Papa broke his leg the other day and I am chief nurse, next to my mother, besides being farm boss now. So you see I'll be somewhat closely confined for some time to come. I hope you'll let the invitation be a standing one though and I shall avail myself of it at the very first opportunity.

I guess Ethel and Nellie have been busy with their exams is the reason you haven't seen them. I got a letter from Ethel the other day saying she was suffering so from cramming, both mental and physical, and from "epizootic" (whatever that is [an epidemic especially affecting Missouri mules]) that she and Nellie would be unable to come out this week. You know they always spend a few days at Christmas out here. It was just as well, as I would have had to cancel their date anyway after Papa's accident. We haven't quite got over the excitement yet. A horse pulled a big beam over on him in the barn. We were so glad he wasn't killed we didn't know what to do.

If you see fit to let me hear from you sometimes, I shall certainly appreciate it. Farm life as an everyday affair is not generally exciting. Wishing you and all of you the very happiest New Year, I am

Very sincerely,

Harry S. Truman

Grandview, Mo.

My Dear Bessie: January 10, 1911

You see I haven't learned to write 1911 yet [he had crossed out 1910]. It's hard to form the habit suddenly. It is also hard to acquire the habit of early rising of your own free will and accord on these chilly mornings. You see Papa could never sleep after a certain time in the small hours of the morning and he always

The first letter. *Harry S. Truman Library*

arose and then called me. Now I have to get up myself and start fires, milk cows, and do other odd jobs around while it is yet dark. Vivian takes turn about with me though so I can gradually come to it. I don't think I'll ever make much of a mark as a farmer or anywhere else but some times I have to come across. This is one of them.

Ethel was out last Friday and I put her to work immediately. She helped me haul a load of baled straw (she sat on top of the straw), and then we got a load of hay out of the stack. You should see her pitch hay. She said she had always been taught never to take big bites on her fork. I told her she could unlearn that on a haystack. She still has that terrible malady I told you of.

My reading has been no heavier than yours—maybe not so heavy. It has been confined to *Everybody's* and one or two other fifteen-cent or muckrake magazines and numerous farm publications. You know if one farm paper gets your name, you'll get a dozen before the year is over.

I thank you very much for your invitation and shall certainly take advantage of it as soon as I can. I suppose skating is fine. I haven't the time to go see at present. I have only a few things to do such as feed hogs and cattle, build a mile of fence and a barn, and be at the house as much as possible, which isn't very much. I forgot to say I have been reading Mark Twain. He is my patron saint in literature. I managed to save dimes enough to buy all he has written, so I am somewhat soaked in western slang and Mark Twain idioms. My mother has been trying to persuade me to read Alexander Pope. She got a copy of his poems for her birthday. I haven't been persuaded yet, except a few of his epitaphs, which are almost as good as those we used to read of Bobby Burns'.

When it comes to reading though I am by it as I am by music. I would rather read Mark Twain or John Kendrick Bangs than all the Shakespeares and Miltons in Christendom.

I have some cousins in Kansas City who affect intellect. They once persuaded me to go to a season of Grand Opera with them. It happened to include *Parsifal* and some others which I cannot spell. Well I haven't recovered from that siege of Grand Opera yet. Perhaps if they had given me small doses I might have been trained, because I do love music. I can even appreciate Chopin when he is played on the piano. But when it comes to a lot of would-be actors and actresses running around over the stage and spouting song and hugging and killing each other promiscuously, why I had rather go to the Orpheum. Perhaps if I could understand Dutch and Dago I could appreciate it better for I did hear an opera in English once that sounded real good. They say though it isn't good form to appreciate singing in English. I am sorry.

I suppose you'll be sorry too when you see the conglomeration I call a letter. But I do like to get letters, and if you can stand mine yours will be immensely valued. My father is doing nicely thank you and I hope he'll be up in four or five weeks.

Wishing you all the best of health and sincerely hoping that you will honor me with another epistle soon. I am

Sincerely yours,
Harry S. Truman

Grandview, Mo.

My Dear Bessie: January 26, 1911
Don't you think Ethel was good to me? She gave me this stationery for Christmas. They always give me a necktie and a book or some stationery, and I give them a box of candy or something else that does not require much study. I positively know that I will get a necktie from them and they know the kind I like, so I don't have to buy one ever. You see a farmer don't need but one a year and he won't wear that out. You know when we have a "shindig" out here someone blows a horn or takes down a receiver on a pumpkin-vine phone and halloos in it and we all go. You know a pumpkin-vine phone is a ten-party line. When you want to use it you have to take down the receiver and listen while some good sister tells some other good sister who is not so wise how to make

butter or how to raise chickens or when it is the right time in the moon to plant onion sets or something else equally important. About the time you think the world is coming to an end or some other direful calamity will certainly overtake you if you don't get to express your feelings into that phone, the good sister will quit, and then if you are quick and have a good, strong voice you can have your say; but you know confidently that everyone in the neighborhood has heard you. If someone would invent a contraption to shut out the other nine when a person wanted to use the tenth, he would be richer and more famous than Edison. But he'd be forever unpopular with us farmers for we'd never know each other's business.

They are endeavoring faithfully to better the farmers' condition though all the time. You know our friend Roosevelt appointed a country life commission to spend the extra cash in the U.S. Treasury. Some fellow with a good heart has also invented a soup spoon that won't rattle. I know he had farmers in mind when he did that. Some other good fellow has invented peas that are cubes instead of spheres so they won't roll off the knife when you eat them. If I can get the seed I shall certainly raise them. It is very embarrassing to take up a nice big knife full of peas and carry it carefully to your mouth and then have the whole works roll off and go under the table, down your sleeves and neck and perhaps spoil someone's nice red tablecloth. You see, the man who invented cubic peas is a benefactor to the farmer. Now if someone would invent a fork with a spring, so you could press it and spear a biscuit at arm's length without having to reach over and incommode your neighbor—well he'd just simply be elected President, that's all.

Farmers get all kinds of experience in lots of things though besides the best table manners. This morning I was helping to dig a grave. It is not nearly such a sad proceeding as you'd think. There were six or seven of us, and we'd take turns at digging. Those who weren't digging would sit around and tell the one who was how it ought to be done and tell lies about the holes they'd dug and the hogs they'd raised. We spent a very pleasant forenoon and then went to the funeral. It was a Christian Science funeral. I never saw one before. They are very impressive. You know we have a cemetery in our front yard and some of us usually get to help dig the graves. Our front yard is a quarter of a mile long and about half as wide so you see there is room for the cemetery without crowding.

I sincerely hope you won't get disgusted with my excuses for letters, for I sure do like to hear from you. I am glad you got to go skating. I should certainly have liked to see *Mrs. Wiggs* [*of the Cabbage Patch*]. Everyone who saw it says it was fine. Several from here went down. I think the Ne'er-Do-Well [from a Rex Beach serial] is fine, only I don't like the idea of falling in love with another man's frau. It always causes trouble, in books and out of them. It sounds too much like Pittsburgh, Pennsylvania. I do hope he'll behave himself for he seems to be a fine fellow. I wish *Everybody's* would come every day. I don't like to wait.

My father is doing fine thank you, and I think he'll walk in a short time by using crutches. I shall be in Kansas City next week sometime and if you have no objection or are not otherwise engaged I shall call up and come out in the evening.

Please don't be discouraged when you get here for I am going to quit, just read the signature then you'll know you owe me a letter and that I am looking for it and I'll be satisfied. I am
                                    Most sincerely,
                                    Harry S. Truman

                                                            Grandview, Mo.
Dear Bessie: February 7, 1911
    You were right. I was about to send you another epistle but thought I had better wait, maybe you would remember that you were indebted to me for one.
    I certainly enjoyed myself the evening I was there and you may be assured I shall repeat the offense as often as I can or you will allow me. That cake and coffee couldn't *be beat.* I am like a girl that once boarded where I did. She said there was nothing better than cake but more cake. I heartily agree with her. It makes no difference about the variety just so it's cake.
    I think you and Nellie could probably get up some religious excitement on Ethel's part if you would do as a certain woman did Aunt Susan was telling me about.
    You know they used to hold outdoor meetings when the weather was good and everyone for miles around attended and stayed sometimes for weeks. Along in the fifties they were holding a meeting not far from here and the preacher had exhorted and ranted and done everything else they usually do when they try to get something started as they call it, but it was no use. He wasn't a quitter though. Finally down one of the aisles one of the good sisters jumped out and began screaming and dancing up and down as they usually do when they get religion. The preacher made a dive for her with his hand extended saying, "Oh! Sister I am so glad to see you come out and say you have religion." Her answer between screams was, "I haven't got it. I haven't got it. There's a lizard on my dress," and she kept on dancing until Aunt Sue and someone else took her outside and one of these little lizards fell off her dress. Try it on Ethel. It will work I think.
    I remember Miss Southern very well. Your opinion of her is good. Mary said that the preacher was giving dancers, card players, and theater-goers fits. Well he has done all these things until he is tired of them. Now he has taken to no preaching for a change. I also have strayed from the Presbyterian fold, though I remember my Sunday school days very well. I am by religion like everything else. I think there is more in acting than in talking. I had an uncle who said when one of his neighbors got religion strong on Sunday, he was going to lock his smokehouse on Monday. I think he was right from the little I have observed.
    We had a neighbor out here who could pray louder and talk more fervently in meetin' than anyone I ever heard. He'd say in every prayer, "O Lord help this congregation to stop and think where they's a going at." We finally found that he beat his wife and did everything else that's "ornery."
    I think religion is something one should have on Wednesday and Thursday as well as Sunday. Therefore I don't believe that these protracted meetings do

any real good. They are mostly excitement and when the excitement wears off people are as they always were.

I like to play cards and dance as far as I know how and go to shows and do all the things they said I shouldn't, but I don't feel badly about it. I go when I feel like it and the *good* church members are glad to hear what it's like. You see I'm a member but not a strenuous one.

I suppose I am getting to be a bore by this time but I like to get letters so well, especially from you, that I do the best I can to deserve them. I shall be in Independence on the fourteenth to attend the probate court (think of it), and if you are at home I should like very much to come around again.

I am glad your mother likes my efforts on the piano. I am ashamed of it myself. But you know a farmer can't be a pianist much as he'd like to be. Mary is getting to be a pretty good piano player. Ivory tickler, as Shorty Short says. He says his piano has a wheelbarrow movement and a fire escapement. It was an old-fashioned square.

Write when you can to

Yours sincerely,
Harry

Grandview, Mo.

Dear Bessie: February 16, 1911

I caught the train I was after Tuesday night. I got off at Sheffield and walked about a mile and a half north to Air Line Junction. I was scared to an icicle almost, but it was all for nothing. I didn't even see a hobo. You know not so long ago a man was held up on the Kansas City Southern tracks right where I had to go. They made him exchange clothes and then knocked him on the head for luck. I would not mind the knock on the head so much but I certainly wouldn't enjoy the other. I am not going where I'll even get knocked in the head though if I know it.

I certainly did enjoy myself Tuesday night. That stew couldn't *be beat.* You know I have always had a kind of a desire to be a chafing dish artist, but I never even had the dish. Ethel had one you know and I got so I could make fudge on it. Farmers though have no use for chafing dishes. They have to plow, put up hay, and trade horses.

A fellow traded me a horse yesterday. That is, he parted me from a hundred dollars and I have a horse. You know horse trading is the cause of the death of truth in America. When you go to buy they'll tell you anything on earth to get your money. You simply have to use your own judgment, if you have any. I haven't much but I think I got my money's worth. Can't tell though until I work him a few days.

A neighbor of ours once had a sale of his furniture and stock. He had a great many horses and some that were no good. He had one that was probably an octogenarian in the horse world. He was very aged anyway. This horse he wanted to sell to a poor lame man who had tried to buy it before the sale. So he took a quart of bad whiskey and soaked the poor lame one and then told him he wasn't going to put the horse up. Well that fellow begged so hard that the horse was sold to him for $170. Just about $100 more than it was worth. The owner had a "buy bidder" to run him up. So that between the booze and the bidder he was mulcted for $100. O hé the honest farmer. I have found that they sell gold bricks now. That is what rural delivery and party-line phones have done for our uplift.

I am not a pessimist though. There are some honest ones and they are always well thought of even by the crooks. They are always the last ones you get acquainted with too.

We have moved around quite a bit and always the best people are hardest to know. I don't know why that is either.

My ink is in the same condition as yours. Mary has ordered ink for the last half-dozen times. I have been where it can be bought. But I can never remember it until I go to write. I sincerely hope you'll forgive this excuse for a letter. You know I am somewhat behind on sleep and the wheels that constitute my brain refuse to run smoothly and therefore I cannot write a decent letter. When a person has hired help he has to be up and thinking all the time to keep them busy as well as be busy himself all the time. If they can draw your money and do nothing, they are all willing to do it. I know because I've been there myself. You've probably heard of George Ade's man who bothered the directors so much for more money that they made him a director, and he was the best man to browbeat the clerks in the whole establishment ever after.

That's usually the case. It's all a matter of viewpoint. A man's mighty lucky if he has two.

I am not going to bore you any longer. I hope you'll answer it though.

> Most sincerely,
> Harry

Grandview, Mo.

Dear Bessie: March 19, 1911

I sincerely hope you enjoyed the playing of that musical editor as well as I did. He was simply great. You know that I think when good music is played in his style it is always enjoyable. Hope I didn't cause you to do anything against your religious principles. You know that I know nothing about Lent and such things and when I was urging you to go with us to dinner at the Baltimore I was merely thinking of giving you all a good time. That was the first "time" I was ever at an Episcopal Church and I like the service very much. But I guess I'll have to remain a Lightfoot Baptist for a while yet anyway. You know I told you that I also had strayed from the Presbyterian fold; but I went in the other direction. In place of more form we haven't any. But there are many things I do not like. For instance they do not want a person to go to shows or dance or do anything for a good time. Well I like to do all those things and play cards besides. So you see I am not very strong as a Baptist. Anyhow I don't think any church on earth will take you to heaven if you're not real anyway. I believe in people living what they believe and talking afterwards, don't you? Well hang religion anyway; it's a dull subject, but I'll not ask you to dinner any more till after Easter Sunday. Will that be all right?

Mary has not arrived home yet. The last I heard of her she was in Independence. When she gets down there she never knows when to come home, and I don't blame her. I like Independence and if I ever get rich enough to retire (be a retired farmer ah) I think I'll land in Independence.

We go to sowing oats in the morning. It will take a week or two as we have about eighty acres to sow. Mr. Hall wanted to know of me if we were *planting* wheat now. You know a town farmer always gets his verbs mixed. We sow wheat, oats, and grass seed and plant corn and potatoes. See the difference?

I did certainly enjoy Miss Dicey's (I guess that's how you spell her) excitable conversation. I bet she is a person who enjoys life. You know when people can get excited over the ordinary things in life, they live. You know a good author makes common things seem great in books, and people who can live them that way always enjoy life. I never did know but one boy that way and only one man. Neither of them can cross the street without having an adventure worth telling of.

When she was telling about those chickens and that trip to St. Louis I thought I'd go up. I guess they thought I was a perfect chump because I forgot to tell them and you too that I enjoyed the evening, but I most certainly did and you please tell them, will you? Next time I'll do better provided I can have a *next time.*

Mamma has seven little chickens and more coming. They looked rather out of place when we had that snow. I told her she would have to begin knitting socks if she was going to raise chickens in the winter. The last few days have been fine on them though. One of my numerous cousins was over this evening and she had seventy-six chickens big enough to fly. They were incubator chickens. I hope you don't cook yours before they hatch. They say that is generally what happens the first time. So be careful.

Did you get your suitcase all right? I wish we had thought and taken it to the N.Y. Life Building and then we could have got it. No one ever thought that man would play overtime. They don't generally.

Now please don't wait so long to write as I do enjoy your letters even if you do call them *notes.*

What do you think of Mrs. E.C.W[hite, a student of Theodor Leschetizky and teacher of Harry Truman]? Isn't she a caution? Some time when she has a swell recital if you care to go out, we'll go and then you'll see her show off proper.

Well I'm going to quit because I have run overtime but if you don't want to read, remember you owe me a letter now and I am looking for it.

Sincerely yours,
Harry

After graduating from high school, Truman worked six months as time-keeper for the L. J. Smith Construction Company, which was double-tracking a line of the Santa Fe near Independence. Every other Saturday night he paid off the four hundred men in a local saloon. Only because they drank away their money did they show up for work on Monday mornings—hence his derisory labeling of them below as hoboes—and himself a "hobo paymaster." As he wrote many years later, a worker received $1.50 per day for ten hours' work and paid $3.50 each week for board, so they netted $11.00 every two weeks. "That," said Truman, "is where I learned about minimum wages!"

Grandview, Mo.

Dear Bessie: April 1, 1911

April Fool Day. Mamma says it is always customary to send blank sheets of paper today instead of written ones. Well perhaps you'd rather get the blank ones, but I am going to fill these and spoil the spirit of the day.

You see I have been sowing oats all week, got done Thursday night, and hauled about six tons of hay yesterday. My face is a sight, as the girls say. You know the wind blew something "fierce" last Tuesday and Wednesday and the sun also had some effect. Between them I look like raw beef or a confirmed "booze fighter." My voice is also somewhat weary from yelling at the horses. You know we drive four plugs to a drill—have them abreast. It is an impossibility to have four with inclinations alike. I had four whose names may be some index to their character—William, Samuel, Jane, and X. X is a bronc—if you know what that is—and he has an insane desire to arrive at the other end of the field in the shortest possible time. You dare not touch him with a whip or let him hear one if you can help. William—Bill we call him of course—is an ex-buggy horse. He hasn't much idea of work but to get out of it if he can. I yell at him in my sleep sometimes. When I am not hallooing "Bill, Bill go on," I am saying the same to Sam. Sam is a very large ex-dray horse and he never hurries under any consideration unless I poke him with a sharp stick or land on him with a baling wire whip. Jane, as Mrs. Barclay would say, is just right. She goes as she should. Well when I land on Sam and Bill, Jane and X want to run away. So I have to take it out in lung work and unprintable names. You can just bet that I am glad I'm done. I always sow Vivian's and mine too. This time I sowed seventy acres in five days. That is moving some. Vivian is well and has been hauling hay for me while I sowed his oats. (I do wish I had your new bottle of ink.) Did you get an invitation to the high school reception for Professor Bryant? I did but I can't go. I have a "previous engagement" to a tacky party. I am going as I usually go when at home and I bet I take the cake. My very best friends would refuse to recognize me if they ever saw me in town in my farm rags. They are dirty and tattered and torn with hog snoot marks, splashed milk, and other things too numerous to mention in their makeup. You ask Ethel what a pretty figure I cut when I pretend to work. Mamma ropes me in once in a while and makes me exchange for a clean set, but they don't feel right until I wear them a day or two.

I am glad your "umbrell" is a useful as well as ornamental article. You know they generally are not both.

I would certainly be glad to attend church with you in Independence and hear your choir.

I guess you will have a fine time at the river tomorrow morning. I haven't been down on those bluffs since I was a timekeeper for L. J. Smith. You know I was once a hobo paymaster. Not a pleasant job either.

I am sorry to hear of Miss Dicie's illness but I guess she'll soon recover. Lively people are never sick long. I hope your mother is well by this time. Our whole family is in good health. Papa only has to hop on crutches but he'll soon be over that.

You say you have gone back to W. D. Howells, well I have never come to him yet. He must be all right for he was a particular friend of Mark Twain's. It's luck I guess but I have never read one of his books. I certainly did enjoy *The Mistress of Shenstone*. I have read *The Rosary* since I read it and they are both good. I have also been reading the history of Jenghiz Khan the Tartar. He is the only great man in history who had no effect on American history, according to Miss Phelps. You know she began with Adam and came down. But I never heard of Jenghiz till recently. Well I am wound up but shall quit here. Please write me when you have the time as I enjoy your letters very much. I am

Sincerely,
Harry

Grandview, Mo.
Dear Bessie: April 12, 1911

I got your good letter yesterday and will answer it later. I have some tickets to Sothern-Marlowe [Edward H. Sothern and Julia Marlowe, Shakespeareans] for Saturday night and if you will help me use them I shall be very glad. I tried for *Macbeth* for Saturday matinee but everything was gone. It is *Taming of the Shrew* and I think is as good as Mac.

If you can't go, why my phone number is Hickman No. 6 and it costs ten cents. So you'd better save the dime and go. It is a Home [local telephone system]. If I don't hear from you, I shall be around at 7:00 P.M. Saturday.

Sincerely,
Harry

In 1905, at the age of twenty-one, Truman joined the Missouri National Guard. For two three-year terms he was a member of Kansas City's field artillery unit, Battery B. In this letter Truman refers to one of his officers, Arthur J. Elliott. A sizable, even corpulent man, he was never an object of Truman's affection. Also referred to below are Mary and Myra Colgan, daughters of Aunt Emma.

Grandview, Mo.
Dear Bessie: April 17, 1911

Well I ran almost to Kansas City, or would have if a car had not come, all
to meet a Battery sergeant and the ornery whelp didn't show up. I called up his
wife, and she said he had made a trip to Moberly for the firm. There I was
downtown on Sunday night and nothing to do. I made a start for church and
landed at the Shubert. Maybe you think I won't tell that person my state of mind
when I see him. You know about ten or fifteen of those boys want to come out
here some Sunday horseback and stay for dinner. Mr. Elliott was to meet me and
make arrangements. They were out here last spring and I tell you they ate more
than harvest hands. That's saying as much about their gastronomic ability as is
possible without stretching the blanket. It's quite a job for Mamma but she says
let them come.

I most certainly did enjoy myself yesterday. I liked that church service very
much. It is the first time I ever saw one on Easter. I am afraid I thanked your
mother too much and you not enough for the pleasure of the day; but you know
I appreciated the invitation from you both. I shall remember that dinner for a
mighty long time. Were you tired last night? Nellie and Ethel were about all in.
It seems to have done me good, for although I didn't turn in until 1:30 A.M. and
got up at five-thirty I don't feel a bit sleepy or tired either. If I had known I wasn't
going to see that man, I most certainly would have stayed in the good town last
night, whether you would have let me come over or not. Course I could have
looked across the street.

See the change in my ink? I have poured in some green fountain pen ink.
It makes a fine combination.

I went to a party at Grandview a few days ago and they tried to teach me
the "hoe down" or country dance. I sure had a circus learning. There is a widow
up there who particularly adores Vivian and he of course abominates her. Well
when he isn't around she takes her spite out on me. Well when they started the
dance she of course took it upon herself to teach me. Did you ever hear them
call a "hoe down"? It goes something like this: "Swing the girl with the pretty
brown hair and now the one with the face so fair. Swing the gal with a lantern
jaw and now the one from Arkansas. Balance and turn and left and right and all
promenade." Then you do it over. You can get most gloriously dizzy and it's a
lot cheaper than booze. There are four couples in a square and you take turn about
until you are through with each one. When you have been around once you feel
as if you had been sent for and couldn't come.

When we get our new barn done we are going to have a barn dance, and
if you and Ethel and Nellie will come out I'll ask Myra and Mary Colgan from
Kansas City and all the country boys in seven miles and show you what they can
do when a bunch of us farmers get together for a time.

There will be a smooth floor fifty by seventy-two, and I think that is large
enough. The barn probably won't be done though until about July. Now please
don't forget a week from Saturday, and if you care for one we'll go to a ball game
in the afternoon and then to Mrs. White's in the evening—or would that be

seeing too much of me in one day? I intended bringing your book home but Mary was reading it and I didn't think you'd care if I let her finish it. I forgot to tell you Mamma has taken off fifty-four chickens this morning and they are fine. That fine batch of yours was certainly a wonder with their ten eggs. How did you manage it?

I was very sorry to hear of Lizzie Gossett's death. I always liked her too. I guess Miss Dicie will make California a land of adventure when she gets there. I'd like to hear her tell it when she comes home.

This letter is lengthy and I hope won't bore you to death but please remember you owe me a letter and that is what I am after. I am always glad to get your letters. Please send one soon.

Sincerely,
Harry

Grandview, Mo.
April 24, 1911

Dear Bessie:

You sure are all right, as they say in Texas. I was simply pining for *Everybody's* and mine hadn't come. The Ne'r-Do-Well is behaving beautifully this time. The story of course lets up at a very interesting point and leaves you on needles for the next issue. By all means send me *Keith of the Border* as I have never read it. It sounds mighty good. I am grinning and shall continue to only at stated intervals and they are only of short duration. That is when a pain runs up and down my leg [see May 9 letter]. But I am doing really fine. I slept all night last night without a break and that is unusual to say the least.

I am somewhat of a philosopher I guess as I am not worrying any, although it is the very busiest time and there are one hundred things I could do to advantage. We happen to have two of the best hired men to be had anywhere and Vivian still has two legs so we can run as usual almost. I intend to exercise my fingers again and be a pianist for six weeks anyway as soon as I can get to it. It will be three weeks though before I get up.

You know I am like the Irish woman Uncle Joe tells about. She lived down here north of us a short distance long before the war. Her husband was drowned in Big Blue one night as he was coming home drunk. At the wake the woman would howl out every once in a while, "To think that Mike should a crossed the great ocean and thin he drowned in a hole like the dirty Blue. Tis a disgrass inded it is."

That's the way I feel about that calf. To think that I have had some really respectable falls and came off without a scratch and then have a sucking calf knock me down and actually break my leg. Tis indeed a disgrace. But perhaps I can live it down.

I had thirteen callers yesterday and the telephone bell is almost worn out. I really didn't know I had so many friends. It does me good to find it out even if I do have to stay penned up.

People out here are kidding me about following in the footsteps of my father.

They say I do it in an altogether too literal manner. It was not intentional in this case by any means.

Mrs. White has postponed her recital. Not on my account but because some of her girls are not ready. Maybe she'll put it off long enough that we may go yet, because I intend to be well by July anyway.

Your letter did me lots of good, so please send another when you have time and I am most thankful for *Everybody's* and shall look forward to the book. I hope your incubator behaved well. Mamma has 112 young chickens and more coming every day. Write when you can to

Yours sincerely,
Harry

Grandview, Mo.
Dear Bessie: April 27, 1911
. . . I shall be worse spoiled than an only child when I get well. Papa buys me candy and fruit as if I were a two-year-old, and Mamma spends half her time making me comfortable and making my favorite pies. You really don't know how much you're thought of until you get knocked out. I shall try and keep my head though.

I am very thankful that I'll have two feet when I'm well as usual. I do certainly feel sorry for Edward Paxton [who lost part of a foot in an Air Line train accident]. I would rather be the poorest laborer in Christendom and be physically whole than be John D. and have some of me gone, wouldn't you?

Such things as broken legs are only chasteners anyway. I shall know exactly how to sympath (I've lost my dictionary and forgot how to spell the last syllable, ain't it awful) with my friends when they have like accidents. I didn't before.

I am sitting up today in a Morris chair and I tell you it is restful to get out of bed once in seven days. I had been thinking all along how nice it would be if I could only sleep for seven days straight. I have the opportunity now and can scarcely get in six hours at a time. That is always the way, we are never exactly satisfied with what we can get.

I shall continue to look for the book. I have been improving my mind with Harold MacGrath the last day or two, his *Splendid Hazard.* It's fine.

I got a note from Ethel saying she would write me in a day or two. I guess they are very busy now and haven't much time for correspondence. I hope you will take this for what it is worth and consider it worth an answer as I most certainly do appreciate your letters. I'll try and do better next time but my pet [Mamma] won't let me sit up long at a time, much as I want to.

Write when you can soon to

Yours sincerely,
Harry

Grandview, Mo.

Dear Bessie: May 3, 1911

I don't care what kind of paper you write on. I should be just as pleased to get a letter from you on wrapping paper as on the finest stationery built. So write whether you have any stationery or not although that last looked good enough for anybody to me.

I am sorry to hear of your chickens dying. Mamma has lost quite a number though. She says it is the cold, damp weather more than anything else—and then some of hers she says have been supporting families upon themselves. She is going to dip them as soon as the weather will permit and then she says they'll be all right.

I had a letter from Nellie saying she was going to quit teaching in Independence and go down to Sugar Creek. They offered her a larger salary. I told her not to fall in love with a bohunk but if she ran across a Standard Oil Magnate to nab him.

Your remarks on the petting and privileges of the oldest one of a family are absolutely true as I can testify from experience. Although the other two back me down that I am always the petted one.

I have been reading *David Copperfield* and have really found out that I couldn't appreciate Dickens before. I have only read *Oliver Twist* and *Tale of Two Cities*. They didn't make much of an impression and I never read anything else. A neighbor sent me *Dombey & Son* and *David C.*, and I am glad for it has awakened a new interest. It is almost a reconciliation to having my leg broken to contemplate the amount of reading I am going to do this summer. I am getting better fast and I am afraid I'll get well so soon I won't get to read enough. Isn't that an awful thought?

I really don't mind staying in the house on rainy, cloudy days like this but when they are nice like last Sunday I can hardly sit still. I begin to think of corn to plant, gardens to make, grass seed to sow, and a hundred and one things to do, and then I pick up a magazine and forget it. I am not worrying much I guess for they tell me I am getting fat. Then Papa is able to get around now and will soon throw his crutches away and then things will hum.

I guess I won't get rich this year although we did break up a field that hasn't had a crop raised on it since 1873. I was figuring on raising five thousand bushels of corn and at least paying my debts, but as Mr. Micawber says, my creditors will have to wait. I do think that Mr. Micawber is the killingest person I have run across in any book anywhere. He is exactly true to life. I know a half-dozen of him right here in Grandview. They are always waiting for something to turn up or for someone to die and leave them something. I never expect to be rich but if I can't make what I get myself without waiting for someone to leave it to me, I hope somebody will knock me on the head and put me out of danger.

I am sorry Ethel didn't get out Sunday as I'd like to see her as well as get the book. I told Nellie to tell her if she didn't bring it out next Sunday I am going to get in an ambulance and come after it.

I guess you'll have a good time with your bridge club. Speaking of people crying at plays, I don't think there is anything funnier. That is the only way I enjoy a tragedy is to laugh at those who cry. Uncle Harrison says he'd rather go to the Orpheum and laugh all evening than sit and grate the enamel off his false teeth to see Mansfield or Sothern or any other big gun. He is very near right I think. Well I hope you'll consider this worth an answer as I'll be glad to get one. Am hoping to be around in ten days anyway.

Sincerely,
Harry

Grandview, Mo.
May 9, 1911

Dear Bessie:

You may be very, very sure that your letters cannot possibly come too often or too regular for *me*. They are the most pleasant and agreeable (to me at least) of all the correspondence or reading I do. So there, if it pleases you any to have me say it. I am glad you have laid in a good stock of stationery and hope you'll continue to use some of it on me.

Speaking of that calf. It had the impudence to come up and look at me through the window a day or two ago and then kick up and bawl, as much as to say, "See what he got for monkeying with the bandwagon." He had three or four more calves of his own age with him. I have the sincere satisfaction of knowing that he will someday grace a platter—perhaps my very own. He is a very obstreperous individual in the cow world anyway. They have had to put a chain on the young man to be able to handle him at all. And he doesn't weigh over three hundred pounds. Calves are like men, some have sense—and some have not. Evidently he has not as he can never find his meals unless someone is kind enough to assist him. Even then he's ungrateful, as behold what he did to me. I only grabbed his tail and made a wild grab for his ear in order to guide him around properly when he stuck his head between my legs, backed me into the center of the lot, and when I went to get off threw me over his head with a buck and a bawl and went off seemingly satisfied, I guess, for I didn't look. I set up a bawl of my own. Uncle Harrison says there is more honor in having a fine calf boost you skyward and break your leg than to have a plug horse do it. (He was heaving a brick at Papa I think and so I don't take much stock in it.) Well, hang the calf anyway. I hope I never am unlucky enough to meet another the same way.

Mamma gave me her prescription for dipping chickens and it's a dinger I tell you. She says it won't hurt the chickens and if it don't it sure ought to get the other fellows.

She takes twist tobacco and steeps it in hot water as if you were making tea. Put in cold water enough to cover the hen and make it the right temperature. Then she puts in a tablespoonful of melted grease. She says she puts her hand over the chicken's bill and eyes and then souses him good. Young and old alike can go through this process without harm. She says she takes four twists of tobacco to one bucket of water. Now if you can get a clear idea of that recipe it is more than I can after reading it. But it will make chickens healthy, although I wouldn't fancy the job of dipping them. Maybe you can force that negro you have working for you to do it. Be sure and pick a warm day to do it.

My opinion of Dickens is not so rosy as it was. I read *David Copperfield* with delight and not a stop. I was so pleased I started immediately on *Dombey & Son*, read a hundred pages and have read the *Manxman*, the *Pursuit of the Houseboat on the Styx*, and *Lorna Doone* and still have 500 or 600 pages of *Dombey* to read. *Oliver Twist* must have done you the same way. *Lorna Doone* is a fine story but written in such a style that it takes about 700 pages to tell what might be told in 250 with ease. I have nothing to do but read and so I waded through it. I guess I'll even get *Dombey* read before I get up for good. I stood up on one foot yesterday and this morning but was mighty glad to get back in bed. The doctor is going to bring me some crutches the last of the week and then it won't be long till I can hop around.

My good friend, the cashier of Bank of Belton, bought him a new seven-passenger auto the other day. He was in to see me yesterday evening and said he would be around and drive me over the country soon as I am able. So if you see me drive up in a big auto you'll know it is not mine, though I'd almost give ten years off my ninety-year existence for one and call it a good bargain. I don't believe Esau would have been blamed if he had sold his birthright for an auto in place of something to eat do you? Jacob was an ornery Jew or he wouldn't have taken it anyway. (I mean the birthright, not the auto.)

I am very sorry to hear of Everett Hall's death but I guess he is better off, poor boy. I went to school with him in Miss Myra Ewin's room at the Noland School. He and Cleve started together. . . .

Keep on writing oftener and more regularly and please me more and more.

Sincerely,

Harry

The Mexican Revolution began in 1910, and soon that country was in turmoil. Below we see that Bess's brother Frank had contemplated a visit to Mexico. Wisely, he changed his plans and went to Panama, an American protectorate.

Grandview, Mo.

Dear Bessie: May 17, 1911

I am sitting up at the desk writing this and it makes me feel a lot more independent. Crutches are certainly the most inconvenient conveniences I have ever run up against. You've no idea how experience teaches sympathy. I have thought many a time that some of the antics of people on crutches were unnecessary to say the least. I don't think so now. It really takes an expert to accomplish anything with them. It is necessary for me to wear my uncle's overalls because I can't get my plaster cast through the leg of mine. He weighs 240 and a large part of his weight is around the waist. You can imagine the beautiful profile I make. I don't care for looks now though. I want to get out of bed and I'd almost wear a dress to do it.

I certainly thank you for the book you sent. It is fine. I haven't quite finished it yet. I sent you a copy of *Life* by Ethel. It is so good. I thought that I could not keep it all to myself. I had wrapped it for mailing when Ethel and Aunt Ella showed up. I hope you hadn't seen it. The center cartoon is particularly entrancing. I should certainly like the opportunity of being a joyrider. I really don't think I'd be one, but I'd just like to have the means to be one.

I was very glad to see Ethel and so I didn't attempt to remove her back hair as I had threatened to do. Anyway I don't believe I could have done it just yet so I let well enough alone. She was perfectly willing for me to try.

You said Frank was anxious to go to Mexico. You tell him he'd better stay out of Greaserdom right now anyway. If a fellow could go as the rearguard of a victorious American army it would be all right, but right now the chances are good that he'd stop a bullet. I am like Mark Twain. He says that if fame is to be obtained only by marching to the cannon's mouth, he is perfectly willing to go there provided the cannon is empty, if it is loaded he'd get over the fence and go home. Sometimes the cannon's breech is as dangerous as its mouth. A member of the Battery got his fingers connected with the breech block on one of those three-inch guns not long ago and left one of them in the gun. I think I shall quit the military stunt in June. My time is out then. I have been a member for six years and have had lots of fun, learned a little bit, and made some friends, so I guess I'd better quit while I am all in one piece. Out at Ft. Riley once while the outfit was out there, a shell exploded at the mouth of the gun and killed seven or eight who were standing too far front. So you see a person is not absolutely safe either in front or behind the gun. Mark's advice is best.

One of Mamma's cousins is visiting us now who was in the real Confederate Army. He was at the Battle of Vicksburg and Corinth and also up here at the Battle of Westport. He thinks that General Price was the greatest man that ever lived. Of all the hair-lifting war tales Cousin Will can sure contribute his share. It really seems funny that in this very country, even right where we live, people should have been afraid to go anywhere unless there were several together. Then maybe the Redlegs or Bushwhackers would kill them. Grandmother once routed a whole band of Indians with a big dog. She was all alone except for a negro woman and two of her children. These Indians told her they wanted honey and if she didn't give it, they would take it and her too. So they sharpened their knives on the grinding stone and then she turned loose a large dog. Away went Indians, some leaving their blankets. If I had been Grandma I'd have disappeared out the front way when they came up the back. But she didn't and finally made them go.

I guess you'll think this is a mighty tiresome attempt at a letter but it is the best I can do today. I read some Chinese poetry this morning and I guess that is the reason I can't do any better. It was rendered into English but even then it sounded as bad as the hen tracks they make for writing look. So if this is too dull to read, I hope you'll consider that you owe me a letter for it anyway.

I want to thank you again for *The Mistress of Shenstone,* as I sure enjoyed it and so did the rest of us.

I hope your calico chickens will be a success and I am really glad you didn't have to use that awful dip. Vivian has to dip chickens out here. I eat them. Well write when you can and if I land that machine [automobile] I'll *try and use it right*.

Sincerely,
Harry

Grandview, Mo.
May 23, 1911

Dear Bessie:

I guess there is nothing for me to do but wait until I am able and then remove Ethel's wig. I sure thought I was consigning your book and *Life* to a safe messenger when I gave them to her. Vivian hasn't said a word about them to me. I shall corner him tonight. I have an idea a certain lady friend of his could tell me where they are if he doesn't. I shall try and make reparation for the book anyway if it doesn't eventually reach you.

I have enjoyed *Nicanar* immensely. I suppose it depicts Norman life realistically but I like for them to be more cheerful about it. I am going to read the book again. I found out the name of a Roman Emperor that history never says anything about in it. He really existed too. You see I haven't anything to do but run down historic rumors, and every book I read since I have been laid up that mentions anyone at all in history I never heard of causes me to look him up. I always forget him five minutes afterwards but I have the satisfaction of knowing [who] he was anyway.

I really wish Rex Beach would do something with that Ne'er-Do-Well and be done with it. It makes you feel like the end of the year instead of the middle the way he draws it out.

I've an idea the poor boy'll lose his job now and his girl and then have a love feast with her old man, come back and get the girl and the Pennsylvania Railroad and live happily until alimony time. What do you think?

Mary's (mine also) cousin in Texas sent her two horned toads in a box by mail the other day. She thought it was a box of pills. It was all wrapped up and very small. You ought to have heard her squawk when she opened the box. You know they have tails and horns on their heads (their tails are not on their heads) and are furious looking little brutes, but are harmless. They feast on flies, ants, etc. I don't see how these two lived for the box was air-tight.

Mary and Vivian went to the Ruskin High School Commencement Thursday night. Said it was fine.

I guess they are all fine the first few times but when very many pass they get old don't you think? They sure must be getting nifty in Independence if the ushers wanted to wear claw hammer coats. That's spreading things thick. The Kansas City *Post* has offered ten dollars for the prettiest graduation dress not to cost over five dollars. Do you suppose one can be made for that? . . .

I have an illustration of what happens to people who set grocery store eggs. I am enclosing it. Did any of yours come out that way? Literature, etc., do not go very well with poultry, do they? One good gang of poultry does more for the country though than all the art Charles Yerkes [the late Chicago streetcar magnate] could buy. You know I think a man artist or pianist is the last thing on earth. They do no good for themselves or anyone else. I never did see one who paid his debts if there was any way to avoid it. That shows his artistic temperament, that, a lot of long hair and a kangaroo walk. Sometimes they go dingy or get two or three divorces. That also is a temperamental sign. Some French artist says that geniuses are insane anyway. I guess he is right in some cases anyway. It is all right to be an artist or pianist if you are a real genius like Lhévinne or Hofmann or Turner or Whistler, but the ordinary run of everyday artists and pianists who imitate these men won't do.

I really thought once I'd be an ivory tickler but I am glad my money ran out before I got too far. Who knows, maybe I'll be a Cincinnatus and be elected constable someday.

If you had called up the other day I'd have made it to the phone some way. I can get around the house to some extent. Soon as ever I can persuade the M.D. to take the cast off I'll do fine. I hope you'll consider this worthy an answer. I'd like to see [illegible] Smith. I bet it's fine. This is the end of my stationery.

Sincerely,
Harry

Truman distrusted the Kansas City Star *and considered its publisher, W. R. Nelson, a malign force in Jackson County. Below he jokes about the* Star's *criticism of Senator Reed and Congressman Borland, both of the K.C. Democratic machine.*

Grandview, Mo.
Dear Bessie: May 32, 1911
You'll notice that I have dated this May 32. If I scratch May right at the beginning, it won't look good and it is easier anyway just to give the month another day. Julius Caesar or Augustus you know could add or subtract days from any month they chose and I guess I can do the same to the one that holds my birthday.

I am dying slowly of curiosity. What on earth is the job I'll have? Of course I'll have to *sit tight* and wait I guess, but it's mighty disagreeable to burn up slowly with a strictly feminine prerogative. I have really got anxious to work since I can't. I once thought if I could only lay off I could sleep at least two days at a stretch but I simply can't do over five hours now to save me, and I believe I'd really pitch hay with pleasure. So come on with your job. I am getting to be something of an organ-grinding pianist myself now and I can't appreciate your torture at the neighbor's hands at all, because if we had any neighbors close enough to listen I'd be doing them the same way. I can play "Happy Heinie" and "Yankee

Doodle" to a fare you well. I suppose it is sometimes good for the neighbors when you have to use an opera glass to see the front gate.

Don't you think Dr. Cyrus Townsend Brady is a fine fellow? I do. When a man has the ability and courage to tell old Bill Nelson what he is, he sure is all right with me. He'll make a success in Kansas City too. The *Star* never did win a political or any other kind of fight of any importance. You know they made a special fight on Jim Reed and W.P. Borland. The *Journal* said the *Star* had won an old-time victory when Borland was elected. When a man wants to win in this end of the state, he wants the *Star* against him. . . .

Say, when I am able to walk like a gentleman again will you go to a ball game with me? I mean a real professional game at [illegible] Park. I am so crazy to walk I don't know what to do. I have been buggy riding a time or two and can go around on three legs. I am like the mathematical dog. I put down three and carry one. That infernal calf is veal now.

Vivian and Mr. McBroom are plowing corn just north of the house and their language is forceful to say the least when they go to turn here at the house. A horse when he is hitched to a cultivator can make a religious crank use profanity. It is not possible to reach him as your hands are full holding the plow, so you have to take it out in strong talk. I have found on investigation that Vivian was entirely responsible for your book going astray. He put it under the buggy seat when they started for Dodson, and Ethel and Aunt Ella had to run for a car and he never mentioned the book. He took both the book and *Life* to his girl that evening and never said a word until yesterday when he brought the book home. I'll bring it myself next time. Well I hope you'll consider this worth an answer. Don't keep me waiting long or I'll die of curiosity.

Sincerely,
Harry

Throughout the letters Truman refers to his Masonic interests. He first learned about the Masons from his cousin and early in 1909 joined the Lodge at Belton, a half-dozen miles south of Grandview. Another Lodge member taught him the basic ritual. Each Mason progressed through a system of degrees. Advancing rapidly, Truman soon organized a Lodge in Grandview and became its first Master. In the thirties he entered the Grand Lodge line of the Masons of Missouri and in 1940 became Grand Master.

Grandview, Mo.

Dear Bessie: June 16, 1911

. . . A new Masonic Lodge is being organized at our town and they have given me the principal office. I have the big head terribly. The Deputy Grand Master was out to see us Wednesday night and handed me an awful lot of hot air. I haven't quite recovered from the effects yet.

Do you really think Minnie would want the clock set back now? I thought it usually took some time before they wished things undone. They tell me that the first few months she can burn the biscuit every morning if she chooses and

Harry Truman behind a one-row cultivator, c. 1910. *Harry S. Truman Library*

it's all right, but after that she learns what a good cook her ma-in-law was. And the first few months he can be as no-account and good-for-nothing as he wants to be but he soon learns how his pa-in-law made his money. Then it's ho for Reno or South Dakota. It is certainly awful what pessimists those two places have made of people. I am a Catholic when it comes to divorce. I believe people could generally settle their differences if they weren't so all-fired selfish.

I guess you do miss Frank. I bet you he don't find any surplus wheat. We'll probably eat cornbread this season. That is provided it rains even in time for corn. I hope he has a good time while he is gone.

We are living on bread and bacon with some canned goods thrown in. I can sympathize with those western rummies now who can never raise a garden. Ours is a total failure. We had one measley little mess of peas and there was more soup than peas then. One of our neighbors who has a big orchard says that all the apples are falling off green. I am doing the usual farmer act now. They are always starving to death. . . .

Write when you can to

Sincerely yours,
Harry

The following letter gets right to the point. Marriage was his goal, and he chose a letter to propose it. But present-day readers will not find it entirely charming, for here again are the racial slurs common to Truman's time.

Grandview, Mo.
Dear Bessie: June 22, 1911

From all appearances I am not such a very pious person am I? The elements evidently mistook one of my wishes for dry instead of wet. I guess we'll all have to go to drinking whiskey if it doesn't rain very soon. Water and potatoes will soon be as much of a luxury as pineapples and diamonds.

Speaking of diamonds, would you wear a solitaire on your left hand should I get it? Now that is a rather personal or pointed question provided you take it for all it means. You know, were I an Italian or a poet I would commence and use all the luscious language of two continents. I am not either but only a kind of good-for-nothing American farmer. I've always had a sneakin' notion that some day maybe I'd amount to something. I doubt it now though like everything. It is a family failing of ours to be poor financiers. I am blest that way. Still that doesn't keep me from having always thought that you were all that a girl could be possibly and impossibly. You may not have guessed it but I've been crazy about you ever since we went to Sunday school together. But I never had the nerve to think you'd even look at me. I don't think so now but I can't keep from telling you what I think of you.

Perhaps you can guess what my other eight wishes are now. If they had no more effect than the one for rain, I am badly off indeed. You said you were tired of these kind of stories in books so I am trying one from real life on you. I guess it sounds funny to you, but you must bear in mind that this is my first experience in this line and also it is very real to me. Therefore I can't make it look or sound so well as Rex Beach or Harold Mac[Grath] might.

I am going to send you the book number of *Life*. There is a page of books in it that look good. Don't get *Ashes of a God*, for I am going to get it and I'll let you have it. Every review I have read on it says it is fine. I have thrown my sticks away and use only a cane now. I told Ethel I am going to get me a gold-headed one and an eyeglass, if some one of my friends lent me the coin, and pretend that I had been to Georgie V's crowning. Don't you abhor snobs? Think of such men as Morgan paying to be allowed to dance with royalty. You know there isn't a royal family in Europe that wouldn't disgrace any good citizen to belong to. I think one man is just as good as another so long as he's honest and decent and not a nigger or a Chinaman. Uncle Will says that the Lord made a white man from dust, a nigger from mud, then threw up what was left and it came down a Chinaman. He does hate Chinese and Japs. So do I. It is race prejudice I guess. But I am strongly of the opinion that negroes ought to be in Africa, yellow men in Asia, and white men in Europe and America.

I guess if Frank won't be satisfied with Kansas City, Memphis is as good as any of them. It is at least in a good old Southern state. Then it only takes one night to get back home. That is better than Mexico or California. I hope he has all kinds of success.

Everybody's came at last and there was plenty of action, wasn't there? I am dying to know if he got her. Say, Bessie, you'll at least let me keep on being good friends won't you? I know I am not good enough to be anything more but you don't know how I'd like to be. Maybe you think I won't wait your answer to this in suspense.

Still if you turn me down, I'll not be thoroughly disappointed for it's no more than I expect.

I have just heard that the Masonic Lodge I was telling you of is a success. There won't be two in our town. The one I belong to is in Belton six miles away. This one is in Grandview, only one mile.

Please write as soon as you feel that way. The sooner, the better pleased I am.

More than sincerely,
Harry

Grandview, Mo.
July 10, 1911

Dear Bessie:

I have just about come to the conclusion that I must have offended you in some way. If being in love with you is any offense, I am sorry but it can't be helped you know. Anyway that shouldn't keep you from being real civil anyway.

Won't you at least let me know you are not "mad," as Shakespeare would say. I was in Kansas City the other day and attempted to call you up but your phone wasn't working or something.

We have given up all hope of rain out here. I guess we'll have to eat canned goods from now till next year or else live on wheat.

Would you object to my coming down Saturday evening? I walk like a wooden-legged man but will probably not be so bad Saturday.

Sincerely,
Harry

Grandview, Mo.
July 12, 1911

Dear Bessie:

You know that you turned me down so easy that I am almost happy anyway. I never was fool enough to think that a girl like you could ever care for a fellow like me but I couldn't help telling you how I felt. I have always wanted you to have some fine, rich, good-looking man, but I knew that if ever I got the chance I'd tell you how I felt even if I didn't even get to say another word to you. What makes me feel real good is that you were good enough to answer me seriously and not make fun of me anyway. You know when a fellow tells a girl all his heart and she makes a joke of it I suppose it would be the awfulest feeling in the world. You see I never had any desire to say such things to anyone else. All my girl friends think I am a cheerful idiot and a confirmed old bach. They really don't know the reason nor ever will. I have been so afraid you were not even going to let me be your good friend. To be even in that class is something.

You may think I'll get over it as all boys do. I guess I am something of a freak myself. I really never had any desire to make love to a girl just for the fun of it, and you have always been the reason. I have never met a girl in my life that you were not the first to be compared with her, to see wherein she was lacking and she always was.

Please don't think I am talking nonsense or bosh, for if ever I told the truth I am telling it now and I'll never tell such things to anyone else or bother you with them again. I have always been more idealist than practical anyway, so I really never expected any reward for loving you. I shall always hope though.

As I said before I am more than glad to be your good friend for that is more than I expected. So when I come down there Saturday (which I'll do if I don't hear from you) I'll not put on any hangdog airs but will try to be the same *old Harry.*

You need not be afraid of bumping the proprieties with me. You couldn't. So send your package along. My new book has come and it is a dandy. A Hindu myth and really fine I think. I sent you *Mollie Make-Believe* by Nellie this time. I hope you got it.

I was at the stockyards yesterday and a fellow offered to buy a bank down here in the south part of the county if I'd run it. I don't know if I could be a banker or not. You know a man has to be real stingy and save every one-cent stamp he can. Then sometimes he has to take advantage of adverse conditions and sell a good man out. That is one reason I like being a farmer. Even if you do have to work like a coon you know that you are not grinding the life out of someone else to live yourself. Still if this man makes the call loud enough, as the preacher said, I may take it. I can stay at home and help run the farm anyway.

Don't you know of some way to make it rain? We need it so badly that if it does not come it will be a real calamity. They say it rains on the just and the unjust alike but it is certainly passing some of us this year. Twenty miles south they have had plenty.

I hope you will continue your good letters as I really enjoy them and will try to answer them to the best of my ability, and although I may sometimes remind you of how I feel toward you I'll try and not bore you to death with it.

Very sincerely,
Harry

Truman seems to have enjoyed children immensely. The young boy mentioned below, Robert Truman Ragland, was the son of Ruth Noland Ragland— sister of Nellie and Ethel. Mrs. Ragland had three children, "Trumie," who died in early 1983, Ardis, and Josephine (Jodie). Mrs. Ardis Haukenberry presently lives in the Noland house at 216 North Delaware.

Grandview, Mo.
July 17, 1911

Dear Bessie:

I brought the boy home with me and he is having a bully time, as Theodore would say. I have been playing boy with him ever since we arrived. We put up a kite and had a real good time. It seems funny to have a kid around. Papa was so tickled I thought he'd go up when he saw Robert. I suppose we'll spoil him completely. If Ruth hadn't promised he could come, I think she'd have gone back and kept him at home. Ruth gave me his photo too and it's nearly as fine as the other one. None could be really as fine. I have some of those tin soldier pictures yet and if you would care for a cat chaser I'll send you one.

Nellie and Ethel went with me to Aunt Emma's, and Myra said she never was more glad to see anyone because she'd have an excellent excuse to stay home from church. It is really "scanluss" the way people like to stay away from church. I guess that is the reason we are having a drought.

I told Ruth to tell Houch [Fielding Houchens, high school classmate] if he called up that I had taken Nellie to the Empress. You'd have thought we'd been there if you could have seen the stylish and refined bunch we came home with. It nearly made me tipsy to breathe in the car. I never did know that Independence could boast of so many beer-drinking *ladies*. We caught the farm aunt crowd. If anything on earth is disgusting, it is the odor of stale beer and limburger cheese or any other booze combination. People who go to amusement parks on Sunday try to tell me that the nicest people go, but they don't look good to me even if they are the nicest. I am not what you'd call rankly religious (you really would not think I had any religion if you'd hear me address a cranky mule or an obstreperous calf) but I don't like Sunday baseball or other forms of rowdyism on that day.

I can't write you a nicely worded letter somehow. The wheels won't turn good. But if you'll consider that you owe me a letter now I'll try to do better. Mary Colgan has decided to stay a week. So I guess she's not angry at Mary and me for running away when she came. I shall look for you to come out in that auto soon, and when the [illegible] come again I hope you will go with me to a game.

Sincerely,
Harry

Grandview, Mo.
July 29, 1911

Dear Bessie:
    ... I have been working like Sam Hill on our Masonic Hall ever since I came home. We had our First Degree work last night and I conferred the first one that was put on. You see some time in the far distant future I'll be bragging about having performed that ceremony. There were about a dozen high moguls out from Kansas City and some from Belton. We had a good Ladies Aid Society time.

You most certainly may keep *Ashes* and *Mollie* as long as you like. You see how promptly I am returning yours. I always leave home either between two suns or in a great rush and can never think to bring them. I'll try to next time. I have found that Mamma had two big maps of my face stored away and I lifted one of them. I am confident it will keep the cats away. It looks as solemn and sanctimonious as your former pastor. When I come in I'll also tote it.

I sincerely hope you'll have a magnificent (is that how you spell it?) time when you go camping. Really, though, if I were you I'd stop handy to a hotel. Send me a postcard while you are gone if you can't write.

Sincerely,

Harry

Truman would do almost anything to win Bess. Because she was a first-rate tennis player he even built a court on the farm to entice her. Here is the first of many references to this plan of attack.

Grandview, Mo.

Dear Bessie: August 14, 1911

Got your letter yesterday but came near not getting it after it arrived. Nellie went after the mail and she decided that I shouldn't have it or anything else. I finally wheedled her out of it. They have been having a big time. We had fourteen for dinner yesterday. Almost threshing day. Everybody helped some though and it wasn't so hard.

Say, I had the --est (you can put any adjective you think strong enough) time getting home you ever read. The southbound train stood on the siding in Noel until my train passed because a freight was off the track. I got to Sulphur at 12:00 P.M. and of course had to stay over. Next morning I decided I'd get you some films down there if I could because I couldn't get to Kansas City in time. Well after going to three places (as many miles apart) I got them and was very thankful I tell you. Then I thought I'd come on home, for if the train was on time I could still see to the clover seed. Well it came into Sulphur one hour late but made up some time to Joplin—but about twenty-five or thirty miles this side of Pittsburg [Kansas] a freight train ran off the track while trying to get in the clear for us and we sat there three hours. I got home at 9:00 P.M. Maybe you think I didn't wish I'd stayed. I've been kicking myself ever since because I didn't. Sorry you didn't get your hay ride. It must have been some fierce booze if it was the Arkansas variety that Frank used. I feel sorry for him. I hope he's well now. I sure do want to see those pictures and would like to have some of them if you'll let me pay for 'em.

Will you please send me the plan of a tennis court. I am going to try and make one. We have a dandy place for it. Wish you could all come out in the machine while all these girls are here. If I get my court built you can come out Saturday afternoons and play in the shade all the time.

I am very glad you enjoyed the eggs, and glad I took them if it caused such a good feeling toward me afterwards. I am going to try and get in toward the end of the week, will call you up from the city if it is all right. Write when you [can] as I always like to hear from you.

Sincerely,

Harry

Grandview, Mo.

Dear Bessie: August 27, 1911

Your letter came day before yesterday and I have been searching for something to write on ever since. I found Mary's stationery box this morning and am robbing it. We haven't even a tablet in the house.

Thank you very much for the tennis court directions. I shall try and follow them as nearly as I can. For the rest of this year I'll just make a grass court. We have a heavy field roller and I can make it as hard as the road and mow the grass real short and it will answer. I bought the outfit the other day. Went to Smeltzer's and tried to buy and they asked me $25.00. Got on a car and went out to Montgomery Ward's and got the same outfit for $13.20. How is that for five cents? I am going to have it ready by Labor Day.

Mamma said tell you she is going to have a chicken dinner that day and shall expect you all to attend. Be sure and remember that. We'll look for you in time for dinner on Labor Day. Not town dinner but midday meal, see? So be sure and come.

Yes, of course Ethel had to take me to church. She always does her sisterly duty by me, but I don't care. I had to go home that day and tried to get the Southern at Sheffield but missed. So I went to Dodson and phoned and Papa came for me. Houchens didn't leave until 12:00 P.M. that night.

I looked for Aunt Ella to tell him to set the milk bottle out or throw the morning paper up the steps, but she didn't. I guess I'm not telling tales for he had a foghorn cough and all the neighbors could tell when he left.

Now be sure and come out on Labor Day. I saw Bill downtown Friday but didn't get a chance to talk to him. If you think it is necessary, I'll send them a special invitation with a map of the road.

Let me know if you decide not to come. You owe me four pages.

Sincerely,

Harry

Grandview, Mo.

Dear Bessie: September 2, 1911

I am enclosing you a rough map of the road. You'll notice that there are two rock roads branch[ing] off going east before you get to Grandview.

Remember to go south every time the rock road goes south and you can't miss the place. Start from 47th and Troost and come as directed, and when you have come eleven or twelve miles you'll come to a long maple grove on the left of the road with a cemetery in front—and that is where you get off.

Wish you'd come to dinner. We'll be looking out for you so be sure and come.

This is all I could find to write on and the low-down, ornery paper hangers (who promised to come two weeks ago) came today and I have to run.

Sincerely,

Harry

Grandview, Mo.
Dear Bessie: September 5, 1911

It was quite a disappointment when you couldn't come yesterday. I really worked all day Sunday getting that court ready for you. We also had a supply of watermelons on hand. But you can make it some Saturday and Mamma says you must come to dinner next time. The weather was fine out here. It merely sprinkled in the forenoon and after dinner it was cool and nice as could be. The autos were thick. I guess Independence must be better than we anyway. They seem to land more moisture anyway.

It seems as though it is impossible for me to ever get to an Independence fair. I have never been to one. I had made up my mind to be present sure this time. Mamma made up her mind she'd have a couple of rooms papered about two weeks ago—so she had 'em emptied and all torn up, and the paper hangers came last Saturday. I went after them every day in between and so, of course, missed the fair. I had made up my mind to go Saturday and let the hangers go hang and they came. Maybe if I'd done that before we'd have had them sooner.

My insurance company settled for the broken pin the other day and now I shall have to go to work in earnest. We begin sowing wheat next week and it is a job. I guess we'll sow about 160 acres.

Say, be sure and save me a piece of those cakes. There is nothing better than cake but more cake and the same is true of pie! So be sure and save me a piece. The devil's food you know would be doing its full duty if I ate it. Don't you think?

I told you before you owed me four pages and you sent them, but you didn't seem to know what I meant. I had sent you four, therefore you owed me the same, see? You do this time too. Although I'll not object to eight or nine.

I am trying to rake up some business in town the end of the week, and if I do I'll phone you.

Write when you can to

Sincerely,
Harry

Telephoning Bess seems to have been complicated by more than just the problems of party lines. The Kansas City area had a dual telephone system, and subscribers to the Home Telephone Company could not connect with the Bell system. Public places had to provide not only both lines but also the corresponding phone books. (Wise businessmen advertised "We're on both phones.") At the outset of their courtship Bess and Harry each had the Home system. By 1918 Bess had switched to the Bell. Telephoning in those days also meant going through an operator, and after waiting as long as five minutes one was likely to get a wrong number. Direct dialing came in only after World War I.

Grandview, Mo.

Dear Bessie: September 15, 1911

You owe me a letter and I am going to write you a note and tell you so. Do you know what has been hurting me all week? I actually came away and *forgot* that *Columbian* you gave me. I thought of it as soon as I got on the car and kicked myself from there home. I suppose I shouldn't tell you I forgot but should cook up some long-winded excuse for not taking it. But forget I did and I am sorry. Save it for me and I'll get it if you'll let me have it.

Do you know I believe His Majesty himself has a special grudge against us. A horse fell on Papa Tuesday and broke one of the small bones in his left foot. He'll be laid up for a month the M.D. says. I suppose as soon as he gets around again I'll take another turn. I am going to have the blacksmith make me some cast iron shoes and sox. They will name us the Insurance Grabbers Association sure now. Don't ever take out any accident insurance. Things begin to happen at once when you do. We'd worried along all our lives without any and a certain gentleman with a large vocabulary and a bent for using it roped us last December. We've been having accidents in job lots since. I really don't know but what those policies had something to do with the dry year.

Bess Wallace, around the age of twenty-five, on the porch of 219 North Delaware. *Harry S. Truman Library*

I got a copy of that red *Life* last Saturday night and am sending it to you "under another cover," as the ad men say of a particularly heinous offense in circulars.

I was in K.C. today buying small pieces of a grain drill. If you buy a whole one, it costs $75; if you buy it by the piece, it costs $275. A binder whole costs $150, in small bits $600. They always intend to sell as many repairs as they can, too.

I tried to get into connection with you over the Bell but couldn't and didn't have time to try over the Home. You owe me two letters.

Sincerely,
Harry

Grandview, Mo.
September 16, 1911

Dear Bessie:

I got your letter this morning and you should give me a mark for being prompt, to say the least. I wrote you a note day before yesterday to thank you for the magazine I didn't take. By all means save me *Kennedy Square*. It sounds good. I shall try to keep my mind on it and not forget it. Don't you dare offer me forty cents. I hadn't thought of it. You may give me some of the pictures in payment if you must pay.

By all means bring Bill's cousin when you come out. I shall have to give that court another discing and rolling before you come. You see I have suddenly become "boss" again, all against my will and inclination, and tennis is a dream for the present. The grass grows though, always, and the court is beginning to turn green. Grandviewites are too lazy to come down and play after I have done all the work. Besides, we are an ignorant bunch and will have to have some expert instruction before we play to do any good. A person might as well read Green's *History of England* to learn tennis as to read Spalding's book when you know nothing of the game. We'll produce some champeens though someday.

It flatters me terribly to have the Miss Macks inquiring about me after this long time. I should like to see them. Which reminds me that Vladimir de Pachmann and Lhévinne are going to play in K.C. this winter. Lhévinne is the best on the globe, I think, and when they come if I have a sound walking machine and you have the inclination, we'll go hear them. One is a Russian and the other a Dutch Pole. So they can tear up a piano from the keyboard side.

There is yet another week of wheat sowing and then some maybe. We didn't get started until Thursday on account of Sunday's rain. It sounds like a joke for the fields to be too muddy to work this year.

I am glad Frank landed the job but I am sorry it prevents him from coming out. Maybe he can get off that day. If you'll let us know in time, we'll give you buttermilk that's real for lunch.

Miss Grace Waggoner went home yesterday. Her beau goes to Kansas U. and she said he only got home twice a month and she'd promised to be there. I tried to get her to let me phone him to come out here but she wouldn't. Mamma says she is going to build a Young Hotel and hire a chef pretty soon. We have two cousins coming out from K.C. in about a week to stay a week. We have a gent and his kid billed for dinner today but they haven't arrived yet at 3:00 P.M.

I like to have company, for we'd die of lonesomeness if no one came. If a Sunday passes without someone coming, it seems like there is a screw loose or something gone wrong.

I shall have business in Kansas City this week if I have to make it. I shall call up and if it is all right shall come over.

Miss Maggie Phelps owes me a dinner and I am going to try and get that in sometime soon. She wrote me from Texas that she is an excellent cook and I told her I didn't believe it. She is going to show me.

Well I hope you'll consider this worth an answer and keep my magazine and book till I come for them.

Sincerely,
Harry

Grandview, Mo.
September 26, 1911

Dear Bessie:

I am glad you and the rest had a good time Saturday. If we'd known soon enough, we'd have tried to make it better. I hope you can come out some afternoon and try our hilly tennis court. If I could only persuade the road overseer to come in with the grader we [would] have a level court. I am sorry you got laid out on the road home.

I have been taking a layoff with tonsilitis since Sunday. I had to go to K.C. yesterday and get a new pair of glasses. I get stung for a new pair about every two years. This time it was for ten good dollars. Just carfare to St. Louis. I don't suppose I'd have gone if I could on account of my sore throat. I went around to Volker's to take Ruth to lunch and she couldn't go until one o'clock. I sat around for about fifteen minutes and then told her I'd go home at 1:45 and take her some other day. Soon as I got home Mamma began doping me and I can neither hear nor see to do any good today. The deafness is from quinine and blindness from new specs. It is necessary to get used to a new pair, and I always wish for the old ones for a week. If I could get them, I'd throw these away. But I can't. Mary has another girl visiting her. She is from Chicago and has asked Mary to visit her next winter. Her brother was cashier in the Martin City Bank for a while. He conferred all the Masonic degrees I have upon me.

I fear this is a very, very dull epistle but it is the best I can do today.

Say, sometimes I have to go to K.C. at 9:00 A.M. and come home at five-thirty. Would you ever care to meet me and go to the Orpheum and then discharge me at Sheffield? The show is always more enjoyable if you have someone along to help appreciate it, don't you think? I like high-brow shows sometimes but I like the Orpheum all times. We had a fat man and his fat wife for dinner yesterday. He ate ten biscuits. He's my Battery friend, Elliott. His wife is a good cook, if she is fat, and I sometimes eat with them. They treat me just as fine as can be and we were glad to have them out. Next Sunday we have a bank teller and cashier billed for dinner. I really don't know what would happen if we didn't have someone for Sunday dinner.

Next time you come out, come on Sunday morning, stay for dinner and play tennis all afternoon. That is, if your religion is not against it. I see no harm in Sunday tennis provided there is no admission fee. Lee's Summit is a pokey town if they ran you out at ten-thirty. I bet the owner of that big car consigned me to regions noted for heat when he broke down. But it would have been nearly the same had you gone by K.C., for you weren't over six miles from here when you broke down. An auto is an unstable conveyance at times.

My head aches and I've run out of juice, as the electrician would say, and I hope you'll consider this a half letter—if not a letter and a half—and worth an answer.

Sincerely,
Harry

Grandview, Mo.
October 1, 1911

Dear Bessie:

I got your letter day before yesterday and I certainly appreciate it. I hope your finger has healed all right.

While I think of it, *A Man Without a Country* was written by Rev. Ed. Ev. Hale. I am sure because I saw an extract from it Friday night. Would you care to see *Pinafore*? It comes to the Shubert next week I think. I thought if you cared to go to a matinee, we could go out and see the Miss Macks afterwards. I don't know on what days they'll have their afternoon shows but whichever one suits you best would be all right with me. You know, being a farmer I am partial to Saturday.

Vivian and I went to the dedication of the new Masonic Temple in K.C. last night. The Grand Master and all the big guns were out. The Grand Master always wears a tall plug hat and a large gold jewel on his left breast. When he happens to be a large man he makes a very imposing figure, but a short one or a fat one is funny. The present one is tall and slim. With the high hat he looks to be about seven feet. But he's not as tall as I am when I got up against him last night. The one last year was a G.M. every inch. He was about six feet and weighed over two hundred. He also had a foghorn voice, a young-looking face, and lots of gray hair.

They unwound yards and yards of pink tape last night and it was all very solemn. They always dedicate a Masonic Temple with corn, wine, and oil, pouring each one on with solemn invocations. This one is the finest in Missouri or most anywhere in the west. It is a York Rite Temple.

I hope you and all who were with you can come out some Sunday. We are going to have a whole bunch of cousins out here either the fifteenth or twenty-second, I don't know which. If you'd come then, I could assure you something to eat for I'd make each cousin prepare a dish and they are all fair cooks. That is when Ethel and Nellie are coming. We'll sure have a roughhouse then.

You need not worry about our front lawn. There wasn't a scrap on it. You know we rolled up the paper and burned it (that is, we burned it next day), and the wind and chickens took good care of anything else that was left. It didn't look as if you'd been here at all the next morning.

I am glad you like the Orpheum idea. I'll put it into execution the first day I am in. I guess I'll have to change my eyes again. They don't work worth a cent. I wore an old pair of rimless nose glasses I have last night in preference to the new ones. They nearly pinched my nose off, too. With all that, they don't stay on good. They'll stay on awhile and then they'll begin sliding forward and my head will begin going back until finally I look like a grenadier in Napoleon's armee [sic]. The specs fall off and I take a new start and do it all over again.

I cut corn all day yesterday. That's a job that causes a fellow to earn his keep. We don't cut it all by hand, but two rows have to be cut on each shock row. Then we hitch a horse to a machine and cut. I was cutting the first two rows. I scratched my face and wore out my overalls at the knee.

Bankers like men with overalls worn out at the knees and elbows. Uncle Harrison said there was a stranger went into the bank of Lee's Summit in the panic of 1893 and told the cashier he wanted to borrow $400 and he wanted it right away. He got the money and when the president asked the cashier why he let the man have it, he said that the man's knees and elbows were worn out through patches but the seat of his trousers was perfectly good—and he knew he'd be good for $400, and he was.

My cold is nearly gone. I can almost hear a coupling pin fall at three feet on a wooden floor.

Please let me know what you think of going to *Pinafore* and then the Miss Macks'. They say DeWolf Hopper and a whole constellation are in the cast.

Please remember you owe me a letter and answer as quickly as you did last time.

Sincerely,
Harry

Grandview, Mo.

Dear Bessie: October 7, 1911

. . . I went to Lodge last night and conferred a Second Degree. It was in the New Temple and Temple Lodge, the largest Masonic Lodge in Missouri. There were only about twenty-five present though. I immediately bought a *Star* when I found I could not come over—to see if there was a Lodge meeting, because I felt not like a show after the chuckled-headed way I talked to you about not getting to come down. You can surely bet on Harry to say the wrong thing in the right place. Of course I was disappointed in not getting to come. After, I thought it sounded as if I didn't care or not from what I said. But I merely had in mind that any entertainment you might go to would be more enjoyable to you than trying to get a conversation out of me, see?

Corn, wine, and oil came down from King Solomon. He used them in his dedications and therefore so do we; and the Masonic fraternity does everything in form, and by ritual, that is why I said they'd unreel some pink tape.

Mamma and I went to the parade. She took a notion she'd go on Monday and we went to Dr. Lester's and sat on their front porch. They live at 10th and Forest, so we saw the parade at about eight-thirty and weren't crowded a bit. It looked just like the first one I ever saw on streetcars. I wouldn't give a copper cent to see it anymore. There were people who paid fifty cents just to see a ten-minute electric show pass. Dr. Lester rented his yard to a man for ten dollars and he charged people twenty-five cents to stand up and look. I told Mamma we had our nerve to go to Dr. Lester's for supper and then help fill up his front porch, and she said he also had his nerve to come out here at 8:00 P.M. and tell her he'd had no supper, as he had done several times. So she let one cancel the other. They treated us fine and had a good spread too.

I have to go to a sale today and I'd as soon take a beating. All a person does is stand around and bemoan the rotten crop year and figure on how much corn he'll have and whether it will be best to feed the hogs as run them over until spring. Then when he takes a notion he'll buy a bargain, his good neighbors will take the same notion—and the auctioneer will sell him the bargain five dollars higher than it ever will be worth. Anyway I am going. There is a fellow who wants to go to South Dakota and register for a claim. He had me get all necessary information for him yesterday. He is trying to get me to go with him, but I think it would just be fifteen good dollars thrown away. I am also going to try and buy a hog but I bet I don't.

Vivian Truman and Luella, on the Grandview farm. *Harry S. Truman Library*

Noel is quite a distinguished place now. Did you ever notice that if you suddenly get acquainted with a place you never heard of, it will always be bobbing up and you will be continually seeing it in print? Be sure and make me some of those pictures, for I sure want them. Myra Colgan gave Mary a Kodak album last year, and I am sure those pictures will materially add to its look and distinction.

I am dead sure I can make those cousins cook if you'll only come. I am going to tell you a deep, dark secret. Please don't let it out until you hear it from Ethel because dear brother might manhandle me. He is going to get hooked up on the twenty-eighth. Has already rented him a farm and is going to start in business right. He sure is getting a fine girl. She has red hair. It is very dark though. We can't get a thing out of Vivian without just pumping and prying, and then what we get isn't worth the trouble. But I know it's going to be the twenty-eighth. I suppose they'll tell everyone soon anyway.

Don't you forget *H. M. S. Pinafore*. I have never seen it either. So I am sure we can enjoy it immensely. I think we'd better have dinner downtown, don't you? It will take so long to go to Independence and back so many times.

You sure are prompt with the reply and I thank you. Keep it up. I am going to try and come in one day next week and will let you know at least two days ahead, and then maybe I can have some luck.

Sincerely,

Harry

Grandview, Mo.

Dear Bessie: October 16, 1911

You see I am writing that note with very exact promptitude. How do you like that for stilted English?

I have forgotten whether I told you I enjoyed the dinner yesterday, but I most certainly did. It was so good that I did not want any lunch until I arrived home at 1:15 P.M. I don't ever remember of having enjoyed myself more than I did yesterday and Saturday. I hope you'll let me repeat the offense at no very distant date.

I am getting ready for South Dakota today. I rather think I'd better hunt up my overcoat this morning. I saw my Colgan cousin yesterday after I left Independence and he is going with me. We'll have enough to play a good game of cards anyway tomorrow night on the train.

I bet there'll be more bohunks and "Rooshans" up there than white men. I think it is a disgrace to the country for those fellows to be in it. If they had only stopped immigration about twenty or thirty years ago, the good Americans could all have had plenty of land and we'd have been an agricultural country forever. You know as long as a country is one of that kind, people are more independent and make better citizens. When it is made up of factories and large cities it soon becomes depressed and makes classes among people. Every farmer thinks he's as good as the President or perhaps a little bit better. When a man works for a boss, he is soon impressed with how small he is and how great the boss is until he actually believes it is so and that money makes the world go round. It does I guess in very large cities.

Say this *letter* is as dry as a Baptist preacher's sermon. Just skip it and write me one—that is what I am after. We have a preacher out here now who never did see a grammar: He talks South Missouri in the pulpit. It makes a great impression on his hearers, I tell you.

Please consider coming out on the last Sunday in this month if the weather permits and let me know if you can. Mamma said it would be all right, the more the merrier. But any Sunday that suits you will be all right with us. Only let me know in time so I can plow and *harry* [harrow] the tennis court.

Now you owe me a letter.

Most sincerely,

Harry

Grandview, Mo.

Dear Bessie: October 22, 1911

Your good letter came along with some postcards I sent from up north. I beat the U.S. mail by a day. That new stationery certainly does look good. I don't blame Frank and George for helping themselves.

Would you like to hear what we did going and coming from notorious Gregory? I am going to tell you anyway because it is on my mind and I shall have to unburden it.

To begin with, it was just like riding a crowded streetcar for a day and night. We took a sleeper to Omaha going and coming. From Omaha up, trains were running every hour or so all day Tuesday, Wednesday, and until Thursday noon. You see, the R.R. companies from one end of the country to the other give special rates on first and third Tuesdays of each month. We got to Omaha Wednesday morning at a quarter to eight and left at eight. They had to call special police to handle the crowd at the Union Station. We managed to get seats in the last coach. There were 687 people on the train and nearly all were nice-looking Americans. I only saw about a dozen bohunks all the way there and back. I never got so tired looking at yellow cars in my life. The Chicago and Northwestern uses all yellow coaches. We played pitch and seven-up all day, taking turn about at each eating station because we didn't dare to leave our seats all at once. Murray Colgan's wife [Murray was a brother of Mary and Myra] fixed us the finest lunch a person could want anyway, so we didn't get hungry.

At nearly every station, we met trains coming back. People on them would yell Sucker! Sucker! at us and men on our train would do the same. One fellow hollered for us to go right on through to a very hot place. It sounded like a pretty good place to be up there, it was so cold.

We got to Gregory at about 10:30 P.M. Then began a chase for a place to sleep. The *hotel man* finally agreed to give us a cot apiece in the writing room, which was some luxury I tell you. There were people who sat up all night. After we'd cinched our rooms we went and registered at the Cow Palace, a wooden shack. It takes about one minute to do it. There were about twenty notaries inside of a hollow square. I bet there was more swearing going on there than there ever will be in one place again. I really don't know what a Quaker would have done. They didn't ask you to swear, but just filled out the papers—and you were sworn before you knew what was happening. I registered for a soldier friend so that I have a chance to get a 160 and half of another. There are about four-hundred claims that are worth from $8,000 to $12,000 each. Of course I'll draw one of them. Then there are several thousand worth from $40 to $4,000, depending of course on location.

There is an old Sioux Indian woman on the reservation who is 123 years old. She looks like Gagool in Rider Haggard's *King Solomon's Mines.* I didn't see her but I have her picture.

I saw all of Gregory I cared to in about an hour and a half. It is a strictly modern town of about 1,500.

We left there at 6:00 A.M. the next day. Played draw pitch all day to see who'd pay for orchestra seats at the Orpheum in Omaha that night. I had to pay of course. Only won one game in seventeen, as eighteen played. The other two broke even on the balance. We saw a fine show though. The headliners are in K.C. this week.

I could have called up your Omaha friend easily because we were there from 7:00 P.M. until 10:45 Thursday evening. Omaha is a fine town I think. Every street is as wide as Grand Avenue.

I was so sleepy when I got in the train coming from Omaha to Kansas City that I thought nothing could keep me awake. But there was an old woman and her daughter had the berth opposite me. The old lady had asthma or some wheezy complaint. When she wasn't wheezing or snoring she was quarreling with her daughter about whether she could sleep on a Pullman or not. They almost came to blows over it once. The wheezy one was very fat and had an upper of course. The porter had to labor manfully to get her up and down. He managed it without disaster though.

I am glad I went. I have as good chance to win as anyone. Even if I don't I had fun enough to pay for going. A person can have a good time most anywhere when he has two congenial spirits along. I sure did. Murray and Homer Pittinger are both all right. They are both strictly temperance and enjoy about the same things I do so we had a good time.

Please remember that I had to get this off my mind, and if it is not a good letter it is all I had to offer this time. Write when you can. I am going to be bro Pete's [Vivian's] best man next Saturday.

Most sincerely,
Harry

Grandview, Mo.
October 27, 1911

Dear Bessie:

Pipe de stationery [sic]. Mary got very tired of my using hers so I had to invest. I never have time to wait for an initial and I always think I'll never be in town for a month (I am generally back in a couple of days), so I just take it as it comes.

It seems that I did not even get in on the forty-dollar claims. I never could draw anything though. Not even the lady I wanted. You see I am born under Neptune or some other far distant and unlucky star. I guess it's good for me that I haven't Houch's pessimistic disposition. It seems best to be silly and grow fat. Just keep imagining that my luck will change someday.

We are in one fine flurry out here today. I wish I had an omnibus or a moving van. There will be six cousins and an uncle for me to haul tomorrow, besides all the family. Papa and I bought out the butcher shop in Grandview this morning. He decided that we could not kill a pig until next week, so we had to stock up. He sold seventeen dozen *pimkins* (not pumpkins) in K.C. yesterday. One of the hired men is going to take them in tomorrow morning. He'll leave here at 4:00 A.M. Wouldn't you like the job?

We have about a carload [of] the mussy pie fruit so we won't starve this winter if we have to live on nothing but pumpkin pie. Dockstader says he just hates to eat pumpkin pie because it musses up his ears so. He has enormous ears, and I don't blame him for being shy of getting them mussed up because it is a job to thoroughly clean an ordinary pair. I went to town with Ruth this morning. She said for me to kiss the bride for her. Aunt Ella told me to do it for her and I'll have to do it for myself. I'll get her between Vivian and me so he can't sock me one during the operation. Don't you feel sorry for that poor girl? I wish I'd thought and grown me a nice soup strainer. There is a man out here who has one that he can tie behind his neck. A man with such a mustache ought to be in Barnum's show nowadays.

I am sorry that Miss Nellie's rich friends had to come on next Sunday. If you'd all have come out we could have a toy charivari. (Is that how you spell it?) Pete and his frau will be here to dinner. It is the custom of the creeks and hollows to have one of those barbarous things whenever anyone gets married. I guess everyone in south Jackson County will come to this one. I went to one once and got a good enamel dishpan belonging to the man's mother and simply beat it to death. She is the third cousin of mine by marriage and I had to buy a new one. It is the right thing to have shotguns, cowbells, circular saws, tin pans, and every other known noisemaker. The racket has to be kept up until the gentleman and his bride show themselves. He must pass cigars and she hands around candy or cake. Everyone is satisfied then, a good social time is had and we all wonder who'll be next. Woe be unto the man who fails to show up and set up. He'll be visited night after night with noise and finally branded a snob and a cheap screw.

It is an ornery custom but it has to be stood for out here. Everyone goes, girls and all. We always have a good time and generally land a very fair feed.

They had one north of here one night. Vivian went but I didn't. Someone stuck a fellow with a sharp stick and he jumped into a pail of swill. He has been constantly reminded of it ever since. He got married himself last night.

I hope you have a good time at the Soldier show. I know you will though. My head hasn't quite gone down yet at what you said when I left.

This letter is too long-drawn-out, nevertheless you owe me one.

Sincerely,

Harry

Grandview, Mo.

November 1, 1911

Dear Bessie:

I am most awful glad you think a letter to me worthwhile. They are more than worthwhile to me. You can never guess how glad I am to get them.

I really didn't mean to put my principal desire in the past tense. That is something that will never be past with me. My grammar was at fault, that's all.

I suppose Ethel has told you all about the wedding. I was scared nearly to death and so was Vivian. Luella was as calm as if she'd been married a dozen times before. She is more like my Grandmother Young than anyone I know. If my dear Pete doesn't make a success with her to help him, he should be blotted out. Everyone is so well satisfied with the match something surely will happen. Even

Ethel and Nellie Noland, in the yard of 216 North Delaware. Bess's house, 219, is in the background. *Harry S. Truman Library*

her grandmother thinks Vivian is almost good enough for her, and Mamma says she's too good for him. They are down to pa-in-law's tonight. Vivian actually told me that they were going to town tomorrow to buy the furniture they need. I guess they'll be at home about Monday or Tuesday. The charivari is set for Saturday I think. If it is, I'll not be present for I am coming to Independence if you'll be at home. I am going with Mary and Ethel and Nellie to the Shubert Saturday afternoon and I'd like very much to come down that night, provided of course that you have nothing better to do.

I want an auto so badly tonight I really don't know what to do. I have a special invitation to assist in the dedication of a new Lodge at Swope Park [in Kansas City]. I shall stay at home because I'd simply be a chunk of ice by the time I drove to 67th Street in a buggy. I couldn't go on the train because Papa and I had to pull up the carrots and beets and bury them this afternoon so they wouldn't freeze. If ever I get my debts paid and then have something left, I'm going to invest it in a benzine buggy, as the hobos say. Then I suppose I'll have the debts to pay over. Just imagine how often I'd burn the pike from here to Independence. I guess you'd better be glad I haven't one for I'd simply make myself monotonous to you. I guess there'll not be much danger of my coming too often this winter for I'll have to work for true, Ethel to the contrary notwithstanding. I always make it a point to invite them out when things are arranged so I haven't anything to do but tease and torment them. That is how Ethel arrived at her conclusion.

The W.M. series begins soon I see. Don't you forget you have pianist dates to go with me. Pianists are all I can stand this winter. I am crazy about any kind of pretty music but of course I can appreciate pianists most. Mary has been practicing on a Mozart sonata that has the most beautiful melody I know of. It makes you think of Greek and Roman fairy stories. Did you ever sit and listen to an orchestra play a fine overture and imagine that things were as they ought to be and not as they are? Music that I can understand always makes me feel that way. I think some of the old masters must have been in communication with a fairy goddess of some sort. That is, Mozart, Chopin, and Verdi were. Wagner and Bach evidently were in cahoots with Pluto. Did you ever know that some of those men wrote the worst trash imaginable for potboilers? Raff has over a thousand compositions and about nine hundred are fit for nothing. He'd write one every time he got hungry. I guess you can't blame the poor man. That is the reason rulers should be wise enough to pick the geniuses and pension them so they can do their best. It seems to me that they would be easy enough picked out because they always beat their wives, or run away with some other man's. Wouldn't Reno be full of pensioners?

I hope you'll be at home Saturday. If you're not, it'll be my loss of course. I'll phone in the morning sometime after I get to town.

You see, I am sending you the other half of that sheet I tore in two before.

I want you to show me some stenciling when I come down. I never saw any I guess, even [though] it is ancient. If I have, I knew it not. You owe me a letter now. Next time I'll wind up and fill two full sheets. Now you know what's coming, so beware.

Sincerely,

Harry

Grandview, Mo.

Dear Bessie: November 14, 1911

I made a threat to send you two full sheets when I wrote last. I doubt my ability to do it now. Anyway you'd better be glad I can't. Some people can write oh so entertainingly but I am not one of them. My thoughts arrive in jerks if they ever arrive. Jerks cannot be put into very excellent English.

When your letters come they always run along so smoothly that I wonder how you do it. I can't.

I got home Monday afternoon and found everyone holding down a good seat around the fire. Sometimes you can do as you please on a farm. Except about 5:00 A.M. Then I never do as I please. My dear pap can never see why anyone should want to sleep after that unearthly hour. It doesn't make so much difference in summer but winter it's as dark as Egypt, and on a cold morning the bed is a mighty good place. I played one on him Friday night. Mary and I went down to Aunt Emma's to supper (dinner she said) and I came back on the midnight train. I took everything, even my hat, upstairs. Next morning I came down after breakfast and went out to the field to shuck corn and Papa was as surprised as I wanted him to be. Sunday morning and Monday he went up to be sure I was not present.

I managed to get a couple of seats for Mr. Whiteside yesterday morning, for Saturday night. So be sure and don't forget it. If press notices amount to anything I guess he'll be worth seeing. We ought to take out a little fire insurance though because he's a hoodoo on fires. He was at the Coates when it went up. The Auditorium caught fire once when he was there and he was also present at several fires in adjoining towns. They always put on an extra fire guard when he comes.

I forgot to tell you how much I am enjoying those books you lent me. The Indian story was great. I have just started Mary Johnston's and am saving *My Lady of Doubt* for a climax. I am going to bring the first ones you let me have home Saturday evening if I have time to work my brains before the train goes. Generally I have just five minutes less than time to get the train, and leave in such a rush that memory does not exist at the time.

I have been to Belton and back since I wrote that last sentence. Papa wanted to go look at some hogs up on Mr. Johnson's place. We arrived there before the owner and found several pigs gone to the happy hunting ground. We did not buy any of those still on four legs because our own are healthy and it would be pocketbook suicide to bring home sick ones.

People who are fond of prating about exhilarating (I looked in the spelling book for it) drives in the autumn air should have had one this morning in a spring wagon. The wind blew about fifty miles an hour from the southwest while we were going up and switched to the northwest coming back. My fingers are as stiff as ten-penny nails yet. Really though it is a fine day. A person can sit by the fire and admire the beauties of nature all right. I suppose these nature fakers use limousines with oil heaters to do their riding in. If they had to face a gale in a spring wagon it would soon dampen some of their enthusiasm.

Vivian and his frau took Mamma and went to Belton this afternoon to buy a cooking stove. They will be ready to move in when they get back with it. I told him he should have bought as important a piece of furniture as that the very first thing. A well-fed person is generally a happy one. I once read a story about a band of socialists who were going to buy an island for ideal purposes. The crew of the ship on which they sailed became socialists and the dear idealists had to go to work and sail the ship or starve in mid-ocean. It knocked their theories into a cocked hat. Parlor talk and bedrock-work or starve are different propositions.

I bet you think I am working awful hard to make a letter out of this. I am. But I am doing it to get one from you. Please remember that.

I shall see you Saturday evening about seven-thirty. I guess that will be soon enough to start because we have aisle seats unless the salesman prevaricated. So if we arrive at the end of the overture we won't be walked over.

I should be very glad to go out to Mr. Pritchet's (is that how you spell him?) sometime. When I get my black ponies broken I am going to come down overland and take you a drive if you'll go behind as slow a thing as a horse. That will probably be next summer. I am about to run over [the page] so I'd better quit. You owe me a letter.

Most sincerely,
Harry

Grandview, Mo.
November 22, 1911

Dear Bessie:

Your letter was a very agreeable surprise this morning. I really didn't expect it so soon. I am awful glad you took the notion to be so prompt.

I did miss that chicken and egg special on Sunday night by a very small margin. The girls were up and I stayed fifteen minutes over there. They generally have their clock about half an hour fast. I was going on that and it was only a quarter fast. I was too lazy to consult my own timepiece so I got left. It was just 11:55 when I got to 8th and Wyandotte so I stayed uptown. If I had been right sure I wouldn't be in the way, I'd have tried to meet you. As it was, I went home just thirty minutes after I got up, without any breakfast. So you see how very energetic I am.

I am very sorry to hear that Miss Dicie is still not looking her best. I hope her heart will soon mend so she can use it for its real purpose. I wish I had her gift of gab (don't ever tell her I said it that way) for the next few weeks. I'd certainly talk money out of friends and enemies alike. I believe if Mary can get fifty or sixty subscriptions, she can win the car. If I see she is going to come pretty close on the windup, I am going to use a little graft but what she gets it. It would be worth fifty or sixty dollars even if it is only a Ford.

I was assistant wash lady yesterday. You ought to see me in that role. Since our nigger woman busted a beer bottle over her old man's head and ran away, we have had to do our own washing. There are some drawbacks to farm life. That is one of them.

We had a four-legged visitor to our hen house Monday night. He killed a chicken and then walked into a trap put there for the purpose.

The hired man skinned him for his fur. I wouldn't skin one for forty dollars. This fellow's name is Booney McBroom. You can search George Eliot, Mary Jane Holmes, and Augusta J. before you find a name that sounds as well or fits so nicely. Ethel can give you an excellent description of him.

Please don't let Nellie know you have one of her Sappho pictures. She'll most certainly murder me. I only borrowed that one when she wasn't looking, intending to return it the same way. I forgot it as I might have known I would. It certainly is a good thing my head is securely attached. If I could get it off, I'd forget it somewhere. I'm just scared to death all the time for fear I'll forget to do something I say I'll do. When a person gets to that stage he evidently has college absentmindedness. It is a sign of age they say. Ethel says she took a vase of flowers from her desk and threw the water in the wastebasket and the flowers in the sink. That probably was only concentration on some other subject. Maybe I can say the same about Nellie's picture.

I hope you'll get those pictures done without interruption tonight. Still, I don't blame the boys for coming. I know what I'd do if I lived where I could. Just wait till Mary wins that dinky car. I can do a day's work and then go thirty miles in an evening without inconvenience. I hope you enjoyed the nickel show.

I read *My Lady of Doubt* on the way home and enjoyed it immensely. Mr. Parrish is a big, fat ugly slob who you'd think ran a saloon instead of a charming love-story factory. His picture was in one of the papers not long ago as a rival of George Barr McCutcheon in the best-seller line. They say that George can write a novel with both hands at once and dictate another to a stenographer.

I have been reading the encyclopaedia (I have to look on the back to see how to spell it) to find out how to get the Dominical letter and the Roman indiction to a year. I don't know any more than I did before. Except that it takes a Newton or Archimedes to figure it. It talks of cycles, moons, and Julius Caesar until I don't know whether Caesar invented time or not. If a man wants to get his name everlastingly before the public, he ought to monkey with the calendar. Caesar did, so did Augustus and Napoleon and a lot more. Really though, this letter business is very interesting and dates from the year one and before. Every year has one, and leap years two. Next year it is G and F. The letters are used to find out when Easter comes and why.

Are you going to take me to church next Easter? It's a long ways off but you'd as well have a date way ahead. Tell your mother I enjoyed the supper Sunday evening very much, as she could very well see by the way I ate. I wish you'd let me come to see you sometimes on Sunday evening because I can't leave always on Saturday.

You owe me a letter.

Most sincerely,
Harry

Grandview, Mo.
Dear Bessie: November 28, 1911

Your letter came this morning and I am being *very* prompt. I hope you'll take notice.

Thanks for the Easter invitation. You probably know that 1912 is Leap Year. Easter is April 7. I did not find out by Julius' and Pope Gregory's method either, but from a patent medicine almanac. Farmers all still read them. I was digesting one when I ran across those Lunar Cycles, Roman Indictions, etc. ad lib. In Freemasonry we all learn that by the use of geometry astronomers fix the duration of years and cycles. I could never figure what cycles meant until I read the other junk.

You certainly must be some housekeeper to be able to loaf from nine till noon. I'll bet your mother doesn't worry about how things will go. I offer you my sympathy for the five relatives for Thanksgiving. I guess you'll enjoy it though. The sympathy is for you, not them.

Mamma's new daughter-in-law gave her a birthday dinner on Monday. Her birthday was Saturday, but Mary couldn't be present that day. We all jollied Luella so about not being able to get dinner by herself that she wouldn't allow Mary or her own sister to help her at all. She had one fine dinner too and I did it justice. So did her father.

How are you enjoying this cold wave? I am not enjoying it. We have some stock and I tell you it is some cold job to feed them every morning and night. I put as much off on the hired men as I possibly can, but still I have to get out every morning by myself and feed the horses. Papa does the milking. I don't mind after I get out as it isn't cold to work, but my it's awful to start.

What have you to be thankful for this year? I am thankful that we have an immense pile of wood *already sawed up*, have some coal, hogs enough to eat all winter, about two bushels of debts to pay (they say debts give a man energy— I ought to be a shining example of that quality if they do), and numerous other things too small to mention. I come of a worrying family but I do my best not to worry about anything. I believe that if a person cannot be happy in his present condition, he'll never be in any future one he may be in on this earth. That's my Aunt Susan's doctrine, and she's fat and happy at seventy-two with more on her shoulders than two men could ordinarily carry.

I got awful busy yesterday morning making a new gate for the back lot. I had it all cut out just like a dress pattern, got its insides all painted green before knitting it together, and was just about to give it an outside cast of the greenest green paint you ever saw when I had to go to dinner and then came the storm. My gate is still an unfinished product. I shall finish it the very first day paint will run, and then I am going to make two more. I always create quite a lot of comment when I go to use a saw and hatchet. People think what I make will be a left-handed job when it's done as well as in the making. Very often it is. Don't you think a violent green gate will look good with these white stone posts? I do. Besides I haven't any other kind of paint. Only have green by accident. Someone left a can in the smokehouse. I thought it was white and wished it was, too, until I opened it. It just matches bluegrass and will be all right for a back gate. It would never do for the front one. White is the only color safe to use there because sometimes it gets so dark out here that if a man was anyways dizzy at all, he never could see a green gate.

Do you think you could stand some Grand Opera? What? I have a desire to hear *Lucia di Lammermoor* or to see it, whichever is proper. Would you go? I don't believe that just one yelling match would be unenjoyable. I have never seen *Lucia* and I am curious to know how much torture one has to endure to get to hear the sextet. I hope not anymore than in *Florodora*. The whole works could be endured in that. If you would rather hear some other one though I'd just as leave. There are several good ones on the list. *Lucia* is Wednesday night I believe. I'd like to come in next Sunday evening if you don't object and you can say then if you'll go to any of them. If you are not going to be at home Sunday, you'll have to phone me for I am coming if you don't.

Papa is reading the farm press aloud for my benefit. I haven't heard a word for ten minutes. He always stops and asks what I think when some exceptionally large lie has been read. The farm papers are run for the advertising money and not for the subscriber. Their farm opinions are mostly rot. They'll tell some long-winded tale about the great record some guy has made feeding cattle and at the end you'll find that he's only fed three and that took all his time and a hired man's. What we want to know is how to feed a carload and not have anything to do.

Have you read the last *Everybody's*? The best story in it is by O. Henry and stops in the middle because Mr. Henry died before he finished it. I wish the publishers had done it for him. It is so unsatisfactory to have to use your own ending on somebody else's story. I have an idea that Mr. Mac got the hook, what do you think?

I'd give ten years off my life if I could handle the English language as O. Henry did. He and the immortal Mark (there are three, but I have only one) could just land the proper word every time. I do hope you won't find this letter as dull as it sounds to me. You should have had a good one this time but I fail as usual.

Tell George [Wallace, Bess's brother] that he can hunt rabbits out here whenever he wants to. He asked me about rabbits and I don't remember whether I asked him out or not. There aren't many but the few there are, are fat. Hope to see you Sunday.

Most sincerely,
Harry

Grandview, Mo.
Dear Bessie: December 14, 1911

I have been dissipating this week in Pleasant Hill. The town is wet and I really could. The Grand Lecturer of Missouri was there and Mr. Blair wanted me to go learn a lecture for him! I have a hard enough head so that when anything is pounded into it in a strong manner, it stays. That's why I got called on.

I am very glad I was, for one of the good old brothers down there took me home with him Tuesday night and gave me quail on toast for breakfast—all I could possibly hold, with a plate full of them still on the table when I left. It was a downright shame to leave them. Even the old Lecturer himself looked at them with regret. He came over specially for breakfast. This good brother begged me to stay Wednesday night, too, but I just had to come home. Papa says I only visit at home anyway. I am trying to make use of my time before we fire the hired men, for it'll be home for me then, sure enough. One reason why I attend these instruction Lodges is because when I visit K.C. Lodges or Independence [Lodge] they make it a point to call on the farmer Master to do something—and if it is bungled they say, oh well he's from the woods; it's to be expected. If it isn't, they won't believe I'm a farmer. I am though and I'm glad I am.

Miss Betty is very good to ask me to dinner next Sunday and I shall be glad to go, more than glad, because you are going. Then I'll still have a dinner at your house to look forward to. Tell your mother that I will be pleased to have lunch there Sunday provided it won't cancel a future dinner.

Do you suppose Allen Bros. could be persuaded to take us out and come for us without a J. P. Morgan fee? It would be much more convenient than a rig because there'd be no horse to look after.

My sister has an old beau in Pleasant Hill. I accidentally ran into him and it entered my head to play a joke on her. I got one of the boys in the instruction school to write her a card and sign the fellow's initials. I beat the card home, so I don't know how it'll turn out. She has never seen his pen ability, so if Vivian gets the card we'll have a circus for a while.

It certainly is nice of you to say that you enjoyed Lucy more than [*Il*] *Trovatore,* and I am glad. I enjoyed it more than any Grand Opera I ever heard. The Christmas wish hasn't struck me yet. But it never does until the day before. I guess everyone will be happy when it's over with. Life would not be worthwhile without a Christmas, though. Be sure and save me a fig. An atrocious pun could be made here but you must give me credit for not doing it.

Nellie Noland called me up the other day and her voice sounded as if she were in the last stages of acute excitement. The cause was a visit from some people who had entertained her at Standardoilville [Sugar Creek, Missouri]. She wanted me for tomorrow night and I have a Lodge election and Third Degree that night. The people decided not to come until next week and I am very thankful. I could neither turn Nellie down nor miss the meeting. I don't know what I'd have done. Probably sent my astral body one place and my temporal the other.

Girls go to an awful lot of work and worry for Christmas, don't they? They'll sew and paint and do fancy needlework for weeks and weeks just to give away. It just takes me about thirty minutes to do the whole stunt. I go grab two or three boxes of candy with pretty pink ribbons (I don't know if ribbon has one *b* or two) and holly on them and a piece of tin "joolry" for Mary and the job is done. I usually have to take my four girl cousins to a show Christmas week and then I'm square for a year.

Ethel says men have no business giving girls things to wear, even cousins, because they use such horrid taste in selection. I think she's embittered because a fellow gave her a solid gold bracelet with an amethyst (I wish Theodore Roosevelt spelling were in use) as big as an English walnut in it. It really wouldn't do for Liza Carilen to wear on the stage.

I have been reading *The Shuttle*, by Mrs. Burnett. It is not so good as *The Rosary*, by Mrs. Barclay, on practically the same subject. *Life* and *Adventure* are my standbys. *Adventure* is the only magazine printed on cheap paper that I can read. Some people like realism in their reading for entertainment but I want refined Diamond Dick in mine. I would nearly as lief read geometry as George Eliot or Browning. Sometime I am going to read *Daniel Deronda* though.

I hope to meet Mary in K.C. Saturday for the purpose of being bled for Christmas and will call you up about going to Mr. Pritchett's.

I certainly appreciate your making my Sunday invitation a standing one. Remember please that you are in debt to me for a letter, which I shall expect after I see you.

Most sincerely,

Harry

The following letter refers to a burden that was to distress Truman for several years: a family argument over the estate of Grandmother Harriet Louisa Young that developed into a nasty lawsuit. She had died in 1909 and left the farm to her son Harrison and daughter Martha Ellen Truman, cutting off the other children with the insult of five dollars apiece. Much to Truman's disgust and irritation, he watched the lawyers consume the hard-earned income of J.A. Truman & Son, Farmers.

Grandview, Mo.

December 21, 1911

Dear Bessie:

You cheated me out of two pages. Aren't you ashamed? If you only knew how glad I am to get them, you wouldn't be so short with them. I suppose I am too crazy about you anyway. Every time I see you I get more so, if it is possible. I know I haven't any right to but there are certain things that can't be helped, and that is one of them. I wouldn't help it if I could you know.

I guess you are lucky that you don't care—as even the best of fellow, which I am not, couldn't very well make a girl happy on nothing a week and a hat-full of debts. You see, I was fool enough or good enough, whichever way you look at it, to go in with daddy even on his debts. Say, don't ever mention that as no one knows he has any, especially his relatives. See?

Really though if I thought you cared, I bet I could win out anyway in spite of all the kin in creation.

This is a mighty poor Christmas letter but our dear relatives have succeeded in giving us the bluest Christmas since grandmother died. If you could see the allegations in the brief, you'd think my mother was the prime lady villain. It makes me so mad I could fight a boilermaker. They even accused our grandmother of being weak minded and most everything else—when she was the best businesswoman I ever expect to see. If we'd ever mentioned property to her, that itself would have finished us—as it should have done.

Bessie, if my dear men friends who invited themselves to dinner here Christmas go home on the afternoon train, I am going to try and see you Christmas evening if you are at home. I'll call up if I can, or if I can't, about five-thirty. But don't stay at home on my account because I may not get to come. I'll bring you a copy of *Richelieu* if I come. I got Edwin Booth's prompt copy for fifteen cents. It's a stirring play I tell you. Mamma and Mary are going to see *Julius* in the afternoon. Maybe you'll run into them.

I sent you a piece of tin jewelry the other day. I got it some time ago but found a busted link in the chain and had to have it renewed, so when I got it again I just sent it—that's why so early. With a Merry Christmas, I am, as always,
Your Harry

TWO

JUST ANOTHER YEAR

The year 1912 brought steady, if repetitive, activity to the Grandview farm. Harry Truman was busy from morning to night with endless rounds of plowing, planting, cultivating, and reaping, cutting hay and shucking corn. When the weather precluded these tasks, he butchered pigs, all the while caring for cows and horses and mules. Evenings he wrote to Bess, and when he could he made the long, tedious trip to Independence and back.

But the work did not seem to go anywhere. The year 1912, itself, which marked a half-dozen years on the farm for Harry, was the sort of even number that pointed only to more of the same. He was twenty-eight years old, and routine hung heavy on his young shoulders. Moreover, his courtship of Bess had settled into a pattern, with no prospect of the speedy culmination he had envisioned the preceding year. There were other disappointments; he went off to New Mexico, where he hoped Uncle Harrison would be tempted to invest in cheap, good farmland as others had who were making quick fortunes. Uncle Harrison, however, was not much interested in faraway New Mexico. The year was marred also by the continued argument over the will of Harry's grandmother.

Grandview, Mo.
Dear Bessie: January 3, 1912
    . . . Where were you Tuesday about eleven-thirty? Someone was evidently talking the receiver off your phone. I had to go see our lawyer in the forenoon and I tried to call up to see if you'd go to the Orpheum, but for some reason never did connect up. I guess I'll not be able to come down Thursday, much as I'd like to. I fear you might carry out your threat about the speech and then I'll have to work today and tomorrow and Friday so I can say I got in half a week anyway. This new route around the sheet is entirely unintentional. I didn't discover until I went to turn it over that I was going backwards.

I am too lazy to start again and, besides, this variety of paper is getting scarce.

I shall have to come to Independence Saturday to swear that I have lived in Jackson County for the last five years, and if you will be at home that evening I'd be most awful glad. I went to Belton from K.C. yesterday and helped them install the officers of Belton Lodge. We will do the job at Grandview on Friday. If I hadn't already lost two days this week (and will lose another Saturday) and if it were not for that speech, I would see the same performance at Independence, but I have to stay at home sometimes.

I was Grand Marshal last night at Belton. You can see how it should be done on Thursday. I didn't do it that way. When the show was over I sneaked off to the hotel and stayed all night so I would not have to arise at an unearthly hour. Some one of the good brothers always takes me home with him when I stay in Belton. They are nearly all in business that requires their attention at an early hour. I have not had more than four hours sleep at one time since last Friday night. Therefore, the hotel.

Did you ever have a house party mostly girls? Well if you have, you know whether they sleep or not. You never heard such a racket in your life. It sounded like the ten-cent store on bargain day from Saturday morning until Monday afternoon. Of course I contributed my share of the noise, but my share was mostly in daylight. Five of the girls stayed in one room at night, and mine adjoined it on the east. It sounded at times as if a young earthquake had escaped and was endeavoring to enter my room through the solid wall. The girls said that one set wanted all the covers and the others wouldn't stand for it. We had a fine time, though, but as Macbeth would say, house parties murder sleep. I wish people wouldn't all try to have their parties on the same day. You know Miss Dicie and Miss Maggie hit the same date, and on Monday evening Mrs. Frank Blair at Belton had a dinner party and Miss Whiteman at Grandview also favored me with an invitation for a party that day. I already had her invitation when you called up. She doesn't know it, though, I am happy to say. If people at Grandview find out I pass them up to go to Independence, they'll think I'm stuck up. I'm not though because I'd pass up the whole state when I get a chance to come down there. Especially between now and February, because after that I'll have to stay at home every day but Sunday. Maybe you'll be glad of that but I won't.

How would you enjoy Mizzi Hojos on Saturday P.M.? That is, provided I am able to land some decent seats. Would you mind balcony no. 1, provided downstairs is all gone? I believe you said you were going to see Blanche Ring on Saturday afternoon. What is the reason I couldn't meet you somewhere after the show and go to dinner in K.C. and then to the show? Provided of course you could stand the Tea Cup Inn, for I'm too near busted for the Baltimore. Besides, they serve a tabled [table d'hôte] whatever-it-is dinner there, and I wouldn't have to bother my ear about what to order. I shall call you up tomorrow and tell you I can't come down tomorrow evening, and then we can discuss this arrangement. I hope you can go. Now you owe me a letter and a half. Be sure and answer the half.

Sincerely,
Harry

Grandview, Mo.

Dear Bessie: January 12, I think [1912]

My South Missouri Limited left Sheffield on the dot and was two hours late at Grandview, which I think is a record that would be hard to beat. There were only about twenty passengers and we had to do acrobatic stunts up and down the aisle and take turns at an old stove in one end of the car to keep warm. I didn't get cold, but there was a woman and a baby that did, at least the kid made a noise as if it was. Coming from the depot I really got too hot. You know I had a cap, mittens, and overshoes waiting for me and I walked as if His Majesty was behind me, which made me feel as if he was. Do you know they had quit looking for me and had eaten all the hot mince pie. That made me wish more than ever that I had stayed in Independence. Mary finally went and got me a piece that was cold and I managed to eat it. Just a half pie was all. Not all I ate—just all the pie I ate.

I have something I want to say now while it's on my mind. I think you look better in that black dress you wore Thursday evening than in anything I ever saw you wear. I intended telling you so when you wore it to the show in K.C. but the proper opportunity didn't appear. The *strawberry* blond isn't in it with you when you wear that dress. Or any other time for that matter. That sounds awful mushy don't it? It's not though when it is meant. Will you please tell me how you made that caramel dessert you had for dinner the time before this last when I was there? I can taste that from memory yet. It was undoubtedly nectar of the gods. I am going to coerce Mary into making me enough to founder on if you'll tell me how it's made.

How did Miss Jessie and Miss Dicie enjoy the show?

I guess the kids spread themselves on Friday night. I wish I'd stayed and gone again. It was so cold I had to postpone our Lodge meeting anyway. I really don't know what I am going to do if people take me for Mr. Brightman. I can't get over it some way. Aunt Ella said someone took me for Tom [illegible] when I was in Emery, Bird, Thayer's [K.C. department store] with Ethel just before Christmas. I really don't see what I've done to merit such treatment. Of course the other people may feel as badly over it as I do, but that doesn't help matters. How would you like to be taken for Miss Jennie? Really it will be dangerous to your good name to be seen out with me if they keep it up. I'll have to hock my overcoat and buy a black one and get a monocle for each eye, then I'll be a person all myself.

I just got a fine letter from Miss Maggie. She forgave me for not coming to her dinner party and said she'd give me a dinner yet and I need not take her to a show just because I didn't get there. I'm going to take her now, sure. Miss Maggie thinks too well of me, that is, she has too good an opinion of me. I wish she didn't. It's awful hard to live up to good opinions and do the right thing at the right time, especially when you have an insane desire to do something real ornery. I have always had that desire but never the nerve to put it over *publicly* yet. Some day perhaps I'll create a small stir among my friends and acquaintances by robbing a bank (the clock stopped when I wrote that) or doing some other Diamond Dick stunt. You know, I like *adventure*—when it's somebody else's adventure. I may even persuade you to run off with me someday when you're not in your right mind exactly.

Now you owe me a letter on the strength of that last statement if no other. Please send it along. The lawyer's coming tomorrow and Harry stays at home, so be sure and write.

Sincerely,
Harry

Grandview, Mo.
January 25, 1912

Dear Bessie:

This is the third letter I have started to you since Tuesday night. You know I took a fool notion not to go over to Aunt Ella's after all and went back to K.C. I figured that I had rather lose an hour's sleep while I was up already than to get up to do it. That sounds like a Dutch Jew wrote it. I was talking to Abie Viner's pa this morning and that's the reason. Abie and his pa belong to the Scottish Rite. They are in the chandelier business. I never saw so many varieties nor such pretty ones as the old man showed me this morning. His store is at 1110 McGee, right back of the Empress. Abie has been married seven years. Think of it. The Scottish Rite has done its best to make a man of me, but they had such a grade of material to start with that they did a poor job I fear. It is the most impressive ceremony I ever saw or read of. If a man doesn't try to be better after seeing it, he has a screw loose somewhere.

I simply can't get "I Dreamt I Dwelt in Marble Halls" [out] of my mind. I think it's the prettiest waltz song of the whole bunch. Mary has gone dippy over "Day Dreams" and won't let me have the piano to play it 'cause she wants to herself. I wrote you the craziest letter after I got to K.C. Tuesday evening you would ever read. I didn't have the nerve to send it next day. Did you know you made a most excellent joke Sunday evening and neither of us laughed? I had asked you if you weren't tired of my hanging around so long at a time. You of course said I was [the one] who would get tired and I said I'd never get tired. Then you, thinking I suppose that something was coming sure enough, grabbed the weather and said, "Oh heck I wish I had some rubber boots!" And we never laughed. I'm glad, for I meant it. You shouldn't have been afraid of my getting slushy or proposing until I can urge you to come to as good a home as you have already. I don't think any man should expect a girl to go to a less comfortable home than she's used to. I'd just like to be rich for two reasons. First, to pay my debts and give Mamma a fine house to live in, and, second and greatest, I'd make love to you so hard you'd either have to say yes or knock me on the head. Still, if I thought you cared a little I'd double my efforts to amount to something and maybe would succeed. I wouldn't ask you to marry me if I didn't. Say, now, ain't it awful— I have already burned up two perfectly good sheets of stationery to keep from saying that, but this one goes. If you don't like that part skip it, which you can't because you won't know it's there. Well, it's just what I think and I mean every word of it.

Won't it be fine if Miss Dicie has her dinner and her party on the same Saturday? I am just dying to see Mrs. Polly and that baby. (Kid, I almost said, but I believe you said it was a lady.)

I am afraid that I won't get to take you to hear DePachmann because he comes on the first Friday in the month. Save me the date as close as you can though, and if I can get away and you care to hear him, we will.

Mamma is raising sand with me to come to dinner and I believe she said there was caramel custard, or was going to be, this evening so I'll have to stop. I guess you'll be glad anyway for I'll frankly admit that this is a bum excuse for a letter, but I hope you'll send me one in return. I'll be highly pleased with any kind on any kind of paper. So just send me a letter.

Sincerely,
Harry

Grandburg [Grandview]

Dear Bessie: January 30, 1912

Give me credit for a *very* early response. You certainly did write me one fine letter (put emphasis on fine, not on one, because they're all fine) and I am going to answer it immediately.

I am going to start in real earnest now to get some of the dirty pelf, for what you say sounds kind of encouraging, whether you meant it that way or not. I am glad Mary Paxton and I can agree on *one* subject [even] if it is unintentional. We never could when we were kids. But Mary's correct this time. I hope she gets her millionaire someday. I am not resting up to go to work—I have been working up to get in trim. Shucked shock corn all day Saturday and got my eyes so full of dust that I could almost scoop it out. They looked like a professional toper's the next day. We have about four hundred shocks left yet to shuck before we are done. It is a job invented by Satan himself. Dante sure left something from the tenth circle when he failed to say that the inhabitants of that dire place shucked shock corn. I am sure they do. I hope never to see another year when it is necessary to save so much of it. We are lucky, though, to have it, as it takes the place of hay at twenty dollars a ton. Papa pretends that he doesn't mind doing it, but he does just the same.

I went down to Drexel last night with Mr. Blair and acted as assistant district lecturer. Went down on the K.C.S. and got back at 5:50 A.M. Got four hours sleep. You ought to see me teach blockheaded Masons how to talk. (Don't ever say that to anyone, for we don't admit that there are any of that kind.) They'd have to be blockheads if I taught them. We had lots of fun. There was a big, old fat guy present who got me tickled and I lost all my high-and-mightiness in short order. We met an old fellow at the hotel who was a cow buyer and a character. He'd quarrel with anybody on any subject. He bet a dollar that Taft would be nominated and then bet two that Teddy would. He fussed with the hotel man because the damper in the stovepipe was not turned at the proper angle. I guess he must have been seventy, but he was six feet tall and straight as a boy. Everybody thought he was funny. He didn't mean half he said but it sounded mighty mean when he said it.

I have to go help Mr. Blair out when it is possible for me to get away, because he has paid my expenses a couple of times to State Lodges of Instruction. I saw his wife on the train the last time I was in town, and she said he had gone off somewhere that day. Said she guessed it was on Lodge business because he always told her where he went except when he went to Lodge.

I won a pound-box of candy on your name the other day. What do you think of that? I went up to Grandview and a man in the confectionary business had one of these cards all full of girls' names. Each name had a number under it on a slip. I took a shot at the best name in the bunch and won a sixty-cent box of Louney's for a dime. That's the second time I've done it. Before, I tore off Elizabeth and won two pounds. I was going to bring you that box but those cousins of mine came out, and Mary knew I had the box and so I had to give it up. They never knew how I got it though.

I shall sure be glad to go to Salisbury's for dinner Sunday. But don't you think people would think I am a terrible tightwad if we walk? I'd like to walk all right and would certainly enjoy it, but please be sure I am perfectly willing to invest in a rig for one day. I hope Miss Dicie does loosen up for Saturday evening, because my time is getting short and I am dying to see Mrs. Polly (as I said before). I hope this baby hasn't whooping cough. She would think her visit was hoodooed sure if anything was to happen to it.

If Miss D. takes a notion for Saturday, will you call me up? Have it reversed because I'll be the one who benefits. I wonder if her ears burn. Maybe writing doesn't have the same effect on a person's ears as talking. If it does, Miss Dicie's ears ought to be about done enough for sandwiches. Don't you think? I ought to be helping Vivian and Luella to move, but Papa sent the hired men and I am putting my time to better use—at least I think so whether you will or not. Maybe you'll wish I had helped more. I hope not though. And I also hope you'll think you owe me a letter. Two of these tablecloth-size sheets are equal to almost four of your size, so I send more words if you do send more sense. I'm glad to get them though, any size or style. Hope to see you Saturday and shall Sunday *anyway*.

Sincerely,
Harry

Truman's mind ranged to all sorts of subjects. One of the more arcane is seen below as he refers to Theodore Roosevelt's advocacy of simplified spelling. The leader of this proposed reform was Andrew Carnegie, who, critics said,

wanted not the King's English but Carnegie's English. He went so far as persuad-
ing VIPs to sign a pledge to simplify. Examples are dialog *for* dialogue, thoro *for*
thorough, *etc.*

Grandview, Mo.

Dear Bessie: February 13, 1912

Since this is your birthday and tomorrow is St. Valentine's and I have
neither a present nor a valentine good enough to send you, I shall try and make
some amends by sending you a very ordinary letter. Which all sounds very
stilted and set just as if it was copied from some ancient work on how to write
letters. Doesn't it? Well any*how* (with emphasis on the how) I wanted to send
you something but hadn't brains enough to think of anything decent enough
that would properly fit my present assets. So I thought I would get nothing and
just tell you about it. That probably won't do you any good but then a good
intention ought to count for something even if Pluto does pave his front yard
with them.

Would it be the proper thing, do you think, for me to buy some *Pink Lady*
tickets for you and your San Antonio friend for some day next week? If you think
so, I would be most happy to do it. I told Mary this morning that Aunt Ella is
expecting her to stay all night at Independence Friday, and now I shall have to
call up my dear Aunt and tell her Mary is coming down Friday evening. When
they come together they'll compare notes and consign me to the Ananias Club,
I guess. Anyway Mary jumped at the chance to go to Aunt Ella's, saying she was
mighty glad she was asked because she hadn't made up her mind where to stay.
Aunt Ella is always glad to have us come down there, so there is no harm
done and I won't have to stand an unmerciful grilling from now until
Friday just because I want Mary to go to Independence with you. Mary
doesn't know yet that we are to be present at the recital. She has already
wanted to borrow my glasses, and I am going to be very generous and lend
them to her so I won't have to make my pockets sag with them all day. I fear
this letter makes me appear as a very sordid and unscrupulous person—but
in some cases, you know, the end justifies the means. Miss Maggie would be
terribly shocked if she knew I had any slick Jesuit beliefs in my system. She
did her very level best to impress us with the fact that the end never justified the means if a person had to overstep the ten great laws to obtain his
end.

I think most people are like the man I read of the other day who was waiting
to see a friend and picked up a Bible. It fell open at the twentieth chapter of
Exodus and he just read the commandments while he waited. When he got
through he thought awhile and then said, "Well, I've never killed anybody
anyway." I heard a man tell another one on the train last night, that he would
have stolen a Bible if he could have gotten it to go into his pocket. Then he went
on to describe what a fine one it was with a red leather back and fine wood
engravings. Said he wanted it most awful bad but the owner watched him so
closely he couldn't get away with it. Now, I think a man ought to draw the line

at stealing a Bible. Of course I suppose it is no worse to steal one than it is to steal any other book or piece of furniture, but it sounds rather sacrilegious, to say the least. I am sure if I were in the stealing business, I'd be rather superstitious about stealing one.

Say, it sure is a grand thing that I have a high-school dictionary handy. I even had to look on the back to see how to spell the book itself. The English language so far as spelling goes was created by Satan I am sure. It makes no difference how well educated or how many letters a man can string to the back of his name, he never learns to spell so he is exactly sure *i* shouldn't be *e* or *a*, *o*. I can honestly say I admire Roosevelt for his efforts to make people spell what they say. He really ought to begin on his own name though.

Tell Frank that so far as I have sounded, which is only very little, Mize has the bilge on Chrisman, and Gentry is not so well thought of as formerly. I am sure that George would make a good race in this township because he has a great many personal friends around here.

The heavenly geese are certainly shedding feathers around this neighborhood this morning. About two inches of them have fallen already. I guess old man winter is going to stay until March, sure enough. We sure ought to produce a crop out of all proportion to former ones if hard winters count for much! All the oldest inhabitants say they do.

I didn't get any breakfast this morning but I told Mamma I didn't want any because I had some most awful good waffles at 10:00 P.M. They sure were good.

This is one bum epistle (emphasis on the bum) and I have no excuse to offer for I am doing my level best. As the country newspapers say, news in our burg is on the run and I can't catch up.

Anyway, I hope you'll live a thousand years if you want to and never get a day older than you are.

I shall call you up Friday as soon as I can get to a phone and you can decide if I shall come for you or not. It seems as if I should since I shall desert before Mr. DePachmann gets done throwing fits. He is going to play Mendelssohn's "Spinning Song" and Chopin's great A♭ waltz.

Please, I think you owe me a letter even if this concoction is a substitute for something else.

Sincerely,
Harry

Grandview, Mo.
February 19, 1912

Dear Bessie:

That's an awful smear, but my Santa Fe de luxe stationery is on the wane and every sheet counts. Mary has just come in here like a cyclone. She says Vivian was going to dip her foot in the garbage bucket to sweeten it for the hogs (the garbage to be sweetened, not the foot). Mrs. Conrad said that word should be pronounced as garage—the spelling being practically the same. I agree with her.

What I want to say is, *you owe me a letter and a half*. Don't forget the half. I can always think of lots of nice things to say to people after leaving. Your friend surely has a fine, fine voice and it is very pleasing to hear, besides. I don't think I even mentioned the fact that I enjoyed her singing. It was a rattled condition, not a rude intention. You will remember that she and George had some smart remarks to make and I forgot what I had to say. I'd give four dollars for her accent. It's the best I ever heard. Still, for everyday listening, plain Missouri English can't be beaten. (Scratch off the en on beat.)

I found your fortune in my cough-drop box. I am enclosing it. You will notice that people with February birthdays have a quieting effect on the insane. I suppose that means those they have caused to become dippy. Don't you?

I think more of my stickpin every day. The card says it's your birthstone.

I was assistant wash lady again today. It is getting to be chronic with me. Papa went to Joplin this evening and I am boss. I made one of the hired men stay all night so he can get up at 5:00 A.M. and help do the feeding. I had rather be stung for two meals than do all that tearing around by myself so early in the morning. I am getting to be real aristocratic. It will take all summer's hard work to purge my soul of last year's loaf. I hope I never have to loaf with the same excuse. Please tell Miss Andrews I enjoyed her singing but just forgot to say so. I am dying for Thursday evening to arrive. I know we'll have a dandy time. I hope they won't use the same topic of conversation though they did before.

It pleases me mightily to be teased about you but I don't suppose you care to suffer the inconvenience on my account, and it's terribly embarrassing. Please send me the letter anyway, if you don't the half.

Sincerely,
Harry

Grandview, Mo.
Dear Bessie: February 27, 1912

. . . Did you have a good time at Miss Nellie's? I am sure you did though. I am scheduled to appear in Belton this evening as assistant to the Deputy Grand Master. I am going to begin forgetting from now on. The calls are coming too thick entirely. I have to go to Freeman on Saturday, and Friday our own session comes off. That dispenses with three nights on which I receive nothing but hot air and get my hatband sprung. I am hoping that the said hatband will soon reach its greatest diameter, in which case I can stay home on at least every third evening. I am hoping to be in town tomorrow, in which case I shall call you up —and if you feel inclined, we can go to a show. I have forgotten how to spell the word for afternoon performance. I shall have to go out to my Colgan cousins in the evening and discuss wedding marches and such things. Of course Myra says she won't need to worry about such a thing until June or September but she appears very anxious that I know the march right away quick. The cousins are all going to chip in and buy her some silver. I think it would be better to do that than for each of us to give her something useless, don't you? My working days are slowly and surely approaching. Vivian moves on Friday and on the following Wednesday, it is goodbye hired men. Then Lent sets in for a year and a day with Harry. But work is the only way I see to arrive at conclusions. This thing of sitting down and waiting for plutocratic relatives to decease and then getting left doesn't go with [me] much. I intend making my own way if it takes ten years, which sounds like Mrs. E.D.E.N. Southworth or Mary Jane Holmes [novelists]. Some Gillis [a K.C. theater] expressions are good anyway, aren't they? Mary Jane Holmes was my grandmother's name before she married a Truman but she was no kin to the famous one. A person would feel better and could wear a much larger hat if he made his own change than he could if someone gave it to him. If we can just settle our lawsuit, this farm will produce about six or seven thousand a year clear and that means about three more than that in town. Such things, though, take bushels of time and barrels of money. Such things make awful dry letters, too, but I am hoping that when the seven-thousand stage is reached I can persuade you to help spend my half of it. Our dear relatives may take the whole works yet and then we'll have to begin again. That sure would be awful, but I guess we'd live through it.

Don't forget a grand opera some night next week. How would you like to see the Orpheum road show in the afternoon and then go to dinner somewhere and then go to the Shubert? We could end up the season in one big splash, for there is no telling when I'll get to a show after the sixth of March.

I don't suppose Miss Andrews would care if you ditched her for one afternoon and evening, would she?

I hope to see you tomorrow but if I don't, you'll know I couldn't come in until four o'clock.

You owe me a letter. When I send you Montgomery Ward's catalogue you'll owe me a 1,250-page one.

Sincerely,
Harry

The Montezuma Hotel, Santa Fe, N.M.

Dear Bess: March 4, 1912
We are in the ancient and historic capital of New Mexico. It is everything they say it is, so far as peculiarities of people and architecture are concerned. I haven't seen much of this town yet but I saw some mighty pretty and very no-account country today.

Willard is situated in the most beautiful valley I ever saw. On the west is a range of mountains called Manzano, which means apple. They are called Apple Mountains because there is an orchard at the foot of them which has been bearing for three hundred years and is still doing business in the usual style. Bears, deer, and wildcats are said to be plentiful there. They tell a story of a black bear having been run into the town of Mountainair by a freight train. He got on the track and couldn't get off. Citizens of the town killed the bear.

On the south of Willard at about an equal distance as the Manzano is a range of straight up and down hills about a thousand feet above the plain, or plane. Then to the north, the valley extends just as far as you can see.

We took the New Mexico Central R.R. at Willard this morning and came here. It splits the valley from north to south. The view from the back end of the train was fine. We were about twenty-five miles from those said Apple Mountains and in going north we left them behind, but more took their places. We came to the Ortes group—a few peaks extending about twenty-five miles from north to south. They belonged to Stephen B. Elkins and Robert Ingersoll. They obtained them in settling the Star Route Graft. There are gold, silver, copper, and lead in them in large quantities. They have been mined by the Spaniards for over 150 years.

To the north of the Ortes Mountains are the Pyramid (hills I'd call 'em) Mountains. They belong to Tiffany, and the finest turquoises in the world are mined from them. One old man told me that Tiffany controlled the market in those beautiful stones by having these New Mexico mines. When the supply is large he closes the mines, and when they are in demand the mines run.

We also saw a range of mountains belonging to the Amalgamated Copper Co., another range called Sandea, which means watermelon. It is named on account of the shape and not the melons raised there.

As we came up the valley from the south the sun shown on us, but in front it was raining—and the most beautiful rainbow was in front nearly all the way. I wanted to get off and chase the end of it down, thinking perhaps it really might be on a gold mine out here.

It is raining to beat Sam Hill here this evening. The legislature is going to meet—I guess that's the reason. I hope tomorrow will be a nice day for we want to go to the old missions and the penitentiary (how do you spell it). If we don't have to stay there, we are going to start home tomorrow evening. If no bad luck occurs, we'll be in K.C. Friday morning. So be ready for Orpheum and G.O. on Friday.

Maybe you've seen all I've told you but I had to inflict it upon someone and of course thought of you first. Now you owe me a letter, don't you?

Hoping to see you Friday. I am

> Sincerely,
> Harry

Grandview, Mo.

Dear Bess: March 12, 1912

Your letter came this morning and as usual I was awful glad to get it. It seems like two weeks since I've seen you. I got in the buggy and drove to Aunt Emma's to dinner Sunday, and it was only because I couldn't find a Home phone that I didn't call you up and see if I could come over. You know the reason I didn't call up Friday morning? I was afraid you wouldn't be up! And since I'd rather sleep than eat myself, I didn't want to cause you to get up just to talk to me over the phone.

Uncle Harrison went straight to a phone and called up Mamma Thursday and told her that he had met me on the street—and that I was with a Miss Wallace from Independence. Mary almost had hysterics. I guess Uncle thought he was doing me a favor, which he was. The people at home considered that they had one on me and I got off without a raking for not letting them know I'd arrived. . . .

They are trying to persuade me to join a band out here. I think I'll draw the line though. I can stand Lodges, militia, and most anything but I guess a band is going too far. I sure would be Har-rar-ry then, broad *a* to match sor-ror-ry. I like Irish Hă—ry better than any other way. I am called Herry Hääry Hāry and most everything else. Miss Mamie Dunne first gave me the Irish way. She was my second-grade teacher at the Westside.

I haven't begun the 5:00 A.M. business yet, but I have gone to work. We are commencing at six now. But that is because we don't have to do anything but feed a dozen cows and twenty horses and about seventy hogs. I dug a load of fodder out of snowdrifts three feet deep yesterday. Will do the same stunt in the morning and every one thereafter until the snow melts.

Mary went down to Vivian's Sunday and couldn't return until today on account of the snow and rain. I had to go after her in a big wagon. In places the snow is drifted six feet deep. Where hedge fences are along east and west roads they are level full of snow. The only way to get through is to drive up against the south fence. Mr. Dyer started to K.C. in a Ford car and it took four mules to extract him from a big drift this side of Blue Hill. That road is open now though.

Grandview is still a dry town in spite of Judge Gilbert. The council refused the license. I am glad because it would have been a tough place. All Kansas and Cass County would have congregated here for their weekly sprees. Then K.C. auto toughs would have had a relay station too. So everything considered, it's best for Grandview to be dry. If they had K.C. police protection, then I'd say give 'em booze all they want, because they bootleg anyway. When they buy on the quiet though they have to drink that way, and that helps some.

I sincerely hope you can go on March 30 to see a *Shakespeare play*, because it may be the last show this season I'll get to attend. Did you get the Kodak pictures and what did they cost you? Let me know when you write *right soon*.

Sincerely,
Harry

Among the many activities Truman related to Bess was his playing in the Grandview village band. He does not seem to have spent much time at it. In their heyday, before World War I, town bands provided fun for players as well as listeners. The music was invariably bad; often the band knew only two or three tunes, but the leader would confuse audiences by assigning different names to the same piece.

Grandview, Mo.

Dear Bess: Monday, 11 P.M. [Mar. 18, 1912]

That's a horrid hour for a well-behaved farmer to be up, especially when he didn't turn in until one-thirty the preceding evening. I have been to Grandburg watching the amateur band perform. It was a circus (unless a person happened to have tender eardrums). They've been trying to inveigle me into it. Being unsuccessful on every other point, they got me to help them read their music. Now I have a clarinet here on the desk. It looks like a Chinese puzzle to me. Had to take it though or make the bunch mad. I may even be crazy enough to learn to play it. They practice at the schoolhouse at Grandview and I tell you the noise they make is positively unearthly. It isn't heavenly either. The kid with the slide trombone got on top of a desk and became so enthusiastic that he socked the tuba player in the nose with the slide. Our town will be on the map when it has a thirst emporium, *brass* band, and a suffragette club. They all go together.

Uncle Harrison stayed all day today. I had nothing to do but play Pitch and Cooncan to keep him entertained. It was so muddy that I hitched up and hauled him to the station about four o'clock and came on back home because I had some work to do. The agent said the train was twenty minutes late. I went back up town at seven and the train went just as I got there. I'll bet the roof of the station was a decidedly fiery color if Uncle Harry's language could have painted it. . . .

Now I'm going to display some tall nerve and remind you that you promised me your *Munsey's* when you were through. Don't forget that I am still wanting to read Mr. Sixbestsellers' latest. That doesn't sound very nice, but I'll have to leave it because I can't scratch it out and my stationery is on the decline. So don't pay any attention to it if you don't want to.

I hope your attack of grippe and threatened meningitis has disappeared. I have been sunburning my face to keep healthy. Got my hat out today and shall bleach it (my face) now. Snow sunburn is anything but pleasant I tell you. My nose looks like a headlight.

I really must draw this to a close. I guess you'll be glad but please oh please don't say so, because I'm hoping for a mile-long letter on the strength of it. Someone is raising sand in the back of the house. I hope it's not a burglar.

It was not; Papa ran into the dining-room door—he came down after some water. Please write quick.

Sincerely,
Harry

Grandview, Mo.

Dear Bess: March 23, 1912

I suppose the gink who wrote *Beautiful Snow* has received a genteel sufficiency of it today. I wish he could spend eternity in a big drift. John Greenleaf Whittier, the old nigger lover, also went into spasms over snow. I guess maybe he wishes he could see some now. It probably would be great comfort to him to spend a few days in a drift. . . .

If this snow keeps up I don't suppose the streetcar company will turn a wheel this evening. If I'd known my relatives were not coming, I'd have been in Independence this evening. I guess I'll have to stay home tomorrow and dig out a load of fodder for the benefit of a lot of beastly old cows. I'm so glad we haven't enough to eat two loads. Nothing is so bad it couldn't be worse. Cows have an insatiable (?) appetite for fodder when it is hard to get. When it is possible to get it without any trouble, they won't look at it.

That band concert will be a peach. I'll let you know all right. Some night when I can persuade them to practice in our grove, you can happen along accidentally and hear the noise. You will probably not come any closer than the front gate after hearing one bleat from the trombone artist. His name is Hank, which is almost Hen-er-y.

The *Apple of Discord* is making a good start all right. I have been reading it. Mamma read a hair raiser in *Adventure* the other evening after we all went to bed. She got about halfway through and got scared and went upstairs herself. We've been kidding her a lot about it. She's not much on the scare order in real life let alone in a yellow story. It must have been a humdinger. I don't get the *Star* now. You'll please excuse any of my expressions that sound a little bit as if they originated in the Kansas City *Post.* I haven't renewed the *Star,* and the old tightwad stopped it on the day my subscription expired. I guess I'll have to renew on account of the free ads [illegible].

I got a letter from Mr. Mize asking my support for his candidacy. If it'll do him any good, he'll get it all right. Couldn't possibly vote for the other old duffer but I do feel sorry for him.

I shall certainly be thankful for those *Munsey's* but really you oughtn't to give them to me after what I said before. . . .

Please, you owe me a letter I think. Send it by U.S.M. and not by any messengers. Don't forget next Saturday. Wish it were today. Pray for rain and maybe it won't snow that day.

Sincerely,
Harry

Grandview, Mo.

Dear Bess: April Fools' Day

This is my day. Ask Ethel if you don't believe it. I wonder why April 1 is called All Fools' Day? I suppose it means court fools or humorists and not our present-day idea of the word. Those court fools usually had more sense than His Majesty. Of course I never met one, nor a majesty either, but Shakespeare makes them very wise and I guess he knew. Which sounds as if I read Shakespeare. I get my idea of Shakespeare from Mark Twain. Mark knew all about such things. Just read *Connecticut Yankee at King Arthur's Court* if you don't believe it. . . .

I have been to the lot and put about a hundred rings in half as many hogs' noses. You really haven't any idea what a soul-stirring job it is, especially on a day when the mud is knee deep and about the consistency of cake dough. Every hog's voice is pitched in a different key and about time you get used to a squeal pitched in G minor that hog has to be loosed and the next one is in A-flat. This makes a violent discord and is very hard on the nerves of a high-strung person. It is very much harder on the hogs' nerves. We have a patent shoot (chute maybe) which takes mister hog right behind the ears and he has to stand and let his nose be bejeweled to any extent the ringer sees fit.

I don't like to do it, but when a nice bluegrass pasture is at stake I'd carve the whole hog tribe to small bits rather than see it ruined. Besides it only hurts them for about an hour and about one in every three loses his rings inside of a week and has to endure the agony over again. If someone would invent a hog that wouldn't root he'd be a benefactor to suffering farmers and a multimillionaire in no time. I hate hogs myself except in the form of ham, sausage, and bacon, but they bring the dollars faster than anything else on a farm, so they're a necessary evil. . . .

I sure did enjoy myself yesterday and can hardly wait for next Sunday to come. I am sure a play is better or worse depending upon whom you see it with. *Twelfth Night* was far and away better than *As You Like It.*

Papa says he's going to adopt a boy if I don't stay home on Sundays. I told him to go ahead.

Please send me a letter on the strength of this. My brains are no good; they are clogged with discordant hog squeals.

Most sincerely,
Harry

Grandview, Mo.

Dear Bess: April 8, 1912

Here goes for another start on your letter. Maybe I'll get it finished this time. My dear brother had to go and get his shoulder dislocated when I started the other one, and I was shaken up so on hearing it I couldn't write. That sounds rather feminine, doesn't it? Mamma says I was intended for a girl anyway. It makes me pretty mad to be told so but I guess it's partly so. When it comes to pulling teeth I always yell and I have an inordinate desire to look nice in a photo. You see I have some ladylike traits anyway. If ever you accuse me of having any, though, you may be sure I'll prevaricate and say I haven't. I told your mother I was going to get her a lily for Easter but couldn't carry it. Of course I couldn't possibly have paid a messenger to deliver it, could I? It was my intention to get it when we came home from the Rev. Cyrus Townsend Brady's, but as we didn't go of course no lily appeared. I hope she'll give me credit for good intentions. There goes another piece of Hellenic pavement to my credit. (I'm not referring to Greece, either.)

Will you please persuade George to persuade the alumni committee of the senior class to forget that they ever had any intention of giving me nervous prostration? If I get to come to their meeting and they should ask me to speak, I'd die of elevatoritis because I'd go right through the floor. It was my hope that I'd get to come and enjoy myself but I sure wouldn't if that calamity were hanging over me. I wouldn't mind making a botch on my own account but I'd so hate to humiliate my friends. Besides, the meeting is on Friday night and unless something happens to annul a Masonic meeting I'll have to stay home. If I get to go, will you honor muh [sic] with yuh company? If I don't show up by 8:00 P.M., you'll know I couldn't kill the Masonic goat and that I'm not coming. If you want to go with any of the *other* good-looking fellows, you'd better, then you'll have a sure escort. Then if I come, I can suffer from the little green god as well as from luck ague. There are more I's, me's, my's in this than I have succeeded in putting into a letter for a long time. You know I am of a rather retiring disposition and it hurts me to blow my own trumpet so much (?). I wouldn't only you know that I'm horribly anxious for you to suffer from an excessively good opinion of me! If you should happen to do that and at some date in the distant future I should get to acting up, can't you hand me one by just telling me what I've said on paper? (Provided you don't consign these to range, as Agnes's flame said.) I really don't care a hoot what you do with my letters so long as you write me—that's what I'm laboring for, a letter from you. You may read them to anyone you choose, put 'em under the parlor carpet, or start fires with 'em—just as long as you send me an answer, which by the way won't be used for any of the above-mentioned purposes.

Well, let's change the subject what do you say? Not that I'd ever get tired of it. I shelled corn by hand all day today. That is as long as I could hold my eyes open. I was sitting on the floor in the sitting room shelling seed corn as hard as I could, when pretty soon Papa came in and yelled, "Harry, dinner's ready! Why don't you come on, you going to sleep all day?" I'd been asleep for an hour and didn't know it. You see, I got up at 4:30 A.M. and turned in at 1:30 A.M., which is rather a long stretch between naps. A freight train got in front of the passenger last night and I got off in our pasture and only had to walk about half as far as usual. The moon was just getting up as the train came round the bend and it looked exactly as if our barn was on fire. I was scared stiff. When I got to the jumping off place I decided it was a neighbor's house and only came to the moon conclusion when I got to the house. Some poor fellow was stalled in an auto about two hundred yards from the gate but got started about time I got to the house. Wouldn't it be pleasant to be laid out about twenty miles from home about 1:00 A.M.? You ought to know for you tried it once. I hope you'll take the risk again sometime soon. Send me a letter immejate.

Most sincerely,
Harry

Grandview, Mo.
April 29, 1912
Dear Bess:
Your letter came yesterday but I was so all fired lazy I didn't answer it. Do you know those ornery cousins of mine came out Saturday morning and *went back*

Saturday evening, after I'd already made arrangements with the hired man so I couldn't leave Sunday. Wasn't that the height of pure cussedness? I guess they had a good excuse though. Aunt Ella was sick. We had a barbecue and land auction at Grandview Saturday and *I had to stay home and work.* Doesn't that sound unusual? So I didn't get to see the girls at all. I was just about to finish sowing clover seed and as all indications pointed to rain I couldn't stop. I finished at five o'clock—115 acres, which means that I probably rode 120 miles on the drill. If you'd only prayed a little harder Thursday, I'd have got off but as it was it only stopped me an hour. Now I'm done and will have to go to plowing. It takes a deluge to stop a plow so I guess I'll have to wait until Sunday. This time Mr. hired man stays if all the relations in the county choose to come.

There were about a thousand people at Grandview Saturday. Everybody and his brother was present. If he didn't happen to have a brother, he brought his mother-in-law. That's what mine did. (My brother.) Mr. Davidson's feed was the most scrumptious affair you ever saw. He had roast cow and several roast hogs with salad and pie and all the trimmings for the whole bunch. He paid $10,000 for ten acres and got $16,500 for it. Probably made $3,000 clear in a month. Wish I could coin money at that rate. You know he made $3,000 on Jost's election.

This letter is a sort of "continued in our next." I started it at noon, then went and plowed a half day, and now I hope to finish it if Mary doesn't announce supper too quickly. I raked all the hide off the end of my left thumb this afternoon while trying to punch a hole in a strap. It wasn't my Sunday knife, so you needn't be afraid to use the one I carry on holidays. You have no idea how very inconvenient it is to try to wash your face with one hand, especially if that one is the wrong one. I did mine as Tom Sawyer did his—gave it a lick and promised it a better one Sunday maybe. Won't I be pretty by then? I'll come down and let you see how I look if you will be at home. I'll stop at a barber shop on the way though and except for an immense amount of sunburn I'll be as usual. . . .

I hope you and Mary had a good time on the chaperon job. I suppose the reason they take you two is because they don't need any, isn't it?

"The Jingo" is a story with a brazen moral I guess and, like "The Squirrel Cage," won't be fit to read in a few numbers. Did you read the article on "Getting up Pinafore" in *Everybody's*? It's a killer. Please send me a letter for this, and may I come Sunday and also May 19 to hear the Bishop and a few other times if I get a chance?

Sincerely,
Harry

Grandview, Mo.

Dear Bess: May 12, 1912

I got your letter this morning and was very glad. As I have to go to the burg after Mary this evening to bring her from church, I will try to write you one and mail it as I go up. The reason you got the other one in such good time is I gave it to Uncle Harrison and he mailed it in town. I gave it to him so those ornery girls couldn't see it. They led me a dog's life while they were here. I guess I about kept even though. I caused Aileen to take a header in the yard and get her shine spoiled and her dress muddy. Grace [Truman, a cousin] upset a glass of milk at the table while trying to put butter on my face, which I had smeared on her arm. We told her she'd have to stay over Monday and do a day's washing, but her beau was coming Friday so she had to go home that evening. Aileen said she was going to send her dress to the cleaner's and the bill to me and that I could set 'em up to a shine the very first time she caught me downtown.

They played their stunt Thursday evening. Two Grandview girls came down to call and find out who was here. When they came in Grace and I happened to be at the piano trying to sing the words to "I Dreamt I Dwelt in Marble Halls" in the front of the libretto and play the music in the back. We found it couldn't be done and were being roasted by Mary and Aileen for creating a disturbance when these girls came. Mary didn't introduce Grace as Miss Waggoner from Independence, but the frying pan she gave me was hanging up in the parlor— and Mamma made an unintentional break by saying it was too small for Grace and me to fry eggs in. She said she meant it because Grace gave me the pan. Those hens took it the other way and I blushed like a school girl at a play party. Aileen had been reading a story in *Ladies Home Journal* called the "Twenty-four of June" and she and Mary kept up a conversation on the subject until those girls had it all figured out that Grace's amethyst (How do you spell it?) ring was a present from me—and the next twenty-fourth of June, the day. I was so mad I could have busted open. I had to take them home. When they went to leave, one of them said she guessed these girls must be the cousins I went to see in Independence. The girls never said anything only just yelled and laughed, which was all the evidence they wanted. My strong denial only made them surer. I told them going home that Grace's father was a paint manufacturer in K.C. and she was only a friend of Mary's, but they only asked if amethysts were her birthstone. I could only say yes because Grace's birthday is in February too. They think they're awful smart. Let them have their good time. I'll get even with the whole bunch, Grandviewites and all. You needn't ever be afraid of meeting them because if you do they'll only get more thoroughly balled up. They seem to take more interest in attending to my business than in anybody's around here. . . .

My Uncle accomplished his errand, and if there's not a slip between now and Tuesday we will probably be able to bring up our case and dispose of it. I hope so because when you pay a lawyer $100 a month and court costs and trip costs it certainly bends your finances badly when they are limited anyway. Mary Colgan called Mary up and told her not to let me make a date for Saturday, May 18, as she is going to have a party. She called on last Monday. I told Mary to tell her to have her party on some other day—I couldn't possibly come because I was going to another one. She nearly bit the phone in two. I don't care, I'd rather see *Manon* (that's the worst one I can think of) with you than go to two of her parties, and I know that Margaret has *Manon* as badly beaten as Mark has Geo. Eliot.

Well, you see I told you about the stunt. Of course it is my point of view, but Mary's or Aileen's couldn't be much different I don't think. You know, people see what they want to see.

I guess you are glad Frank didn't take that grounded boat. I hope he arrives safely. I'd like to see what a card mailed on the high seas looks like.

Please send me a letter, and I wish tomorrow were the eighteenth. I'll get done planting corn on Thursday at noon, if it doesn't rain, and will be my own boss Saturday at noon. So pray for clear weather this time.

Sincerely,
Harry

Although Truman's relationship with Bess seems to have been mutually respectful, he was not above making fun of suffragettes as he does in the letter below. Demonstrations toward passage of the Nineteenth Amendment inspired many men of this time to taunts such as "Go home and wash the dishes!"

Grandview, Mo.

My Dear Elizabeth: Monday P.M., May 20, 1912

How does that look to you? I just wrote it that way to see how it would look.

You know we have associations for every name. England's great Queen always goes to Elizabeth for me. When I was a very small kid I read a history of England and it had a facsimile signature of hers to Queen Mary's death warrant. I'll never forget how it looked if I live to be a hundred. But that didn't put me against her, for I always thought she was a great woman. I never think of you as Elizabeth. Bess or Bessie are you. Aren't you most awful glad they didn't call you the middle syllable? It is my pet aversion. There is an old woman out in this neck of the woods who is blest with enough curiosity for a whole suffragette meeting and a marvelous ability for gratifying it—to her own satisfaction. She has a wart on the end of her nose and a face like the Witch of Endor. Her first name is Liz. She is an ideal person to carry the name. I am sure it is not a nickname but her real one as no one of her caliber could possibly be Elizabeth. I have a very belligerent (spelled right?) cousin whose name is Lizzie. Therefore I care not for Liz and Lizzie for these two very good reasons. I have an idea, from the Lizzies I've seen, that Proserpina's middle name is Lizzie. The last syllable makes an entirely different combination. It is a name fit for a goddess (since you wear it) and I suppose it is a part of Venus's or Pallas's.

I don't know what got me started on this line of talk, but I hope you won't be offended because I don't like some of the nicknames of your good name. But please remember that I like yours muchly—anyway—as well as the real one.

I had the best luck getting home yesterday evening. I caught a car going to the barn. It overtook a Mt. Washington car at Sheffield. I jumped off and caught that car making the through trip to 8th and Wyandotte in just forty-five minutes. I got to the depot in about five more, so I had about fifteen minutes to spare. I had the livin' scared out of me as I came through the burg. Some guy evidently got off the train as I did. He followed me clear through town a quarter of a mile.

Every time I'd whip up he would too, and if I slowed down so did he. I guess he thought I was a bum and I'm sure he was. He finally went south and I went north. I was very much relieved when he did.

I did another job of painting today. Gave the front gate another coat. It looks like one of the pearly ones now, but it's made of cypress. If you'd read an ad of the Southern Cypress Assn. you'd think that the gates of heaven were made of it. I wasn't satisfied with painting the gate. I gave the pump a good coat. I did that because it stands immediately in front of the back door, and in one of those horribly dark nights I was telling you of when the Nolands were here I was endeavoring to get out of Ethel's way in a hurry and collided with the pump. I dislocated my specs and gave myself a black eye. For this reason I decided to paint it white. Now it can be seen on the darkest nights.

I hope your grandmother and grandfather got started all right. Tell Fred to hurry and get well. This is mighty fine weather and I know he hates to spend it in bed. I have at last discovered the trouble Mr. Cobb had. He punched a spectator's head for calling him an ugly name.

You said you were afraid I wouldn't appreciate your last letter because you were so prompt about answering. If you knew how glad I am to get them, you'd send 'em quick every time. I hope you'll consider this worth an answer in a hurry.

Sincerely,
Harry

Grandview, Mo.
Dear Bess: May 30, 1912

Ten-thirty P.M. and I'm going to answer your letter. I've succeeded in packing Mary and Nellie off to bed and now maybe I can have some peace. Nellie got your letter this morning and I almost choked her to death before I succeeded in getting it. . . .

I have been plowing corn, have enough to run me the balance of the week. Then I'm going to put up hay, then plow again and still some more, then probably put up the wheat, or, harvest it would be the proper way to say it. I hope you get to go to Platte County and will let me come to see you while there. I can then forget any jobs I may have on hand.

Do you know I've put in a whole day and a half getting my court in shape? It is pretty good for a rube affair. I guess at a pinch a person could play tennis on it. I'm going to keep fiddling with it until it gets in shape. I don't suppose I'll ever get to use it myself. I'm always up to my neck in work every time it is ready, and when it rains it's too muddy. I don't care whether I ever get to use it or not because I'd never make a shining light as a tennis player, but I don't begrudge the labor I put on it if it helps keep anybody that comes amused. Farmers ought really to have such things and if they'd spend more time on recreation and brain development and less eating and whittling to a lie accompaniment, they'd be much better off. Most of them, you know, eat like hogs and spend quite a bit of time at the stores swapping prevarications. They'll ship a load of hogs or cattle and spend enough of the proceeds on booze to buy the whole family a good time at some brain-developing show. Then they'll beef around worse than if they'd been sold a gold brick if their wives want a few dollars for a church fair. I can't see why men are so constituted. To preach hard times and retrenchment at home and then be a good fellow among the boozers.

This one is worse than the other, isn't it? It's not quite so personally offensive anyway. I guess you won't get over the fact that I'm so averse to Liz will you? Well, if they called you that I'd forget the rest and like it.

Now, does that please you enough to forget the other one? . . .

I'm just dying to see Weber and Fields and I want to ask you to go so badly I don't know what to do, but I know I simply cannot leave. I hope you get to go. If it rains Wednesday and you should happen to be at home and I could think up some excellent reason to leave, would you go? If you get a chance to go, don't count this because I am sure Wednesday will be an ideal June day. Please remember though that this is my busiest busy season, and since I laid off all last summer and the crops failed besides I must work to make up. You know when a person is not blest with plenty of change he's got to work like the tarnation bowwows to get it. That simile is like the one I heard the other day. A fellow said it rained at his place harder than seven hundred dollars. I wish Weber and Fields would come when there is snow on the ground anyway.

I sincerely hope you'll consider this worth an answer, and will send it immediately.

Most sincerely,
Harry, without any alias so far as he knows.

Dear Bess: [Grandview, June 18, 1912]
I had all kinds of luck getting you over the phone this morning, didn't I? After I got on the car going to Sheffield it struck me that it might be a good day to go on to town and get you to come over, go to lunch, and then take in a half dozen picture shows. Luck was agin me though. I bet I called up six times on the Home and once on the Bell—at Paxton's. . . .

Your last letter was a most excellent one (they all are), but it was very injurious to my head. A thirty-two–inch belt would hardly buckle around it after what you said about my eligibility. I don't care what the balance think if you'll only think so yourself.

I have an invitation from Belton Lodge to come up there Tuesday and confer a Third Degree. Mary gave me one to go with her to town that day also and invest in a dress for her. I think I'll go the other way, although I won't have any peace until the thing is bought. I guess she deserves it because she is making her last year's suit work again this summer. I'm a pretty good buyer of feminine wearing apparel by this. Mamma entrusts hers to me (and Mary takes me along and pretends to go by my judgment). Mary Paxton told me her show was to be next Friday. Hope she'll postpone it. I'd like to see it very much. But I have to have a show of my own that day.

I hope you'll consider this worth as much as two sheets and as many more as you care to fill.

Most sincerely,
Harry

Dear Bess: [Grandview, June 24, 1912]

S.V.B.E. [Si vales, bene est], as Dicie's brother would say. It is about all I have the ability to think of now. Not that I ever have the ability to think much, but at times my brainstorms are worse than others. This probably won't be a violent one because *we've* been putting up hay all day. I ran the buckrake. Therefore I had to pail the cow when I got in, which is a job I hate. There is only one cow on the place that will let me milk her and not create a disturbance. She is the old standby and the old rip gives about a bushel at a milking. Her name is Nellie Bly. I call her Purple for short. Ethel has a favorite poem which runs "Did you ever see a purple cow. No, I never want to see one, although I'd rather see than be one."* Entrancing, isn't it? That's why I call her Purple. (The cow, you understand.) There are two more that have to be milked after calves obtain a share. One of them is a most perverse creature. She has to have her feed in and you must approach her in a gentle and smiling mood. I always do until she's tied. It's "Whoa you nice cow. That's a nice cow," until the rope lands. Then it's "Now get away you blankety-blank speckled rip. Let's see you chase around the lot now." I make Mr. McBroom attend to her when I milk, which I don't very often. Papa stacked hay today and didn't feel like doing the job was why I did it. You see, the rake is not quite so strenuous. He wouldn't let me do the stacking, though, and he positively won't run the rake. It is a cussin' job. Ours is one of the kind where the horses are hitched behind the rake. If you desire to go to the right, it is necessary to make the left-hand horse move and the right one stand still. It works like the tiller on a boat—wrong end to. Sometimes you aim for a pile of hay and get one some distance away. I have arrived at the stage where I can generally go where I'm looking, therefore it's my job. . . .

This letter ought to be most awful good, there is a gigantic Bible being right close to it. I am writing upstairs in my room. It always creates so much comment when I sit at the desk on Monday evening to write that I came up here where I could have some peace. I have one on Mary though. She got a picture from a guy down here in Central Mo. the other day. I had business in her room Sunday while she was away and saw it on the bureau. His brother and sister-in-law were here just as I left. They have a four-year-old boy who wanted to go upstairs and they wouldn't let him. I said, "Oh let him go. He wants to see the picture of his uncle." Mary was sure enough sold out all right. Also it was necessary for me

---

*I never saw a Purple Cow,
I never hope to see one;
But I can tell you, anyhow,
I'd rather see than be one.
    —*Gelett Burgess*, The Purple Cow, *1895*

to beat it suddenly, which I did in good order.

Please write me a letter on the strength of this. Let's hope also for rain Saturday evening so Salisburys will have to postpone their do another week. I'll be along about seven-thirty Saturday if it will be all right. Answer—quick.

Sincerely,
Harry

[Grandview, Mo.]
July 1, 1912

Dear Bess:

Isn't it funny how many nice, bright remarks a person can think of after he gets out of a conversation? It seems to me that I never manage to say the proper thing in the proper place. I don't believe I even thanked you or your mother for the fine dinner you gave me, and I know I didn't thank Agnes for her pie. She ought to know it was very much appreciated though because two pieces disappeared in my direction; and you know I always enjoy dinner at your house.

I have been working over an old binder. My hands and face and my clothes are as black as the ace of spades—blacker, because the ace has a white background. Papa and the men are finishing up a small patch of plowing, therefore I have some time to write. I hate the job I have before me. If the machine goes well, it is well; if not, it is a word rhyming with well(?) literally because when the thing breaks down it is always in a hollow where the sun does a warming act equal to any His Majesty can possibly put up.

This is surely a long-drawn-out letter. I started it yesterday morning and I am going to finish now. I was in your city a few minutes last night. Arrived at eight-thirty and left at ten-thirty. Beginning Friday night I have gone the great Napoleon one better and managed to do with three hours sleep in twenty-four. Yesterday I put in a day's work and then drove to Dodson in order to get to help confer a degree on Murray Colgan. I feel as if I could appreciate some sleep. It looks much like rain and I'm hoping for it, though I shouldn't. I saw Frank just as I was ready to get on a car last night. He wanted to know what the mischief I was doing down there. It did seem like something was wrong when I didn't see Delaware St. Papa says he supposes if some of the family were dying and they'd send for me to put on a degree, I'd go. Murray and also the Hon. Allen Hoyt called me up yesterday to come down and I just couldn't resist going.

But I'd give fifty cents for a nickel's worth of sleep. I met an old man from Arkansas on the train last night who was the most interesting talker for a man that I've seen lately. I don't suppose he used the first person singular more than twice in the whole hour coming out and we talked on everything from religion to politics. He is an intense Bryan man, a good Mason, and a farmer, so you see we could have a most agreeable time. He told me that there would be some six thousand cars of Elberta peaches shipped from his neck of the woods. I hope some of them will land here. We have one lone peach. Mamma says she's going to have that when it gets ripe.

Bess, I hope you'll think a box-headed letter like this is worth an answer. Remember my intentions are good anyway and my sleep account is overdrawn to such an extent that the bank's about busted. It's always a little cracked though.

Please write me as quickly as you did before. Here's hoping it'll rain and it won't (I told you I had a feminine brain).

Most sincerely,
Harry

Political rallies were certainly one of the popular entertainments of the day. Here Truman reflects on a particularly good time he and Bess had hearing William Jennings Bryan, unsuccessful Democratic candidate for the presidency in 1896, 1900, and 1908. He was one of the great orators of his generation. When he toured the country in 1912 supporting Woodrow Wilson for president he drew huge crowds. Part of his attraction was his stentorian voice. A leather-lunged speaker, he could shout for three city blocks in an era when there was no mechanical amplification ("loudspeakers" came in about 1920). His principal concern was the plight of farmers. Withal, he was full of quips, many of them spontaneous; one time, Truman recalled, Bryan appeared at a farmers' rally and having nothing else to stand on clambered up on a manure spreader. Once there, he grinned and told the crowd it was the first time he ever stood on a Republican platform.

Grandview, Mo.
[July 17, 1912]

Dear Bess:

. . . You really don't know how much I enjoyed Mr. Bryan. I am one of his staunchest admirers. Mr. B. would not have been half so good though had you not been present. You know any show is good to me, unless it's positively rotten, if I can only see it with you. Let's hope that some rainy, cool day soon, real soon, the sooner the better, that we have lunch in K.C. at—well, the Hinkydink? on Tenth and Grand or some other place equally as good or better, and then see all the pictures that can be crowded into four hours. What say you? That'll be a regular Twelfth Street stunt but if a person don't have a good time doing what everybody does, he'll live a mighty bored life, won't he? I'm sure you must like picture shows or you wouldn't go every night in the week. My conscience still hurts me a little yet for keeping you from going to the Chautauqua in the evening Tuesday. If I'd only kept my head shut about K.C., I'll bet you'd have gone. Well a person must do the wrong thing sometimes just so he can have something to be sorry for. I can positively assure you, though, you missed not much. Thought it might have been better than what you did see. I'm no judge though and thought that show pretty good.

Do you know I did the orneriest thing this afternoon. I was cutting oats right here close to the house and amputated the left foot of an old hen with five chickens. I felt badly about it too. She was over in the oats, where I couldn't see her till I'd already done it. Mamma says she'll get all right. I hope so. I'd rather do most anything than to hurt something that can't tell me what it thinks of me for doing it. That old hen was more worried over what became of her chickens than she was over her foot. There are people who could very well profit by her example.

Please forgive the Sunday school book story, but it happened and that's what I thought of it.

Please "borrow" more of George's paper when you write, not because of the silver letters but because it holds more and makes a longer letter. He maybe won't miss a few sheets and besides I bet he used lots of yours last winter.

Tell your mother her fine dinner made me entirely well and I'm as good as new. That Sally L. was sure fine, as good as if you'd made it. That's some compliment too. Write quick.

Sincerely,
Harry

Throughout we will hear Truman refer to His Majesty, that is, the devil— whom he blames for all ill luck.

Dear Bess:

Grandview, Mo.
[July 22, 1912]

His Majesty's reign has begun for us. The thresher arrived this evening, *after supper* thank goodness. We will have men and boys roosting from cellar to roof (we have no attic) and over the front yard too. I helped the owner of the machine thresh his own wheat this afternoon. It wouldn't be any trouble to thresh if the bloomin' thing would run.

Just as we get to going and the thing begins to behave, why some pinhead with a young team will run into the belt and throw it or dislocate some of the innards of the thresher itself by backing into it. Both happened today. I didn't happen to be the pinhead either time. If that doesn't happen, some gink who is tired will throw a half-dozen bundles in the seemingly insatiable maw and choke her down. Then it's time for the owner to cuss and the engine to buck and snort. Any blockhead can choke a machine, but it takes a smart man to feed it all it'll eat and still go a very rapid gait. I am not one of them, but Booney is.

Since I started this I have had a most strenuous time. You know of course that 2:00 A.M. is my bedtime on Sunday. Well Papa of course called me as usual Monday morning. I decided to go to bed at eight-thirty Monday night. So I went up and started this letter to you. The phone rang three times and each one was for Harry. The question was invariably, "Are you going to thresh? How much help you want?" I went back upstairs and wrote a sentence. Papa came and wanted me to go show the water boy where to put his team. I did that and then Vivian came up. He wanted me to help him get some corn—at 9:00 P.M. now mind you. After he left I ran up and got in bed as quickly as I could and decided if anyone else called I'd play possum and not hear.

The old machine is humming this morning. I ought to be in the field but

Mamma has no help, therefore I am a filler in the house. You notice I say *filler*. I mean thresher men filler-up.

It rained within a quarter of a mile of our field and never a drop in it. Wasn't that luck? Good, Papa says, I didn't say.

Our wheat is a nice quality. I wish Frank could have used it. My dear uncle is coming out this morning and going to bring a girl to watch the machine run. She may get pressed in as cook and then she'll be sorry she came. It's best for visitors to fight shy of harvest time. The temptation is always too great to make 'em work.

I'd fill this sheet but I've got to get busy, also meeting dear uncle and it's train time. Please answer quick as you did before.

Sincerely,
Harry

[Grandview]

Dear Bess: July 30, 1912
. . . I had an adventure yesterday. I was putting on a load of wheat down at Mr. Babcock's. It was at the back of his farm close to Lee's Summit rock road. Had about half a load on when a most awful good-looking girl came driving down the road like mad and said her dog had jumped in an open well up the road and would we come and get him out. The pitcher and I got in the buggy and went with her, got a ladder, and I went down and got the dog—a fox terrier. There were about a half-dozen women tearing around the top of the well all the time trying to get the dog to climb ropes and jump in the bucket. They were a most awfully pleased bunch when "Dudley" arrived at the top in as good condition as ever except for a good swim. The ornery cuss shook himself while I helped him and I looked as if I'd been rained on. They were very profuse in their thanks and I believe the old lady and the girl would have kissed us if we hadn't made a hurried getaway. . . .

Have you won your tennis match yet? I hope you put it all over them. Both of our former neighbors have invested in autos. I am crazy to but can't. Hornbuckles [Roy Hornbuckle was engaged to Myra Colgan] came up and took Mary for a ride last night. They wanted me to go too but I wasn't home yet when they came. May I come Sunday? You must answer quick please, for I'm a day late.

Most sincerely,
Harry

Grandview, Mo.

Dear Bess: August 6, 1912
I caught the train all right. My conductor and engineer were both on. It was very, very good for my health that I did, too. Mr. Craig began threshing as early as he could and got done by noon. If I had not been present, he would have been short and wouldn't have been able to get done. I did hate to leave though. If I

had my way, I'd be around every evening, provided of course you'd let me come. But if I ever expect to have any change, you know business has to be attended to. Mark says and he's right that if business interferes with pleasure, throw business to the winds. I'll do that when I am financially able.

I wish I'd asked Frank about the other circuit judges but I guess I can pick a man with a pretty name. I am going up and hammer Winstanley and Chrisman pretty soon. Papa says I can land two votes to the opposition's one and I must come. Politics is all he ever advises me to neglect the farm for. I have other ideas. For instance, if I only owned a car, there'd probably be some very serious neglect. . . .

I am wishing for a slick tongue now because I'll have to use every argument at my command to down Mr. Chrisman. Roads promised to farmers are hard to down. If I can only prove he's seventeen kinds of a crook and prevaricator then I'll win. There are some citizens who will take my word anyway; they wear a square and compass.

You've no idea how swelled up I was when you told me you turned down other engagements for me Sunday. I felt real mean about it too. I should have called up. I hope you'll turn them down next Sunday, too, because I'll want to come if you'll let me.

I have to go put the hired men to work and then go to the polls. I hope you'll consider this worth an answer. You'll notice I'm getting this off on time and at 6:00 A.M. to do it.

Sincerely,
Harry

Grandview, Mo.

Dear Bess: [Aug. 12, 1912]

I am writing this on Monday evening. It won't amount to much because I haven't been to bed since Saturday night. It was a very good thing (so far as getting the train is concerned) that I went to 2nd and Wyandotte last night. It (the train) left one hour late going out to Leeds over the Missouri Pacific. If I'd gone to Sheffield to catch it, I'd have been there yet. The thing stood at Leeds until six o'clock this morning and then came home. There were several carloads of lumber upset at Swope Park in such a way as to block both the Southern and the Pacific. Why on earth the rotten thing should go and stand all night at Leeds I don't see. They could have stayed at 2nd and Wyandotte as well and we could have gone up to the Jefferson and slept some maybe. There was a bunch of hoodlums behind me and a fellow that goes to see Jesse Davis, and every time we'd get to sleep they'd let out a roar and wake *me* up. Mr. Galt seemed to sleep placidly on. We both called ourselves some bad names for not going into the Pullman. But I thought every minute would be the last and it would only take them thirty minutes to get to Grandview. Well, you could put all the sleep I got last night under a postage stamp. I got home at 7:00 A.M., which by the way is the latest yet for me, and changed my glad rags for my sorry ones and went to

Harry S. Truman, c. 1905. *Harry S. Truman Library*

loading baled hay into a car. That is the hottest job there is, I think, except shoveling coal for His Majesty. We finally managed to get 289 bales into the car at seven-thirty this evening. I came home and put on my clean overalls and a white soft shirt, had supper, and was just getting ready to come up and start this letter when Papa came in and said it was lightning around and that we should go over to a haystack some three-quarters of a mile away where the baler had been at work and cover up the hay. I almost told him we'd let the hay go hang, for you can imagine how very much I'd feel like going three-quarters of a mile across a stubble field with low shoes and silk stockings after being up all night and working all day—at 9:00 P.M. besides. I went though and handed up thirty-two boards a foot wide and fourteen feet long while Papa placed them on the hay. I'll bet two dollars to two cents it doesn't rain now, but it sure would if I'd refused to go.

It is as I told you. Life is one —— thing after another. But if it were not, what would we do anyway? A person must have something to beef about and his busy-ness is as good as anything I guess. Anyway, he doesn't have time to form himself into a class and put the rest of Americans into one beneath him, as J. Townsend Martin of N' York and Los Angeles did the other day. He said that there were so many common people in our American cities that people of culture could find almost no one to associate with. I class him with Poland Chinas [hogs],

Herefords, and Shorthorns. He belongs in a glass case with a plain label: the Most Exclusive Snob or Slob in America, as an old Mason in St. Joe said to me about some tall guys in the order. The old farmers in his district had more good in the dirt on their boot-heels than a certain old Dr. in K.C. had under his vest. It would apply to that geezer anyway.

I got off the subject you see, but I was only going to say that you can see now that I can sometimes go a pretty good gait, even if Miss Mary Ethel [Noland] does say I don't work. She merely does it to tease me, I guess. They're not out with me, as I thought, because I never had anyone treat me nicer than Aunt Ella did Sunday. But then she always would anyway. The girls were asleep and I didn't see them.

I am hoping that I'll have to go to town tomorrow to collect for the hay and see about some wheat weights. If I do, I'll call up and you can simply throw this letter away, after reading this far of course, and write me one on the strength of it. You see I should have put this direction in the first part, but no convenient place came along to work it in until now. I guess if you go this far, you had as well finish and then be sure and use the pen. Here's hoping I see you before you see this. If His Majesty takes a hand in my plans and I don't, may I see you on say Sunday?

Most sincerely,
Harry

[Grandview, Aug. 25, 1912]

Dear Bess: *Blue Sunday*

I guess you are having a fine time in the evening. I'm not. I'm mad. The K.C.S. went down at seven o'clock and the Frisco at six. Both too late for me to arive at a reasonable hour. I tried to call up but for some reason best known to Independence central I didn't get you. She said you didn't answer. I know she told a mistake, to put it mildly. Do you know I left on Friday fifteen minutes too soon? When I got to Union and Delaware the car was coming and I hopped on. It was the 10:25 car. I looked at my watch after getting on. I was leaving by your clock. It was 10:30 by it when we went out on the porch. When I heard the car go uptown I just supposed it was the 10:37. Wasn't that luck? I had so much to do this A.M. that I didn't go to Grandview at all, therefore I'd have had to go downtown and see a hand-scraper face-scraper maybe. Uncle Harrison intended going to town also, but the trains were so late he decided to stay out. He went down to have a look at the babies [Vivian's wife, Luella, had given birth to twins]. He's highly pleased over them.

I wish Mamma would hurry and come home. It's mighty lonesome without her. We don't expect her for a month and then we probably won't see her but for a day at a time. She's plumb dingy over those twins.

It seems that there has been a runaway in the neighborhood. Anyway two boys were here awhile ago to warn another one that his prospective father-in-law was on his trail. They wouldn't believe me when I said he wasn't here. The old man was moving to California to prevent the match. It seems like he's hastened it. Maybe that was his intention. Very mean remark. I'm sure it was not, for the boy's kinda 'hornery. (Do you spell ornery with an h?)

I keep wishing I were in Independence. I hope you didn't let my uncertain date keep you from any others. (But I really hope you did.) I am expecting to come to the fair on Thursday. But there is no telling what will happen. Mr. Hall said he expected to thresh here on Wednesday. I hope he chokes if he does. When he says Wednesday of this week he means several days after. The unexpected might happen though. Thank you very much for the Orpheum list. I hope we'll get to go see some dozens of the good things. Please send me a letter for this. I ran out of good paper upstairs and that is why this is short. Also I'm not in a good humor, as I said before, and can't write a decent letter. Don't work too hard at the fair. Can you show me around when I come in? I hope you can. Answer quick.

Most sincerely,
Harry

Grandview, Mo.
[Sept. 5, 1912]

Dear Bess:

Your excellent but very short epistle came this morning. I was on the point of phoning to see if it had been missent. Your Wednesday note was almost written but even if yours are worth two to one, I don't want to establish a precedent.

I am all alone this afternoon. Papa's cutting the pasture with a mowing machine. Mamma's down to Vivian's, and Mary's gone to see her. I'm holding the house down because the sun gave me a most excellent headache. It will be a new set of specs I guess before it's done. I have an idea that if I could get no magazines or books or newspapers for about one year, I'd probably not need any glasses at all. But I'd rather be half blind than totally ignorant. Wouldn't you?

I am glad Frank and Henry had such a good time. I was afraid it was rather slow. They only got a few birds and then it rained to boot. Mamma was highly pleased that they liked her feed so well. If they'll come when rabbits are ripe, maybe they'll have better luck as to eats and game too. Mary said that they got the same Independence car she did. I knew they got the same Dodson car. Those boys really don't know what a favor they did me by coming out Monday. The most unbearable man I know had a picnic for Myra that day, and it did me as much good to turn him down as if I'd been a girl. He's the only person I know that I think is really detestable. He's one of these old bachs who's set in his ways and who's endeavoring to be a sixteen-year-old in order to get a girl about half his age. . . .

You said you might go to Dicie's to stay all night. If it would alleviate your suffering any to have a caller that evening and if you'll give me a tip, perhaps I can accidentally appear on the scene. That is, of course, if I could make the evening any more pleasant.

I shall call you up on Sunday. Be sure and save me that Rex Beach story. I know it's good.

I hope you think you owe me a letter. If you'll write it tomorrow evening then you'll get yours on Wednesday as usual. Please do.

Sincerely,
Harry

Grandview, Mo.

Dear Bess: [Sept. 9, 1912]

I am going to put in this Monday evening properly. I have practiced on Polly's wedding march, read a short story, and am ending up by endeavoring to obtain a letter from you.

Today has been the most satanic we've had, to my notion. I took an energetic spell last week and decided to clean out the barn cistern and put a pump on it. Well, last Friday evening Boon and I began draining water about four o'clock I guess. Well, we took bucket-about until after six. I guess we must have taken out some hundreds of gallons—and it looked as if there was as much water as ever. We finally quit because it got dark. I took it on myself to finish getting the water out of the cistern by this afternoon. I'll bet I drew some two hundred gallons more or less, and there's still some water in the blooming thing. I'll get its goat tomorrow though. Then I want it to rain about three inches and fill the thing up. I was on the east side of the barn where breezes were scarce and sunshine was plentiful and exceeding hot, as Moses has remarked about the future residence of some of us. I haven't been much warmer since I sat on Mr. Slaughter's hogs while they were being vaccinated. He had some weighing about two hundred and as strong as mules. It was necessary to sneak up and grab a hind leg, then hold on until someone else got another hold wherever he could, and then proceed to throw Mr. hog and sit on him while he got what the Mo. University says is good for him. A two-hundred-pound hog can almost jerk the ribs loose from your backbone when you get him by the hind leg. It is far and away the best exercise in the list. It beats Jack Johnson's whole training camp as a muscle toughener. I helped at that job all morning Saturday and was supposed to get back this morning and finish. Maybe you think I wasn't glad when I called up and found out he'd done the job yesterday without my assistance. I'm most glad he was so scared. He is our important neighbor. That is, in his own estimation. He is a good neighbor but there is a difference in opinions, you know. We have another one that's a caution. He came up and helped us thresh oats. Along four o'clock he said to the man who was pitching bundles up on the wagon to him, "Do you suppose this man pays every night? I'd like awful well if he would, because I've got to stop by the store and get a little coffee and sugar for breakfast." The pitcher was a poor man and came very near lending that old codger a dollar. He's worth a hundred thousand dollars and probably had a wad on him big enough to choke a mule. To look at him you'd think he was a Dago ditchdigger or something of the kind. He always has about a thousand dollars in bills in his pocket, too. Papa told him someone would cave his head in sometime, but he says no one would think he had any money. You wouldn't either if you didn't know him. He is always trying to appear as a very hard-up poor man and makes out like he's powerful ignorant, while the one I mentioned first wants to appear as a leading citizen with a bushel of brains. Maybe you can guess which is the more popular and also which has the basket of brains.

I'm hoping that Boxley or Cox will get me some good seats for Friday. If he don't, there is going to be a grand row. I think I'll take my grouch out on Polly if things don't hitch just to suit. She had no business coming to see me when I want to go see someone else. Now has she? We'll make Friday as joyous as Saturday would have been anyway. Let's go try your new lunch counter, what do you say? I can meet you somewhere and we can have a whole long, fine evening if you would care to. I hope you will. Answer quick and let me know.

Most sincerely,
Harry

Grandview, Mo.
[Sept. 17, 1912]

Dear Bess:

It is 2:00 A.M. and I am going to write you. If I don't, I won't get a chance in time for you to get it on the right day.

I was in your burg this evening conferring a Third Degree. I wanted to call you up but when I got to a phone it was too late. Murray Colgan got his degree and of course I had to be on hand. Papa is about to hire a substitute for me. He says I am losing interest in the farm. I told him he had another guess coming, that I am only now getting very thoroughly interested. I think that every month will see me stay home more, but it gets worse. What I need is a sixty-horse-power motorcar. Then I could do a day's work and run around all night. We are still performing the last sad rites over dead hogs. I'll be most glad when they get done wanting to be planted. I have become disgusted with the perverse things. Of course they had a perfect right to kick the bucket, but they ought to allow some packing house to do the honors and not force me to it. Really I guess we have no more moral right to murder a horse, cow, or hog than we have one another. There really is something to be admired in a South Sea Islander after all. They eat one another, making the chances equal, while we take life we raise for the purpose. Sometimes I have a notion to swear off on meat. Especially right after dinner, when I have had a sufficiency. Like the fellow in the book you lent me. He swore to St. George that if he'd spare the life of his friend, he'd quit drinking entirely except for a gallon of ale before dinner, a gallon during dinner, and a gallon after. Wasn't that some temperance vow? That man was the original Women's Christian Temperance Union.

That was a good story, too, about King Ed. III and the Black Prince. Couldn't help but be good when it's about them, you know, if it is any way readable at all—and it is very readable.

I have to go practice Myra's weddin' march someday this week. She wanted to know if she should have the preacher present. I told her, sure he ought to earn his money and it wouldn't hurt to have him.

I am a perfect dumbhead and so sleepy my head won't stay up. Won't you please count this worth an answer and send me one? I'm hoping to see you Sunday evening. I wish every day were Sunday. Do you suppose it ever will be?

Sincerely,

Harry

[The American Hotel, St. Louis, Mo.]

Dear Bess: September 23, 1912

You see, I've followed Frank's advice and hung up at The American. It looks as imposing from the sidewalk as it does in the illustration, too, which isn't usual. The dummy [railroad] that brought me here was exactly on the tick but it ran so fast I didn't get much sleep. I've already been stung on a vaudeville show at the Columbia. It was either that or Mr. Shea in *A Man and His Wife*, which seemed from comments and pictures to be an ultra highbrow "drammer." I took the punk vaudeville. Also, I saw the divine Sarah [Bernhardt] in a movie. It was also necessary to suffer some extra acts to see her at the Hippodrome. She was worth it, though, even if she did play Queen Elizabeth as a very emotional person. Imagine a woman like that great Queen making love as Sarah can and does. Still, I hoped against my convictions that Elizabeth was like that. I also hope that she is.

This evening I attended the session of the Tuscan Lodge out on Kings Highway. They have the finest individual building in the state. All of the big guns were present and performed to the best of their ability in the limelight. Some fine highbrow time was had. I came downtown with Judge C. A. Mossman of St. Joe., who is Junior Grand Warden for this state. He is just a nice old man and not one bit stuck up.

Every time I come to this sleepy old town I am more thoroughly convinced that K.C. is a live one. It may not contain square miles or so many Jew jewelers, but it's far and away ahead of this place for things doing. *Louisiana Lou* is the leading show at the high-class theaters, and I wouldn't go see it because it's already been to K.C. The Shubert is putting on some other musical comedy, and every other show house in town has moving pictures! Except the Gayety, and Gayety shows are not *always* good. Real business begins in the morning. Tomorrow afternoon I can go on a two-mile parade if I want to and help dedicate the new Home Building. Little Harry thinks he'll skip the parade and go to the St. Louis Fair. I can do that and get back for the dedication. I guess I'll have to turn this sheet or ring for more. It is forty minutes after 12:00 P.M., and as I'm on the twelfth floor I'll not ring this time.

I am wondering if you'll consider this worth anything. I hope you will. I had a bad dream this morning. I thought I went back home from here immediately on arriving to get something I'd forgot and the folks wouldn't let me come back. I was almost ready to do some desperate trick when I woke up. I've been wondering all day if something's gone wrong at home. I never did have a more vivid dream and really thought I was home when I woke up. I am hoping to see you sometime Thursday if I can. Please send me a letter for this.

Most sincerely,

Harry

Grandview, Mo.

Dear Bess: [Sept. 30, 1912]

It is said not to be the proper thing to start a letter with an apology, but here goes. By some unreasonable freak of the mush with which my head is filled I came away and left the book you loaned me lying beside the box of candy. I was so all fired anxious to get in every second I could that I left the book in the rush—and missed the car. Caught the train though by a very narrow margin. I hope you'll still let me have the book because I'd really like to read it. I didn't think of it until I was on the car or I'd have come back for it. Also don't forget the Rex Beach you saved for me. I'd like it, too.

I came very nearly spending $4 today. *Everybody's* offers itself, *McClure's*, *Cosmo* [*politan*], and *American* for one year for that. I don't believe I'd be so badly stung as if I paid $4 for *Harper's* do you? I'll have to skin Mamma out of the farm first. She has some butter money around loose, and perhaps I can arouse her taste for muckrake magazines. I hope so, for I'd hate to spend $4 for prospective literature. I'd rather have *Life* than any of them but the bloomin' thing costs $5. I can take that and buy a whole library of hair-raising literature that is eminently proper and thrilling. I guess really it'll have to go for sugar or show tickets. Maybe both.

I worked *all* day today. It took two trials to get me started though. Papa came after me at the usual hour and he says I answered and talked rather sensibly. I know nothing of it. Anyway, he came again in about an hour and I very distinctly remember that. He was decidedly on his ear, as Vivian would say. It didn't take me long to get downstairs. After breakfast I officiated at the burial of five hogs, dumping the whole works into one hole and one ceremony. Thank goodness there are only about a dozen left. We sent thirteen healthy ones to market this morning. When the dozen die, then our hog population will be zero, from ninety to start. That beats Mark's record from affluence to poverty, doesn't it? He says politics is the quickest way. I say hogs.

I am hoping that next Sunday will be as fine a day as today was so we can have that outside breakfast. Here's hoping it will be a good one for I'm hungry now. No telling what I'll be by Sunday and a three-mile walk thrown in. It's a shame I told you all about the wedding. Just think what a letter it would have made. I had awful luck at that wedding. Only got to kiss two girls, and both of them cousins. Had to kiss one of them on the neck and got a mouthful of talcum for my pains. That's what everyone ought to get for kissing a cousin. Though I'll admit that it has to be done sometimes.

I hope you'll let me come over next Sunday evening whether you have that breakfast or not. Also please write me as long a letter as your last. It was most highly appreciated. I guess Dicie will be willing to save us that fifteen cents again Saturday, wouldn't she? Get her to let me know if I'm to get the early train Sunday please. In the meantime, *write.*

Sincerely,

Harry

The presidential election was heating up, Woodrow Wilson against the incumbent, William H. Taft, and both of them against Theodore Roosevelt, who was running on the Bull Moose ticket. Wilson came to Kansas City in the company of Champ Clark, Speaker of the House of Representatives and a Missourian, who had been Wilson's rival for the nomination at the Democratic convention in Baltimore. Clark's son, Bennett, was to serve with Truman in the Senate in the thirties and early forties. Truman, of course, would be President at the end of World War II, as Wilson would be for World War I. But, as Truman writes to Bess below, he was too busy to hear Wilson and the elder Clark in October 1912.

Grandview, Mo.

[Oct. 7, 1912]

Dear Bess:

Here goes for a punk epistle. I have been pitching and stacking hay today and my thought factory won't work. "Friar Tuck" seems to be some good story. I have merely got the introduction, you might say. To make another sudden and uncalled-for change to another subject: Do you remember my telling you about the two fellows in *Adventure* having a terrific fight on the balcony with six others when the rail gave way and then came "To be continued"? Well, those guys lit all right, all right. You'll remember I was worrying considerably about them being suspended in mid-air for thirty days. They not only landed on the ground but the six villains landed on top of them and very nearly pulverized not only the heroes but themselves as well. It's a great relief to have those fellows off my mind, I tell you. It ought to be against the law to stop a story at a place like that. Suppose a person should kick the bucket in the succeeding month. Wouldn't it be calamitous to go into the great beyond in all that suspense? I've an idea a person would suffer some of the torments of Mr. Dante's *Inferno* sure enough. I am reading another continued story that has stopped with a guy kissing his wife on the ruins of Persepolis just as they were called to breakfast. Of course the agony isn't quite so great, but a thirty-day kiss is at least a little overdone, and if they have eggs for breakfast in that hot, Godforsaken country I'm sure they won't be edible in thirty days to say the least.

To retreat again to hay. I put up my first stack today and it's a cuckoo. You've no idea what a job it is to put up a stack unless you do it once. Papa has always done it but turned the job over to me today. I reckon I must have walked some thirty-five or forty miles around a stack some thirty feet in diameter. It is necessary to keep tramping because if you don't, the stack will settle in a sort of shrunken manner and spoil. Then you're in for all manner of jibes and insults which it is necessary to take as good advice. I have always been a good stack adviser. It remains to be seen how well I can take it. We only have some ten or twelve more to build. I suppose the job is mine too. Just think of me on all the nice days of this week as runner-up for a hay marathon. I shall have probably gone some thousand miles by Saturday night, and a plush chair will sure feel good. Mr. Cox has agreed to get those seats for me and mail them. Here's hoping he gets good ones.

I'd give nineteen cents to hear Woodrow and Champ tomorrow but I can't. Cusses on the hay. I don't suppose I could hear any of their remarks anyway even if I went. That's a good sour-grape consolation anyway. You must tell me about it when you write. That is, if you are willing to consider a nonsensical scribble such as this worthy of an answer.

I shall be on hand Saturday in time to eat, unless the heavens fall or I slide off a haystack or ride a calf between now and then—very unlikely calamities.

Most sincerely,

Harry

Grandview, Mo.

Oct. 14, 1912

Dear Bess [he wrote "Bss"]:

You see my ability to leave out letters has begun early. Generally it is because I know no better, but this time I'll have to admit it was the rush. My pen is in a very dilapidated condition too. It is a new (supposedly) gold fountain one I bought to take to New Mexico. Don't suppose I have used it more than twice, and the bloomin' thing is plumb whopperjawed. I'd go down to the desk and get another but Aileen and Mary are holding down that end of the house and I'd never have any luck getting a pen. Aileen and I are getting on beautifully. Outside of the fact that I have frankly told her she will in all probability be an old maid and that she has told me I'm a boor and egotist and a chump, we have had no fusses whatever. Aileen is the finest girl to fuss with on Mary's list. It is only necessary to say one word or two at the outside and I'm in for a ten-minute word war. Trouble is, I usually get the worst of it, but I always grin and that makes her so mad she'd chew me up if she could, but as she only weighs one hundred pounds I guess I'm in no danger whatever. She's going to stay till Saturday. The probabilities are I'll be wearing a wig by Sunday. If you'll let me, I'll come over and show you how I look in one.

How did you feel this morning after the walk? With the exception of a blister I was as fit as could be this morning. I'll admit though that I was tired last night and I'll bet you were too. I hope you'll give me credit for having a little sense and leaving a half hour early although I didn't want to a bit. I had the best luck with the train last night. A freight got in front of it and it slowed down so I could jump off right close to home. It got me to bed a whole half-hour earlier than usual. I was sure thankful, I'll tell you.

Mary has just been up here to get a bottle of Vaseline. She saw that picture of you on the bureau and she's having one fit after another to know who it is. She's taken the picture down to see if Aileen knows who it is. Of course she doesn't, and it's created a sensation. I told Mary I got the picture where I was last night and that's made things worse. She's confident I'm a two-faced scoundrel, etc. ad lib. I'm not going to tell her nor Aileen either who it is for a week anyway. I hear them now discussing it downstairs. I told Mary I am writing to "her" and I just heard Aileen say she'd see the address in the morning. I'm going to mail it myself and not let them see so I'll have a disturbance soon enough.

Have Nell and the rest recovered yet? I'll bet you had no tennis today even if it is the finest one we've had this month. I am going to push a pitchfork in the morning. We have about sixty acres of hay cut.

Do you know I promised to bring you H. Rider Haggard's *Ayesha* and forgot it entirely. I am going to tie it to my coattail right now so I'll not forget it next Sunday (provided, of course, that it is agreeable to you that I should come). Here's hoping it is. I wish I had some of those ham sandwiches and grapes now with a little bit of that pudding and [illegible] sauce to top off on. I guess I'll go down and glean the leavings from supper before I go to bed. My appetite has come back in full force. Hay stacking is doing me good. I am hoping to lose my job tomorrow. We hired an extra, and if he can stack he's sure going to. I hope you can read this and will send me an answer. I arrived at the end of my paper before I intended, hence the abrupt ending. This is all the paper until a trip to town.

Most sincerely,
Harry

Grandview, Mo.

Dear Bess: [Oct. 21, 1912]

Look what I found—two whole sheets of paper. They were in the drawer upstairs and I just accidentally ran into them. I'd made up my mind to use tablet paper and a stronger envelope. I guess I'll have to next time if I don't get to the city soon. Here's hoping I have business there some *morning* soon. Papa has decided we won't cut any more hay, so I can probably chase off someday soon without any excuse whatever but my own whim. He'll have something on hand soon though. We started a man to shucking corn this morning. I'm hoping against hope to elude that job. It's one I don't appreciate at all.

I met a fellow at Union Street last night who was going to the Wyandotte depot to catch the Great Western train for Cedar Rapids, Iowa. It goes at eleven-thirty and I told him he'd never make it except by exceptional luck. His grip was at the Sexton Hotel but he said if I'd show him to the train the grip could go hang. We ran from 8th and Walnut to 8th and Wyandotte and just caught a car. Made the train by one minute. He was very effusive in his thanks but was a little on the obese order and had to blow so much he made a very poor out at the thanks. Said he hoped he'd see me again at Union St. So I guess he's some attraction down that way too. I didn't learn his name in the excessive hurry but he wore a pin like mine, so I guess he's all right. Seemed to have plenty of dough, because he was willing to pay Allen's five dollars to take him but decided that by the time he walked uptown and got cranked up he'd miss out sure. It would be some ten-dollar reason that would make me pay Allen's five dollars for a ten-cent ride. Maybe he had the ten-dollar reason, for he sure wanted to catch the train. It was a very fine night last night out here—the moon was about two yards high and it was lightning all along the north. Made very fine scenery I'll tell you. I wanted the rain most badly but not badly enough to want to get wet. It didn't come even after I was perfectly willing. . . .

Please send me a letter as soon as you can.

Most sincerely,

Harry

Grandview, Mo.

Dear Bess: [Oct. 29, 1912]

I had to work the same stunt on Mary you did on George. Only I didn't say by your leave or anything else, just simply went to her box and helped myself. That's the way you should do too.

I had a very good time at Nolands' last night. Played hearts at my table and I beat, that is, I got the most hearts. My score was something like sixty-nine. The other bunch played bridge. Ethel had everyone to cut out a black cat from a piece of paper, just simply cut without any outline or anything. Miss Pavey won. Dick Busch got the ornery prize, which was a cat head full of lemon drops. I tried to win it but couldn't. Ardis and Jody [younger sister of Ardis] thought I was entitled to it and pulled for me but it was no use. They probably had good reasons for wanting me to get it. I've forgotten what the real prize was. I'm having a deuce of a time with this letter. It was started before dinner and now Papa is yelling for me to come on he's going to the field. So I'll have to rush this to an early ending. If I don't seal it up now, you'll never get it on Wednesday morning. I'll do better next time. . . . Please send *me* a *long* answer.

Most sincerely,

Harry

Dear Bess: [Grandview, Nov. 6, 1912]

. . . Nobody talks anything but election. The *Star* says 297 for Roosevelt. The *Post* says 360 for Wilson, and the *Journal* gives Taft a majority only. Q.E.D., Wilson is elected easily. I shall scratch Winstanley and Bradshaw. Vote for one Republican and one [Bull] Moose. I was reading Plato's *Republic* this morning and Socrates was discoursing on the ideal Republic. It was not ours. You see, I sometimes read something besides *Adventure*. Please, will you mail it to me if I don't see you tomorrow? I have left a hero and his wife down under the ruins of Persepolis and I'm dying to know how they got out. This is the same two that I left kissing each other last month.

Here's hoping I see you tomorrow and that you'll answer this horrible mixture.

Most sincerely,
Harry

Grandview, Mo.

Dear Bess: [Nov. 11, 1912]

Now you are going to see an *in*coherent letter in opposition, or answer I should say, to your good one of last Friday.

I have been scooping corn today, probably some three hundred bushels this afternoon. That is to say I scooped 150 bu. twice—into a wagon and out again. (I changed pens here—notice any difference.) Ask George if you don't believe it's some work. As you probably know I didn't get my full allowance of sleep either last night, only from two to five. Sounds like an afternoon reception, don't it? But Napoleon said five hours in twenty-four is enough anyway, so I guess it'll make a man of me. I had it all doped out to write you as much as the squeaky wheels in my head would turn out this evening and then put in enough sleep to last Napoleon three days all at a stretch. But one of the McBrooms got it into his head that he wanted a few dollars, so I had to begin figuring from way back in the middle of the summer and multiply, add, and subtract for some time, finally coming out almost even with the board. He's satisfied though and now it's over I don't care much either. I was cussin' mad when he first came though.

As you have probably concluded by this time I was not held up. It was dark as pitch clear to the car line though. That Galt guy ran out of Davis's just as I came along and nearly scared me green but it was a double pleasure when I found who it was. I don't think it ever was any darker out here. All my fright was for nothing—not one thing happened.

I guess George and Frank got in safely, as I see nothing in the *Journal* about any holdups last night. . . .

My inclination was not to work today. The Scottish Rite had one grand banquet at noon. The man who nominated W. J. Bryan in 1900 at Kansas City presided and some more distinguished members of A.A.S.R. spouted oratory. I wanted to be present so bad I almost busted. But I knew if I went today I'd never come home till Thursday evening and maybe be out some $125 and four good days' work, so I resisted the temptation and stayed home. If our porkers hadn't been so inconsiderate as to die before their time, I'd been there with both feet without a qualm (he! he!). You didn't think I had that word in my system did you? I'll tell you what A.A.S.R. means if you don't already know; it is no deep, dark secret.

Do you want to see *Mikado, Pirates of Penzance, Pinafore,* or the other one? Pick your choice and I'll order tickets by mail if you'll let me know right away quick. If I could be in town so often this busy time we'd see them all on account of my big saving at the Scottish Rite, but I can't leave so often if I'm ever going to get any dollars ahead.

Please write me a nice letter for this spurt and I'll sure know you are good-natured and easily imposed upon.

                              Sincerely,
                              Harry

                                                          Grandview, Mo.
Dear Bess: [Nov. 26, 1912]
        I am going to get this one off on time or bust a hamstring. That is a classic expression because that said string holds the key to the whole set of harness. If it breaks, away go the horses and you stand in the road. Also it is the last piece of harness to break. It is either very rotten when it breaks or the rest of the harness is very strong.

        I've spoiled my excessive effort but I'll get the letter off.

        It was well I left when I did the other evening because that car was uptown. It is a "most" uncertain quantity. No wonder people swear at the Met. They had a transfer out Sunday which said that the car ride is the cheapest thing in town and gets more knocks. A man will go to dinner and tip the waiter for five rides and then whip the con[ductor] when his transfer is overdue. Mr. Ed Howe of Atchison was the composer of that. I suppose the Met will give him a life pass for it. They ought to. I wish I were a railroad attorney or some other kind of grafter so I could ride free. The depot agent at Grandview has worked for the Frisco thirty years. He gets a pass for himself and wife over the whole system for the balance of his days. He's only fifty, so he can ride some thousands of miles yet. He says he's going to California December 1 and stay a month and then to Penn. and stay a month and then go to work again. I really don't believe, though, I'd want to be a station agent until I was fifty in order to get a pass. Rather be something else. Section boss for instance. I guess I'll be a clodhopper and pay the grafters. That's his privilege.

        I have to write this on the installment plan, as usual Papa keeps wanting something. Also he's anxious for me to get to work. We are going to haul some tons of hay today. It is a backbreaking job. Fine exercise though. I just wish I could get some of these white hopes and black champs in on the usual routine farm exercise. You'd hear them howl about being stale and overdone along about four o'clock the first day. They'd do their country and also their morals much better service if they spent their time producing something with their tall muscular force. I hate a prize fighter worse than a packing-house employee. They are both butchers and barbarians under the hide. Worshippers of Woden I guess. Anyway they attempt to imitate Thor when he drank an ocean of booze.

        Which makes me remember that there was a Latin Bible called the Vulgate which King James used in his translation along with the Septuagint and Hebrew. I am not writing an essay or connected letter—my trains of thought are scattered as were those of Mr. Brian O'Cree's mother in perpetua. For another jump, I have diligently searched for authority to translate *mores* [as] death but I can't find it. Guess I'll have to come in and say it means bad manners or something along that line. I guess we could say O horrors and make it modern couldn't we? Hang Cicero, Hebrew, Thor, and all the rest. You owe me a letter. Send it quickly.

                                    Most sincerely,
                                    Harry

                                                            Grandview, Mo.
Dear Bess: [Dec. 10, 1912]
        Here goes a bid for two letters. Fact is I'd bid for one every day in the week if it would bring it. . . .
        I am not shucking corn this morning, as you have probably surmised by this time. You see Mary has not arrived as yet. We are expecting a man to mend the kitchen flue, therefore I had to empty the kitchen and do some other tall stunts —start a fire in the parlor for instance. The parlor stove is the most pigheaded one on the place. I had a roaring fire in the bloomin' thing, departed to the coal shed for more fuel, and when I came back the whole shebang was as cold as a tomb. Now stove, pipe, fire and all are endeavoring to up the flue. I gave it some encouragement with a little John D. extract. I have hopes that the flue is good and that the wind won't get any stronger, in which case we'll still do business at the old stand. I must chase in and see what's happening. It may be necessary to scale the roof and dump a bucket of salt where it will do the most good. It's all right and behaving as a good fire should. You know salt has a most quieting effect on a roaring flue. It is also very quieting to a conversation mill when thrown in in huge quantities. Mamma said that Uncle Harrison once got an unsuspecting neighbor boy to lie on his back, open his mouth, and shut his eyes with the expectation that said uncle would raise him up with a straw. Mamma was standing by with a handful of salt and when the poor fellow got his mouth widest open she dashed in the salt. From all accounts he riz up all right. It seems that he had heated a penny and gave it to Mamma. She enlisted Uncle Harry to help her even up, hence the salt episode. He gave Mamma no more hot pennies. . . .
        I must quit but be sure and send the *two* to
                                    Most sincerely,
                                    Harry

                                                            Grandview, Mo.
Dear Bess: [Dec. 17, 1912]
        I've got it—oh, job well done maybe. It's not a rope of pearls or a limousine. It took me seventeen and one-half minutes by the clock to decide and seven weeks to think of. Then of course it's not half good enough. I really couldn't get anything good enough, not even if I had a million. You can exchange it for something if it's not agreeable. It didn't come from Cady's or Jaccard's nor E.B.T.'s nor any hardware store nor Monkey Ward's nor the ten-cent store. I'll

give you three guesses and if you guess, I'll send it back and get the other one, which happens to be the same thing. The guy brought the wrapper from gay Paree in the bottom of his trunk. He gave me that and it's better looking than the thing itself. You can't guess it, so you needn't try. I'm only building up your expectations so they can be keeled over at one fell swoop. You know a grand disappointment is as much fun as a good surprise—to the lookers on.

That lowdown dentist kept me for one solid hour and nearly drilled into my gray matter, fact is some of it must have leaked out. . . .

Did your flowers ever arrive? I should have sent a messenger but did [not] think of it at the time. I suppose you carried the prize home. I was in your burg again last night to a Lodge of Instruction. I told Polly that's where I was going but they didn't believe me, neither did Ethel and Nellie or the folks at home. It doesn't pay to tell the truth even occasionally to some people.

We are going to kill hogs today, oh what a mess when the meat comes home. It's always my job to stuff the sausage into sacks. It is a very agreeable one too. Always I put in some good hide off my own hands along towards the last because they blister and the blisters wear off. It doesn't injure the flavor of the sausage.

May I come Sunday, and are you going to let me go shopping with you Monday or?—and?—Tuesday, whichever suits you best—and I wish that wedding was in kingdom come on Saturday night, for that's the only one this week that I can get off to go to a show. Perhaps it is as well for I'll have a few more cents for Christmas presents and lunch Monday and, or, Tuesday.

> Sincerely,
> Harry

> Grandview, Mo.

Dear Bess: [Dec. 31, 1912]

Behold this gorgeous stationery. Some I traded from Nellie. I gave her two sheets of white and she gave me this. Some man gave it to her, because she won't tell me who did. I have decided *not* to send that letter I wrote on Thursday night. It has melted and ran down in my pocket. You've no idea how very glad I am I didn't send it. I'll try and make up for it in this one. First and foremost I get more pleased with that chain on every occasion I wear it. Vivian has already attempted to purloin it. Ethel says she's going to take it for a necklace. It just fits her. They'll have to go some if any of 'em get it. We are going down to Hornbuckle's to dinner. Then I have to go to Dodson and meet Mary Colgan. I have hopes of spending some strenuous day. Have already hauled thirty gallons of water. Our well has a pigheaded streak. My dear nephew and niece are raising sand in here. Luella has gone to town and Mamma is having the best time she's had for a week. Those kids are as fat as all get out. They ought to be though. They do nothing but eat and sleep.

I got your glasses engraved. A very fine job I think. You know I stayed over and had it done. It was a good thing I did because Papa wanted me in town anyway. I have those *Get Rich Quick Wallingford* seats. It seems that good shows are as scarce as hen's teeth. I am betting this one is punk. Here's hoping I'm wrong. Those ornery girls are squalling for me to come on and take them to Myra's. I'll have to go. Make it three next time.

Most sincerely,
Harry

THREE

. . . AND ANOTHER

The somewhat pale kaleidoscope of life on the farm continued through *1913*. What matter to Harry Truman that this was the last year of peace Europe and the Western world would enjoy in the twentieth century, or at least for seventy years thereafter? He did not even sense the downward course of diplomacy in faraway Europe, the imminent tragedy for world peace—the tragedy in which before long he would be involved, and in which many years later he would play a major role. The round of farm responsibilities went on. He developed a stiff neck and visited an osteopath. After seeing the latter, who, Harry tells Bess, almost wrung his neck, he went to a physician who prescribed iodine. Troubles with the Home Telephone Company arose when owners of that enterprise tried to gouge the farmer subscribers. His father ran for road overseer, a township job; Harry dutifully campaigned, but, as he says, he wished John Truman would not have run. The Eastern Stars, a sister organization of the Masons, of Grandview, including Mary Truman, needed assistance from Harry in his role as Master of the local Masonic Lodge, and that took up some time. The farm lawsuit continued, with Aunt Susan on the wrong side: "One hates," wrote Harry, "to see a white-haired old lady one likes and respects tearing up the truth just for a few dollars."

The courtship progressed smoothly but slowly. Hoping to cut loose from farm duties, Harry tried to stake a claim in distant, cold Montana, where the federal government had raffled off Indian lands to settlers. The more he thought about the prospect, the better it sounded. "Who knows," he asked of Bess, "I may be His Excellency the Governor of Montana someday (hee haw). How would you like to be Mrs. Governor?" This proposition came to naught, as doubtless he sensed it would. Travel to Independence continued. A friend who had ended his own agony of courtship by getting married told him, Harry said, of "what an awful mistake I was making to go chasing over to Independence so often. Said he'd never do it. He'd go get her and make one trip do." But Bess stayed in Independence—and when she gave Harry a set of cuff links for Christmas, he told her they were the finest he ever had.

The name Fred Boxley recurs often in Truman's letters. Boxley, a Kansas City lawyer, had been a member of the National Guard in Battery B with Truman. At the time of this letter he represented the Trumans and Uncle Harrison in the suit over Grandmother Young's will.

Dear Bess: [Grandview, Jan. 6, 1913]

I was all kinds of a fool for not accepting your invitation to stay. When I got home the hired man was here. I didn't get cold but it was not the most agreeable walk in the world from Grandview. Besides instead of being thanked for getting home to milk I got nothing but jibes. Papa had the impudence to ask me if your mother kicked me out. Pretended he was anxious for me to stay because he wanted me to go see Judge Mize on business. Any old time I ever let grim duty interfere with my inclination or pleasure it will be a warmer night than the last one was. You know Mark or Bill Nye or some other smart man has said that when business interferes with pleasure, by all means let business go hang. It seems that people who do are as well off. Anyway they're not pursued by bad hoodoos as I told you I am. Some day I shall whirl on that hoodoo and knock it into a cocked hat, then things will begin to come right.

I bought an *Adventure* last night and entertained myself with bloodcurdling stories on the train so I'd feel nice and comfortable coming down the road. This month's number sure contains some hair raisers. I took your watch chain and hid it in my hat band. I was going to tell my good holdup man to take my dollar and a half but leave such chain provided he'd found it. I wouldn't lose that for a farm. It's my good luck piece now. I'm not one bit superstitious, oh no. But you know there is always a part of the giver along with a present and that's what makes it precious. I'd be most tempted to eat that chain rather than let someone get it.

My letters are like the ones Agnes's [Agnes Salisbury's] flame used to send her. They are candidates for the kitchen stove. These sheets are large enough to start a good fire. I think I shall follow your stunt and get some very, very tiny note paper then they'll go down the register easily anyway. You ought to use some larger paper. You get the best of me in that. One of my sheets is as big as your two. I'll admit that one of yours is worth all mine but you should give as much paper anyway.

You sure punctured my head in your last. Mrs. Southern was most awful nice to say what she did. Even when you know such things are mistakes they make you feel good. I was on the point of buying a new hat and having my picture *took* and all sorts of things. Really now, won't you get me a picture made for my watch lid? I want it most awful bad. You know I only have two of you and neither of them is half as good looking as the original. Now, you ought to give me one anyway. If it'll help any I'll say they couldn't make one that would be, though I'd like you to let them try.

Are you going to let me come over next Sunday? I hope so. It'll be a mighty long week. There are no holidays in this one and not a good show in town that

I've heard of. Besides I'm busted anyway. Boxley is going to New Mexico and has politely informed me that two hundred dollars are in order. That guy keeps me busted from month to month. If it keeps up much longer I'm going into the hands of a receiver in Judge Pollock's court. That seems to be a money-making proposition. It wouldn't work in my case for I'm not a public service corporation. I have nothing I could raise the price on except hot air, and that's too high already.

You owe me a four-sheet notepaper letter. At least I think you do. Here's hoping I get it. You are going to get this on Tuesday. Ought I to send one so you'll get it on Wednesday too? I'll have to know pretty quick if I do.

Today is another good day to *contemplate* a walk to Courtney. I dreamed the other night that you and I took a longer one than that. I was afraid to tell it 'cause it's a bad sign. But I hope it comes true. Not the sign.

Most sincerely,

Harry

May Wallace, mentioned in passing in the letter that follows, is the daughter of Colonel William Southern, Jr., onetime owner of the Independence Examiner. *She married Bess's brother George in 1916 and is the last surviving Truman in-law. Ever since her marriage she has lived in a bungalow behind 219 North Delaware, which she calls "the Big House."*

Dear Bess: [Grandview, Jan. 21, 1913]
   . . . I wish you had consented to go to hear that Russian pianist. I believe he'll be worth hearing but I guess I'll not go. I'll save the money to go to some other show with or else throw it away on a hat. Four dollars ought to get a pretty good one. I wish I could get an overcoat for that much. It seems to me that it would be an excellent thing if people wore the same styled costumes for the seasons instead of changing. There's China and Holland. They seem to be as well satisfied with their clothes as we are with ours. If we could do that way, think how much we'd be ahead for booze and other luxuries. I'm for it especially because I need the money for booze. I shall probably be in town the day you get this. If I am, I'll call up.

My head is empty and I am slated to milk and feed. Papa has gone to Belton to get himself tortured by a dentist. I'm glad it isn't me. I hate dentists as a class and as individuals until I get a swelled up jaw and then they're fine people to have around. Mamma is sitting here in the room. She insists on telling me a lot of things and then asking my opinion. I've gotten in bad two or three times because I said yes where no should have been. She finally decided that I am a very poor stick to talk to. Wasn't a bit backward about telling me so either. I only grinned. She said she hoped I paid more attention to other people when they were discussing things. I told her I'd rather listen to her than anyone and that mollified her to some extent. Of course I made a mental reservation when I said that. Of course you could never guess who that would be, unless maybe you happened to have a mirror handy. Did you ever pay any attention to my humble request for another picture of you? Why don't you do like May does George and give me two or three. They'd be as highly appreciated I assure you. Just try me and see. You've no idea how crazy I am about you and you won't have until I get somewhat richer than at present. Do you suppose that time will ever arrive? I guess not as long as lawyers cost like they do.

You probably owe me a letter. Anyway I'm of that opinion. Please send it and say I can come down as usual on Sunday anyway. I sure did enjoy myself last Sunday and I certainly appreciate Frank's sharing his sleeping quarters with me.

Most sincerely,
Harry

Below, Truman describes his mixed feelings about politics, in this case his father's candidacy for road overseer of Washington Township, which included Grandview. As such, John Truman would supervise the repair of local roads. A minor political office, it usually involved friendship with one of the county commissioners (known in Missouri as county judges). Since the state was overwhelmingly Democratic, the contest for most offices occurred in the August primary.

Dear Bess: [Grandview, Feb. 4, 1913]
Here goes for an attempt at answering your good letter. Thanks very much for the Kodak print. As you remarked about my Arkansas letter, that doesn't count on the photo deal. I shall still expect one. You know you really couldn't get one too cheap to be good. The picture couldn't help but be good. You ought to give me two for that.

My stayover was of no consequence. I couldn't find the country lawyer who was to present that petition. I don't know whether it was presented or not and I don't care. If my dad would listen to me he wouldn't have the job. Politics are very bad for men's systems anyway.

This old duck who holds the job really ought to have it again, but he was fool enough to be for Chrisman and to vote for Sheppard therefore off comes his head. As no one else can be found who can run the job, Papa must needs go for it. I am rabidly for him in public and got his petition signed by some of the other guy's signers but I honestly hope he gets beaten. He'd be as mad as a wet hen if he knew I thought that.

While wandering around hoping to run into my country lawyer I went into Boxley's office and he opened up his heart and his pocketbook—took me to lunch and a five-cent show. The lunch was good but I'd unfortunately eaten two chocolate eclairs and a bowl of custard about fifteen minutes before and couldn't do it justice. The show was also good. Most things are good when someone else will do the paying. A person really doesn't feel like kicking. That of course is a payer's privilege. I wouldn't have kicked anyway even if I'd paid.

I've an idea that rube lawyer got into a thirst emporium somewhere and is there yet. He's a perfect tank for booze. He's one of the Grandview saloon's best customers but he's a good fellow. As the saying is, it's such a shame he drinks, he'd be such a help to his mother. Wife and children would be better, for his mother is of the step variety and they usually drive kids to drink. His pa's rich and I've an idea if ever he gets any of that money he'll paint things a most violent rainbow tint. I got tired searching for him about 1:00 P.M. and came home on the Kansas City Southern. It was very well I did for I found Booney has the grippe. I gave him a half a glass of toddy and a vinegar gargle and sent him to bed a few minutes ago. If he gets sick, I'll be up against a stay-at-home proposition sure enough. Can't even leave on Sunday. I'm hoping the booze will take the kinks out. I'm no advocate of whiskey as a steady diet but on occasion it can do heaps of good. . . .

Bess, please don't give up shows after February 5. Something extra fine will be sure to come to the Orpheum sure as you do. You know Sothern-Marlowe and Faverchain [Faversham] (Is that how to spell him?) don't count as shows—even rabid Baptists go to see them. They're supposed to be educational and not entertaining. But the Orpheum is different—sometimes. Remember you have a date with me for said Favaperson and Divine Sarah and I wish you had one for Sothern. I guess you've seen them in everything though. I'd like to have a date with you for every day in the year. May I have one for next Sunday evening anyway? If the hired man's sick and Papa's gone I may not arrive before 9:00 P.M. but I sure will come if Dodson cars still run. I can catch the six-thirty car and get over there by eight-thirty. Oh for the six sixty *limmersine* [limousine] or even a four forty or a motor cycle. I'd better be glad I've got a saddle horse and a plug and ramshackle buggy. Some poor guys haven't even that and still they have a good time.

Please get some *big* stationery (some of George's) and write me a nice long letter. I shall want one awful bad this week.

Most sincerely,
Harry

Dear Bess: [Grandview, Feb. 10, 1913]
You have succeeded in enlarging the size of my hat. The idea of anyone, especially you, ever wanting to decorate my striking likeness with a silver frame has almost made me unable to contain myself with any degree of satisfaction. I even smiled when Mary informed me we were out of water at 6:30 P.M. after a hard day's work too. You know it is necessary for us to haul water a half mile. Also it was dark at six-thirty this evening. I had to hitch up a horse to get that water and eat supper all alone. I can only attribute my good humor to that request. Hang the chaperon. She generally (he I should say) doesn't know straight up about common sense. She (he) can write piffle about how many fingers to stick out when you eat salad and if it's proper to eat pie à la mode with a spoon when ice cream is slushy but for good sense she (he) is no authority. You may be sure I'd never have the effrontery to offer my photo to you because that, it seems to me, would be a case of rank egotism. You want one, you ask for it, you swell my head, make me feel good which is a good deed anyway Q.E.D. Hang the chap-

eron. I have had a very strenuous day—my reason factory is not very good, but you'll get that tintype if I have to bust one dozen cameras. A silver frame! I can't live it down. Now don't forget I want yours worse than ever.

My dad arrived with his two loads of cows last night at seven o'clock. Mamma said he was on his ear in proper fashion when I wasn't there to meet him. He called me in the morning from Lowry City, and the K.C. central had to repeat the message, and instead of leaving that town at 5:00 P.M. he left at noon. She called at twelve o'clock [and] five o'clock. I'm glad she did. There was no harm done and I spent the evening where I wanted to. We have more old cows now than you have chickens I guess. Fifty-two new ones and thirty we already had. It sounds like the stockyards on a busy day. Of course there are some calves and the cows have more trouble sorting out their proper calves than the people did their babies after the Virginian's mixing them up [*The Virginian*, by Owen Wister, 1902]. Instead of being two hours night and morning tending to the cows it is now twelve hours all day. I am of the opinion it will grow pretty old before grass comes. Anyway Papa is very happy he can get up at unearthly hours and cipher around with a lantern and stay out at night long enough to use one. He would rather yell at a cow than eat a meal. I would rather eat. His being away from home has caused me to get in bad with the W.C.T.U. The mayor of Grandview arrested the saloon man for selling whiskey. He asked me to go his bond to keep him out of jail. I went it same as I'd go a preacher's if he asked me to. This man's a pretty good fellow only he sells booze. I don't suppose it would have done him any good to stay in jail and I'm sure he likes me better. The only ones who will have it in for me are the "backyarders," as Uncle Harrison calls the North Carolinians. I'm not hankerin' for their friendship anyway. They yell temperance and want to lynch a saloon man but they'll go to the city and get gloriously stewed. I told them if they wanted really to shut up the saloon to do as I do and drink no booze, then the saloon man would have to get a pick and shovel and go to work.

I am going to send for Mr. Faversham's tickets for Thursday evening of the week he's here. Will that suit you? We have a man from St. Claire County here. He came home with Papa. It is my duty to show him K.C. tomorrow. Do you envy me my job? I don't. He's a fine man and I like him but I'd rather do something else. He's never been to K.C. and I don't know what to show him except Emery, Bird, Thayer's Eleventh Street entrance and the Shubert (*from the outside*). Maybe he'll get down to the stockyards and be so interested we can spend the day there. Let's hope so.

You owe me a letter. Also may I come Sunday as usual? Wait till we sell a cow and I'll get you that tintype.

Most sincerely,
Harry

Dear Bess: [Grandview, Feb. 18, 1913]
I am having a hard time finding a pen. There are some half dozen around but none that will write. The folks insisted on my going to see an osteopath today.

I went but thank heaven he wasn't in. I am totally cured by just having been at the office. I stole a book on theosophy off his desk and I've an idea that had something to do with the cure. It has an article on India in the year 11,182 B.C. telling about the birth of Jupiter, Saturn, and the Indian god Siva the destroyer, a letter from Mrs. Annie Besant, and various other stuff. They contend that we are born until we become perfect, then we enter the bosom of some god or other. It is a very convenient and satisfying system if a person could subdue his brains and make himself believe it. It would be about as easy to believe Greek and Roman mythology. I guess I'll have to plod along with the four Gospels as my foundation for a while longer. They are the best yet. The trouble with the churches is that they don't teach enough of those books. They're too strong on St. Paul and the rest of the Apostles. I don't believe there'd ever have been any split if the teachers had stayed by the original four books. . . .

I busted a camera into four pieces today. I told the lady manager I wanted to get my face in a small enough space to go inside the rim of a silver dollar. I can tell you if I succeeded or not day after tomorrow. It always makes me feel embarrassed to get in front of a picture machine. I suppose a person who can keep his poise in that position makes a good actor or public speaker. I notice they all look very much at ease in their pictures anyway. I am positively confident mine will look very scared or very mulish, one. In either case I'll not find fault with the cameraman for my own shortcoming. This picture is going to be as small as you want it to be. It sure would be a shame to waste any good money to frame it. It will be too highly honored just by your accepting it. I'll show you the proof Sunday if I get them before then.

I'm very glad you liked the roses. I wish I'd had brains enough to think of something really worthwhile but I didn't. I thought of stationery and then decided that would look like an Indian present, at least one with a string to it. I'm glad you got some though and I hope you continue to let it come my way.

Mary can't get over my bringing *Keeping up with Lizzie* home with me. She wants to put something in the name. She and Myra Colgan both had a great deal to say about that book. I'm not going to let either of them read it for that. They both know how I love the name and how thoroughly pleased I am to have them call you Lizzie. They're both in bad for the balance of the week anyway. Lizzie sure was a goer in this case. Would you care to have me extract that East Indian story from the back of *Adventure* and send it to you? I like it a lot. I'd offer you the whole magazine but I'm afraid you like it about like you do Nick Carter. It is lots better than Nick and not nearly so bad as *Ainslee's*. The only thing about it is the tough paper it is printed on.

Please send me a letter for this and I'll do better next time. I've had a strenuous day you know, almost saw an osteopath, got my phiz mapped, and did a half-day's real work.

Most sincerely,
Harry

Dear Bess: [Grandview, Feb. 24, 1913]

I am starting with a new pen. It runs so smoothly that there is no telling what I'll write before I'm done. You'll probably get this a day sooner. I'm going to East Lynn tonight and, if Papa doesn't seriously object, to Garden City tomorrow night. Home Wednesday and Independence Thursday. Last week I stayed home and tended to business, this week I'll try Mark's system and not allow business to interfere with pleasure, provided always I can keep the boss in a good humor. That is some job too. I'm generally successful at it but the rest of the family sometimes fail to have any luck.

My grandstanding ability for sympathy is plenty large. I usually work it on the home folks to a fare you well, but I am generally in such good spirits when I arrive in your vicinity that I forget to play for it. (Quarter please.) I shall add that quarter to the asset side of the ledger and let it run as an open account. If I go into bankruptcy or an estate you'll have to pay it or stand suit. My thought factory as usual is in a decidedly clogged condition. One lobe of the brain is cold and the other warm; the cold side is the one I think with. The other contains my penmanship. You can see that both are rather mushy. The reason I know one side is cold and the other warm is because I have a warm hand and foot and a cold one. Can't account for it unless it's because one side's next to the fire. It was about seventy-five degrees below zero last night when I got home. The hired man stayed all night and has the fresh-air habit to an extreme. He had all the windows in the room skyhigh. I piled on some additional covers but I nearly shook the bed to pieces before I got warm. It did go down to eight above. With wind. in the north that is cold enough for all practical purposes. I hope Easter Sunday will be as cold as yesterday. I would just like to know if all the girls would wear straw hats, white dresses, and no coats if Easter were a zero day. I bet they would. Your remarks about ancient styles suit me. I'd kind of hate to abide by the then prevailing costume on a day like today though. If there is anything I do hate, it's to buy new clothes. I always imagine everybody can hear me coming. I guess it will be absolutely necessary for me to borrow or steal enough for a spring suit. If the coats are going to strike halfway up the back they ought to take off some for the saving in cloth. Also the balance of the suit will be saving as to cloth. Therefore I have hopes of getting one. I think I'll get a green one. So it will match up with rural scenery.

Did you enjoy that Indian story? Don't say you did just for politeness. I'd really like to know if you liked it. I did but then my access to reading matter is limited and therefore I'm no good judge. If I can find a card in the City of East Lynn I'll send you one. I'll get Frank Blair [cashier of the Bank of Belton, Deputy Grand Master of the Masons of Missouri] to write one to Nell and sign it 'Uncle' if you'll not let her know you are acquainted with the fact. Do you suppose she will get very mad? Mr. Blair writes a perfect copybook hand and she'll never connect me with East Lynn. I'd hate to have Nell to start in to lift my back hair. I have a notion she'd manage to get at least one handful. I've got a surplus of hair but I don't care to have it removed in that way.

I hope Mr. Faversham is good. If he proves rotten I'd feel like heaving an egg at him because I'm anxious to see a good show. Haven't seen a picture show for two weeks, think of that. I am expecting you to remember that Bernhardt and Eva are on your date list with me. They are in the far distant future but I'm going to manage to see them or bust a hamstring.

You owe me a letter. You can make it two if you want to, this is such a *good* one.

Most sincerely,
Harry

Dear Bess: [Grandview, Mar. 4, 1913]
I am endeavoring to make this arrive on time. The car got laid out at Sheffield and I missed my train. There was some more holdups down in that end of town and I wasn't sorry it was too late to go down there. I got home this morning on the ten-thirty train. Papa was in a very bad humor because he was away from home yesterday. There were several buyers here for cattle. I wanted him to stay at home, but he said he wanted to go to town as well as a certain other person whom he named. Anyway he was sorry he went, and I said I told you. He finally got in a good humor. I think [the] thing the matter with him was that Mamma is down at Vivian's. Their hired girl skipped without notice and the grandmothers are doing duty turn about. I hope they'll soon find help because Mamma still has two children of her own. You'd really think I am jealous of those infernal twins but I'm not at all. If Luella ever finds that I used such a strong adjective in describing them I've an idea she'll let me know what a redheaded woman can do when she's on her ear. I wouldn't blame her a bit. Of course I wouldn't allow anyone else to use it, but being one of their only two uncles I guess I have some privileges. One of them is going to be to teach them meanness and [the other] to sass their daddy. I've already informed Luella that we're going to make a tough citizen of the boy. There are getting to be too many moral mollycoddles in the family. We ought at least to make a white hope or a big leaguer out of him. If not that then maybe I can get him to whip his pa and get the family name into good repute again. I am sorry to say that their mother doesn't look with favor on my plans for their future. Neither does Mamma. Someone will have to see that that boy is not an effeminate piano player though, so why not me. I shall buy him a sawbuck and saw as soon as he's big enough to use it and also a G. Washington cherry tree tool. I'll bet he'll make a piano hard to catch when he gets so he can use them. . . .

Vivian is going to the post office and it's my only chance to get this off. Have to stop. You owe me a letter.

Most sincerely,
Harry

Dear Bess: [Grandview, Mar. 10, 1913]
You are muchly mistaken if you think I was in a bad humor when I penned your last epistle. It may have sounded as if I was because I laid such emphasis on having no mammy at home or because I was at the time disgusted with

pinheads in general and myself in particular. You see I'd just succeeded in bringing on my stiff neck again and I was sure it was a mollycoddle stunt. I'll try and be more cheerful this time. For one thing I've been to see Mamma this morning and she's promised to come home and visit us a few minutes tomorrow. I took Uncle Harrison down to see his grandnephew and niece. The girl laughed at him and was glad to see him, but the boy yelled every time he came near. I guess the girl was flirting young, showing plainly that she is a girl by smiling sweetly on an old bachelor. Ethel says widows and old bachelors have the fun anyway.

I sealed your letter and the thing came unsealed after it started. The stickum on these envelopes is not of the best. I shall put some extra paste on this one. (I said paste because I can't spell the other word.) If there is any other apology I ought to offer, except for a lack of brain power which I can't help, it is hereby offered for that last spasm of mine called a letter.

I don't know what I was intending to prove by your letters. It was something important at the time. I guess I'll read them back for six weeks or so and then tell you. I was reading of a girl not long ago who read a letter to her mother and told her it was from one of her young man friends. The mother raised sand with her and told her she never heard of such gush. The girl showed her her father's signature and it is said you could hear the snow falling out in the backyard. I think that was a most awful mean and undutiful daughter. My dear uncle is sawing logs on the couch. Every once in a while he hits a splinter and such a choking and scraping of saw teeth (false teeth) you never heard. He holds the record for snoring. He was cussing the jail system this morning. He said if he had his way he'd close every church and jail in the country. Just build a stockade and head the criminals into it and give them a hundred stripes with a whip for the first offense and hang 'em for the second. Then he said judges and marshals and all other such truck would be unnecessary and useless. I don't know why he included churches in the destruction but I guess it's because he hates preachers so badly. He says a highwayman is a gentleman alongside of a preacher or detective. He can almost convince you that it's so, too. I don't think they are quite so bad as a class but there are individuals among preachers who ought not to be able to look a good highwayman in the face. There was once a Presbyterian one in Belton who was a quack doctor and a genuine dinky hoss trader. He's the only really great character that burg ever produced. They tell a story about him when he was going to medical college in St. Louis. He was very hard up for cash and went away from school for two or three weeks, when he came back he had plenty of money. One of his classmates asked him where he'd been and he said, "Oh I'se been down here in Kentucky preaching like —— for the last three weeks." He'd been holding a camp meeting and industriously passing the hat. It is said that he could preach a sermon that would make a marble statue weep. He could also make a horse trader weep over his bargain. He finally did some shady medical practice and they fired him. And do you know every woman and kid in the church cried and the men hated to see him go. I guess he was a genius with a screw loose.

I wish you'd go to the Orpheum Saturday, but if you won't I guess I'll give

Boxley a hint to take me tomorrow. I have to go see him tomorrow. Will try and call up this time. Our lawsuit comes up next Monday and I guess I'll be busy as a cranberry merchant on the twenty-fourth of December for the rest of this week. Here's hoping Warfield has a comedy show instead of one to make the caryatids weep as he did last season.

You now owe me a letter. You can let one of them come Wednesday and the other Friday.

Most sincerely,
Harry

Dear Bess: [Grandview, Mar. 12, 1913]
Your most highly appreciated letter arrived this morning. I certainly was glad to get it. My head is still swollen over the remark you made about my photo.

There was a man here to buy the cows Tuesday. I had to come home at one o'clock or you may be sure I'd have tried 64 [Bess's phone number] before the Orpheum. He bought the cows so it was a good thing we came home. I am riding around in all this rain getting testimony in our lawsuit. You know it comes up Monday. I certainly wish I was like Gaul *divisa in tres partes* because I'm needed at home, in K.C., and in Belton this afternoon. I just called up Blair telling him I couldn't come up and he jumped about a foot high. The lawyer won't let me go, and Papa wants me to help drive the cows to Belton. So there you are.

I got the Orpheum tickets today. They are in the fourth row but on the side. I guess if we understand French we'll hear it all anyway. Dinner is waiting on me and if I don't run and eat a bite I'll surely starve this P.M.

Thanks awfully for that Friday letter.
Sincerely,
Harry

[Hotel Victoria, Kansas City, Mo.]
Dear Bess: March 26, 1913
I am writing you anyway although I sent you a substitute for a letter. I sincerely hope you don't freeze to death tonight in the bowling alley. I guess you can keep warm by playing baseball with the bowling balls.

I don't know when I have felt so ornery. It seems to me that I have spent two whole weeks of work and worry to no purpose. My head is about the size of a barrel. I have a notion to go out and have a glorious whiz. They say that when a person is loaded he sees things in a much rosier way than when he is merely sober. This letter is a rank failure. You know I don't care for money nor appreciate its value when I have it, but the things that lawyers and some people will do to obtain a little of it are certainly astonishing. I have sincerely wished that Grandma had died a poor woman then we'd have seen who cared for her. Some of those stoneheaded Dutch on that jury argued that Mamma forced her to make a will in her favor and that her letters were merely saved for just such a contingency as this. They were also of the opinion that Mamma was mean to her sisters and kept them from going to see their mother. The more I think of it the worse I feel, and the more I feel like punching the heads of those old lawyers and the young Everharts. There really doesn't seem to be any use in a person trying to give his worldly goods to those he wants to have them. If he thinks he's going to die and deeds his property away he'll live to be ninety-nine years old and get kicked out by those he gave it to, and if he wills it some jackleg lawyer will leave a flaw in the will so he can halve the property with the heirs or divide it with the opposition lawyers. That's rather a pessimistic view but I know that if I could arrange an income of about six or seven hundred a month I don't believe I'd strive for any more money. I'd make it my business to spend that scientifically—and thoroughly. I believe I could make quite a number of people enjoy life on that much.

Have you ever had that photo made? I am very anxious for it. If you will remember I asked for yours before you said you would accept one of mine. Please hurry it up. I want it worse than ever as well as the original.

You may consider that you owe me two letters if you so desire. Hope to see you Sunday. I feel better after having bored you with my troubles. I hope you'll feel no ill effects from reading them.

Most sincerely,
Harry

Dear Bess: [Grandview, Apr. 2, 1913]
You perhaps have guessed that the letter will be a day late. I have been trying to sow oats and therefore have been most awful busy. On Monday I had to go to K.C. for a seance with Boxley. You can perhaps guess what the gentleman wanted. Just a thousand on account. On Monday night we had an anti–Home-telephone meeting at Hickman Mills. I am sure that if the managers of that concern had heard all the nice things that were said of them on that evening they'd at least have been sorry they raised our rates, or else they'd have been in a fighting mood. Probably the latter. There were eighty-seven phones ordered out that evening, and from what I have heard since every one they have out here will be taken out. The farmers are going to organize a phone company of their own. It is the talk that they will make the whole county one system and then try and force one of the city companies to exchange service with them. There will be a farmers company in Washington Township anyway whether it gets any further or not. The Home Company wanted to charge us $3.50 a month and ten-cent toll to K.C.—that would make our phone about $10.00 a month. We simply can't stand that, so we're going to do without.

Tuesday night I had to go to Belton. They had a blowout and eight of us went from here in two autos. They sure had some spread. Conferred a Third Degree on Joe Weston's son.

I walked about seventeen miles yesterday behind [a team and] a railroad-iron, breaking [corn] stalks—and then stayed up till 12:00 P.M. at Belton. You can imagine how very bright I feel today. Have been riding a drill this morning. It was almost necessary to tie myself to it to keep from being blown into the Missouri River. Today is nearly as bad as Easter. Every time an oat comes out of the drill [planter] it goes five miles before it lights. (Profitable half day's work, isn't it?)

I am heartily ashamed of this excuse for a letter but I hope you'll take pity on me and answer it. May I come over Sunday on the K.C.S.? We have no help yet and I can't leave until the late train. I'll try and get there by eight.

Please answer *quick.*

Most sincerely,
Harry

Dear Bess: [Grandview, Apr. 7, 1913]

I am going to try and get this letter off on time or bust a hamstring. I have been to Belton today, also to Kansas City. My dear uncle owed me some money and I had to accompany him to Belton to get it. Then he wanted me to go with him to K.C. by the leaky-roof route [railroad] and since he paid the fare I went. Arrived in town at five o'clock and left at 7:40. Got to try on that suit though and Brer Marks [Theodore Marks, a Lodge brother] has half promised to have it ready Friday. Hope he does. Had quite a time with Uncle Harry coming to town. You know the leaky-roof branch of the Frisco runs to Belton via Olathe and goes through some very pretty farming country. It runs through a farm of some 1,400 acres that once belonged to John Bartleson, you know he was Aunt Susan's husband. (My Arizona aunt.) Uncle Harrison showed me the place where he killed a wolf with some hounds when he was a very small kid and a place where he said a New York doctor once chased a deer twenty-five miles—not because he wanted to but because Mr. Bartleson had given him a thoroughbred horse trained to hounds and he ran away with the said Doc. He was in at the killing but he had to get a couple of Indians to show him the way back. He had to walk as he was in such a condition physically he couldn't ride. I suppose he had something to brag about all the rest of his life. If I'd been him I'd have tried assault and battery on my host as soon as I was able. People sure did enjoy themselves in those times. It seems to me from what I hear that the men spent all summer chasing foxes and all winter going to dances. Uncle said it snowed once about three feet on the level and he got a couple of wagon boxes full [of friends] on sleds and had a dance every night for a week. Everyone at a different place. They'd dance all night and spend all day getting to the next place. He was in a fine humor today and offered to give me something for helping get the [law] suit ready. I told him that I'd be paid if we won out, and he said I'd be more than paid. So I guess he's pleased with the efforts Boxley and I put forth anyway.

That piece of lemon pie was still on deck this morning at one-thirty. At 1:32 it had completely disappeared. That and your mother's good cake made me take a trip to Honolulu between two and six. The nice part of the trip was I thought you were along and we were having a dandy time. It's wonderful what an amount of territory a person can cover in a night when he has had the proper incentives earlier in the evening. I was across the Pacific and half the American continent in four hours. That was a fine trip. Here's hoping I get rich enough to take it as per above.

I sure am lucky this evening. I had not been home but a short time when it began raining and I had on a suit just pressed and was carrying my blue one in a paper box. I barely escaped a soaking this morning too. I hope it rains Friday morning about seven o'clock then won't have to have a scene with my pa because of something I ought to be doing when I leave. From the way it's coming down now I guess we won't farm any more for two weeks. I told Mamma that I wished we'd hung our big washing out and let the rain do it. . . .

I know your letter was worth two of mine, or three for that matter, but I gave it a double amount of appreciation. You ought to let that count for something, don't you think?

Please send me one for this anyway. See you Friday at two at E. B. T.'s Eleventh Street entrance. I missed the phone meeting but I guess they didn't me.

Most sincerely,
Harry

Dear Bess: [Grandview, postmark illegible]
Your letters are always so good and so readable that I am ashamed of my attempts. But since mine are made to get those from you I guess their purpose is accomplished. Some people you know are naturally good letter writers and some are not. I am one of the *knots*. So long as you answer them though, why I am going to keep spoiling good paper. In order to start you on a sympathetic line of thought I'll inform you that I have a kink in my neck for a change. This is probably the line of sympathy I'll get, "Oh I told you so, you crazy boy, why didn't you go see that osteopath?" Well I am going someday when I have time. . . . I most sincerely wish I'd been born with Napoleon's ability to do without sleep. You know five hours was his limit on all occasions. Ten or fifteen suit me. I have been averaging about three out of twenty-four. Perhaps that is what put the first kink in my head. Someday I am going to put in about thirty-six hours straight and catch up. When I was laid up with a broken pin I could only sleep from about one o'clock until five in the morning. Now I am sure I could go from one till one and back again. Morpheus is a perverse god anyway, almost as contrary as Eros I guess. I can remember when I stayed in town of being utterly unable to sleep beyond 6:00 A.M. on Sunday morning, but on any other morning I could travel right on through until 8:00 A.M. if no one pulled me out. I was never known to miss breakfast on Sunday (you couldn't get it after eight) but on week mornings I've had to chase off without it.

It is now close to twelve o'clock and one of our infernal guineas is squalling like it was midday. It is surely an awful insult to be called one of those things. There is absolutely nothing can keep up the clatter they can through every hour of the twenty-four. I don't even believe Mrs. Pankhurst can. . . .

May I come Sunday evening and some day sooner if I get a chance? You'll have to send a letter to let me know yes or no to that double question. I am looking for it!

Most sincerely,

Harry

Dear Bess: [Grandview, Apr. 23, 1913]

. . . It is raining to beat the band now. I hope it keeps up and then perhaps I can gush over on two sheets. Don't you hope it stops? The hired boy has been sent to help bury a fellow. Grave digging isn't exactly in my line and I shirk it whenever it comes my way. You see I don't care whether I'm buried or not. I'd as soon not be for a while yet. Anyway it's one job I'm not worrying over.

I have been nearly blown away today. I suppose there is another jimmy case somewhere. Let's hope Omaha escaped this time. We had a young horse hitched up this morning. She kicked like a starving suffragette. Maybe she is one in a second incarnation. It will be a job to break her but it is said that a hard one to break makes the most tractable horse. I hope it does. It's going to quit raining and I've got to go plow. I am waiting as patiently as I can for that promised photo. Don't you think your new blue dress would make a dandy picture? I do. Please try it.

Hope to see you Sunday if not sooner. You can answer if you want to. I always want two for one if I can get it.

Most sincerely,

Harry

Tish and Lizzie, referred to below, were characters in Mary Roberts Rinehart's Adventures of Letitia Carberry *and of numerous short stories. Tish was an intrepid old maid and the heroine, and Lizzie one of her companions.*

Dear Bess: [Grandview, Apr. 28, 1913]

I have put the two hired men to work and am stealing an hour to write you. You'll get this a day earlier if I succeed in getting it mailed this afternoon. I suppose you are house cleaning for fair this morning. Mary would like to be but she is so everlastingly busy concocting a dinner for four hungry men that house cleaning has been very happily pushed aside. I'm hoping it'll stay pushed until Mamma comes home. Then I can dodge it perhaps. Luella is a lot better this morning. Neither of the kids have shown any signs of being sick yet. I hope they both have the measles and be done with it. I can't see what anyone wants to wait till he's grown to have kid ailments for. You know Ethel succeeded in having mumps after she had been a school teacher some years. I have always been sorry I didn't see her when she was at her worst. She has always considered it an act of Providence that I didn't show up.

It is up to me to distribute some three hundred pounds of timothy seed over a good-sized patch of the landscape this afternoon. It seems that sowing things is a continued [task] in our next process on this farm. It seems to me that we sow from March to September and reap between times. I am looking forward with agony to haying time. There will only be some 150 tons to put up. I suppose I'll be strong enough for a big leaguer when that job is over. It is a back-breaking job but very good appetite developer. Almost as good as tennis but somewhat more long-drawn-out. Here's hoping you got your court rolled today.

I have read Miss Tish's adventure with the Syrian. She's a grand old maid. I hardly know which to admire the most, Tish or Lizzie. If Lizzie didn't smoke, I'd favor her without hesitation.

I am hoping to get to town this week but if the weather stays good I fear I won't make it. I have a date with Dr. Witmer on Wednesday or Thursday but I may not keep it. You know I am not very reliable on doctor dates, especially when it's time to pay. I have a notion though that Dr. Witmer is almost honest —a bad failing in a doctor. . . .

Please consider this worth an answer. May I see you Sunday if not sooner?
                              Most sincerely,
                              Harry

Dear Bess: [Grandview, May 12, 1913]
Here goes for another letter. I am sincerely hoping this one gets into the mail and also that it arrives after it gets there. . . .

There is the finest copy of *Motor* out this month. I saw it this morning. It has thoroughly convinced me that I want a Peerless, Lozier, Pierce Arrow, American, Locomobile, Fiat, Marmon, or some other equally cheap car. There are the finest pictures and most convincing ads on those cars you ever saw. I am like the nigger who was asked to change a five-dollar bill when an agent asks me to buy an auto. He said, "No sir, boss, I can't change it but I thank you sir for the compliment." If autos were fifty cents each, I wouldn't be able to invest in a hind wheel at present. Tire factories ought to give autos away in order to sell the tires.

Hope to see you some day this week and also to get a letter from you. Please remember that I most highly appreciated that birthday letter. The picture only could have been better.
                              Sincerely,
                              Harry

Dear Bess: [Grandview, May 19, 1913]

How do you appreciate my ability as a weather prophet? We had a small rain out here this morning. I hope you had none and that we'll have more. . . .

I started this letter before breakfast and had to quit because there were so many congregated around the desk to see what I was about. We have the freshest hired man that ever hopped a clod. He has to know where every letter comes from and to whom every one goes. I informed him that I was writing a business letter and it was none of his affair where it went. He immediately got the Sunday *Post* and said he would peruse the personal column and see if he couldn't find a reason for a business correspondence. He found one which said a rich widow desired to hear from a bachelor of some means, object matrimony. I suppose he is going to investigate. I told him he was no bachelor; he's only twenty-one—a perfect infant. He thinks he's older than I am. I told him I was forty-two my last birthday. He had to go to work with a post auger this morning.

I am sorry the picnic note didn't arrive, but I shall look forward to another one later. Uncle Harry pulled out this morning. He's going to Monegaw Springs in the morning. He says they have the finest set of hillbillies in America down there. They give a formal dance every Wednesday evening during the summer. Full dress consists of a hickory shirt and blue overalls for the men, and red calico dresses for the ladies. They must have a good time. He said he showed them how to dance the pigeon wing and crawfish wire, evidently two very complicated steps if names count for anything. I have an idea that he would make a better instructor in poker and seven-up than in dancing. He's too pigeon-toed to dance. It is all he can do to walk without getting tangled up.

I am going to Harrisonville today and Wednesday night too if nothing happens here at home and it will keep on raining. It looks very much like we were going to have a trash mover. I suppose you and the Southern girls will have another party if it rains. You ought to have played tennis yesterday afternoon. It was an ideal day for it. You couldn't possibly have gotten too warm at it. Mamma has a broom just raising sand in here. I never saw anyone but Aunt Sallie who takes any more pleasure in creating a disturbance with a broom than Mamma. The coldest day in winter she'll raise all the windows, get a broom and a dust rag, and just be perfectly blissful while the rest of us freeze. Whenever the dog and cat see her coming with a broom they at once begin hunting means of exit. They know by sore experience that Mamma's broom is a poor implement to get in front of. When eating time comes though they forget the broom as well as the rest of us do.

Please now you owe me a letter if you'll let the stationery count for one. Do you approve of Electric Park? If you do we'll go out when the weather gets warm enough. Mary saved me a dish of strawberries. I can't imagine what she wants, a new dress or hat I bet. See you Sunday if not sooner?

Most sincerely,
Harry

Dear Bess: [Grandview, May 26, 1913]

Here goes for an attempt at a letter. You'll probably be in debt to me for several extra sheets when this is done. I have been in the house nearly all day as the result of a very stiff neck. Not an unusual occurrence for me lately. I suppose I caused it by trying to raise up a rock weighing some four hundred pounds on Saturday morning. (I've an idea the rock will still weigh that much on Monday evening.) Anyway I have been getting particular fits both from Papa and the rest of the family but I can't stand around always, neck or no neck. We are afflicted with a talkative plasterer these days. I am hoping he will get through and leave us in peace by Wednesday. As I told you, it is impossible for anyone to mention any subject that he is not very well acquainted with. He has been endeavoring to teach us the rudiments of Spanish this evening. Everyone has left him talking but Mamma, and I have an idea she is trying to escape. He's a very good plasterer but I suppose everyone has some redeeming quality. Even His Majesty is said to be very energetic. Luella and the kids have been here all day. They are the best (I wanted to say cutest but I hate the word) babies I ever saw. They can both almost talk. The girl is the most curious of the two. I told Mamma she naturally would be and got slapped for my pains. They sure will be a pair when they get to walking and talking. The boy looks like our family and the girl like Luella's. They are both pretty as babies can very well be. Boys you know are generally best looking at five or six and girls after they are grown up. I never could rave over the beauty of babies because to my notion they all look alike, unless there's something radically wrong with them. I was unfortunate enough to say that babies were like pigs—simply small human beings, as pigs are small hogs—and that they never looked like anyone until they were three or four years old. Luella asks me every now and then if her kids look like pigs. I suppose I should have said colts or chickens instead of pigs and it would have sounded better. Papa is very sick of his road job and I am very glad. I hope he gets sicker yet because I didn't want him to take it. The Belton *Herald* has written him up as one of the "henchmen of the Jackson County court" because he has been giving some of the inhabitants of this district particular fits over the way they do not trim their hedges and cut their weeds. He made a trip to Belton to whip the editor but couldn't find him. It's as well he didn't. I told him that was a very mild remark and should be accepted as a compliment to a man who has a political job. I read the Mary Roberts Rinehart in *McClure's*. It is a grand story, really good enough to appear in *Adventure*. Could I possibly compliment it more highly? I suppose I'll have to renew my subscription to *McClure's* now so I won't miss a number. There are several good stories in this number. The *Saturday Evening Post* has an infallible Godahl story this week. I thought *Pearson's* had a corner on them. They are always pretty good.

I am going to be a good little boy all this week and go to bed at nine o'clock every night (perhaps). Last week beginning Sunday I went to bed at from twelve to two every night. It doesn't seem to bother me any, only I hate awful to pull out at 5:00 A.M. Do you think this worth an answer? Say yes and send me three

sheets and I'll write you a real nice letter next time. That's an awful threat. Hope
to see you this week before Sunday.

Sincerely,
Harry

Dear Bess: [Grandview, June 10, 1913]

I was in K.C. again yesterday for about two hours to get my bones knocked
into place. It has almost gotten to be a habit. The doctor of course wants to keep
up the performance indefinitely. You know that as long as the two dollars come
forth he'll be perfectly willing to keep going. When I decide that I've had enough
I'll ask for credit, and you'll see a remarkable recovery. He says that there are three
sections of my head supporter about a quarter inch out of line, and that as soon
as he's pulled them back everything will be all right. I told him to do the job up
in a hurry as I had no time at this season to be going to see him. He told me
that if I was going to carry any more cows on my head, to begin when they were
calves and then let them grow up thus raising a little more weight every day and
then I wouldn't get jerked in two. . . .

I suppose you'll have a good time this week playing tennis. It's evidently not
going to rain because we have hay down. My reputation as a prophet won't
amount to much now if it rains. A prophet is a man who can't afford to make
mistakes and keep his reputation. I hope it rains sometime soon but not today
or tomorrow or the next. . . .

I'll bet you don't get this letter until Thursday but please remember I've had
two arrive on Tuesday lately. Your last letter was sure a good one. If I could stand
the financial strain, I'd give you a Pym racket every week to get a letter like that.
I had no idea that Pym rackets were such fine pieces of tennis furniture or I'd
have come along with it sooner. Here's hoping it makes you champ of the courts.
I hope to see you some day this week if that man Lindberg leaves me any
disposition to go anywhere. I have to see him again soon. Hope to see you Sunday
anyway. *You owe me two sheets.*

Sincerely,
Harry

Dear Bess: [Grandview, June 30, 1913]

As a weather prophet I guess most any old farmer has P. Conner beaten to
a frazzle. It is sprinkling rain now and prospects are good for a trash mover. I
caught the Limited last night all right. There were five or six got off at Grandview.
Most of them were well diggers for Mr. Johnson. It's nice to have company when
you are scared, even if you don't know the company extra well. It was as dark
as a stack of purple cats last night, and both dogs attempted to eat me up as I
came into the gate. I told Mary that I intended giving the collie to you. She nearly
had a spasm. She pretends to be very much attached to it. I think that two dogs
are generally two too many. We have a good neighbor up the road who has three

big fat ones and his horses and cows are so poor they can hardly navigate. One dog is a sufficiency on a farm and one too many in town. They say that when an assessor doesn't want to be reelected, the best thing for him to do is to enumerate all the dogs in his district. I have an idea that it would be very effective if a person had a desire for unpopularity.

Aileen and Uncle Harrison are both here. I have had a fuss with Aileen already. I didn't do anything but throw a small piece of bread at her. It had some pea soup on it, but I wasn't aware of that fact until it landed on her neck. She has been very cool ever since that chunk of bread took her one in the neck. Some people are touchy anyway. She'll get over it if she stays long around here. What Aileen needs is two or three brothers to pick on her turn about [one after the other]. I guess you can appreciate what a fine effect brothers have on girls.

My dear uncle is squalling for me to come and entertain him at a game of cooncan. Can you play it? It's some game if you play for fun, or if you have plenty of money and are lucky. I only play for fun with him. I'd be hopelessly broke forever if I had to part with a dollar every time he beat me. That's the usual price of a game. I hope most sincerely that it will rain itself out before the Fourth, and also that it will rain enough Saturday that Bill can't think of Warrensburg and yet leave the roads good too. I shall be on deck at your house about nine o'clock or 8:45. It will be necessary for us to leave at not later than nine because the train leaves Sheffield at 9:33. We will then arrive at Pete's [Vivian's] at about eleven, a very proper hour for country-style.

It's necessary that I draw this to a close. Uncle Harry is having a fit to play cards and he's gotten to the point where he has to be concilliated (can't spell it). I hope your knee got well. I forgot to ask about it Sunday. You should have limped a little to remind me. Well I hope to see you Friday evening as well as Sunday morning. You owe me a letter. Please use tablecloth-size, like this.

Sincerely,
Harry

Dear Bess: [Grandview, July 7, 1913]

I caught that train this morning by nearly as narrow a margin as we did yesterday. It was across the track when I got off the car. The agent remarked that I was making trains on the minute this summer. To tell you the truth, I was not caring much if I missed it. I wanted to go down in town and see the Kodak man and incidentally let Dr. Miller try his luck on my other wisdom molar. According to Mr. Blair, I will be in a very poor way indeed when I lose that one. It will be three. You know I can't afford to part with much wisdom and still run loose. Tell your mother that Mary said she answered the phone last night and Central said that the girl at Independence refuses to connect her again. We have been getting most ornery service since March. I haven't paid the bill for the last three months and I don't think I shall. I was mighty sorry your mother got worried about us last night. You tell her that I am a very lucky person and that accidents never happen to me when I have company and am off the Blue Ridge farm. It is only when I am in argument with ostreperous cows and calves that I get worsted. Do you suppose she'll ever let you come again? I hope she will if you enjoyed it, for I certainly had a very pleasant day. If ever I gain credit enough to own an auto then we can arrive on time. Papa and Aileen beat Mary and Bill one game and then got beat one. You see you were the expert in the other games. Did you go to the city today? We are all pleased this morning, I guess, and are satisfied that biting flies mean wet weather. . . .

I hope to see you Sunday if not sooner, and you owe the letter.

Most sincerely,
Harry

Dear Bess: [Grandview, July 14, 1913]

I came very nearly being in your burg again today. A delegation of roadseekers went to see the [county] court this morning. They wanted Papa but he was nowhere to be found until the very last minute. I had my glad rags on but got left at the post. . . .

My head feels like a barrel this A.M. I had it all doped out to stay in bed till 10:00 A.M., but my dope wasn't worth a cent. Six is as long as I was allowed to stay in peace. Had to go to the phone and then I just stayed up. I sure do pity a boozer on the morning after. I suppose in addition to the barrel for a head, he'd probably have a taste in his mouth like a burnt boot. At least I've heard them remark that it resembled that article. I can think of no more disagreeable a taste, especially if the boot happened to be rubber and tastes as it smells when cooked. I know one fellow who used to drink ink and coal oil to allay the burning thirst of the next day.

I suppose you are exercising a tennis racket today, that is if you saved Luke's scalp. It would be rather windy for a game out here. I guess the breeze must be blowing about forty miles an hour. It's hot, too. We are hoping for rain. I guess we'll get some in a short time—the flies are working overtime.

This stationery you are complimenting so highly is a Christmas present from Mary Colgan. I have had it in a box in the desk and just ran across it the other day. I wasn't especially fond of it but would have used it sooner if I'd known it was here. I gave her a grand lecture on where to buy stationery about two days before Christmas in an accidental conversation on the subject, telling her how much nicer the Jaccard brand is than any other in town. I suppose she had this already on hand and decided I should take it anyway. I did Ethel the same way once and she had bought me some at Peck's and had it monogrammed. I felt like thirty cents when it came. I usually show my knowledge of things where it will do me the least good and make me feel like a fool afterwards. We used to have a Dane working for us who said his mother told him to see, hear, and say *nawthing*. It's a most excellent theory but mighty hard to practice. I sometimes feel as if I'd surely explode if I didn't get some bright remark off my chest. Nine times in ten I'd feel better afterwards to have been silent.

I hope we can arrange to go fishing with Agnes and Earl some nice day soon.

Also I think we have a date to ride over to Excelsior Springs some evening when the weather's fine. I have not forgotten it. Also there is one important date you haven't filled yet. It is with a photographer. I am still hoping for the picture to go in my silver frame. I am hoping to see you some evening this week if we don't thresh too strenuously. You owe me a tablecloth-sized letter anyway.

Most sincerely,
Harry

Dear Bess: [Grandview, July 21, 1913]
    . . . I hope the creek will hurry and arrive at the proper stage for us to go fishing. By then I shall be leather-hided and tough enough to resist attacks by any kind of insect in this state. I suppose we shall have to take some liquid bait along. The kind that Hamlet always labeled "Danish Snake Bite Cure." You know that a fishing excursion is never complete without at least a small bottle. That's what makes the fish that fall back look so large. I have even heard of cases where after using a little of this liquid bait a person could dump his can of worms and catch fresh ones as they came to hand, provided they were not too large. I suppose pieces of pink and purple snakes would make acceptable hook food for fish. I suppose also it would be well for us to come home by the river road so we can buy a few fish from the fishermen. That also is entirely customary. I am going to bring a pair of khaki overalls for wading purposes. There's no use going to the creek if you can't go into it.
    Did you ever see the Madonna in the moon? I imagined I saw her. The proper directions are to think of your girl's countenance and then you can see it. I don't know how the girls are supposed to see it. Probably imagine that they are gazing into a mirror. I'd rather look at the real thing than to hurt my eyes and pain my head gazing into the moon's face. Not that I'd ever have to put forth any effort whatever to conjure up your face because it's always in plain sight. I never see a pretty girl or the picture of one that I don't think, well if she didn't have this imperfection or that one why she'd look like Bess. You know perfection can only be reached once. You're it. So what's the use of imagining you in the moon when I can see yourself at Independence.
    The threshermen won't come today but perhaps tomorrow. I hoped they would come today so I could get to town some day this week but I guess I won't get in. Hope to see you Sunday though. You now owe me a tablecloth-sized letter.

Sincerely,
Harry

Dear Bess: [Grandview, July 29, 1913]
    This is Tuesday morning, therefore you probably won't get this effort until Voden's day [Wotan's, or Wednesday]. I was in this city yesterday and could not write. I made a call on Dr. Lester. He advised me to keep rubbing iodine on my stiff neck. I suppose I shall in all probability turn to a bottle of iodine, that is if

I keep following M.D.'s instructions. There is a slight probability that I may not. You know Doc Jones gave me a whole lot of dope to use, but I didn't use it only about a week. Aspirin doesn't appeal to me anyway. I have about come to the conclusion that there is absolutely nothing the matter with me anyway. It is merely an error between the shoulders. If I correct the error I am well. (I haven't been to any Wednesday evening meetings.) Dr. Lester said that he was sure coming out next Sunday. He said he'd come Saturday only Mrs. Lester got mad at the old man they had staying there and fired him. Doc said the Mrs. didn't have much patience anyway. He said, "You know how a woman is. The old fellow just got a little too much Kansas toddy and decided to make Mrs. Lester a political speech. She's not interested in boozy politics, therefore I am now the chore boy." He said the old man was perfectly harmless but would insist on taking a little tea once in a while. For my part I think Mrs. Lester treated him absolutely correct. Now, if he'd used Missouri booze, it might have had a different effect. Aggie Thompson was at the doctor's. She's a cute little thing but so affected I couldn't tell whether she thought what she said or not. She's just a high school kid and, I suppose like all the rest of them, has things all figured from the beginning to eternity. She'll be a nice girl in about ten years. Her dad used to have my glasses made but he got to charging such outrageous prices that I quit him. I guess he had to charge though because his family goes to Europe once in a while and I suppose do the high-society stunt too.

I'd have called you up yesterday only I thought perhaps you were playing tennis. It was surely hot enough for a good game of tennis. Mr. McLaughlin is the world's champeen after all. Americans are like the prime minister in the *Mikado*. They are champion tennis players, baseball players, fighters, and most everything else. I suppose it's on account of the conglomerate population. We can suppose we got the best of the European population, although there's an old man out here who says it's always the trash that leave a country. He not only said it but proved it too. I couldn't agree with him.

There's a three-hundred-pound ice cake at Grandview awaiting my attention. The man just now phoned. It sure is something awful the way ice does melt. I got three hundred pounds on Thursday. Uncle Harrison says things are fully equalized in the end. Rich men have all the ice they want in summer and the poor men all they want in winter. My dear uncle got rolled Sunday night. He was sleeping with his door open and someone lifted his pants. He lost a solid gold watch and some small change. He usually has a roll of money that would choke a calf but I suppose he had sense enough to put it in his safe. He has one in his room. Next time I see him I'm going to say I told you so. I was there not long ago in the afternoon and he was asleep with the door open. I asked him if he wasn't afraid of being robbed and he gave me a horse laugh. I'd have liked to have heard the choice American he used when he got up. I'll bet it would have made a South Sea ship captain sound like a Sunday school meeting.

I am going to try and get in one day this week for I may not be able to arrive on Sunday, although I am going to beat a sneak if I can. I'll have to quit because my three hundred pounds of ice won't be over half as much if I don't go after it. You owe me a letter anyway. See you Sunday if not sooner.

Sincerely,
Harry

Here, Truman expresses the hope that His Majesty will convert to oil. The figure relates to the widespread use of coal at this time, so that if one went to Hades, he or she would be put to work shoveling coal.

Dear Bess: [Grandview, postmark illegible]
    I suppose that by this time tomorrow there will be a horde of people here to work on the road (table). For my own part I've a notion to beat it to some quiet place and let 'em work. The closer field would be a fine place for me to spend my time. The hay needs to be cocked up so it can be threshed. Independence is a nice, quiet place to spend a holiday also. In fact if I could get anywhere I believe Independence would have the preference over any other. You know I am so seldom in that burg that it would be an immense pleasure to spend the road days there. Since my Daddy is making such strenuous efforts to place this district in prime condition I suppose I'll have to help. I'm going to get out and make speeches against him if he attempts to run for any political office on the strength of this job. Next time the road man is appointed I don't think I'll help him. Politics sure is the ruination of many a good man. Between hot air and graft he usually loses not only his head but his money and friends as well. Still, if I were real rich I'd just as soon spend my money buying votes and offices as yachts and autos. Success seems to me to be merely a point of view anyway. Some men have an idea that if they corner all the loose change they are self-made successful men. Makes no difference to them if they do eat beans off a knife or not know whether Napoleon was a man or a piece of silver.
    Some others have a notion that if they can get high offices and hold up themselves as models of virtue to a gaping public in long-winded, high-sounding speeches that they have reached the highest pinnacle of success. It seems to me that an ability to hand out self-praise makes most men successes in their own minds anyway. Some of the world's greatest failures are really greater men than some of the other kind. To succeed financially a man can't have any heart. To succeed politically he must be an egotist or a fool or a ward boss tool. To my notion, an ideal condition would be to have to work just enough so if you stopped you'd not go busted at once—but still you'd know if you didn't work you couldn't live. And then have your home and friends and pleasures regulated to your income, say a thousand a month. I am sure I'd be satisfied then to let vile ambition, political or monetary, starve at the gate.
    Even if a person attains all there is to attain he's got to leave it all, probably right when it's most pleasure to him, and probably go to shoveling coal. (I hope they'll be using oil furnaces when I arrive.) Do you suppose that Alexander, Hannibal, Caesar, Napoleon, or Artemus Ward will have any better standing

before the Great White Throne than St. Cecilia or Billy Sunday? I don't think
so. . . .

I sincerely hope you'll answer a day early, as you did last week, because I
have a better excuse than I had last week for being a day late.

Sincerely,
Harry

Dear Bess: [Grandview, Aug. 5, 1913]

I am writing this at six o'clock in the morning. We have had breakfast but
Mary, Ethel, and Nellie are still unconscious. I don't suppose they'll show up
before nine. . . .

I suppose Madge has arrived by this time. I hope she won't care about our
going fishing. Maybe you can get *Frank* to entertain her that day by going to the
K.C. Chautauqua! I hope you'll get to go anyway. It looks as if it might rain this
morning. I hope it does. That's what we need, also it'll make the fish bite better.
They say that liver is the best bait. Perhaps you wouldn't object to baiting your
hook with liver. It is necessary to bury it three days. That might cause it to be
as objectionable as worms. There's an old man by the name of Moore living at
Hickman Mills who is an expert in the fishing line and he says liver is the best
bait on earth. I don't know what effect the burying has on it but I suppose it adds
to the flavor. English are said to have buried their deer meat to make it good.
I'd prefer mine to stay on top of the ground.

We can come home by way of the Missouri River and buy a few fish if we
don't catch any in Blue. I think that is the usual mode or procedure anyway. . . .

Well I hope to see you Saturday anyway. I shall look for a letter real soon
this week.

Most sincerely,
Harry

Dear Bess: [Grandview, postmark illegible]

I saw George today in K.C. I might as well have stayed in town for all the
time I spent at home. It was necessary for me to see Boxley, principally to get
touched for some money. It seems to be a very charming habit of his. In fact,
as Bill Bostian said in his famous high-school speech, touching seems to be the
proper description of interviews with lawyers. If dollars were tears, those gentlemen would certainly have their clients praying for a larger reservoir. Besides the
visit to Mr. B., I made one to the office of the Burlington Railway Company.
Got about six volumes of literature, and some information. Also I visited the
offices of the Rock Island, the Chicago, Milwaukee & St. Paul's, the Chicago &
Great Western. At each one I hid all the books I already had and received a new
supply. I brought the literature home in a market basket. (There were apples in
the bottom of it.) At each office I learned that the railroad had the best and

quickest way to go, although there was a difference of six hours in some of the schedules. I have had half the fun of going now anyway whether I get off or not. I've a notion that my name will be no. 9002 if there are 9,001 claims, but I reckon I'd as well blow sixty dollars for carfare as for booze. Since I don't drink I can charge the sixty dollars off to unrequited thirst and know that at least I'm obtaining more nearly value received. I haven't any excuse to offer for not having called you up except that I went to Federman's twice to do it and couldn't get a phone. That is another time my intentions were good. Please credit. Of course I couldn't possibly spend five cents. I hate to talk over a pay-as-you-enter phone because every time just as conversation is going good, down comes the key with a "Time's up, another nickel please." To tell the truth, I hate to talk over the phone anyway. I'm always rattled and can never say what I want to. I like to use one only when I'm driven to it. I don't even answer one here at home when Mary's handy to it. . . .

Bess, I can't write a good letter tonight. I'm mad because I had to come home. The threshers were expected this afternoon and they *didn't* arrive. I might just as well have been at Independence, provided always of course you'd been home. It was most awful nice [of you] to say the breaks in the middle of the week are a pleasure to you. You bet I'm glad. They're seventh heaven to me.

Can I come Sunday? If we don't thresh, I shall have urgent business in town —I hope about Friday. Please consider this worth an answer.

Most sincerely,
Harry

Dear Bess: [Grandview, Aug. 22, 1913]
    . . . I have been cutting clover for seed. We have an immense crop of it but it is so short that it is almost impossible to save it. There is always something the matter with a crop. It's either too dry or too wet or too short or too long or too much or not enough. *If* is the largest word in a farmer's language. *If* we could save all our clover seed, there would probably be two hundred bushels. It will probably be only one hundred that we'll get. I suppose I ought not to kick over that much because it mightn't have been any like the corn. We had a sprinkle out here last night. It thundered and raised sand around. You'd have thought a deluge was falling. It only settled the top layer of dust. I have hopes of another one some time in the next month. There's an old gink living down north of us who says it won't come a real rain until October. He says we had a "Comic" in 1901, 1911, and that there's one this year. I almost told him that it was anything but comic, but he really thinks that's the proper word and I didn't say it. He's also an A.P.A. and it takes him fifteen minutes by the clock to say, "The cow crossed the road." He has a confidential way almost like Judge George Clinton's. It's funny once but the second and third times become very, very tiresome—especially when he tries to tell me that the *Star* is a good, honest paper politically and that Bryan and Wilson are crooks in direct communication with the Pope. It is honestly surprising to find someone with a sixteenth-century mind in this day.

You should have seen what was in that box Ethel sent Mary. I fear very much you'd have never let it get by. It was a pink (really) girdle and a beautiful one. I think Mary is figuring on sticking me for a dress to go with it. I shall absolutely refuse to be stuck this time though for the very good reason that I'm busted. . . .

Dinner's ready and I've got to go eat and get to work. You can imagine this blank space full of all the nice things I haven't the brains to say. See you Sunday, I hope, if I don't have to put up hay.

Most sincerely,
Harry

Dear Bess: [Grandview, Sept. 2, 1913]
You are going to get your letter on Tuesday if everything holds together and ink don't play out. It's only ink that needs to play out, as you know. I have an abundant supply of words. Trouble is I can never string them together so they mean much. Some people can take an empty tomato can and write an essay worth forty dollars on it, but I can't take a train wreck and get fifteen-cents worth out of it. The ink didn't give out, but I went to a picnic and did a half a day's work besides yesterday—and therefore the words ran out. Myra had a lot of her friends out and asked Mary and I down. Elsie Coon was there. She had lost the upper half of her teeth and therefore you'd think she wouldn't be quite so long on conversation. She is though. The funny part about her is that she can talk so you can't tell she has no teeth. She gave me the last of the pear preserves, and I told her she was almost sweet enough to kiss even if she had no teeth. She tried her best to break my head with a watermelon rind. It seems that some people can't appreciate a real compliment. Her little boy thought she was endeavoring to kill me and intervened in my behalf or she would I guess. Elsie can thoroughly appreciate Mark Twain, so you see I can forgive her for losing her teeth. She said she was going to unname the Embroidery Club, call it the Clatter Club. It would be a very good name for it. Those girls, or women for most of 'em are married, all talk at once all day long, and you can't tell what anyone says and none of them seem to care what's being said just so long as each one can say something herself. Myra and Mary Coon hold the record. Either one of them can talk for two hours without taking a breath. Mary sang "I Dreamt I Dwelt in Marble Halls" as we heard it sung by that blond prima donna last winter. I almost went up. She imitated her to perfection.

I saw a silo being filled yesterday. It was down close to Roy's. Talk about a dirty job now. There's one that can give any other job you can think of cards and spades and beat it out for real downright dirt. The man who was feeding the machine had a bandana handkerchief tied right over his face. It didn't even have eye holes in it. He looked like some of Captain Kidd's victims must have looked after that gentleman got through with them. Then the man inside the silo has to walk and walk and then walk some more. It is just the same as being in a jug. You can imagine how very nice that would be on a day like yesterday. I told the fellow inside that I'd dispense with all the clothes I could if I were going to work in it. I hope I'll never have to work in one.

I have a cornstalk in my eye now and can't see how to write very well. I was out in the field this morning tying skeleton shocks for the corn cutters when I stuck a blade in my eye. It didn't hurt much then but it smarts somewhat now. A corn blade will cut like a razor if it hits you just right. The men who are cutting wear gloves and scarves all the time. . . .

I am hoping to see you Sunday and before if I can. It seems like a hollow week if I don't arrive at 219 Delaware at least one day in it. I've got to take Mamma to Monegaw someday this week but I don't know which one.

Anyway you *owe* the letter now.

Most sincerely,
Harry

Courtship of Bess, and perhaps the seemingly interminable work on the farm, inspired Truman to sign up for a land raffle in Montana. The beginning of his journey by rail to Glasgow, in the northeastern part of the state, is described here. The raffle drew farmers from near and far. His father and Mr. Hall, the threshing-machine operator, went along too.

Dear Bess: [St. Paul, Minn., Sept. 17, 1913]
If my ink holds out I'll try and send you something to read. I have already sent you a package from St. Paul—minus enough postage I very much fear.

We stopped here in the yards, the porter saying we'd probably stay three hours. Two of the boys ran off just as hard as they could go toward town. The rest of us went a little way up the street and got something to eat and a basketful of eats. When we came back the train was gone somewhere. We found it in the Union Station about ready to pull out we thought. The front half went and left our cars but the two boys who had run off hadn't shown up. Papa and Mr. Hall were having one fit after another. Finally just before the train pulled out we found them ciphering around the yards trying to find their car. Now we are all fixed to leave. There are about fourteen Tourist cars in our train. That many have already gone and there are more to follow. I am very sorry George didn't come. The expense is going to be very little more than forty dollars apiece. We are loaded with enough grub to last to Glasgow, and I suppose we'll find enough to load up with there to come home on. I guess we'll stop in Minneapolis when we come back. Hope to send you a package from there too. Don't let it get out that I didn't know how much postage it takes to go from St. Paul home.

You owe me a half a letter anyway.

Most sincerely,
Harry

Master of the Masonic Lodge at Grandview, Truman was in charge of the piano committee and could spend anything up to and including $100 to purchase one. As this letter shows, he enjoyed shopping for it. He seems to have sensed *what all piano lovers know, that there are as many different pianos as there are horses—and sharp dealers to match. Perhaps he did not take with him that sine qua non of the prudent secondhand-piano buyer, Michel's Piano Atlas, which lists the "breeds" by year and serial number. But he knew enough to bargain, and probably did all right.*

Dear Bess: [Grandview, Sept. 30, 1913]

. . . I was in K.C. again yesterday piano shopping. I visited Jenkins', Hoffman's, Kimball's, Smith's and Olney's. Afterwards I learned that there was a company on McGee. If I'd known it, I'd have seen them too. We finally bought one from Hoffman for $125. There was a Bradbury at Olney's for $175 that was as good as new. It was surely a bargain but the tightwads out here had said we shouldn't pay over $100. I have an idea that there'll be some strong, loud talk when the bill comes. The salesman at Jenkins' was bound to sell us a piano any way. We found them to be higher and fuller of hot air than any other house in town. Hoffman's man tried to sell us an old banged-up Hinze piano for $145. We'd just been to Kimball's and they'd offered us a new one for $195. When I told the guy that he nearly fell over. He'd told us it was a $250 piano. There's more thieves in the music business than there are crooks in the horse trade. That's going some too.

I got into it something fierce last night. I called Mary up to see when she was going home and she said that I was invited to Duvall's for supper. I told her I was going home. The two boys who were on the piano committee had driven to town and I was going out with them. I had had a session with the dentist, who had taken away some more of my wisdom. Dinner therefore didn't look good to me. When I got out to Waldo—almost half home—I remembered a package I'd left at Eighth and Walnut. Then since I had to stay downtown till 11:00 P.M. anyway I went after Mary and Aileen. Mrs. Duvall and Clara came also. Didn't I have a nice handful? They wanted to meet Mrs. White at Eleventh Street entrance to E.B.T.'s. Well when I'd shoved, pulled, and cussed as far as that, Mrs. W. was not to be found. We got out of the crush and I steered the whole mob over to Thirteenth and McGee, spent a dollar for five seats, and sat in the Hippodrome until the show was over. Then we went around and saw some of the windows—they went home and I went to 2nd and Wyandotte. If ever I do it again I hope I choke. Every time I put my foot down some woman would yell Ow! You're on my foot. One good thing, mine seemed to land on top most every time. There was a punk show at the Hip. Tillie Zick was fairly good, but she insisted on changing her duds right out in sight, which is rather embarrassing to say the least. She's about the best toe dancer I ever saw. The balance of the bill wasn't fit to appear at Yale's. Don't get stung there this week if you're in town. Go to the ten-cent store and see a better show for nothing.

I have been working like Sam Hill this morning sowing wheat. Papa has a fit every time I heave on a one-hundred-pound sack of wheat. I guess I can stand it though, I'm not hurting yet. Get to lay off on the wheat this afternoon and pitch hay while they thresh.

I got an official notice today that I'd drawn No. 6199 at Ft. Peck and would be given a chance to take it sometime after April 1, 1914. I guess I won't have to go to Montana for some time yet. Hope to see you Saturday if wheat sowing doesn't hold on too well. If not Saturday, Sunday morning sure. You do owe me a letter now.

Most sincerely,
Harry

Dear Bess: [Grandview, postmark illegible]
   Have you recovered from your walk yet? I am just now up to date. The beautiful K.C.S. limited arrived in Grandview an hour late on Sunday night. There was a wreck at Leeds and the passengers had to go over the Missouri Pacific. Therefore I got in at two-thirty instead of one-thirty. Quite some difference when you have to rise at 5:00 A.M. This morning I am somewhat more awake than yesterday. I have hopes of being in K.C. tomorrow or Thursday, in which case I'll call up. There is nothing sure about it because we are baling hay and I've got to start a plow this morning. There's a fellow over south of us whom we are going to have to sue to collect $125, and I suppose I'll have to do it. I am going to see him this morning. Try and make a collector of myself. I've an idea it won't amount to much. I shall be the most surprised person if he pays. Some people just won't pay their just debts. I've a notion to go into bankruptcy myself sometimes only I'm scared I'd die of shame. I was at the big city of Belton yesterday. Frank Blair's bank has a nicer set of fixtures and has the building all stuccoed up like a new one. Frank has a little pen all his own just like Ferdinando P. Neal and E. F. Sweeney. I asked him how much larger hat he was wearing and he got sore. He soon got in a good humor though. I was wishing for some of those good sandwiches yesterday about noon. Missed my dinner. You ought to have seen me break for the eatables when I got home. There's a big fat good-natured old lady in Belton who runs a lunch counter. I went there and asked her for some pie. She said she had none just then but if I'd wait she'd bake me one! She would have too. I didn't wait. . . .
   You must please consider this a letter and send an answer whether it's worth it or not.

Most sincerely,
Harry

Dear Bess: [Grandview, Oct. 6, 1913]
   Mamma and Mary are suffering from an attack of house cleaning. They have my desk in the hall locked up with all the drawers gone somewhere and most everything else gone somewhere too. I found two sheets of paper and a dirty envelope. You must suppose that it got dirty in the mail. Haven't any blotter and have to hold each sheet over the lamp before I can turn the next one. It is injurious to your train of thought. There was a wedding party on the K.C.S. last

night. Think of getting married on Sunday! It would spoil half the fun. A person would hardly feel like a breakneck joy ride to catch a train on Sunday night. I am sure the rest of the hoodlums wouldn't put on as good a show as usual. They were on deck last night, throwing rice and beans in confetti. Think of being wished on a happy honeymoon with Boston's famous food! It is the first time I ever saw 'em used. They are pretty good though. The very next wedding I go to I shall take a pocket full of navies. This crowd didn't seem to take much enthusiasm in their work at all. (More drying process before turning the page.) They'd just pitch a handful of stuff every now and then just like clockwork. The married people didn't seem to mind at all. The porter only got about a half a gallon of rice, beans, and confetti mixed when he swept. Very tame I thought. Comes of being married on Sunday. I shall be disappointed if my friends don't invest in at least two bushels. When Myra left, Mary Colgan and I put two gallons of rice and salt in her suitcases, besides about a bushel we threw at them. . . .

I put in about thirteen acres of wheat today. If I keep it up I hope to get done by Saturday evening. Then comes baled hay, baled hay, and some more of it. There are four stacks that will make six hundred bales, each weighing about eighty-five pounds (you can make Fred tell you how many tons that is). I shall be most awful happy when everything is over. There'll be something turn up about time we're done. A farmer's life is like the doctor's motto: "Life is just one ——— thing after another." I guess it's a good thing. You hardly ever hear of farmers being hanged or in any other kind of scrapes when they stay at home. It's when a man hasn't anything to do that he's into ornery things such as Reno and Sing Sing.

You need never apoligize (can't spell) for your letters. They're always good, only sometimes they're not long enough. I'm looking for a long one—not that this deserves one. *Be ready to walk Sunday.*

Most sincerely,
Harry

Every once in a while one of Truman's letters was a grab bag of anecdotes and potshots. Here he and Uncle Harrison have met in Kansas City for the purpose of investigating a small business venture, an ice machine company. In this case they may have been on to something, but the two of them backed off. One recalls Alexander Graham Bell's offer to Mark Twain of stock in a telephone company at fifty on a par value of a hundred; the humorist said he wouldn't take it at half the price.

Dear Bess: [Grandview, Oct. 22, 1913]

Here goes for a Thursday letter. I spent all day today in the city. Would have called you up but thought you had a bridge party on. I paid my respects to Judge Goodrich. He mulcted me for some money and flattered me somewhat and, I suppose, forgot I'd been in the office until he went to get the check cashed. It would serve him right if it went to protest and he had to pay the money back. All that lawyers care for is money. I've an idea that most any one of them would pay a visit to the lower regions for fifty dollars. It seems to me that justice ought to be rendered without any money. There'd be very few lawyers and fewer judges if the government dispensed justice as it does garden seeds and agriculture reports. I can say that I like the manner in which the judge accepts what I have to offer. There are people who make me feel as if they were conferring a favor by allowing me to pay them money. But the judge made me believe I'd done him a real favor.

I met Uncle Harry at Thirteenth and Grand. While I was talking to him a hobo came up and wanted to sell me his pocketknife for fifteen cents. Said he wanted the money for a bed. Claimed to have had thirty dollars the day before but had allowed the barkeeps to get it all. He told Uncle Harrison that he was an honest man, very emphatically an honest man, and that he'd had money the day before. Uncle H. told him that he (uncle) was a crook and that he'd had money some fifteen years ago but riotous living and race horses and ten-cent beggars had got it all. The fellow looked very foolish and cheap when he got through. I didn't buy the knife.

Nothing would do Uncle H. but that I must go and investigate the qualities of a patent ice machine and see if the corporation was worth putting myself into. The machine is a wonder and will make someone rich but the corporation had best be let alone. It's merely a scheme to get people's money and then sell the machine to some big concern, leaving the stockholders with an empty bag. I don't really think that Uncle Harry had any intention of putting money into the thing. He just wanted something to talk about. . . .

I am hoping that this won't stay in your neighbor's mailbox and keep me from getting a nice *long* letter this week. You certainly owe me one.

Most sincerely,
Harry

Dear Bess: [Grandview, Oct. 29, 1913]
. . . We are due to have a card party at our house tomorrow night. Some of the Grandview folks are coming down to *learn* to play 500, with me to tell 'em how. Won't that be a joyous job. I am going to have a good time at it anyway though. They are all rather hilarious and you know I'm not very backward myself when it comes to making noise. If I could only make money as easily as I can stir up a racket, I'd have begged, persuaded, or cajoled you into thinking Harry was the nicest boy in seventeen states. But never mind, my ship's going to come in yet and if it doesn't have you aboard it'll only be a charred hulk and not worth the candle. You know, I told you once before that I thought you the superlative of excellence in everything and I think it harder all the time. I've been crazy about you ever since I can remember. I hope it's a mutual admiration society because then I can work harder and not get half so tired. You know, when the motive's strong enough a man can do most anything if he's got the stuff in him. Perhaps I haven't got it but there is nothing like trying to find out.

Who knows, I may be His Excellency the Governor of Montana someday (hee haw). How would you like to be Mrs. Governor?

I dreamed that I owned a *German* silver mine in Wyoming last night! Wasn't that a grand dream on a piece of bride's cake? I guess the spangles and white fronts gave me the silver suggestion, but where under heaven could I get the German part? From my granddad on my mother's side I guess. He was a Dutchman.

Papa has gone to sleep in his chair. He's waiting very patiently for me to finish my letter so he can go to bed. He occupies the couch down here by the stove. I don't feel a bit like going to bed now I've got the habit of staying up I guess. But my oh me, how I hate to arise at 5:00 A.M. It has to be done though when Papa's around home. If he goes to bed at half-past four he gets up at five and so do I. Mamma is a sleepyhead like me. She never wants to get up but she can stay up till the small hours at night.

I guess this letter is a mixture and doesn't amount to much. I hope you'll answer it though. My letters get one day later every week. You'll get this one Friday unless I mail it on the K.C.S. at six-thirty tomorrow. I lost one by doing that and I'm not going to do it again.

Hope to see you Sunday evening and get a letter Sunday morning.

Most sincerely,

Harry

In the following, Truman is "puffed up and hilarious and happy. . . ." Bess had finally given her word!

Dear Bess: [Grandview, Nov. 4, 1913]

Your letter has made a confirmed optimist out of me sure enough. I know now that everything is good and grand and this footstool is a fine place to be. I have been all up in the air, clear above earth ever since it came. I guess you thought I didn't have much sense Sunday, but I just couldn't say anything—only just sit and look. It doesn't seem real that you should care for me. I have always hoped you would but some way feared very much you wouldn't. You know, I've always thought that the best man in the world is hardly good enough for any woman. But when it comes to the best girl in all the universe caring for an ordinary gink like me—well, you'll have to let me get used to it.

Do you want to be a farmer? or shall I do some other business. When Mamma wins her suit and we get all the lawyers and things out of the way I will then have a chance for myself. We intend to raise a four hundred-acre wheat crop, which if it hits will put us out of the woods. If we lose, which I don't think about, it will mean starting all over for me. You may be sure I'm not going to wait till I'm Montana's chief executive to ask you to be Mrs. Governor, but I sure want to have some decent place to ask you to. I'm hoping it won't be long. I wish it was tomorrow. Let's get engaged anyway to see how it feels. No one need know it but you and me until we get ready to tell it anyway. If you see a man you think more of in the meantime, engagements are easy enough broken. I've always said I'd have you or no one and that's what I mean to do. (This darned pen has it in for me.) Luella and the kids are here today. They are sure a fine pair. I haven't told Luella my Sedalia and Regalia story yet. I have the most awful job ahead of me you ever heard of. It is necessary for me to pay a visit to six country schools and make a speech at each one about the Washington Township Fair. It is going to be at Grandview and I am on the committee to get exhibits. The schools have to be notified because the school that has the best exhibit of schoolwork gets ten dollars. Also the Commercial Club, of which I am also the representative, is offering a prize for the school with the biggest attendance. Don't you feel sorry for me? You know I've got a timid disposition anyway and school kids, especially country ones, haven't very much sympathy for a person. It has to be did though. Washington Township is trying to beat Prairie, which contains Lee's Summit. I hope we can. Mr. Ikenbury is the man who is having the fair for the benefit of the farmers. I am going to *borrow* a cow and see if I can't win ten dollars. Mr. Makin is pasturing the finest Hereford cow I ever saw, here. There is ten dollars offered for the best cow. If I enter her and win, there'll be ten dollars toward a show or diamond ring. Twenty-five premiums like that might get a real pretty one. I'm going to get you one as soon as the change is forthcoming. Bess, why am I an enigma? I try to be just what I am and tell the truth about as much as the average person. If there's anything you don't understand, I'll try and explain or remedy it. I feel very much stuck up at being called one, especially by you, for I always labored under the impression that it took smart people to be one. This letter seems to me to be more erratic and incoherent than the last, but you shouldn't blame me very much because I'm all puffed up and hilarious and happy and anything else that happens to a fellow when he finds his lady love thinks more of him than the rest of the beasts. Send me a letter quick. If I can raise business reasons enough to please Papa, I hope to see you before Sunday.

Most sincerely,

Harry

The manner in which Truman describes below his political ambition was hyperbole, but strangely prophetic.

Dear Bess: [Grandview, Nov. 10, 1913]
      . . . I have been cleaning seed to show at Grandview tomorrow. We have about fifty bushels of clover seed to sell. I cleaned a peck so beautifully that it's simply a perfect sample. If anybody buys seed from us on the strength of that peck, he'll be sorely disappointed when he gets his seed. I wouldn't spend so much time cleaning it for sale. It would be just as good only there'd be some dirt and trash left in it. We have a peck of wheat, the same amount of oats, and timothy seed to show along with the clover. They are all extra fine because I spent some three hours cleaning them. I suppose there'll be a big crowd at the show. I expect to have a very busy day. You'd think I was running for office if you'd see me chasing around shaking hands with people and displaying a classic cat grin. I will simply be acting as one of the township committee to show people around.
      I suppose you had a fine game of tennis today. The weather has been ideal

if it'll only keep up. Mary has gone riding on Ben. We are going to lend a couple of horses to girls in Grandview and then have a riding contest. If you'd have come to our fair you might have won the five dollars for the best lady rider. You could have ridden Ben. I am hoping to be one of the judges in that contest so I can tie the ribbon on a plug and then laugh at Daddy because his fine hoss got beaten. He'd never get over it and Uncle Harrison would simply go straight up. I fear I'd have to leave home if I did the trick. I saw an overcoat downtown this morning just like I want but I won't get it. Why? Because it was seventy-five dollars. I can use three at that price and still have money left.

You were most awful nice about the other girl but don't suppose there'll ever be one. If a fellow can pick his idol at ten and still be loyal to it at thirty, there's not much danger of his finding another. One or two of my aunties and good matron friends have sought to arrange things for me several times but could never understand why they never had any luck. Maybe they will before long. How does it feel being engaged to a clodhopper who has ambitions to be Governor of Montana and Chief Executive of U.S. He'll do well if he gets to be a retired farmer. That was sure a good dream though, and I have them in the daytime, even night, along the same line. It looks like an uphill business sometimes though. But I intend to keep peggin' away and I suppose I'll arrive at something. You'll never be sorry if you take me for better or for worse because I'll always try to make it better.

I am hoping to see you Wednesday evening. I suppose Mamma and I will have to be present at Aunt Susan's grilling. If she'll only stick to the truth I won't mind, but if she does like the rest I sure will hate to be present. One hates to see a white-haired old lady, one he likes and respects, tearing up the truth just for a few dollars. It has a tendency to make a pessimist out of a person. I like money as well as anyone but I think I'd do without it if I had to cast aspersions on my mother's character to get it. I suppose you are tired of hearing me harp on our old suit but it means so much to us if we lose that I can't help it. You owe me a letter anyway and I hope it'll come early. You'd better send it if you don't want me to have another spasm in the middle of the week like I did last time.

Most sincerely,
Harry

Dear Bess: [Grandview, Nov. 18, 1913]

Here it is, Tuesday morning and your letter's not in the post office yet. Usually it goes up Monday night but I went to the Scottish Rite meeting last night and didn't get to write. It was some meeting, too. There was a class of fifty-nine. I wanted to go ahead and finish up most awful bad but I'm not going to. Old man Thalman told me he'd lend me the money for ten years without interest if I wanted to go ahead, but I turned him down. The Scottish bodies bought $8,000 worth of new costumes this year. They are most certainly fine. A person thinks he's back in the days of the Wise King. The Eastern Star ladies served supper at six. It was a good one, too. There was some good-looking woman who was sure a pianist. She played everything from Chopin to "Peg o' My Heart," while we ate. After the meal the men were as thick around that piano as flies around a loaf of sugar. Some duck who thought he had a voice got her to play "The Rosary." He sang it with all the twists and quirks of Schumann-Heink. It turned out that she was a little old wizened guy's wife but I didn't get to find out who he is. I learned another lecture last night. I can begin talking at eight o'clock and buzz right straight through until 1:00 A.M. now without a break if I had to do it. . . .

I got a long-distance call from Belton yesterday to come up there to some kind of party a ladies club is giving Thursday. I had been a filler at this club once before when they were shy a man. They always have fine things to eat. That's one thing worth going for anyway. The lady I must go for wears a big diamond on the third finger of her left hand. She said her rich uncle gave it to her but I can't see why she'd wear it on that finger, can you? As George Ade remarked, maybe she's in the third summer of her twenty-ninth year and is starting something. You won't mind, will you, if I'm merely an extra at this party? It's made up mostly of married women and nice maiden ladies from twenty to thirty-four. There was a red-haired one invited me before so you see I'm kind of general help all around. Did I tell you that my nemesis was on the car Sunday evening? Well, she was and she rode up to Union, too. I waited until she started off at the back and then I made a rush for the other end, beat her off, and ran up the street before she could ask where I was bound for.

There was a man and a girl sitting behind me as I came to town Sunday evening. They were having the most beautiful quarrel you ever listened to. It sounded just like the conversations Nellie Noland and Fielding [Houchens] used to have ages ago. This man would inform the girl how she'd smiled too sweetly at someone else and she'd tell him about the other girls he had taken to dances. They were evidently very much in love with each other but I thought once he was going to choke her. You know Eva Tanguay's leading man used to choke her almost into insensibility and then remark, "Oh, how I love that woman." For myself, I'd prefer some other means of demonstration and I fear you'll have to get along without being choked by me. Maybe I can show you how much I think of you some other way. My demonstrative bump is very small. The lack of that said bump covers up some very strong feelings sometimes, anyway.

I've managed without any effort on my part to get this week all taken up. I suppose I'll have to live through it until Saturday night but you never can tell what opportunity is going to turn up for a visit to Independence. Tonight's Eastern Star; Wednesday, Ft. Peck Settlers Association; Thursday, Belton; Friday, a degree in Masonry at Lee's Summit—but thank heaven Saturday is as it should be.

There's some danger of a spasm this week, so you'd better answer early.

Most sincerely,
Harry

Dear Bess: [Grandview, Nov. 19, 1913]

I've been at the installation of an Eastern Star chapter. The woman who did the job is Julia V. Freyman of Kansas City. She's a Past Most Worthy Grand Matron of Missouri and the nicest old lady. (Say the old in a low voice.)

She had on a lace dress and two of the biggest diamond earrings with the most beautiful diamond ring. I never saw one like it. If old Dr. Freyman gave it to her for an engagement he surely had an eye for beauty. It's evidently a joy forever to Julia for she wears it continually—along with several others. Besides all this array of regular adornment on her left breast she wore the jewel of a P.M.W.G.M. (There are so many letters I forgot one myself). It is a five-pointed star of solid gold suspended from a bar with a Masonic pin set with diamonds attached by a tiny chain. All this array is what you see at first, but when you get acquainted with her you forget that she has a loose screw for gew-gaws and like her immensely. Not a single woman there had a mean thing to say of her. They all said, "Just isn't Mrs. Freyman lovely!" That speaks for itself. What I started to say is that Sheffield Lodge has informed our aggregation that they are going to come out on Friday to show us how to put on a Third Degree. On Wednesday evening the W. M. has asked me to conduct a Lodge of Instruction, on Thursday evening as president of the Commercial Club I had to call a town meeting to get ready for the Township Fair, and on Saturday I have to call a meeting of the Woodmen to get them to donate their half to the farmers for their exhibition Tuesday. Ain't that an awful array for one pigheaded farmer to have in a November week? Especially when he'd rather be some twenty miles away on every single night. I'm hoping for a flood or snow or some other disaster to take place for I'm dying to come to Independence. I know your last letter word for word and then I read it some forty times a day. Oh please send me another like it. I wear it in my left breast pocket. I'm going to put it in a safety vault to keep from wearing it out. You really didn't know I had so much softness and sentimentality in me, did you? I'm full of it. But I'd die if I had to talk it. I can tell you on paper how much I love you and what one grand woman I think you, but to tell it to you I can't. I'm always afraid I'd do it so clumsily you'd laugh. Then I'd die really. When a person's airing his most sacred thoughts he's very easily distressed. No one ever knew I ever had any but you. You are the one girl I'd ever want to tell them to. I could die happy doing something for you. (Just imagine a guy with spectacles and a girl mouth doing the Sir Lancelot.) Since I can't rescue you from any monster or carry you from a burning building or save you from a sinking ship —simply because I'd be afraid of the monsters, couldn't carry you, and can't swim —I'll have to go to work and make money enough to pay my debts and then get you to take me for what I am: just a common everyday man whose instincts are to be ornery, who's anxious to be right. You'll not have any trouble getting along with me for I'm awful good-natured, and I'm sure we'd live happy ever after sure enough. I'm writing this at 1:00 A.M. just because I can't help it and if you get tired of it, as Agnes' beau said, put it in the kitchen stove. This is all the stationery I have upstairs and Papa's sleeping where I keep the other and I can't get to it. If you don't like mushy letters, just tell me so. I never had any desire to write them before or to preach my own good points so strongly. Do you suppose your mother'll care for me well enough to have me in her family? I'm freezing and must quit because my paper's run out.

Most sincerely,
Harry

Dear Bess: [Grandview, Nov. 25, 1913]

It's Tuesday morning again and I am just starting your letter. Yesterday morning Papa went out on the road and I started to read the November install-ment of "Kidnapping Colleen." I went to sleep over it and Mamma didn't wake me up until 3:30 P.M. Isn't she a nice mammy to let me spend a whole day asleep when I ought to have been in the cornfield? About five o'clock a bunch of Masons called up and wanted me to go to K.C. to Lodge. They wanted me along so they could get in. I happened to be acquainted with the big gun of the Lodge they wanted to visit. I tried to call you up but for some reason or other couldn't make connection. That was about seven o'clock. The next time I got to a phone it was 10:10 and I thought I'd better not try so late. I have broken the record for late hours in the last two weeks. The average has been 1:00 A.M. since a week ago Friday, and yesterday is the first extra sleep I've had too. My head feels like it is empty this morning; that is, it has a ringing sound and the Scotchman said that meant emptiness. I heard a most excellent address on Freemasonry last night by Dr. Smith, pastor of the Central Congregational Church. He's a real orator and an extemporaneous one. He told a pretty good story about a young lady who went into a bookstore to get a present for an old man's fiftieth wedding anniversary. She asked the clerk for something appropriate and he turned to the bookshelf without any hesitation whatever and gave her Greeley's *Fifty Years of Strife*. He was telling that story to show that a man should be familiar with his subject. There were about four hundred present. You never saw such a rush when refresh-ments were served. It was like a football rush. The Eastern Star served in the banquet room. It has a dancing floor. There were several disasters to coffee cups and striped clothes. We had to eat standing up there was such a crush. Evidently some were not used to such slick floors. They give dances there about twice a month. I suppose they have a good time. It's one of the best floors in K.C.

I met Val Brightwell Sunday night and rode home with him in his auto. We almost had a year's growth scared out of us at Dodson. There were three men standing at the end of the Blue Ridge right where several holdups have taken place. They didn't stop us but they might as well have for all the difference in our feelings it would have made. Val said he was sure glad that I was along and I was the same as regards him.

I suppose you saw Independence in motion last night. I wish I could have been along. I couldn't ditch my crowd or I would have been. There were ten of them in two machines and they kept me in tow pretty close.

I suppose you'll go to Platte City next Sunday. I hope you have a good time.

I guess I'll hold a Masonic Lodge of Instruction that afternoon or go to the Orpheum, one. I'll certainly have to do something. I was wondering if they had a Home phone over there. If you didn't mind, I might call up and tell you where I go or what I do to get through the evening. Do you suppose you'll get to stay the whole week? It sure will be nice if you can but I hope you're back by a week from Sunday anyway. Two in succession would be a calamity. The box supper out here Saturday night will be some diversion. Mary said that Aileen Duvall and Nadine Blair will be here. Maybe I can make them believe I'm staying home on their account. I'll have to put some strong bluff anyway. You must write me a long letter this week to help fill the gap. There is a good-for-nothing coming for a load of hay and we've got to quit.

Most sincerely,
Harry

Dear Bess: [Grandview, Nov. 29, 1913]

I got your letter this morning. I was sure glad to get it. I suppose you are on your way to the City of the Platte. (Which really means Buenos Aires.) You must not forget to mail me a card from that burg, so that Miss Duvall will speedily discover her mistake. I have made up my mind to stay home on Sunday in order to *help with the evening work.* It will be the first Sunday that the men leave and you know my staying at home will look grand to daddy until he sees your card from Platte City.

The Noland girls have never said anything sassy to me about you. They are well aware that they'd better hadn't I guess. They always talk to me as if they were of the same opinion that I am regarding you.

The hired men are paid off. They beat me badly when I paid them. Wornall hadn't had a settlement since July. He had over forty dollars coming. The other fellow got thirty dollars. Just think what a lot of Christmas presents that would have bought. I wish I knew what you want for Christmas. My brain refuses the task of thinking up something really worthwhile and within my financial ability. Were I a Jawn D. [Rockefeller], there'd be no trouble whatever. There's autos and jewelry and most anything in a millionaire's line, but there are so few things an ordinary person can get that are really worthwhile. Maybe I'll have an inspiration of some kind before midnight, December 24. You may get anything from a needle to a threshing machine. I could use a threshing machine in my own business. It might be good policy to give you one. It is said that a man to be absolutely ornery must own one and a fiddle. I haven't reached either yet. . . .

Mary's in an awful stew. Her Pleasant Hill beau has written that he'll be here one day this week. Today is all that's left, and she's got someone else for tonight I think. Then there are three extra people and I bought her the wrong kind of cheese for the sandwiches. I guess she'll be a wreck by Sunday evening. I told her I am going to stay home tomorrow evening and she said she knew I'd

stay till 4:00 P.M. Won't she be surprised. You might send me about an eight-
or ten-page *note* for this and I'll try and send you a good letter Wednesday.
Most sincerely,

Harry

Dear Bess: [Grandview, Dec. 2, 1913]
    I suppose you didn't get the special I sent to Platte. It was marked too late
to arrive I guess. I spent a very quiet Sunday. The auctioneer, Colonel Andy
James, lives about twelve miles from here over in Kansas just south of Overland
Park. I drove him home and got a most excellent dinner for my pains. He has
a most agreeable wife and a daughter about sixteen. The colonel drove me around
over his four-hundred-acre farm and showed his fine cattle and barns. I was
supposed to arrive home in time to take Nadine Blair to Belton, but Mary and
Aileen decided that I'd gone to Independence after all when I didn't get back
at exactly four o'clock, and so they drove Nadine home. I got home about thirty
minutes after they left. I was very glad they'd gone because I'd had all the driving
I cared for.
    The box supper was a grand success. They made $64.90. There were fifty
boxes and the average price was $1.25. The high price was $2.25. There were no
real bad cases present and therefore no extremely high bids. I got stung for three
boxes. Of course I had to buy Nadine's because she went with me, and when Val's
Grandview girl's box was sold I bid on it to spring the price. He let me have it
for $2.00. Then I got a little six-year-old girl's box. She had expressed the hope
that I would and there was nothing for it but to do it. I got so full of cake and
pie and flossy sandwiches that I thought I'd never want any more. You never saw
such a collection of boxes. There were moons and stars, diamonds, hearts and
every other shape. The auctioneer had some smart remark to make about each
one. We had a dance after it was over. I furnished the music and the rest danced.
Even Papa got gay and fixed up an old-fashioned square dance. Mamma wouldn't
go at all. We all told her she'd just about lose the old gentleman if she doesn't
watch him closely.
    I don't suppose you had much tennis at Platte City if it performed over there
like it did here. It rained like the mischief about twelve o'clock Saturday night.
Val Brightwell and Delbert Weston came down in the car and took Aileen and
Clara and Mary to the box affair. When they came back the car stopped at the
front gate and I had to bring them to the house in installments. You've no idea
how nice a good top buggy is on a rainy night when there is a dirt road. Val's
auto curtains were home in the barn. He got wet and so did Weston. They, of
course, had to sit next to the rain and keep the girls dry. Nadine and I didn't
get a drop of rain on us, only going from the buggy to the house.
    The hired men have gone and I am the man of all work now. I bragged to
Papa last night that I could get up this morning and do all the work they and
he both did before breakfast in the same length of time. I had made some

arrangements before I said it. So I got up this morning and did all the two men were supposed to do and then milked a cow for him. He couldn't understand how I made it and I didn't tell him. Besides, hired men generally take double time to do everything. I expect to put in a strenuous winter from this out. We have about seventy cattle to feed and it's no small job or nice one either on a rainy day like this one. I am hoping to see you Sunday. Papa can't possibly expect me to stay at home two in succession. If he does, he'll be sadly disappointed anyway. I am looking for an extra long letter this week. You should count the note even if you didn't get it.

Most sincerely,
Harry

Dear Bess: [Grandview, Dec. 9, 1913]

Here it is Tuesday morning again and I am just starting your letter. Yesterday was the most strenuous day I've put in for a year. We shipped some cattle and sold some and also sold some hogs. The whole works had to be delivered in Grandview by noon and it was a rush to get there. Of course the hogs had to cause all the trouble they were able to. You know, it's a hard and fast rule that a hog's head is always turned opposite the way he is to go. There were twenty-nine to be loaded. I tried to get them in the barn and did get fifteen in. Usually when I have the barn door open and don't want them in every one of them will be right there. We loaded the fifteen and then tried to get the others in. I put some corn in the barn, and they all went in when one extra smart one grabbed an ear and ran out between my legs before I could shut the door. I went down without a struggle and the hogs all ran out. I finally got them in a little pen and when Papa came back we loaded them without any more trouble. . . .

I've got to bring this to a close in order to get it off this morning. You owe me a letter anyway and I hope to see you Friday evening.

Most sincerely,
Harry

Dear Bess: [Grandview, Dec. 15, 1913]

This letter or attempt at one will not amount to much this morning because Papa is in a hurry to go to Grandview and my thought factory is empty. I very nearly missed the limited last night. Kansas City was in the clutches of another fog. It was impossible to see six feet. The cars just had to creep. It didn't extend only to about Woodland. At Troost it was so thick you could cut it with a knife. The K.C.S. just barely moved until it got past 15th Street. Then it whooped up and arrived at Grandview exactly on the tick. There was a new engine on, and it sure did ramble. There wasn't any fog here last night but there's a humdinger on this morning. It was almost equal to a plunge to feed fodder this morning. I have one disagreeable job ahead of me today. We killed hogs Thursday, and it is necessary to put the sausage into sacks and hang it this morning. That is always my job. Mamma always wants to do it but when she does, it makes her sick. Mary and Papa won't, so it falls to me. I usually get sausage in my shoes, on my clothes, and in my hair, and over the kitchen floor. It isn't an agreeable job at all. But the sausage is worth the trouble later when it comes time to eat it. Then I am absolutely sure there's nothing in it but hog and the dirt off my own hands. It sure is fine for making hands clean and bright. Also I usually have some blisters from squeezing the sacks so hard. There'll only be about a dozen sacks not blisters I hope. I sold fifty pounds and Papa sold seventy-five. That leaves us fifty still, and I don't suppose we'll more than use it up before it ought to be, especially if it turns a little bit warm. . . .

You really owe me two letters now and you said you'd send them. Remember you said you were a woman of your word. You've no idea how blank a week is v. :thout a letter, so you'd better make this one extra bright.

Most sincerely,
Harry

Dear Bess: [Grandview, Dec. 22, 1913]
I have been sending some Christmas cards to various old aunts, uncles, and others who I've an idea don't give a continental whether they hear from me or not. I have never hurt myself sending them before and I do not think I shall again very soon. The cards were here though and needed using very badly, and in order to make them come out I used them on everyone that's had me to dinner in the last year. I don't think I overlooked any. There are still some cards left if I did. They're the [illegible] kind that go in envelopes and look excessively formal and wedding like. I know very well some of those people will have a notion they're getting an invitation to something. It'll be an awful comedown to find that it's only a "Wishing you a Very Merry Christmas," "Mr. Harry S. Truman." Some of the comments will be, "Well what do you suppose ever possessed that guy to send me this?" Then there'll be a scurry for a return to arrive here December 25. I sent 'em today so they have ample time to send me one. Most of them went to Belton, one to Lenexa, and one to Olathe. Of course Aunt Ada and Aunt Emma get one every year and they'll not be surprised. I hope you got everything ready on time. I'm trying to figure out some way to get Uncle Harry's parasol without going to the city. I don't see how I can do it. The thing's got to cost not more than a five and still be pretty good. I've an idea it'll be a hard proposition to make that agree. My box of apples never has come and I've been putting in the morning trying to call up the commission company. It's a Dago and an Englishman I guess. Ginnochio-Jones is the name.

Papa's starting to Grandview now and if I quit you'll get this on Tuesday. Wouldn't you rather have it come a day sooner than to get another sheet? If you'll write quickly, I'll get it before Christmas.

Most sincerely,
Harry

Dear Bess: [Grandview, Dec. 30, 1913]

Your note won't come so soon this week for the reason that I did a day's work for a change, and the train left on time. We hauled two loads of hay to the cattle and horses and then went two miles and a half and hauled two loads of straw. I got my dinner at 4:00 P.M. and I sure wanted it. Mr. Delbert Weston and a Grandview bride and groom were on the K.C.S. train. Delbert said he was very anxious to get married if he could only be right sure he could make a lot of money. He said he knew a very rich girl he thought he could get but he was afraid she'd spend the rest of her life reminding him of his good fortune. I told him that it was my opinion that if people were real crazy about one another, a little coin one way or another wouldn't make any difference but that a fellow ought at least to have a good living assured before he asked any girl to leave a good home for him. He's a good kid all right because he said that there were very few girls who were not too good for the best of men. He's absolutely right on that all right. This kid who got married at Grandview was telling me what an awful mistake I was making to go chasing over to Independence so often. Said he'd never do it. He'd go get her and make one trip do. It hasn't been two weeks since he was driving down six miles south of Pleasant Hill and getting home at 3:00 A.M. instead of 1. It's funny how they reform after one day's married life. He was married Saturday. I was informed some two months ago that he was going to be, but he made me promise not to tell it. Mary was very much put out when I calmly informed her that I'd known it so long. The boy's name is Hall and the girl's was Garrett. (No kin to Lloyd.) He's my very good friend, one who is of the opinion that whatever I do is exactly correct. Naturally I am his good friend. I suppose I'll have to buy a present for him to show my good feeling. I don't know what it'll be. A small, very small piece of silver I guess. People are very foolish to get married at Christmas. Don't you think so? I'd rather get all my Christmas presents at that time and be sure someone wasn't killing two birds.

Papa's going to St. Clair County in the morning and says he's not coming back for three days! Ain't it awful. Just think of me arising at 5:00 P.M. and making three fires on these chilly mornings. Papa sleeps with a fire and so he doesn't mind starting another one. I sleep with the windows up and shake for thirty minutes every morning when there's a fire already going. I guess it'll mean another thirty for three days anyway. What under the sun he wants to stay down there three days for I can't see. Perhaps he'll buy some more cows and string out the feeding process some more. It will be such a nice job while he's gone. The fodder is all covered with snow and it's a hard job to keep warm loading it. Generally I have snow up my sleeves and down my neck when Papa's on the wagon to pile it up. I guess I'll just pass up the fodder and feed hay while he's gone. There's a stack open and he'll never know the diff. Maybe the cows will. There's one thing, I'm not a gentleman farmer and if any of the cows get funny, they'll get a board instead of seeing my hat come off.

Everybody is crazy about my cuff links. I am going to have to keep them under lock and key. They're the finest ones I ever had and you may be sure I'm not going to let anyone else wear them if I can help. I suppose if Ethel needs them she'll just commit assault and battery and take 'em anyhow. I'm going to hide them and my chain when they come. They usually get 'em, and then I have to bribe them to get my own belongings. Hope to see you New Year's Day if the company goes and Dad comes. Please send me a letter that day anyway.

Harry

FOUR

FROM FATHER TO SON

---

*Two more years or so of farm life, from the beginning of 1914 into 1916,
and a decade had passed since Harry left the Kansas City bank to help his folks
near Grandview. His father's death late in 1914, the settling of that tedious family
lawsuit, and Uncle Harrison's interest in enterprises to advance both their fortunes forced a rearrangement of affairs. At last Harry Truman's prospects began
to improve. He so wanted a better future that he once wrote to Bess, "There's
no one wants to win half so badly as I do."*

*The death of John Truman came after that aging head of household strained
himself lifting a huge boulder while performing his duties as road overseer. The
resultant operation was unsuccessful, and after lingering for weeks he died. His
son was grief-stricken. In times past John Truman had pushed Harry hard,
especially when the courtship of Bess detracted from farm work. Sometimes he
poked gentle fun at Harry for being sleepy, other times he was almost cruelly
critical. But when he sickened and the faraway look came into his tired eyes, the
father-son bonds strengthened quickly. Harry missed him terribly, as the few brief
references in the letters show.*

*John Truman's death left Harry as sole proprietor of the farm, and he
eventually persuaded Uncle Harrison to consider a few outside investments. One
opportunity to buy land near Fort Stockton, in western Texas, fell through: Harry
was ready, but Uncle Harrison was not. Clearly, however, the uncle was loosening
up, and that meant (so Harry told Bess) as much as forty thousand dollars to
invest. The prospect was exhilarating.*

*Meanwhile, for only six hundred dollars Harry bought a 1911 Stafford car.
It made his visits to Bess immeasurably easier. He could forget the Frisco railroad
and the Kansas City Southern, along with the streetcar between Sheffield and
Independence. The car posed its own brand of inconvenience—the constant
changing of tires, the wearing out of this or that mechanism—and Mary Jane
insisted on learning to drive. She learned well enough to run into the gate in front
of the house. Still, Harry could get back home from Bess's house at a decent hour,
midnight or 1:00 A.M. And he and Bess could explore the countryside, driving*

as much as 120 miles in a single day, which was great fun for a farmer and even for a town girl. Life was looking up.

Economic recession in 1913–14 caused great numbers of unemployed men to "take to the rails"—traveling on "side-door Pullmans." The downturn came to an end after World War I began in August 1914. But for a while the railroads were full of hobos; a farmer found it scary to be followed by several of them, as Truman relates below.

Dear Bess: [Grandview, Jan. 6, 1914]
    . . . If you don't think it was dark last night, you're very much mistaken. I could barely see ten feet in front of me. I was scared pink for the whole mile for fear someone would hold me up and get my watch chain and cuff links. That's all I was afraid of losing. I turned into the cemetery gate instead of ours but I was not fussed over that. It pleased me to think I was so near the house. It would have been an ideal night for some old antebellum ghost to rise up and turn my hair gray but it never appeared. That cemetery is the best behaved I ever heard tell of. I have been passing it at midnight and 1:00 A.M. since 1906 and never have I seen even so much as one piece of sod turn over or one gravestone behave other than it should. It's the live ones I'm scared of. There were three hobos I'd never seen before got off the train when I did and came out through town behind me. I don't know where they went. You may be sure I didn't stop to inquire. Also over on the railroad right opposite our southwest course is an old depot the hobos use as a hotel. I imagined I could see a light over there as I came along but I guess I couldn't because the fog was so thick you could have cut it with a knife. I guess a fellow's pretty dippy when he has an insane desire to go through hades every night to see his lady love, don't you think so? (You'd better not say yes.)
    This proposed note is gradually stringing itself into a G. B. McCutcheon (hang the pen) story if length counts. . . . You owe me a *letter* anyway. Hope to see you some day this week, don't know which. Papa goes to town tomorrow. Jim comes Thursday and our blowout, Friday. That leaves Wednesday and Saturday and *Sunday* sure.
                                    Harry

Temperance is the issue of this letter. Prohibition became nationwide in January 1920 with the Volstead Act, which enforced the Eighteenth Amendment. In the growing agitation for prohibition Harry Truman was unsure of his stand. He never drank much, and while on the farm may not have drunk at all. He found saloons, "thirst emporiums," to be amusing, however, rather than dangerous, and liked to tell jokes about booze. Most of all he detested hypocrisy. As a youth he had worked evenings and weekends in Clinton's Drug Store in

Independence, and often observed God-fearing, church-going town fathers fur-
tively apply to the druggist for shots of whiskey, which Clinton served up for
medicinal purposes. He never forgot this spectacle.

Dear Bess: [Grandview, Jan. 12, 1914]

Here it is Monday night again before I get started on your letter. I intended
getting it off in time for you to get it Tuesday but I never did get back to the
house after I went out this morning. After we got the cows fed, a man came and
wanted to buy one for $42.50 and have us deliver her at Grandview. We told
him that if we decided to take him up, we'd be there by two o'clock. The cow
was caught after a half hour's tussle all over two acres, and we decided to weigh
her and see how much we were being skinned. She was attached to the rear of
a wagon and dragged on the scales. She weighed 930 and would bring about
$54.00 in K.C. Papa decided that $10.00 was too much of a present to make so
we turned her loose. I was mad as I could be after all that trouble, and then keep
her. She's a horrid beast, always has her nose where she's not wanted. She's like
Uncle Harry's four work steers. He said a fellow had two yoke of cattle named
for the different churches. One was called Catholic, one Methodist, one Baptist,
and one Episcopalian. He had good reasons for calling them that too. He said
the Episcopalian wouldn't eat at the proper time and would try to horn the rest
away so they couldn't eat. The Catholic wanted all there was to eat and didn't
want the rest to have any. The Methodist was always battling and wouldn't pull
a pound, and the Baptist wanted to run and jump in every hole of water he saw.
This cow is of the Catholic persuasion. It was 2:00 P.M. when the cow episode
was finished. I started to the house and had just got myself comfortably seated
when a man came after a load of hay. I had to put on fifty-two bales for him and
some of them would weigh all of a hundred pounds apiece. There is no reason
on earth for me to belong to the Kansas City Athletic Club for exercise. I can
probably get my money's worth out of the pool and barbershop on Sundays, and
the *bar*—I was about to forget the bar.

I have made up my mind to quit the Grandview Commercial Club because
they sell booze and then, to be consistent, I join the K.C.A.C. because they do!
Most people are about that consistent in their actions. I'll not try to drink up
all the K.C.A.C. has on draught the first time I go anyway. I'll endeavor to go
by easy stages. It sure would be a strain on the breweries if everyone drank as
much as I do—at least a strain on their dividends. It makes me tired to hear a
lot of holier-than-thou people yell temperance and try to make me vote dry, and
then when I'm in the city with them they make fun of me for drinking buttermilk
instead of rye. I was in town on the Thursday before Thanksgiving with some
of Grandview's strongest drys. On the way home we stopped at a lunch stand
to get a sandwich and then every one of them had to have a cold bottle and I
got bawled out because I didn't take one. I never did hear a remark that suited
me better than "What you do speaks so loud, I cannot hear what you say." If
the drys were all really dry, there'd be about half the booze drank and sold that

there is. Excuse me. I didn't intend to get on a Women's Christian Temperance Union subject but it just intruded itself.

I met a cold wave last night as I came down the road. It was a breeze right off Lake Winnipeg coming from right under the south star. I didn't appreciate it a little bit. My north window was up and the bed was cooled down to about absolute zero. I was hot when I got in the house but it didn't take me long to cool off. It was an awful task to arise this morning in that ten-degree room. I finally did but I believe some of the enamel is cracked on my teeth.

I hope to get to town this week but I don't know what day. If I get in I'll call you up. See you anyway Sunday, which will be a long time to wait. Anyway if I get a long letter pretty quick it'll help some.

Sincerely,
Harry

Dear Bess: [Grandview, Jan. 20, 1914]
My mind is full of nothing but figures and double entries this afternoon. I have been spending the whole morning trying to get the books of the Commercial Club straightened out. They called on me to do it, and I'm going to resign from that club. I don't like the job or the club either for that matter. My official position ended January 1 anyway and I hoped to drop out without causing any disturbance, but they went and voted me an honorary life membership. Now I have to resign to get out. It doesn't please me to be tied up with a booze-selling crowd. I don't have any use for it. You never did see such a mess for a person to fix up as those books were. The fellow who helped me was thoroughly disgusted. We finally padded them with twenty-two dollars on the debit side and made them balance. He is going to quit same as I am and no one but us could find it, so I guess we're safe. Anyway the books prove to a penny. Never again an auditing committee for [illegible]. I have to hold an instruction school tonight for the Woodmen. That is, I have to call it, the other boys [are] to do the instruction, because I'm not hunting learning any Woodmen foolishness. My head's nearly bursting open from the strain that's been put on it by the Masons, and that's a plenty for one rube.

It has been just a half a day since I started your letter. If there had been no interruptions, you'd have received it on Tuesday instead of Wednesday. I had about a dozen extra jobs at the barn and Papa insisted on my doing them yesterday instead of this morning. We have to go to Dodson to the justice court and try to collect a pasture bill. There's an old curly headed windjammer who has been keeping three horses here since last January. They have just about eaten themselves up and we've got to collect them in order to get pay for the feed. There's a long string of red tape to be gone through with before we can get them, but I guess we'll start to unwind it this morning. I sure do hate to collect a bill by force. I know how hard it is to pay bills myself. If this man would come and offer to pay about half what he owes, I think I could persuade Papa to let him off. He has promised to come and get these horses every week since September but has never showed up.

I dreamed last night that your mother and you and Mary and I were trying to buy tickets to *Paddy* at Convention Hall, and that every time I'd go to pay for them I'd get a lot of extra tickets and a roll of money out of one of my pockets. Do you know what it means to dream of having a bushel of money? I don't. I am hoping to get over to see the *Prisoner of Zenda* this week, but if the weather stays fine I have an idea I'll have to help the road overseer build some culverts. I am wishing for snow and ice. Be sure and send me a letter anyway because, as I said before, it's a long time till Sunday.

I'll copy the Assyrian poem [see Sept. 1, 1918, letter] and bring it home when I come over.

Most sincerely,
Harry

Dear Bess: [Grandview, Jan. 26, 1914]

I am going to stay home from a drill meeting at the Woodmen tonight in order to write you a letter. I came very near spoiling that nice remark by another qualifying it. I usually make a mess of my nice remarks both written and verbal. My intentions are always good, though, and there is no malice aforethought because I haven't the brains to aforethink it. My remark about a week's sleep was one of those boxed-headed kind. You may be sure that I would never want to waste an evening in sleep that could be spent at 219 Delaware Street. That's one reason I want an auto so badly. I could do a day's work and still arrive in your town at a reasonable hour. I suppose if I did have one, I'd learn to do my sleeping between stops. There's no doubt that it would not be worn out standing still.

The *Redbook* has some good short stories in it, and Mr. Glyn's continued one starts well. I hope I'll not forget to buy the magazine on February 23. Old Mike Sullivan, the conductor on the K.C.S., swiped it last night while I was in the back of the car talking to Delbert Weston. He stuck it under a pillow when he got off at Grandview and I got it back. I'll not leave my belongings, particularly magazines, lying around loose after this. If I hadn't seen him take it, I'd have been out fifteen cents for a K.C.S. conductor. Mr. Weston seems to have the Sunday night habit as badly as I have. I'd like to see the girl. Bet she's not over four feet ten high. He is about six and a half feet tall. When he and Val Brightwell are together they look like Mutt and Jeff. He's a mighty nice kid though, and his pa has some change. Not enough to be rich but I've heard about fifty thousand. There are three boys and a stepmother. I guess she's young and agreeable though. Delbert calls her Mrs. Weston and seems to think she's all right. I'd hate to have one though—if she were the nicest person in the world. Mamma is a person for whom there is no substitute. I hope she lives to be a hundred and one. She may do it, for she's a mighty healthy person right now.

Do you think you'll go to Platte City Friday? I hope you'll have a good time.

If you don't come home Sunday, you ought to send me a letter so I'd get it that day. I shall probably send you one. (If you want me to.)

Papa has announced that he will go to the city tomorrow. That leaves me an awful big day's work and in all likelihood means that I shall have to keep it up the rest of the week. He is going to see the county judges and says he's going again before the week's out. I suppose he's trying to get even with me for being gone Thursday and Sunday. I don't care if he does. I can attend to the cattle as well as he can anyway.

My idea of what's coming to the theaters seems to have been rather hazy. I was absolutely sure Peg was coming next week, but the papers say not. We'll see her anyway when she does come if you want to. Maybe we'll have a man by then and I won't have to hurry home. If I were rich and had an auto, we'd go every week. I shall look for a letter early this week so I'll know if you go to Platte.

Most sincerely,

Harry

Dear Bess: [Grandview, Feb. 3, 1914]

I fear very much your letter is going to be a day late. I have a very excellent excuse though, been on the go steadily on account of certain litigation. I have an idea that I will perhaps have to go to the city early in the morning, in which case if I find I can't come over I'll mail it—then perhaps it'll get there on time. I went nigger chasing again on Monday. Right through Central Africa: Vine St. There was no trace of that Nelson nigger. She has as completely disappeared as old Tom Swope's good qualities. Pretty far gone, isn't she? I drove to Belton this morning to see Mr. Blair. It was very cold coming back, I am shaking yet. He is going to establish a new Masonic Lodge down at Archie in Cass County and wants me to be there. It's going to be tomorrow night and I doubt very much whether I can go, but I sure want to. Maybe I could cop some more of his jewelry. He seems to think that I'm the goat in the jewel deal and not himself. I am perfectly willing to be the goat as long as they unload real gold on me.

I got onto a new brand of pie down in Marshall the other day. I forgot to tell you about it Sunday. They called it transparent pie. Why I don't know because it looked like pumpkin and tasted like sugar and water with clay or something to give it body. It had a mussy top—one of the kind with a French name that goes on a "leming pie." The top was very good. I'd like very much to know what the balance of it contained and why it was transparent.

When the Marshall Central girl called me to say you'd be in at six o'clock, I like an idiot said, "Hello! Bess?" She said, "No, this isn't Bess. It's Myrtle, but the Bess you want will call at six." Then I told her to please cancel the call as I was leaving town at five-forty. She was an awful fresh Central. I have been entertaining my dear uncle at double dummy bridge. It's some game. He beats me so badly that it's not much fun for me. He gets lots of enjoyment out of it. Mrs. J. F. Blau has very kindly invited Mary and me to a Valentine party at her house on February 13. Mary has been kind enough to R.S.V.P. that we'll be

there. I am going to take a red-headed woman who plays the "pannanno." I don't
know what they'll do for entertainment—play rook, I guess, or some kissing game.
I'd prefer the former as I'm not very strong on the other one. Rook is a kind of
church member's bridge. The cards are numbered and are different colors. It's
a very good game. Tricks and fines are counted. Our Grandview outfit will have
to switch if things get too warm.

The will case has been set again for next Monday. So I don't suppose I'll
see you before Sunday unless I go to town Thursday as well as tomorrow. I bought
some G.O. tickets. They are in the ninth row of the arena balcony on the west.
Do you suppose we can see anything from there? I hope they'll be all right. Uncle
Harry is crazy for more bridge and I've got to go. You owe me a letter anyway
even if this is a bum one.

Most sincerely,
Harry

*The following two letters show, for the first time in his writing to Bess, that
Truman's emotions were not always under control. The death of someone close
to him proved difficult to accept. Below he refers to the funeral of Aunt Ada,
his mother's youngest sister. His attachment to her began in the summer of 1901,
when after high-school graduation he visited her in Murphysboro, Illinois. He
wrote a half-century later in his memoirs that everyone liked Aunt Ada.*

Dear Bess: [The Alton-Burlington Limited, Feb. 17, 1914]
I expected to see you this evening but, as has been the case all week, His
Majesty has interfered and I am somewhere else.

Aunt Ada died yesterday and I am on my way to her funeral, which is to
take place tomorrow morning at nine o'clock. On account of her death the will
suit had to be postponed. We are hoping to be rid of it before another trial. I
just barely had time to run to the train after we learned the case must be
postponed or I'd have phoned you. I haven't even got a clean collar with me.
Expect to be home on Thursday, will call up as soon as I get in town.

The next stop is Mexico [Missouri]. I hope to be able to mail this at that
town so you'll get it on the regular day.

I am very much cut up over auntie's death and therefore can't write a very
good letter. The train is so rough I can hardly write anyway.

If you should happen to see any of the Nolands, please tell them where I've
gone and why because they were expecting me down to stay all night some day
this week. I am hoping to see you Thursday if I don't have to stay longer than
I expect.

I just got back to the courthouse in time yesterday. Jim Buchanan was
waiting and Papa was chasing all up and down the courthouse for me. Tell Agnes
and Earl I'm very sorry to miss the ball game. This is all the paper this train
affords, so I'll have to stop.

Sincerely,
Harry

Dear Bess: [The St. Louis-Colorado Limited, Feb. 20, 1914]
     I missed the morning train from St. Louis and had to take the awful Wabash
(not any more awful than the Missouri Pacific) and therefore can't arrive in K.C.
until after 10:00 P.M. The train is now fifty minutes late and we're due at
nine-fifty. I had hoped to arrive in time to call you up but can't.
     I am going to take the K.C.S. home and will see you Sunday. As I told you
in my C. & A. [Chicago & Alton Railroad] note I had no time to get other
clothes, and the ones I'm in are a fright. Also my face is a sight from a copious
shedding of tears. Don't you hate to see a man weep? There's nothing I hate
worse, but this time it couldn't be helped. I'd almost as soon have attended
Mamma's funeral. I barely got there in time. If I'd arisen at 4:00 A.M., I could
have caught the daylight train on the Missouri Pacific, but Mary would have
insisted on getting me breakfast at that time of day, so I caught the seven-thirty
train and didn't get into St. Louis till eleven o'clock—one hour after the train
had left. I hope you'll forgive me for the great number of unkept appointments
I have made in the last week. I'll try and not make any more I can't keep. I shall
see you Sunday sure if it is all right.
                                        Sincerely,
                                        Harry

Dear Bess: [Grandview, Feb. 24, 1914]
     Well, here goes a letter from home once more. My dear sister is about to
have a fit. She saw whom I am writing to. Your note about Aunt Ada was very
much appreciated, and I feel the same way about wishing it had been some of
the rest of them. She was the nicest sister Mamma had, and I thought more of
her than any of them. I think she liked me pretty well too.
     I have got to take the nigger to town this evening but I won't get to stay
because Papa is on the jury. Wouldn't it be good if we had him on our own jury?
I guess we'll have all the performance to go through with again in thirty days.
That is, if we can manage to satisfy the lawyer's rapacious appetites for money.
I see where I made a grave mistake in studying music when I could have studied
law and bought canned music. I could have grabbed a piece of the Young estate
without having to wait my turn at all then. Now it looks very much as if there
won't be any turn. Every trial costs about $3,000, whether it goes or not.
Wouldn't it be grand to run a department store on the court plan? Sell a piece
of goods and make a mistake, and then sell the person another piece off the same
bolt to correct it and have that wrong, and so on ad lib. That's court procedure
all right. If you win, you lose. It's like the board of trade. The only sure winner
is the middle man, the lawyer. Goodrich said he made $2,500 week before last
giving advice! I wish my conversation was worth that much.
     If I get in town in time this afternoon, I am going to get the tickets to that
Slipper show. I'd be willing to bet that that lawyer, whose name begins with box
but whose head I can't hardly call that, will want me to run some errand for him
on the night I pick. He can unreservedly go hang or somewhere else.
     Uncle Harry says he's going back to town this morning. I've an idea he's

hankerin' for about three fingers on a small glass and some chips to rattle. It'll be my job to drag him out of town next time he's wanted. It seems to me that it's a most awful mistake to begin taking any responsibility on yourself. He always has let someone else do his worrying and there's always been someone to do it.

I hope you'll not be too much put out by this dry, personal opinion letter but I've been chasing from point to point for the last month not knowing half the time whether I was going or coming as far as accomplishing anything I could see was concerned, and I've almost got a case of nerves. That sentence is good enough to go in a German grammar. Mark says that German literary lights travel all day in one sentence and that makes them celebrities. He evidently knew, for he gave a sentence covering four printed pages to illustrate his point.

I have been reading the *Redbook*. I hope never to begin another continued story. They always leave off right at the edge of things and make you wonder if you can possibly wait a month without bursting, and when the next number comes you run across a continued story and wonder what the first of it was about.

I hope you and Helen enjoy the Orpheum and I wish very much that I could come to Independence to the show but, as usual, there's an obstacle. If Papa should happen to get off then, I'll come and this letter will be for sale at a discount. You can write me one though in return for a box of candy I'll bring with me and in answer to this if I don't come.

Sincerely,

Harry

Dear Bess: [Grandview, Mar. 20, 1914]

I have a few minutes so I'm going to write you a short note. Mamma has had an operation called hernia. It is somewhat akin to appendicitis. At least there was a long incision made in her right side and some parts removed. She is getting along as well as we can expect.

I have to stay with her all the time, Mary has so much else to do. The doctor is with her now. We were very much surprised when the doctor said he wanted expert advice on the case. He just supposed at first that she had a slight rupture. The specialist came at five o'clock Thursday, and at six they decided to have the operation. I had to stand and hold a lamp while it was going on. I hope never to witness another one.

It will be necessary for me to stay with her right along for three or four days. I am awful sorry that I can't come over Sunday but I'll try and come over the very first day I can leave.

The doctor has come down and he says she is doing very well. Her temperature and pulse are normal, so I suppose that we have nothing to worry about. Hope you had a fine time at the wedding today. I am sending the Nolands a note but theirs won't be special so I guess they won't get it till Monday. I'd have written yesterday only I didn't get a chance. Hoping to be able to see you in a few days, I am

Sincerely,

Harry

One can guess from the following letter that settlement of the family lawsuit would enable Truman to buy a car—his 1911 Stafford. Terry Stafford of Topeka made, altogether, some three hundred cars, and had moved his factory to Kansas City by the time Truman bought one. New, the cars sold for $2,350. Hardly any have survived. Truman was astonished to find one in Rhode Island in 1953—and also pleased, for his car had long since disappeared. As he described his former car to the Stafford owner in Rhode Island, Floyd Clymer, it was "a five-passenger open car with straps attached to the top that buckled to the front part of the frame, although it was usually driven as an open car. I had it remodeled into a hot sport roadster and took it to Camp Doniphan with me in 1917, where it was used by Battery 'F' as a kind of transportation truck for ice and whatever else was necessary to be hauled around the Battery." He sold it in March 1918.

Dear Bess: [Grandview, Mar. 24, 1914]
    Your note came Sunday morning. I was very glad to get it. It helped to get the day by to some extent as it should have gone. Mamma said thank you for your sympathy and kind expressions. She is getting along fine. The doctor said he'd never had a case like hers to do so well.
    I am still staying with her and will have to for a few days yet. Vivian was here yesterday, and I made a flying trip to K.C. to see Uncle Harry and Boxley about our infernal suit. There is a prospect of settlement now. It will stretch our finances until they crack, but I guess we'll get over it eventually.
    I made an effort to call you up but didn't even succeed in getting Independence. I didn't get another chance because I had to go with Mr. Ferson to buy a carload of hay and when I got to the train there were only about four minutes to spare.
    Ferson wants to sell me a Stafford car for $650. It's an old one but will outlast and outlook some of the new ones they are selling now. I told him that unless I could filch the amount from the Young estate while the settlement was being made there was no prospect of my owning a car. It sure is a bargain though. Uncle Harrison thinks we'll have to sell some of the farm, but I hope not. It will bring probably $200 an acre now but in four or five years it may be worth three times that. I hope I never have anything more to do with an estate like this one. It is a hoodoo from start to finish. If there are any other pieces of bad luck loose, I suppose they'll come our way before long. There's no use bothering about what may happen though. I've got my hands full looking after the results of what's already taken place. The gamblers say that fate can't always hand out one brand of luck and I'm hoping strongly for a change in our brand. A bigger crop than ever was raised is what would convince me we were in good again. I got that oat sowed as I told you before; the hired man is just now finishing up with the harrow. We thought we were going to lose him Sunday. I gave him $15 Saturday night and he said he was going to pay some bills he owed. I guess he must have hit a crap game first because he didn't get home until Sunday morning. He came up here about noon looking rather dilapidated and said his wife had given him a round with the poker. Said he guessed he'd have to leave as it looked as if he wasn't going to be able to stay home. I guess they must have patched things up

because he hasn't said anything more about leaving. He's a great big man, and his wife won't weigh over a hundred pounds. I'm going to work your mother's system and pay on Monday after this. I wouldn't have this fellow leave for anything. He's the best man we ever had. Mamma is of the opinion that he needed braining, but there is always a bond of sympathy between women when a man has been shooting craps and every good man has his failings. I mean good hired men. Luke, for instance!

Vivian is going back to Cass County this morning. He rode up horseback on Thursday night and is going to drive back. I think it is safe for him to leave, Mamma is doing so well.

I am hoping to see you before the week is out. As soon as she can have company there'll be someone here all the time, but we don't allow her to walk any yet to amount to anything.

Please send me a long letter as it has been some years since a week ago Sunday.

Sincerely,
Harry

Hotel Mercer, Kansas City, Mo.

Dear Bess: [Apr. 7, 1914]

I am in the city again. It looks as if I am going to get to stay here for a few hours and if I don't send you a letter now, another week will go by without my getting one. Uncle Harry is sick and I am trying to get him to go home with me. He says he'll go at one o'clock but he has to vote. Yesterday he wasn't able to be up but is better this morning. Vivian was in town and went to see him and phoned me I'd better come for him as he was down in bed. You may be sure I got a horse and made haste to get there. Got wet, too, and as my only other suit was wet also I had to bring it in to be pressed. This piece of paper happened to be in the suitcase. It has been to New Mexico and back. I wanted to come over last night but didn't get uncle persuaded to do as I wanted him to until it was too late to go anywhere. Besides, my clothes were in soak. I suppose you got wet yesterday if you came to town. It was no day to buy spring hats anyway, was it? Let's hope that Easter will be somewhat different.

There was a big shine on the K.C.S. the other night, all decked out in her Easter duds. She had a gold bracelet on each hand and a lot of red beads around her neck, also she was studying some play. She was as black as a John B. Stetson hat, and I've an idea would be somewhat of a disappointment as Portia or Desdemona. Gilbert Strode was with me and we came to the conclusion that it would be worth Shubert prices to see a show with this coon as the beautiful star.

We almost had a moving picture show in Grandview the other afternoon. I forgot to tell you about it Sunday. There's a nice old maid and her sister run a millinery store in Grandview. This old maid was elected a delegate to Sedalia to the Royal Neighbor convention. Well, on the day to go, which was Wednesday or Thursday I forget which, she got very busy in the store and when train time came she wasn't ready. She made a flying start from the store right down the center of Main Street just as the train pulled in. When she got in front of the hardware store, the gallant merchant ran out to carry her suitcase so she could run faster. When he grabbed it the thing came open and spilled lady's wearing apparel all over the street. The merchant fell down. They got the things together and finally caught the train. All this performance was in plain view of the train and of the whole town. I saw her yesterday and she said she only lost a silver thimble and someone found that and gave it to her. Uncle Harrison put me up at a new place last night, as you can see by the headline. It's a nice place, too, all brand-new and clean. He sometimes eats here. I much prefer the Vic but he told me to come here and I did.

I am hoping he won't die until a settlement in our suit is reached. I don't want him to die at all, but it would merely be filling our bad-luck cup full for some such calamity to overtake us. If things keep happening with the regularity of the past six months, I shall be a nervous wreck in another year. I am always looking for a change of luck and I guess it will come sometime. I try to work harder every time there's a reverse but I haven't arrived yet.

I'm going to work Ferson for a ride home this afternoon. He's trying to sell me an auto and he ought to be willing to demonstrate it, don't you think? Please send me a long letter, as it looks as if I won't be able to see you before Sunday.

Sincerely,

Harry

Dear Bess: [Grandview, Apr. 1914]

I've got another brand of stationery and must send you a sample [Jackson County Farm Bureau]. There is so much heading that the space for correspondence is rather limited but I suppose a person can use more sheets. I have placed an X at the reason of my having this so you won't fail to see it [Harry Truman, Bureau president for Washington Township]. The job was wished on me without my knowledge. I wasn't even present when it was done. There evidently was a scarcity of material. I was informed by the farm adviser that I might use the Bureau stationery in my correspondence to advertise the Bureau. Since you are my principal correspondent you are getting some of the stationery merely as a sample.

When a person gets his stationery and stamps furnished him he is beginning to arrive at the boodle stage. The stamps haven't been donated yet, but I have hopes. I could steal them from the Masonic Lodge but since I usually have to buy Lodge stamps myself I'd simply be in the same boat with the conductor who built himself a railroad with what failed to hang to the bell rope when he worked for the company. He became a conductor on his own railroad and knocked down so much that he broke himself up in business.

I arrived home Sunday night at twelve o'clock. That is, I had the rattler housed and was in the house at that time. I was scared all the way home that I'd have a blowout or puncture or something. But not a single thing happened. I took Uncle Harry to town yesterday. It began raining at Forest Hill and he wouldn't let me put the top up until we got wet. Kept saying he didn't think it would rain much. I've got to go get him Thursday. Went over to Ferson's yesterday and tore the engine up and put it together again. I'm going to tear it some more this morning and see if I can get it to work again. I went up Dodson hill so fast I had to shut off the power before I reached the top. Took Mary to Belton last night to a piano recital. Got home at 11:00 P.M. If we'd driven [by buggy], it would have been twelve. . . .

Will call you Thursday if I arrive in town in time. Uncle Harry just now called and said he didn't want to come home until Friday, but I'm going to get him Thursday if I can. You are going to get your letter on time this week anyway and I'll look for mine.

Sincerely,
Harry

Dear Bess: [Grandview, Apr. 18, 1914]

I am going to send you that letter I promised. It is not the delayed one but an entirely new brand. Also it is on a new brand of stationery [J.A. Truman & Son, Farmers]. I kinda like the looks of this, so I thought I'd use it.

Our disappeared man was on deck this morning madder than a Mexican pirate. Claimed he'd been down with his daughter all these days. He seemed to think it an impossibility for us to make connection with Belton. Papa let him go to work. The man we hired is a good one too, so I guess we'll have two for a month. Then the best one gets to stay. I am hoping they'll manage to get along all right.

I caught that car all right and got down in town at five minutes to one. That was a record trip. I had to go to E.B.T.'s this morning and part with the price of a pair of white silk gloves. I sure made a nice picture buying gloves elbow length. I must be a great little feminine shopper by this time. It is rather embarrassing sometimes to have a fresh clerk ask me if my wife is a large or small woman. I always say it's for my mother but I'm never believed.

Bess, I'm going to beg you for a photygraft again. I wish you'd have yer pitur took in that hat, even if it is only a stamp. This is the couple of dozenth time I've asked for one, but I'm still hoping to get it just the same. I've been wanting you to have one taken in that hat if it's only one and that one for me. Please do. I'm going to get cheated out of a letter this week but the picture will do for a substitute. That's almost the same request I made in the other letter and that's all I didn't tell you last night. I know I'll get there Sunday evening and Monday evening now with two men.

Sincerely,
Harry

Dear Bess: [Grandview, Apr. 1914]

I am two days late on the letter but I guess you have some slight idea as to the reason. I have been endeavoring to learn to push an auto. My head is rather thick I suppose. Anyway I'm not an expert chauffeur as yet. It is to be hoped that

Summer 1915, Harry and Bess in the front seat of the 1911 Stafford. *Harry S. Truman Library*

there will be some improvement by Sunday. Have had a puncture already, killed the engine times without number, and got the batteries all worn out by running on them. It is as old man Fred remarked, when you have an auto there is nothing else to cuss about. Your mind is entirely occupied cussing the auto. I managed to get up Dodson hill on high and then killed the engine, getting up about a 2 percent grade. There is only one thing I can brag about and that is that I can stay in the road. Got by some thousands of telegraph poles without disaster and then ran over a horseshoe full of nails. You can imagine the result of that.

Have you recovered from the big dose of music? I made the K.C.S. limited all right. It was exactly on time and I only waited about three minutes. Mary arrived the next morning and all she could do was talk music and auto. She has an insane desire to drive. She'll soon get it gratified for it's not much pleasure to me to drive. It's an awful amount of bother.

It is as I told you it would be when the car came home. It is raining like Sam Hill this morning and Papa wanted me to drive him to Independence! Ain't it awful what the weather can spoil sometimes. He seems to be fairly well pleased with the purchase. So does Uncle Harry, but neither of them are very anxious to let loose of any money. Papa is starting to the big town up the hill and I'll have to quit in order to get this mailed. I hope to arrive in Independence Sunday afternoon if nothing busts. Please don't expect the arrival too early but I'll get there some time if I have to take the train! Send me a letter this week since I'm behind almost two. Did you get the special Mary mailed?

Sincerely,
Harry

Dear Bess: [Grandview, May 4, 1914]

I am going to get your letter off on time even if I am a sleepyhead this evening. I have to go to the city in the morning after the hired man's daughter and I know very well I won't get a chance to do another thing. I almost did a day's work today! Put away all the meat. We have ten hams and three shoulders and some bacon. Here's hoping it lasts till hogs are ripe again, because gasoline is spot cash.

I got home before the rain and only thirty minutes after Mary did. It was just ten minutes after twelve when I came into the front gate. It rained like the mischief at about 12:45. If I'd had to take the K.C.S. I'd have gotten soaked. It will be an awful comedown if that old machine ever refuses to go. I don't know how I could manage to walk from Grandview. The tires are standing up fine. (I have my hand on wood.)

Almost I went to Montana tomorrow. Mr. Hall is going and was very anxious for me to go. But on account of our *picnic* Saturday and for reasons of expense I have decided not to go until two weeks from today. My claim doesn't come up until June 3, and I don't want to pay over two weeks' board if it can be helped. I haven't much hope of getting a good claim. I've heard a lot of adverse criticism on Ft. Peck in the last month. I'm not going to be bluffed out by conversation though. I'll have to be shown. I think every real estate man in Montana has written me a letter to offer his services in locating me—for fifty dollars. They are very liberal and they all know every foot of the reservation. You know it is only fifty miles by a hundred, and there are only 1,200,000 acres to be homesteaded. So, you see, these men are exceptionally bright and capable and their services ought to be cheap at the price. Think of holding a platte of Jackson County in your head. Ft. Peck is some six times as big. I doubt very much whether it can be done. Anyway I'm not going to part with my fifty dollars until I'm absolutely certain it's a safe proposition. I've an idea that a person will have as good luck just to shut his eyes and put his finger down on the map.

One of our hired men (the other one) is off on a toot. He's been gone since Saturday. He's drawn all that's coming to him too. Also it's all he'll ever draw I guess. No boozers for mine. Our hand of help is almost equal to Luke. First one and then the other has a tantrum. No man that's any good would be a farmhand, though, so it's not to be expected that good ones can be found: One good thing, they are plentiful and are not hard to break in. . . .

I shall look for a letter early this week as there's not much chance of my getting in. I'll have to work! *(Maybe.)* Please send the letter anyway.

Sincerely,
Harry

Dear Bess: [Grandview, May 12, 1914]

My [automobile] riding yesterday was more worthwhile than Sunday's. I suppose everything will be fixed by tomorrow evening. I now have checks payable to my order in my pocket for $9,500. Wouldn't that buy a lot of gasoline? Also, couldn't I have some time should I take a notion to be a crook? There is nothing to keep me from getting the dough if I choose to do it. I don't choose. I'll have some title to this place when I turn the checks over. They're all going to deed their shares to me, and I'm supposed to deed them over to Mamma and Uncle Harry. I could just prosecute the suit to its termination and then I'd own five-sevenths of the farm anyway. There have been enough suits in the family to date so I'll just very meekly deed the thing over and let it go at that. I think though that they ought to compensate me for my trouble in some way. I haven't any notion of getting a cent but I'll be very well satisfied if Mamma gets her farm, and then maybe I can do something for myself. Four years of litigation have been some strain both physically and financially. If Uncle Harry will only let me act as his agent in selling some of his property, though, things will be fine. Also, there is Montana. I'd almost forgotten Montana. I go there next Tuesday. It has snowed seven inches in South Dakota but Montana isn't mentioned. I don't suppose a snow would have the impudence to come to South Dakota and miss the great state of Montana. It is such a beautiful climate up there. Only forty-seven below last winter. The wind sometimes blows sixty miles an hour right from Alaska. I guess I can get me a cowskin cloak and a beaver cap and manage to keep warm. Coal is only two dollars a ton too, but I've an idea a person can burn some seventy tons a week.

Mary is beefing to have me teach her to run the car before I go away but I hate to do it. I know very well there will be strife when two people in the family can run it. I guess I'll have to do it, though, since Mamma paid for the thing. Also, I know how to jim the thing so it won't go at all and then suddenly fix it. It almost jammed on me this morning. I had to spin it about ten minutes to make it go. The handle flew off the crank shaft and sprained my wrist and I bumped my head on the radiator. My chances of heaven get slimmer every day I have the thing if every cuss word is to be counted against me. I just now discovered that my supply of decent stationery is exhausted. I guess Mary has tapped the box. This half-sheet is all there is left. She is practicing the wedding marches for Virginia Kritley. She thinks I don't know who it's for but I happened to hear a phone conversation that was supposed to be strictly personal. Hope to see you sometime this week after Wednesday. I heard Mary making a date to take the Duvalls for a ride just now but that can be easily attended to if it interferes any. Hope you'll send me a letter even if I am shy a half a sheet.

Sincerely,

Harry

Dear Bess: [Grandview, May 26, 1914]
. . . We got home at ten o'clock last night. I went downtown and got my gray hat. The hat works had made it look like a 1914 model with a dark gray band and a hand-tied bow. I put it in the back seat to keep it from blowing away, and do you know those two women lost that hat. It is reposing somewhere on Park Avenue between 76th Street and Linwood Boulevard. The car door came open

along there somewhere, and they are both of the opinion that it must have been lost out then. I was very much disappointed when I found it gone for I did want to wear it just once. I'll have to buy a straw now, I guess, or another two-dollar cap. Maybe I can go to George's place and get one for a dollar. . . .

Please do send me a letter this week as it has been some ages since I have had one. I still have your frying pan and spoons, also a fruit jar and a basket. I guess I'll just continue to tote them around until they're needed for another picnic. Anyway I shall try and have them aboard when I get over again.

Most sincerely,
Harry

Dear Bess: [Grandview, no postmark]

I am still using the farmer brand of stationery. It seems that I get no chance anymore for my own purchases. I have made two flying trips to the city this week and both of them were for someone else and I had no time to do as I wanted to. I succeeded in getting Uncle Harry to divide the farm with Mamma. I guess he got somewhat the best of it but I'd rather that than fuss with him. This family have had fusses enough for one generation. Uncle Harrison is going to rent us his share just as he always has, and I don't suppose we'll know it's divided unless he should happen to die.

I was at Virginia Kritley's wedding Wednesday evening. I saw Miss Carry and Mrs. Wallace. Mrs. Wallace was very glad to see me. She kissed me before the whole houseful and said she was conferring such favors on all her relatives. I nearly shrank to nothing. It was a very nice wedding. Mary caught the bouquet when it was thrown. The man looked like a simp but I guess men always look that way at their own weddings. They are going to live down in Cole County close to Jefferson City on a farm.

Tuesday evening I went to the Battery banquet at the City Club. It was a very nice affair and there was really something to eat. Roast beef and potatoes and such things, ending up with a pineapple sundae and a million cubic feet of hot air. Hon. W. P. Borland made a spread-eagle speech that would have done W. J. Bryan credit as did also Mr. Pugh, his opponent. . . .

I have thought I'd see you each evening and something has always interfered. See you Sunday anyway and hope for a letter before.

Most sincerely,
Harry

Dear Bess: [Grandview, July 1914]

Here goes for a letter. It seems that I won't be able to arrive in Independence tomorrow. Vivian is up against it for hay help and two of our neighbors are threshing. We must help them both if we can and Vivian too. . . .

A bonehead dropped his pitchfork into the mouth of the machine, and since the steel in the fork was the harder something in the thresher had to bust.

Babcock has a new machine [automobile] too, but he doesn't know how to drive it. He said he was going to learn when they first bought it but didn't have time to. Now he is going to learn to drive sure enough.

I was at home fifteen minutes Sunday night before Mary and Val arrived. Didn't drive over twenty miles an hour either. It just took me fifty-five minutes to go about nineteen miles. Mary claimed that they stopped in town and got a soda but I'd have beaten them anyway. The Auburn can't climb hills like a Stafford, even if the Stafford has been around the world. I got my spring fixed yesterday so I'm ready for most any kind of journey.

It's a long ways to Frisco but if you go and stay too long, I'll have to buy 150 gallons of gas and get across there somehow. It has been done and I'm willing to bet that Sal can do it. It would be cheaper than railroad fare if I didn't eat. I don't see how I could manage not to for two weeks though, do you? If I couldn't arrive any other way, there are the rods still left. Another way is to ride on top of the passenger coaches. It's almost as disagreeable as the rods though, on account of the smoke. If I go that way, it won't be by Arizona, Montana, and the northern route for mine. I am talking from a summertime point of view. If it's winter, then I'll give Arizona more consideration because the rods or on top wouldn't be very agreeable at 40 degrees below any more than they would at 117 degrees above. It's a good thing that the country is large enough north and south so a person can have some choice as to the climate he wants to go through as he goes to the West Coast. If everything holds together, I hope to see you later in the week. Work is so plentiful around here though that I don't know what I can do, only work, and from twelve to four is very short hours for a laboring man to sleep. I can stand it though for a trip to Independence. Please send me a letter for this anyway.

Most sincerely,
Harry

Dear Bess: [Grandview, July 1914]
    . . . We brought Uncle Harry home with us, for another short visit I suppose. I have to take the car to the factory but am almost afraid to start because I know he'll want to go to town. No, there's nothing really wrong with the car, Mary just ran into the gate and bent the front axle. I was fool enough to let her drive it to Grandview by herself, therefore and consequently I am solely to blame. The thing will run all right only I can't make it turn to the left to do any good. That would be a rather embarrassing situation if a large truck were coming around a corner from the right. The gate looks rather sickly. I am very thankful that she hit the gate instead of a stone post. She took it a sideswiping lick and yanked it off the hinges. I suppose she must have been going too fast and didn't straighten up the wheel soon enough after making the turn. Of course she says she was only barely moving. It is a very sore subject with her. She had gone to Grandview after Vivian and Luella. They are going to stay with us a few days. I sure did take a drive Sunday evening—only ninety-seven miles after five o'clock. When we got

home I thought I'd never want to drive anywhere again. Jim Wright said he never expected to get so much riding in an auto in his whole life, let alone one day. I have arrived at the place where I can't appreciate his point of view, because it seems like no drive at all if I don't make at least one hundred miles before the day's over whenever I start out. Roads in Jackson County are becoming as familiar to me as the two blocks from Union to Delaware formerly were, and that's a fair acquaintance. I am getting so I don't object to driving like I did to begin with. Getting sort of used to it I suppose—five thousand miles in three months is moving around somewhat. That's one thousand miles more than Frank Blair went in three years.

Vivian says I ought to sell the machine and buy cows with the money. I suppose I ought but I'm not going to, not just yet anyway. It sure would be a calamity to have to do without it. If it doesn't rain very soon though, I guess maybe, will have to sell it to get money to buy gasoline! . . . Hope to see you the latter part of the week if Vivian goes home *on the train*. You owe me a letter anyway.

Sincerely,
Harry

Dear Bess: [Grandview, July 28, 1914]
. . . Coming home last night we met a small Packard truck with its last tire blown out. It had a hole six inches long in it. They were going to get a poor guy who busted up his hind wheels. We couldn't do anything for them because their tires were thirty-six by five and mine are only thirty-four by four. We went on about two miles and came to the man who was broken down. It sure was comforting to him to learn that his trouble shooters were in trouble too. He persuaded the hired man with me to give him all the cigarettes he had and very philosophically (awful word) made up his mind to spend the night where he was. Someone in a little old Ford was taking his girl in. He evidently tried to turn a corner at a high rate of speed and had succeeded in smashing a hind wheel. I suppose it doesn't pay to get in a hurry. Frank Blair's system is best. He says that whenever anyone is in such an awful hurry he ought to start a little sooner and go a little slower. . . .

Hope to get a letter Friday this time because you know I want to be there Friday night. We'll go to Lee's Summit to the Chautauqua, unless you'd rather go elsewhere.

Sincerely,
Harry

Dear Bess: [Grandview, 1914]
. . . I may have to go to Independence today to take Papa in and also to take Uncle Joe Noland some of Mamma's blackberry cordial. Maybe the cordial will never arrive. It is so good to drink that I'd as soon have it as water or a little

sooner. We don't get any unless we're sick. This bottle that I'm taking in is about seven years old and very fine.

I got home without a disaster last night and without meeting a single machine. The road was almost entirely deserted except for a buggy or two that was taking home a sleepy swain. Country boys always tie the lines to the whip and let the horse drive himself home. They know very well that the old man is going to make them arise an hour earlier on Monday than usual so they put in the time going home in sleep. I have had to get clear of the road several times to keep from dislocating a wheel. Vivian used to drive a little old pony that wouldn't turn out for anything. He met a fellow driving one of the same kind one night and they woke up standing with the front wheels locked. They simply backed up, untangled the buggies, and went to sleep again.

Hope to see you before Saturday and surely on that day. This doesn't amount to much as a letter but you must remember that I'm a sleepyhead this morning. It was just ten minutes after midnight when I drove into the shed—*garage*. (The first one's right.) Here's to Little Blue and a fine rainy day next Saturday. Cheese the rain until Monday. I'll call you up if I come after my aunt across the street.

Sincerely,

Harry

Dear Bess: [Grandview, Aug. 18, 1914]

Here's where you get your letter on time. This is Good Roads Day and I am hoping to escape the road. There seems to be no interest in good roads out here this year. The Kansas City *Star* and Judge Gilbert are not at all interested. The *Star* because it has its road, and Gilbert for personal reasons I suppose.

I actually put in a day's work yesterday unloading a car of hay. It seems funny for us to be buying hay but when it can be bought for $8.25 a ton and then we can sell what we have for $12.00, it raises money. It seems that I am really going to have a right steady job the rest of this week running a new plow. It will be somewhat slower than pushing Sal around but I can stand it. A riding plow gives one a chance to think of all the meanness he ever did and all he intends to do. I have memorized a whole book while plowing forty acres. When I run out of something to think of I count the revolutions of the plow wheel and figure how many acres there are left. I have learned how many square feet and square yards there are in an acre.

Papa's raising a rumpus for me to take him out on the road in the auto! Imagine working the roads in a machine. It suits me. I hope to see you this week anyway if the plow doesn't come. You really owe me two letters!

Sincerely,

Harry

Halfway into the following letter Truman refers to the "post-office case." *Since 1914 was an election year, it was a good time to apply to Congressman* *Borland for the position of postmaster of Grandview. He got the job but did not profit from it financially; he appointed a widow as acting postmaster and gave her all the money.*

[Grandview]

Dear Bess: August 31, 1914

You are going to get a piece of a letter this week anyway. I'm not very good at letter writing. You know, the doctors have given Papa only a short time to decide on an operation or the grave. We are still hoping that there is some mistake but I am afraid there isn't much hope. You know he is sixty-three and an operation at that age is nearly always fatal. The X ray showed that the lower entrance to the stomach is almost closed. It has probably been going on for ten or fifteen years. The doctors say that if the operation is successful, he can probably live ten years. So as a last resort I am going to try and persuade him to do it.

Mary and her Santa Fe were exactly on time. They were a very much sunburned bunch. The Ford was not on deck but it is tonight. You know, Aileen got her wires crossed and sent her mother a card saying they would be home Saturday at 5:05. It was necessary to show her the card before she'd believe it. Mary and I got home at ten minutes to seven. I did want to go back to Independence so badly, but Papa wasn't feeling so well and Mamma was almost done up. A great aunt of mine, cousin (third), Vivian and Luella, and Mr. Campbell and Mrs. too were lucky enough to push themselves on her for dinner. I suppose if Luella hadn't been in the church, she'd have given up the ghost right there. It was a very good thing for my Sunday that I got started at ten o'clock instead of eleven. For it could have been stay at home sure enough if that bunch had pulled in before I got away. The great aunt is still here. She's a fine old lady, Grandfather Young's half-sister. She's lost her only son and is trying to forget it. She has a daughter but the son was her support and an old bach so she misses him keenly. I'm very much a favorite of Lee's also.

I wrote the Hon. W. P. Borland this evening and stated the post-office case to him. You ought to see what a grand piece of political guff I can hand out. I didn't ask him to appoint me straight out but asked him to make the appointment that the majority of the patrons of the office wanted.

I can't write you a good letter, Bess, this evening. I am somewhat worried and continually thinking of what I'll do without my pappy. It doesn't seem at all possible to get on without him. It sure was nice of you to call up, and as usual I couldn't think of anything to say over the phone. I guess I can't get in this week. I have to take Papa to town tomorrow and next day and run the farm. But remember I want to come over and sure would if I could.

I hope to see you Sunday but I doubt if I can go picnicking because there's no telling what'll take place between now and then. There is no immediate danger of fatality except in case of the operation, and we may not decide on that for a week.

Please send me a letter as I'll sure appreciate it this week.

Most sincerely,

Harry

Dear Bess: [Grandview, Sept. 8, 1914]

This is Tuesday again and I'm going to send you an excuse for a letter. I am hoping for better luck getting one this week. I have given the postmaster a good raking and he has faithfully agreed to produce the goods this week.

You know, he's the guy that's to be my deputy if I am made P.M., therefore he is very anxious to please me.

I just did beat the rain home Sunday night. It began sprinkling when I was fifteen minutes from home and I had to put up the top. About an hour after I got in it sure did pour. The lightning struck a barn north of us and the new automobile club building. The barn was burned but the club only had the flagpole damaged. A shock of corn was also struck and burned up in a field south of us. Monday morning I had to take Papa in, and Brush Creek and Blue were certainly on a rampage. The Federal Ball Park was almost washed away. . . .

I have been to see the Chinaman [physician] and am now on my way to be road overseer awhile. We are building a bridge for Jackson County and it has to be inspected once in a while to be sure the pay will be forthcoming.

While Papa is sick I have to do a good many extra jobs. He is feeling better today but he looks very weak. I am half worried to death for fear he'll not get all right. It is necessary to see the Chink Doctor every day this week. He is confident that he can make a cure but all doctors are that. It's part of their ethics to fool the patients into confidence, I suppose. The Yellow Peril of course is no exception but I honestly believe that he's more honest and trustworthy than most white M.D.s.

He told Papa that whenever he failed to improve under his treatment the best thing for him to do is to quit coming. You never did hear an American advise his patients that they'd better quit coming even if they are entirely well.

I hope you gave the coon a good wigging about that letter, because I began haunting the P.O. Thursday and still had hopes until Sunday noon. Then I thought perhaps mine had failed to connect. It's a long week to have to stay at home every night and not be at all sure that I won't be able to leave even Sunday. I am going to coerce the hired man into staying at home if Mary takes a notion not to this Sunday. He went to see his sister last Sunday.

That book was sure a fine one. No one would ever guess that the Baroness Xyzsky [sic] was a Hungarian by the brand of English she uses. I read it clear through at one sitting, from seven to twelve-thirty last night. It was good enough to appear in *Adventure* ('nuf said).

Be sure and send the letter by someone else this week.

Most sincerely,
Harry

Dear Bess: [Grandview, Sept. 17, 1914]

Your letter is going to be a day late, maybe two. I've had a circus and then some this week. Papa was worse Monday and Tuesday but insisted that he must go to town on Monday. He couldn't get up on Tuesday. Today he's better. Went to town again and strenuously declares he thinks it helped him. I don't. I'm of the opinion that he really gets weaker all the time. But as long as he thinks the Chink's doing him good it's as well for him to keep going, because he won't let the operation take place.

To cap Tuesday off the hired men had a fuss and almost came to blows. I had to threaten to take a hand myself to restore peace. Today I put one of them to plowing in one place and the other in another place. They seemed to be rather ashamed of themselves this morning. If they'd fought, I'd have had to can them both and then wouldn't I have been in it. I also discovered that the seed wheat I saved won't grow. It got hot in the [illegible] and I'll have to sell it and buy some more. The nemesis constellation must be in conjunction with my star this year. I don't care though, I've a notion that perhaps I can beat even a combination like that, but it takes a little time. Your good letters sure help to put that backbone into me to accomplish what I've set out to do in spite of the devil and all his angels. That's some job too. When the finest girl in all the world has faith in a fellow's ability to win he's simply got to do it, that's all. You know sometimes things do look awful discouraging and just one little word of encouragement will clear the whole horizon. I guess I'm rather simple anyway to have expected to get the world by the tail in five years on a big farm. It never even occurred to me that crop failures ever came here and as for operations and doctor bills and lawyer fees—well, they were never even remotely possible to me five years ago. Well, as you know, the whole bunch has happened in one year and in almost every year at least one of them has occurred. But, as I said before, I think I can win yet and I will, the Lord willing and you thinking so.

This is not much of a letter but I hope you'll think I meant well anyway. I was very much disappointed not to be able to arrive in Independence last night, but Mamma thought I ought to stay at home and she has never yet wanted me to stay home unless it was really necessary. So I stayed. I am hoping to arrive Friday night though, party or no party. Please send me a letter if mine is late.

Most sincerely,
Harry

Dear Bess: [Grandview, Sept. 28, 1914]

I am going to try and send you a letter anyway this week. Sunday was Papa's worst day. He very nearly got so weak he could hardly talk. Today he is better but he hasn't eaten anything since Saturday morning except a little eggnog. I am very much afraid he isn't going to last so very much longer. I tried to talk to you over the phone today but you were not at home. Our phone here isn't working so very well today. Brownie tried to talk to his sister at Independence tonight but could not get a connection. I couldn't talk very much to you anyway because Papa insists on having the door from his room into the hall open so he can hear what is said. So I didn't try to call you from here this evening, although I told George I would. I have been very busy today trying to be in several places at once. I have been to Belton and Kansas City and have bought 100 bushels of wheat in one place and 150 at Dodson, and a new drill down in the west bottom, besides getting a tire fixed and purchasing a quart of whiskey! You know, I ran over a piece of glass with my brand-new hind tire and cut a hole an inch long right through to the tube. It was sure a piece of very bad luck. The tire had only been about fifty miles. It is as good as ever now though.

I have also sent a man down to Vivian's to bring me up four mules of his to work. I am going to run two drills, two plows, and a harrow and roller the rest of this week and next week also. It is absolutely necessary to make things hum to get in two hundred acres of wheat. I have been so busy hauling Papa back and forth to K.C. that things are 'way behind here. He says he's not going in anymore but that he's going to cure himself. If anyone asks him how he's feeling, he always says fine, even if he can't raise up his head. We can't put any faith in what he says about himself but have to watch him all the time. He was not able to get up today until about three o'clock and then he could only sit up about an hour at a time, yet he insisted that he was able to go see some cattle and wanted me to take him to help buy the wheat. He didn't get out of the house though.

Yesterday was the longest day I ever saw. There was absolutely nothing to do only sit around and pretend that there was nothing to worry about, and then of course when evening came I had to stay at home. Mary was down at Aileen's, and I phoned her to come home on the K.C.S. at three o'clock. She was expecting me to come by and take her to Independence and then bring her home with me that evening. I was hoping that Papa would be well enough by seven o'clock for me to leave but he was still very weak, and Mamma thought I ought to stay at home. These Sundays that I don't get over to Independence are almighty dull Sundays, I can tell you. It seems as if I've seen very little of you in the last month but it hasn't been because I didn't want to, you can be very sure of that. I am *hoping* Papa will get well soon and then perhaps I can have better luck. I am really very much afraid he won't live a month. It's a road we all have to travel, though we are never ready to let those we love depart if we can help it.

I shall look for a letter this week sure, and if Papa gets better so I can leave at night I'll be over.

The Masons are having a Grand Lodge in K.C. and I'm supposed to attend night and day, but I'm not going at all. It is the first one I've missed for a good while. The rest have been in St. Louis. This one is close at home and I can't go.

I have done Uncle Harry a mean trick. He's been sitting around in here waiting for me to go to bed so he could tap that quart I spoke of awhile ago. I outsat him. He gave up just now and went to bed without his nightcap. I guess he'll make up the difference on an eye opener in the morning. He says he's going to stay with us. I hope he does. I hope you'll consider this worth an answer anyway.

Most sincerely,
Harry

Dear Bess: [Grandview, Nov. 1914]

. . . One of my auto wheels refused to turn in the proper manner and I had to spend two good hours at the factory. I was also an hour chasing up Uncle Harry and then didn't get to see him.

This bunch of Star women up here also made a dray out of me again last night. They had to go to Belton. I was so sleepy I could hardly hold my eyes open all evening. There were some very good eats at the end though, and that paid partly for the trouble. One reason that I had to go was to take Mary. It seems that Val called her up and she told him that I was to take her and so I had to. I had a race with him coming home. He had a half-mile start of me, and just when I got within about a hundred yards of him one of my lights jarred out and I had to stop. He'll never get done blowing about beating my Stafford with his little old Ford. The women in my car had already begun to tell me how many children they had at home and what an awful thing it would be to make orphans of them before the light went out. They were very glad of an excuse to stop, I suppose. You can imagine that I was rather hitting the high places when I tell you I gained the half-mile in driving two and a half. It was rather chilly moving at that rate too. I almost froze before I got clear around the circle yesterday. . . .

Do you suppose you'll have your picnic next Sunday? I'd like awfully to go. I think if you'd ask me to again I would. From the looks of the sky out this way I don't think anyone will get to go. The oldest inhabitant of Grandview has prophesied snow and it seems that he may hit it. I hope not because I'll have to haul feed to a lot of unthankful old cows if it does. It is a nice job to dig shock corn out of snow about two feet deep. Every time an armful is lifted on the wagon a bushel of snow goes up or down your coat sleeve. It would be fine work for July but it's not so nice in winter. I am almost up to date on work now. Soon as three hundred bushels of wheat get to Lee's Summit I'll be in pretty good shape for snow or any other brand of weather.

I shall look for a letter on schedule time this week.

Most sincerely,
Harry

From the following letter we have some indication of how deeply Truman felt the death of his father (Nov. 3, 1914). His expression of grief takes the form of recollected stories.

Dear Bess: [Grandview, Nov. 1914]

Here I am a day late sending you a letter but I had a most awful time with a load of hogs today.

They were shipped yesterday evening and I drove down to the yards and stayed all night in order to be there when they were unloaded this morning. I went over to the yards at half past seven thinking I was very late but the hogs did not arrive on the market until 2:30 P.M. There were 34,000 on hand and the yardmen couldn't handle them all. Mine were finally sold about fifteen minutes before the market closed, at 3:00 P.M. I just now arrived at home and I expected to get in at about 10:00 A.M. I suppose I'll carry some of the malodorous dust from those hog yards in my clothes for sixty days. I wouldn't work down there for fifteen dollars a day.

I have quite a job on my hands now trying to make things run as smoothly as they formerly did. You know, I've been in the habit of running the farm for some time, but Papa always made it go. He could make the men step lively even after he was sick a great deal better than I can or ever will. It surely makes me feel a loss that is quite irreparable, I tell you. There are things that I don't suppose I'll ever learn that were entirely natural to him. I have got to arrange to get some cattle to eat up a lot of feed I can't sell, and I'm morally certain that I'll be skinned on the deal. When Papa did those things, the other fellow was never sure that he had all his hide when the deal was over. About six weeks before he died he bought ten cows from an old tightwad here in the neighborhood that no one else can do business with for $500 and sold them for $900. If I could only make deals like that, there'd be nothing to worry about. You've no idea how much he appreciated the flowers you sent him when he was at the hospital. He wouldn't let the nurse throw them away until they were entirely gone. He was very particular to point them out to Aunt Ella and tell her where they came from. We certainly appreciated the flowers that you and your mother and Frank and George sent to the funeral. Your good letter also helped out wonderfully. I can't tell you how much good it really did me.

I can't write you a good letter either for as you can probably tell I can't talk of but one subject. It is probably a very good thing that I have more work to do than I can possibly get done because I have something else to think about. I hope you will consider this worth an answer, and if Ferson gets his new car and will let me have it I hope to ride you around in it Sunday. Would like awfully to see you sooner but can't very well leave home.

Most sincerely,
Harry

Dear Bess: [Grandview, Dec. 1, 1914]

If this paper has any finger marks on it, they were there when the paper came from the shop—not because my hands are soiled. I have been putting coal and wood in reserve against morning and I haven't taken time to go to the wash basin.

I am afraid your letter is going to be a day late unless I can get up soon enough to mail it on the K.C.S.

I hauled Uncle Harry to Belton this morning and didn't get back as soon as I expected. Then I had to have some pasture cleared of brush, and now it is night before I get your letter written.

You needn't ever be afraid of my being jealous of your having a good time with some other fellow. I may feel badly because I'm not there but I don't believe that is jealousy. I am always glad when you have a good time whether I help furnish it or not. It's my opinion that when people come to the point where they are jealous of each other (which is nothing more nor less than distrust), it is time to quit. I never intend to arrive at that stage myself—i.e., I never intend to quit. . . .

Mr. Cox told me to sell his cow for him for $75. I am not a good cow salesman. If Papa were alive, he'd sell her for $85 and make the fellow who got her believe he was stealing her at that price. My line of trade talk has never been fully developed. I guess I'll have to practice up on this cow. When I buy a cow for $30 and then sell her to someone for $50 it always seems to me that I am really robbing that person of $20.

I have seen Papa buy thirty head of cows for $40 apiece and then unload them on a fellow for $1,900. The guy thought he was getting a genuine bargain too, which he was.

I must be an easy mark to work for. No less than four men have asked me for a job since I let the other fellows quit. I am going to develop a mean disposition and begin browbeating my help. It seems that the best and richest men got most of their money skinning their help and cheating ignorant people. The banker at Grandview wanted me to help him cook up a job on an old man who can't read once. That is the reason I do business with Frank Blair. His doctrine is squeeze the rich ones and give the poor man a chance. He has the biggest country bank in western Missouri as a result too. He was in Grandview yesterday evening holding a Lodge of Instruction. He says every man has to have a hobby and his is Freemasonry, about as harmless a one as he could possibly have I guess. He says that the only trouble he has with his hobby is his wife getting after him for being away from home so many nights.

I do wish you'd express a desire for something for the twenty-fifth of December. My brain has completely run out of ideas worthwhile. The things worth getting for you are beyond my reach and those I think I can get aren't worthwhile, so there you are. I guess if you don't the twenty-fourth at 10:00 P.M. will have to decide. Hope to see you tomorrow night anyway.

Sincerely,
Harry

Dear Bess: [Grandview, Dec. 29, 1914]

. . . I got home Sunday without a puncture and also took Uncle Harry to town yesterday and got back without a disaster. He began urging me to go to town as early as seven o'clock—I got him in by noon. As soon as he alighted he had to quench his thirst with fire water. About Friday or Saturday I'll have to rescue him again. . . .

There's one little old five-cent show between Grand and Walnut on the south side of the street that has the best shows there are. I've never seen a Pathé weekly or a World travel picture there yet. They have only one fault. On Mondays they will run a continued-next-week but they are so thrilling that they can be tolerated. The one yesterday had a fight on the highest building in San Francisco in which one of the combatants was pitched headfirst to the sidewalk.

It also had a chase through the fairgrounds. You get all this for the whole sum of five cents too. . . .

You owe me a letter anyway, really two but one long one will be very acceptable.

Most sincerely,
Harry

Shortly after John Truman's death Uncle Harrison was, as Truman describes below, "almost on the point of cashing in." For the next two years he had his ups and downs, and died in August 1916.

Dear Bess: [Grandview, Jan. 26, 1915]

I am going to try and send you a Wednesday letter. I have been chasing to town every day on account of Uncle Harry. He has been almost on the point of cashing in. I can't get him to come home. I took Mamma in yesterday and she couldn't even get him to come. I took her to the Orpheum in the afternoon. She sure enjoyed it. It is a fairly good bill, but if Martin Beck pays Liza Abarbanell two thousand dollars a week he'd better save his money and buy booze. She claims to be the Bernhardt of song. She has the movement all right but not the voice.

You don't know how sorry I am to hear you are confined to your couch. I am very sure you'd rather be in most any other place. I had our tickets exchanged for next Saturday evening. If you're not well enough to go then I'll trade them off again etc. ad lib. until you can go.

Your letter has never come yet. I suppose Uncle Samuel is reading it at Washington or some other wayside station. I had purchased a foot warmer and had two more side curtains put on so that Old Lizzie was as warm as a church. I think she was right disappointed at not getting herself tired out. I am going to have to take her back to the factory though as she is suffering from a worse knock than before she was fixed. I have an idea that the "expert" who worked on her jimmied her innards a little to get her brought back. He wanted to put on a new piece and I wouldn't let him. If I can make Stafford believe he fixed it wrong, I can get it fixed over for nothing.

I am going to send you a *Life* for last week. The cover is very good if the insides are not.

I am hoping to see you soon.

Will split this letter and write another the end of the week.

Most sincerely,
Harry

Dear Bess: [Grandview, 1915]

I got your letter this morning and I can tell you I most certainly appreciated it. I am very glad you like the flowers and only wish they could have been more. If I could have been in town I'd have sent you some fresh ones every day. I am hoping that you'll be up very soon so I can get to see you. It has been so long since I last saw you that it seems like a year. If you don't hurry and get well, Mr. Warfield is going to get by. They tell me that Blanche Ring is as fine as ever at the Orpheum.

I have finally succeeded in getting Uncle Harry home. He remarked when he got here that he was either awful sick or awful drunk, one. It was a combination. The doctor has succeeded in getting him sober and we hope to keep him that way for some time to come. I was in the city Saturday and it did seem entirely wrong not to go to Independence anyway. I sent you a little bunch of homegrown sweet violets. They told me that they are more fragrant than the California variety. I like violets better than any other kind of flowers both to eat and to look at. I shall try and send you some more before the week is out.

We are having a most lovely snow out this way. I am hoping it keeps up. Mrs. Chas. H. Lester has asked Mary and me to come out there to dinner tomorrow evening but I fail to see how I'm going to make it over roads like they are now. Old Liz hasn't been out since Thursday when I brought Uncle Harry home. This is the longest rest she's had for some time. I've got to put her back in the factory. She is suffering from a worse knock than ever. It seems that experts are experts only in getting money out of people. They expert an engine all to pieces and do it up again only to find it won't run any better than it would before. They also charged me up with thirty hours labor at seventy-five cents an hour. I don't know how they got it in as the car was only there a day and a half. Charging and getting are two altogether different processes. I am going to jaw with them some even if I have to pay in the end.

I am supposed to take active charge of the post office today but I haven't done it. The thing is a white elephant on my hands. Every person in Grandview who could possibly run the thing has asked me for the privilege of doing it. I have had the efficiency gag, the poor widow who is the only support of her family, the plain, easy-money one, and every other hand drawn on me to get the job. I have so far turned a deaf ear to all of them and allowed the boy I promised it to to keep it. There's no telling what I may do if they keep on. Political promises are no good anyway and I may break mine yet. I have an idea that I'll simply resign and let 'em fight it out all over again among themselves.

I am hoping to see you before the week goes by again. When you get well you've simply got to give me another picture of yourself so I can have one downstairs and one up. It's right unhandy to chase upstairs every day to see how you look. Here's hoping to see the original before long.

Most sincerely,
Harry

Dear Bess: [Grandview, April 28, 1915]

It has been so long since I sent you a letter that I've almost forgotten how to write one. It seems that I'm going to be at home this week very much—hence the letter. The hired man is going up to help Vivian plant corn from now to Saturday evening. I shall have to run the farm all alone. Mary is also going to leave for her throat operation. We'll be a very slim family. I'll have to take her in tomorrow.

I almost got done planting corn this evening. It will take me a couple of hours tomorrow. I was in the field at six o'clock and quit at seven. Nearly a day's work. There will be several of them before the summer's over. I've simply got to make things come across this year if I have to work night and day.

Did you discover from Miss Paxton if the Orpheum is a good place to go this week? I thought that if you had no objections to Saturday night I would be glad to have you go then. The reason I say Saturday night, Sunday comes next and we don't have to get out so early in the morning. I find I can't stay out all night and get up at 4:00 A.M. and work all day and do any good at it. Things have come around so that I must do as much work as anyone here or the hired men will soldier on me. They were all afraid of Papa but they are not of me a bit. I suppose the only way to get their goats is to fire 'em, but I hate to do that.

Things surely look fine now. If the crops only turn out as well as they appear now, there won't be anything to worry about. I hope they do. . . .

I guess you think I'm a funny sort of guy to urge you so on paper to become engaged to me and then not follow up things with the proper sort of jewelry. But some way I can't talk of things that are of such vital importance and interest to me. You know what happened to me immediately after that most valued letter came from you. Financially I'm $12,500 worse off than nothing. But I'm not going to be for long, and if you'll only believe it I know I can make things come right yet. To lose your good opinion would be the last bitter drop in a cup that has been pretty full of disappointments in the last year or two. I hope never to lose it and the rest won't amount to anything. They can all be overcome.

Mamma's for me hammer and tongs and so's Uncle Harry now and you know they can put me on top if I try myself.

This is a bum letter—and I hope you'll forgive it and hope for a better next time. Maybe the Orpheum Saturday can help make up what it lacks. Hope to get a letter from you before the week's gone.

Most sincerely,
Harry

From late April until early November 1915 either few letters were sent to Bess or they have been lost. During this period Truman went to Texas with a group of farmers for another try at making money by expanding his farm holdings. He sent two postcards from Dallas, views of the Adolphus Hotel and the Columbia Club. The Adolphus, he related, was the "Baltimore" of Dallas; on the Columbia Club card he said he would have wired Bess the preceding Sunday but was afraid it might alarm her ("you'd think I'd broken my neck").

Dear Bess: [En route to Fort Worth, Tex., Nov. 4, 1915]
Since I forgot my fountain pen I suppose a pencil will have to do. I have taken another sudden notion to go to Texas. There is some chance of my making something this time though. If one of the men buys, I am to get a hundred

dollars. You should hear me talk Texas land. I am almost an expert salesman by this time. We are now in the center of Oklahoma going south at sixty miles an hour. If nothing breaks we'll arrive in Ft. Worth at 8:05 P.M. I am hoping for the best. *The Birth of a Nation* I suppose will keep another week. I was hoping you'd consent to go about Thursday. I shall be home next Wednesday and hope to see you that evening—if you are home. . . .

I shall mail this at Denison, Texas. I think there's a gink watching me do this—as he's my intended victim (can't spell it) I'll have to stop without insulting him. May have more luck later. Wish I could get a letter from you but I can't.

Sincerely,
Harry

Between trips to Texas, Harry, Uncle Harrison, and Mamma went to Monegaw Springs, eighty miles southeast of Grandview, twenty miles below Clinton. The springs were and are attractive to young and old, less so now than formerly —they were a place where the young came to hold hands, and the old to think back when they too had come for that purpose. As Truman discovered, and relates to Bess in this letter, when he drove the Stafford half the fun was in getting there, and the rest in coming back.

Katy Flyer [on the Missouri-Kansas-Texas Railroad], Okla.
Dear Bess: [no postmark]
I am going to send you a penciled note to let you know how I came to be here.

I suppose that you remember that I started for Monegaw Springs on Sunday. Mamma went along and we almost reached the springs without an accident. We got within a half mile of them and ran over a stump. I spilled Uncle Harry over the front seat and threw Mamma over my own head. Neither of them were hurt, except Uncle Harry renewed his profane vocabulary. I backed Lizzie off the stump and ran her into town with a badly bent axle. Mamma and I started for home at 6:00 A.M. on Monday. Got within seventy-five miles of it and it began to rain. Had the nicest slipping time you ever saw. What with a crooked axle and a bent steering wheel I could hardly stay in the road. Five miles south of Harrisonville Lizzie took a header for the ditch and got there, smashing a left front wheel into kindling. I phoned to Ferson and he sent me his front wheel. The accident happened within a half mile of a R.R. station, Lone Ture by name. Mamma and I sat there from 1:30 till 8:00 P.M. waiting for the wheel. It arrived all right and I couldn't get it on. Then it began to rain in real earnest. I got soaked. A good farmer came and took us up to his house and we stayed all night. Next morning he hitched his team to Lizzie and pulled her out of the ditch. (I had tried to put the wheel on wrong end to, the night before.) He would not have a cent for keeping me nor pulling the car out. We started for Harrisonville and get about five miles north of there when we ran through a puddle and get the mag wet. Had to phone back to Harrisonville and get a man to come and tear it up—cost a five-dollar bill. Another good farmer took us to dinner free. Finally got to Grandview at 3:00 P.M. Tuesday. Mr. Hall called me and said if I wanted to go to Texas and New Mexico free, R.R. fare sleeper and meals, I could. Took Lizzie to town and gave Ferson his wheel, left her at the factory, and I'm on way to Ft. Worth and the Pecos Valley aboard a special Pullman with a nice crowd of farmers. Several of my close neighbors are along. I endeavored to call you last night but your line was busy. I wanted to come over and see you before I left and also borrow your Kodak. Hope you'll excuse this scrawl as I forgot my pen and stationery.

You are the only one getting any letters this trip. Hope to be home by Sunday and get a ride in the new car while Lizzie has only three feet. I'm headed for Ft. Stockton, Texas, clean off the map on the western border.

Most sincerely,
Harry

[Hotel Stockton, Fort Stockton, Tex.]

Dear Bess: February 4, 1916

We are staying at a very very fine place (at the expense of the United Land Co.) and having a fine time. I have seen some of the finest irrigated country in the world. The money some of these fellows are making sounds unbelievable. One fellow paid $125 an acre for land three years ago, sold enough seed and hay off of it to pay for it this year.

Another made $80 an acre from cotton. It is warm enough to go swimming this evening and we are three thousand feet above sea level. The heat record is 95 degrees and the cold one 15 degrees above. That was made night before last.

Enough climate. I am convinced that I can make some money down here. It is now the hard part to convince that uncle of mine that he should give me a boost. If he only would, I know as well as I'm alive that I could make $25,000 in three years and have a farm that would bring $150 an acre. There's a man by the name of Grove down here who paid about $100 an acre for 240 acres of land here to get it in condition to use. That was one year last April. He was offered $48,000 for it a month ago and refused to sell because he is absolutely satisfied. The climate is ideal. The land will make him $100 an acre every year and there are fish and game in reach all the time. We saw at least one thousand quail today, twice as many jack rabbits, and some cranes and wild ducks. (That's as good a one as a real hunter can tell.)

I have been attempting to make a Victrola with a busted spring run. Another fellow and myself decided to tear it up and see what was in it. As soon as we got thoroughly into it the proprietor came in. We expected Texas trouble right off, but he said he'd done the same thing himself and if we could make the blamed thing go he'd be much obliged. It wouldn't. He has to send to Kansas City or Dallas for a spring. I don't suppose it will arrive before morning.

That makes me think we have a real observation Pullman this time. It has a big Victrola in the parlor but there are only about half-dozen records. We've worn out two packages of needles on them. I suppose another package will be gone when we get to K.C. There are two porters and a cook along. We are living in real millionaire style. I have been about 120 miles in a machine today. It is possible to see—well, just as far as you can look. The Davis Mts. are 80 miles one way, Castle Gap is 60 the other, we can see in both—that makes 140 miles. If my eyes were better and [illegible], I could see the whole distance at once.

Hope to see you Wednesday evening, if the TP and Katy stay on the rails.

Most sincerely,

Harry

Once again the Grandview farmer went to Texas, this time with Uncle Harrison in tow.

Dear Bess: [En route to Fort Worth, Tex., Feb. 16, 1916]

This is the roughest road in Texas I suppose.

We are approaching Ft. Worth an hour late, hence the reason I am endeavoring to write while we move. (If we were on time, I could write after we arrive.) The car is supposed to stay there an hour.

Uncle Harry seems to be enjoying himself. He is able to lead every big lie that is told in his presence by a bigger one. When he can do that he's happy. He's begun to cuss Texas though, which isn't so happy for me. I doubt very much if he allows me to do anything down here. If he doesn't, I'm going to try and make him loosen up at home. It is springtime here. They are plowing and burning just as we do in May. It is certainly fine weather down here. I want to stay but I can't. There's a month's work at home to be done in a week. Vivian and Mr. Blair seem to think that I am badly in need of a guardian for even suggesting west Texas. I have converted Blair but Vivian never. He can do nothing but quote his paw-in-law. You know the old geezer has just sold a one-third interest in a Joplin mine and made some more money. The mine cost the three of them $30,000. They sold it for $105,000. He has another one that brings him $1,000 a week. I wish him some more luck. That won't keep me from trying my luck if I can. You are well acquainted with my very urgent reasons for wanting some kind of good luck. I shall send you another letter from San Angelo.

I am sending Nellie a grand collection of jails, libraries, and schools. You should see them. Here's the city. I must quit.

Sincerely,

Harry

Dear Bess: [Fort Worth, Tex., date illegible]

We are at Ft. Worth this evening. The Katy was three hours late and we missed connection on the Texas & Pacific and are staying over here until eight o'clock tomorrow, when we will begin our journey across Texas. I suppose you think that I am somewhat erratic in my Texas trips. I am, but there is method in my madness. Mr. Oscar K. Herndon has offered me 160 acres of land on my word for five years or a section of land on the same terms if I want to take it.

I am here to look it over and see what can be done. I am getting very impatient of my slow progress at home. You know my prospects there were of the brightest at the outset and one disaster after another has almost put me to the bad. I still have a good fighting chance to make things go on the farm if Uncle Harry will manage to live about five or six years yet. I am hoping he will. But this proposition I am looking over has a fine face on it, and if as Herndon says I can take it on and get someone to run it for me, I can make a very large stake in a short time. You know I am most anxious to do that for the most excellent reason that I am crazy to marry you. In the last year my finances have seemed to put me farther from that happy event rather than closer to it. Sometimes, in fact nearly every time I see you, I want to urge you to throw prudence to the winds and take me anyway just as things are and take a chance on my ever making good and then I think of all the debts I'm saddled with and of my present inability even to buy you a decent ring and I haven't the nerve to do it.

I want you to keep backing me to win though and I will. When I see how happy Frank and Vivian are and how easily they seem to do it I am mad with envy. Then I see myself in an ideal country home with everything as it should be and you to run it and me and it's almost unbearable to wait. Then I wake up and see our old house going to wreck for want of paint and repairs because I must pay interest on a debt I had no hand in making and my dream has to keep waiting. Sometimes I am nearly persuading Mamma to sell the whole works for what it will bring and pay out; and then I think how she loves the old place that's been home to her so long. Then I think maybe next year will be a rousing crop and I can pay the major part of things and build me a bungalow.

Uncle Harry talked favorably of allowing me to dispose of some forty thousand dollars worth of his property. If he does it we'll all be on easy street and you'll have to run mighty fast to get away from me.

I hope you got my letter in time to use the Orpheum ticket. I was sick because I missed getting to go with you and I hope it's only a postponement. I'm afraid you'll come to the conclusion that I am a poor person to make a date with but you know I'd never missed this except I had thought of doing something to make our permanent date closer per hopes. Then we can see several shows on the twenty-five dollars I am getting out of the trip.

I am hoping to see you as soon as I arrive in K.C. and let you know the luck I have.

I am writing this at 1:00 A.M. in the Union Station yards at Ft. Worth. Everyone is in bed but me. I had to wait until now so I could write in peace. Some of these guys are mean enough to read every bit of this as I write.

Here's hoping for an early settlement of my financial ills and an early arrival of a certain event which I hope will make us both forever happy.

From the one who thinks you the whole world and heaven besides,

Harry

Dear Bess: [Fort Stockton, Tex., Feb. 19, 1916]

We are in Ft. Stockton today. I didn't get to write at San Angelo because we didn't stop long enough. It is about to rain here for the first time since November. Uncle Harrison and I were driven out to a big alfalfa farm this morning and he got cold. Said if he ever thawed out he'd never freeze again in this country anyway. I have about given up hope for this proposition now. There's no harm done, though, because the old gent feels better than he has for two months. My only task will be getting him home from Kansas City. He's feeling so well that he'll want to stay there.

There are several Dutchmen aboard who think the country is very fine. They are all going to buy.

The stock agent of the Orient Road is with us. He's a real Southerner, raised on a plantation at Marshall, Texas. He's been arrested by Villa and had all kinds of experience. His home is San Angelo. He says that town has more millionaires than any other town in the country its size. They are cow men. One of them owns a couple of Texas counties. This county we are in has an area equal to two Rhode Islands. It's about one hundred miles long and seventy from north to south.

I just heard a Dutchman make a joke. Someone asked him to have a drink. "No dank you," he said. "I nefer drink between drinks."

The train has made another start. My most excellent penmanship is made almost illegible by the motion. It affects the spelling also. It is nearly impossible for me spell correctly at any time and when the train rocks, the alphabet becomes jumbled completely in my head. I hope to see you on Wednesday evening. Hold the thought for my good luck. There's no one wants to win half so badly as I do. Will call up when I arrive in town. Dreamt I was taking you to the show last night. Had a new machine (not a Ford either). I can make the show part come true but not the machine. There's one waiting for me.

Sincerely,
Harry

FIVE

AIMING TO GET RICH: LEAD, ZINC, AND OIL

———————————

An almost forgotten chapter in the life of Harry Truman is set in 1916–1917, just before America entered World War I. Uncle Harrison may have at long last turned loose some money, for Harry took a flyer in a lead and zinc mine near Commerce, Oklahoma.

This adventure deserves telling in the words of the principal entrepreneur —Harry was secretary-treasurer of the T.C.H. Mining Company and related the whole story to Bess, letter by letter. His two partners were far less active in the venture. Jerry Culbertson was the guiding spirit and resident enthusiast; he could be called the promoter. Mr. Hughes, as Truman spoke of him, seems to have been a rather timid farmer who hoped, like Truman, to double or triple his money in short order. Instead, lightning struck his barn soon after the mine opened. He rushed back home to repair the damage, and that was the end of him as a mining partner.

Truman sought to get the mine in running order. He hired and fired bosses, got the big engine going, and secured enough water to wash the ore as it came out of the shaft. The mine was a difficult, unwieldy project, its management made all the more frantic for Harry by conditions at home. The farm was in Mary's charge, and the farmhands did not like working for a woman. At one crucial moment Mary had to fire one and the other quit; Harry rushed home from Commerce to help her.

As the mine slipped toward disaster, the irrepressible Harry tried another enterprise that might allow him to "win"—an oil company. It was essentially a fancy letterhead on which he and two partners (Culbertson, again, and a wildcatter named David H. Morgan) offered stock to investors in Kansas City. During the winter of 1916–1917, Truman worked out of the company's downtown office and welcomed any investors he could entice. Unlike the lead and zinc mine, the firm of Morgan & Company had promise; it had at least one partner, Dave Morgan, who knew the business. The company put a well down in Kansas on top of what years later proved to be the famous Teter Pool; they could have tapped into it had they drilled a bit more. Truman and his associates, and all the stock purchasers, would have gotten rich. Instead, the company had to sell its leases.

Time had run out, for in April 1917 the United States entered World War I—and Truman signed up.

Dear Bess: [Yates Hotel, Joplin, Mo., Mar. 5, 1916]

This is a very dull Sunday. I am at this hotel waiting for a mill expert to come and tell me how much money to spend on our mine. He was over and looked at our proposition yesterday. We are very much pleased with his opinion. He thought there was $4,000 in waste ore lying immediately around the mill. We have to spend $1,500 to get it, but it will be a paying investment.

My money is in now and I am feeling better over it every minute. After next week the money will begin to return.

When *our* mill is properly repaired we can grind enough ore to make $1,000 a day (half profit). Some pipe dream that. I have been prowling around trying to find someone who thinks the Eureka mine is a fake but I can't. They all say it's all right only it needs about $3,000 spent on it. We are doing that. I suppose in about ninety days we'll be turning out about $500 a day if present prices prevail. In six months we expect to be on velvet and an income of about $400 a week apiece.

I wish I was in Independence this evening but it can't be done now. I almost came home at noon today but decided to be economical until the $400-a-week days begin anyway.

I suppose you are tired learning of the mine and how much I'm going to make but I've just got to tell someone about it and you're the only one I care to tell. I even tell Jerry Culbertson that I expect to lose all I've put into the blamed thing but I don't expect to—not by a jug full. If the bloomin' thing fails to connect I'll be so disappointed I won't know straight up from crossways. Jerry says the "hinges of destiny" are greased for our door of opportunity to open. Jerry has oratorical ambitions I think.

I'll take a shot at something else if this loses (I have a loose head) and win anyway. You know I've got to win. Hold the thought. I'm going to have the best farm in Jackson County and one in the Pecos Valley for winter with a Pierce Arrow to ride in—and be a rube.

Does that suit you or not?

If you write me at this hotel before Friday, I'll get it. I'll most certainly appreciate a letter.

It's mighty lonesome down here where I know not a soul. I've lots of work to do tomorrow and Tuesday. I'm coming home Saturday or bust a hamstring trying. See you Sunday.

               Sincerely,
               Harry

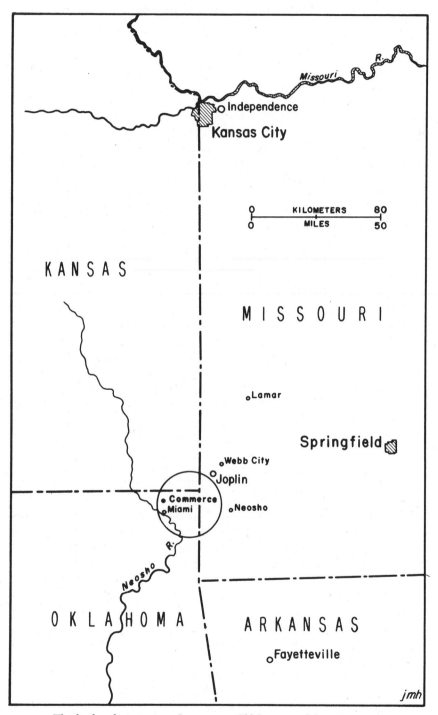

The lead and zinc mine, Commerce, Oklahoma, and four-state area.

The mechanics of opening the mine are revealed bit by bit in Truman's letters. The operation proved a far more difficult task than he and his two associates had anticipated. The mine itself comprised only a shaft with tunnels at the bottom. A mechanical hoist took men and equipment down and brought up unseparated ore, or "dirt." To dig the tunnels, the men used an air drill run by a compressor up above and then applied charges—gunpowder or TNT. When the dirt got to the mill, it had to be crushed. Then, using an "ocean" of water the crew above ground separated ore from worthless rock. Truman and his associates calculated that at current prices, from $80 to $120 a ton for separated ore (the price fell rapidly during their mine's operation), they could do all right. None of the partners knew much about mining but they went ahead—and even dug a pond when someone cut off their water supply. Their hiring practices were haphazard and got them into labor trouble. Under the best of circumstances the mine could run only by the grace of God. Otherwise, which was almost all of the time, it remained under control of His Majesty.

[Hotel Ruth, Commerce, Okla.]

Dear Bess: March 15, 1916

I am stopping as you see at the best hotel in town. Mr. Hughes and I have to occupy the same room. The partition walls are just boxing with paper over them. We are in Room 9 at the west end of the hall. We dare not whisper because the show girls in Room 1 at the other end of the hall can hear us. It is a first-class hotel when it comes to eats and it is far above the street when it comes to sleeping.

There will be a house at the T. C. H. [Truman, Culbertson, Hughes] Mining Co.'s property very soon and then we'll live in comfort. The mine is going to be all right. We have as good or better dirt than our neighbors. I was down in it today.

Three men are working down there getting things in shape to raise sand (ore I mean) by next Monday. We are not going any deeper just yet because there is plenty of good zinc in sight to make a binful of ore without much expense. That's only twenty-four thousand dollars' worth. Maybe next time I write the blasted thing will have gone dry. They do sometimes. The new part of the mill will be done by Saturday, that is, the building will. The thing won't have the wheels going round until the next Saturday. That's the day I've planned to come home. Hope to have things humming so my eyes'll really shine for two reasons when I see you. We have a good mine boss and I hope a good manager. One man told me he is all right and another said he'd steal the hose off the engine if we leave him with it. I am going to make a special trip to Webb City Friday to look him up. I suppose I should have done that first. He looks honest and he acts honest but so do I, therefore I'm going to find out.

A nut at Grandview, who is a contractor, told me that he was under the impression for a long time that I was a gentleman of the cloth, a preacher. If I can only retain that holy look, I can sell the mine by the blue-sky route and get rich anyway. I'm going to buy me a checked suit and a cane if I win and I'll bet I'll overcome my sanctified way.

Mr. Hughes is nagging me to quit writing and write him a check so he can go to bed. I guess I'll have to do it but I don't want to.

Please write me a long letter for I'll sure be homesick before I see you again. Will write again Saturday or sooner if you like.

Most sincerely,
Harry

[Yates Hotel, Joplin, Mo., Mar. 18, 1916]

Dear Bess: The Day after St. Pat's

I am almost sober this Sunday morning. I looked long and hopefully for a letter but I guess that cross-eyed post-office girl is still holding out on me.

I had to come to Joplin yesterday evening to buy some supplies and look at a piece of machinery. Some day I hope to be able to quit buying and go to selling. Our mine (I finally got to it, you see) will be going I hope by Wednesday. It is getting better and better underground. Every shot shows up fine ore and we have a new vein in sight that will probably show up better than any yet. We won't work on it until later though because there is already enough in sight to keep us going for a month. We consider that we have a proposition worth sixty thousand dollars anyway. Our foreman says we have a much better mine than he expected to see when he went down in it. I have been in it twice this week. When we get to going good I want you to come down and ride the bucket to the bottom. It is iron and about three feet across and four deep. It goes round and round as it goes down. When I get to the bottom I can't tell north from straight up. We carry little carbide lamps that give about a penny's worth of light.

That's plenty though in a place of total darkness.

I sent you a package last night in place of the letter I promised to send. I am hoping to see a letter when I get back to Commerce this evening. When I see you next Sunday (it seems like next year) I hope to be able to tell you that we are going full blast and making ore so fast it makes our heads swim. It is now worth $115 a ton. Five tons a day soon amounts to something.

Send me a letter quickly. If you knew how badly I wanted one, you'd send it every day.

Sincerely,
Harry

Dear Bess: [Commerce, Okla., date illegible]

I suppose you must have been displeased with the brand of Commerce stationery and the pink ink I use; or else the new P.M. has held out on me. I haven't had a letter from anywhere since I have been here this time. Duns don't count. We got the water situation adjusted after a fashion, and something else had to come loose. The ground boss got drunk yesterday and got the rest of the help to quit us because we fired him. The mill is standing still today. Not on account of the drunk boss, but for some further improvements. We decided to finish the thing up before we made another effort to run. The dirt is very rich as far as we did run. We got a ton and a half of ore out of three hours run. Should it keep up that fast I'll need an expert accountant to keep my individual books. I am getting a very liberal and very expensive education. I am hoping it amounts to something. I have given instructions for Grand Opera tickets. I hope they are in a place where we'll be able to see and hear.

I don't know if I'll get home Saturday or not. Should I fail to get things in a position so I can leave then you'll certainly see me Wednesday. I am hoping to get away so I can be home both Sunday and Wednesday. This place down here is certainly one beyond the limit. They have smallpox in town. The pest house is just a half a mile from us here at the mill. When it rains there is water six inches deep over everything. When it's dry the dust is as deep over everything. Mr. Hughes and I board across the street with a poor woman who has eight children. Five of them are under ten years and the other three are married. She's a good cook but is very shy of table furniture. She used a bottle for syrup and a glass for a cream pitcher today. She's good and means well so I guess we can put up with it.

Please send me a letter. I am very lonesome down here when I'm not busy and letters from you look awful good.

Most sincerely,
Harry

Dear Bess: [Commerce, Okla., date illegible]

Your good letter came last night. I suppose that cross-eyed woman held it out on me Saturday. I was sure glad to get it. You evidently had a very busy day that day and I feel stuck up that you took the time to write. If you knew how I appreciate your letters you'd send one every day. I am writing this in the mill over behind the air compressor. It's a machine about the size of the water pump down at the Missouri River pumping station for Independence. It runs like the mischief when the men are working in the ground, and when they stop it slows up. We can always tell how much they are doing by the way the compressor runs. The drills are run by air. We haven't started the mill yet but the time gets closer when we shall.

I have gotten real penurious and am now staying at the plant nights. Last night was the first night. I tried to hire a watchman and he wanted $2.50 a night just to sleep here. I was paying fifty cents a night for someplace to sleep so I bought me a cot and mattress for $4.50 and now I consider that I'm making $3.00 a night by sleeping in a better place than I was paying fifty cents for. I expected all sorts of haunts and things to bother me, but if they came around I never saw them. A man fell down the shaft of this mine about three months before we got it, and I thought maybe he might come and inspect the boilers or tell me how to do it (he was a night engineer) but he didn't. The ore veins are as good or better than ever. I am going down in the mine again at noon to see what showed up after last night's shots. Jerry wanted me to give him a thirty-day option on my share for $10,000 but I didn't. I would take that much cash but not wind. Hope to hear from you *several* times this week and see you Sunday. How do you like my St. Pat's ink? It's guaranteed fountain pen kind. Couldn't get other. My stationery is limited, so are my ideas. You can suppose another sheet of nice things said and meant.

Sincerely,
Harry

Dear Bess: [Hotel Ruth, Commerce, Okla.]
                                                              March 23, 1916

You see I have to go back and borrow from my friend Ruth again. I eat here all the time though and he shouldn't feel badly if I use his stationery.

I was sure glad to get your letter. I have been almost homesick since Tuesday. You know Mr. Hughes went home Saturday and left me in charge. I've had lots to do but still I'd rather be home. I am sure coming home Saturday night and I'll be in the capital of Jackson County on Sunday evening or blow up the K.C.S. Railroad. I hope your mother has a good time at Platte. I know she will though for that's the place to have a good time. Do you really have to get up at 5:00 A.M.? I have to get up at that time down here and light up the gas under the boilers. I'll be thinking tomorrow and Saturday that you also will be lighting gas at that time. I wish I could come to breakfast instead of going to the Hotel Ruth. We have oatmeal (I don't because the cream's condensed) and bacon with eggs fried greasy. Doesn't it sound appetizing? The coffee's nice and black and bitter. We usually have a good dinner. They changed cooks the other day and the new one is just learning how to do the trick. . . .

Our mine still continues to hold out good. The foreman estimates that there is enough material in sight to run us for four or five months when we get started. If such is the case I can pay all my debts and have something left over. There are all kinds of good opportunities down here, but a fellow has to have anywhere from $10,000 to $20,000 to handle them. Jerry was over yesterday and said if we could clear $15,000 apiece on this job that we have the chance to get a piece of property that will make bushels of money when ore is $35 a ton. I hope we can do it. The dirt in our mine runs about 5½ to 6 percent, now. It may be richer as we go back and it may be poorer. We can make money on 3 percent at the present price of ore.

I always talk shop before I get done but you asked me what it made.

Hope to see you Sunday evening. I surely appreciate your letters and could stand them at the rate of half dozen a day.

Sincerely,
Harry

Dear Bess: [Commerce, Okla., Mar. 1916]

While ciphering around in my suitcase just now I ran across another sheet of stationery. I am going to send you another letter if I do beat it home. Your answer to my green epistle came out of the hands of the cross-eyed woman after I'd mailed you one this morning. I was sure glad to get it too.

That was a real mean insinuation about the show girls, especially as I was in Joplin sending you a package on Saturday evening and that particular bunch of 'em left the hotel on Sunday. I came out to the mill from Joplin Monday. So you see I have a very clear conscience. It is too bad you couldn't go to the party but I'm glad, because if you'd gone I wouldn't have the letter till tomorrow. I don't have a double-barreled shotgun or any other kind here with me. I'm more afraid of a gun than a possible intruder. I haven't lost any sleep yet worrying over cutthroats. There are two mills in less than 150 yards that run all night. They make an awful racket, but it's comforting to hear 'em. My cot is much better than the Ruth Hotel bed I had and I have a lot more exclusiveness, really too much. The wind blew so hard here the other night that I expected one of our old tin smokestacks to fall across my bed. If it had, I'd not be writing now because the thing weighs some tons or more. I was all wrought up about it for about an hour and then I went to sleep and it was 5:00 A.M. before I remembered it again. I must be noiseproof when it comes to sleeping. There's a 135-horsepower gas engine in one of these mills that's running all night. It makes a racket like the German army. The other one has a shaft hoister going all the time. It makes a noise like a rattletrap Met streetcar. Occasionally some water or something runs down out of one of the boilers here in the room, making a sound like a rat sliding off a tin roof. None of 'em affect my sleeping powers after 9:00 P.M.

The mill isn't ready to run yet. There are so many little things that take time and show up unexpectedly, but I am hoping for Monday or Tuesday sure. I was down in the mine again today and also yesterday. It's getting better all the time. If I just don't run out of money before the wheels go around I'll have the financial end of things nearly whipped to a standstill. The payroll last week was $387.50. This week it'll be $440.00. That sure eats money. But I'm not worried. Things couldn't get this close to a win and then drop for the want of $2,000. I'd sell my gray horses first (or Lizzie!). I shall see you Sunday night as I said if the K.C.S. stays on the rails. I sure appreciate your letters and am hoping they'll keep coming.

Most sincerely,
Harry

Dear Bess: [Commerce, Okla., Apr. 2, 1916]

This is Commerce stationery, the very best brand [it is blank paper]. Twenty cents a ream or whatever quantity it is they sell paper by. I got to this place about ten o'clock yesterday. Everything was all right except that the mill was not running and had not been. It is running now. I hope to see it run like Sam Hill for some time. They made another rich strike in the mine while I was away. The ground boss had a hole drilled down eighteen feet below the bottom of the present level and it went through fine lead and zinc all the way. If it only runs all over the bottom the same way I fear we'll get rich too fast.

There always has to be a scoundrel in every mining story. We have ours. The two fellows above us have agreed to shut off our water. You know a mill can't run without an ocean nearly to separate the ore. We all get our mill water from one mine. This mine pumps all the water from this district so that all the mines are dry. It comes down a ditch similar to an irrigation ditch and the mines along it help themselves to as much as is necessary and send their waste water back. The two guys above us have split what comes this way between them and are sending the waste away so we can't get it. I am going around the gentlemen and build us a ditch from headquarters and then they can whistle for water themselves. I think they want to buy us out at a discount. There will be a decided mistake before they connect. The rain was sure a good thing for us. We caught enough water in our pond to run on for a couple of weeks and by then our ditch will be in.

I'll have to run—the first 1,000 lbs. of ore is ready to come out and I must be present. Please write as many times as you did last week. If I could get to Joplin, I'd send you a package but I can't.

Most sincerely,

Harry

Dear Bess: [Commerce, Okla., Apr. 9, 1916]
Your letter came yesterday. I was sure glad to get it. There is now a very decided blond who wears specks and chews gum in the P.O. She chews the gum, I guess, to help her sort the letters because she always moistens her thumb when she goes to hand out the letters. She sent some of our mail to Miami [Oklahoma] and I had to make a trip over there after it. Your first letter came Thursday and the second one yesterday. I tried to get to write you last night but had two lumber bills and a supply account to check. The discount on them is good only until today so I had to work for the company.

We fired the ground boss as I told you before and all the rest of the gang but two carpenters and the superintendent. He thought he was going to get it too because he went to work himself. I don't know whether I told you that we made another rich strike in the ground just before we fired the bunch or not. Struck lead and zinc better than has ever been taken out here. We have been working like sixty and will go right [on] Monday. Found a very good man for boss who doesn't drink or talk about himself so I suppose we'll have no more trouble there. It was necessary to buy some more new pieces for the mill as we found out by the run of four hours we made. . . .

Be sure and send some more letters.

Sincerely,

Harry

Dear Bess: [Commerce, Okla., Apr. 16, 1916]

Here I am in the edge of the world on this fine Easter morning. I certainly wish I was home. You know what an awful stew I was in for this week's payroll. The banker down here let us have it without a word. The shaft went down through the limestone and into fine lead and zinc. I am so well pleased I could almost sell some stock this morning if it weren't Easter Sunday. We are going to have a real mine, even better than expected in the first place. I had almost come to the conclusion we were stung properly but it is evident that luck is with us.

We are going to have a fight with the crooked superintendent in the morning. He is a crook right. Has cost us nearly one thousand dollars to find it out. Maybe I'm not learning something in this game. I hope I am though.

I ordered a package sent to you this morning. I hope you got it. I wish I could send myself in time to go to church. I suppose I'll go to Miami to church or more than likely not go at all.

Mamma was still in bed when I left. I am so uneasy about her I don't know what to do. I phoned Jerry last night to find out how she is. He has a Bell phone and we haven't. It only cost me $1.61 to talk five minutes. . . . Be sure and send me a letter or two or three because I expect to be here nearly all week. Will send you another tomorrow.

Most sincerely,
Harry

Dear Bess: [Commerce, Okla., Apr. 24, 1916]

I tried to call you up Thursday but your line was busy and I couldn't wait. I left home on the K.C.S. and made the road or somebody a present of my new raincoat. Left it hanging up on a hook in the car. I guess it's either in Joplin or Port Arthur by this time. The agent at Joplin wired to Neosho for the conductor to send it back on the next train. I couldn't wait to see if it came back. My presence was badly needed here. Jerry was to go get it for me and bring it over last night but he forgot to go see about it. I am the boss today. Mr. Hughes went home last night. Jerry is coming Monday and I hope to get home Tuesday.

The superintendent we have is a crook I believe. He had Mr. Hughes scared to death when I got here. Told him we'd worked clean out to the line and there was nothing else to work.

I got hold of the ground boss today and gave him some very explicit orders. We didn't expect to work the old diggings. There is a new vein of ore in the bottom of the shaft we expect to turn out better than anything we've had yet, or that has ever been taken out here.

The mine is worked something like that. [Truman enclosed a sketch of the mine.] The two dots are drill holes. . . . The ore hoist of the shaft seems to point to them and if a new drift starts out that way we can mine for years and make money. It will take four more days to tell the tale. I'll know then whether I ride in a glass machine or walk the balance of my days. It is something like sitting on a pin to wait but it has to be done. If that drunken ground boss had done what he was ordered to do, we'd know now. But he went down there and got drunk and broke up a lot of dead dirt and sent [it] up to us instead of doing what he was ordered.

I guess you get tired hearing [about the] mine but it is uppermost in my mind right at present and I have to talk of it. You know how much I want to win and how very badly I'd hate to lose. If I lose though I guess I'll take a whack at something else. I can't possibly lose forever. If I just knew which god or goddess had it in for me, I'd try and appease him somehow. I hope it isn't Venus. I'd rather have Mars or Jove himself after me than her. She could make a pessimist of me and the rest can't.

Please send me a letter. I may not get away from here before Wednesday and I'll appreciate hearing from you, oh, several times. Our box is 54. I got Turner's and Troutman's and Freeman's mail yesterday. I think that's pretty good for a start. Shows we have a really good P.M. Nearly as good as I made.

Hope to see you the middle of the week.

Most sincerely,
Harry

[Commerce, Okla.]

Dear Bess: April 27, 1916

Your letter came today. I have been looking for it since Tuesday. I think this postmaster is nearly as bad as the cross-eyed woman was before him. He held out a letter of Mr. Hughes' in the general delivery this week. If I had not asked for it, I guess he'd never have gotten it. We have been very busy this week firing the superintendent and sinking the shaft. The superintendent won't fire worth a cent. Says he is going to stay until Saturday and draw his fifty dollars. I suppose I shall have trouble with him on that day.

This mill is running full blast today. We'll probably have a car of ore by the middle of next week. My worries as to where next week's payroll is going to come from will be over then. I have been very much worried about Mamma, she was very sick the first of the week but I had a letter from Mary saying she is better now. I wanted to go home most awful bad but couldn't leave here. . . .

I hope I can get home and get invited to that choir picnic. I had a good time at the last one. If things go well and I get by this week's payroll without being mobbed, I'll be home Sunday. It is necessary for me to stay home all next week and plant corn. Running a farm and a mine so widely apart is some job. If they were on adjoining lots, I could manage very well. Mines are not usually in a farming country but this one is. There is a wheat field and a hayfield on our west line. I was down in it yesterday twice. There is a lot of lead and zinc in sight. If I get home Sunday I'll call you. Write me anyway on the chance that I won't. Things are somewhat mixed here and I'm the official straightener.

Most sincerely,
Harry

One of the most remarkable traits of Harry S. Truman, and perhaps this is the case with anyone who manages to "get ahead," was his refusal to remain discouraged. And so, while the following letter admits defeat in his lead and zinc project, he soon recouped with typical enthusiasm. But the moment was a bad one.

Dear Bess: [Grandview, May 19, 1916]
    It was my intention to see you at the Orpheum today but Uncle Harrison was taken sick yesterday and I had to stay up all night last night, so therefore I must stay at home.
    The mine has gone by the board. I have lost out on it entirely. If Uncle Harry had not been sick I should have gone down there Tuesday evening. It is a setback from which I don't suppose I shall very soon recover. If I don't lose all the livestock I have, it will only be because I shall turn it over to Mamma. I shall join the class who can't sign checks of their own I suppose. It is a hard nut to crack but it has to be done. There was never one of our name who had sense enough to make money. I am no exception.
    I shall endeavor to make the farm go as usual but I'll have to stay on it. My finances are completely exhausted and I suppose they'll remain so for some months to come. Perhaps at some future date I'll get a mine or something that will make money.
    We are very uneasy about Uncle Harry. It would just be our luck for him to die now and leave everything he has in a mess. It is to be expected.
    I hope you will have some patience with me and let me come down sometimes (when I have the carfare). You would do better perhaps if you pitch me into the ash heap and pick someone with more sense and ability and not such a soft head. My position seems to be that of following a mule up a corn row rather than directing the centers of finance. I hope I never send you another letter as foolish as this one but I thought I ought to tell you, and if Uncle Harry does not improve I'll have to stay with him.
                                                    Very sincerely,
                                                    Harry

                                                    [Commerce, Okla.]
Dear Bess: May 23, 1916
    The T.C.H. Mining Co. may be a reality yet. The chances are better than they were last week. Had Jerry have come down when I wanted him to, we'd have avoided all trouble and perhaps have been on top. The scoundrel didn't come Sunday night. He was at the train and I supposed he had a ticket. After I'd bought mine he said he wouldn't go. I felt like hitting him. Our grand superintendent had all the supply men in town form a combination and tie up our pile of ore. They both told me yesterday that they were sorry they did it. We have some reputation in the community anyway.
    If we connect now, inside of ten days we stand a show of getting our money

back. The men we have to deal with are very nice men. If the folks at home had been well so I could have been here, I am satisfied that my gift of conversation would have stood them off. But His Majesty has had a hand in this thing ever since we started. I am still hoping for the best though. We put too much confidence in Jerry's ability to raise money or we'd never have been in this condition.

There is a good chance of our not having to sell out our farm stock anyway. I may be able to continue business as Harry S. Truman yet. (You see I slept all night last night for the first time in several nights and I feel hopeful as usual.) I am hoping Mamma didn't stay up all night with Uncle Harrison anyway.

We are going to see the former owners this morning and if they treat us as well as the rest of the billholders have, we are going ahead and make something. I shall write you and tell what happened tomorrow. Send me a letter because if I don't get a wire from home there is no telling when I'll return. I must save something if I can.

I read your last letter every little while and it makes me feel better every time I do it, so send me another one.

Most sincerely,
Harry

Frank Blair, who appears below, came to the rescue during one of the mine's many near failures. He was cashier of the Bank of Belton and not merely a leading figure in the Masons but someone whom Truman instinctively trusted. Blair's sentiments, Truman once said, were to skin the rich and help the poor.

[Commerce, Okla.]

Dear Bess: May 26, 1916

Your good letter came today. I was sure glad to get it. I have been home since I wrote you, but had no chance to call up or see you. The T.C.H. Mining Co. is on its feet again. You would never guess who did it either. Mr. James Frank Blair. I just couldn't see the thing go clean to pieces without some effort to save it. Jerry quit us cold and I was so discouraged I didn't know what to do. (As you very well know.) Jerry assigned me his right title and interest in the concern and I went to Blair with my tale of woe. He told me I deserved to lose the whole shebang. Said I deserved a bump for going in with Culbertson. He knows him well. He finally said that if Culbertson assigned me his rights until I got my money back, he'd help. I called Culbertson and he agreed. I have paid all debts today, fired the sheriff, and we go right off the reel Monday. I tied up the superintendent's bill so he can't possibly collect before October. I am hoping he won't collect at all. If he was worth anything we'd sue him and get something back. But he's not and we have to hold what we owe him to get anything. He was the whole cause of our trouble. . . .

Will be home as soon as I can and tell you all about it. Send me another letter because it may be a week before I arrive.

Most sincerely,
Harry

[Commerce, Okla.]

Dear Bess: June 3, 1916

Your letter came day before yesterday. I tried to answer it the same day but I was so tired I couldn't write. I have been doing the heavy [work] over at the mill in order to save expense. I am hoping to have the thing going so I can go home this week. I doubt very much if I do though. The gas engine has been balking on us this week. An expert has been working on it seven days at $4.50 per day. I suppose it will go today. We made two tons of ore Friday and Saturday from the sand on top of the ground. The banker down here sent us a man who says we have a mine if we can only develop it. I am hoping to do that this month. This is some job. Jerry has never shown up yet. He is ashamed to come now I suppose. I bet if we make some money he'll be very much on the job.

I am sorry I missed the picnic. I had rather be plowing and going to picnics once in a while than doing what I am. I don't suppose I'd ever have been real pleased if I hadn't tried just once to get rich quickly. I tried to call you up twice since last Sunday, once in Joplin and once in Commerce. Had no luck either time. I had to run for a train in Joplin and the operator could not make the connection from Commerce.

The mills around us are running full tilt. They are piling the ore up in big piles. The price is down about $40 a ton lower than two months ago and everyone is holding for high prices. It is estimated that there is about $5,000,000 (I guess I have enough o's) in the bins. About 1/5,000 of that is ours. What a grand showing for three months work. I am crazy to be home now. The corn needs going over and I am sure it'll never get a good tending when I'm away.

Here's hoping I am present at the next picnic and that I see you not later than Sunday. Please, another letter. They sure look good. I have to go to work much as I hate it.

Most sincerely,
Harry

[Commerce, Okla.]

Dear Bess: June 10, 1916

Your letter came last night and I was most glad to get it. It is very lonesome down here doing nothing but work. I am engineer now. We are sinking some holes in the bottom of the mine trying to find out which way the best of the zinc leads. I am hoping to find a good mine before we are done. We spent the whole of last week trying to make a gas engine run. Next to an auto engine a gas one is the most pigheaded in the machinery line. We finally hit the right spot and got ours to go. Don't know what it was, we did so many things but it is shooting now at the rate of 190 times a minute. It is making about $50 a day at an expense of about eleven. We hope to be able to find the dirt to make the big mill go very shortly. I have to get up at 5:00 A.M. and come over here to the mill and light the gas under a boiler and then start two pumps and an air compressor besides that gas engine. I am at present a very greasy specimen of humanity. We use three or four different brands of oil on the different machines besides cup grease. I have some of each brand on my overalls and usually on my hands. I washed 'em before I started this letter but if I have to go fill a lubricator or run off something, you may get a sample before I'm done.

I am most awful sorry I'm not present to meet Mr. Bee but as you see I am in a fix I can't get loose from except by keeping my nose to the grindstone. I am hoping to see you tomorrow evening and if I do you can dispense with this letter. I have been mailing them the day they are written. This P.O. is on the blink. You know the P.M. took poison and we've had to do with whatever service we could get since. Jerry sent me the assignment I told you of but it's in the mail yet. Had a letter from him saying it was sent. I am crazy to be at the picnic today but it will be an impossibility. If it is raining up there as persistently as it is down here, I don't suppose you'll have it anyway. I am hoping to attend one soon anyway though if I have to get an aeroplane to do it. We have finally found an honest man to work for us and he has hopes of our making something.

The old guy we bought the shebang of was here yesterday and he told me to go ahead and endeavor to make something out of the thing and he wouldn't be hard on us. If the farm doesn't go to ruin while I'm doing it, I have hopes now of making something yet.

You'll probably get a phone call from Grandview tomorrow, I hope so anyway. If you don't get one you'll know I was not able to leave this unwholesome joint. I'll be lookin' for a letter anyway. The blooming boiler is about to blow off and I must run. (I'll lose a dollar's worth of steam if it does.) Here's hoping to see you Sunday.

Most sincerely,
Harry

[Commerce, Okla.]

Dear Bess: June 24, 1916

I arrived in town this morning at 5:00 A.M. on the Meteor from K.C. The corn plowing was so badly needed that I stuck by it until 7:00 P.M. and then had Jimmy drive me to Dodson so I could get the Frisco at 11:30 P.M. I got down there at ten-thirty and went right to bed but didn't sleep any only by jerks. Having had some three hours sleep the night before, I am a live bird tonight.

The mine is going to be a dinger I guess if I can believe the ground boss and I guess I can. It is not as fine as Hughes told me but the boss says we can probably make thirty tons of ore a week after next week, which is pretty good at $80 a ton. The expense will be about $700 or $800. I am hoping it is that good. I am busier than a cranberry merchant in the summertime now, hiring men and making other kinds of expenses. If we blow up this time it sure will scatter the remains far and wide. I am forgetting that a blowup (not out) is possible. We are supposed to have enough dirt in sight to make two hundred tons of ore so I can get my money and interest back anyway and enough surplus to invest in some platinum ware. They say it is bad luck to buy that kind of ring on time or with borrowed money, hence my long wait about getting it. I am not superstitious about most things but I am certainly not going to fly in the faces of the fates in this case if I can help it. I believe they are beginning to weave me a more kindly brand of luck from this [point] out anyway.

Would you care to help run this shebang if it does win as greatly as they say it will? You can have my share of it except enough to pay Mamma out of debt and give her a house if you'll take me along with it and help me run it. I know that's some promise but I'm hoping you wouldn't let it stand in the way of an acceptance. I shall be crazy to hear from you.

Most sincerely,
Harry

Through all of the mine's vicissitudes Bess supported Truman's efforts, as the following letter indicates.

Dear Bess: [Grandview, June 29, 1916]
You'll not recognize the letter I know when it comes in a civilized envelope written with black ink. The mine took another balky spell and has absolutely refused to go to date. I was on the point of making a strike again yesterday when Mary wired me that the boys had quit. Jimmy got so very smart to her that she had to fire him and the other boy quit. I suppose they were just tired and saw a large job coming on therefore they left. I had to drop the mine at once and run for the train. Mr. Hughes is in bed with a slight fever and I'm thinking things will go hang down at Commerce. I'm not going to worry over it. It is necessary to save wheat, oats, and clover now. I am going to do it. There are two men and a boy helping me today. It will take me the rest of the week to catch up. Farm work sure is a pleasure beside a mine. I'm for the rube stunt every time.

You perhaps can guess why I'm feeling so elated and all that even if the mine does go hang. Your last letter was enough to make me see rainbows in the darkest kind of sky. I have another thing to be glad for too. That uncle of mine has disposed of his property. I don't know how but he had Mr. Blair do it and from what he said I'm sure it's right. He's been improving ever since he did it too. Seems to be something off his mind.

I am hoping to hear that the mine didn't go smash this week and I'm going to work so hard I can't worry about it. I am going to see you Sunday too if I have to walk over, which I won't.

Most sincerely,
Harry

Dear Bess: [Hotel Muehlebach, Kansas City, July 13, 1916]
I have been trying for the last hour to call you (but I guess you are down in the yard or out riding). I received a wire from Oklahoma this morning saying, "Come at once prospect is good." I hope it is. I am on my way and expected to get to see you this evening.

I shall get back to Kansas City at about nine-thirty Saturday evening and if you don't mind will call you up. I am counting on Warrensburg you see. Lizzy is at Stafford's having her stopping machinery arranged.

If your courage doesn't run then we can fall back on mine. That is I think mine will go that far again. I do wish I could have seen you this evening. My train leaves somewhere around ten o'clock. Do you suppose His Majesty has decided to take his finger out of my affairs at last? The farm is going beautifully. I got all the wheat, oats, and hay saved in grand style and my cow prospect was never better. If the mine only will turn out then—but it's really too great to contemplate. See you Saturday night or Sunday.

Harry

[Commerce, Okla.]

Dear Bess: July 25, 1916

You probably have cut me from your list by this time but I'll tell you what I've done and maybe you'll put me back again.

You know I've got some politics mixed up in my affairs along with mines and a farm. On Friday I was at Horseshoe Lake with about seven Grandview citizens of voting age and Mary. The first part of the week I threshed every day except Monday afternoon. On Saturday the gink who is running with me [for township committeeman] called up and said he wanted to see the south part of the township. I went after him and took him around from Dodson to Dallas by way of Holmes Park, Hickman Mills, Grandview, and Martin City. I was supposed to get home by six o'clock but it was half past ten and there was a wire from Commerce saying to come at once or the mine would shut down. Old man Hughes gets scared stiff every time I leave. I got up on Sunday at 4:00 A.M. and drove Lizzie down here. It was some drive—192 miles and about 92 of them are as rough as a road can be. There are four river bottoms to cross and they are full of chuck holes and everything else. Jerry came down with me and then went home at midnight Sunday night. Wasn't that some stunt for him to pull off? I was mad enough to break his head. The mine was in a dickens of a shape. Mr. Hughes was fussing with the ground boss and had a couple of old nuts on the mill that don't know how to run a coffee mill. I fired them both and got the boss in a good humor. He's found us a real mine. If the people we bought off don't foreclose on us for a couple of months, I'll have all my money back and more besides. We'll make five tons of ore tomorrow. It is going up every day. I am very much encouraged even if I have got $5,500 due and unpaid today. I'm going to make the thing run for one week if I bust everyone inside. I'm only about $5,000 behind the board now and a couple of thousand more won't make much difference in the final settlement.

I hope you'll send me a letter, though I'll admit I don't deserve one. I didn't intend to leave for here until Monday if I hadn't got the wire. There would have been no mine if I'd waited. It looks as if I'd have to stay for some time now. Please send me a letter and when you are dissatisfied because I didn't phone you

Saturday just remember that if this old mine does make good, you'll have a chance to see me all day everyday if you want to.

Sincerely,
Harry

[Commerce, Okla.]
Dear Bess: July 28, 1916

Your letter came yesterday evening. I was certainly glad to get it, even if it was a short one. I had written you Tuesday morning but I guess you hadn't received it yet. Your news was sure exciting. Made me awful homesick. My prospective building operations seem to get farther away instead of closer up. The bloomin' mine had had one crazy spell since I've been here. Mr. Hughes was on the point of shutting up shop and going home when I got here. We have been running since Tuesday and have made about six tons of ore. We ought to have made that much every day. The ground boss has been telling us every day we'd certainly come ahead the next day. I am going to keep trying to make it because it means everything or nothing to me. If it does fail I'll be so far behind the board I'll have to take a flyer in wheat or something to ever catch up.

I am so crazy to make things go I can hardly stand it. I had expected by this time to have all my obligations met and more besides. I am still hoping to win yet. You have probably gotten tired reading my troubles but I always feel like telling you just how I'm situated and what I expect to do.

The car came through without any trouble to speak of. One hind tire came off and spoiled a brand new tube (rear tire? I've been in Oklahomy so long I talk like 'em—be saying you 'ens and us 'ens pretty soon). It happened just outside of Butler. The engine didn't miss a shot the whole way. You certainly deserved to get stuck about one mile north of Grandview when you came to Camp Shawnee and didn't let me know. I certainly wish you'd have broken down somewhere out there. Maybe you'd have called me then and I could have seen you or perhaps towed you in with Lizzie.

I wish I had the Kodak. There are some more pictures of this awful town I'd like to have. I took the whole Throop family (people I board with) and went to the Neosho River the other evening. We met a threshing machine and I ran off in the ditch. Had to unload to get out. The roads down here are so rough that shock absorbers would wear out in one day. There are five Throop kids and the old man and old lady. She's fat but good. He's redhead and half cross-eyed but he's stuck to us through thick and thin. If the T.C.H. Co. makes good I'm going to give him some stock. The dog ran along behind the other evening and we had to pick him up to keep him from running himself to death. You see I had a load when the dog got aboard.

There isn't any telling when I'll be home. I'm going to make this thing go or bust it one. If I make it go I'll come home in a new car and we'll beat May and George to it yet. If I don't make [it] I'm not thinking of how I'll come home. Wish heavy for me to win.

Mrs. Hughes is sick. I have to go get her some medicine and I'll send this off so you'll get it tomorrow. Write me a *long* letter please.

Most sincerely,
Harry

[Commerce, Okla.]
Dear Bess: July 30, 1916

Your letter came last night. I had already started you a second one telling you all that had happened. I am most awful glad you were not very angry with me. About those auto races—I'll have to admit that I forgot them entirely. I had them set for yesterday instead of last Saturday. I guess my memory is failing. I dreamed of you last night. Thought we were going down a grand street in some very big city. Evidently were trying to find somewhere to eat when I discovered that I had no hat and then I woke up. I hope to see that place in that manner some day with a hat on.

The mine is picking up. It may amount to something. Took all the Throops and went to the ball game this afternoon. It was a good one even if Commerce did get beaten. Score was 2 to 1. Talk about hot. It's about 111 degrees in the shade all the time down here. We also have a very active brand of mosquitoes. They work all night every night. The flies work in daytime. Mrs. Hughes has had some kind of fever for the last two days. She insists that it's malaria but I doubt it. I never felt better nor had less in my life. Still I'm hoping the last complaint will be remedied before long. Jack and lead are still worth enough to make lots of money. There is one mill down here that has over $100,000 worth of ore piled up. The Royalty Co. refuses to sell for less than $100 a ton. This mill belongs to them. They have six mills and all of them have big piles of ore. I suppose about a quarter million dollars would about cover what they have piled up. There are four men in the company, each worth a couple of millions. Ten years ago they couldn't pay grocery bills. The president now owns an airship factory and a Packard 12 roadster. Hope to see you next Sunday. I suppose I'll get beaten for committeeman. I can't be there to work on election day. I'm glad Frank got so much for the wheat. Wish I'd had 6,000 instead of 600 bushels. I wasn't drunk when I wrote those last lines. It got dark and I couldn't find a match.

I do wish I was home tonight so I could go to Independence. It seems like a part of His Majesty's own domain down here tonight—and that Sunday night too. There are a couple of mills running over east here that could very well be mistaken for his coal shovelers from the noise they make. As for heat we have that in sufficient quantities, although we had a rain and a cyclone Friday. It blew Miami into a cocked hat. Tore up about one hundred trees, smashed plate glass, and upset some Fords. Nobody was hurt. It missed Commerce. If I make a grand strike in the mine this week I'm going to wire you. So don't think I'm killed if you get one. We are expecting to set the world on fire or fail one right soon. I

hope for the best. Be sure and send me a letter. Wish I could see you this evening
—and every evening.

Sincerely,
Harry

*The would-be miner's mother was every bit as supportive as was Bess. Here
Truman praises one to the other.*

[Commerce, Okla.]
Dear Bess: August 4, 1916
    I am still working in July [he had started the date with *J*] you see. Bill day
comes on the tenth and I don't want it to arrive. If I could make the clock run
backwards for about two weeks, I'd be glad to have it that way.
    You didn't get any wire because there was no reason to send it. There is no
bonanza as yet. We are still hoping and clinging by our fingertips. The pond
broke loose last Sunday and we lost all our precious water. It has taken us all week
to catch up. We have made about ten tons of ore instead of thirty or forty as
I expected the first of the week. I am still hoping for better luck but I'm not so
sure it will come. I am not going to go dingy over the thing though. If the thing
fails I'll go completely and entirely to the wall. Mamma tells me that that won't
hurt me if I'll keep right on pulling. That's what I intend doing. Anyway it hasn't
happened yet. Lots of things can take place in seven days and I have that many
until the tenth. Your letter was as good as a strike in the mine. I've felt a lot better
ever since it arrived. I hope George and May find a plan that meets all the
requirements. You'll have to instruct me as to a wedding present. I am still hoping
to buy a joint one, but the prospect is not so bright today as it was when I wrote
before. Mary thinks that I was beaten in my political dabbling. It will do me good
to get my drubbings one at a time. I have been told that reverses make a man
or a mouse. We'll soon see. Some of my best friends threw me over because I
wasn't present election day. They thought I ran away on purpose. They'll find
out differently when I go home with enough to purchase the townsighte (how
do you spell it?) [town site] or without enough even to ride the rods; won't they?
Your good wishes are going to make me win if redoubled efforts count for
anything. I won't be home Sunday I'm sorry to say because I must go to Carthage
to see a prospective buyer. Keep wishing me luck because it means everything
to me. Will write again tomorrow.

Sincerely,
Harry

[Commerce, Okla.]
Dear Bess: August 5, 1916
    I wrote you yesterday and promised to write again today. Mr. Hughes got
a wire from home yesterday evening that his barn had burned, hay, oats and all.
He and Mrs. Hughes had to go home and see about it so I am in full charge.

I don't seem to be in charge of much. The mine all but shut blind last night. So I shall probably have to ride the rods home instead of the new car. I'm going to give her one more week and then take the consequences. If Jerry Culbertson would get busy and raise some money, we could go ahead yet, but I doubt if he'll ever take any more interest in the thing now. I may go into the auto business down here if I can make the old mine produce even a reasonable amount. There is no Ford agency here. One would pay about $5,000 a year. They sell about two hundred cars every year here, besides supplies and tires.

I have only gone in the hole on this hole about $11,000. Do you suppose I'll ever catch up? I think I will. Uncle Harry will probably cut me off his will but that can't be helped. If you still have faith in my poor judgment I can still win. You know a man's judgment is good or bad accordingly as he wins or loses on a proposition. It seems to me that it's one big guess and the fellow who guesses right is the man of good judgment. I am going to keep guessing. Mamma says that Grandpa Young was cleaned out three times that she can remember but he came up every time with something else. This is only once for me, but it's a once that I surely hate to contemplate. I am still hoping the next round of shots will make us a Blue Goose. There's nothing equals this business for making Micawbers of men. They really and truly expect something to turn up. Please send me another good letter right away. I make two trips a day to the P.O. looking for your letters.

Most sincerely,
Harry

[Commerce, Okla.]

Dear Bess: August 19, 1916

Your prophecy about my coming home is going to be correct. I can't come. We are still hanging on by our eyebrows. I am not certain for just how long. There is only an overdraft at the bank and I have made it about $330 bigger today by the payroll. If that good-natured banker refuses to pay, I shall probably get thrown into the shaft. I am hoping he'll pay. There is good prospect in the ground, even better than I expected to see. It would most certainly be awful if somebody else gets this hoodooed hole and makes a million out of it. . . .

You probably get awful tired reading my continual babble on this hole called mine but I've had considerable worry and much to think of concerning the thing and I've got to tell you about it. Just think what a win would mean. All my debts paid (something that no one of the name ever accomplished), a city home, a country home, some automobiles and flying machines—and who knows but maybe a yat (yacht? what?), and you to boss the whole layout. I'd be cruising in Greenland waters today under those circumstances, for it's 120 degrees in the shade down here and there is no shade.

I'm feeling better than I was when I started this because I've handed out some checks and the bearers haven't come to pitch me in the hole, so I guess the banker's going to bust the National Bank Act to save my hair. He's some banker sure. I do wish I could borrow one of Mr. Robinson's flying machines and come to your city tomorrow but I can't. Besides, I couldn't drive it if I could get it but I'd sure try. Please send me a letter of consolation. The last one you sent me down here was worth seven trips after it instead of one. Here's wishing you a nice, cool pleasant Sunday *without* any gentleman callers.

Sincerely,
Harry

[Commerce, Okla.]
Dear Bess: August 26, 1916

Your very good letter came day before yesterday in the morning but I have been so hard pushed trying to raise this week's payroll that I couldn't write. I succeeded in doing it, although I hope I never have such another time doing it. The banker had broken the National Bank Act by paying me out last week and it looked as if he'd either have to bust it wide open or turn me down today. There is a lead buyer here who has a heart, and he happens to be a friend of my ground boss and also of the banker. They succeeded in having him advance me a payroll on the expectation that I would get out some lead by fourteen days hence. He wasn't my last resort though by any means because Old Man Bigham had already promised to let me have it if I failed to make connection. Everyone says he's a hoss thief and a pussyfoot but I wish I knew some more of that kind. You know he's already paid my gas bill to save me $35. He may have an ax to grind but I can't find it. If he has, I'll certainly try to grind it.

The mine is a mine now sure enough if my eyebrows don't give way before it pays out. Every shot makes things come better. More lead and more jack every shot.

The old gink I went to see Tuesday was as lenient as he could be. He told me to go right ahead and do what I could to run because he is for me. I shall get to the point after a while when I can ask Morgan, himself, for a loan and not even think I'll get a refusal. If the mine could only be persuaded by conversation to yield something, I guess I'd surely get a bonanza. It is totally deaf to all my entreaties so far but I am still hoping for the best.

I am the sole boss and proprietor on the job now. Hughes hasn't returned or written me. If the thing goes, I suppose I'll have plenty help to run it. Perhaps I won't need it. I am surely sorry to hear that your mother is sick and I am hoping that she is well by this time. The fair I know is fine. I hate to miss it but it can't be helped. Do you suppose I'll ever get to come over every Sunday and twice a week? It seems a year since I saw you. Mr. Hughes will surely come so I can get home for Labor Day. I shall certainly scalp him if he doesn't. I hope you are having a good time entertaining Walter. Please send me a letter quickly because I spend a half-hour daily going to the P.O. and it's some disappointment when your letter fails.

Hope to see you very soon.

Most sincerely,
Harry

Uncle Harrison's death does not receive much attention in Truman's letters, but here he mentions it in passing. To his surprise, the older man had left him part of the farm—creating a modest rise in Truman's finances.

[Commerce, Okla.]
Dear Bess;   August 29, 1916

Your letter came yesterday and I was sure pleased to get it. It seems like ten years since I was at Independence. Mr. Hughes is evidently paying me back for the three weeks I spent at home. I wish I'd stayed there permanently and let the whole shebang go to grass then. We are still getting some good lead and could make money if His Majesty would only let the machinery alone. One of the boilers went down yesterday and will cost about a hundred dollars good money to fix. It not only costs to fix but knocks us out of two days' run, which is a dead loss. We made two tons of lead and two of jack on Monday and would have done as well today.

Your dog is growing right along and I hope to have him at home very soon. If I can only succeed in getting Hughes down here, I'll most certainly even up with him. I shall probably have war with the Throop kids when I go to take that greyhound away from here. They think he is the finest thing ever. He is as ugly as a bulldog. If he ever grows to his feet, he can outrun a locomotive or Locomobile either. He is very thin now but I'll have him fattened up before I take him home. Greyhounds are supposed to be thin though, and he may be only running true to type, because I am certain he gets enough to eat.

I can't write you a very good letter this time. They are always poor but this one will be worse than usual because I've got the dumps and am homesick and can't think well—if I ever do. This may be great for experience but it's mighty hard on my feelings. I'd not care if the mine would only pan. But if it doesn't, I'll simply have to suffer from a grand chorus of "I told you so." That wouldn't bother me so very badly if I'd only not gone and lost so much money. I'd sure have been right if I'd stayed at home and worked the farm this time. But how did I know Uncle Harry wouldn't live twenty years? And that he'd lease us what he had when he did die. I'd done given up hope in that direction. The unexpected happened and now I'm all balled up and have gotten Mamma in the same fix. I am going to find a way out though if it takes the hide off both my hands to do it. The worst is surely here now and things will surely brighten up directly. I must quit this, it's not nice to tell your troubles, is it? It makes a person feel good though if he can get a little sympathy, and I'm sure I'll get it. I am going to come home for that Labor Day picnic if the whole thing blows up here.

I do hope your mother is well by this time. I am sorry that we didn't have a picnic and some cookies for the fair, too. Maybe we can do better next time. Please send me another letter quickly.

Most sincerely,
Harry

Dear Bess:

[Commerce, Okla.]
September 7, 1916

Your note came today. I have been thinking you didn't get my last Saturday's special; now I know it. I have been holding a post mortem over the mine; closed it down yesterday after paying out the last cent I've got. There's nothing like going entirely busted while you're at it. Hughes has never arrived and of course Culbertson hasn't. We are at the point of making good. Made five tons of lead Monday and Tuesday, but I couldn't raise another payroll on it. It is evidently best to close the thing up and take a new start anyway. I've put up all the money and would only get one-third, so if the thing goes up I can perhaps take a new start and win by myself. The banker who has been so good to me down here is in bed sick because his assistant cashier and his wife were killed Sunday in an auto accident. I went to see him today and he told me he still had confidence in me and thought I'd make a go of the thing yet.

I am most awful sorry I wasn't present Monday. I spent the day in a most homesick manner. I simply couldn't run away when things are going to wreck, because they'd all say I was a quitter and couldn't stand the gaff. I have failed to pay this week's payroll up to Tuesday and am still alive. I hope to have enough to pay by Saturday. I hope to come home in a very short time but I can't leave until I've satisfied everyone I owe down here that I'm not trying to beat anyone out of his money. I am getting gray-headed doing it but having pretty good success.

I hope you'll get this letter and send me one right away. I have been feeling very badly because I hadn't heard from you. I was going to send you another letter today anyway. I am crazy to see you and hope to very soon.

Most sincerely,
Harry

Even as the lead and zinc mine was failing, Truman launched into another venture—the oil business. By November 16, 1916, he had gotten himself an office in Kansas City and a fancy letterhead.

[Kansas City, Mo.]

Dear Bess: November 16, 1916

As you can see, I am fulfilling my promise to send you a letter from the office of the above company [Morgan & Company, Oil Investments].

I am simply on needle points today waiting for a wire from Morgan. I have one from him saying that he had wired New York for confirmation of the $300,000 Healdton deal we are on, and that he is expecting the confirmation. I have a long-distance call in for him at Tulsa, but have been unable to get him for the last hour. I suppose he is out showing old man Walker the $3,500,000 Cushing property. Should he succeed in selling that, I shall simply float away on air. People seem to think our promotion project has some merit, too, or else they are convinced by Culbertson's salesmanship. We got $225 yesterday and sixty so far today. If it comes at the rate of $50 per day, we can pay rent anyway if we never drill a well.

If Morgan makes his sale, we shall be so far on easy street that I can come out strong for the oil business. Nearly every person I have talked with lately is interested in some kind of an oil deal. I nearly bust to tell what kind of one I'm in and then don't.

I have had a small war with the Standard in the last two days. They are putting down a pipeline across us and I gave them orders not to come in until they'd paid crop damage. They came anyway and I told the hired man to tell 'em we'd have shotguns on deck this morning and the contractor refused to go to work. They had an adjuster out there in a hurry but I'm in town. He's coming to see me. I am hoping to get enough out of him to buy some more gasoline for Lizzie, then I'll bring your dog home. I have been calling him Don Juan of Austria, but you can name him Tige [sic] or Caesar or any other that you wish if you consider the first not suitable. If you are an English sympathizer you would hardly call him after anything Austrian, even if Don Juan was a Spanish Grandee. You might call him Kitchen (short for Kitchener). You could even name him Willy [after William Jennings Bryan], and be Democratically right. Villa would be a grand name. As I said before, you use your own judgment. Hope to see you Sunday, and be so full of oil that I'll float.

Sincerely,
Harry

[Kansas City, Mo.]

Dear Bess: January 23, 1917

It is now 8:30 P.M. and I haven't been to supper yet. We sold 636 shares and collected $1,592.50 today. I have just finished getting out yesterday's receipts. We got about $800 yesterday. The refinery is bought and so is another 200-acre lease adjoining it with some nine producing wells. Your shares now have 1,500 acres of deeded land and 1,300 acres of leases at Chanute, besides a 200-acre lease in Allen County and a contract for 5,000 acres in Sumner County, Kansas, and 5,000 acres in Garfield County, Oklahoma. The money is coming in by the basketful and it looks as if the Atlas Okla. Lands Syndicate should be in the pictures before many days. I'm afraid to be glad for fear something will drop. I was just as sanguine over a certain hole in the ground location at Commerce, Oklahoma. If this venture blows, I'll know I'm hoodooed. I don't want to be a bloated plutocrat, but I would like very much to have enough to tell my creditors to take my liabilities off the books and then have something left over. As old man Holmes would say, just enough for a country place, a machine or two, and a couple of new dresses a year for the lady. I'm going partners within it all. That's not an extravagant wish, is it? If some hard knocks and a little overwork will accomplish it, I hope to win. There's one thing, my mother is for me, first, last, and all the time—and I know you are. Why shouldn't I win? Such backing should overturn the worst of hoodoos, I think.

Hope to be able to call you and say we're over the rocks very soon. Here's wishing you all the happiness on earth and hoping to share it.

Sincerely,
Harry

[Westgate Hotel, Kansas City, Mo., May 27, 1917]

Dear Bess: Sunday night

The train was late. It didn't arrive until ten-fifteen. Should have been in at nine. I didn't call up because I know you don't appreciate midnight calls. This letter should have reached you at ten o'clock this morning but the one I had written sounded so badly that I didn't send it. In fact it was both blue and mushy. They don't go well together or singly. This one may be as bad before I'm through. If it is, I won't send it either. I have written you dozens of epistles you have never seen. Whenever I'm particularly happy, or particularly the opposite, an insane desire to tell you about it possesses me and I write you about it. Generally I'm never half so badly, or so well, off as I at first thought, and you are therefore not worried with knowing what a very erratic and unstable person I am.

You know, I have been badly disappointed today. That dad-blasted mine has been sold twice and has come back to me both times because the brother of the man who owns the land the thing is on happens to own the adjoining mill and wants my mine to run through it. (Can you comprehend that Dutch statement?) There is a Bertha M. Clay plot connected with the thing. The men from whom the magnificent Mr. Culbertson made his purchase are bitter enemies of the Commerce Mining & Royalty Co., the richest outfit in the Oklahoma mining district. The Royalty Co. owns the land. The people we bought from owned the lease. Now the lease is going to quit very shortly and I had been led to believe that I could get another if the mill were running. I went to see the president of the Royalty Co. yesterday and he told me that he was of the opinion that he'd let his brother run the dirt from that mine through his mill, which is the adjoining one to mine and called the Lost Trail. My sale fell down because he said that, hence my happy feeling this evening. I still hope to arrange another lease because the former Grandview banker whom I never cared for very much is going to work for the Royalty Co. in the capacity of cashier of their new bank. I hope to be able to hand him a line of conversation that will cause him to make Mr. Robinson see me on this lease. (Robinson is the Royalty Co.'s president.) Maybe he can;

Harry Truman, secretary-treasurer of Morgan & Company, Oil Investments, 1917. *Harry S. Truman Library*

maybe he won't. If not then it's the sheriff for the mine, unless I can ring in our friend J. S. from Ardmore. He hates mines and at present seems to love oil. Hope he stays that way except in one instance.

I seem to have a grand and admirable ability for calling tails when heads come up. My luck should surely change. Sometime I should win. I have tried to stick. Worked, really did, like thunder for ten years to get that old farm in line for some big production. Have it in shape and have had a crop failure every year. Thought I'd change my luck, got a mine, and see what I did get. Tried again in the other long chance, oil. Still have high hopes on that, but then I'm naturally a hopeful, happy person; one of the "Books in brooks, Tongues in trees, and Good in everything" sort of guy. Most men are liars—I'm one myself on occation (I'm not sure but that's sion)—and they all are where there's money in it. I was very, very impressionable when I was a kid and I believed all the Sunday school books and idealist dope we were taught and it's taken me twenty-odd years to find that Mark is right when he says that the boy who stole the jam and lied about it and killed the cat and sassed his ma, grew up and became a highly honored citizen and was sent to Congress, is absolutely right. The poor gink who stands around and waits for someone to find out his real worth just naturally continues to stand, but the gink who toots his horn and tells 'em how good he is makes 'em believe it when they know he's a bluff and would steal from his grandma.

I don't believe that. I'm just feeling that way now. If I can't win straight, I'll continue to lose. I'm the luckiest guy in the world to have you to love and to know that when I've arrived at a sensible solution of these direful financial difficulties I've gotten into, that I'll have the finest, best-looking, and all the other adjectives in the superlative girl in the world to make the happiest home in the world with. Now isn't that a real heaven on earth to contemplate? I think it is and I know I'll have just that in the not far off future, unless it is necessary for me to get myself shot in this war—and then I'll still find you somewhere. I dreamt that you and I were living in Rome when togas were the fashion. I am always dreaming of you. I'm never anywhere in a dream or out of it that I don't imagine you there, too. Last night I thought I was in an airplane in France. I fell about 17,000 feet and didn't get much hurt and I was idiot enough to weep because I couldn't see you in the hospital. It seemed that you were outside and they wouldn't let you in. Some dream, what? (I had a cheese omelet for supper.) I'm going to eat one every night.

You'll sure enough be bored when you get this if you do. But I just had to have a conversation with you. I can never say what I feel when I see you and anyway when a hardheaded American citizen gets to spouting his heart actions in Laura Jean Libby periods he just simply feels like an idiot and I do, but I mean all I've said about you and I'll keep hoping that J. S. Mullen stays by us till we get a gusher—and I can really show you how much I care.

Hope to see you right soon. Will have to go home tomorrow night to get a new set of collars, etc., as my grip has all second-handed ones. Can I come over Tuesday night? Just remember how crazy I am about you and forget all the rest.

Most sincerely,
Harry

II

YOU'RE IN THE ARMY NOW

✻ ✻ ✻

WHEN HARRY TRUMAN joined the army in 1917, becoming one of the 4.5 million Americans who fought in World War I, he discovered a camaraderie that had been impossible on the farm. The loneliness of work with horses and mules gave way to incessant, close contact with men of the regiment. In this setting his remarkable ability to lead flourished, and the experience was to change the entire complexion of his life.

Truman had had a small taste of the military in his twenties as a member of the Missouri national guard. It had been a lark. He may even have enjoyed the fuss Grandmother Young raised when, decked out in a blue uniform with red stripes down the trouser legs, red piping on the cuffs, and a red *fourragère* over the shoulder, he showed himself off at the farm. His grandmother, however, only remembered how Yankee raiders had killed four hundred of her hogs. "Harry," she said, "this is the first time since 1863 that a blue uniform has been in this house. Don't bring it here again." But Harry enjoyed the guard and rose from private to corporal. When President Wilson called up the troops in 1916 to protect south Texas towns against the depredations of Pancho Villa, Truman ardently wished to go. But that was the year he tried to run the Commerce mine as well as the farm, and he could not spare the time. In 1917 he was managing his oil business when the call to arms came; this time he opted for patriotism and what probably seemed the larger adventure.

Missouri's national guard expanded, and Batteries B and C, the field artillery units of Kansas City and Independence, became a regiment. As a former member of Battery B, Truman helped them sign up recruits. He proved so effective that, to his surprise, he was elected first lieutenant. (The election of officers was common in the Civil War and lasted until the federalizing of national guard units in 1917.) After entraining for Camp Doniphan, a tent cantonment set up within Fort Sill near Lawton, Oklahoma, the Kansas City and Independence field artillery regiment was taken into federal service in August; Truman and other officers carefully removed the gold insignia on their shirt collars, exchanging "Mo." for "U.S."

The reasons for U.S. entry in the war against Germany were far more complex than Truman and most of his army friends understood. Although they sensed the reactionary nature of the German government under Kaiser Wilhelm II, they did not linger over political nuance. Their individual decisions were based on patriotism—an outlook that may seem today emotional and antiquated. The typical rhapsodies against the Kaiser and Germandom show up infrequently in Truman's letters, for the routine of army life was foremost in his mind—along with the exhilaration of leadership as he rode at the head of a column of 194 men and officers. He had become captain of Battery D, 129th Field Artillery in July 1918. When the war ended, Truman spent month after month in wintery France, ensconced in a village with manure piles in front of each house, bedeviled by regular army officers who wanted him and his men to feed the Battery horses oatmeal, not oats, and to spend the rest of their time currying the horses, oiling harness, and having foolish inspections. Truman wished—as did most American Expeditionary Force members after the war—that "Woodie" would quit his "galivanting" and go home. Europeans, they now felt, could impose upon themselves whatever boundaries and governments suited their fancy. Truman even said he hoped the Czechoslovaks would put themselves under the King of the Lollipops if they wanted to. Eventually, however, he received permission to go home, which meant addressing the project that was most important to him— marrying Bess.

The war letters show little about the home front of 1917–1918, save occasional references to buying bonds. Truman's French francs came flooding in, but the supply was depleted so rapidly—partly because of expenses, partly through loans to his impecunious men—that he had no money to buy bonds. Bess seems to have been a prime mover in organizing the women's auxiliary of the 129th Field Artillery, which among other good deeds financed Christmas dinners in 1918 for the regiment. For Truman, the home front meant only his concern for Bess and her family (Fred Wallace was suffering through college at Columbia, Missouri; Grandfather Gates sickened and died; Mother Wallace's health was unsteady). In the autumn of 1918, coincident with the war's last weeks, a dreadful influenza epidemic had spread, from its perhaps Spanish origin, throughout Western Europe and thence to the United States. Within two or three months it caused perhaps ten times as many American deaths as did World War I itself. Harry's fear for Bess's life was justified.

Truman's duties as first lieutenant—and after promotion, captain—appear in the letters, and in only one particular did they vary from those of other officers. In 1917 and the first months of 1918, prior to going overseas in April, Truman ran the army canteen with the assistance of Sergeant Eddie Jacobson. He had known Eddie since shortly after the turn of the century, when they met while working in the bank. It was a natural combination; Truman kept the books, and Eddie bought the merchandise. Eddie had been a men's furnishings buyer in civilian life and knew about purchases in large lots. Together the captain and sergeant bought all the items the army did not furnish, including large quantities of a soft drink called Puritan; theirs was the best-run canteen at Doniphan. With the disregard for individual inclinations that marked the army of that time, Truman and Jacobson arranged for a levy of two dollars from each man in the regiment (no one would dare make such demands today). With it they paid for stock bought in Oklahoma City and elsewhere. After a proper mark-up they took precautions with their military help by employing a cash register; they also kept a close watch on their assistants among the so-called enlisted men (the army persisted in this solecism for all soldiers, even draftees). The canteen paid ten thousand dollars in dividends to the original investors, which ensured Truman's promotion to captain.

As commander of Battery D, Truman took his unit through the war, bringing every one of his men back to Kansas City for their parade. The Battery was composed of "Wild Irishmen" (as Truman described them) and an admixture of Germans, such as Sergeant Eddie Meisburger, later a newspaperman in Kansas City. Actually the "boys" of the Battery were no unruly group of desperadoes but decent enough fellows who enjoyed wild drinking expeditions—partly to taunt their commanders. The Battery had broken three commanders before Truman took over. When the new captain stood before his men and told the sergeants to dismiss the Battery, they disrespectfully gave Captain Truman a Bronx cheer, and later that evening created bedlam by stampeding horses and knocking down tents after reveille. Next morning on the bulletin board was a list of those— mostly sergeants and corporals—who had been demoted to privates. As a Battery member recalled, the men suddenly realized their new commander was "a different breed of cat." Eventually they came to revere their captain, willing to do anything he asked, never to forget the man they called "Captain Harry." In the Harry S. Truman Library in Independence today are hundreds of letters between the men and Captain Harry over the many years after demobilization. To each the captain responded, usually with a typewritten letter and handwritten postscript. In the inaugural parade of January 1949 the men of Battery D, a middleaged group, balding, paunchy, with enormous pride, walked in single file on each side of President Truman's limousine, jauntily swinging canes. They turned out, what was left of them, for the President's funeral in 1972. And when Bess died in the autumn of 1982, a half-dozen of the boys, four of them in wheelchairs, came to Trinity Church and attended her burial in the courtyard plot of the library next to Captain Harry.

SIX

CAMP DONIPHAN, OKLAHOMA

In 1917 the Germans thought they had made all the calculations necessary to win World War I, even if it meant fighting against the United States. Strategists in Berlin were concerned about the uncertainty of winning on the Western Front. They decided to starve the British, whose grain came mostly from India, Australia, and Argentina, and to do so by submarine blockade. This would also close off American commerce and risk America's entrance into the war. Although not especially irritated with the Americans, the Germans did not admire them and considered the 100 million people in the New World not so much a nation as a hodgepodge of immigrants, nothing but—to use the term of ex-President Theodore Roosevelt, who worried about the depth of American patriotism—a group of hyphenates (Irish-American, German-American, Polish-American, and so forth). This potpourri of people, however, was inevitably affected and angered by the German submarine blockade of England.

The Wilson administration detested what was known as unrestricted submarine warfare, sinking of ships on sight, and took immediate offense, dismissing the German ambassador. The President waited to see whether the Germans would attack American merchantships. When they did, America retaliated. On the evening of April 2, 1917, President Wilson drove up Pennsylvania Avenue to the Capitol to ask Congress for a declaration of war. Troops stood at attention along the avenue as the beflagged presidential automobile swept up the hill. Street lights gleamed in a light spring rain, and the great dome of the Capitol shone with tragic splendor—floodlighting had just been installed. Wilson entered the House Chamber shortly after eight o'clock and gave the greatest speech of his life. His voice, intensity of expression, and the sheer eloquence of his words brought the audience on the floor and in the galleries to its feet. The country, too, cheered his words to the echo.

Then began the work of making American intervention effective. Could America raise and train an army and transport it to France before either the blockade or the French front decided the war? German leaders thought it impossible. In 1917 the U.S. Army was a minuscule force of 127,000 men and ranked seventeenth among the world's armies, behind that of Portugal. But quantitative *assessments were misleading, for in the United States the declaration of war released a demonic energy. Immediately the country adopted the draft. In the summer, huge cantonments went up, tent camps in the South, wooden barrack camps in the North, and beginning in autumn the draftees poured in. Meanwhile Truman's regiment entrained for Camp Doniphan, a tent camp in Oklahoma where, he wrote to Bess, the devil himself had a hand in the dreary arrangements.*

The amateur manner in which the new artillery regiment chose its officers is evident in the letter that follows.

[Densmore Hotel, Kansas City, Mo., July 14, 1917]
Dear Bess: 11 P.M., Saturday night
I have just finished the Regimental Banquet. It was a very solemn affair. Colonel Klemm made us a speech on our duties to God and country, and

Lieutenant Truman, summer 1917. *Harry S. Truman Library*

Lieutenant Colonel Elliott made one on the duties of an artillery officer. They were both from the shoulder and gave us something to think about. I had thought somewhat on both subjects, but not as far as these gentlemen went. According to them, we have placed ourselves in a position of placing the American Government above everything, even our lives. We are expected to do absolutely as we are told. Evidently, if we are ordered to go to Berlin, go we must—or be buried on the way.

I hope Russia saves us the trip, although I'd like to be present when Berlin falls. I tried to call you up this evening hoping that perhaps I'd get asked over to dinner tomorrow but I had only one chance at the phone and it failed. Maybe I can have better luck in the morning. I thought about you all evening, as I hope this letter proves. It was absolutely necessary for me to be present, as the colonel gave us our commissions from the governor. I am going to give you mine to keep because someday it may be very valuable to someone—at least I hope it will. I have felt like a dog all week. It seems that I have caused you to be unhappy by my overenthusiastic action in getting myself sent to war. Two big tears came in Mamma's eyes last night when I started off to Lodge in my soldier clothes. You are the two people in the world that I would rather see smile and that I like to cause to smile, and here I've gone done the opposite to both of you. Perhaps I can make you all happier for it. I'll try my best. Some way I seem to have an ability for getting myself into things by my overzealous conduct or anxiety to see them a success and do not seem to see the consequences to myself or others until the

First Lieutenant Truman of the Missouri National Guard, 1917. *Harry S. Truman Library*

conclusion comes. The Joplin mine is a shining example. My brilliant farming experience is another. Just the other night when Major Klemm gave his battalion a banquet for making him major, I arose in my zeal and fulness of heart and announced that I was for him for colonel; for Captain Elliott for lieutenant colonel; and for Captain Miles for the new major. Someone chased right off to Major Stayton and informed him of my brilliant speech and he ceased speaking to me. I didn't care, for I'd have informed how I stood if he'd asked me but I shouldn't have been so loud in my remarks. Since Stayton got beat all along the line there's no harm done because he can't reach me now, but if he'd won either high office I sure would have caught the dickens. Maybe a little war experience will tone me down and make a man of me. I hope it will anyway.

Bess, I'm dead crazy to ask you to marry me before I leave but I'm not going to because I don't think it would be right for me to ask you to tie yourself to a prospective cripple—or a sentiment. You, I know, would love me just as much, perhaps more, with one hand as with two, but I don't think I should cause you to do it. Besides, if the war ends happily and I can steal the Russian or German crown jewels, just think what a grand military wedding you can have, get a major general maybe.

If you don't marry me before I go, you may be sure that I'll be just as loyal to you as if you were my wife. I'll not try to exact any promises from you either if you want to go with any other guy, why all right, but I'll be as jealous as the mischief although not begrudging you the good time.

Bess, this is a crazy letter but I'm crazy about you and I can't say all these nutty things to you without making you weep. When you weep, I want to. If you'd looked right closely the other night, you might have discovered it, and a weeping man is an abomination unto the Lord. All I ask is love me always, and if I have to be shot I'll try and not have it in the back or before a stone wall, because I'm afraid not to do you honor.

Sincerely,
Harry

Caldwell, Kansas
September 27, 1917

Dear Bess:

We left town about seven-thirty and I had no chance to get to a phone. The colonel succeeded in getting us a Pullman but the steam refused to work and I almost froze. I heard Lee tell Hale that he reached up into the upper and got a blanket. Hale said that that was why he nearly froze—he was in the upper.

We are running along fine. The train is about to pull out and I'll have to mail this.

Will write you all about it tonight.

Sincerely,
Harry

Dear Bess: [Lawton, Okla., Sept. 29, 1917]

We are here and are almost fixed up. Except for nearly freezing last night I am all right. The train made good time all the way. C and E [Batteries] are just pulling in. Everyone seems to be happy and in good health. We have the choice of the whole post for a camp. Batteries and flying machines, balloons and doughboys are as thick as girls in petticoat lane. Major Stayton was over and paid *me* a call. He seemed as glad to see me as if I'd been his long lost brother, invited me to dinner, and instructed me to wear a white collar because their dinners are formal. Har! Har! I am going to put on a white collar and go down just the same. I can't see any reason for missing a good dinner. They won't allow a woman in this camp. The married men are at liberty to go to Lawton from 7:00 to 10:00 P.M.—from seven o'clock Saturday evening until six o'clock Sunday. There seems to be nothing to do for us but work from 5:00 A.M. to 10:00 P.M. and then nothing to do till morning.

It sure is a good thing I brought Lizzie. The cooks and carpenters and tentmakers have begun to run the wheels off of her already. I am going to have a special tent for her. The Battery pays for the freight, tires, etc., so I should worry.

I am looking for a letter, a picture, a cake, and *you.* Please don't forget the

Camp Doniphan, near Lawton, Oklahoma, and surrounding area.

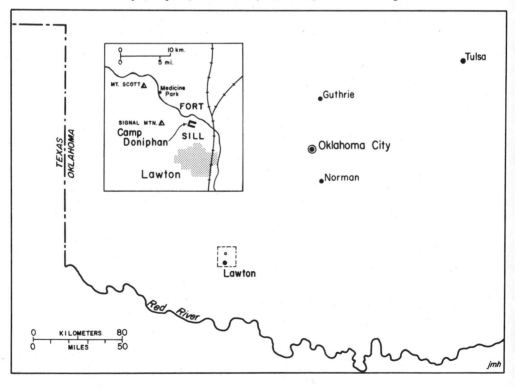

picture. Captain Pete's father-in-law died last night and he has to go home. This letter will go by him. I suppose I'll have to resurrect a grandmother or something in November. Pete is about ready to leave and I've got to quit. Wish I could see you now and every day.

Most sincerely,

Harry

What is now called the army post exchange (PX) did not exist in Truman's time. Each unit had to organize its own "canteen." Within days of reaching Doniphan, Truman was appointed regimental canteen officer. His was one of the few canteens that survived financially. In the following letter he describes some of the logistics involved in buying and selling.

[Lee-Huckins Hotel, Oklahoma City]

September 30, 1917

Dear Bess:

I am writing you from Oklahoma's capital tonight. The colonel sent me over here to buy some soda pop and shoestrings and several different other things, as the Walrus would say. . . . No one can leave the reservation, except to go to Lawton, without the brigadier's permission, but since Colonel Klemm is acting that capacity I had no trouble getting away for he sent me. The rest of the guys sure are green with envy. They want my brand of blarney but I can't transfer it. You should see the business I do. I am called Lieutenant Graball by Captain Carr. I took in $100 before dinner today, which makes about $450 in two days and a half, with nothing to sell but tobacco and Puritan and a few apples. I'd rather own that canteen than the trapshooters. We called a meeting of the Battery commanders today (we means *me* and the colonel) to make up a fund for the canteen from the Battery funds. Olney and Sermon and one or two others had so much to tell me that I finally got disgusted and asked Captain Jobes if he would lend me three thousand dollars on my John Henry to start one and he said, "You doggone bettya." I then told the outfit that I didn't want their blooming funds. The colonel wasn't present and when he learned what I'd done he simply reared up on his hind legs and threw a fit. Actually came down to my tent to tell me that he would issue an order making the outfits put up and ordered me not to borrow any money. So I didn't, but I'm going to get what I wanted out of those captains.

We are all as happy as can be expected for a bunch of house plants who have their wives and sweethearts to think of all the time. I am as brown as an Indian already.

They all want my horse. He's the best-looking plug on the job so far. If some nut offers me three hundred dollars, he's going to buy something. Drill starts in earnest tomorrow and no one is excused for any reason but a dislocated leg or neck. Both happen occasionally, but not as often as on streetcars and automobiles. Did I tell you that they simply dislocated all the principal inner workings of Lizzie? Busted the universal joint and some other contraption whose name I never heard all to pieces on the first trip out. I think they had her loaded to the guards [guard rails] with ice and potatoes and such other necessities as camp cooks need. I am hoping to see a letter as long as the moral law from you when I get back to camp. This one is almost that but I'm so crazy to see you that I have to say my say on paper. Nothin' but Indians in Lawton, and ugly ones at that, so you have no reason for thinking that anyone else but you ever enters my thoughts. You wouldn't have anyway if all the Lillian Russells and Pauline Fredericks in this Republic were down here for I don't like but one style of beauty and that's yours.

You should send me two letters the day you get this one for that last remark. Please get acquainted with Mrs. Klemm somehow so you can pay her a visit down here if it's only for twelve hours. I used all the stationery on this desk and I guess I'd better quit. Remember I'm the smiling kid when your letters come, so let 'em come often.

Yours always,
Harry

Dear Bess: [Lawton, Okla., Oct. 1, 1917]
You sure made me feel good this evening. Your letter came at a most opportune moment. I have put in a very hard day. The canteen opened up last night with cigars and tobacco. I bought twenty barrels of Puritan and sold it by noon today. Then bought fifty barrels more. My sales today amounted to nearly three hundred dollars. Not a bad day's business for a new man in a new town, what? It has nearly run me wild though getting started. The major doctor has my building and won't move. I have to use a tent. When he moves out I'll have a store that will make Emery, Bird's look like a jay-town store. . . .

Hope Frank will be blind the day of the exam. I'm sure crazy to see you.

Harry

Dear Bess: [Lawton, Okla., Oct. 3, 1917]
This is the banner day of my stay here so far. I got two letters from you. One of them was postmarked the twenty-ninth, and the other the second.

I was on the point of wiring you but was afraid it would cause you more worry than gladness and so I didn't do it. I slipped up a day on writing you but couldn't help it. You no doubt got my spasm from the Lee-Huckins written on Sunday night. Monday was my most strenuous day. I began having callers at eight-thirty, and from then on until twelve-thirty salesmen nearly ran me ragged. At two-thirty I got a car and began making the rounds, trying to buy some pop and get into connection with a laundry. Pop seems to be unobtainable. I could only get fifty cases and I wanted a carload. The laundries have formed a combination and advanced the prices 40 percent for our benefit. I told them that we would do our own washing. It would cost fifty-four cents to get a shirt, pants, and socks washed. Colonel told me to send the laundry to Kansas City. I am hiring a man here in the Battery to do mine. After I'd seen the laundries and wholesale house to the tune of seven dollars worth of auto hire, I had to run to catch my train back here and get into camp at 12:30 A.M. The canteen is a whiz. I did four hundred dollars worth of business today. It gets bigger all the time. Sold six hundred bottles of Puritan in two hours this evening. It takes six men to wait on the trade and keeps me phoning all the time to keep in supplies. I am writing this at 11:30 P.M. after my day is over. We had a grand time yesterday selecting our mounts from the issued horses. There were one thousand to pick from and we took turns on precedence. I am the seventh first lieutenant from the top and had a grand allotment to pick from. Picked a sorrel with a flax mane and tail. He proceeded to pile three men on the ground one after the other. I am going to get another horse to rest up on when he gets done with me. It was like a bunch of six-year-old kids turned loose in a candy shop when those officers were told to select their mounts. The chaplain was given first choice. He picked a beautiful black with one white hind foot. Everyone was offering him advice but I don't think he needed any. We all had lots of fun and I think everyone is happy with the choice he made.

I can't understand why you haven't had my letters. I have written one to you every day but yesterday. All our mail goes to Lawton then comes over here, and I suppose they haven't their system properly arranged as yet. . . .

Don't forget the picture for I'm sure lonesome to see you. Thank your mother for her love and give her mine if there is any left from you.

Your Harry

Father L. Curtis Tiernan of Kansas City, mentioned below, was chaplain of the regiment. He became a lifelong friend of Lieutenant, later President, Truman.

[Lawton, Okla.]

Dear Bess: October 5, 1917

Another fine day—got your letter of yesterday. I can't understand what has happened to my letters to you and the home folks. I have only missed one day writing you and I have written home twice this week. It seems like I have been here a year.

Was in Lawton today and mailed my letter to you over there. It is a nice little town, but they have arranged their prices as usual for our benefit. It seems that the whole country is organized to sell the soldiers at a fair profit plus all the traffic will bear from 40 percent to 100 percent. I have been cussing the laundries out down here. They added 40 percent to their prices for our benefit and I told the association over in Oklahoma City just what I thought of it. They called a meeting yesterday and a committee is coming over to talk the matter over with me. They got the impression some way that I am the canteen manager for the whole shebang down here and I didn't spoil it. The way they were charging, it would cost a man fifty-four cents to get a shirt and pants and socks washed. It doesn't seem right to me for a bunch of stay-at-home plutocrats to take all the money they can get for washing our clothes. When a man does a day's work drilling he doesn't feel like doing a night's washing. The outfit have already offered to take off 25 percent, but they've got to do better or we'll do our own washing.

I also tried to buy a carload of pop from the Coca Cola bottling works in Oklahoma City and Lawton. They refused to let me have more than fifty cases. I wired the Seltzer bottling works in K.C. to take care of us because we are a Kansas City organization, and they referred me to the Coca Cola bottling works of Oklahoma City. So there is another combination in restraint of trade. I'm not going to sell pop.

I suppose you are tired reading of my storekeeping experience, but I have nothing more to write about at present. . . .

I took some pictures today and if they are good will send you some. They call me Lieutenant Trumanheimer now instead of Graballsky. You may just address my letters as usual because if Father Tiernan, who sorts the mail, came across a letter from you addressed that way, I'd never hear the end of it.

Here's hoping tomorrow will be another grand day. Had a letter from Mary today too. Remember me to your mother and all the rest of the family and yourself first, last, and all the time.

Your Harry

Dear Bess: [Lawton, Okla., Oct. 11, 1917]
        . . . I have been branding horses today. We take a red-hot iron and put 129 F.A. on the right front hoof and the number of the horse, beginning with I and F, on the left foot. Then I had to take a complete description—with his age and weight and his government number, brand marks, etc. It took me about two hours to do thirty head. One hundred forty-eight had already been done.

Speaking about eats, we have everything we want. Cream of wheat, steak, potatoes, coffee, preserves, hot biscuits for breakfast. Then more vegetables and pie for dinner and supper. So you see we do not suffer for lack of eats. I don't know if I told you, I ran a grader day before yesterday to round up our picket lines but I did and everyone was surprised that I knew how. No one else in the Battery did, so I had to grab hold and go to it. It came out a very good job, too, if I do say so myself. . . .

I am hoping to see you soon in some way or other.

Lee's in bed and Pete's at the barn. I have to take reveille in the morning so I'll have to crawl in too. I am and always will be

Your Harry

Dear Bess: [Lawton, Okla., Oct. 15, 1917]

You certainly will have some reason to give me thunder because I have missed two whole days writing to you. I had to work until ten-thirty both last night and night before, and was so near all in that I couldn't write. As I promised before, I'll not let it occur again. We are certainly putting in the days here. They have begun to teach us the English and French methods of artillery fire. I think we are going to get our equipment very soon. I hope we are anyway. They have begun to issue winter clothes. The boys are sure glad to get them, too. It is a real summer day today. The wind has been blowing a gale from the south. When it gets cold enough, the boys are going to have stoves in their tents. The colonel doesn't want them put in yet because he says the men are more healthy without them. I think they are too. My canteen is still running in its grand, rushing manner. Some of the other canteens are started now and my receipts have fallen off somewhat. About three hundred dollars a day is my average. I caught one of my men stealing money out of the cash drawer night before last and had him put in the guardhouse. It took me all afternoon yesterday to draw up the charges. I guess he'll get about two years. I backed him into a corner and made him admit that he took the money. He had ten dollars in one pocket and three dollars in another, and two in another, and three in another. Did it all in about an hour. I was at school when the canteen steward came up and called me out and told me about it. They say the poor fellow is a good soldier but so much money in sight all at once was too much for him. There has been someone stealing constantly from the till for the last two days. I suppose he was the guy. . . .

Here's hoping to see you soon.

Most sincerely,

Your Harry

About this time Truman's letters begin to reflect the routine of army life. Many of them have been left out of the pages that follow.

Dear Bess: [Lawton, Okla. Oct. 18, 1917]

. . . When we came back at midnight the weather was as fine as could be wished for. About the time I got in bed it began all of a sudden to blow from the northwest at about sixty miles an hour. Mr. Lee jumped up and tied up the tent and began to yell, "Captain Allen, Captain Allen." I turned over and asked him what the heck was the matter with Captain Allen. He said he just merely wanted to see if the captain was in his tent and awake so he (Lee) wouldn't have to go to the picket line. The old boy has a head like a tack. It very nearly blew our tent over and has been getting fresher and fresher ever since. I went to the picket line this morning and it was almost impossible to see a horse from one end of the line to the other. The dust storms we have had before have been mild breezes compared to this one. . . .

I'm going to stay right here in the canteen and keep books. The dust isn't quite so bad in here. A tent fifty yards away is invisible. Dust is in my teeth, eyes, hair, nose, and down my neck. The cook next door brought me a piece of apple dumpling and it was sure fine, but when I ate it there was a grinding sound as if a butcher knife were being drawn across a piece of crockery. I ate it anyway, sand and all. I have sold a whole case of goggles and could sell two more. . . .

Please write me because it's a bright day, sand or no sand, when your letters come.

Sincerely,
Harry

Dear Bess: [Lawton, Okla., Oct. 21, 1917]

. . . We have an oil stove and the cussed thing smokes like Vesuvius. It smells like a refinery and tastes like quinine in here now. I guess if we get good and smoked and eat about a peck of sand every day, we'll be hard-boiled and bomb-proof when we get to Berlin. The wind isn't blowing today and we are all very happy. Had chocolate pie for dinner. I am sure sorry about that sugar but I guess I can steal enough Hersheys from the canteen until you can send me some fudge. Our board is only going to cost us forty-five dollars a month. That's not at all high, is it? We ought to live high on that. I think it must be a mistake. I hope it is anyway. It won't make any difference, though, because the government doesn't seem to be inclined to pay us anyway. I'll eat as long as my credit is good. I guess I must be increasing in weight somewhat because my wristwatch got too tight for me. So have my leggings. I don't feel any heavier though. . . . Write me when you feel in the mood but please feel that way often.

Lovingly,
Your Harry

Dear Bess: [Lawton, Okla., Oct. 23, 1917]

I failed to write yesterday because I had a severe case of indigestion to put it politely. In my younger days, I'd have called it something else. Father Tiernan came to my rescue with a big drink of whiskey. The last one he had and also the last one on the reservation. We also had another dust storm yesterday, worse than any previous one. They seem to be progressive in their actions, getting worse all the time. . . .

Hope to get a letter tomorrow.

Most sincerely,
Harry

When the army had nothing else to do, it ran inspections. Here Truman is complaining about how the army wasted time with what he considered such nonsense.

Dear Bess: [Lawton, Okla., Oct. 28, 1917]
    . . . We have inspection every Saturday morning by Colonel Klemm and I
have to get the canteen in apple-pie order. We had things in fine shape inside
but he kicked like a bay steer because the Puritan distributor hadn't returned for
his empty bottles.
    I have a Jew in charge of the canteen by the name of Jacobson and he is
a crackerjack. Also the barbershop is run by a Jew, Morris Stearns by name. He
formerly owned the Ridge Barber Shop, does yet but the guy he left in charge
is stealing the income because Morris says he gets nothing from it. What I started
to say was that the colonel inspected the barber and everything was shipshape.
Morris had it all scoured up and shining like a new pin. The colonel couldn't see
anything outside to kick about so he made Morris open his cupboard doors and
then he said, "Just as I expected, you simply stuffed the dirt out of sight." The
rest of the bunch sure rawhided Morris. . . .
    Hope to get two letters tomorrow. Send that picture as soon as you get it.
                                                Yours ever,
                                                Harry

Dear Bess: [Lawton, Okla., Nov. 2, 1917]
    I am sure in bad with you I guess but there are extenuating circumstances,
as the coon partner in Lawton's tonsorial parlor would say. The men had a payday
last Tuesday and I have been sitting on a money bag ever since. I also had to
spend the last two nights until 1:00 A.M. invoicing this devilish place—and I was
so infernally tired I simply could not write. I thought of you all the time just the
same and would have sent you a day-letter telegram but was afraid you'd think
I'd been messed up by "Dynamite," our bad horse. . . .
    I have a letter from Miss Nellie inviting me to her wedding and I surely am
coming home if there is any way to manage it. It looks good now. The salesmen
are eating me up and I've got to go to Lawton. Will write another later today.
                                                Sincerely,
                                                Harry

Dear Bess: [Lawton, Okla., Nov. 3, 1917]
    This is Saturday night and I have been going like a steam engine ever since
I wrote you last. I would like very much to know just what you were doing that
you can't tell me until I arrive home. You ought to tell me because something
might happen that I couldn't come and then you'll have to tell me. . . .
    Captain Salisbury put a good one over on the officers yesterday. An old billy
goat has been parading up and down our street for several days, sleeps on the
windward side of the colonel's tent and doing other unseemly things such as
walking into the mess hall while dinner is in full swing. Salisbury caught him
in the horse lot today and cut his throat and took out a good piece of him and

fed it to the officers telling them it was beef. They thought it was fine until they found out what it was and then it didn't taste so good. The goat was the property of the 1st Kansas Infantry, now the 139th, and if they discover what has happened to their mascot, I'm very much afraid Uncle Sam will be minus an artillery regiment. I don't suppose they'll ever know what became of him though.

I also enlisted another man in Battery F today. He's a fifteen-year-old nigger boy. Works in the regimental barber shop and shines shoes. He's a good one too. We had our photos made again today and as soon as they are finished I'll send you one. If I have any luck getting away from here, I'll probably see you very soon after you get this; if I don't, you'll hear from me again. I'm hoping to see you.

Most sincerely,
Your Harry

[Telegram, Lawton, Okla., Nov. 7, 1917]

PERMISSION TO LEAVE REFUSED AT LAST MINUTE. WILL WRITE YOU FULLY. WISH I COULD BE THERE. NO TRUTH IN RUMOR THAT WE ARE LEAVING. HOPE MISS NELLIE HAS A FINE WEDDING. IT IS NEARLY IMPOSSIBLE FOR AN OFFICER TO GET AWAY FROM HERE. HARRY TRUMAN

Uncomfortable with army regulations, Truman found himself equally annoyed with regular army officers. His particular nemesis was Brigadier General Lucien G. Berry, commander of the 60th Field Artillery Brigade. It included three regiments—the 128th, 129th, and 130th—together with a trench mortar Battery and an ammunition train. The brigade numbered 6,300 men and officers and was attached to the 35th Division, drawn mostly from Missouri, Kansas, and Arkansas. Berry's relations with Truman were never more than frostily formal and were, to Truman's relief, infrequent. The general was very strict over leave policy and seemed to Truman to take pleasure in other seemingly arbitrary acts.

Dear Bess: [Lawton, Okla., Nov. 8, 1917]

I expected to see you this morning but General Berry was in a bad humor yesterday afternoon and refused to let me off. I was all ready to leave, had my grip packed and Colonel Klemm made a special trip over to division headquarters to get me off for five days. He told the general that he was sending me on regimental business and still there was nothing doing. He's a hard-boiled cookie and sure loves to sit on a national guard officer. I think he's going to make artillerymen out of us though if work counts for anything. I'm off him, he's no friend of mine, but I reckon it's a lot he cares. I have been so downhearted ever since that I couldn't write you until this morning. I sent you a telegram telling you of my bad luck. I didn't even get to buy Miss Nellie a wedding present. I

do hope she had a grand wedding and that she'll be happy ever after. . . .
I will write you later in the day and then perhaps I'll feel better.

Yours always,
Harry

*Choosing a wedding present for Nellie is a concern in the letter below. Had
she gotten married, Truman would have had an excuse for asking General Berry
for a leave. For some reason, however, the wedding never took place.*

Dear Bess: [Lawton, Okla., Nov. 11, 1917]
I had a letter from you yesterday and one today. The one yesterday gave me
an awful fit of the dumps. I wouldn't have you think for anything that I was
stringing you along about coming home to Nellie's wedding. I was the most
thoroughly disappointed person you ever saw. It didn't even occur to me that I'd
be turned down, because I had a job for the divisional canteen officer to perform
in Kansas City. The colonel also has things for me to do, and I had my grip all
packed on Tuesday at noon to catch the three-thirty train. The colonel went over
and asked General Berry himself to let me off and there was just a curt no for
an answer. A first lieutenant who has been attached to us and who has been in
the Philippines for the last five years asked for a ten-day leave to go see his mother,
who has three boys in the army, and General Berry turned him down without
comment. They are letting no one go home. I thought that by working regimental
business and pulling wires to get a job for the division I could surely get away
for three days but, as you perhaps know, couldn't. Your remark hit a very tender
spot because I have not been so completely disappointed for some time. . . .
Yesterday was my busy day. I had a case in the general court. They tried
one of my thieves. Convicted him but I don't know how hard, for the court won't
tell until the judge advocate general of the division reviews the findings of the
court. I guess the poor kid will get about three months hard labor. Pretty
expensive eighteen dollars.
Well, I wish I were in Independence this afternoon. What would you
suggest that I buy Nellie for a wedding present? Write as often as you can, for
the days your letters come are brighter.

Yours always,
Harry

Dear Bess: [Lawton, Okla., Nov. 17, 1917]
I am writing this Saturday morning because we had to go to school last night
after a ten-mile hike in the afternoon and I didn't have pep enough left to write
last night. The lecture was on shoes and what goes into them, and how to make
a soldier walk farther than he can. I nearly went to sleep but I guess I got
something out of it. We dug trenches yesterday afternoon about five miles west
of here and got wet coming in. What do you think of that for a country that

hasn't had a rain in two years? It also rained last night. Came down in sheets. This morning is as fine a spring morning as you'd care to see.

I told the whole canteen force they had to go dig yesterday and they went. It nearly killed the barber and the tailor. The tailor said there was some difference between a number 10 needle and a number 2 shovel.

We had some inspection this morning. The colonel was all wrought up. Made everyone do setting up exercises until they were black in the face. I got the canteen all rigged up and he never even came around. I've got to eat up our mess sergeant because our kitchen had some dust on one two-by-four alongside the stove. Knives and pots and pans have to be polished and shined like a Christmas tree. Yesterday was a grand day in spite of the rain because I had a letter from you and one from home.

Mrs. Klemm was here yesterday. She sure thinks you are fine. I think so too so we had a fine agreeable conversation. I am hoping you can come to see me before we have to go to Mineola, New York, or some other shipping point. There are all sorts of rumors running wild down here about going to France in six weeks, but I don't pay any heed to them until I am officially informed, which will no doubt be at least two days beforehand. I have a chance to get this mailed special delivery and will have to quit. Write often to

Yours always,

Harry

Below, Truman refers briefly to a French officer at Doniphan. Allied officers visited all the training camps in the United States to teach the Americans tactics of warfare suitable for the Western Front.

Dear Bess: [Lawton, Okla., Nov. 24, 1917]

I got your picture last night and I have had such a wide smile ever since that everyone has remarked about it. It is sure a speaking likeness and I really can't tell you how glad I am to have it. Unless you'd come yourself you could have sent me nothing that I'd like better.

Otto has just handed me your letter and I admit that I deserve a call-down but I can only plead work from 6:00 A.M. till 10:00 P.M. We had a payday Wednesday and you can guess what that meant to me. I counted money until my head ached. Changed five thousand dollars in ten-dollar bills in about a day and never lost a penny. Today I had to go to the trenches and dig or see to the digging and also have some timbers cut down. We are under the direction of a French officer and actually playing a real war game. It is very interesting but also very hard work.

The piano you have asked me about so often and which I have failed to tell you about (because I didn't know myself) was drawn by someone out on the south side of Kansas City. I can't remember the name because I've never heard it but once, but I'll find out from the first sergeant of the supply company and tell you. If there are other questions I've left unanswered, it's by accident

The photograph of Bess that Harry Truman carried to France. *Harry S. Truman Library*

and not intention. The pictures are not done, because picture paper is not obtainable, so the photo man tells me, but we are expecting them any day. . . .

Write me as often as you can and come to our dinner if you can. Had you have come down the other day, you'd not have had to be any waitress or waiting maid either nor would I have done any dodging.

Yours,
Harry

Dear Bess: [Lawton, Okla., Nov. 24, 1917]

I am making up for lost time by writing you two letters the same day. I am dizzy tonight from counting money but I am going to write anyway. I handled seven thousand dollars in change and never lost a penny. Mamma sent me a baked chicken and it is sure fine. Things seem to be showering in all at once. I had a letter and a picture from you yesterday and a letter and a chicken from home today. Tomorrow is Mamma's birthday. I wired Boxley to send her some flowers and I guess he will. I am urging her as well as you to come down Thanksgiving. . . .

If the war continues for a year or two, we'll all be hard cookies. Won't you please come down and knock off some of the rough edges? Jacobson says he'd go into the guardhouse thirty days for one night on Twelfth Street. I'd go in for forty days if I could see you thirty minutes.

Tomorrow is Sunday and I'm to be officer of the day. Sounds natural doesn't it? Remember how regularly it used to come on Sunday when we were at Convention Hall? Everyone who pays me a visit nowadays remarks on what a beautiful girl I have on my desk. I swell up like a pointer pigeon and my hat won't stay on at all because I think how lucky I am and Julia Sanderson's song runs through my head.

Please write as often as you can to
                                    Yours always,
                                    Harry

Dear Bess: [Lawton, Okla., Dec. 14, 1917]
    . . . They say I have the best canteen on the reservation, and every regiment has one. I declared a dividend to the Batteries of three thousand dollars last week. The regiment appointed a committee to audit me. I came out with flying colors. Even the colonel couldn't find anything wrong. The sanitary inspector came around and told me I had the cleanest place on the job too. . . .

I have found a good hard-working soldier who evidently hasn't any friends or relatives to look after him. His name is Stanley Hackinsky. He is Russian but not Jew. If your mother wants to send him something, I am sure he'd be very highly pleased. His address is Battery F, 129th F.A. I hope Mrs. Bundschu comes. I want to see you so badly I don't know what to do. I am wiring you today too.

                                    Yours always,
                                    Harry

                                    [Telegram, Lawton, Okla., Dec. 15, 1917]
HOPE YOU HAVE MY LETTERS BY THIS TIME. MAIL SOMEWHAT DELAYED DOWN HERE. MARY AND MAMMA ARRIVED TODAY. MARY TELLS ME YOU ARE SICK. WIRE ME HOW SERIOUSLY. NO CHRISTMAS LEAVE. HOPE TO SEE YOU. THAT WOULD BE THE BEST CHRISTMAS PRESENT. HARRY S. TRUMAN

                                    [Telegram, Lawton, Okla., Dec. 24, 1917]
MERRY XMAS. WISH I COULD BE PRESENT TODAY. WE ARE HAVING SOME XMAS DOWN HERE BUT IT'S NOT LIKE HOME. HOPE ANOTHER

WON'T PASS WITH ME AWAY. BEST WISHES TO YOUR MOTHER AND
ALL THE FAMILY. HARRY S. TRUMAN

Dear Bess: [Lawton, Okla., Jan. 10, 1918]
   Got your letter today and was sure glad to hear from you. I sent you a note
from the train but you evidently had not received it yet. We were hours late and
there were so many people to get on at Oklahoma City that some of them got
left. I was not among them. We got into camp at ten minutes before midnight.
That is all the time of my leave that I wasted in camp. They put me on as officer
of the day right off the bat and I didn't get any sleep for another day. This colonel
is working the socks off of us. My cold kept getting worse and worse until today.
I couldn't talk yesterday and I went out and stayed all day mounted, very nearly
froze to death and came in feeling better than I have since I got back. They
sent me a general order closing all canteens until they had paid their debts and
shown that they are solvent. I passed out the word that last night would see
the finish of the canteen and they almost mobbed the place. Sold six hundred
dollars' worth in three hours. I have been working like a nigger ever since getting invoiced and billed out. It seems like you're never up with the hounds in
the army.
   There is a terrific blizzard going here. It began raining this morning from
the east. It turned to snow and the wind got around in Hiawatha's corner and
ice balls began blowing in straight lines like bullets right from Medicine Hat's
worst mixture. You can't see ten feet from you now and the wind is blowing about
sixty miles an hour. This must be one of the kind I've heard my grandfather speak
of when he crossed the plains. This place just sticks up high enough to catch every
misting air current that goes from the Arctic to fill the holes in the Gulf of
Mexico. In summer it catches all the dust in the whole of North America. Now

Camp Doniphan, Oklahoma, 1917–18. *U.S. Army Signal Corps*

we are getting some of Klondike's surplus snow. We were to have been inspected from cellar to garret and clear to the top of the chimney tomorrow but on account of the storm we won't be. This colonel inspects, too, believe me. There are eyes in the back of his head and nothing, absolutely nothing, gets by unseen. Then he congregates the whole regiment and gives a lecture on what you didn't do so the rest can profit by it. Makes you feel like crawling in a hole and pulling it after you but it gets results.

You've no idea how short five days are. I have been pinching myself every day saying, well what a grand kidding you gave yourself. I sure wanted to stay another week. If I only could. But I suppose it would have been just as hard to come back in another week as it was in five days. When I counted up I was only home one hour and thirty minutes one afternoon, four hours another, and part of two nights. Didn't get to talk to Mamma over an hour and never saw you much over that at a time. I didn't know how crazy I was about you until I went to leave. I'd give all I have or ever expect to have to see you tonight. We are getting closer to a move all the time. No telling when it will come. Write as often as you can and I'll do likewise.

Yours always,
Harry

After the end of the year rumors began about the regiment's moving to an East Coast port and on to France. Most, of course, were false, but Truman reported all of them. Bess was never quite sure whether he was leaving or not.

[Lawton, Okla.]

Dear Bess: Sunday, January 27, 1918
I am keeping my promise although my hands are so cold I can hardly write. It does no good to sit on them and you are so far away that old Dr. Miller's remedy can't be worked. We are having a blizzard in real Western Plains style. It began yesterday at noon, coming out of the northwest as suddenly as a thunderclap. The weather was warm as springtime, the sun shining and everything fine, by night it was zero and snowing, sleeting, doing everything else it shouldn't. Our tent is usually as warm as a house but for some reason our stove refuses to draw this morning and we have a cold tent. I am writing to Mamma this morning for the first time in two weeks. I guess she thinks I'm already in France or at the bottom of the Atlantic.

We are sure a disappointed bunch. Got our goods and chattels all packed, weighed, and marked and then turned right round and unpacked 'em. The King of France had nothing on us for we'd already arrived in Paris with a through ticket to Berlin, and now we've got to stay in this magnificent training camp and in all probability get benzined [dismissed from the army] and sent home. We'd all figured that we'd beaten the benzine board by a nose when we were ordered abroad. They are most certainly giving us an intensive course of training. We study drill regulations all week and take an examination on Saturday. I have been closing out the canteen, doing Battery office work, drill, and going to school. It is a strenuous life. Don't hurt me any unless I get mad at someone or something and then there's a blowup. I have also been teaching school for noncommissioned officers most every night until nine-thirty. If I won't be a go-getter when I get out of this place, there's no one that will.

The present understanding is that our special detachment won't go now until March. So you may have the pleasure of seeing me permanently located in Jackson County before then. I would most certainly like to be there for some very excellent reasons but I would hate to get sent home by a benzine board, although there'd be some satisfaction in knowing that I'd tried my best for the old stars and stripes.

We heard a lecture by an English cclonel from the Western Front last night and it sure put the pep into us. He made us all want to brace up and go to it with renewed energy. He made us feel like we were fighting for you and mother earth and I am of the same belief. I wouldn't be left out of the greatest history-making epoch the world has ever seen for all there is to live for because there'd be nothing to live for under German control. When we come home a victorious army we can hold our heads up in the greatest old country on earth and make up for lost time by really living. Don't you think that would be better than to miss out entirely? I am crazy to get it over with though because I wouldn't cause you a heartache for all there is in the world.

You'll never know how badly I hated to leave on the night I started back down here. I can most certainly sympathize with an enlisted man who stays over his time. A man sure ought to have some extra credits in the judgment book when he leaves the strongest ties in the world to do what is called duty, don't you think so?

This is a fun letter and it is a bad day. Perhaps you'd better follow the advice of Agnes' suitor who always instructed her to put his epistles in the kitchen stove. Anyway I love you just the same and more than ever and I'm working hard to finish the war quickly so we can make up for lost time.

Yours always,
Harry

Dear Bess: [Lawton, Okla., Feb. 1, 1918]

I have your letter today and I sure am glad to get it. As I have told you, the day is always bright and fine when your letter comes. We are working as usual. I have a regular schedule. From eight to eight-fifty I teach physical exercise (it is to laugh), from nine to nine-fifty I teach communication, semaphore, buzzer, and wigwag. Had to learn the international code in one evening to do it. In the afternoon I teach foot movements of artillery, and then more communication. Every lieutenant has a definite thing to do at every hour and he's got to be on deck or something drops on him. In addition to my regular drill periods I have to see that every man in Battery F has all the clothes he is entitled to and that he wears them. Also they reopened my canteen because it is solvent. That has to be run. I don't have very much to do, no not very. Every day we have a regular officer's school on how to fire a battery, and Saturday a written exam on the week's work. . . .

I'd liked very much to have been at Miss Elizabeth's wedding. I know it was a grand affair if you had anything to do with the arrangement. Couldn't be any other way. Hope she lives happily ever after and that the Germans haven't made any bullets for the man. I know they haven't made any for me. We have had two blizzards since I wrote you before but today is a fine day. Just about zero and sunshiny and no wind. I am hoping we have some warm weather very soon now. The natives say we have spring in February but they are such liars I don't put any faith in what they say. I am writing this at noon. The bugle has blown and I have to run.

I wish we'd had the nerve to beat Lib to it. We'll know better next time.

Yours always,
Harry

Dear Bess: [Lee-Huckins Hotel, Oklahoma City, Feb. 3, 1918]
     I am at Oklahoma City this time sure enough. Wired you this afternoon. I am like a parrot out of his cage. We have been hitting it up at such a rate down at camp that some of us almost have nervous prostration. The Scottish Rite are putting a class through, and General Wright issued a bulletin allowing four-day passes to Guthrie. It came out yesterday morning and was revoked at noon. I got mine before the cancellation intending to go to K.C. on it, but after they recalled the privilege I thought perhaps I'd better not risk it. They are always hunting for some good excuse to rim a N.G. officer, and if they should suddenly take a fool notion to call me at Guthrie and I not be there, it would be all up but the signing. It is most surely a disappointment because I was planning on stepping into your front hall this evening at about seven-thirty and perhaps causing you heart failure for one minute anyway. I have been doing squads east and squads sideways, arms up and hands down until I can't open my mouth without telling someone to straighten up or get in step. "Hold your head up. Look at the back of the head of the man in front of you, if he isn't there look anyway. This ground's level, you won't fall down if you don't get your feet tangled. - - - - x x straighten up, step out like a man, put some snap into" etc. etc. ad lib. Then after some hour or so of that I go count nickels and dimes up to four hundred dollars a day more or less. I guess I should be very proud of my Jewish ability. My thirst emporium is the only one in camp that's open. The rest are insolvent or can't make a clear statement of their financial standing.

I am going to forget drill-book exercise and all of it for three days anyway and occupy my mind on higher things. Perhaps that won't hurt me any because I have acquired an ability to swear like Sam Jones or Captain Kidd, and there may be a high reckoning on it sometime. I think not soon.

We have exams every Saturday. I have passed every time yet but the next one I'll probably blow up on. The hotel is full of soldiers and first lieutenants. Some going to Guthrie and some going to the School of Fire and some, I fear, just playing hookey. I sure wish I could have happened in this evening, but I can't. I look for a letter every mail even if I don't send one.

Yours always,
Harry

Dear Bess: [Lee-Huckins Hotel, Oklahoma City, Feb. 7, 1918]

I am back at the Lee-Huckins after a grand vacation at Guthrie. I tried to get myself to write every day while I was there but the Guthrie citizens wouldn't let me. They kept us going from 8:00 A.M. until midnight.

I stayed at the home of Governor Haskell's daughter, Mrs. Neblack. She is a grand woman and he is a fine man. She entertained us royally, taking us driving in her Hudson lim, introducing us to all the girls in town, and doing her level best to see that we had an enjoyable time. We did. I looked every day for a letter or a wire but none came. I am hoping there'll be one when I get back to camp.

They put on all the Scottish Rite in as grand a form as I ever saw it from beginning to end. The Temple is fine and well arranged. They have a pipe organ and an organist that can play as well as Krieser I think.

They fed us three meals a day that would make Hoover [Herbert, then food administrator] blow up if he'd see them, and at the end they gave a dance, last night, and would let no one but soldiers dance. Then's when I wished I was a dancer. There were girls from Norman, Tulsa, and all-around pretty girls, fat girls, tall ones, and short ones—and they were all doing their best to see that every soldier had every dance that went. I tried my luck at a one-step with my hostess and with Lieutenant Rainey's wife. They were both very kind to me and pretended that it didn't hurt when I stepped on their toes. Mrs. Neblack was all lit up in an evening gown as were most of the girls. The citizens had on soup and fish, and from every standpoint it was a grand occasion. I sat out most of the dances with some of the good old married sisters and the best-looking unmarried ones I could. We left at twelve o'clock last night, and I don't know what Mr. Neblack's initials are and I suppose it's up to me to find out some way and write him a letter of appreciation.

And now it's back to slavery of the worst sort, but I guess we can do it better now.

The boat that sank today I am informed is the one we'd have gone to England on if we'd got off on our special detail. I don't believe it though because we couldn't have made it to New York in time to get on it. Anyway the one I go on isn't going to sink. I do wish I could see you. Every girl I met last night I tried to think looked like you if she was nice, only none of them could be as good looking. There's only one best-looking girl in the world to every man. You're that to me. Write as often as you can for I sure appreciate only a line.

Most sincerely,
Harry

Dear Bess: [Lawton, Okla., Feb. 11, 1918]

Your letters were all waiting for me when I got back and I got one last night. I hope you got my last Oklahoma City letter Sunday. (Filled my pen here. It's always dry when I need it.) I have been going like a horse since I got back. Went over and took some special instructions on gas protection. Had to take a mask like a diver's and get into it and then go into the gas house and sit there ten minutes. Some of the men were very uneasy about going in. They were afraid they'd get gassed and never see the Kaiser. I don't see that it makes any very great difference where a person gets gassed or shot either provided he's slated for either one, because the same result takes place. Still I reckon there's more honor in getting battle wounds than training ones. Don't you worry about what's going to happen to me because there's not a bullet molded for me nor has Neptune any use for me. Had I have been on the boat that went down, I'd have been in Dublin by this time with some Irish woman at a dance (if she looked like you) or taking a look for the man who invented corks and corkscrews. Ireland's a great country so they say. . . .

Please send me a wire or letter to let me know you are all in good health and spirits and not doing any worrying over a good-for-nothing person like me. I am awfully glad you think I'm well enough without a D.S.O. because I'll never get one. The Huns can't run fast enough to catch me. I don't think they could make another like yourself because perfection comes but once.

Yours always,
Harry

[Telegram, Lawton, Okla., Feb. 13, 1918]

BIRTHDAY GREETINGS. MAY YOU HAVE MANY MORE AND GROW NO OLDER. WROTE YOU YESTERDAY. HARRY

Dear Bess: [Lawton, Okla., Feb. 16, 1918]

I haven't heard from you for five days and I am getting terribly uneasy. I am going to wire you today if I don't hear. I got a letter last Tuesday saying that you didn't feel well and I have been expecting every day to hear you were worse. I hope that you are not and that everything is all as it should be. I haven't heard from home for a week either. They played me a bad trick at the bank up there the other day. My good friend Booth called a four-thousand-dollar loan on me. Maybe you think I didn't unburden my mind on him. I am going to show him a thing or two some of these days.

I went out to fire the other day along with the rest of the regiment's officers and by some hook or crook I was unlucky enough to observe more shots correctly than anyone else and now I have to fire next time. I'm scared green because General Berry always eats 'em alive after they fire. He's very expert at making a person shake in his boots. Captain Pete was second and Lieutenant Paterson was third. There was evidently some mistake in grading the papers because you know very well that a person with a half-baked eyesight like mine couldn't see more shots correctly than one with real eyes. Anyway I'm the goat. I guess it's very good experience though.

If I don't hear from you very soon I'm going to disgrace the service by going A.W.O.L. and finding out what's the matter. There was some joy in life when I got letters from home and from you, but when they come from bankers and I am ordered to show my ignorance before the whole regiment, there's not much left. If I could only see you, I'd be all in heaven.

Yours always,
Harry

The following describes Truman's certainty that he would not be promoted to captain. General Berry was a member of the promotion board and showed no evidence of passing him. Truman did not learn of his promotion until May, when he read about it in the Paris Herald. *(He later applied for back pay, and the army typically refused to give it to him, because he had not "accepted" his commission earlier.)*

Dear Bess: [Lawton, Okla., Feb. 23, 1918]

This day has been a bright one. So was yesterday. I got your letter both days, and I have been the delinquent party this week. I hope you won't blame me when I tell you what has been happening. The overseas detachment is again having spasms of preparation to leave. I am still on it, thank heaven, and so of course I am having spasms too. I had a regular one yesterday when Colonel Danford ordered me up before an examining board not for efficiency but for promotion. I think I failed miserably because General Berry was so gruff and discourteous in his questions that I forgot all I ever knew and couldn't answer him. He said, "Eh huh! You don't know, do you? I thought so. You don't know. That'll be all, outside." He kept me and the two others, Lieutenant Paterson and Lieutenant Marks, standing out in the cold so long that we took a terrific cold and I couldn't get up this morning for reveille. I got up for breakfast and outside of a slight headache I am all in good health and spirits. That is as good spirits as could be expected in a man when he falls down on an examination. We had no opportunity for preparation and I suppose that it would have been no better if we had. I have been looking for them to say that it was a mistake and that an efficiency board is what I needed instead of an examining one. Please don't say anything about it until the announcement is made as to whether I get the promotion or not. If I don't get it then we won't say anything. If I do then we can tell it. I guess it is a compliment anyway to get ordered up even if I didn't pass. They almost sent me home on a physical, too, yesterday but I talked past the M.D. He turned my eyes down twice and threatened to send me to division headquarters for a special examination and then didn't. I guess I can put a real good conversation when circumstances demand it. You see by taking everything together if I hadn't gotten your letters, I'd sure have been a blue person. In addition to all the other things I did yesterday I turned the exchange over to Captain Butterfield and sat on a general court martial. Some day, wasn't it? Can you wonder that I didn't get up for reveille and still have a slight headache?

I shall cable you as soon as I arrive in Europe. I thought I told you I would once before. I intended to anyway. I am glad Uncle William was landed safely and I hope to see him when I get across. I don't know much to tell you about leaving, but I'll let you know immediately I start. I shall also let you know if I get the two bars. Please don't say anything about that though until I hear that I'm turned down, which is what we all think. I am no longer Trumanheimer. Did I tell you I met a very pretty girl in Guthrie who was nice to me until someone told her my name was Trumanheimer, and then she wouldn't look at me anymore. She thought I surely must be of Hebraic descent with that name. She of course didn't know that it is little I care what she thinks or doesn't.

Please write me as often as possible because the days are sure brighter and not so hard when your letters come.

I think of you always.

Yours,
Harry

Dear Bess: [Lawton, Okla., Mar. 3, 1918]
Your letter came today twice, making this some grand day even if I did nearly freeze this morning going out to watch the Battery fire. We get out and fire every other day now. I think I told you I fired Wednesday. I did not fire today but had to watch some captains and lieutenants from the 128th fire our Battery. They made quite a mess of it principly (I don't know how to spell any more, never did in fact) because they were scared green. It is some job to get up before some dozen of officers and perhaps a couple of generals and three artillery colonels who are experts at the game and tell a Battery just exactly what to do with itself. You know that every time you open your mouth the Battery is going to do something and that there are seven separate and distinct things you've got to do exactly right or the colonel who is conducting the problem will blow the whistle on you. If you get those seven things off without a bobble, the Battery shoots bing, bing, bing, bing, at two-second intervals and all four of the shots insist on staying in the air about an hour and when they do burst maybe they are crossed up like a cross-eyed pup and No. 1 is going where 4 should be. It takes exactly seven and one-half seconds for the shots to go three thousand yards, but it seems like hours. Well you look at the target and the devilish crossfire and lick your lips and look at the target again and cuss a little very quietly to yourself and bust out with some wild command and the colonel blows the whistle on you and then the general

summons the whole world around to pick you to pieces and perhaps ask if you have any brains. He wasn't there when I fired so I got away better than some, but the foregoing is the usual procedure. It's really heartbreaking the way some awful smart men simply blow up when they fire the first time. After doing it once you don't care a hang what happens and it usually comes out as it should. . . .

I'm sure glad to get your letters and I hope I can go to Hoboken by way of K.C. and come back the same way.

Yours always,
Harry

Dear Bess: [Lawton, Okla., Mar. 5, 1918]

Your letter came today and evidently my Sunday special did not arrive as a Sunday special. One of the barbers went to Oklahoma City and I gave it to him to mail. I hope he mailed it. We haven't gone yet on Monday evening although they say the cars to take us have arrived. There was a special order came out today saying that if the special detail were here the next muster period (April 1), they would be carried as if they were not a special detail. I don't much care whether we leave so soon or not because we are getting some very good schooling. Had an examination yesterday in which we had a problem like this: a scout measured the angle found by two trees on the opposite bank of a river, it was 150 mils, he walked back fifty yards and the angle between the same two trees was 120 mils. How wide is the river? I got the right answer, what do you think of that. It is two hundred yards wide. A mil is the 1/6400 of a circle, which is the measurement we use instead of degrees. That was one of five we had to work besides several on drill regulations. We'll sure be wise birds when the war's over if we don't get shot first. I got an underground intimation that I passed my captain's examination all right. I don't believe it though until I see the evidence from Washington. I am telling you only because I thought maybe it would be nice to share good news with you if it is only a rumor, and I know you won't kid me about it if it's false. To tell you the honest truth I'd rather be a first lieutenant than anything else in the army except a buck private in the rear rank. He's the guy that has no responsibility and he's the guy that does the real work. I heard a good one the other day which said that a lieutenant knows nothing and does everything, a captain knows everything and does nothing, a major knows nothing and does nothing. Very true except that a captain has to know everything from sealing wax to sewing machines and has to run them. He also is responsible for about $750,000 worth of matériel and 193 men, their lives, their morals, their clothes, and their horses, which isn't much for $200 a month and pay your own expenses. I shall probably get the swell head just as all captains do if I get it, and it will be lots better for me if I don't. . . .

This is Tuesday and I'm still here. I got as far as that last night and got called on a court martial case. I am a member of the general court, which doesn't mean anything—only to hear evidence against some poor son of a gun who has used government funds for his own use or done something against the 4 million regulations you're supposed to know and don't. I got done so late that I went right to bed because I was afraid I'd have to fire today and not be able to see to do it. Luckily I did not have to although Pete and Mr. Lee did. They did very well. I acted as an onlooker and fire observer. There were four Batteries firing, and it was very hard to tell which was which. The weather has been so nearly ideal the last three days that I think the devil or whoever else hands out Oklahoma weather has overlooked a bet. Don't you worry about my leaving because I'll certainly wire you when I start.

Pete is hollerin' for me and I've got to run.

Yours always,
Harry

Dear Bess: [Lawton, Okla., Mar. 10, 1918]

This is Sunday morning and a magnificent one but we all have the blues. They have taken Colonel Danford away from us, sent him to Washington to report to the artillery commander-in-chief. I don't know what for, unless it is to be a general or something because he knows more artillery than Napoleon Bonaparte himself. The whole regiment is feeling badly over it. Captain McGee told his first sergeant about it as they were walking to the stable. The sergeant stopped and said, "The H--l?" The captain told the colonel about it and it nearly pleased him to death. He sent for me yesterday and practically gave me his horse, a fine Kentucky-bred saddle animal, pretty as a picture and gentle as a dog. He's a very dark sorrel with a dark sorrel mane and tail and a pretty, little intelligent head like Rosa Bonheur puts on her horses. I got him for one hundred dollars. He'd be cheap at three hundred dollars. Colonel Klemm and Major Miles were both peeved because they didn't get him. Colonel Klemm said to me the first thing when he found I had the horse, "You lucky Jew you get all the plums that fall, don't you?" I told him I took them when they were thrown at me. I don't know why the colonel picked me for the bargain, but he did. I am going to ship the horse home along with Colonel Elliott's and Colonel Klemm's and keep him. He's too fine to take to war.

I have made Masons out of both Colonel Klemm and Colonel Danford since we've been here, so I guess maybe that helps my *drag* [influence] somewhat, although it's not supposed to. General Berry is one and I am going to help make General Wright one next Wednesday if he shows up as expected and I'm still here. That's the one thing I've studied in the last years that has done me more good than anything, except artillery study. This letter doesn't seem very nice to me. I haven't been able to talk of anything but myself and then have said nothing. I sold Lizzie to a poor sucker yesterday for two hundred dollars, which I consider as a find in the road, because I'd already charged her off to profit and loss, less the profit end. My former Jew clerk in the canteen watched me make the sale and then told me that he still had something to learn in salesmanship. The canteen declared another three-thousand-dollar dividend the first and paid back the investment besides. That is only earning at the rate of 621 percent a year. Sounds like Standard Oil. Colonel Danford told me I had made a reputation in the devilish thing that I'd have a hard time living down. I am going to horseback ride over the Medicine Park this afternoon and look at it because I don't ever expect to come back to this place again if I live to be a thousand.

I am very glad that Chandler Wright thinks well of me. I always try to treat all the men in the Battery just as I'd like them to treat me if our places were reversed, and it seems to work very well.

Write as often as you can because I may stay here another month. Dinner is ready and I must run.

Yours always,
Harry

Dear Bess: [Lawton, Okla., Mar. 17, 1918]

. . . Our new major commander isn't so worse after all. He sat on General Berry the other day, and I am for him strong. The general told him to examine some second lieutenants for firsts. He asked the general if he expected them to know as much as a regular army first lieutenant. General said yes. Major Waring said, "All right I vote no on every one of 'em. I can't waste my time on a bunch of cockeyed lieutenants that are not professionals so I'll just kill 'em now." General then told him to fix up any kind of exam he saw fit. So he fixed one they could pass. I understand now that our promotions are indefinitely held up because there are no vacancies. I am glad for I'd rather go to Europe a lieutenant than a captain on this special detail. I can't plead guilty to having taken anyone horseback riding last Sunday but my orderly. He and I rode about twenty miles out to a copper mine and to Medicine Park. The mine looked like the one I already own so it wasn't very enticing. I hear indirectly that Morgan and Company has a gusher camouflaged in Texas and is trying to lease the whole northeast corner of the state. I hope so. I'd like to be a millionaire a few days before I go to Europe so I'd be used to it when I come back. I sure appreciate your letters and I'm crazy to see the box. Will write immediately it arrives. This is my last sheet. Next time you'll get scratch paper.

Yours always,
Harry

Lawton, Okla. [telegram, Mar. 19, 1918]

WE ARE MOVING TODAY. YOUR PACKAGE CAME ALL RIGHT AND WAS VERY FINE. WILL WRITE YOU FROM TRAIN. HARRY S. TRUMAN

SEVEN

SOMEWHERE IN FRANCE

The very idea of traveling to Europe intimidated most Americans of Lieutenant Truman's time. It was, after all, a long way across what the soldiers called "the pond." Such army braggadocio, however, belied a fear that American ships might well be sitting ducks for German submarines. Once safely across the Atlantic the men faced new uncertainties—the foreign language and customs, and all that one finds disorienting in an unfamiliar culture. Finally, and fundamentally, each soldier was unsure how he would behave under fire, facing the enemy, pitting his enthusiasm and brief training against the German army's mastership of the art of war.

Truman went over on the George Washington, *a converted German liner that later took President Wilson to the Peace Conference. A large, fast ship, it made the crossing in a few days, fairly secure against attacks by the slow-moving submarines of that time. The lieutenant and his companions found France both attractive and awkward. Nothing seemed so lovely as the slow, miragelike looming up of the French coast, followed by the definition of harbor, town, and countryside. The soldiers were to remember years later the somewhat absurd railway cars marked* Hommes 40, Chevaux 8 *that transported them to a bewildering series of camps or to villages and farms where they were "billeted" in houses or barns and other outbuildings. The number of men to be put up was perhaps a shock to the little country. American divisions, made up of regiments and brigades, totaled twenty-eight thousand men each—much larger than a European division. Attached troops, including field artillery regiments, brought the divisional slice up to about forty thousand. When it came time for billeting, the attractiveness of French villages and farms paled. Primitive arrangements and interaction with peasants who had been forced to offer hospitality to Allied troops since 1914 began to wear on the American visitors.*

"Somewhere in France," read the heading of American letters home. Men tried to give clues about their locations to family or sweethearts. Truman, for example, wrote Bess about a particular issue of the Saturday Evening Post *that celebrated a French locality. Once in a while a free-wheeling censor resorted to common sense and allowed men to say that, well, they were in a training command in a specific town—for what good would that petty fact do the Kaiser? But*

then security regulations would resurface, and it was back to "Somewhere in France."

The officers censored letters of doughboys and vouched for their own episto-lary purity, but both men and officers played games with the censors—to the point of insulting them. Since this could trigger retaliation, some writers num-bered their letters.

Most letters from the American Expeditionary Force were dull in the ex-treme, apostrophes to weather and food and relatives, sermonettes about French ways and, especially, French prices. Truman's, however, show remarkable range, willingness to see fascination in the banalities of life behind the front, wry speculation about people, whether civilian or military, and always the fondness for Bess and the fervent exhortations that she write, write.

Dear Bess: [En route to East Coast, Mar. 20, 1918]

We are moving out at last. Sat up all night last night waiting for the train. It pulled in at 1:30 A.M. this Wednesday morning. We have a fine Pullman observation car with all 129th officers except five or six. They are 130th. We are going north and hoping to hit Kansas City. They say we'll go around the outer edge if we do. Your package was just in time and sure was fine. I never tasted such good candy in my life and the cakes were just as fine. This train is so rough I can hardly write but I am afraid if I wait I won't get to mail it. We are sure glad to leave Ft. Sill but we may see the time when it will look good to us. They turned down Lt. Lee at the last minute. I was so mad I could have cussed all the doctors in Christendom off the map if I could have done it. They sent him before a physical efficiency board and he beat them there and got his baggage loaded into the car after spending all day chasing back and forth to division headquarters. Then they made him stay behind and sent a substitute. He was the most thoroughly disappointed person you ever saw. I hated it almost as badly as he did. We don't know where we are going but it looks like we might come through Kansas City now as we are going north on the Rock Island. I'd give anything in the world to see you and Mamma and Mary before I go across but I doubt very much if that is possible except by good luck. I shall keep you informed by wire where I am until I leave this country. All cables will come to Boxley through the chief cable censor so you will be informed immedi-ately on my safe arrival across. You can write me Detachment 35th Division, 129th F.A., Camp Merritt, New Jersey, and I'll probably get it. The train is slowing and I'd better quit, will write some more tomorrow and wire you today.

Yours always,
Harry

Heading east with part of his regiment, Truman took advantage of a stop in Kansas City to call Bess. It was a brief, early morning layover in the rail yards with no public phone in sight. The switchman let him use his phone, saying, "Call her, the phone's yours, but if she doesn't break the engagement at five o'clock in the morning she really loves you." Bess, to be sure, was delighted.

Dear Bess: [En route to East Coast, Mar. 21, 1918]
    We are rolling along through Iowa at Washington now. I think I shall mail this at Rock Island, Ill. That is where we are going to eat supper. They have been kidding me pretty strong today because I called you out of bed to the phone. Major Gates said he expected to see in the society column where you were engaged to someone else because of it. I told him not to worry his head about that. It was not a very pleasant thing from your point of view I don't suppose to be called out at that unearthly hour, but it gave me lots of pleasure to hear your voice once more even if it was only over the phone. Besides it may be a whole year or more before I'm in Kansas City again and if it had been two o'clock instead of five I'd have done it. I am sorry to have disturbed your mother but I hope she'll forgive me this time. There is only one chance that I won't go to France and that is a strict eye test at the port of embarkation. I guess I'll get by though. We only stayed in K.C. about twenty minutes and I spent fifteen of that hunting a phone. I do wish I could have seen you. I suppose Mary will have a fit when she finds I was in town and didn't call up. There were no Home phones in a mile. We were over in Armourdale in the Rock Island yards and one Bell phone in the yardmaster's office. I am terribly thankful it was there and that it was a Bell. Be sure to write me at Camp Merritt, 129th F.A. Detachment, 35th Division.

                                        Yours always,
                                        Harry

Dear Bess: [Hotel McAlpin, New York City, Mar. 24, 1918]
    Would you believe it? I am here at this joint along with four other Missouri guys. We are having the time of our innocent young lives lookin' out the window up Broadway. We got here or at Camp Merritt at eleven-thirty last night. They assigned us quarters and we put in a very pleasantly cold night. Got up this morning, had breakfast of ham and eggs at a cafeteria in the camp, and then got permission to come to the city. Got a taxi, five of us did, and drove thirteen miles to 130th Street, rode the ferry across, and then began hunting for the subway downtown. They told us it was only a block from the ferry. We walked around and hunted and finally decided to take the elevated, which was nearby about four stories up. Well the elevated turned out to be the subway! The devilish thing runs out of the ground about 120th Street and runs over a low place on stilts. We couldn't recognize it as the subway. We have all had shines, shaves, baths, and are now in here to go to church somewhere this afternoon. We haven't decided whether it will be Al Jolson or George Cohan. I have an idea we'll flip a coin and decide. Camp Merritt is a cantonment with steam heat, hot baths (when there's a fire) and private rooms for officers. We missed the boat and may have to stay

a week. That will be awful, won't it. As it is we don't have to go back to camp until 4:00 P.M. tomorrow (Monday).

They are waiting on me and I've got to run. Will write tomorrow.

Yours always,
Harry

Dear Bess: [Camp Merritt, N.J., Mar. 26, 1918]
Your good letter came yesterday evening when I got back out to camp from New York. I was sure glad to hear from you. I suppose you got my night letter and my regular letter from the McAlpin. We went to the Winter Garden Sunday night and saw the rottenest vaudeville show I ever saw or ever hope to see. It couldn't even play at the Globe and get by in Kansas City. New York is a very much overrated burg. It merely keeps its rep by its press agents' continually harping on the wonder of it. There isn't a town west of the Mississippi of any size that can't show you a better time.

We walked up Broadway after supper. The street was all torn up and as far as bright lights go they looked no brighter to me than Twelfth [Street in K.C.] most any night. I went to the top of the Woolworth Building, 792 feet and 1 inch above the street. Saw the whole town for fifty cents. It was a grand sight. Could see the whole of New York, Brooklyn, Jersey City, Hoboken, Weehawken and all. I am going to see Central Park today. We will sail this week. I can't tell you the day but will mail you letters right up to the time, and when they cease coming you'll know I've gone. I must run. Keep on writing—the letters will be forwarded.

Yours always,
Harry

Dear Bess: [Camp Merritt, N.J., Mar. 27, 1918]
Your telegram and letter were both waiting for me when I returned from New York this afternoon. I was in on strictly business today. Bought two pairs of glasses, which make me six pairs so I don't suppose I'll run out.

I accidentally ran into an honest optician who happened to belong to my goat tribe (i.e., Scottish Rite [Masons]) and he sent me to the best or one of the best oculists in the city. He gave me a complete and thorough examination, a prescription I can use in Paris or Vienna, and lots of good conversation all for the whole sum of $5.00, and then he asked me if I thought I could stand that. How is that for the crookedest town in the universe? Then the optician, who also gave me lots of good advice, only charged me $17.50 less 10 percent for two complete pairs of regulation aluminum frames and glasses, throwing in an extra lens that he happened to chip on the edge in the grinding. I can't understand it. Watts stung me for $22.00 for two pairs, and Dr. Leonard charged me $10.00 the last time I bought any, and they were supposed to be friends of mine too. This place is on Madison Avenue just off 42nd Street and I know he pays more rent for a week than Watts does for a month. Evidently these men are patriotic men if one of them is named Haustetter. That's the optician's name and he says it loses him business, although his son has made some wonderful inventions in observing instruments for the U.S. Navy since we went to war. I sent you a small package today for Easter. I hope it arrives intact. When you wear it think of me out on the Atlantic thinking of you and seeing your face in the moonlit waves of Old Neptune, and wishing wishing oh so badly that I could only see you. Really I'm almost homesick for you and Mamma and Mary. If I could only have stayed these two days in Kansas City instead of this —— Kike town, I'd have felt much better. I am crazy to leave because I know that if the British stem this tide there'll not be another and I do want to be in at the death of this "Scourge of God." Just think what he'd do to our great country and our beautiful women if he only could. That is the reason we must go and must get shot if necessary to keep the Huns from our own fair land. I am getting to hate the sight of a German and I think most of us are the same way. They have no hearts or no souls. They are just machines to do the bidding of the wolf they call Kaiser. Old Julius Caesar's description of the senate exactly fits the Germans of today and to think that Wilhelm should call himself Caesar! Attila or Tamerlane would be nearer the truth.

As I told you before, I've seen this town from cellar to garret and from the Battery to the north end and I can't do much for it. When a New Yorker shows you the Woolworth Building or Senator Clark's house or Grant's Tomb or the Hudson River he expects you to fall dead with admiration, and if you don't he's confident your education has been overlooked. When one of our N.G. lieutenants showed me Grant's Tomb from the Hudson Ferry I did him like Mark Twain did the Dago who showed him the paintings of Michelangelo. I said, "Well! Is he dead?" The nut didn't even think it was a joke. He thought I wanted to know sure enough. Anyone from west of the Mississippi can make these people believe anything. I believe I could sell gold bricks on Broadway and make 'em cry for more.

I shall try my best to find White's and spoil a photographic plate if it will please you. This is Wednesday evening and Friday we leave, so I don't know whether I can make it but I'll try.

Don't you worry about me not taking care of myself. I'm not out for V.C.'s [Victoria Crosses] or a Croix de Guerre. I'm going to use my brains, if I have any, for Uncle Sam's best advantage and I'm going to aim to keep them in good working order, which can't be done by stopping bullets.

Agnes must want my fine plug pretty badly, but she doesn't want to pay what he's worth. He has a pedigree that would make the King of Spain green with envy. He's worth $300 for a saddle horse and being himself he's worth $500. If Agnes wants to make an offer like that I might listen to it, although I promised Colonel Danford that I'd keep him until the war is over and let him have him if he wants him. That was the only way I'd take him because it would have been stealing to buy him for $100. Agnes must think I want $50 mighty badly. I do need it and badly but my grand saddle horse isn't for sale. This letter is not what it should be but I'm trying to make up for what I didn't do at Ft. Sill. I hope you'll forgive me because my intentions were the best but I was trying hard to make good for Uncle Sam. I did down there and if I can only hold up on the other side perhaps I can do him and you and everyone some small service. A telegram just came from Gates Wells to know if I can see him. I shall try to meet him at the McAlpin tomorrow if he can come up there and I can get away. It's fine of him to want to see me. Tell your mother I love her almost as much as I do my own, and if you ever throw me down I'm going to call her mother anyway. I'll write you tomorrow and wire you Friday.

I shall cable you direct when I land. My cable censor address is Boxley and I can cable often because it's about half the cost. Keep on writing to the same address—the letters will be forwarded.

Yours always,
Harry

Truman's description below of what the army called a Sam Brown belt suggests that he was fond of this aspect of the American Expeditionary Force officer's uniform. A leather belt, which circled the waist and passed diagonally over the right shoulder, it had been invented by Sir Samuel Brown of the British army in India in the late nineteenth century.

Dear Bess: [Jersey City, N.J., Mar. 28, 1918]

It is eleven o'clock and I've got to arise at three in order to get my goods and chattels in readiness to go on the boat, but I am going to write you one last letter on this side on the last day I can. I didn't get to see Gates because they kept me here until nearly two o'clock reading orders and instructions as to how we must act, what we must say and not say when we arrive in General Pershing's jurisdiction. About all we can write is "I am well if you are well it is well," and if we were to put that down S.V.B.E.V. they'd destroy the letter and probably hang us for spies. I don't suppose I can even say I love you, because some heartless censor would cut it out as a state secret and spoil what was on the other side. If you get any letters with strips cut out of them you'll know that is what I said and that I'm always saying it. I am awfully sorry but I didn't get to go to White's for the same reason I didn't get to see Gates. It was too late by the time I got through here to do anything whatever in town. If I'd stayed here another week, I'd be writing home for money and I haven't got anything for it either—only a very uncomfortable pair of feet because of their not being well acquainted with hard pavements. Have two immense blisters, which I never had in all my Ft. Sill marching and countermarching. Bought me a Sam Brown belt today and I look real fussy in it. They're the kind that have a strap over the shoulder and a broad red leather belt in the center with loud brass trimmings. Have to carry a can of brass polish to keep it looking well. It has a hook for a saber but I never expect to wear one.

I didn't get a letter today and I'm terribly disappointed. I know it's Uncle Sam's fault on the delivery and I may get it on the boat anyway. Hope so.

My new address is 129th Field Artillery Detachment, 35th Division, A.E.F. via New York. It will take two envelopes to get it all on. Wired you today and as you are reading it I'll probably be going out of Sandy Hook behind a warship.

Remember that I've always loved you and shall continue to no matter what happens, and when the Great God Ammon Ra weighs me for good and for bad I'm hoping that will be for the main and principal cause of the good outweighing. I am hoping to cable you from Berlin soon.

Yours always,
Harry

Dear Bess: [Aboard U.S.S. *George Washington*, Apr. 1918]

We are about to arrive and I am going to write you what purports to be a letter. There are so many things we can't write about that there is practically nothing left but the weather and the scenery to talk of. The weather has been fine all the way across, ideal submarine weather so they say, but I prefer it to the rough kind. We had one day that made me and several others pretty much disgusted with life on the sea. I can't see what a man wants to be a sailor for. Except for the one day, I've enjoyed all the meals I could get. Some of the officers have been sick all the way and, I am sure from my one day's experience, have spent a very unpleasant time. Everyone has a remedy and none of them work but Christian Science and sometimes it fails in a rough sea. We have had a very pleasant time except for the monotony of it. There are six lieutenants in our cabin, all congenial spirits. We play cards awhile then go on deck and hunt for submarines awhile and sleep the rest of the time except when we're on guard.

There is no scenery to write about, nothing but blue water everywhere when the sun shines, lead colored when it doesn't, and copper colored at sunrise and sunset. The sunsets on the sea aren't half as good to see as those on our prairies at home. You see just as far as the rim, which they tell me is twenty miles away. The funny part of it is we never catch up with that rim. If we could only get over it I'm sure we could go twice as fast because it would be downhill. One fellow remarked to me the other night that according to his map of the Atlantic Ocean we'd have a hard pull of it from here to France because it would be uphill all the way. Some of the things the crew pull off are a caution to hear. Most of the best ones are unprintable but are not so bad as humorous when you hear them. I am enclosing you a copy or two of *The Hatchet*—our daily paper—which will tell you lots that goes on on board every day. I didn't get any of your last letters at Camp Merritt. The telegram about the picture was the last thing I got. I am hoping they were forwarded on this boat and that I'll get them when I land.

Shall write again tomorrow.

Yours always,
Harry S. Truman

Dear Bess: April 14, 1918

I landed today and have been trying to find a cable office that hasn't a U.S. censor in it. They won't let us cable for things like informing our people we landed safely because the wires are so crowded they can't send them. I guess you've got my cable I left in New York by this time anyway. My cussed pen went dry right up there and I had to get up and fill it. I am in a French hotel room about as big as your grandmother's room and the front hall combined and the floor's as cold as the top of a lake when it's frozen and the grip [suitcase] with the ink had to be as far from the bed as it could be. The electric switch turns off the light in the center of the room, and another turns lights on over the head of the bed. You can't light both at once—when one's on the other goes off automatically and as the bed is the warmest I am writing this in bed. We go to work tomorrow and I have been seeing this town, which is quite wonderful to

Battlefields of the American Expeditionary Force, 1918.

me. It isn't Paris, but if Paris is as much livelier as it is bigger, Paris is some town. Wine and beer are sold here and most of the 35th Division have been in Oklahoma so long that they are trying to drink all there is here. They can't as the supply seems to be inexhaustible. Prices are marked strictly on the American plan in French money and they skin us alive. Our dinners cost us 10 francs apiece, about $1.80, so you see things are not so cheap. One fellow bought him a Sam Brown belt for 40 franks (I don't know why I spelled that with a *k*) and gave the man a ten-dollar bill. He got 60 francs in change and the belt so he made a belt and 3 francs by the deal and didn't know it until someone told him that ten dollars was 57 francs.

This is a beautiful place. I wish I could tell you where it is. (Call Boxley up.) The room I have at the Hotel des Voyageurs is furnished in mahogany with double lace curtains at its windows. It has a picture of Henry IV and his children on one side and Henry VIII of England at some state function on the other. This is a fine place (no fine) with a white marble mantelpiece, which has a Dutch clock under a glass case. (The clock doesn't run, probably on account of its age.) It is a beautiful gold affair with a couple of seventeenth-century pikemen on top of it. It is flanked by two exquisitely beautiful lamps and there is a large mirror over the whole thing about four feet square. The chairs are upholstered in red plush. It looks more like some count's bedroom than a hotel room.

I went to a picture show and saw Pearl White in one of the sections of a spasm that has been running a year or so over in U.S.A. The name and explanations were in French and I've forgotten its name but it was good old mellerdramer and I had not seen this episode. There was a comedy and another complete film that was good and a dancer named Miss Theer. We got tired and left before the show was over or I guess we could have been there yet. It began at two-thirty and we left at five-thirty, all for 1 franc 45 centimes—about 35 cents.

We had a most pleasant voyage and found a well-formed rumor that we were sunk when we got to port. The navy has the army beaten forty ways for wild stories.

I've got to quit because it's 10:00 P.M. and lights go out at nine o'clock and I'm liable to get arrested.

Write me as below.

Yours always,
Harry S. Truman, 1st Lt. 129th F.A.
Det. 35th Division, A.E.F.

One theme of the early letters from France is the schooling that General Pershing required of the American Expeditionary Force so it could learn more about tactics used on the Western Front. Although Truman, at the age of thirty-four, found classwork difficult, he himself was eventually teaching.

[Somewhere in France]

Dear Bess: April 17, 1918

How do you like the stationery? It is French or Swiss or Belgique or some foreign kind. They do things in great shape over here. Everyone tries his level best to treat Americans better than the one before, hoping that there will be a greater consideration forthcoming. We find a nice restaurant where we can get a fine meal for 3 or 4 francs and when we go back after spreading the news it costs 10 or 12. I suppose it serves us right though because our buck privates get as much money as a captain over here. My check was for 1,007.40 francs and next month it'll be about 1,100.00. Nearly enough money to retire on over here and plenty to start in business with an immense stock of goods, all of two counters full. The people generally treat us fine and seem very glad to accommodate us in any way they can.

I am not in school yet although I shall be very soon. Have been walking around the town and country seeing the sights and there are lots of them. If the sun would only shine, it would be a beautiful place. It never has been shining except on the day we landed. I guess that was a good omen. Hope so anyway.

I have been trying to cable you ever since I landed but as I told you in my letter day before yesterday the wires are so crowded with official business I haven't been able to do it. I left a letter for you in New York to be mailed when we arrived which I suppose you have gotten by this time anyway. I have been going through the art gallery with Major Gates and some of the other lieutenants today. It has lots of pretty pictures and statues and things but nothing of note. We are going to Grand Opera tonight—Ambroise Thomas' *Mignon*. I don't reckon it'll amount to much but we are going to try it anyway. Saw Clara Kimball Young in a spasm last night entitled *Femmes des France,* but couldn't see any connection between title and show if *"Femmes des France"* means "Women of France," as they tell me it does. She was a Red Cross nurse and married an Englishman that she'd been dingy over before the war, after nursing him through a wounded spell. Very touching when Clara Kimball does it and caused the French audience to clap very loudly when he took her in his arms in the last act. All the explanations were in French, so I just guessed the thing out. They put on a real American picture the other night, Douglas Fairbanks, and everything was in good United States language. It was sure some satisfaction too I tell you. I sure do get tired of *Oui, Oui Monsieur* and *Cinq Francs, Merci Monsieur*. All I can say is *je ne comprend pas,* and I'm not sure of that.

Wish I could step in and see you this evening. Have only seen one good-looking French woman and she was married to some French general or admiral or something, anyway he had seven or eight yards of gold braid on him. Might have only been a second lieutenant for all I know.

Be sure and write lots of letters for I'll appreciate them when I get them if it won't be till next summer sometime. I am thinking of you all the time and dream of you always.

Yours,
Harry

Perhaps Truman's enthusiasm about the French landscape, so evident below, resulted from its contrast to Missouri farmland. The Missouri system of square-mile surveys devised by the Northwest Territory Ordinance was completely different from those meandering boundaries originally set in medieval France.

                                                                    [Somewhere in France]
Dear Bess: April 23, 1918
    You have no doubt wondered at not receiving a cable from me when I landed, but the orders were very strict against sending cables saying that we were safely landed and therefore I couldn't send one. I tried every day for three days after getting off the boat to get one off but was refused every day. I left a letter in New York that was to be mailed as soon as the boat arrived and I suppose you have it by this time.
    I have been touring France quite extensively at the expense of the American Government and haven't gone to work yet. The country is very pretty and I don't blame the French for wanting to keep it. I wouldn't trade any of U.S. for an equal part of France but if I had to give up being a Missourian I'd be a citizen of France by second choice. Every inch of the country that is at [all] equal to growing anything is in cultivation. Their boundary lines run every which direction, and I don't see how they ever describe a piece of property when they want to transfer it. The cities seem to be just as bad. The fields make an irregular patchwork of the landscape when seen from a distance and if I were a painter I'd surely want to go to work on the scenery right away. It's a shame that our business is to tear up all the pretty places and villages we can instead of putting something more to them. They tell me that the part of France that Germany has mussed up was just as pretty and well taken care of as what I've seen and that now it is a desert. They (the French) seem to think that we are going to help them very materially to get it back. . . .
    Haven't seen any good-looking girls yet.
                                                    Yours always,
                                                    Harry

                                                                    [Somewhere in France]
Dear Bess: April 28, 1918
    The fourth Sunday after Easter and I am just now ready to go to a real artillery school. Have had a splendid tour of the Atlantic Ocean and France. Have seen France as no civilian tour could possibly see it and now have a room with four of the most congenial first lieutenants in the regiment at an old chateau with a beautiful garden, a moat, a fine park, and a church with a chime clock and the most beautifully toned bell I ever heard. The hardships of this war are sure easy to bear so far.
    Major G. and I took a walk yesterday afternoon and turned off on a

road that said *"Chemin Particulier."* Neither of us knew what that was. Evidently it means private road, for we ran into another chateau. There was a man at the gate who invited us in and showed us a park with a pretty little stream running through it. There was a swan on it and some green and white ducks. The gardens were things of beauty. There was an old mill in the park where they made flour (before the war), their own ice plant, electric dynamo, and every other convenience. There were six kinds of horse vehicles (no horses, gone to war), three autos in a garage that looked like pictures of Swiss homes you've seen. The whole thing was surrounded by a six-foot wall. Take it all together, the major and I had a very pleasant walk. It belongs to a French colonel. . . .

Went to church this morning. Catholic in French. Couldn't understand a word but I reckon it was all right because they took up a collection, and Major G. told me that the drift of the priest's little French talk was that the ration should be adhered to and that the girls shouldn't flirt with the gay Americans. Like to froze in the church, but it is nice and warm outside.

Be sure and write real often. I hope to get them someday. Will write as often as I can.

Yours always,
Harry

[Somewhere in France]

Dear Bess: May 5, 1918

. . . We work so hard during the week we don't have time to think of anything but work. Sundays are sure dull though if we don't get letters to read.

Be sure and write and keep writing and I'll do the same. We sure appreciate letters and more letters from home. France is France and a grand place for Frenchmen. I don't blame them for fighting for it and I'm for helping them, but give me America, Missouri, and Jackson County for mine with the finest girl in the world at the county seat. French girls are pretty and chic but they cannot hold a candle to American girls. Every man in this room agrees with me too. It's raining today for a change after starting out with a grand sunrise and a fine morning. We've seen the sun about four days since we've been in France. The weather doesn't bother us much, but I'll bet a Frenchman would suffocate if he got into a heated room. They're never warm from September till June. They thrive on it though. Be sure and write to me much and often, for I can always put in another week happily if I get at least one letter. The more, the better. I'm sure crazy to see you.

Yours always,
Harry

[Somewhere in France]

Dear Bess: May 19, 1918

I am still somewhere in France going to school like a darned kid, and I guess I'll keep on going for some weeks to come. No letters yet since the first week I was here, but I know there are a bushel of them somewhere. They send them just as the mailman feels when they come. If he's facing the south bag when he gets our mail that's where it goes, and if he's facing the north bag, why it goes north, etc. ad lib. I guess we'll get 'em sometime. I went off on a truck ride this morning over to the adjoining town. It wasn't any different from the other French towns I've seen, but the ride was beautiful. The French know how to build roads and also how to keep them up. They are just like a billiard table and every twenty meters there are trees on each side. I have raved over the scenery in every letter I've written and it is worth raving about, but it was particularly beautiful this morning because the sun was shining. It has shone for two days together—a really unusual occurrence. I didn't take my raincoat because it was so pretty and bright, and as was to be expected it rained to beat thunder. We were lucky though and got home between showers. It's sure pouring down now. If you'll read the letters that came out in *Collier's* about a month ago, you will get a very good and vivid description of France as we see it.

We have been working harder than ever. I had an examination Saturday that would make the president of Yale University bald-headed scratching his head trying to think of answers. I think we'll all be nuttier than an Arkansas squirrel if we study this hard much longer. I am now an orienting officer (whatever that may be). From what I can gather in a casual survey of the situation, I am supposed to go out on the earth somewhere and find out where I am and then tell everybody else. It's a nice job as far as I can discover if I can get a little surveying, geometry, astronomy, and a few other things into my noodle inside the next three or four weeks. If it doesn't bust, I guess I can do it. . . .

I am hoping to get some letters this week sure, so keep on writing. Remember that I'm thinking of you all the time anyway if I don't write every day. Every fellow in this room is engaged to some fine girl back in the States and the French girls haven't a chance. None of us have ever seen any worth raving over yet. I guess all the pretty ones are in Paris anyway. I'd like to go see but I guess I won't anyway soon.

Yours always,
Harry

[Somewhere in France]

Dear Bess: June 2, 1918

This is another Sunday and it must be Saint's Day or Pope's Day or something because the bells on our church have been going since about 5:00 A.M. to the tune of an immense amount of swearing on our part. The priest or someone evidently gets up in the tower and plays a regular tune on them. The church has two bells and after beating on them drum-style for a while he comes downstairs and rings them a half-hour church-style. He's been doing that ever since 5:00 A.M. at two-hour intervals. We'd be happy to see those bells melted into cannon, I tell you. We won't have to be bothered by them for more than one Sunday more though because I fear they are going to send us to our regiment next week. . . .

If I tell you more than I have about the country the censor'd cut it out, so I can only say as always

I love you,
Harry

Angers, France
June 14, 1918

Dear Bess:

I am back with the regiment and a sure enough captain. Have been, it seems, some six weeks. I'll have about a bushel and a half of francs back pay coming next payday. I reckon I can go out and have a real time with it. I just barely slipped through the artillery school, as did some of the others. One or two made names for themselves and were promoted out of the regiment as instructors, which means that they'll be second lieutenants until the end of the war, and that they'll not get to the front. I am very glad that I didn't make any such record. I am the adjutant of the Second Battalion, 129th F.A. A right hefty job and one that gives me precedence over all the Battery captains, even if they do outrank me. I've got to organize a regimental school and teach the balance of the officers what I learned (which won't be a whole lot). . . .

I will write a longer letter tomorrow. I think of you always. Counted the leaves on a locust limb the other day and they said "this year," which I am hoping is right.

Yours always,
Harry

Angers, France
June 27, 1918

Dear Bess:

Another banner day. Got four letters. Hooray! Also a box of candy from Paris on which it said it was sent by order of Miss Bess Wallace, Independence, Kansas City, Mo. It was grand candy, too, and very much appreciated because candy is hard to get. I guess they sent the candy instead of the cake because cake is under the ban. All flour is used in bread. The candy was just as well and lasts a heap longer. I have been working as usual—the regimental schoolteacher, along with Captain Paterson. You should hear me hand these fellows bunk and make them like it. It's rather funny for an old rube to be handing knowledge (of a sort) to the Harvard and Yale boys, but it's happening now. The hardest work I ever did in my life too. I'd rather saw wood or pitch hay. You can never tell what will happen to you in this war. May be a farmer superintendent before it's over. They say that if you can't pass an exam in trig. and logs, they'll keep you on the horse lines and won't let you up front. I hope it's only a rumor. . . .

I was mighty sorry to hear of Rufe Montgall's death. Hadn't heard until I got your, and Mary's, letters. He was a fine boy and his mother's only child. The French say, *"C'est la guerre."* One old lady over here had eight sons killed. She asked that the ninth one be sent to the reserves. Her request was granted but before the order got there he was also killed. They are stoics though and are satisfied to give all for the principle they are fighting for.

I'm for the French more and more. They are the bravest of the brave. If there were only millions more. They and the Americans hit it off fine. The people we are billeted with seem unable to do enough for us. They appreciate the least friendliness and if I had the time I could learn French from them. But I don't know any more now than when I landed. Too much artillery to learn.

No I haven't seen any girls that I'd care to look at twice and when I'm happiest I am dreaming of you, so that ought to be the right and proper condition of mind, oughtn't it not? If you'll just keep writing so I'll get letters and lots of 'em I'll write every time I have a minute.

Yours always,
Harry

Somewhere in France
Dear Bess: July 14, 1918
I wrote you several letters from the last town I was in and told you how I came back to the regiment, am a captain, and a lot of things like that. Now some other censor has decided that we should not have mentioned places and I am much afraid all that mail is destroyed. Someday they will get the things all straightened out.

Your letters of the fourteenth and nineteenth of June were here at camp when I arrived and you may be sure I am most happy to get them. You couldn't possibly write me a silly letter. I am disappointed that you should think of tearing up one, they are so very valuable. We work like thunder and cuss the things we have to do sometimes, especially when some chappie who's been to school since the war began and has never seen a man or a horse tries to make things clear and easy for us, when along comes a letter from home saying we are heroes and puffing us all up until we don't have a worry in the world but to make good and win the war.

We moved from our billets at the beautiful old French town I told you of and are now at a large artillery camp with the whole brigade. We are going to shoot every day for a while and then we hope to shoot some Huns.

You've no idea how sorry I am to hear of your mother's illness and I most sincerely hope you have succeeded in making her well again. I should certainly like to see Fred washing dishes. I bet he can't do it any better than I can. Your cornbread, I know, would be the finest to be had, as would anything else you'd make. I wish I could only have a hunk of it. We get plenty to eat but of course it's not like your, and mother's, cooking. I hope your grandfather is much better now, and that by the time you read this letter you won't have a thing to worry about but how quickly I'll be home to march down the aisle with you.

I am a Battery commander now. They made me captain of Battery D after letting me serve as adjutant of the second battalion for thirty days and try to teach the other officers what I'd learned at artillery school. No, the school you mentioned was not the one I went to. That one was an officers' training camp like Funston. Ours was a high school for artillery officers. Tell George that little Higginbotham is in my Battery. I have the Irish Catholic Battery but they seem to like me pretty well and I am satisfied that, if I don't blow up with too many worries, I'll have a good Battery. I hope the best in the brigade. The one that does the best work here gets to fire the first shot of the brigade at the Hun. I shall do my very best to win the honor, although I may fail to get it as there is hot competition.

You've no idea the experience I'm getting. I've been most everything and done most everything in this man's army since August 5 and now I have attained my one ambition, to be a Battery commander. If I can only make good at it, I can hold my head up anyway the rest of my days. . . . Please keep writing and remember I love you

Always,

Harry

The death of Bess's Grandfather Gates (maker of the family fortune) got little attention from the busy Captain Truman. Here he mentions it only in passing.

Somewhere in France

July 22, 1918

Dear Bess:

This is a banner day sure enough. I have your letter of July 1 telling of your grandfather's death and remarking that I would probably have to take a day off to read your letter. I have read it over and over. It is certainly a grand day when letters come. I am most awfully sorry to hear of your grandfather's death but it is something that we can't help and that we can only accept the best way we can. . . .

They gave me a Battery that was always in trouble and in bad, but we carried off all the credits this week. I hope to make a reputation for myself if the cards fall right and I don't get wounded or something. It is the Irish Battery I have and the adjutant has decided to put an O in front of my name to make me right. They seem to want to soldier for me and if I can get them to do it, I shall consider that I have made the greatest success there is to make. If I fail, it'll be a great failure too. That's always the case though. The men are as fine a bunch as were ever gotten together but they have been lax in discipline. Can you imagine me being a hard-boiled captain of a tough Irish Battery? I started things in a rough-cookie fashion. The very first man that was up before me for a lack of discipline got everything I was capable of giving. I took the Battery out to fire the next day

Captain Truman of Battery D, summer 1918. *Harry S. Truman Library*

and they were so anxious to please me and fire good that one of my gunners got the [illegible] ague and simply blew up. I had to take him out. When I talked to him about it he almost wept and I felt so sorry for him I didn't even call him down. Tell George that little Higginbotham is one of my shootin' men. He pulls the hammer on No. 1 gun and he sure rides it. The other day it nearly bucked him off. The thing wasn't set solidly on the ground and as he has to pull the hammer from the right-hand side of the gun he insisted on riding it every time because it was easier to reach the lanyard. . . .

I don't imagine that Columbia [Mo.] would be a very grand place to spend the winter, although I hope Fred goes there because I never knew how very valuable a university education is until now, even if I did help Slagle shut up the chappies by telling them that I was a graduate of Moler's Barber College. We told them at artillery school that we belong to the Q.T.F., which meant Quinine Tonic Fraternity, and we never heard any more college yells at that school.

I am going to send you a picture postcard of me next week if the camera stood the strain.

Please keep writing and remember I am

Yours always,

Harry

Somewhere in France (still far from the front)

Dear Bess: July 31, 1918

Your letter of July 5 came today and I, as usual, had a fit of gladness. I hope you had a good Fourth but I know it couldn't have been a glorious one with the death of your grandfather so close to it. I do wish I could be there to help you decide whether you'd stay in a huge house or a small one. It wouldn't take me two minutes to decide.

I am going to buy you an iron cross or German helmet or something like that and send it to you as soon as I can get where they are for sale. You can tell 'em I captured it or anything you like. Most war trophies are bought afterwards or picked up on the field after the battle. Nowadays battles are just sort of a "You shoot up my town and I'll shoot up yours." They say that Americans don't play fair. They shoot 'em up all the time. I hope so because I want to finish this job as soon as possible and begin making an honest living again.

My Irish Battery went out on the range the other day and outfired the others in the battalion, on account of which I am rather swelled up. The major remarked that "D Battery is all right" and then he proceeded to tell the others why they weren't. I was awful lucky and they say that a smiling face goes a long way toward getting things looked on in the right way. Anyway, I feel right encouraged. As I told you before, if I am a success as the commanding officer of a Battery of field artillery I shall have accomplished the best thing I could do in this war. I have my doubts about my bravery when heavy-explosive shells and gas attacks begin. I am like a fellow Uncle Harry used to tell about. I have the bravest kind of head and body but my legs won't stand.

I hadn't the slightest notion that I was causing you a heartache when I wore my uniform to the party last Fourth. I was so proud of myself for having it that nothing would do but I must wear it. I wouldn't make you an instant's unhappiness for all the glory in the world. But I've got to put my ability (if I have any) to its very best use now so we can really enjoy our great country and real happiness when it's over. I am sure you wouldn't want me to be anywhere else than where I am now.

I certainly appreciate your putting a star on the church flag for me. I believe in all churches, even the Roman Catholic can do a man a lot of good. I had a Presbyterian bringing up, a Baptist education, and Episcopal leanings so I reckon I ought to get to heaven somehow, don't you think so? . . .

I am hoping most sincerely that they don't send me to the service of supply, or home, before I get one chance at the front.

It is sure a great game if you don't weaken. Be sure and write to me as often as you can, because I think of you always and can never tell you how much I do think.

Yours always,
Harry

EIGHT

ACTION AND AFTERMATH

For the most part, World War I was fought along stationary lines; there was little movement of the opposing armies. Each side was protected by two or three trenches—a buffer of as much as a few miles. The trenches, however, provided only minimal protection and then only if one were in a dugout. From 1914 to early 1918, the French, British, and German troops all endured frequent machine-gun fire and almost nonstop shelling. The Americans sought to introduce more movement to this war of position.

The greatest numbers of General Pershing's American divisions arrived in France in the summer and early autumn of 1918. Truman was among an advanced section of the 129th Field Artillery Regiment. He first saw action in the Vosges Mountains in one of the more stable fronts where neither side had disturbed the line in more than ritual ways for nearly four years. Like most American units, Truman's was impatient with this arrangement. Following Pershing's advocacy of offensive tactics, they fired five hundred gas shells at the German line. Retaliation was quick. Truman described the exchange in his November 23, 1918, letter to Bess: "I shot my gas barrage at 8:00 P.M. The first sergeant failed to get the horses up in time, and the Hun gave me a good shelling. The sergeant ran away and I had one high old time getting out of that place. I finally did with two guns and went back to my former position, arriving at 4:00 A.M., where the cooks had the best hot meal I've tasted since I arrived in France without exception. The boys called that engagement the Battle of Who Run, because some of them ran when the first sergeant did and some of them didn't. I made some corporals and first-class privates out of those who stayed with me and busted the sergeant."

Second, third, and fourth of his regiment's engagements were the Battle of Saint-Mihiel, September 12–16; the Battle of the Meuse-Argonne, which began on September 26 and lasted until the Armistice, November 11; and an attack on the old Verdun sector, which commenced on November 6. Truman's Battery was part of the opening barrage at Saint-Mihiel and the Meuse-Argonne. When it got to Verdun it found itself on territory where shelling often churned up new corpses left from the battle of 1916.

At war's end, Truman, like many officers, had ambivalent feelings—desiring to march straight to Berlin, yet willing to call it quits because the Germans had surrendered. As weeks of armistice stretched into months, and the Peace Conference slowly got under way, Truman's irritation with critical regular army officers —especially their well-known rule that "what looks right is right"—mounted ever higher. He pronounced a series of curses on the regular army and all its works, and speculated on what national prohibition would mean for the unquenchable thirsts of boozing regulars. Surely if the government dispatched the regulars to civilian life, they could no longer hope to run booze emporiums, one of the two professions for which they were suited. The other, serving as restaurant waiters, was also likely to fade out because of the increasing popularity of cafeterias. No number of passes to Paris or Nice or Monte Carlo could compensate for his increasing desire to go home, get married, and do as he pleased—the specifics of which were inchoate. He wrote to Bess of possibly running for eastern judge of Jackson County. He considered running for the House of Representatives so he might sit on the Military Affairs Committee and consign all regular army colonels to damnation. He also spoke of going back to the farm and staying there, letting the world go by until he could retire to Independence (surely a not very subtle ploy to attract the attention of Bess). Always, however, was the desire to "walk down the aisle." He envisioned Bess's coming out to New York, where they might be married in the Little Church Around the Corner. This notion gave way to Bess's request because of her relatives, to be married in Trinity Church in Independence. But he could not arrange to marry Bess until the army released him from its occupation purgatory. The army at last served up a long, seasick voyage back to Hoboken, New Jersey, aboard the German liner Zeppelin, *a decent enough ship but, alas, impressed into service without being filled with ballast, so that it slipped and rolled for ten days before tossing itself up the Narrows into New York harbor. After that it was a long trip by train back to Doniphan and mustering out.*

Somewhere in *Parlez-Vous*

Dear Bess: September 1, 1918
     I am the most pleased person in the world this morning. I got two letters from you and have accomplished my greatest wish. Have fired five hundred rounds at the Germans at my command, been shelled, didn't run away thank the Lord, and never lost a man. Probably shouldn't have told you but you'll not worry any more if you know I'm in it than if you think I am. Have had the most strenuous week of my life, am very tired but otherwise absolutely in good condition physically, mentally, and morally.
     It has been about two weeks since I've written you because I haven't had the chance. They shipped me from school to the front *in charge of Battery D* and the Irish seem to be pleased over it. We went into position right away and fired five hundred rounds at them in thirty-six minutes. Two of my guns got stuck in

the mud, it was dark and raining, and before I could get away bing came the reply. I sent two of the pieces to safety, the horses on the other two broke away and ran every which direction but my Irishmen stayed with me, except a few drivers who were badly scared and my first sergeant. We covered up the two guns I had stuck with branches and things, and one of my lieutenants—Housholder is his name—and myself then collected up all the horses we could and got the men together, caught up with the other two pieces and went to safety. I slept for twenty-four hours afterwards and am now back of the lines awaiting another chance. I went back the next night and got my guns. Every man wanted to go along but I took only the two sections who belonged to the guns.

My greatest satisfaction is that my legs didn't succeed in carrying me away, although they were very anxious to do it. Both of my lieutenants are all wool and a yard wide. One of them, Jordon by name, came back with the horses off the other two pieces to pull me out, and I had to order him off the hill. Four horses were killed, two of them outright and two had to be shot afterwards.

I am in a most beautiful country and it seems like a shame that we must spread shells over it, but as the French say Boches are hogs and should be killed. Please don't worry about me because no German shell is made that can hit me. One exploded in fifteen feet of me and I didn't get a scratch, so you can see I have them beaten there. I would give most anything to see you this Sunday morning. The piece you sent me about Mary is very fine. She is a very able sister and I hope sometime to send her to Europe or anywhere else she wants to go in return for running things as she has.

I am so sleepy I can't hardly hold my eyes open but will write again as soon as I can.

Keep writing. They are like stars seen in the blue waves that roll nightly on deep Galilee (your letters)—as my pet poet says of the Assyrians (not a very appropriate application, but you know the meaning anyway).*

Yours always,
Harry

Somewhere in France
Dear Bess: September 15, 1918
I am well, happy, and somewhat rested up and very, very lazy this morning. It has been raining almost continually for a week and today is sunshine. Day before yesterday was a grand surprise for me. I got a letter from you. I don't know how it ever caught up with me because I have been moving around some. It is the great adventure and I am in it. We haven't done anything but be in reserve

---

*The Assyrian came down like the wolf on the fold,
    And his cohorts were gleamimg in purple and gold;
And the sheen of their spears was like stars on the sea,
    When the blue wave rolls nightly on deep Galilee.
    —Byron, The Destruction of Sennacherib, *1815*

but I am hoping for a shot most every day. My Battery was examined by the chief ordnance officer the other day and he said it was in the best condition of *any in France*, and he has seen them all. That referred to the guns. I was somewhat swelled up but the chief mechanic deserves the credit. His name is McKinley Wooden and he is the straightest, stiffest soldier I have. It almost hurts me when he stands at attention to talk to me. I am plumb crazy about my Battery. They sure step when I ask them to. We had to get ready for a night march a day or two ago and my bunch beat the regiment by nearly a half hour. At Coëtquidan we always won every competition there was to win and then the colonel gives me h (excuse me) every chance he gets. He says that is what he is for and I guess it is. There is no other need of him that I can see. He likes me pretty well though and I get along fine with him.

I am having some very interesting experiences, some of which will do to tell of at a later date. They gave me a new lieutenant yesterday, a second, from the school at Saumur. He's been in France a year, has two gold stripes, is a fine looker, and seems to have horse sense (a hard thing to get in lieutenants). I now have four, two first and two seconds. They are all efficient and that is the reason I have such good luck. Lieutenant Housholder is from Kansas and is also a training-camp man. Lieutenant Jordon is from the plains of Texas, has a Southern drawl, is tall, and has brown eyes. He can ride anything that has a back to sit on and is my horse lieutenant. He moves the Battery with skins and cripples when it has to be done that way. My other second lieutenant is named Eagleton. He's from Oklahoma and has not as much training as the rest but he's a good man and runs my kitchen and supplies. My Saumur graduate is from Chicago and is named Zemer. I sit back and inform them (the lieutenants) and my sergeants what I want done, and it is. My noncoms, now, are whizzes. I sorted 'em over, busted a lot and made a lot. They've gotten so they don't know whether to trust my smile or not, because I smile when I bust 'em and the same when I make 'em. . . .

Remember me to everyone, especially your mother, and keep on writing.

Always,

Harry

In the following Truman excuses his two-week lapse of letter writing by relating how busy he has been—in the battle of the Meuse-Argonne, which opened on September 26 with a massive artillery bombardment. In the first few days American divisions pushed forward rapidly, but soon a slugging match developed against cunningly prepared German positions.

[Somewhere in France]

Dear Bess: October 6, 1918

This is the first opportunity I have had to write you since the day I wrote from the woods before the big drive began. I am very sorry to have been so long but things have happened to me so rapidly I couldn't write. There was no chance to mail them if I could have. The great drive has taken place and I had a part in it, a very small one but nevertheless a part. The experience has been one that

I can never forget, one that I don't want to go through again unless the Lord wills but one I'd never have missed for anything. The papers are in the street now saying that the Central Powers have asked for peace, and I was in the drive that did it! I shot out a German Battery, shot up his big observation post, and ruined another Battery when it was moving down the road. My excellent Second Lieutenant Zemer and myself were in the front of the infantry lines while I was doing it, and I saw tanks take towns and everything else that there is to see. I brought my Battery forward under fire and never lost a horse nor a man. Had shells fall on all sides and I am as sure as I am sitting here that the Lord was and is with me. I'm not yet dizzy although one or two men in the regiment are.

We are in billets now resting up and I suppose we'll go back in when they need us. I am as fat, healthy, and look as well as I ever did, so don't worry about me because there is no German shell with my name on it. I am glad Fred is going to the university as I believe it is a necessity to a man these days. I've had a university education and then some in the last year. Being a Battery commander is an education in itself. I don't know if I have made a successful one or not, but we've been in and out a couple of times together and I still have the Battery. There were a couple of men hurt this last time but they were not with me, they were on special detail with the ammunition train.

If this peace talk is true and we do get to come home soon, I can tell you a lot of things I can't write about. You will probably hear more than you wish. . . .

Would you meet me in New York and go to the Little Church Around the Corner if I get sent home? We can then go east or west or any old direction you wish for a tour. I have an idea if peace comes that it will be six months before we can get home. I got three letters from you today and I surely did appreciate them. I got three also while I was right up under the German guns and I tell you it sure bolstered up my nerve. We were on the most famous battlefield of the war, in front of the town the Germans couldn't take, and were against the Kaiser's pick but they ran just the same. I hope the censor don't see that.

Write often and I'll write just as often as I can.

Yours always,

Harry

Here Truman mentions the frequent night marches that he found so exhausting. The only way, however, to move the hundreds of thousands of American soldiers from Saint-Mihiel to the Meuse-Argonne without danger from German air attack was by night march. Strategically it was also necessary to keep the Germans from knowing the strength and position of the Americans.

Somewhere in France

October 8, 1918

Dear Bess:

I wrote you yesterday [or the day before] kind of a dizzy letter and I am going to do the same thing today—trying, you see, to make up for lost time. There were some three or four weeks from September 10 to October 6 that I did nothing but march at night and shoot or sleep in daylight. I thought of you every day and had I been able to write or mail letters even after they were written, I would certainly have written.

I came through absolutely unscathed—didn't even lose a man in the Battery, although every other Battery had from one to a half-dozen fatalities. A couple of my men who were on special duty with the ammunition train were slightly wounded and that's all. The whole thing was a terrific experience and I'm glad I had it, but I'm also [glad] that it's over with. We are now resting up and I guess we'll go in again when our turn comes. It isn't as bad as I thought it would be but it's bad enough. The heroes are all in the infantry. When a man goes up with them he really does something. We are only their supporters and don't get much real action. The easiest and safest place for a man to get is in the air service. They fly around a couple of hours a day, sleep in a featherbed every night, eat hotcakes and maple syrup for breakfast, pie and roast beef for supper every day, spend their vacations in Paris or wherever else it suits their fancy, and draw 20 percent extra pay for doing it. Their death rate is about like the quartermaster and ordnance departments and on top of it all they are dubbed the heroes of the war. Don't believe it, the infantry—our infantry—are the heroes of the war. There's nothing —machine guns, artillery, rifles, bayonets, mines, or anything else—that can stop them when they start. If we could keep up with them, they'd go to the Rhine in one swoop. The Prussian Guards simply can't make their legs stand when the word comes to them that the Yanks are coming. They move on, what's left of 'em. . . .

Please keep on writing because it helps put the pep into me. I love you more and more and shall continue to pile it up at compound interest for future payment.

Yours always,
Harry

Truman writes from the quiet of a village some distance back of the front. The 129th Field Artillery Regiment had been pulled out of the Meuse-Argonne on October 2. Later, when he had time and energy to reflect, he described the experience more fully, saying that the regiment went "back to a little dirty French town to rest and I'll say we all needed it. Every one of us was almost a nervous wreck and we'd all lost weight until we looked like scarecrows." (Letter of Nov. 23, 1918.) The Battery stayed at Signeulles about a week.

[Somewhere in France]
Dear Bess: October 11, 1918

Your good letter dated September 9 and numbered 19 came this morning. You undoubtedly are right in giving me the dickens for not writing oftener but my duties have been so strenuous and my work so hard in the last two months that I have hardly had a minute to call my own. If I'd written you every time I have thought of doing it, you'd get several every day. . . .

I wish I could have gone to Lone Jack with you on your hunt for a chicken dinner. I'd have taken you back through Lee's Summit and about eight miles west, where I know there are chickens—and a good old mother who can cook them—and we'd have had a real chicken dinner without any expense whatever, although from what Mary tells me it is necessary for each one to carry his own sugar. When we go anywhere to dine out over here we carry both bread and sugar. Sometimes we forget it and then it is necessary to use all our arts and wiles to persuade the proprietor of the place to let us have some. If it happens that the proprietor is feminine, there is normally a chance of success by an added compensation of some francs. These people love francs better than their country and they are extracting just as many of them from us as they possibly can. There are parts of their country that are very beautiful and worth fighting for, but most of it would be a punishment to inflict on the Germans to make them take it. I suppose Germany though is the same kind of country only with a different brand of smells. You can always tell a French village by day or night, even if you can't see anything. They are very beautiful to stand off and look at, nestling down in pretty little valleys, as they always do, with red roofs and a church spire. But when you arrive there are narrow dirty streets and a malodorous atmosphere that makes you want to go back to the hill and take out your visit in scenery.

Please keep on writing even if I am delinquent and shouldn't be. Your letters put pep into me and make me want to finish the job and get to New York as fast as possible. I have about come to the conclusion that the Statue of Liberty is going to have to turn around if she ever sees me again after I land in U.S.A. once more.

I'll never cease to think of you,

Always,
Harry

After leaving Signeulles, the 129th went to the Verdun front, to a position about three kilometers from the famous Fort Douaumont, north of the battered city. Here they were shelled almost every night, and it was a dreary, desolate place.

[Somewhere in France]
Dear Bess: October 30, 1918

Your letter dated October 2 and numbered 28 came last night and you may be very sure I was more than glad to get it. We sit around these Battery positions and wait for something to shoot at and make maps and do so many things that are necessary and a lot that are not that I sometimes don't know straight up from crossways. You know the Battery commander is the man to whom "the buck" is passed both going up and coming down, and he's got to watch his *P*'s and *Q*'s mighty smartly if they don't succeed in getting something on him. So far I have been very lucky in that I have had no one gassed, have not been shelled in any of my positions (and I've occupied several in the last month), and I haven't shot up our infantry yet—at least haven't done it so they could catch me at it. I went out to the front-line trenches yesterday and adjusted my Battery for range and deflection with ten shots. It used to take at least forty-eight when I was at school. But when you know that some Hun plane is just laying for you to catch you shooting so he can run home and tell a gas Battery about you, it does not take so long nor so many shots to adjust with as you'd use under other conditions. There is an old Battery of 155 long guns across the road from me whose date of manufacture was so long ago that no one knows it. They shoot gas at the Hun every time he fires this way and it seems that their work is very effective because the Hun usually ceases to fire when this antique outfit starts. The Frenchmen say that the old guns shoot very accurately. I have paper windows in my dugout and the concussion from the guns has completely ruined it. You should see the palace I live in. It is a different one from that in which I was when I wrote you last. I have a very large arched room which contains the Battery kitchen. On one side I have a small room with a stove, a table, a chair, some boxes, a lot of maps and firing tables and other necessary Battery commander junk. On the other I have a sleeping apartment with room for myself and two lieutenants and a stove. The Battery is up the road a couple of hundred meters and so well hidden that I can't find it myself after dark sometimes. I have a telephone right at my bedside and one on my desk so that when barrages and things are called for I can be immediately informed. I have all the comforts of home except that I'll have such a habit sleeping underground that I'll have to go to the cellar to sleep when I get home.

I was in the most famous war town in France today, unless it's the one where the King of France was crowned. I walked in and I've never seen a more desolate sight. Trees that were once most beautiful forest trees are stumps with naked branches sticking out making them look like ghosts. The ground is simply one mass of shell holes. They say the Hun shot them 1 million a day when he was trying under the Crown Prince to come through. The French simply put 75s hub to hub and mowed them down like hay when they started across. When I arrived in town there was not a building that hadn't a shell hole in it, although the old arched gateway is still standing just as it always has. Both towers of the cathedral are still intact but the rest of it is a mass of ruins. There is not a civilian in town —nothing but soldiers, mostly Yanks.

When I was going in I saw some railway guns firing. They can shoot fifteen or twenty miles and not start to strain their ability to shoot. I am hoping that these were sending messages to Metz.

The news sure looks well today. When Austria *begs* our grand President for the privilege of peace it really looks like something. I'm for peace but that gang should be given a bayonet peace and be made to pay for what they've done to France. I am sure that this desolate country was cultivated and beautiful like the rest of France and now, why Sahara or Arizona would look like Eden beside it. When the moon rises behind those tree trunks I spoke of awhile ago you can imagine that the ghosts of the half-million Frenchmen who were slaughtered here are holding a sorrowful parade over the ruins. It makes you hope that His Satanic Majesty has a particularly hot poker and warm corner for Bill Hohenzollern when his turn comes to be judged and found wanting. . . .

I am just as homesick to see you as you can possibly be to see me. I hope the time is short when we'll see each other. I love you more and more and shall continue to be

Yours always,
Harry

[Somewhere in France]
November 1, 1918

Dear Bess:

I have just finished putting 1,800 shells over on the Germans in the last five hours. They don't seem to have had energy enough to come back yet. I don't think they will. One of their aviators fell right behind my Battery yesterday and sprained his ankle, busted up the machine, and got completely picked by the French and Americans in the neighborhood. They even tried to take their (there were two in the machine) coats. One of our officers, I am ashamed to say, took the boots off of the one with the sprained ankle and kept them.

The French, and Americans too for that matter, are souvenir crazy. If a guard had not been placed over the machine, I don't doubt that it would have been carried away bit by bit. What I started to say was that the German lieutenant yelled *"La guerre fini"* as soon as he stepped from the machine. He then remarked that the war would be over in ten days. I don't know what he knew about it or what anyone else knows but I am sure that most Americans will be glad when it's over and they can get back to God's country again. It is a great thing to swell your chest out and fight for a principle but it gets almighty tiresome sometimes. I heard a Frenchman remark that Germany was fighting for territory, England for the sea, France for patriotism, and Americans for souvenirs. Yesterday made me think he was about right.

I got a letter of Commendation, capital C, from the commanding general of the 35th Division. The ordnance repair department made a report to him that I had the best-conditioned guns after the drive that he had seen in France. The general wrote me a letter about it. My chief mechanic is to blame, not me. He knows more about guns than the French themselves. As usual in such cases, the C.O. gets the credit. I think I shall put an endorsement on the letter stating the ability of my chief mechanic and stick it in the files anyway. I am going to keep the original letter for my own personal and private use. It will be nice to have someday if some low-browed north-end politician tries to remark that I wasn't in the war when I'm running for eastern judge or something. I'll have the "papers" and can shut him up. If ever I get home from this war whole (I shall), I am going to be perfectly happy to follow a mule down a corn row the balance of my days—that is, always providing such an arrangement is also a pleasure to you. I think the green pastures of Grand Old Missouri are the best looking of any that I have seen in this world yet and I've seen several brands. The outlook I have now is a rather dreary one. There are Frenchmen buried in my front yard and Huns in the back yard and both litter up the landscape as far as you can see. Every time a Boche shell hits in a field over west of here it digs up a piece of someone. It is well I'm not troubled by spooks.

I walked out to the observation post the other day (yesterday) to pick an adjusting point and I found two little flowers alongside the trench blooming right in the rock. I am enclosing them. The sob sisters would say that they came from the battle-scarred field of Verdun. They were in sight and short range of Heinie and were not far from the two most famous forts of his line of defense. You can keep them or throw them away but I thought they'd be something. One's a poppy, the other is a pink or something of the kind. A real sob sister could write a volume about the struggle of these pretty little flowers under the frowning brows of Douaumont the impregnable.

Please keep writing, for I look for letters eagerly even if I don't write them as often as I should. I love you

Always,
Harry

[Somewhere in France]
Dear Bess: November 2, 1918
Your letter of the eighth came today written on Treasury Department stationery, and I am sure glad to get it. You must be a wonderful solicitor and money getter to be made manager of the drive. Should we decide to promote some of my numerous oil leases when I return, I shall know whom to elect secretary and money getter. . . .

I am sending you (under separate cover, as the mail order house says) a package which I hope some postal clerk in the A.E.F. doesn't steal, because it is supposed to contain a Christmas present for you. It is not a good present but it is the very best I can do since I can't go to Paris. It is a pair of bronze vases (they're bronze looking anyway—really they're plain old brass) made from German 77 shell cases by a Frenchman here on the front. They will be rather unusual anyway, whether they are pretty or useful or not, and I hope that you'll think of the thought and not look too hard at the present, always considering that it arrives at all. I am hoping that I can give you a better one next time, or make up for the lack of this one on February 13.

I am enclosing you, also under separate cover, a *Stars and Stripes*. It is a very hard thing to get papers up here but I sent my efficient second lieutenant to town today and he succeeded in landing one, as well as some *Saturday Evening Posts* and some late Paris papers, all of which we appreciated highly. Mary tells me that she was elected to be treasurer of the 129th Auxiliary without a dissenting voice, which is very nice. She also seems to be on the point of purchasing a Dodge coupe. Well, I don't care if she does, but I'll bet four bits she backs out when it comes to handing out the money for it. I am sending her a piece of German brass also made by a Frenchman into a powderbox. Face not guns. She said she purchased a couple of Liberty bonds. Did you solicit her? I have never bought any Liberty bonds yet because I've always seemed to need all the francs and centimes I could rake together to lend to worthless birds in this regiment. I'll have enough to start a French bank or buy a Paris lot or something if I ever get it all collected up, which I don't ever expect to do. Maybe I can make them collect votes for me when I go to run for Congress on my war record—when I get tired chasing that mule up this corn row, as I told you, I am going to.

I am glad you don't hold it against me when I can't write but there have been times, and there will be again, when I couldn't possibly write. I have gone as much as sixty hours without any sleep and for twenty-two days straight I marched every night. You know that's not conducive to letter writing however badly you want to write. I thought of you just the same and still think of you,

Always,
Harry

[Somewhere in France]
Dear Bess: November 5, 1918

I am trying to keep up the record and write you every day or at least every other day while I have the chance, because if we take a fool notion to go on another drive there's no telling how often I can write. I don't know if I told you or not but we marched every night for twenty-two nights straight in September and then some over into October and it was a hard proposition to write, especially when there was nothing to write on and no place to get anything.

I am still sitting down in a position, sending over a few shells occasionally and receiving a few. My sleeping apartment is practically bomb proof, so I sleep soundly and well—unless there's gas, and I've almost gotten so I can sleep with a gas mask on. Next time I send you a picture it will be with a gas mask on and then you'll be disappointed sure enough.

That helmet picture was a dickens of a looking thing but I thought perhaps you'd like to see what I looked like as a real fightin' man. It was taken in a little town at the foot of the Vosges Mountains where I got some jelly custard from a French woman that tasted exactly like United States? I'll never forget that place.

I wish you would send me a Kodak of yourself. I have your picture in my pocket now you sent me to Doniphan and it sure makes me homesick sometimes when I look at it. Here's hoping I'll see the original before Easter. I dreamed last night I was going down Delaware. It was a disappointment to wake up and see the same old iron shack and rock pile over me I tell you.

I was censoring letters today when I ran across this sentence by one of my best sergeants. He said that he and the Battery had been in some very tight places and came out all right but that they had a captain that could take them to h--l and bring them all back. I nearly blew up. He didn't know I was going to read it, I guess, because I make my second lieutenants censor all the mail but they got behind. I took it for a compliment anyway.

A rumor, which I hope is so, says K. Bill has abdicated. I hope so because we won't have to dodge shells much longer if he has.

Keep writing for I can't get too many letters. I love you

Always,
Harry

[Somewhere in France]

Dear Bess: November 10, 1918

... I am still holding down a place in a quiet sector and I'm getting fat on it. Also that helmet is not going to make me baldheaded, at least I don't think so.

The Hun is yelling for peace like a stuck hog, and I hope old daddy Foch makes him yell louder yet or throttles him one. Throttling would be too easy. When you see some of the things those birds did and then hear them put up the talk they do for peace it doesn't impress you at all. A complete and thorough thrashing is all they've got coming and take my word they are getting it and getting it right.

This has been a beautiful Sunday—the sun shining and as warm as summer. It sure made me wish for Lizzie and five gallons of gas with her nose pointed down Blue Ridge Boulevard and me stepping on the throttle to get there quickly. I wonder how long it will be before we do any riding down that road. Easter? Maybe, if not sooner. Heinie seems to be about finished. Just to make the day interesting one of their planes came over and shot down one of our sausage balloons and came near getting shot down himself. I shot away about five hundred rounds of high explosive shells myself. Not at the plane but at some Hun machine guns about seven miles away. I don't know if I hit them, but I have hopes as I laid the guns very carefully. A Hun plane dropped some bombs not far from my back yard last night and sort of shook things up. They made him run home in a hurry too. There is a big railroad gun about a kilometer behind me that shoots about every fifteen minutes and I heard one of the boys remark that "There goes another rolling kitchen over to pulverize Jerry." The projectile makes a noise like a wagon going down the road when it goes through the air, so the remark was very good.

I have been censoring letters today and it is some job. I had no idea that there were so many accomplished liars in any organization on earth as I have in mine. They are eternally trying to get by the censor with some big tale of their heroism and accomplishments in this war and they do it too, sometimes, especially if they put in something nice about their commanding officer and the part he took in the tale. Usually though I have to tear 'em up or send them back when they tell too much or stretch the truth even beyond literary license. Some of them write very good and very interesting letters and some of them do not. It is a job to censor them and when my lieutenants get too far behind I help them out.

I hope the base censor doesn't laugh at mine as I sometimes have to at theirs.

Hope I get that letter tomorrow. Also hope the Hun signs the peace agreement. Write as often as you can to one who thinks of you,

Always,
Harry

[Somewhere in France]

Dear Bess: November 11, 1918

I knew Uncle Samuel was holding out on me when your letter came not with Boxley's and Brelsford's. Two came this morning and I am of course very happy. We are all wondering what the Hun is going to do about Marshal Foch's proposition to him. We don't care what he does. He's licked either way he goes. For my part I'd as soon be provost marshal of Cologne or Metz or Munich or Berlin as have any other job I know of now. It is a shame we can't go in and devastate Germany and cut off a few of the Dutch kids' hands and feet and scalp a few of their old men but I guess it will be better to make them work for France and Belgium for fifty years.

Their time for acceptance will be up in thirty minutes. There is a great big 155 Battery right behind me across the road that seems to want to get rid of all of its ammunition before the time is up. It has been banging away almost as fast as a 75 Battery for the last two hours. Every time one of the guns goes off it shakes my house like an earthquake.

I just got official notice that hostilities would cease at eleven o'clock. Everyone is about to have a fit. I fired 164 rounds at him before he quit this morning anyway. It seems that everyone was just about to blow up wondering if Heinie would come in. I knew that Germany could not stand the gaff. For all their preparedness and swashbuckling talk they cannot stand adversity. France was whipped for four years and never gave up and one good licking suffices for Germany. What pleases me most is the fact that I was lucky enough to take a Battery through the last drive. The Battery has shot something over ten thousand rounds at the Hun and I am sure they had a slight effect.

I am returning the enclosure from the Kansas City *Post.* It is a good thing I didn't censor Bill's letter or I probably would have thrown it out. It was evidently not quoted correctly even as it is. He was promoted for bravery by me but he was not mentioned in orders. Of course the remark about his captain is pleasing but there are no vacant sergeancies now so he won't get promoted for that.

It is pleasant also to hear that Mrs. Wells has adopted me as a real nephew and I shall certainly be more than pleased to call her Auntie Maud and I hope it won't be long before I can do it.

You evidently did some very excellent work as a Liberty bond saleswoman because I saw in *The Stars and Stripes* where some twenty-two million people bought them and that they were oversubscribed by $1 billion, which is some stunt for you to have helped pull off. I know that it had as much to do with breaking the German morale as our cannon shots had and we owe you as much for an early homecoming as we do the fighters.

Here's hoping to see you soon.

Yours always,
Harry

When the war was over, rumors started, as they had at Doniphan when a similar question of "moving out" had arisen. Captain Truman would not have minded going via Germany.

                                                                [Somewhere in France]
Dear Bess: November 15, 1918
    Your good letter of October 26 came today and you of course can guess how happy I am to get it. I am enclosing the forty cents for the very nice things you said to me. Being written with red ink reminds me of a letter I censored for one of my Irishmen the other day. He started out with blue ink and ran out so he said well here goes with a little blood and went on and finished his letter with red ink. I suppose his girl thought he really used blood. A letter from you written with charcoal, chalk, or clay would be fine enough to send me into the seventh heaven. I don't care what they're written with long as I get them.
    I am very glad that Pike Sands holds no malice for my having busted him. You know it is the hardest job a man ever undertook to be absolutely square and just to 194 men when you have good ones and bad ones (very few bad), smart ones and dull ones. I love 'em all and if anybody wants a fight or a quarrel with me he can get it suddenly and all he wants if he says anything derogatory about my Battery or one of my men. I wouldn't trade off the "orneriest" one I've got for any other whole Battery. While I'm not a braggart I believe I can take my outfit and beat any other one in the A.E.F., shooting or doing any other kind of Battery work (every Battery commander in the regiment says the same thing). I recommended one of my kids to go to West Point and he was one out of seven in the A.E.F. to go. I was as proud of him as if I had done it myself.
    You know I have succeeded in doing what it was my greatest ambition to do at the beginning of the war. That is to take a Battery through as Battery commander and not lose a man. We fired some ten thousand or twelve thousand rounds at Heinie and were shelled ourselves time and again but never did the Hun score a hit on me.
    There are rumors rife that we will go to Germany to do police and rioting duty. I'd rather go home but if your Uncle Samuel needs us in Germany, to Germany we'll go and be as happy as we can. We got in on the last drive and fired up to the last hour and I suppose that is the reason they'll send us if they do. Shall I bring you some German spoons and tableware or just some plain loot in the form of graft money? I hope they give me Coblenz or Cologne to hold down; there should be a good opportunity for a rising young captain with an itching palm, shouldn't there? . . .
    Please keep writing to one who thinks of you
                                    Always,
                                    Harry

    Touring Paris was fun for World War I soldiers, who appear to have made the rounds in traditional directions.

[Nice, France]

Dear Bess: November 29, 1918

What think you, I am at Nice! I have been to Paris and to Marseilles and I hate to think that I have to go back to slavery again at the end of seven days. I put in for a leave and got surprised by getting it. It was necessary to go to Paris in order to get here but time spent on the road doesn't count on the leave so I spent twenty-four hours in Paris and twenty-four hours at Marseilles. I saw a lot of places in that twenty-four hours in Paris. I dined at Maxim's, went to the Folies Bergères, saw Notre Dame, Napoleon's Tomb, the Madeleine, and could have seen King George V but didn't. I rode around in a taxi all afternoon from one end of the Champ Ellesee (I can't spell French, or English either for that matter) to the other, down the Rue Rivoli, across the famous Alexander III Bridge over the Seine, saw the Palace of the Luxembourg, Luxor, Tuilleries, Boulevard de l'Opéra, and a lot of sidestreets besides. It was a very full twenty-four hours. None of the galleries were open so I didn't see any art treasures. Napoleon's Tomb was all covered up with sandbags and so were some of the statues on the Arc de Triomphe.

At Marseilles I saw Gaby, and she threw me a bunch of violets. They weren't intended for me personally, but I happened to be in the line of fire when she threw them and I got them. She is prettier than ever and some dancer. She has a fine chateau at Marseilles, so I was told, and owns the theater she was playing in. Marseilles is some town. It has Paris beaten for crowds now.

I am stopping at the Hôtel de la Méditerranée, a dandy place overlooking the sea. I have a room about the size of a town lot with furniture enough in it for us to go to housekeeping on. All it lacks is a range.

The view from my window is simply magnificent. There isn't a painting in existence that could do it justice. There is no blue like the Mediterranean blue and when it is backed by hills and a promontory with a lighthouse on it and a few little sailing ships it makes you think of Von Weber's *Polacca Brilliante*, which I am told was composed here.

I am getting very heavy (fat I should say). I'm afraid you won't love me when you see me with cheeks all pushed out and a double chin. My uniform fits me like the skin on a sausage and I weigh 174 pounds. When I came out of the Argonne drive I weighed about 135 but plenty of sleep and a good allowance of bacon and beans have had their effect. I hate to think what I'll be like after seven days of chicken and dumplings and "Haut Sautern" down here. There is only one thing that could make the place real heaven and that would be to have you here, but I suppose every place must have its drawbacks and I am going to try and overcome that one the next time I pay a visit here. Of course I'll need your entire cooperation to achieve it. Be sure and keep writing and I hope to see you at no very distant date. I love you

Always,
Harry

[Monte Carlo, Monaco]

Dear Bess: December 3, 1918

I am having a very enjoyable vacation, as I told you in a letter day before yesterday. The whole bunch of us went to Monte Carlo day before yesterday and stayed all night. They won't let soldiers into the casino, nor will they allow anyone who lives or works in any of the towns along the Riviera to play. It is a gaudy, gorgeous place, just what you'd expect in a place whose sole income is from fleecing tourists and making them gamblers. The fleecing isn't done at the casino but at the hotels and cafés. The gambling is on the square but the probable error has been so closely figured that the house wins in the long run. They let us go in and see the great gambling rooms before ten o'clock in the morning and they are surely furnished in a style you'd expect to find in a place of the kind. There are velvet hangings, beautiful paintings, and mahogany chairs and tables, a beautiful mahogany bar in a drinking saloon which has Brussels carpet a foot thick on the floor and leather chairs to sit in. No French theater is complete without a fine bar and a beautiful room to drink in. Everyone, men, women, and children, are frequenters and every show gives thirty-minute intermissions between each act so the audience can go out and quench its thirst, which it does en masse. I'll bet that this country drinks enough wine to float the British navy every month. They use water only to wash in and if a man wants water to drink with his meals, they think he needs a doctor or something. . . .

I have to go back to slavery day after tomorrow and I'd almost rather be shot. Most of us are endeavoring to get the flu so we can stay here. The trouble is that the flu or any other sickness doesn't work here.

I am hoping for a bushel of letters when I get back. Be sure and keep sending them. How I wish you were here.

Yours always,
Harry

Verdun, France

Dearest Bess: December 8, 1918

. . . I stopped in Paris again on my way back to the regiment and went to the opera, the real one, and heard *Thais*. It was beautifully put on and well sung. The building was worth the price of admission to look at. Major Gates and I went. The rest went to the Casino de Paris to see a gaiety show, which, they said, was very good. Paris has a thousand streets more or less and no two of 'em run in the same direction, nor do any of them have the same name from end to end. Nearly any old street in a small village sports a name for each end of it and in Paris they have from two to a dozen. It is always necessary to hire a bandit in a taxi to take you around or you'll never arrive. They're not such bandits after all, because I rode all afternoon with Major Gates and Colonel Elliott and it was only 15 francs, about $2.75 in honest-to-goodness money.

They made us sign a paper the day we returned stating whether we wanted to become regular army men with our same grades, go into the reservist army, or have a complete discharge from the army at once. I naturally took the last event. I don't expect to go into anything where I can't say what I please when I please. Anyhow the emergency is over and I am ready to be a producer instead of a leech. If they take me at my word, which I much doubt they'll do, I may want to see you in New York sure enough if you'll come. I am of the opinion we'll all go home and be discharged with our outfits next spring.

How I wish I could see you. Keep on writing. May you have a Joyous Christmas.

Yours always,
Harry

Near Verdun, Camp La Baholle
December 14, 1918

Dear Bess:

It is a dark, unwholesome French day and I am frankly homesick and very, very lonesome. Christmas is approaching and I can't possibly see those I want to and I do so wish I could. I can't even send you a present that I'm sure you'll get, not even a cablegram. This devilish place is about seven kilometers from Verdun in a patch of woods. The sun hasn't shone in I don't know how many days nor does it look as if it ever intended to shine again.

I guess it will though and I know it's shining in U.S.A. and at Nice. I am so glad you are a general. I shall always expect you to outrank me in our household and there is never any prospect of my ever being anything in the military line beyond a captain, although had the war continued, which God forbid, I should eventually have had another promotion. You tell Fred and May that I would have appreciated the major's leaves and the compliment very highly but I'd never have worn them. All promotions ceased in the A.E.F. on November 11, 1918, the greatest day in history. Personally I'd rather be a Battery commander than a brigadier general. I am virtually the dictator of the actions of 194 men and if I succeed in making them work as one, keep them healthy morally and physically, make 'em write to the mammas and sweethearts, and bring 'em all home, I shall be as nearly pleased with myself as I ever expect to be—until the one great event of my life is pulled off, which I am fondly hoping will take place immediately on my having delivered that 194 men in U.S.A. You'll have to take a leading part in that event you know and then for one great future. I've almost come to the conclusion that it's not intended for me ever to be very rich, nor very poor, and I am about convinced that that will be about the happiest state a man can be. To have the finest girl in all the whole world (and to make the statement without fear of contradiction) to share my joys and troubles, mostly joys I'm hoping, to have just enough of this world's goods to make it pleasant to try for more, to own a Ford and tour the U.S.A. and France perhaps, although I've nearly promised old Miss Liberty that she'll have to turn around to see me again, and still have a nice little country home to be comfortable in—well that's really not a hard fortune to contemplate. Maybe have a little politics and some nice little dinner parties occasionally just for good measure. How does it sound to you? Just its contemplation has almost cured me of the blues.

You know when I was a kid, say about thirteen or fourteen, I was a tremendous reader of heavy literature like Homer, Abbott's *Lives,* Leviticus, Isaiah, and the memoirs of Napoleon Bonaparte. Then it was my ambition to make Napoleon look like a sucker and I thirsted for a West Point education so I could be one of the oppressors, as the kid said when asked why he wanted to go there. You'd never guess why I had such a wild desire and you'll laugh when I tell you. It was only so you could be the leading lady of the palace or empire or whatever it was I wanted to build. You may not believe it but my notion as to who is the best girl in the world has never changed and my military ambition has ended by having arrived at the post of centurian. That's a long way from Caesar, isn't it? Now I want to be a farmer. Can you beat it? I'm hoping you'll like the rube just as well as you would have the Napoleon. I'm sure the farmer will be the happier. . . .

You are probably bored stiff by this time but I am writing you just as I feel today. I do wish I could see you Christmas Day. I'll be thinking of you as I usually am anyway. I hope to have a better present for you next Christmas than the one I tried to send you this one. Keep on writing to one who thinks of you,

Always,
Harry

Still near Verdun, Camp La Baholle

Dear Bess: December 19, 1918

This day is a banner day sure enough. Your letters of November 24 and 26 came and I am entirely cured of a case of grippe I was endeavoring to have. Those are two grand letters and I am so happy to get them. You are right about my not getting all your letters but I am certainly thankful for what I do get. Your mother is very flattering when she says I write a good letter. *I write in order to get letters* and if mine happen to appear interesting because they come from France, I'm that much more pleased. I appreciate the compliment anyway. Some time back I wrote you a great long-winded account of all my doings since leaving Coëtquidan. Mr. Lee says he wants to get some of the facts to go into his history of the 129th, but I don't think they would hardly be worth putting in, do you? My hair is not any whiter than it's always been, except for a few gray hairs around the edge and they are not visible unless you look closely. I think I told the Nolands in one of my letters to them that my experience in moving up front that first night of the drive when it took me twelve hours to go a kilometer and a half was enough to give me a set of gray hairs. I don't think I have any more than I've had for the last two years, but my hair is thicker so the helmet must have done it good. I sincerely wish I could have gone to Platte with you and also to the show. There's a good time coming though and I hope not so far away.

We have rumors of going to Hunland and rumors of going to Brest and rumors of staying where we are till peace is signed. I told you I'd signed up for full plus immediate "separation from the army." We call ourselves the F & I's and we kid the life out of those who signed up to stay in. But we'll all probably come home together. Major Gates, Major Miles, Sermon, Marks, McGee, the colonel, and myself are all F & I's. Salisbury, Allen, Paterson, Dancy signed up to stay in. The rest signed up for the reserve. I can't see what on earth any man with initiative and a mind of his own wants to be in the army in peacetimes for. You've always got some old fossil above you whose slightest whim is law and who generally hasn't a grain of horse sense. For my part I want to be where I can cuss 'em all I please when I please, and you can bet there are some in this man's army who are going to get cussed and more if they fool around me when I get out. I'd give my right arm to be on the Military Affairs Committee of the House. It's not an impossibility, is it? You've no idea how the attitude changed when there was no more chance of promotion. It's right laughable sometimes. I got a lot of new horses today which don't look much like going home. I'd about as soon be in Coblenz or Cologne as in this mudhole. If I can find it, I am going to send you a copy of a poem called *Sunny France*. It's a peach.

You've no idea how I appreciated the Christmas card from all the family. I wish I could send them each one but I can't. Remember me to all of them, especially your mother, and wish them each a Merry Christmas for me. *And keep on writing.*

Yours always,
Harry

[Camp La Baholle, near Verdun]
December 31, 1918

Dear Bess:

You see I am ending the year properly by writing you a letter on that last day. Yesterday was a grand day—a letter from you. I am so glad you had such a pleasant visit and I do wish I could have been there with you. You tell Uncle Strother that I shall certainly get him an iron cross if such a thing is at all attainable. Should we go into Germany, there is no doubt but that they will be plentiful and I can get one. My outfit picked an aviator who fell near the Battery position just before the close of the war and I learned afterwards that one of 'em got an iron cross of the observer. He'd already sold it or I'd have made him produce it. Anyway my abilities as a collector of souvenirs are not very great. I can't tell what will make a good one and what won't. Everything looks so very common and useless when you are here and can get most anything for a song. Some of the men have so much unnecessary stuff, like those coal-scuttle helmets, haversacks, etc., that it would be hard for 'em to carry their clothes. They'll undoubtedly have to leave most of it behind. I have the helmet off the first dead Hun I ever saw and I reckon I'll keep that. That's about all I have that's worth keeping. I am going to Verdun tomorrow or next day and shall in all probability get the iron cross. Two of my lieutenants went up to Douaumont the other day and found a helmet out in front of the fort with a skull in it. There was a hole right through iron, head, and all. There are some queer sights up in front of that old fort and also in front of forts Vaux and Tavannes. Except the Somme, it is the hardest-fought battlefield in France. There were days when the Hun held parts of each fort and the French would be at hand-to-hand conflict with them all the time. There were days when enough steel fell on them to fight the Civil War with. They show their wear and tear too. It will take fifty years to make the surrounding country look as it did before the war. The French are gathering up all the duds and exploding them. You know it will be awful for the farmers in this neighborhood when they first go to plowing. There won't be any Croix de Guerre or Legion of Honor badges for the rubes who go skyward as result of plowshares hitting unexploded 77s and 150s. For my part I don't believe I'd do any plowing if I had to do it here.

Tomorrow is New Year's and we are going to celebrate it by a few boxing bouts and wrestling matches. Maybe a basketball game or two if it isn't as muddy as usual and some races. My Battery will be badly hurt if one of the boxing matches goes against us. They have 7,000 francs bet on our man. He's not Tommy Murphy either but another sergeant of mine named Meisburger. Doesn't sound very Irish, does it? I have some Schmidts and a Kuhn. The Irish call 'em the German sympathizers and we always told 'em if we were captured they'd have to protect us. Really they are among the best men I have, especially the Schmidts. There are two of them, brothers, one is a corporal and the other a sergeant.

My boxer on whom the big bet is placed is fighting a gorilla from Battery E. Captain Carranza [Salisbury's nickname] himself has bet about 1,000 francs on his man and I am not laying down on mine, so it ought to be a right good affair. It may be necessary to unscramble the two Batteries after it's over. The chaplain of the 130th is going to referee the bout. He's some boxer himself.

Remember me to all the family, especially your mother, and keep writing.

Yours always,
Harry

[Camp La Baholle, near Verdun]
Dear Bess: January 3, 1919
I intended writing you yesterday as I agreed to do, but things happened so quickly and the day went so fast I couldn't do it. Had a basketball game in Verdun in the forenoon, in which I got defeated or my team did, rather, by a bunch of noncombatant engineers. In the evening we pulled off a boxing bout in which my Sergeant Meisburger lost the decision over a gorilla named Hamby, and I lost 1,000 francs. Of course being the loser I should say it was a rotten decision. I won't say it, but the other fellow had to be carried from the ring and my man walked out—so you can judge for yourself what I think of the decision. Also he's been going to the doctor every day since and my man was for duty the next morning. As I told you before, I think more of that sergeant than if he were a boy of mine and I'd rather have been beaten by anyone on earth than one of Salisbury's outfit. But as the French say, "It is the war," and somebody had to lose. I've paid fifteen dollars to see a fight that wasn't worth half as much as that one was though. It was a fight from start to finish and was really a show.

Oh! loads of joy, my Christmas box came this evening. I started this letter yesterday and had to leave before I got it finished. This pen is a humdinger—writes better than any I ever owned, and those handkerchiefs are certainly the most beautiful I ever ordered. They are certainly grand and I shall use them when I go on state affairs, such as a dinner with the colonel or a trip to Paris, if ever I get another. I'll also save one of 'em to wear to my wedding—which shall it be? I can't decide which is the best looking.

You've no idea what a lot of comfort getting that box was. It was exactly like a small piece of God's country arriving in this forsaken place. Even if it was late, it made no difference because all the days are nearly alike and we can make any one of them Christmas. . . .

I hope I can write you a better letter next time. But remember I certainly appreciate all the things in the box and especially the pen and handkerchiefs. Keep writing.

Yours always,
Harry

[Camp La Beholle, near Verdun]

Dear Bess: January 7, 1919

Such a joyousness—two letters from you last night, one from home, one from Boxley, one from Morgan, and one from some uneasy papa of one of my irresponsibles to know if his son is shot or not. He isn't and never has been over half-shot since he's been over here. (I should be shot for saying that, because the kid's one of my best corporals.)

You've no idea how this muddy spot brightens up when letters come. I was so glad to get yours because I have been scared to death, ever since you told me Frank had the "flu," that either you or your mother would get it. I'm so glad you're getting well. It had been almost two weeks since I had received a letter and I was certainly uneasy. Mary was down with it too so you can imagine how I felt.

George Arrowsmith was in to see me yesterday evening and I told him you had been sick, and he said yes he knew it but wasn't going to tell me if I didn't know it. Considerate man, isn't he? Mary says she is much better and I hope that by the next mail I'll hear you are both in excellent health.

I thought perhaps you'd like to see how I am wasting away, pining to get home and out of the armee, so I'm enclosing you a Kodak picture of me made by Captain Paterson. I am supposed to be engrossed with a letter to you but inadvertently I am holding a pencil instead of a pen. I am thinking of you anyway because Paterson remarked that he'd flatter me as much as the camera would admit because he knew you'd like it that way. Don't you think I am getting thin? It took Pat nearly five minutes to get me posed so my double chin wouldn't show! The colonel says I'm getting thinner. I'm not so obese as I was a week or so ago and I'm still wearing my American uniforms, which by the way are better than any that can be bought over here now. . . .

I do hope you are well and that all danger from that dreadful flu is past. I am hoping for another letter later than the ninth. I'm glad you like the 77s. They don't amount to much as a present but they are worth something for their associations and the Vosges, Saint-Mihiel, Argonne-Meuse, and Verdun are the fronts the 129th worked on.

Yours always,
Harry

Waiting to go home, men in the American Expeditionary Force began to feel that their officers were keeping them in France so as to maintain wartime ranks. Morale slipped, and General Pershing decreed more inspections, more disciplinary action. The men easily sensed when the officers were unsure of themselves and became almost openly rebellious.

Camp La Beholle, near Verdun, France

Dearest Bess: January 11, 1919

This is a nice rainy Saturday night, and instead of going down to Captain Jobes' for an evening's entertainment at penny ante I am going to make an attempt at a letter to you. You know I have a nice boy in my Battery whose name is Bobby (I have three Bobbys, every one of 'em as fine as boys can be) and once in a while he brings me a letter that he doesn't want any second lieutenant nosing into, and it's always addressed to just Dearest and I feel like an ornery, low-down person when I read them—sometimes I don't, I just sign 'em up and let 'em go. But if that girl doesn't wait for that kid I know she's got a screw loose. He doesn't write a thing silly but he's all there and I hope she is too. What I started out to say is that I'd like to write you a real silly, mushy letter that would honestly express just exactly what I feel tonight but I have command of neither the words nor the diction to do it. Anyway I had the most pleasant dream last night and my oh how I did hate to wake up. Of course I was in U.S.A. parading down some big town's main street and I met you and there was a church handy and just as casually as you please we walked inside and the priest did the rest, and then I thought we were in Paris and I woke up in a Godforsaken camp just outside of old ruined Verdun. You've no idea how often and constantly that last part is a daydream with me. It seems that Sam is never, never going to take us home so that priest can be met. We just live from one inspection to the next. You know these regular army colonels and lieutenant colonels who've had their feet on the desk ever since the argument started are hellbent for inspections. Some of 'em haven't been over here but a month or two but they can come around and tell us who went through it exactly and how we did not win the war. Some of 'em are nuts on horse feed and some are dippy on how to take care of harness and some think they know exactly how many ounces of axle grease will run a gun wheel to kingdom come and back. One important little major who had evidently read somebody's nonsensical book on how to feed a horse came along the other day and wanted us to feed the horses oatmeal, cooked! and we don't get enough to feed the men for breakfast half the time. Then another one wanted us to shake all the chaff and dirt out of the hay and give it to the horses and if the horses wouldn't eat the dirt, why we must put salt on it so they would—and we haven't got the salt. A lieutenant colonel was here today who said they were both crazy and we'd better feed oats and hay as usual, which is exactly what we intended to do anyway. This peacetime soldiering is an awful bore and anybody who wants to do it is certainly off in his upper works.

In addition to inspections and more inspections we have to keep our Batteries from going to pieces. Two of my kids were caught asleep on guard last night and I gave 'em the privilege of going before our summary court and getting a fine maybe or taking what I'd give them. They seemed to prefer the latter. Now what do you reckon I'm going to make those poor boys do? Why, clean out stables all Saturday afternoon and Sunday and wash the muddiest, dirtiest wagon I can produce on Sunday afternoon for four weeks. I reckon that ought to impress them that an armistice isn't peace, don't you think? One of 'em is one of my Bobbys, too, and another one is a nephew of the present Grand Matron of Missouri. The better I like 'em, the meaner I have to be to them just to show 'em that I'm impartial. You've no idea how I hate to call a man down. I'd almost rather take a beating than tell a man how good for nothing he is when he's done something he shouldn't. Two of my men overstayed a pass I gave them to Verdun the other day and I talked so mean to them when they came back that one of 'em cried and I almost let him off without any punishment. If we stay in this place much longer, I'll either have a disposition like a hyena or be the dippy one. If there's one thing I've always hated in a man it is to see him take his spite out on someone who couldn't talk back to him. I've done my very best not to jump on someone under me when someone higher up jumps on me, because I hate the higher-up when he does it and I'm sure the next fellow will hate me if I treat him the same way. Anyway I can't jump all over a man for doing something that I'm sure I'd have done myself if I'd had the opportunity and been in his place. Justice is an awful tyrant. Just to show how she works I took all the privileges away from a fellow for a small offense and gave him a terrific calling down and I had to do it four times more when I found out that four more were offenders in the same way. One of 'em was a man I particularly like too and I know he thinks I'm as mean as Kaiser Bill. . . .

I hope you are entirely well by now. Remember me to all the family, especially your mother, and keep writing.

Yours always,
Harry

In the last weeks of the war and after, the flu ravaged army camps. It struck at troops going to France; on every transport dozens of men died at sea. The statistics are surprising: civilian deaths from influenza in the United States in 1918–19 are estimated at 500,000; battle casualties of the A.E.F. were 48,909 dead—and 230,074 wounded—but total deaths in the army, navy, and marines were 112,432, the balance caused by disease, chiefly influenza.

Camp La Beholle, near Verdun
Dear Bess: January 12, 1919
     Last evening was a glorious one even if it was raining. A mail brought me three letters from you dated December 13, 16, 18, one from Fred, two from Mary, and one from Miss Maggie [Phelps]. I am so glad you are out of danger from that awful flu. You've no idea how uneasy I've been since hearing you and Mary had it. We over here can realize somewhat how you must have felt when we were under fire a little. Every day nearly someone of my outfit will hear that his mother, sister, or sweetheart is dead. It is heartbreaking almost to think that we are so safe and so well over here and that the ones we'd like to protect more than all the world have been more exposed to death than we. I am hoping that the worst is past and that from now on we'll never hear of it again. It seems that war and pestilence go hand in hand. If it isn't the Black Death it is something equally as fatal. We hear that the poor Russians are dying by hundreds and the damnable Hun is murdering himself for pleasure. I suppose it will be some time before we have a golden age of health, peace, and prosperity such as the ten years before 1914 were. . . .
     I do hope you are well and all right by this time. Be sure and write when you feel like it. I love you

                              Always,
                              Harry

Camp La Beholle, near Verdun
Dear Bess: January 19, 1919
     . . . Please let me beg of you not to say anything about my letter of commendation. I only told it because I thought I was very lucky and that you'd like to know it. You know the most embarrassing thing that can happen to a fellow over here is to have his enthusiastic friends or relatives publish his private correspondence or hold him up as someone who deserves especial credit. There's not one of us who have done anything that any other one of us could not and would not have done if the opportunity had offered. Most real citations—and citations can only be made by generals in general orders—are a terrible embarrassment to the men they affect. There were three of our lieutenants cited and they are having an awful time living it down. Webster's letter of commendation is causing him no end of kidding just because his folks don't know what a citation is and what it means. General Traub made the fact that I happened to have the best chief mechanic in the artillery brigade a subject for a general memorandum and he wrote me a formal letter of commendation on the condition of my matériel. His statement was that it "showed especial efficiency in the commissioned and enlisted personnel of the organization." Well the enlisted personnel did the work and should have the credit. I sent the letter to Boxley, and if you care to see it he will show it to you. However I don't want it published because it can cause me to be court-martialed for stealing it out of the files of the

organization, and would cause me no end of embarrassment. My chief mechanic happened to be a whirlwind and I happened to be lucky, and that's all there is to it.

Be sure and keep writing. I love you

Always,

Harry

Camp La Beholle, near Verdun

Dear Bess: January 21, 1919

. . . You know I have two breast pockets in my blouse. Naturally you can guess whose picture stays in the left-hand one. I keep Mary's and Mamma's in the other. Yours is the one you sent me at Doniphan and it has never left me from that day to this, nor will it ever. It's been through all the trials and tribulations and happy moments same as I have. I have looked at it many, many times and imagined that you were there in spirit, as I knew you were, and it's helped a lot—especially when things were blue and it would look as if I'd surely blow up if another thing went wrong. I've never blown up and my disposition isn't so very bad. That picture saved it. The biggest worry I've ever had was when I heard that the original of that picture had the flu and the happiest day was when that letter came saying you'd walked uptown. . . .

We are having another spasm of moving. There have been orders out twice to move up back to a dirty, little old French village. . . . It's my opinion that we'll stay there until Woodie gets his pet peace plans refused or okayed. For my part, and every A.E.F. man feels the same way, I don't give a whoop (to put it mildly) whether there's a League of Nations or whether Russia has a Red government or a Purple one, and if the President of the Czecho-Slovaks wants to pry the throne from under the King of Bohemia, let him pry but send us home. We came over here to help whip the Hun. We helped a little, the Hun yowled for peace, and he's getting it in large doses and if our most excellent ex-mayor of Cleveland [Secretary of War Baker] wants to make a hit with us, he'll hire or buy some ships and put the Atlantic Ocean between us and the Vin Rouge Sea. For my part I've had enough *vin rouge* and frogeater victuals to last me a lifetime. And anyway it looks to me like the moonshine business is going to be pretty good in the land of Liberty loans and green trading stamps, and some of us want to get in on the ground floor. At least we want to get there in time to lay in a supply for future consumption. I think a quart of bourbon would last me about forty years.

I hope you have a most happy birthday and that you never see another one without me to help celebrate and then may they go on without end. Remember me to your mother and Fred and Frank and Natalie and George and May and just keep writing when you feel inclined, because I love you

Always,

Harry

Rosières, France

Dear Bess: January 26, 1919

Your good letter of January 6 came last night and of course I was as happy as could be. Now of course if you'd rather be married in Trinity Church at Independence, Missouri, I am perfectly willing. I just couldn't see how I was going to wait until I could get to Independence if I ever got to America again. But I understand that they expect to send all organizations to concentration camps and muster them out as a whole and I've an idea that my chances of getting away from mine at New York would be very slim and I'd better let you make whatever arrangement you choose to—*but don't make any delay.* I get such a longing to see you sometimes that if such a thing were possible I would desert and stowaway home at once and quickly.

I have been rather sorrowful the last day or so. My Battery clerk died in the hospital from appendicitis. I know exactly how it would feel to lose a son. He was the most agreeable Irishman with a sweet tenor voice and an excellent soldier. He ran my office and kept me from paying out my money for the government. He was one of the reasons that my organization is a success. When the letter came from the hospital informing me of his death I acted like a real baby. I had no idea he was at all badly sick until that letter came. I certainly hope I don't lose another man until we are mustered out.

We finally moved and are now living in a dirty little village about four kilometers north of Bar-le-Duc. We moved out of camp on the morning of the twenty-second and slept outdoors that night. It was as cold as the dickens but I had so much cover on my bedroll that my arms would get numb from the weight. Got into town on the afternoon of the twenty-third and got all billeted before dark. I have two rooms, my two lieutenants and myself. One of them has a fireplace in it like old man Grimm tells about in his fairy tales. You build a fire in the center and sit inside the fireplace to keep warm. Out in the room it's about freezing all the time. The old lady we stay with is very good to us, cooking *pommes de terre frites,* or French fried potatoes, and stewed Belgian hare. She's very careful that we don't burn our candles two at a time. They are our own but are so expensive in France that she doesn't like to see them wasted. All French women are thrifty. Be sure and keep writing. I'll write you a better letter tomorrow. I love you

Always,
Harry

Rosières, France

Dearest Bess: January 27, 1919

. . . I was out on a maneuvering problem today along with Major Miles, Captain McGee, and Lieutenant Younger. My part was to pretend that I was a Battery. I guess they give us those things to do to keep us from going dingy and also to have some legitimate employment for the oceans of staff officers running loose. Staff officers, you know, are purely ornamental and utterly useless as far as I can see. They are mostly lieutenant colonels and majors and fresh young captains. They sit close to the throne and promotion comes easy to 'em whether they know much or whether they don't, and mostly they don't. Most all of 'em are either West Pointers or from Dea' old Yale or H'va'd don'tche know. I've an idea if the army shuts up shop and there's no demand for bartenders, and cafeterias run the supply of waiters up, that these poor ginks will actually have to do some useful work or other. That is if the government doesn't decide to keep on taking care of them. For my part I wouldn't trust 'em with a pair of mules or any surplus cash I happened to have, because they'd either let the mules run away or sell 'em and I know what they'd do with the cash if John Barleycorn were handy.

I most sincerely hope you are well by now and have gained as much weight as you desire. I don't care how thin or how much weight you have, I love you just the same. Keep writing to

Yours always,
Harry

Rosières, France, near Bar-le-Duc
Dear Bess: February 1, 1919

It seems as if the first move has been made to take us home. An order has been put forth canceling all leaves and furloughs and setting a date for us to turn in our guns, horses, etc. and start for Le Mans, which is a clearing place for home. . . .

You've no idea how I'll hate to give up my guns, my French 75s, those implements of destruction which the Hun has said were weapons of the devil. You know I told you in a letter from Coëtquidan that if I could only give the command that fired one volley at the Hun I would go home willingly and be satisfied. Well there were some ten thousand rounds—or if fired in volleys, over two thousand volleys—fired by those guns at Heinie and they did it all at my command. They are the same guns that I learned to shoot with and with the exception of one barrel, which I had to leave in the Argonne with a shell lodged in it, there have been no repairs on them. If the government would let me have one of them, I'd pay for it and pay the transportation home just to let it sit in my front yard and rust. Men you know—gunners and section chiefs especially —become very much attached to their guns. They name 'em Katie, Lizzie, Liberty, Diana, and other fantastic and high-sounding names and when they fire them they talk to them just as if they were people. French gunners even cry when their guns are taken away from them. Guns do have an individuality. No two of them shoot alike and weather conditions will affect each of them differently. . . .

I don't suppose I'll ever fire another shot with a 75 gun and know I won't with these I'm so attached to and it makes me rather sad. It's like parting with old friends who've stood by me through thick and thin and now I have to give 'em to some ordnance chap to put away and maybe later some fop out of West

Point will use 'em for target practice and declare they're no good because he don't know how to shoot 'em. . . .

I am hoping to see you by April 1. Be sure and keep on writing on a chance that orders may be changed. I love you

Always,
Harry

[Rosières, near Bar-le-Duc]
Dear Bess: February 18, 1919
I wrote you day before yesterday but I very much fear you won't get it. The mail orderly doesn't know whether he got it or not and I can't find it. I had just gotten some letters from you and naturally told you how glad I was. Also I told you that we are coming home right away. I know it officially now because General Pershing shook hands with me—and told me so. I also met the Prince of Wales, as did every other company and battery commander in the 35th Division. . . . Please get ready to march down the aisle with me just as soon as you decently can when I get back. I haven't any place to go but home and I'm busted financially but I love you as madly as a man can and I'll find all the other things. We'll be married anywhere you say at any time you mention and if you want only one person or the whole town I don't care as long as you make it quickly after my arrival. I have some army friends I'd like to ask and my own family and that's all I care about, and the army friends can go hang if you don't want 'em. I have enough money to buy a Ford and we can set sail in that and arrive in Happyland at once and quickly.

Don't fail to write just 'cause I'm starting home.

Yours always,
Harry

Rosières, France, near Bar-le-Duc
Dearest Bess: February 23, 1919
I have been real good today. Went to Bar-le-Duc and went to Mass. I have a Catholic lieutenant, Ducournau by name ("Ducano" he calls it), who is from Louisiana and who is responsible for my attending Mass. He's not very orthodox and neither am I, as you very well know, but we were curious to see inside one of the old churches and also expected to hear some good music. Our curiosity was satisfied and we were not disappointed in the music. There was a grand organ and a master at the keyboard. He played a most beautiful offertory from Bach and some woman with a grand soprano voice sang a part of the Mass. The church has some very fine paintings and some stained-glass windows behind the altar that are very beautiful. There are four of them and each one had a Boche bullet hole punched in it. Evidently made by shell fragments. Bar-le-Duc was under fire in the first battle of the Marne and was bombed once a week or oftener during the whole war. I don't suppose that those windows will be mended ever, because some

old heathen will want to collect francs from American tourists while he unwinds some magnificent lie about how they came to be busted.

They have beautiful costumes for the priests and choirboys. One old priest who took up the collection had on a lace skirt that most any American woman would trade her husband for. There was one individual whose duties and position I couldn't quite fathom. He had on a Napoleon Bonaparte hat with a white plume running from end to end of it. His uniform would make a Greek general jealous and he had on a rapier or sword, I couldn't tell which. In his right hand he carried a tall cane with a golden ball on top of it like you see in pictures of Louis XIV and Madame de Montespan. He was in the back of the church when we went in, standing like the guardian of the gates of heaven, but when the collection priest started to pass the hat he marched up the aisle and placed himself in front of the collector and marched ahead of him. He'd go about four steps and set his cane down with a bang and then wait while the priest made a good canvass of about two rows of seats and then he'd move the same distance again. Now I can't figure if he was a representative of the French Government to see that the state gets a fair share of the contribution or if he was some part of the Catholic Church machinery. I was afraid to ask for fear it might be an unnecessary inquiry. Anyway, as Mark would say, he impressed me very much and I looked at him as much as I did the whole row of priests and choristers and censor boys it took to put on High Mass. One little old kid was sure an expert at swinging the incense pot. If the main priest had ever backed up while that pot was working he'd have been brained sure. . . .

Remember me to your mother and all the family, and keep writing to one who loves you,

Always,
Harry

[Telegram, Camp Mills, N.Y., Apr. 21, 1919]

ARRIVED IN CAMP MILLS EASTER AFTERNOON. HAVE BEEN EATING PIE AND ICE CREAM EVER SINCE. WIRE ME HERE USUAL ADDRESS. HOPE TO BE IN FUNSTON SOON. NEW YORK GAVE US A GRAND WELCOME. GOD'S COUNTRY SURE LOOKS GOOD. HARRY

Camp Mills, L.I.
April 24, 1919

Dear Bess:

I have been in America just four days and I have been so busy just lookin' at the place and getting some honest-to-goodness food under my belt that I haven't had time to do anything else.

I had the most miserable ten days coming over that I've spent in this war. We had a fine boat, brand new and never used before, but she was empty except for our baggage and ourselves and she did some rolling. I am not a good sailor and you can guess the harrowing details. Of course I could get no sympathy. Even my own Battery laughed at me. I lost about twenty pounds (and I can afford to lose it). For a time I wished most sincerely that I could go back to the Argonne Forest and at least die honorably. I am bravely over it now and I fear that I am gaining in weight.

I've never seen anything that looked so good as the Liberty Lady in New York Harbor and the mayor's welcoming boat, which came down the river to meet us. You know the men have seen so much and been in so many hard places that it takes something real to give them a thrill, but when the band on that boat played "Home Sweet Home" there were not very many dry eyes. The hardest of hard-boiled cookies even had to blow his nose a time or two. Every welfare organization in America met us and gave us something. The Jews gave us handkerchiefs; the Y.M.C.A. chocolate; the Knights of Columbus, cigarettes; the Red Cross, real homemade cake; and the Salvation Army, God bless 'em, sent telegrams free and gave us Easter eggs made of chocolate. They took us off the boat at Pier No. 1 in Hoboken, fed us till we wouldn't hold any more, put us on a ferry, and sent us to Camp Mills, where they gave us a bath and lots of new clothes, the first some of the men have had since they joined. Then we made a raid on the canteens and free shows. I'll bet ten barrels wouldn't hold the ice cream consumed that first evening. I was so busy that I didn't connect until the next day but I've been going strong ever since.

I was down on Broadway night before last with Major Miles and Major Wilson and stopped in at an ice cream joint and who do you suppose asked me if I belonged to the 35th Division? Stella Swope. She asked me where I was from, what regiment I belonged to, and then if I knew you, before she told me who she was. I was somewhat embarrassed but managed to tell her. She was with a sailor but didn't introduce him.

I am so crazy to get home that I'm about to go A.W.O.L. but I guess I'd better not set my Irish a bad example at this late day. We hope to leave here day after tomorrow for Kansas City, where we parade. They'd better keep Klemm [who had gone home earlier] out of that parade too.

I hope you'll forgive me for not writing oftener while here but it's just so good to have U.S.A. under my feet that I have to look at it somewhat. My Dago barber [Frank Spina] gave me an Italian dinner at his sister's house last night— yards and yards of spaghetti, chicken and dumplings, rabbit and peas and all the trimmings. I nearly foundered myself. Hope to see you soon and make up for lost time. Sincerely, I love you

Always,
Harry

[Telegram, Camp Mills, N.Y., Apr. 30, 1919]
LEAVING TODAY. GLAD TO SEE YOU AT THE TRAIN. HARRY

[Telegram, Okmulgee, Okla., May 31, 1919]
EXPECT TO SEE YOU OUT HOME TOMORROW. HARRY

III

POLITICS, LOCAL AND NATIONAL

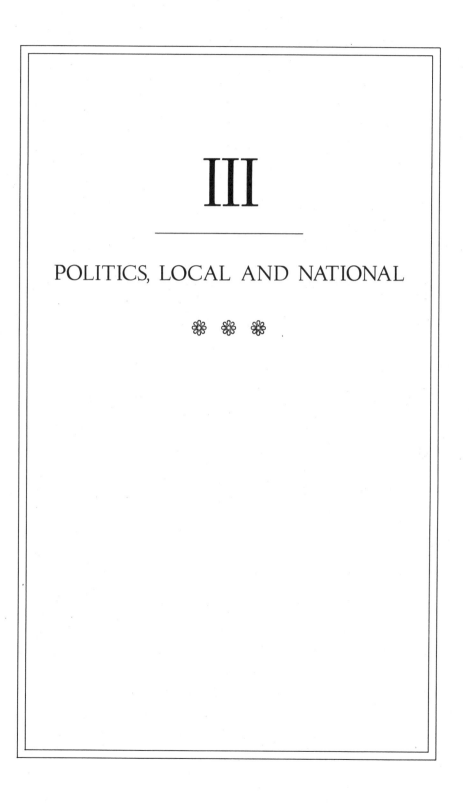

U PON RETURN FROM THE WAR Truman had no idea that he would devote the rest of his life to politics. He married Bess on June 28, 1919, in Trinity Episcopal Church, a few blocks east of Bess's house in Independence. Harry's fellow Battery commander from the 129th Field Artillery, Ted Marks, was best man. Ted was a tailor in Kansas City and produced a splendid gray-striped suit for the groom (see illustrations following). After the ceremonies Bess and Harry took a brief trip to Chicago, Detroit, and Port Huron, Michigan, after which they returned to live with Bess's mother at 219 North Delaware.

After marrying, the onetime farmer undertook to earn his living as a merchant. He and his former canteen sergeant at Doniphan, Eddie Jacobson, opened a men's furnishings store in downtown Kansas City. Their preparations took all summer and autumn; the store opened in November 1919 at a choice location across from Kansas City's major hotel, the Muehlebach. "Truman & Jacobson" read the legend on the store's floor mat at the entrance. The partners stocked expensive silk shirts, ties, and hats; it was a store for the well to do. The partners took turns waiting on customers. In addition, they divided the labor as they had at the canteen, with Harry keeping the books, and Eddie buying the merchandise.

The store's first-year sales were over $70,000. Through 1920 the business was enough of a success so that when offered the chance to sell out at inventory cost Truman and Jacobson refused. By 1922, however, the value of their inventory was cut to $10,000 from $35,000. Their eventual business failure, in 1922, can be attributed to the postwar price deflation; it was perhaps not, as some have said, the result of overextended credit. What may have been an inevitable development was later used to ridicule Truman—a president, it was said, who couldn't even manage a haberdashery.

The debts incurred from this failure were to dog Truman for almost a decade, in particular a five-year lease on the store and a note owed to a Kansas City bank. After the store closed, early in 1922, the partners were still liable for monthly rent until November 1924. Neither partner had much money in reserve, and both became instant candidates for bankruptcy. Eddie went under in 1925.

Wedding party, June 28, 1919, l. to r., Helen Wallace (Mrs. Truman's cousin); the best man, Theodore Marks (former captain, Battery C, 129th Field Artillery); the groom; Frank Wallace; the bride; and Louise Wells (Mrs. Truman's cousin). *Harry S. Truman Library*

Not until the early thirties was the landlord's legal claim settled. The bank loan, over five thousand dollars, pursued Truman through the twenties, interest compounding. When the bank that held the note failed during the Depression, Vivian Truman purchased the paper at sheriff's auction for one thousand dollars and resold it to Harry, thereby canceling it.

Just as friendships in the army were responsible for Truman becoming a merchant, so they made it possible for him to enter politics. During the war he had casually speculated about a political career. Later one of his fellow officers, Lieutenant James Pendergast, remembered this interest. He was the son of Mike Pendergast, political boss of eastern Jackson County, and nephew of Tom Pendergast, who controlled the entire county. In 1921 Jim and Mike came to the haberdashery in Kansas City and asked Truman to run for eastern judge. At the time the store was going fairly well, and he turned them down. The following spring when they returned with the same proposition, he eagerly accepted. He announced his candidacy—a few weeks before the primary elections of 1922—to a cheering crowd of veterans assembled at Lee's Summit, a small town near Independence.

The preceding court, a three-man group, had not suited the Pendergasts, who disliked the presiding judge, Miles J. Bulger. The judge was making a

The "grey stripe" was his wedding suit. *Harry S. Truman Library* personal fortune providing "piecrust" roads for the county and taking kickbacks from road contractors. He was "putting the lug," as Missourians said, on the approximately one thousand county employees, forcing them to give back part of their salaries each month. But what especially bothered the Pendergasts was Bulger's attempt to construct a political machine of his own in opposition to theirs. The Pendergasts therefore allied with another Kansas City politico, Joseph B. Shannon, and went for Bulger. Truman's candidacy fitted neatly into this scheme: the former Battery captain could win the veteran vote, had grown up in eastern Jackson County, had relatives in the area, and as a Baptist could appeal to the many Protestant voters, offsetting any concern about the Catholicism of the Pendergasts.

Truman worked feverishly for the Democratic nomination in the primary. Because politics in Missouri at this time were almost entirely Democratic, August elections usually determined November's winner. Truman won the primary and took office the following January 1923.

In later years Truman's vociferous critics said he had not merely failed as a haberdasher and took refuge in politics but also stooped to join the obnoxious Pendergast machine of Kansas City. The machine produced votes for him for county and national office—first as eastern judge for a single term, 1923–25, and then (following his defeat in 1924) two four-year terms as presiding judge, 1927–35, and United States Senator, 1935–41. Critics claimed that his political success rested on a foundation of fraud.

Certainly Mike and Tom Pendergast used repeaters in Kansas City elections. They not only took care that absent voters had ballots cast for them, they even voted the dead—a well-known quip on election day was, "Now is the time for all good cemeteries to come to the aid of the party." Repeater voting served two main purposes. One was the need of many ward heelers and precinct bosses to display their hard work on election day—sometimes resulting in preposterous majorities. The other was to defend against St. Louis, which was dominated by another Democratic machine and was the perennial rival of Kansas City. The metropolises vied with each other for state and national offices, and a little cheating in St. Louis inspired more in Kansas City. In the senatorial election of 1934 Truman ran principally against a St. Louis candidate; a politician in St. Louis made the mistake of announcing by how many votes his candidate would win. Alerted to the number of votes his candidate would need, Boss Tom produced them.

The Pendergast machine was an insuperable fact of life in Kansas City; anyone who desired to be elected to political office could not ignore it. In one way or another Truman had to cooperate with the Boss. As eastern judge and then presiding judge, whose duties included appointing almost a thousand employees, Truman carefully voted for appointments Pendergast favored. But he had limits; his compact with the Boss was that he, Truman, would support patronage but not graft, and Boss Tom gave him permission to fire any employee who would not work. As principal executive of the county, Truman managed to work within the machine system and yet achieve his own ends. In the late twenties and early thirties he floated two large bond issues. This at a time when Kansas City issues failed because voters feared the money would be improperly used by the machine. Boss Tom recognized Truman's ability to win the confidence of voters and he so admired him as a county executive that he appointed him boss of the eastern part of the county when Mike Pendergast died, in 1929. Since Truman was an honest, attractive figure to the voters it seemed best to let him run county government. If Boss Tom needed money for himself or the machine, he didn't have to pressure Truman for it; he could get it from complaisant businessmen in Kansas City or siphon it out of city government, run by his city manager, Henry F. McElroy.

The machine got into trouble in the thirties. The changing composition of Kansas City's central wards, where Italian immigrants were displacing the Irish, brought to power a ward boss named Johnny Lazia, who was nothing more than a gangster; the machine could hardly control him. Lazia took control of the police department and welcomed gangsters to Kansas City. The result was several well-publicized killings, including a virtual massacre in front of the Union Station in 1933. The gangsters were trying to rescue a friend from a police escort. Lazia's death early in 1934 in a blaze of machine-gun fire came at the time that Truman declared himself for the Senate. The primary elections that summer in Kansas City were marked by violence and voting frauds. Again, Truman's good reputation with the voters enabled him to rise above the negative image drawn by his association with the machine. He won the election, but not long after Truman went to the Senate, Boss Tom himself got into trouble. His health began to fail; he developed mastoiditis, suffered a heart attack, and underwent a serious operation for cancer. All this was followed by his indictment for accepting a massive bribe from fire insurance companies doing business in Missouri. The Boss had been betting on horse races, practically every race in the country; his losses skyrocketed, for he was betting 10-20-30 (show, place, and win)—in thousands. The insurance companies desired a favorable ruling from the state insurance commissioner, R. Emmett O'Malley. Boss Tom told O'Malley to grant the request but in turn got $750,000. A reforming district attorney, Maurice J. Milligan, sent him to Leavenworth for income tax evasion.

Judge Truman, meanwhile, was doing his very best for county government. He dedicated himself particularly to constructing good roads and improving county buildings. He became president of the National Old Trails Association and spent weeks promoting the construction of national roads along the nineteenth-century trails. In Jackson County he attracted attention by announcing that no taxpayer would be farther than two miles from a good, cement road. Toward this end he enlisted two bipartisan engineers who drew up a road plan of grids all through the county. The plan was realized after the presiding judge obtained his bond issues. He also renovated the Independence courthouse into a Georgian-style building that resembled Colonial Williamsburg. In Kansas City he replaced a sprawling courthouse of the seventies with an art-deco skyscraper.

In his initial plans he had proposed to top the skyscraper with a statue of his, and the county's, political hero: General Andrew Jackson. The cost of the topping, which would have had to be paid in the midst of the Depression, and the apparent absurdity of placing a statue where no one but a bird could see it, persuaded him and his engineers to put the general on a horse and place them both on the ground in front of the courthouse. Done in meticulous detail by the well-known New York sculptor Charles Keck, the statue was unveiled in 1934 by Miss Margaret Truman, aged ten.

The birth of daughter Margaret in 1924 was, next to marriage to Bess, the most important event in Harry Truman's life. Margaret, referred to in Truman's letters as "Marg," "Margie," and sometimes "Marger"—all pronounced with a hard g—at once became the light of his life, as his letters to Bess demonstrate. He constantly feared that she would lose her small-town simplicity and openness, that she would not work at her piano lessons, and that (like Bess) she would fail to write when her father was away.

During the twenties "Dad" was not often away from home. He traveled for meetings of the National Old Trails Association, but most of his letters to Bess in the twenties and early thirties were written from reserve summer camp. There was something about army life that continued to appeal to Truman. After mustering out he had been promoted in the reserves to major, and by the mid-thirties was a full colonel. Increasing rank meant more responsibility, which he liked. After a while, however, Truman realized that the army was no longer giving him what he had expected. The reserves were mostly officers, with few and sometimes no enlisted men; training was often too theoretical for his liking. Army trucks replaced horses, and the change was bothersome, in part because primitive trucks of the twenties needed almost as much care as had the horses. The trucks also emphasized the passing of what had been familiar to Truman. Horseback rides across the plains of Kansas at Fort Leavenworth and Fort Riley reminded him of the tree-lined roads in northern France, and he had imagined himself back at the head of Battery D in 1918. Moreover, younger officers began to replace Truman's contemporaries of World War I; now in his fifties, Truman sensed that in any future war, leadership would go to younger men. All he could do now was to try to teach the youngsters all he knew about siting guns, which was a good deal, and color it with tales of battle experiences.

In the mid-thirties Truman's second term as presiding judge was ending. Pendergast's backing of him for the Senate astonished him, as he had thought that his political career was over. The Boss's decision was a tactical one, part of the on-going rivalry between Kansas City and St. Louis. The state's senior Senator, Bennett Champ Clark, who was from St. Louis, wanted a second Senator from his own city, contrary to the custom that gave each metropolis a Senator. He was the son of Champ Clark, who nearly defeated Woodrow Wilson for the 1912 presidential nomination, and believed himself thereby destined to bring Missouri again into national prominence. Throughout the thirties the younger Clark harbored presidential ambitions and might have realized them had not President Franklin D. Roosevelt accepted nomination for a third term. When

Clark hoped for another St. Louis senator Boss Tom thwarted him by choosing Truman. Presiding Judge Truman, let it be said, was Boss Tom's fourth or fifth choice. Several proposed nominees turned the Boss down for various reasons. At least one may have been afraid to ally himself with a machine that had included Johnny Lazia. In the primaries that year, supporters of the machine violently opposed members of a vote reform movement in Kansas City. They also made sure that Truman had enough votes to beat his St. Louis opponent. Truman won the primary and went on to an easy confirmation in November. In January 1935 he marched down the aisle of the Senate Chamber arm in arm with Bennett Clark, who introduced him to Vice President John N. Garner, who swore him in. Having won, and been sworn in, he set out to do a job in Washington the best he knew how.

Letters to Bess increased to flood proportions during the Senate years, for the Senator and Mrs. Truman were so often apart. When they were together in Washington they lived in a succession of small apartments that were hardly convenient: Harry and Bess in one bedroom; Margaret and Mrs. Wallace in the other. The Senator's wife disliked the incessant socializing that went on in the nation's capital. Even an invitation to the White House from Mrs. Roosevelt was not enough to keep Bess and her two charges, young and old, from escaping back to the comfortable, quiet house in Independence each year for months on end. The lonely Senator in faraway Washington could do little but write and scheme to bring about their return. His letters show how hard he tried to lure them back —through finding an attractive apartment, perhaps buying a house, or stressing the importance of the social invitations. Sometimes, in desperation, he simply begged. He remarked from time to time how he had been tempted to get on the train, or even fly (an uncertain adventure in the thirties) to Independence.

During his first term, 1935–1941, Senator Truman was enormously busy. By nature he performed his tasks in an almost compulsive way, whether dictating a hundred letters to office secretaries or moving from one committee meeting to another, or from one Senate roll call to another. He frequently accepted dinner invitations, feeling he had to present himself to the capital's hosts and hostesses. One senses that Bess's absence did not make this task easier. But his major work in the Senate during the first term developed from his acquaintance, which ripened into friendship, with Senator Burton K. Wheeler of Montana. Burt Wheeler was a serious Senator as well as a friendly one and was fascinated by the railroad high finance of New York bankers and lawyers as exposed in the Depression bankruptcies. He found in Truman an avid listener who asked to be present during hearings of Wheeler's Interstate Commerce Committee. His obvious interest persuaded Wheeler to put him on the railroad subcommittee. The result was the Truman-Wheeler Transportation Act of 1940, a milestone in railroad regulation, which bound errant bankers and lawyers to stricter business ethics. The Act protected unsuspecting people who bought railroad bonds and stock in the belief that they were getting certificates of value. As a member of the Wheeler subcommittee, Truman gained a reputation for being a populist, anti-Wall Street. He was just plain furious because of the dishonesty of supposedly responsible people who liked to think of themselves as pillars of their communities.

During the latter thirties Truman also played a large part in reorganization of civil aviation under the Civil Aeronautics Board, headed by a chairman responsible to the President rather than Congress. The latter arrangement, he rightly believed, would have placed the fledgling aviation industry in grave danger, subject to the whims of legislators.

His achievement in the Senate, however, did little for him in Missouri politics, where forces gathered in the late thirties that moved against the junior Senator in the 1940 primary. Truman's problem after the fall of Pendergast was in part the loss of Kansas City's repeater vote, which thus increased the likelihood of attack from St. Louis. Moreover, he had to contend with the danger that Governor Lloyd C. Stark, owner of the world's largest nursery and producer of Stark delicious apples, would try to take his seat. Stark had achieved the governorship in 1937 after asking Truman to secure Pendergast support. But when he saw Pendergast's vulnerability, he allied himself with District Attorney Milligan to bring down the Boss. At the outset he gave no evidence of desiring the senatorial nomination, and during one of his frequent trips to Washington told the junior Missouri Senator's secretary that he, the governor, would never think of running for the Senate. When Truman heard that, he was sure "the self-made S.O.B.," as he later described Stark, would run.

The result was a donnybrook in which for a while Truman seemed to have no chance. The Roosevelt administration virtually threw its support to Stark, although the President refrained from saying so openly. At a crucial point in Truman's preparations to declare his candidacy, a henchman of F.D.R., Press Secretary Stephen Early, called the Senator, who was then in St. Louis. Truman's secretary answered the phone (Truman, present in the hotel suite, cautiously declined to speak), and Early proposed the appointment of a place on the Interstate Commerce Commission, a lifetime appointment at a salary higher than that of Senator. The Missourian indignantly told his secretary that the President could go to hell. Shortly afterward he declared he would run for reelection even if he received only two votes: his own and that of Bess. Then the district attorney, Milligan, entered the race, perhaps enticed by (and certainly supported by) Truman loyalists in an effort to divide the "good government" vote that otherwise would have gone to Stark. The governor's egotism became ever more ¬parent to others as he was seen at rallies in the company of a group of unifo. .d Missouri colonels. People even noticed his state police chauffeur saluting him. He forced all state employees to contribute to his campaign fund. Rumor had it that he was not genuinely interested in the Senate but wanted a Cabinet appointment—perhaps encouraged by President Roosevelt, whom he had frequently visited in Washington. F.D.R. seems to have mentioned Stark as a possible vice presidential candidate to replace Garner, who after two terms was retiring. Milligan meanwhile proved a disastrous public speaker, putting his audiences instantly to sleep. Truman was not much better, but at least his words rang true. He solicited support from Missouri's blacks, and they flocked to his standard. So did numbers of labor unions, especially the railroad brotherhoods, who supported him because of his anti-Wall Street Senate speeches and his co-sponsorship of the Transportation Act. At long last Bennett Clark roused himself on behalf of the junior Senator. Moreover, unexpectedly and for reasons still unclear, help came from St. Louis. A young man named Robert E. Hannegan, a policeman's son who had become a powerhouse in the city's politics, instructed his ward heelers and precinct bosses to go for Truman. St. Louis's slim majority swung the election, giving the Senator a statewide plurality over Stark and Milligan of 7,976 votes. When Truman walked into the Senate Chamber on January 20, 1941, to be sworn in for a second term, the entire body of Senators stood and applauded.

NINE

JACKSON COUNTY POLITICIAN

Harry S. Truman's stewardship of government in Jackson County, Missouri, challenged his administrative abilities, and not merely because the county contained the second-largest metropolis in the state, Kansas City. Truman ran the county at a time when local government was in transition. For many years anyone who presided over a county government had been a sort of caretaker, watching the courthouse, the jail, and the old folks' home—and sleeping through his term until election time. After World War I, however, county government had to meet the needs of the automobile; the demand for good roads was suddenly inescapable. Truman spent much of his time on the issue. Industries, moreover, needed efficient surroundings—cities and towns and villages had to be orderly, people who lived in them had to feel that they were obtaining necessary government services. In the twenties industry made more and more demands of local government; county administrators had to be sharp.

Truman's work as head of a large and important county was complicated by the politics of Kansas City. He had to weigh each situation for its political content, and he never forgot the lessons in governing that Jackson County taught him.

The following two letters are apparently the only ones that Truman wrote to Bess in 1921. They describe a state convention of the American Legion.

[Hotel Robidoux, St. Joseph, Mo.]
Dear Bess: September 19, 1921
. . . It certainly does your heart good to look over these boys. They are the cream of the country, every one of them a man's man. They can do anything from fight a battle (not bottle) to spark a lady. The next twenty years will see them running the country, and it will be in safe hands.

Old Colonel McDonald, the St. Joe police chief, made us a speech of welcome and it was a dandy. He's the man who lost a son in the 35th on

September 26 and asked to be sent to the front at once. His request was granted and he thinks he got enough Dutchmen to escort his son through Paradise properly. The Post here is named for his son.

There's a gang at the piano singing "How Dry I Am," "Madelon," "The Old Gray Mare," and the rest of the soldier repertoire (I can spell it). It makes me homesick for my real Irish gang.

If I only had my honey here with me, my enjoyment would be complete, but I'm afraid yours wouldn't because you'd probably consider this a very roughneck outfit, but they're not. They're just young and full of pep and they have to explode some way.

I wish I were home tonight but the gang want me to see them through and I guess I'll stay until tomorrow afternoon. I'll call you as soon as I get to town. I hope you're feeling fine and can go to the *Four Horsemen.*

Yours always,
Harry

By the autumn of 1921 the Truman & Jacobson haberdashery, shown here, was losing money rapidly. Truman is at left. *Harry S. Truman Library*

[Hotel Robidoux, St. Joseph, Mo.]

My Dear Miss Bessie: September 20, 1921

. . . This convention has settled everything that refers to the ex-serviceman and most of the burning political questions of the country. Our state commander,

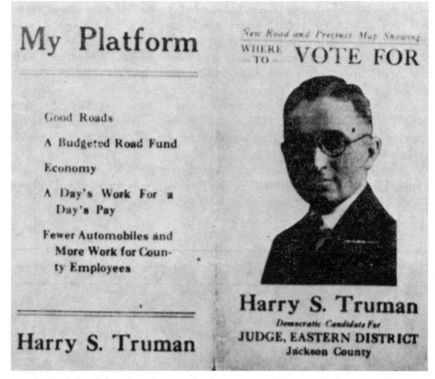

Candidate for eastern judge, 1922. *Harry S. Truman Library*

Jack Williams, is the ideal man for the job. He's a fine-looking, upstanding fellow with blue eyes and black hair, which he parts on the side and combs straight back. He looks as if he could lick anyone here if he chose to do it, but he has the most pleasant smile, makes his rulings in a fair and diplomatic manner, presiding over the conversation as if it were the Senate of the greatest Republic on earth instead of a howling mob of ex-soldiers.

I was so tired last night I could hardly walk. Went to bed at eleven and knew nothing until eight-thirty this A.M., didn't even hear Jimmy Pendergast when he came to bed. Jimmy and myself have the same room. He's a nice boy and as smart as the old man he's named for.

The convention's called and I must run.

Yours always,
Harry

In 1922 Truman was elected eastern judge of the county court. During this year he appears to have written no letters to Bess. His first long separation from her since their marriage was for summer camp at nearby Fort Leavenworth, which he describes below.

[Ft. Leavenworth, Kans.]
My Dear Wife: July 16, 1923
    I hesitated somewhat on that word. I wanted to say honey, sweetheart, Miss
Bessie. But the one I used is in the last analysis the finest and loveliest word in
the world. When a man has a perfect one as I have, what in life is better?
    Mr. Kirby refused to bring me up here until he'd delivered Miss Settle in
Lawrence, so I got stuck for the dinners at Tonagonoxie at a dollar per head. They
were twenty-five cents higher than week-day dinners. We had cold roast country
ham, cold roast veal, old-fashioned country-fried potatoes, three kinds of salad,
pickled beets, oranges, four kinds of preserves and jam, with ice tea and angel
food and orange cake with preserves or peaches for dessert. It was a good dinner
and worth twice the money. I was homesick for you all the way here and after
I got here. It was ten-thirty when we arrived and Kirby, I think, was sorry to leave
me in the camp.
    Colonel Clendening was in the office. He gave me a blanket, *two sheets*, two
pillow cases (think of that) and took me to a tent where I found an iron spring
cot with a pillow and mattress and a mosquito bar to cover it. The tent has an
electric light and I have my individual wash basin.
    I got up at five-thirty, went down to the end of the street in my pajamas
and took a cold shower, ran back, dressed and was ready for breakfast at six-thirty.
We had a half grapefruit, cream of wheat, ham, two eggs, two hot cakes, and
coffee, *and I ate it all*.
    After breakfast I went for a physical examination. Shut my mouth and said
ah! bent over, hopped on one foot and then the other; had my heart tested, my
lungs tapped, and my throat examined; and the old major who did it said that
I sure am a healthy specimen. He looked me over and remarked that he guessed
I'd always been healthy too. Aren't you glad to hear that?
    I hope you slept better than I did last night. My bed was good, the air fine,
but I wanted someone to keep me covered up and to hug. [Illegible] has been
here and given me a job so I'll have to go and attend to it. It is teaching eight
second lieutenants how to read a map. I used to be a bear at it but I doubt my
ability now.
    Please come and see me. We have nothing to do after six. I just can't get
over wanting to see you. I am
                                            Always,
                                            Your Harry

                                                            [Ft. Leavenworth, Kans.]
Dear Bess: July 19, 1923
    . . . Well we are in the midst of a great war between Kansas and Missouri,
and the mean part about it is that I am in the Kansas army and am helping to
lick my own people and doing a good job at it. Say, but this is fine for brain work
and they keep us in such excellent physical shape that our brains really work. I'd
give most anything to take the School of Fire course and then take the year at

Leavenworth. We were out again yesterday watching that Battery work and I've cooked up a deal to put all the second lieutenants here on horses and the guns and take that Battery out once for a real go-around. I guess it will go across and I'll have a real time.

If Jacobson doesn't ask you to come up here Friday, I'll not have anything more to do with him, but I'm sure he'll ask you. He told me he would.

I am going to have to write orders for a whole division today, and believe me it's a real job. I won't have time to think of any politicians or jobs or roads either for the balance of the week.

Don't fail to write, because my day is ruined if I don't get that letter. All the love in the world.

Yours,
Harry

[Ft. Leavenworth, Kans.]

My Dear Wife: July 21, 1923

I am going to have a bum day today because I won't get any letter. It was a treat to see you certainly, but there were so many around I couldn't enjoy your company as I could if we'd been alone. I sure hated to see you go back. Just for a small amount I'd have gone home with you.

You perhaps can see something of the pull there is on a man when he's had some military training to do it again. There is no explanation for it but it's there. He'll cuss the military and all that pertains to it and then he'll go right back and take more punishment. There is something about it that's not to be explained by reason or common sense, any more than why a man loves his wife. We are a bunch of nuts and can't help it, I guess, but we enjoy it. You can see that I'm not the only one affected.

I have to use my brain today sure enough because when you tell someone else something that you know yourself it's a real job.

You be a good girl and I'll be a good boy. I have been. I haven't had a thing to drink nor have I drawn a single card.

I love you an awful lot, can't help it and don't want to.

Yours,
Harry

[Ft. Leavenworth, Kans.]

Dear Bess: July 25, 1923

It sounded mighty fine to hear your voice over the phone but I surely feel like busting a dentist I know of. It does seem to me that he could have extracted that tooth in a shorter time than that. I'm very glad it's out and I hope you'll get the rest of them fixed. . . . I sure feel fine this morning. It is cool and the pep is in everyone. I have been eating too much and I cut my diet day before yesterday. The result has been marvelous. Then we've had a new physical instructor the last day or so and he's been putting us through some real stuff. I'll be able to lick all the rabbits [Shannon Democrats] and the Kansas City *Journal* too when I get home. . . .

That Battery drill today is going to be some exercise. I'll have about forty green men and you can guess what will happen. We are going to show the infantry how fast we can take up a position and start action. If someone doesn't fall off his horse and break his neck or point the gun north when we want to shoot south, we'll be all right.

I've got a good executive and I guess everything will come out all right. Hope to see you tomorrow. Lots of love. I hope your tooth extraction hasn't caused any aftermath.

Yours,
Harry

Ft. Leavenworth, Kans.

Dear Bess: July 28, 1923

I was sure glad to get your letter. If I hadn't, there'd have been a call for you. The rain was very satisfactory and did no damage, except to get your old man a little damp when he tightened the tent ropes. . . .

Last night we had a party at the golf club, without extra charge. The mess fund paid for it. A right good meal and then stunts. A take-off on Colonel Siegmund that was a dandy. Initiated Colonel Clendening into the field artillery to which he's been transferred, a mock court-martial, and a badger fight which was a scream. The boys who were sold on it were nearly scared to death before it came off, and when the badger was pulled one of them jumped over the table and nearly broke his neck. I'll tell you what a badger fight is when I get home if you don't know.

I just got some sad news. I can't leave until after breakfast Monday A.M. I hope to be in Independence at eight-thirty. Be a good girl until I arrive. I hope I'll never be away from you so long again. I love you.

Yours,
Harry

The single letter to Bess that has survived for the year 1924 is notable for what it leaves unsaid. Attending another state convention of the American Legion, Truman doesn't mention his defeat in the Democratic primary, caused by the Jackson County Democrats' split between the Pendergast machine and Shannon. Nor does he say much about the principal event in his life that year, the birth of Mary Margaret Truman.

[Hotel Connor, Joplin, Mo.]

Dear Bess: August 18, 1924

I hesitated a long time over the salutation and finally stuck to the old much used and really the best one. You might accidentally leave the opening statement exposed and someone would be sure to say we were a couple of idiots if I should start off "Dear Hon" or "Sweetie" or "Honey Bunch" or a half-dozen equally descriptive and proper words.

James and I had a very satisfactory trip and would have been here by nine o'clock had we not run into a small chuckhole and broken a front spring. The hole was not half as large as forty or fifty we'd been over before but the old spring broke right in the center just as completely as if it had been sawed with a hack saw, every leaf. I had another put on this morning for $7.50, half of which Jimmy insists on standing so I won't be out so awful much, might have broken it if I'd stayed at home. We had to make a detour and I went through Lamar, the first time I've been there since I was a year old. I couldn't see much change in the town except that Pop's old livery stable apparently is a garage now.

The convention opened with a bang. The mayor turned the town over to us, and a Hebrew gentleman by the name of Herowitz read an address from Governor Hyde. We accused him of writing it himself but he said he didn't. I

With Mary Margaret Truman, 1924. *Harry S. Truman Library*

told him I didn't think Hyde could write as good a speech as that.

We are invited out to a chicken dinner at the club tonight. It is strictly stag so don't get uneasy. Jimmy is trying to get the state headquarters moved to Independence but I don't think it can be done. It looks as if Carl Grey will be the next commander. George Cowls is here. I saw Ralph a little bit ago. He's taken the pledge—says he's not drinking any more. I hope it sticks.

I was pretty homesick last night and am yet. I'd like mighty well to see Miss Mary Margaret Skinny Fatty Sweetness, etc. ad lib. right this minute. It's peculiar how your own wife and children grow on you, isn't it?

I hope to see you Thursday about noon or two o'clock.

Your Harry

The duties of eastern judge continued until January 1925. Thereafter Truman put on what he described years later as a "whirlwind" drive to sell memberships in the Kansas City Automobile Club. The work kept him busy until 1926, when he ran for and was elected presiding judge. Meanwhile summer camp continued at Fort Riley, near Manhattan, Kansas.

Fort Riley, Kans.
Dear Bess: July 4, 1925

We came through on schedule, arriving here at 2:30 P.M. We got to Topeka at 10:00, Manhattan at 12:30, where we had a good dinner on Colonel Elliott. The roads were very good—not a bad place in them. There is only one drawback to the arrangement—I am quartered in the same room with the colonel and Captain *Percy* Fleming. I guess I can stand it though.

I hope your foot is much better and that Miss M.M. is behaving as she should. There is only one drawback to this camp business. I can't have you both with me. I sure do miss you. I hope you are feeling all right. I am rather tired and hot but there is a good breeze blowing.

Claude Sowers let me have this paper [Sowers-Taylor Company, K.C., letterhead] so I could start the week right. I hope you are doing the same thing. My mind is rather blank and I hope I can do better tomorrow.

I love you,
Harry

Ft. Riley, Kans.
Dear Sweethearts: July 7, 1925

Another day gone or nearly so and the pace has been just as strenuous. We had our call on the general and his lady. It consisted of going by them on their front porch and off at the other end and away. He always kids me about my political career and I tell him if there weren't politicians to run the government, he would not be a brigadier general. That usually stops the conversation—at least it did last evening.

We had a horseback ride this A.M. in addition to our other duties. It was not very strenuous. I can use that swimming suit if it isn't too much trouble to send it. This day has been much brighter because of your note. I am very sorry about your foot. If you'd just be as anxious to take care of yourself as you are to doctor me and the young lady, you'd be all right nine times in ten. You should have had the doctor when your foot first hurt you.

I wish I could take you and the baby "bye." I guess it was pretty selfish in me to come off up here and leave you and take the car and I shouldn't have done it. I need the workout though and it's doing me good. Jay Lee is here. I've just had a bath and a fine breeze is blowing from the southwest, but it was sure hot this A.M.

I hope I get that letter in the morning. Kiss the kid and remember

I love you,
Harry

Ft. Riley, Kans.
My Dear Hon and Baby: July 8, 1925

I got your letter at noon today. Where did Miss M. get her bad eye? It sure was a surprise to me to hear that she has a bad one. I do hope it's nothing serious. I am glad your ankle is improving. The box came today and I was very glad to get the stocks as I only had one. Laundry service is not the best in the world here and I only had one white stock. We have to dress up in the evening, either in civies or full-dress uniform. It's a good thing I brought my civilian clothes. They are very handy when it's hot.

I think I told you I went swimming yesterday and it was the coldest pool I was ever in. Minnesota lakes have nothing on it. Our showers are the same way. I can't understand what causes it. I got the colonel to let us ride to work in cars this morning and it has improved the morale considerably. We'd been walking a mile and a half to a lecture, then riding some rough ponies for an hour, and then walking another mile to another lecture and then walking back a mile and a half to the noon meal and then walking to the lecture room and back at three-thirty. Some of these birds looked like a picked chicken after two days of it and now we use the cars. I saw a fellow just now who says he loves his wife as much as I do mine. He writes her every day anyway. His name is Claude Sowers. I borrowed stationery from him the first day. You kiss my baby and

Write me,
Harry

Ft. Riley, Kans.
Dear Sweethearts: July 9, 1925

Today is fine and cool and a beautiful day, but for all that it's a dull one —there was no letter. I got the swimming suit by air and I am very glad you sent it. We have swimming parties every afternoon and while the pool is cold as the mischief it's very good for us. I'm as healthy as a farmhand.

Say, if you want your hair bobbed so badly, go on and get it done. I want you to be happy regardless of what I think about it. I am very sure you'll be just as beautiful with it off and I'll not say anything to make you sorry for doing it. I can still see you as the finest on earth so go and have it done. I've never been right sure you weren't kidding me anyway. You usually do as you like about things and that's what I want you to do.

I hope that you and the baby are both well and not entirely roasted. We've never been uncomfortably hot although yesterday was a stinger. Be sure and let me hear from you. The days are awful dull without the letters. I doubt if I'm to come home Friday or not. If I can't, I can't that's all. We had a fine ride this A.M. and we're going to pistol practice shortly.

Lots of love to you and kiss my baby,
Harry

[The Cavalry School Club, Ft. Riley, Kans.]

Dear Bess: Sunday [July 12, 1925]

Well I got a letter when I went to dinner. The day's brighter. I'm writing you again. I'm glad the baby's eye is better. I did a kid trick last night. I wanted to see you and Skinny so badly after supper that I backed my car out without anyone seeing me and started up the road in the direction of home and with the intention of going there too. After I'd driven about an hour I saw a sign which said Topeka seventy miles and I began to figure that the best I could do would be to arrive about 1:00 P.M. and perhaps scare you all to death so I turned around and came on back. Besides, I had to read all the rules in all the artillery books today so I could give the men who fired a square deal when I check them. Jay Lee, Bachelor, and I have spent the whole afternoon checking up on them. It's harder to keep track of a man and grade him than it is to fire yourself.

How do you like my new stationery? I let a fellow go to church in my car and it was full of gas, he wanted to do something for me, so he stopped by the club and brought me some stationery.

I went down and watched the Missouri national Guard regiment unload just before noon. I found one of my Battery sergeants and one of my corporals in it. I saw the sergeant and he ran a half a block to shake my hand and said hello Captain Truman, I wish I was in your outfit. That makes me feel very good.

Now this is two letters today. You see how badly I want to see you and hear from you. Kiss my baby.

Yours always,
Harry

[Fort Riley, Kans.]

My Dear Sweetheart and Baby: Tuesday, July 14, 1925

We had a storm last night that cooled things off in good style. The lightning killed three mules down at the national guard camp but injured no one else. It was so muddy the war was called off and we didn't go to the firing point this morning. . . .

I've been so afraid my daughter would forget me. I did not know what to do. I'm glad you are keeping her informed on who her daddy is anyway. That bob expert at the Baltimore was in my canteen barber shop. His name is Baker and if you'll tell him you are Mrs. H.S.T., he'll spread himself to do you a good job. He was in Battery A—Keith Dancy's Battery in the war. I'm sorry Natalie and Frank can't agree but I'm satisfied she'll have her way. They always do. I should have made you get your teeth fixed before you operated.

I had a note from Mamma and a report from Miss Reyling. It was a very good week at the club. Just as well as if I'd been present. So my worries were all for naught. Be sure and kiss the young lady.

Yours always,
Harry

Another year passes, and Truman again writes from summer camp.

Ft. Riley, Kans.
July 8, 1926

Dear Bess:

The letter came yesterday before I got to the phone and I was sure glad to hear from my babies. I never wanted to come home so badly in my life as I did last night after the young lady said she'd cried. I can somewhat sympathize with these birds that lose all respect by going over the hill to see their honeys.

Two letters just came but one of them was the insurance company's letter. I'm very glad you sent it. I'm most always easier to get along with after getting your letters; the gang here found it out and usually make their requests after I get one.

We had a fine rain last night and yesterday afternoon and the weather is fine. Regular summer resort weather. I've still got plenty to do. We are having a grand time. The camp is better organized than it was last year and things go more smoothly. Still there is plenty for a regimental commanding officer to do.

I have a chance to get this in the mail at once and I've got to close. Be sure and kiss my baby and tell her to kiss her mamma for Daddy. I'll write more fully tomorrow.

Yours,
Harry

Ft. Riley, Kans.
July 10, 1926

Dear Bess:

Your letter came today. The day is perfect *now*. The weather is cool, regular summer resort kind. I saw that you'd had a four-inch rain. I don't understand why you didn't get a letter, because I haven't missed a day. With all the business I've had I don't let it interfere with your daily letter.

This is a very fine bunch of men. They have cooperated wonderfully with me. They are asking me to take permanent command of the regiment. It makes me feel pretty good. We are going to have an exhibition drill and riding contest Saturday morning. I wish you'd come up. I am sorry you couldn't go to Reed's dinner. I imagine it was a great affair. The Mt. Washington letter was a report for the Grand Lodge. Had a letter from Metzger enclosing a proof of my buttons. Don't like 'em. Be sure and kiss my baby and tell her to kiss her mamma. I'm healthy, sleeping well, and if I had my honey I'd be happy.

Harry

Field artillery Battery at Fort Riley, 1926. *Harry S. Truman Library*

Ft. Riley, Kans.

Dear Bess: July 12, 1926

Your letter came Sunday and I surely appreciated getting it. It made the day really worthwhile. We are on our way to Manhattan this morning to look over and study a G.P.F. 155 Rifle. It will shoot ten miles and make a hole in the ground you can throw a house into. It rained last night and we are going over on the streetcar, hence this shaky writing, so don't accuse me of being drunk as you once did when I wrote you a letter on a French train.

I was in Junction City to dinner last night at the hotel. Captain Milburn took Captain Hyde, Captain Hurd, Majors Bryant and Salisbury, and myself over and we had a very pleasant evening. Colonel Griswold, who is a state senator from Nebraska, has asked us over to the hotel for dinner tonight. I took him over last week. There are lots of politicians here. We have a great time trying to get our campaign funds out of the poker game. Be sure and kiss my baby. Wish I could see you.

Your Harry

The letter that follows contains one of Truman's few references to politics during summer camp of 1926—Colonel Southern, as publisher of the Independence Examiner, *evidently was supporting Truman for the office of presiding judge. The Pendergasts had settled their differences with Shannon, and Truman rightly was unconcerned about victory in the August primary.*

Ft. Riley, Kans.
Dear Bess: July 15, 1926
    Your good letter came this noon and I was sure glad to get it. Mr. South-
ern seems to be taking some active interest in politics. He usually does that
when there is nothing to fight about. I hope your mother is much better. You'd
better have that cistern water analyzed and not let the young lady have any but
boiled. . . .
    We are having a party tonight. The annual banquet of the reserves is some
affair. There'll be a badger fight, some boxing bouts, and speeches by unit
commanders. I was so rushed today that I didn't get to write this at noon, as I
should have, and I doubt if you'll get it as soon as you should.
    There's a rumor around here to the effect that we can't leave until Monday
but I hope it's unfounded.
    Keep writing. Kiss my baby—how I'd like to see her and her mamma.
                              x x x x x
                               50=50
                         From your Harry

    *The next several letters were written on the road as Truman attended
meetings of the National Old Trails Association.*

Herington, Kans.
Dear Bess: Sunday evening, Nov. 7, 1926
    We have kept our schedule to the dot. Got to Council Grove at 2:30 P.M.
and met all the prominent citizens in town, at "the" Building and Loan Association office. You'd think I was the President of the U.S. We discussed the National
Old Trails, cussed Osage City, the next large town to the east (we'll do the same
for them when we go to Osage), and came over here to Herington. Arrived at
5:45, left Council Grove at 5:45. It is twenty-six miles, so we lost no time on the
finest dirt road you ever saw. Had a flat tire at Burlingame. The hotel man called
a garage and had it fixed while we ate the finest chicken dinner you ever saw with
the leading lawyer, the county judge (commissioner they call him out here), and
a couple of other prominent citizens. Tonight we'll do the same here. It has been
misting since 3:00 P.M. I don't know if it is going to rain but I hope not. I am
feeling fine and dandy. My voice is improved. I've eaten a box of the whiskered
bros. [Smith Bros.] cough drops. Be sure and kiss my baby and look in the mirror
for one for yourself. Will write you tomorrow. I wish you and the young lady were
here. Love to you both by the bushel.
                              Yours,
                              Harry

[Hotel Zarah, Great Bend, Kans.]
Dear Bess: Tuesday 10:30, November 9, 1926
    Got up at six-thirty, had grapefruit, bacon and eggs, oatmeal, toast, and hot
tea for breakfast. Took a bus for Sterling and got a Santa Fe train for this place.

Mr. Moses, of the Moses Milling Co., met us in a big Hudson sedan and the president of the Chamber of Commerce was there in his Buick sedan. We are billed to speak to the Lions Club at noon, after which these gentlemen are going to drive us over to Larned for a 3:00 P.M. meeting and a Chamber of Commerce meeting at six-thirty at Kinsley, after which they will drive us to Dodge. This is almost like campaigning for President except that the people are making promises to me instead of the other way around. They sure do treat us royally. The Rumanian Queen had nothing on us.

The weather is ideal, as pretty a day as you can wish for. This a beautiful town and seems to be plumb full of live wires. I do hope I get a letter in Dodge. Bill Francisco was at Lyons. He's straightened up and is making good as a salesman for the Rock Island Imp. Co.

You sure ought to be along. We'd have the time of our lives. I've got a trip all arranged to California for next fall if you want to take it. Kiss my baby and take a carload for yourself. I've got to run.

Love from
Your Harry

[Dodge City, Kans., Nov. 10, 1926]

Dear Bess: Tuesday, 10:15, maybe 9:15

We had a grand meeting in Great Bend and Mr. Moses and the president of the Chamber of Commerce hooked up a fine 1927 Buick sedan and hauled us to Larned where we had a meeting in the Cafe Bon-bon with the town's leading citizens, after which we drove out to Pawnee Rock, which is a rock hill about one hundred feet above the surrounding plain at a little place about twenty miles southwest of Great Bend called Pawnee Rock and from the top of which you can see for miles. It is the only rock in forty miles and was formerly used by Indians as a place from which to jump out and slaughter unsuspecting travelers who were going down the Santa Fe Trail. The D.A.R. have put a fence around it and erected a fine monument on top of it to the early pioneers.

We drove on to Kinsley, where we had another meeting at 8:00 P.M. At Kinsley the road forks going east and the new Santa Fe Trail goes by way of St. John and Syracuse to Hutchinson and Emporia. At Larned the road splits and goes west to Garden City by way of Jetmore and is called North 50. If Larned directs traffic straight west by North 50, it misses Kinsley and Dodge City. If Kinsley directs traffic east over the new Santa Fe Trail, it misses Larned and Great Bend. Larned and Kinsley each have had signs up directing traffic away from the other but they each claimed that some outside town on the other road had put up the sign. The inhabitants of each town are almost afraid to be caught in the other town because of the situation. We have delegates from each place due at our meeting here tomorrow and from the look of things we have reestablished good relations and will have all the cities in this neighborhood pulling for our National Old Trails, which is what we came for.

I have met some real characters on this trip. This Old Man Moses I rode down with on the train from Kinsley and in the auto to that place is not the

Kansas Milling Co. Moses but is a financier of these parts. He owns (or did until he gave them away) four department stores and three banks besides generous portions of the business sections of Great Bend, Larned, Pawnee Rock, and various and sundry other towns. Davis tells me he's worth a million or two. He has two sons and some granddaughters in whom he seems to be very much interested. He gave his department stores to the managers who had been with him longest and organized a finance company to run his banks and gave them to his sons. He still is burdened with his real estate. His wife died in June, but he told me that they had seen everything on the American continent and most of Europe before she died and that he intended to keep their big house in Great Bend running just as if she were alive for they both believed in getting everything out of life there is in it. He came here from Sedalia, Missouri, in 1874 after taking a much shot-up trip across Colorado to San Francisco and Portland. He said his brother was sheriff of Great Bend when he arrived and that the chief deputy killed a man that night and his brother had to kill one the next day. I'm meeting some fine old Kansas Red Legs, as my mother would call them, and they're not half bad.

We came down from Kinsley on Santa Fe No. 5, which arrived here at 10:05, stayed fifteen minutes and left at 9:20 [sic]. You can't beat that and I'm sober too.

I'm hoping I get a letter from you tomorrow. I'll sure be disappointed if I don't. Be sure and kiss my baby. I'll be home Friday evening and gone again Saturday at 10:00 A.M.

Loads of love from
Your Harry

[Dodge City, Kans.]

Dear Bess: November 10, 1926, 5:30 P.M. (or 4:30)
. . . I met Ham Bell, who was mayor of South Dodge at the same time Bat Masterson was mayor of North Dodge. One lies south of the R.R. and the other north of it. They tell me that the Hon. Ham was not so pious in those days as he is now. He's a pillar of the Methodist Church and places a bouquet on the altar every Sunday now, but they tell it on him that in days gone by, when he ran a dance hall in the part of the city of which he was the presiding officer, he was pitched bodily over into his part of town by the invincible Mr. Masterson when he came across the track to meet some ladies from Wichita who were going to work for him. It seems that inhabitants of the two sections were supposed to stay in their own bailiwicks and if they ventured into strange territory, they did so at their own bodily risk. It seems that Mr. Bell thought he could get over to the train and back without attracting attention, but a long scar on his face shows that he failed. He's forgotten it and no one can persuade him to mention it, but gossipy neighbors spilled the beans.

We went out to old Ft. Dodge, southeast of here on the Arkansas River, just to say we were there. It is not a soldier's home and not interesting to look at except that it was an Indian frontier about sixty years ago. The fort is four miles from town because it was against the law to sell booze within that distance of a government post in those days and when the R.R. came they had to start the town four miles away. They showed us "Boot Hill," where they buried the gentlemen who were slow on the draw in an argument. It has a schoolhouse on it, a large brick structure which the city has outgrown. It has been abandoned as a school for a better one and is now vacant. The Catholics built a fine hospital here and some of the "Sheet Bros." bought "Boot Hill" to build a finer one but fell out among themselves, as usual, and it's still Boot Hill with an old schoolhouse on it. I am enclosing you a picture of it.

We're leaving at 7:00 P.M. and will be home Friday. You really don't know how awful glad I was to hear from you. I'm sorry you were so uneasy about me but I was never better in my life. I hate it because you had a poky Sunday. I hope the time will soon come when you never have one. Be sure and kiss my baby and take a carload of love for yourself.

Your Harry

[Hotel Stamey, Hutchinson, Kans.]

Dear Bess: November 11, 1926
. . . This is Armistice Day. Eight years ago, if I remember rightly, I was up figuring a barrage to fire on Hermeville and Grimaucourt down in front of Verdun. I fired at 3:00 A.M. and 4:00 A.M., and at 5:30 A.M. old "Pat" (Paterson) called up from Klemm's headquarters and told me that the firing would probably cease at 11:00 A.M. because he had been reliably informed that Foch had signed an armistice to take effect then, but for me not to tell anyone. I think he did every captain the same way. I went on and fired 163 more rounds through the fog and then sure enough at 11:00 A.M. it turned out to be true. Sermon called and said cease firing. I hadn't fired any since 9:00 A.M., but an old French 155 (6-inch) Battery behind me kept right on right up to 11:00 A.M., shooting as hard as they could just to be shooting. The commander said because they had *beaucoup* ammunition.

Then a few days after that I got a letter from you saying you'd nearly died with the flu and I felt just as I did at Dodge this morning. I hadn't suffered much except loss of sleep and worry for my outfit and here nearly all I had in the world was nearer the great divide than I'd ever been because I never believed my name was on a bullet. . . .

I am ashamed now that I didn't stay at home and fight the job hunters and take you to see the Queen. I'm afraid I'm not as thoughtful of your pleasure as I ought to be. If ever I can connect, you'll never want to do anything you can't. Kiss the baby. I wish I could hear her say "Lo Dad."

All the love to you,
Your Harry

[Thomas Hotel, Greenville, Ill.]

Dear Bess: November 14, 1926

Still it rains. We left Columbia about eight-thirty this morning and stopped in Fulton to see Nick Case, the senator from that town in the state legislature. He invited us out to his house and was very cordial to us. We arrived in St. Louis about one-thirty and came on out here. Found *George's* Hotel, and just now phoned the president of the Chamber of Commerce. He's coming down to see us after a while. We've seen the local newspaperman, who said our names and business would be in the paper tomorrow.

This hotel is run by an old fat codger who is very good humored but he has a tough egg for a wife. She made a couple of kids take their pup out of her hotel lickety-split just now. They were tourists same as we are, but my sympathies are always with the kids. The old lady told them they could take their dog up to the garage and let him stay in the car, which they did.

We are now traveling on the National Pike, which was surveyed and laid out in Thomas Jefferson's administration to get communication with Louisiana Territory. That was done along about 1806. Last year or the year before the road was finally paved into St. Louis. Quick action what? We've gone from wheels on the ground to wheels on steel and now we are back on the ground. What, I wonder, will be the next step?

The National Old Trail is really on the map here. They have hotels, eating houses, garages, and drugstores all named for it. So you see we won't have a very hard time getting things rolling over here. I hope you and the young lady are in fine health and spirits. I'd like very much to see you both tonight. Be sure and kiss my "good girl" and make believe for yourself.

Love by the bushel from
Your Harry

[Hotel Gibbons, Dayton, Ohio]

Dear Bess: November 15, 1926

We arrived here at 8:10 P.M. after an all day's drive, and I find it a rotten town. I thought I'd get a letter as soon as I arrived and I found none. I was so disappointed that I went off to a show before I wrote this. Then I got to thinking that maybe you had so much to do Saturday that you couldn't write and maybe after you wrote Sunday it didn't get off until Monday, in which case that's today and I won't get it until morning. But I sure did want it.

We left Greenville, Illinois, this morning at 7:00 A.M. Old man Thomas, who is the proprietor of the Thomas Hotel, proved to be a right interesting old man. He told me about a former saloonkeeper of his town who was such a good citizen and ran such a clean place that all the high collars and "the ribbon ladies" (Thomas called them that) looked on him with favor. He told me all that to impress upon me how nice it is to leave your widow money, no matter how you get it. The good saloonkeeper died and left his wife rich. In due course of events she married a Baptist preacher and the money personally went to a good purpose.

Davis has just read in a Terre Haute paper that President Coolidge dedicated a $2 million memorial for K.C. and that Will Rogers says it looks like a silo. Other people have the right slant on R.A. Long's monument to himself as well as us perverted people who only fought the war behind a gun.

We passed through a whole string of Illinois towns. Evidently they were all good ones too. We stopped awhile in Greenup to see a former supporter of the Old Trails and also stopped in Casey, another nice little town, to see quite a number of former supporters of the movement. They all seemed to be still enthusiastic.

We ate our noon meal at Brazil, Indiana, at the Hotel Davis. Had a grand lunch for fifty cents. Then we headed for the Hoosier State capitol. Got there about two-thirty and drove around and round the town for thirty minutes trying to find a place to park. They have a fine town, a good-looking state capitol, a federal building, and a courthouse equal to any. The Old Trail runs straight through the town from one side to the other on a big, wide street called Washington. Down in the center of town and a block north of this street is the Soldiers and Sailors Monument erected to the men who fought in the Civil War. It is a beautiful thing and is in the center of a large circle into which run four streets, one from each cardinal point. Around the circle are fine hotels, theaters, and clubs. We wanted to see the secretary of the Hoosier Auto Club, whose office is in the English Hotel. It is on this circle. After driving around about a dozen times and out each cross street and around the block trying to find a place to park, Davis finally got out and I kept going around the circle. Finally I stopped double in front of the hotel and the secretary came out to see me. I told him I'd been around that circle so often I didn't know south from straight up. He set me right and we headed for here. Stopped in Richmond, Indiana, at 6:00 P.M. and had as fine a meal as I ever ate and safely arrived here for a woeful disappointment. No letter.

This is a fine town, however, from a civic standpoint—good hotels, fine buildings, and apparently lots of business. I hope we have good luck tomorrow, and I hope that letter comes. Kiss my baby and lots of love to you from

Your Harry

[Hotel Windsor, Wheeling, W. Va.]

Dear Bess: February 12, 1927

The meeting is over and was one howling success. The National Highway Boosters Association is no more, and the National Old Trails Highway Association is a national organization indeed and in fact. We are completely organized back here and have had our financial situation practically guaranteed. George Washington Lutz, who was the president of the Boosters Association, is our executive vice president back here and Maryland, Pennsylvania, West Virginia, and Ohio are completely organized with two vice presidents each and a bunch of enthusiastic boosters behind them.

George Washington Lutz is seventy-one years old and is *the* leading citizen of Wheeling. He looks like George F. Baker, the president of the First National Bank of New York, has mutton-chop whiskers and everything. He's been president of the Board of Trade, the Fair Association, Chamber of Commerce, mayor of Wheeling, and most everything else. He is a widower with no children and has only one nephew, of whom he is very fond. He told me if his nephew had been a girl, he'd have married him long ago, which was his way of saying that he is very fond of him. He took us to his house just outside the city and gave us of his liquid hospitality and showed us the most complete house I've ever seen under one roof.

Our trip is a success. I've got to go to the train. Kiss my baby.

Your Harry

Below Truman reports what was apparently a business trip combined with pleasure. He had been inspecting the operation of gravel pits, so important to the building of new roads, with a group of public officials.

Branson, Mo.

Dear Bess: May 18, 1927

We had a fine trip down; the good-for-nothing outfit decided to come down here first and see our Osceola gravel bank on the way back. We saw the ones at Carthage and Sarcoxie. The state has some very fine roads down in this country. We were on boulevards nearly all the way. We came by Harrisonville, Butler, Nevada, Carthage, and then south and to Aurora and Branson. At Branson we put up the cars and took a nice little motorboat for about sixteen miles down the lake to the prettiest little seven-room cottage you ever saw. It was about seven o'clock when we arrived and Hunter and O'Malley proceeded to prepare supper. Mr. Wheatley, to whom the cottage belongs, called up a man who came and finished the cooking. We had to carry all our baggage, groceries, etc. up the hill about two hundred yards to the house. It was quite a job. Hunter and I wheeled up one hundred pounds of ice in a wheelbarrow. Supper was ready about 9:00 P.M. It consisted of fine T-bone steaks, one for each person, O'Brien potatoes, oranges, strawberries, and plenty of other things to go with them, such as bread, coffee, water, etc. Everyone else is in bed and I am writing this on my knee in my room. I am one of three who rank rooms. The rest of them are on cots in the big living room. You don't know how great a relief it is to be loose from that responsibility. I'm not going to think of anyone but you and my baby and come home without a headache. It is raining to beat the band but they need it down here.

The lights just went out but the old caretaker lit a lamp for me to finish by. Be sure and kiss my baby and remember I am thinking of you always.

Your Harry

[Ft. Riley, Kans.]

Dear Bess and Margie: Sunday night, July 10, 1927

We arrived on schedule, that is, in time to take a bath and have our noonday meal here at Ft. Riley. We'd have been about forty minutes earlier but for a nail in the right front tire at Manhattan. It happened right in town and only one block from a garage or we'd have been in a nice fix, for there was no jack in the car. I shall probably unburden my sentiments to friend Oliver when I return. If he had my job and I his, I'd expect a good going-over under the same circumstances and I'd probably get it.

I am very nicely situated, have a room with a would-be closet and another with a washstand and toilet. It pays to be a lieutenant colonel. I have Eddie McKim in my room at my request. He promoted me a table, a couple of chairs, and a bureau with a mirror, so we shall live in fine style. . . .

Kiss my baby and tell her to write me and you do the same. Not a sign of headache tonight and I hope you haven't.

Your sweetheart,
Harry

Ft. Riley, Kans.
July 11, 1927

My Dear Sweethearts, Bess and Margie:

The first half-day has gone by with only one casualty. One of the lieutenants stuck his finger into the breech mechanism of a 155 howitzer and a piece of it was amputated. Someone looked at the gun trail and noticed this piece of finger lying there and asked who had lost it. Everyone looked to see if he was the guilty party: in the meantime the man to whom it belonged was hotfooting it across the field toward the hospital. One of the boys picked up the piece and started after him, but in the excitement he lost it and the surgeon over at the hospital found it necessary to graft on a piece of skin, so the invalid won't be permanently injured. He was back on the job in an hour.

We are going out to fire on Friday morning. That is the only part of the performance I care much for. I am feeling fine and I hope you both are. Bess, you kiss the baby and tell her to kiss you for me.

Always,
Your Harry

Ft. Riley, Kans.
Wednesday, July 13[1927]

My Dear Missy and Baby:

I received a letter last night and one at noon today. This has been therefore one successful day. I am getting as brown as an Indian and as tough as Dempsey. I haven't had a headache since I came. It has rained and is cool and probably will rain again tonight. There is nothing wrong except your absence and my inability to tease my daughter.

I appreciate your enclosures, especially the deposit slip. That made your check I gave you good. It was long enough coming. I was afraid it was lost in the mail. The deposit, not the slip. Thanks for the clippings. Everything seems to be going all right in my absence politically. I wish I could see you. I'm glad you missed me at the party. Wish I could have been present. I am taking good care of myself. The colonel is anxious to work and I urge him to do it. I'm having a wonderful time doing a little political maneuvering. Also evening up some scores. The colonel listens to what I say and when I make suggestions about certain regular army officers he immediately flies into them. He's made Colonel Elliott's flunky, Captain Fleming, stand on his head right away, which pleased me immensely. You see politics is never absent when I'm around.

Be sure and keep writing. I look for 'em every day. Kiss Margie and tell Margie to kiss her *mamma* for her daddy.

Your Harry

Ft. Riley, Kans.

Dear Sweetheart and Baby: Thursday, July 14, 1927

I got *your* note today in return for mine. It's what I deserved all right and I am thankful for small favors. I hope you had a good time at Helen's luncheon. She seems to be doing the high social right. I'm very much pleased and flattered that you miss me so. There are two little girls in the other end of this barrack, daughters of a Captain Clayton, who is on duty here. Every time I see them I get so anxious to see you and my daughter I can hardly stand it. They keep us pretty well occupied here and in times past I'd have thought I was being worked to death but being presiding judge of Jackson County has shown me that there is no limit to a man's ability to stand punishment. When I get in this crowd of soldiers out here and they don't make a grand rush for me and begin pulling me one way and another to get my ear for a road or a contract or the right to sell soap or tacks to the county, I'm rather at a loss. My right arm is almost well and my left is sore from holding a dancing horse. . . .

Wish you could see a Battery fire once and then you'd appreciate what a powerful weapon of destruction your old man had in the war.

I'm glad it's cooler there. It is here too. You can't say this is a note, can you? I bought Margie a saber today. I guess I'll have to file the end off it to keep her from poking her eye out. Kiss her and look in the glass for me.

Your Harry

Ft. Riley, Kans.

Dear Honey and Baby: Friday, July 15, 1927

This day has been successful. I have a letter from you, have been horseback riding, watched the Battery fire nine problems, had an hour swim, a good meal, and am tired as I can be without any *headache*. I am certainly glad you and Marg are resting in my absence. We'll have to arrange it so you can keep it up. I never need any breakfast and if that would keep you from having any more indigestion, for goodness sake let's do it. I'm glad Mrs. Ott is satisfied with the court. I am too. I see the said court is functioning. The *Star* said they had ordered Koehler to pave Fairmount Ave. Had a letter from Vrooman saying the court was not taking any chances on anything but holding all doubtful matters for my return.

I called on the old general out here and asked him to our party next Friday.

It's to be a badger fight, so ladies can't come. Eddie McKim is waiting to take this to [Junction City] so I'll have to make it another *note*. Be sure and keep writing. Kiss the baby for

Your sweetheart,
Harry

Ft. Riley, Kans.

Dear Bess: July 21, 1927

Got a letter today with Dr. McConnell's card. I guess they are having a fine time. But it's not doing them any more good than my trip is doing me. We fired shell all morning and all yesterday afternoon. It rained so yesterday we couldn't fire in the A.M. A shellburst is a wicked thing to see. You can't blame people for getting shell shock. It is a very real disease. Some even get it by looking at the bursts without even getting in reach of them. I can't say I blame them. I went to a reception by Colonel Oliver yesterday afternoon. He's the colonel of the Second Cavalry. I should have had cards but they'll never know the difference. At seven-thirty we had a riding contest between the cavalry, engineers, and artillery. We only got two prizes, third in walk, trot, and canter class by Colonel Siegmund and second in potato race. The cavalry won first and second in the walk, trot, canter, first in potato race, and third in jump. Engineers won first and second in the jumps. It was a very good exhibition only I'd have been better pleased if the artillery had won more prizes. Jozack Miller, Dinwiddie Groves, Crabs, and myself are invited to a picnic by a Major Brown over in the post. I'd rather stay home and sleep but I guess I'll have to go. You know how enthusiastic I am about picnics. They are about to leave now and I want to get this mailed so you'll get it. Hope to see you Saturday P.M. if everything holds together. If not it will be Sunday noon. Kiss the baby and love to you. I want to see you both badly.

Love from
Your Harry

Lyons, Kansas

Dear Bess: Tuesday, August 30, 1927

Yesterday as I was driving along west of Olathe I picked up the nicest looking fellow thinking he belonged somewhere around west of town and that I could put him down at home. He told me he owned a cleaning shop in Borger, Texas, and that he had been making as high as eighty dollars a day running it, but that the governor of Texas had ruined his business by sending rangers in there and chasing all the girls and gamblers out of town. Claimed he was trying to sell his cleaning machinery. Told me his name, which I promptly forgot, and asked me mine. I handed him my card and he looked at the Judge on it and said, "Well I wish I'd been in your court in K.C. yesterday, I'd have had you send me to St. Joe." I began to wonder what I had aboard and he said he was a dope fiend and that he had been since the war, got the habit in the army, and that he was either going to quit or die in the attempt. When I went north to Topeka he got out and went south, said if he went to a big town some uplifter would try to sell him dope or hire him to rob a bank. I told him if he'd come into court Monday I'd send him to St. Joe for the cure. I think he was honestly trying to quit.

I saw the big Auburn 8 that those two fellows were killed in at Council Grove. It was some wreck. They were actually driving a hundred miles an hour when they hit. A little too fast. The whole works ought to be exhibited for the benefit of the wreckless drivers' club. . . .

I hope you and your daughter feel fine and that you are having as hot weather as we are. Haven't needed any vest or coat either today.

Kiss the baby and tell her to kiss you for me.

Love to both,
Harry

Dear Bess: [Dodge City, Kans., Oct. 2, 1927]
The Kansas situation is settled. Council Grove won. It was a hard thing to settle but abiding by the rules and weighing all the historical data obtainable, Council Grove won.

We woke up in Lyons this morning to find it raining, and our transportation from Great Bend had stuck in the mud and didn't arrive. We went down in the salt mine, supposed to be the largest in the world. It is 1,043 feet deep and the finest looking I've seen—nineteen feet thick. The deposit was made some centuries ago by the sea. There are fourteen miles of tunnels and a theater down there. They have mules in the mine that haven't seen daylight in six years. We got some fine samples of salt. . . .

Lots of love to you and everyone else in our family (kiss the everyone else).
Your Harry

                                    [Franciscan Hotel, Albuquerque, N.M.]
Dear Bess: Monday, October 3, 1927
I sent you a telegram today but I couldn't tell you what a time we've had. Arizona put up its claim and I want to tell you it was some job to decide. L. S. Williams from Williams, Arizona, made the best plea I ever listened to, but Williams was like Independence—they never had done anything for the National Old Trails. Springerville, which happens to be the residence of J. W. Becker, national vice president of the N.O.T., has never missed an opportunity to boost the road and pay its money. Davis and I voted for Springerville and Mrs. Moss voted for Williams. Kingman had a little old maid here who was a member of the committee and who was supposed to have an unprejudiced mind but who put forward an argument for Kingman every time a point was made for another town. Her name was [illegible] and the man from Williams named her incompetent. She was. She lost her town every opportunity to win.

The state conference of the D.A.R. for New Mexico is being held here today. They invited Davis and me to their reception this evening and I had to make a speech. Then they had refreshments. An old lady by the name of Joyce got hold of me and told me her home had been Pleasant Hill some twenty years ago and wanted me to recollect a lot of people who had been dead before I was born.

After she got done with me the Albuquerque delegation backed me into a corner and tried to force me to promise to vote for this town for the monument. Then a Santa Fe outfit did me the same way, and then Albuquerque started all over. Santa followed us to the hotel and wouldn't let us loose and I am writing you at 1:00 A.M. out here. It is 2:00 A.M. at home. I've got to get up at six-thirty, meet Mrs. Moss at seven-thirty, and at 9:00 A.M. hold another court to hear this town, then drive to Santa Fe, sixty-six miles, hear Santa Fe come to a decision, and then start at Trinidad, Colorado, and hear Las Animas and Larimer and decide Colorado and then I'm coming home.

It will be Thursday before I arrive, but I'd better get this over now than to make another trip. I am crazy to see you and my baby. I don't know how much I love you till I get away for a day or two.

Kiss my baby and tell her to kiss her mamma for Daddy.

Love to you,

Harry

[Fort Cumberland Hotel, Cumberland, Md.]

Dear Babies: April 17, 1928

We arrived here at 5:30 P.M. and the leading banker of the town wanted to take us to dinner, so we just decided to stay here all night. We are only a half-day's march by auto from the Capital anyway and we can get more rest by doing that.

Mr. Lutz came down to the hotel this morning and went over to Washington, Pennsylvania, with us where we met one of our vice presidents for Pennsylvania and had a meeting with him and the Chamber of Commerce and the president of the country club, McGinnis by name, and tried to settle the monument location for Pennsylvania. Then we went on to Uniontown to a Rotary Club meeting, after which we met the president of the Chamber of Commerce and the manager of the Motor Club and found out that Washington and Uniontown are at swords' points because the former got the monument. They've even brought in the governor and the state auto commission. They're worse than Kentucky mountaineers. Same here in Maryland. But Davis and I are going to straighten them out I believe if we can get the feminine part of the row satisfied. The local D.A.R.s in both states are at outs with Mrs. Moss and with each other.

I saw General Braddock's burial place today, was on top of the Allegheny Mountains 2,908 ft. above the sea level and there was the remains of a snowstorm of last night, just enough to see.

It has cleared off and is very pleasant tonight. We'll be in Washington at noon tomorrow. Hope to see at least four letters there from you. Tell Margie to be a good young lady and tell her to kiss her "mudder" for daddy. Wish you were both here.

Yours,
Harry

The letter below refers to Truman's bond issue, without which he could not finance new county roads and buildings.

[Hotel La Fayette, Washington, D.C.]

Dear Bess and Baby: April 19, 1928

Got your letter soon as I arrived and another one this morning. I'm glad they are at last getting the bond business going. If we carry that, there'll be no stopping us from being a real court. I just had to call you last night. Maybe my phone bill will be the biggest bill I have, but what do we live for anyway? Money or nothing else matters when you have a real sweetie and a baby.

Mrs. Moss and an old maid niece of hers had dinner with us and took us to the Congress, where Secretary Davis was the main speaker. I met the president-general and a whole string of women, from Maine to California—every one of them Mrs. Mark S. Salisbury type, but nice to talk with. We go to a reception for the Missouri delegation tonight. Glad to stop here and go down in town with Dave and Davis. We called on Reed, who was gone, and Capper and Curtis and I left a card for Hawes and George Combs. George was out too. He made a speech to the women Tuesday night and they all want to adopt him. His speech was to the Missouri women not to the whole Congress. Only Coolidge, the Cabinet, and a county judge from Missouri do that—he-haw.

Be sure and kiss my baby and both of you be good girls until I get home and after too—I'll bring you a stick of gum.

Your Harry

Ft. Riley, Kans.

Dear Mudder and Margie: July 9, 1928

Eddie and I had a very pleasant trip down. The air was cool and refreshing and we didn't have to drive hurriedly. This end of the road from St. Mary's to Manhattan was somewhat rough on account of rain a day or two ago and because of detours. They are paving the last gap now and next year will have pavement all the way. The road is open from Manhattan to Riley.

We have nice quarters with plenty of furniture and all that it takes to make our existence pleasant while here. They had assigned me to a place over the dance hall upstairs but I had it changed to the same barrack that the balance of the regiment is in. That is the reason it pays to come a day earlier. I'd have probably been uncomfortable all the two weeks if I hadn't got here and made arrangements to suit me yesterday.

I am going over to the hospital for a physical examination and I'll bet you I am 100 percent when I come back, except of course my eyes, which never were any good. I hope you and Margie are having a lot of fun riding around in your new car and that it is giving you entire satisfaction.

I am looking for a letter today. Kiss my baby and look in the mirror for me and do the same thing.

Your Harry

Ft. Riley, Kans.
My Dear Honey and Little Honey: July 10, 1928

We arose at 5:30 A.M., put in fifteen minutes at setting-up exercises and then had breakfast, after which we went to the gun park and hitched up, went to the field and under the direction of George Arrowsmith set up the fire central signal system. At nine o'clock we got on horseback and rode until eleven-thirty. There are copious calls for new skin to be grafted on places where these fat men sit down. The ride was under the direction of a cavalry officer who has, as all cavalrymen have, leather where he sits instead of skin and naturally can't appreciate the tenderness of some of the office-bred boys. They'll get all right in a day or two. I am not the least bit uncomfortable. A lieutenant colonel has opportunities to take care of his hide that the lower ranks don't have. Some advantage in that, even if it is a useless office except on payday.

We are to have gun drill and blackboard firing under the direction of the lieutenant colonel this afternoon.

There was not a letter today. I am looking for one this evening. Be sure and kiss my baby, and tell her to kiss her mamma for daddy.

Yours with love to burn,
Harry

Ft. Riley, Kans.
Dear Bess and Margaret: July 15, 1928

I got your special delivery this morning and I am more than pleased to get it. You should have had a letter from me every day because I've never failed to write a note of some kind every day at noon. I even answered Margie's letters; they were so nice and well written I couldn't overlook them. Everybody I showed them to thought I must have a mighty smart four-year-old girl at home. . . .

I have been intending to tell you about Jay Lee's attempt to clutter up the stag party for Friday night. You know it has been customary for some years for the reserves to have a "badger fight" either on Thursday or Friday night of the last week. Well a badger fight is not a very ladylike affair nor is it intended to be one. But it makes a very fitting climax to two weeks of very hard physical labor and it is customary. . . .

Kiss my baby and take a lot of love for yourself and keep writing. I haven't missed a day in spite of the fact that you've missed *two*.

Yours,
Harry

Ft. Riley, Kans.

My Dear Sweetheart: July 19, 1928

I felt very properly rebuked at what you said about my letter writing being a task and not a pleasure. If I inadvertently implied that it was a task, the implication was not intended. It is a pleasant duty, as you by this time ought to know. I am the only person here who has written his wife or sweetie as many as two a week and because I write every day it is a cause for comment. It is also a cause for comment that I don't go to picnics or dances or any of the other feminine entertainment, but as you ought to know I didn't come out here for but one thing and that is mental relaxation and physical employment. I have gotten both. We have a physical instructor who has loosened every muscle I have and artillery has kept my mind so busy that I haven't had time to think of court or have a headache. There is only one thing that would make the vacation complete and that would be to have you along. It is the most satisfactory vacation to me except for your absence, both from a financial and a physical standpoint, that I could have. I had two letters today as I had hoped I would have. There was also a nice one from my girl. By the way, you didn't mention her in either one. I have written her two letters of her own which you didn't say had arrived. The mail service is rotten. There never has been a day that one wasn't mailed to you, and then two to daughter besides.

I have been grading officers on firing all day today and yesterday and I got

The Truman family, c. 1929. *Harry S. Truman Library*

to fire a real shrapnel problem myself. Never expected it but this colonel is a peach. Quite the smartest man I've been under. The doctor is going to take these to Junction City. So kiss Margie and tell her to kiss her mamma for

Daddy

One year later, Truman was again at Riley.

Ft. Riley, Kans.
Dear Bess and Margie: July 7, 1929
    We had a very pleasant trip up, with no casualties of any nature. Not even a hot motor. We stopped at Manhattan for lunch while it poured down rain and then drove to Ft. Riley in the rain, arriving about 3:00 P.M.
    Eddie McKim pulled in about 7:00 P.M. and several of the boys arrived along during the evening. I slept like a log last night, got up at 5:15, and am in good physical condition. Had a complete physical examination at 8:00 A.M. and they didn't see my cut [hemorrhoid operation], so I got by. They gave my eyes a real test though and my heart too. The heart was all right. They ordered me to be vaccinated for smallpox but I didn't do it. He also told me that I'd never need another typhoid inoculation. . . .
    I came away without my slippers at last but I can use my low-cuts instead, so you needn't mail them. If anything worthwhile shows up in the *Examiner*, please mail it. Kiss my baby and tell her to kiss her mother for me.

Always,
Your Harry

Ft. Riley, Kans.
Dear Bess: July 12, 1929
    I got another letter last night and it made the day perfect. I thought that you and Margaret might want to come and see me while I am out here was the only reason I asked you if you could come, and as to finance that would have been my problem and I'd have solved it. But maybe we'll have better luck next time. My physical condition is almost perfect. I think another ten days and it will be.
    The county farm seems to have made a name for itself while I'm gone and Mr. Bash [T.B., eastern judge] seems to head the column. I wonder what Barr [R.W., western judge] was doing? He never knows when to grab off the lead. I guess I'll have to phone him and tell him something about this case. These people sent this old man out there over my protest alleging that he was not in his right mind and that they could not care for him at home. It seems to be different now. Please keep on writing and let me know how the reaction is.
    I get the *Star* and *Times* and have received two *Examiners* by mail, so I guess they are sending it.
    I hope Margie has been a good girl and that she'll tell me when I get home

that she has minded her mother and never cried a bit while I'm gone. Lots of love to you and kiss my baby.

Your Harry

Ft. Riley, Kans.

Dear Bess: July 14, 1929

Sunday morning and I am feeling fine. Got up at a quarter of six and had breakfast at seven. Some of the boys went over to ride after hounds at 6:00 A.M. I didn't go. There was church in the Godfrey Court dance hall at 6:30 A.M., where they had a dance last night. They opened with "Onward Christian Soldiers" and I wanted to see my girl so badly that I wanted to come home at once. If I could get a plane, I would.

Yesterday was a day of accidents for our organization. Rufus Burrus sprained his ankle and a lieutenant by the name of Carruthers ran into a car at Manhattan on his way home to Topeka and wrecked himself and his car both. He is in the hospital here and it will take a week to fix the car. I think I told you yesterday that I walked a mile and climbed the highest hill on the reservation without serious results. I am eating like a horse, sleeping well, and getting sunburned in good shape. If I had you and Margaret here today, I'd be completely happy. Be sure and keep writing. The letters have come every day and so have the papers. Got the *Digest* and appreciate it a lot. Kiss Margaret and tell her to be a good young lady.

Lots of love to you both,
Harry

Ft. Riley [Kans.]

Dear Bess: July 17, 1929

Well another perfect day. The letter was in the box when I came in from the firing point. I am glad that the baby had a good time at the park and the flying field. I want her to do everything and have everything and still learn that most people have to work to live, and I don't want her to be a high hat.

I took my field glasses to the ordnance officer of the 128th F.A. and had them cleaned. They are just as good as the day I bought them now and I wouldn't trade them for a new pair because of the sentimental attachment. Maybe you don't know it but I guess I am two-thirds damn fool and the other third sentimentalist. Whenever I see a yellow-headed little girl I want to pick her up and squeeze her, when I meet a member of my Battery I don't care how ornery and good-for-nothing he is, he can have whatever I've got, and when I think of school days I always think of a pretty little girl with curls down her back who grew into the best and sweetest sweetheart a man ever had and I wish I could see her now. Kiss my baby and look for me sometime Saturday I hope; will phone you if I am later.

Your good-for-nothing but loving husband,
Harry

The summer of 1930, and it was Riley again—this time with Rufus Burrus.

[Ft. Riley, Kans.]
My Dear Sweethearts: July 18, 1930

Rufus and I arrived quite hot and dusty, as well as somewhat grimy, yesterday afternoon about seven-fifteen. We stuck a wire fence staple into one of our tires just east of Manhattan and had to get out and get under—the first time I've changed a tire in a long time. It was just about such a place as the one where we stuck the stake into the same tire.

The party was in full swing when we arrived and was a grand success. There were a great many candidates to pull the badger; and the engineers tried to give me a lesson in probabilities at five cents ante and a quarter limit. I made them pay me at the rate of about a dollar and a half an hour for the time of the session.

At the horse show this morning Eddie McKim's horse failed to take one of the barriers and both horse and Eddie did a wonderful Prince of Wales. He sprained his elbow and was wondering if he could make his wife believe he had fallen out of bed or something. . . .

I hope you are both enjoying the heat as well as I am. Write me as often as you'd have me do it and kiss my baby if she's good.

Your boy friend and sweetheart,
Harry

Ft. Riley, Kans.
Dear Sweetheart and Margie: July 22, 1930

The day has been fine and ended perfectly—your letter came just before dinner. You say it has been a week from Sunday to Thursday. I say it's been a month and getting a week longer every day. I overslept this morning, which kept it from being quite so long. I usually get up at five-thirty and beat everyone to the shower and shaving trough; today I didn't arise until the whistle blew. I have three majors whom I have to keep busy and it makes my head go around to do it. They are smart and well-informed men. I have them studying now on an order for tomorrow, but tomorrow I'll have to give them another for the next day.

If we have another war, I am going to arrange to take my honey and my baby along. It is a wonderful thing how absolutely dependent a man can become. I don't see how I got along until I was thirty-four [-five] without you. Just think of all the *wasted* years that could have been pleasantly and profitably spent. I might even have been a financial success if I'd started with you sooner.

Went out and watched my former buck private fire his Battery. He's a good Battery commander in the 128th F.A., Missouri national guard. He writes his wife every day too. You see I even trained them right in every respect. Kiss my baby and a regular one to my sweetheart from her
Harry

Ft. Riley, Kans.
My Dear Sweethearts: July 24, 1930

Got your letter today and you can tell Miss Margie that I have not fired the big cannons yet. I will fire them next Tuesday, and if she stays I'll show her how to do it.

I am sure glad you are coming down, and I am also sure you'll have a good time. The sun shone down on us today but there is a fine, cool breeze now and there has been a necessity for cover every night even on the hottest days. Please bring my "Anthony" salve. I have a tender place on my saddle connection. Kiss my girl and don't fail to come down.

Love to you both,
Harry

Ft. Riley, Kans.
Dear Wife and Daughter: July 27, 1930

Well here I am doing what I said I wouldn't. I've been waiting and waiting for the phone to ring, but I've waited in vain I guess. If I remember correctly, I phoned when I arrived (after a four-mile trip) and I phoned you Saturday night (under like circumstances) and just because I don't raise sand and have spasms

Margaret, behind 219 North Delaware, c. 1930. *Harry S. Truman Library*

doesn't mean that I never worry about you or that I wouldn't highly appreciate a phone call—especially tonight. I haven't been so homesick since I went to France. It was almost a tragedy when you left. I guess I am a damn fool but I wanted you to stay, though I thought you'd be cooler and happier at home.

I'd better get a letter tomorrow, at least.

Don Fitch had dinner with me. I guess the fat colonel [Elliott] and all his crowd are in by now. Kiss my baby.

Love to you both,
Harry

Ft. Riley, Kans.
My Dear Sweetheart: July 30, 1930

I missed writing yesterday. It was hot and we'd fired from seven-thirty until one-thirty and then examined a lot of officers on instruments and then came in and went to sleep. Today we finished up the firing with shrapnel and tomorrow will examine the balance, and tomorrow night the regimental dinner, go riding Friday, and the war will be over. I'll be very glad to get home and take on the troubles of Jackson County until fall. I suppose the gang will have spent all the available funds by the time I arrive and it will be my job to find the funds to operate until fall elections are over.

Got a good letter today and was mighty glad to have it. I hope that Barr and Sermon do come down. But I'll bet you they don't come. I'm looking for a letter up to Saturday noon.

Kiss my baby, love to you both,
Harry

Dear Margie: Yes I shot the big guns about four hundred times. They made a lot of noise and you ought to have heard them. I hope you have been a good girl today. Write your daddy again. Lots of love to you.

[Hotel Duluth, Duluth, Minn.]
Dear Bess and Margie: August 9, 1930

I slept fine last night with a breeze from Canada blowing my way. It was about seventy this A.M. at six o'clock when I got up. I walked up the hill about a mile and looked over the town. It's like Eureka Springs, Arkansas. The city is strung along the lake front for ten miles and is about a mile wide up a steep hill. The cars go up in low gear and come down in second. It is a beautiful view out over the lake and if the town were built in the European style, you'd swear it was Nice.

They're all (the people) from the Scandinavian peninsula or Denmark or Finland, all blonds and most of 'em talk with an accent. I've only seen one nigger and he was bleached out to a pale yellow.

There are lots of boats going and coming, mostly long freighters hauling wheat, coal, and iron ore. There are also some fine pleasure boats and passenger steamers that run from here to Detroit, Chicago, and Buffalo. There was a carload of Jews from Massachusetts on my train from St. Paul. They were making a circle tour by train and back to Buffalo on a boat.

How would you like to drive up here, catch a boat, get off at Detroit, and drive home? It wouldn't cost so much and would be a wonderful tour. Think it over.

The *Paducah* came in at 2:00 A.M. and will leave about that time Monday. I am going aboard now in a few minutes and my expenses will cease, unless I get taken in a friendly poker game. (My head doesn't ache, and I don't think they can beat me.)

Please think that trip over. Kiss my girl and tell her to do the same to you. Call Mamma and tell her I'm all right.

Love to you both,
Harry

Duluth, Minn.

My Dear Bess and Margie: Monday [Aug. 11, 1930]
I thought maybe I might get a wire or a letter today but so far no word. Of course I didn't tell you how to send one because I didn't know. If you'll send me one to Mackinac Island aboard the U.S.S. *Paducah* and one to Chicago addressed the same way, I'll get it. We'll be at Mackinac Thursday and Chicago Friday evening. I came aboard Saturday at 9:00 A.M. and have been playing sailor ever since. They surely have a soft life except when they ship coal, which they did this morning. They battened down the hatches, closed the portholes, put us all in overalls, and then poured on the coal from a big crane with a clamshell shovel on the end of it. It was a nice, coal-dusty job. I didn't get dirty but everyone else did. Barr came yesterday evening and seemed to be mighty glad to get here. I am having a good time and no road overseer can see me. The mailman is starting a show, so I'll have to quit.

Kiss my girl and tell her to be good.

Love to both of you,
Harry

[U.S.S. *Paducah*, en route to Chicago, Ill.]

Dear Bess and Margaret: Friday, August 15, 1930
We are now in sight of the big city and it has been a successful cruise. The lakes have been very calm and the weather has been fine. The last two hours on Lake Superior were rather rough but we came into Sault Sainte Marie before I got sick. It is rather rough now but we'll be at the dock in an hour and I don't think I'm going to be sick. They have treated me royally on the trip. I've gained at least five pounds and have enjoyed it immensely. . . .

They have had a lot of fun teaching me naval terms for kitchen, dining room, deck, etc. I wish you and my baby were going to meet me at Chicago. Will see you Sunday. We leave Chicago at four-thirty Saturday.

Love to you both,
Harry

Reelected to a second term as presiding judge and taking office in January 1931, Truman faced increasing difficulties—as the following letter indicates. His two recent Jackson County colleagues on the court had enriched themselves at public expense, and the Great Depression, which had begun in 1929, was making county financing nearly impossible. Moreover, his mother had had to increase the mortgage on the Grandview farm.

[The Lafayette, Little Rock, Ark.]
Dear Bess: February 12, 1931

I hope this reaches you the morning of the thirteenth, because while I'm not there I'll be thinking constantly all day that this is *her* birthday and I'm not there.

I don't know whether you entirely appreciate or not the tremendous amount of strain that's been on me since November. My two former associates as you know were just full of anxiety to obtain any funds that they could because of their positions, the finances of the county were never in such shape since Miles Bulger handled them, and every person I've ever had any association with since birth has wanted me to take pity on him and furnish him some county money without much return. On top of all that, the refinancing of the farm at home has been getting deeper and deeper into difficulties, and if something unforeseen should happen there that good old woman who made me an honest man would pass on.

You and I have had our own difficulties to look after and with it all I was becoming so keyed up that I either had to run away or go on a big drunk. That latter alternative never did have much appeal, so I've taken the other one.

My head hasn't ached and I've slept like a baby because I know the phone's not going to ring, and that no one's going to stop me with a tale of woe when I walk down the street. I shouldn't write you like this but I ought to be home today and, like all men since Adam, I've got to justify myself for not being there with an alibi.

This jaunt would be perfect if you and Margaret were with me. We'd have the best time in the world and see some very good things to see and they'd look a lot better if you were here. I saw Governor Parnell this morning and he inquired what he could do for me, and when I told him not one thing he said I was doubly welcome. He asked that he and Mrs. Parnell be remembered to you and invited me to come back. We go to Shreveport by way of Hot Springs and Texarkana this afternoon, and I am anticipating a pleasant ride.

Tell my girl she must go to school and learn all about everything and someday you and she and I will go see it all.

I hope we see sixty more birthdays *together*.

Harry

Truman's reference below to "bond signing" is not really a complaint, for the presiding judge was delighted that his second bond issue had passed the voters and was being sold.

Ft. Riley, Kans.
My Dear Sweethearts: Monday, July 27 [1931]
Our war has started. We have been drilling to beat the band this morning. I was in the saddle from seven o'clock until ten-thirty and will continue it this afternoon, but not horseback.

How are you two getting along without your dad? I miss you both when I'm not hard at work and wish you were here. Every time I see a little, yellow-headed lady I see in what manner she favors my own pretty daughter, and if she has curls I can always see a resemblance to another pretty little curly-haired lady who went to a Presbyterian Sunday school in Independence about forty years ago.

My arm is still stiff from that last bond-signing and I can hardly write. We are living in the Second Cavalry barrack and they are living in tents out on the parade ground. You know they must love that. I have the choice apartment with Major Snyder and Ed McKim. There are about 160 officers in the building with twelve wash basins all in the basement. There is a scramble in the morning. Write to me as often as you can.

Your loving dad,
Harry S. Truman

Ft. Riley, Kans.
Dear Bess: July 28, 1931
I am evening the score. I've received two and this will make two I've sent. I suppose will have to buy Miss Vrooman a present. It would hardly do not to send one. While I'm not fond of Mrs. Vrooman I do like Howard, and he's crazy about the girl.

I'm glad you missed me. It makes me feel better. I've been so nearly *non compos mentis* in the last four months that I'd about come to the conclusion I was not fit to live with anyway. When I get that courthouse located and the contract let, will take another weddin' tour and maybe I can get back on earth (if I'm not in the midst of a state campaign). Tell my daughter to be a good young lady, mind her mother, and speak respectfully to her grandmother and all her uncles and aunts.

I shall be home Saturday morning and close court, and I hope I can arrange it to stay until Monday. It was very hot out here yesterday but the wind is in the north today and it is more comfortable. Keep sending me letters.

Love to you both from
Your Dad

Ft. Riley, Kans.

Dear Bess: August 5, 1931

I was very much surprised at your peeve last evening, although I expected it. Yesterday was about the world's worst. I had an accommodation spasm all the way down here besides a headache and Halvorson. The courtroom was impassable and every pest in the county was there, including Lester and Stayton. I am just about to blow up and another bellows is turned into the balloon (and it's really the only puff that can count). So I went out to camp, hunted up a friend, took two snorts, and went to bed. This morning I felt better, took the outfit out horseback, and rode them fifteen miles more or less over a terrain problem. I was in command of all the artillery. It was a success, so I guess my head, eye, and pests had cleared up.

You tell my daughter that the next time you choose to spoil two days in succession, for her please to remedy the situation. I hope you've both had a good day and lots of fun. If you don't send me a letter tomorrow I'll neither write nor call you until Sunday morning.

Love to you both,
Your Dad

Ft. Riley [Kans.]

Dear Bess: August 5, 1931

Your good letter came today and apparently you are over your disgruntled spell. Well so am I. We fired today and will do the same tomorrow. It is a hot, strenuous job for me. I fire every problem with every officer and then critique it with the instructor. It looks as if some of them never will fire but we have to have patience. If we can get 90 percent of them so they will be of some use in an emergency in the future, our time and the government's money won't be spent in vain.

It has been a very good camp but the break in it made it seem like two to me. I hope my daughter hasn't forgotten how to write. She wrote me when she was four years old and I still have the letter. Now here she is over seven and can't find the time to write her daddy. I hope to be home Saturday sometime. Most of the men will get out Friday but I have to stay and sign reports, etc.

Kiss my bad girl and tell her I'll not bring her any teeth if she doesn't write me.

From your loving Harry

In an oblique manner the following letter is Truman's celebration of promotion to full colonel in the field artillery reserve.

[Hotel Robidoux, St. Joseph, Mo.,

My Dear Sweetheart and Daughter: July 7, 1932]

I arrived about seven-thirty, went up to my room, a good one, and now I'm writing you. You've no idea how I wish you were both here. It will certainly be an ideal condition when you can go with me everywhere.

I told you I'd forget something. My raincoat is at the office. Please mail it to me at Camp Ripley so I won't have to buy one, and look in my right-hand top drawer and get one of those full packages of razor blades and mail it to me. Margaret must practice her exercises every day. I hope she will turn over to the front of her music book and learn how to read bass notes while I'm gone.

Whatever do you suppose caused Boxley to call me up and have the fit he did about the arrangement of the courthouse? Old man Gunn is in his dotage and doesn't know what it's all about, but I kidded him into believing he is necessary because Pendergast likes him, but Boxley ought to have more sense than to listen to him. I've made Keene, Wight, and Neild agree with each other and with me. Now the counselor is having a fit. I sincerely wish that all professionals could be made to wear a strait jacket when alterations come on them. I'm not going to think of it any more for two weeks. Tell Buck to calm the county attorney down.

Kiss Margaret and tell her to kiss her mother for me. My address is

Colonel Harry S. Truman
F.A. Reserve, Camp Ripley, Minn.

Camp Ripley, Minn.
My Dear Daughter and her Mamma: July 10, 1932

We arrived here at one o'clock yesterday and went through the physical examination and got assigned to quarters. We are living in a tent just like Camp

Colonel Truman in summer camp, 1930s. Second from left, Harry H. Vaughan, later military aide to the President; at far right, John W. Snyder, later Secretary of the Treasury. *Harry S. Truman Library.*

Doniphan—sand and all. The wind is from the northwest and right off the north pole, but the sun is shining and it will be warm by noon. There are about 182 reserve officers ordered here, 40 of them will be in my outfit. There are no horses, everything is tractor-drawn, and there'll be plenty of walking. Ted's car broke down below Minneapolis and he didn't arrive until six o'clock. He and George are over at the doctor's now. It's to be a good camp but no luxuries. We have to walk over two hundred yards to the bathhouse, and it's a hard thing to do at 5:00 A.M. with a north wind blowing your bathrobe over your head. Pajamas are rather thin about that time of day.

Margaret, I bought a St. Paul paper this morning and all I could see in it I knew was *Jiggs*. Sure wish I had a *Star*. Have you practiced your music? I'm hoping you can play all those exercises without hesitation. If you can, I'll teach you to read bass notes when I get back. Kiss your mother, and mother you kiss my pretty girl for me—and write—write—write.

Your loving dad and sweetheart,
Harry

Camp Ripley, Minn.
July 13, 1932

Dear Bess:

Got your second letter today. I don't know where Rufus has his wife parked but it's somewhere up the road. He brought his sister and someone else. They haven't seen much of him because he has been sick in camp two days. These young kids can't stand the physical and mental inconveniences that the old heads take as a matter of course. I often wonder how many of them could go through a Meuse-Argonne or Camp Doniphan training and still be whole. They all live in a machine-convenience age and when the machine doesn't function for them they are out of luck.

I hope that my beautiful daughter is still doing her finger exercises and practicing as she ought. The day is very pleasant, not hot or cold. Yesterday it went to 97 while I was tramping all over six hundred acres trying to put seventeen carloads of tractors and trucks into position as a regiment of 155s. I got it done after a fashion but got a skinning for not doing it some other way. The Nebraska colonel who is Republican candidate for governor went out this morning after I'd made all the mistakes in the book before him and made as many as I did. So I don't feel so badly.

I hope you are all well and happy as I am. I'm brown as an Indian, eating like a horse, and sleeping seven hours a night. Keep writing even if it does get hot.

Kiss Margaret. I had hoped for a letter from her.

Your loving Harry

Unexpectedly Bess Truman, rather than her husband, was absent from Independence in the spring of 1933; Margaret had become ill, and it was necessary to take her to Mississippi. There, warm weather along the Gulf, together with careful diet, restored her health.

[Grandview]

My Dear Bess: Good Friday night, April 14, 1933
    . . . I am in bed at home, have seen Frank, Natalie, and George. Had dinner
with your mother, who by the way seemed really glad to see me, and Fred. Nannie
showed all her teeth when I told her Margaret missed her and was sending her
a card. She's going to the post office tomorrow to see if there is one.
    Frank is still in a turmoil over the mill, however he thinks that there is now
a chance of his voting your mother's stock independently of the others, in which
case he can go in with Arch Waggoner and handle the situation. Old man Dunn
has agreed to resign. Frank has had a conference with the Wellses and with
Henry Jost and he seems to think he has the situation in hand.
    George looks much better, and if we can keep him down another week he'll
be cured. He promised me not to try to get up until Monday and I'll get a further
delay then I think. He was much pleased with the candy and said he would give
Frank and Fred a piece of it. Your mother looks fine and so does Fred. Fred says
he sent another letter to the Colonial. You'd better ask for it.
    I have talked to T. J. and to Jim over the phone. T. J. is much better and
gave me to understand that I could do as I pleased with the county. I am to see
him Monday morning. Will see Jim tomorrow.
    Lou Holland called me and told me that he is being considered for Comp-
troller of the Currency, which is the biggest job under the Secretary of the
Treasury, and wanted me to get Mr. Pendergast to endorse him. Mr. P. told me
to write my own ticket and make the endorsement as strong as Lou wanted it.
    McElroy, with his usual fine Italian hand, has been trying to put me into
a bad political position over the action of the state board on assessments. He has
reduced his assessment 5 percent and has cut the rate somewhat, but I'll still
make him like it before the show is over. As long as the Big Boss believes in me
I don't care what the others do, and McElroy will be kissing me before the month
is out.
    I feel so much better about our daughter that it is almost as if a hundred-
pound weight has been lifted from my head. Make her follow sun and diet as
she should and by the time I come back down there, she ought to be as big and
beautiful as her mamma. The weather has been terrible up here, snowed all day
yesterday and rained today. The wind in the north and very cold. Paper says clear
tomorrow. Hope you all have a good time and don't worry about anything up
here. Everyone is *all* right. I love you and miss you terribly, but if our child gets
all right, I can stand it.
                             Lovingly,
                             Harry

[Grandview]

My Dear Sweetheart: Saturday before Easter, April 15, 1933
    This day will go down as a good one. I got a letter. Even if it was short, I
got one. You said I write letters that are no good, well you don't say much in

yours. But I'm glad to get them even if there were only an envelope with an address to me, written by you. I am in bed in my old room at the farm, and I can remember how I used to lie up here and wait for a letter from you, and then read the old one. Those were the days—why didn't you marry me when I first asked you? I don't know, do you?

Mr. Bill Southern is my friend all right but he'd like to make me quit politics in a blaze of fire and brimstone. I don't want to quit that way. Governor Park made a speech in which he told McElroy—not me—that his, Park's, budget bill for counties would cure Jackson County's going into the red. The dear governor's county budget bill is an extract from my county reorganization bill—just one of the features of it. McElroy has evidently told Park that I am a very extravagant official and need checking. Well anyway, the budget bill is half what I want, and I'm not a partner to any rackets. The *Star* is making a goat of me. . . .

Tell Kicky and Margaret to be good little girls and I'll bring them something nice when I come for them. Be nice and write me as often as you feel inclined.

Your lonesome Harry

[Grandview]

Dear Bess: Easter Sunday, April 16, 1933

It has been sunny most of the day, especially at church time it was as bright as any day you ever saw. But rather cool—had my coat on all day. Ate dinner with Mamma and Mary. J. C. was there too.

Vivian and I went down in the pasture this afternoon and looked at a place for a lake. We could build a fine one if we had the funds. I sincerely hope we can find them. From a financial viewpoint things are getting no better. But I doubt if they can get worse.

The board of appeals on real estate starts tomorrow and I certainly dread it, but it has to be done. That is what I came home for.

The *Star* seems to be softening up somewhat but they have planted a lot of poison.

How is my baby? I want to see both of you so badly. I believe I'm actually homesick, but don't you pay any attention to that. You do your job and I'll do mine and we'll both be all right. I'm hoping for a happy summer when you come home and I'm hoping we'll never be separated again. Remember me to Miss Kinaman and kiss my good girl for me. Tell her I'm still looking for her letter. I am well and feeling fine, physically. George is much better today. He was alseep when I went to see him. Write often.

Your loving dad

The tradition in county officeholding was a limit of two four-year terms for presiding judges. Looking beyond January 1935 when he would be without a job, Truman here presents some possibilities to Bess.

Grandview, Mo.

Dear Bess: April 23, 1933

This is a beautiful Sunday morning the first real sunny day in several, so a sunny Easter is really working. I was not intending to be hard-boiled about the letters. I was homesick and woefully disappointed and may have been a trifle jealous when two days went by and I got no letter and someone else in the family did. The balance of the week was delightful from a letter standpoint and I have nothing but praise for your effort. *Let me say that next Sunday* too.

Fred gave me a party last night and Natalie wanted me to have dinner with them, but the board of equalization was meeting late and I asked her to postpone the invitation and she said she would.

I had a fine talk with T. J. yesterday and I am still *on top.* He told me to do as I pleased with the county payroll, make the adjustments I wanted to, and he'd put the organization in line behind me. He also told me that I could be Congressman or collector. Think of that awhile. Congressman pays $7,500 and has to live in Washington six months a year, collector will pay $10,000 and stay at home; a political sky-high career ends with eight years collector. I have an opportunity to be a power in the nation as Congressman. I don't have to make a decision until next year. Think about it.

Write often,
Harry

In the worst period of the Depression, early 1933, it became necessary to trim the county payroll.

[Independence]

Dear Bess: Thursday, April 27, 1933

This has been a big day. Got a good letter. It is now 10:25 P.M. and I am at the office in Independence. The town clock is right and you can see it on the white faces same as daytime. The building will be nearly done when you get home.

I came to work at seven-fifteen this A.M. to write orders on the discharge of all those employees, went to court, and spent hours going over and over the list. . . .

Please be careful about eating anything that comes in the mail. Someone sent me a cake the other day and I threw it away. With these discharges coming off you can't tell what they'll do. Also watch that water heater in the bathroom. Four people have been asphyxiated in the last week with heaters like it. Leave the window open when you use it. Your mother said she wrote you yesterday. She got a letter from Margaret today. Pleased her very much. I am coming down as soon as I can get away and stay as long as we can. Keep on writing. Kiss my baby and tell her she owes me several letters.

Lovingly,
Harry

[Independence]

Dear Bess: April 28, 1933

Well I did it and the *Post* treated me fine—the *Star* gave me a kick. I had been to see each one of them and expected the same treatment from each one. The *Star* is off me anyway. I think our friend at the city hall has been "helping me out" down there. I'll sure be glad when this job is finished. The court has been working all day every day and I've been going half the night. I'm going to the farm tonight and stay over Sunday and maybe it will calm down.

We are discharging some two hundred people and every one of them and all his friends will try to see me. I was sick last night after the session and lost my supper but I'm going strong again this morning. Gates and Oscar were over last night and I had to run off to bed without saying much to them. Gates was down at Frank's but I don't think either of them changed his position.

Every time I get a letter I wish I was down there. This has been a good week. I've had a letter every day but one.

I wonder if my little girl has been too busy to write her dad? You must have had a grand time going crabbing. I hope you caught some fish. Can't you make reservations for next fall and stay down there all winter? I am of the opinion that our baby would be entirely cured by that. Maybe I could get a job down there. We'll have a talk about the Washington job. There are several angles to it that have to be studied. Kiss my baby and keep writing.

Lovingly,
Harry

Construction of the skyscraper courthouse in Kansas City was a fairly important issue at this time. Truman's involvement is reflected in part in the next few letters.

[Pickwick Hotel, Kansas City, Mo.]

My Dear Sweetie: Friday, April 28, 1933

This is letter number two today so you see I am keeping right up with things. I suppose that by the time this reaches you, you will have seen all the comments in the *Star* on county affairs. I have had to go off and hide. I am now on the seventh floor of the Pickwick Hotel. The manager gave me a room without registering so no job holder who wants to stay on can see or phone me. I'll have a court session tomorrow and then I'm going to Joplin or Columbia or Topeka or St. Joe and stay until Monday morning. Monday I've got a meeting with the architects and Wednesday the tenth I've got to make a talk on the courthouse to the Chamber of Commerce and then let bids on the building, and I hope that after that I can get everything wound up and come to Mississippi about the eighteenth. That will put me there by the twentieth. That is the best thing in life now that I have to look forward to. I am counting days and hours. I'll write you tomorrow and you'll be one up on me. I've never missed a day writing you but sometimes it would be at 7:00 A.M. and sometimes at midnight so you might miss getting the letter on time. You count them. I got one this morning and yesterday morning and the day before so I am feeling good. Should get two Monday. What's the matter with my girl? Has she forgotten how to write? Doc Wilson said he'd write her today when I paid his bill. Be sure and kiss my baby. How are your friends?

Lots of love,
Harry

[Pickwick Hotel, Kansas City, Mo.]

My Dear Bess: Saturday, April 29, 1933

Judge Buck [E.I. Purcell's nickname] brought me a letter to court this morning and that made things a lot brighter, even if I did have to keep on firing Democrats. There will be 202 less of them than there were on the payroll last year. That's terrible but it had to be done, and the tax had to be raised besides, but the income with the raise will be less than it was before by some $100,000.

The papers didn't treat me so very badly. I guess I'll survive—politically I mean. I am hoping the days will fly by now until I can come down. I am going to Topeka tonight to a Legion meeting. I don't think anybody up there can ask me to put him back on Jackson County's payroll. They are expecting Woodring but I doubt if he'll be there.

The wind has been blowing a gale all day—blew down two trees in the grove at the farm. It rained and hailed last night and rained awhile this morning but has been sunny most of the afternoon. I went with Fred Canfil and Jo Zach Miller to a race meeting of the Mission Valley Hunt Club. They were out in red coats, black caps, and white breeches. It would have been fine to see if the wind hadn't blown so much dirt in our faces. I hope Margaret and Kinnie are behaving themselves. You tell them if they don't, I'll take a sharp stick to them when I come down. Be sure and keep on writing, for the day is terrible when I don't get a letter. Has Margy forgotten how to write?

Lots of love from
Harry

[Grandview]

My Dear Bess: Sunday, April 30, 1933

I suppose you'll miss a day on getting letters. But I haven't missed sending one every day and on some days two. I paid my bill at Sands yesterday and he sent you a beautiful plant. I gave it to your mother. She seemed very much pleased with it. I just talked to her over the phone. I am at the farm, have been all day, and shall stay all night.

Well Easter is still working. In spite of wind and rain and hail yesterday and last night today is a fine day. I hope you are having fine weather, and that there are no more sore throats, and I also hope that the water and the other things will become more satisfactory to Miss K. However, most of us are disgusted with a lot of things we never *talk* about and other people are not bored. If my dear old mother has any fault, and I don't agree that she has any, it is an inability to keep her personal likes and dislikes from the world at large. But I pay no attention to it and I know that in nine cases out of ten she is only suffering from a passing whim.

I shall have a great deal to tell you about the two jobs I'm to choose from when I see you. There are excellent reasons for taking either, and the same kind for taking neither, so we'll decide it later. I am going to finish this one before I cross another bridge. Please keep writing and tell my baby I hope she hasn't a sore finger or a paralyzed arm or anything. Give her a kiss.

Love to you both,
Harry

[Hotel Robidoux, St. Joseph, Mo.]

Dear Bess: Sunday, May 7, 1933

This has been a very dull Sunday. I came up here last night to a Legion affair and stayed all night and I'm still here at noon. It was a good party but I had to leave it. As usual they got too rough and I'm still in politics. . . .

Tomorrow I'll be forty-nine and for all the good I've done the forty might as well be left off. Take it all together though the experience has been worthwhile; I'd like to do it again. I've been in a railroad, bank, farm, war, politics, *love* (only once and it still sticks), been busted and still am and yet I have stayed an idealist. I still believe that my sweetheart is the ideal woman and that my daughter is her duplicate. I think that for all the horrors of war it still makes a man if he's one to start with. Politics should make a thief, a roué, and a pessimist of anyone, but I don't believe I'm any of them and if I can get the Kansas City courthouse done without scandal no other judge will have done as much, and then maybe I can retire as collector and you and the young lady can take some European and South American tours when they'll do you most good; or maybe go to live in Washington and see all the greats and near greats in action. We'll see. I'm counting the days till I see you.

Lots of love to you both,
Harry

[Hotel Claridge] St. Louis, Mo.

Dear Bess: May 11, 1933

I am in St. Louis this morning. Got here at seven-fifteen and have just finished breakfast. Will see Judge Charles at noon and Scott Wilson later in the day or tomorrow morning. I should leave here tomorrow night and with luck arrive Saturday evening. I'll wire you when to meet me.

Yesterday was quite a day. Said my speech to the Chamber of Commerce and by working all night they got the model ready and had it on exhibition. It is a beautiful building and I believe I sold it to them. Even old Battle said I made a good speech, but I am always rather doubtful of my ability in that line. There was a place card for McElroy at the table but he didn't come. It was the biggest crowd the Chamber had had this year. They asked a lot of questions but they were all apparently friendly. Keene, Wight, Gunn, and Neild were all there and helped me answer the questions. Everyone seemed to go away sold on the idea that the building should be put up. When I get that job done I can probably retire to a quiet job and enjoy life a little bit with my family. Not that I'm not enjoying it now but it is sometimes pretty hard on head and nerves. I can hardly wait to see you both, but it won't be long now, I hope. Be good both of you until I arrive.

Lots of love to you both,
Harry

In the summer of 1933 Truman went to a camp near Little Rock, Arkansas, where he commanded a detachment of the Citizens Military Training Corps—high-school reservists.

[Camp Pike, Ark.]

Dear Sweethearts: Friday morning, August 18, 1933

I arrived at camp yesterday morning, signed in and reported. Stayed all night in Little Rock—Thursday night. Got a physical and had the usual trouble with eyesight but talked past the doctor, as usual—otherwise, physically sound as at twenty-four.

About one o'clock Captain Buxton, who is a member of my regiment living in Truman, Arkansas, and who is a district engineer from the Arkansas highway department came out to camp and said he had been instructed by the governor to bring me in for a call. I went and met a nice old man about sixty-five who treated me as if I were somebody. Then we called on the state highway commission, and a number of state senators and the chairman of the highway commission and Captain Buxton came back to camp with me to dinner. I will have an entirely strange list of officers and I am really responsible for the welfare of these kids. There are about 350 of them.

In going around yesterday afternoon I saw a couple of them playing tennis in rather unique costumes. One had on a pair of red shorts and nothing else and the other a pair of white shorts and a campaign hat. If I'd had a camera I'd have made me a picture of it.

I was so busy yesterday I couldn't write, but I'm looking for a letter from you today. There are a number of Kansas City officers here who are leaving tomorrow. Most of my bunch come from St. Louis and Arkansas.

I am in perfect health, no headache, and no dizziness. It is a new set of responsibilities and will do me good mentally and physically.

Margy, you kiss mother for me and she can return it for me also. Both of you be good girls.

Your loving dad

Camp Pike, Ark.

Dear Bess: August 21, 1933

. . . I do not need any more underwear or white shirts. I wear khaki and olive drab all the time. Even when I go to town, which hasn't been but once since I came out. At night we may put on a white shirt with uniform breeches but I don't do it. The boys have to stay in uniform all the time and I make the officers do it too. I have everything running like clockwork, even the constitutional gold bricks are afraid to be seen looking. The food is good, the weather fine, and the work interesting. These Arkansas boys are cards, but they are as nice looking and do just about the same amount of devilment as any others. I went to church yesterday morning and sat on the front row. Everyone else had been ordered to go so I had to. The roof didn't fall in, and the red-haired army chaplain seemed to feel complimented. I'm going to have to pin on a lot of medals on other people and make a speech on citizenship besides run the camp, but I guess I'll live through it. One of the orders is no cussing. Never saw it in the army. Tell Margaret to be a good girl. I'm looking for a letter from her.

Love to you both,
Harry

[Camp Pike, Ark.]

Dear Bess: Monday, August 21, 1933

It was certainly a pleasure to have a nice fat letter from you yesterday evening. I was down in the bottom of the dumps because I thought I should have had one on Saturday. Evidently it takes two days for them to arrive. I'm glad you bought the daughter some shoes she can turn black herself. The clipping and the *Examiner* were just what I wanted to see. That letter from that old maid stenographer was just what you'd expect from a rabid dog. They tried me and convicted the county court without a hearing. If I'd opened up on the delegation as I should have, they'd have all been in jail for contempt. . . .

Kiss my daughter and tell her to be a good girl. It is cool enough to sleep under a blanket every night.

Lots of love to you both,
Harry

Camp Pike, Ark.
My Dear Bess: Wednesday, August 23, 1933
Yesterday was one hell of a day. There were no letters, no papers, nothing from home. I had to, as camp commander, chase the Y.M.C.A. secretary off the post and order him not to come back because the provost guard caught him stealing gasoline out of a car with a siphon and a bucket. Two of my young men were caught carrying raincoats out of camp and not returning with them, and to top it all off, I ate some hamburger steak night before last for dinner and contracted a first-grade stomach-ache. You can see that I'm not in a mood to be fooled with this morning.
However there is a brighter side. I'm looking for two letters today. The outfit took a six-mile practice march yesterday morning, made it on schedule, and only one man of the three hundred dropped out. I have inaugurated a competitive standing of the companies and they are at each others' throats to win. One got second place yesterday on account of two flies in the dining room. The company with the best kitchen, cleanest area, neatest tent row, and best formation at drill gets mentioned in orders that day and a ribbon is pinned on the company guidon marked "Best Company." You'd be surprised how they work for it. It beats bawling them out all hollow.
I hope I get a letter today. Is Margy a good girl? I hope she is.
Lots of love,
Harry

Camp Pike, Ark.
Dear Bess: August 24, 1933
I got two letters yesterday after I'd sent yours. They acted as a cure for all ills. You see the only time I have to write is right after breakfast at around 6:30 A.M. We have breakfast at six. I come over to the office (I have a private one and no one can come in until I tell him to) and write you, by that time I hear the adjutant in his office, and routine business begins. I heard a long complaint yesterday about food in Company A. Called in the mess officer and listened to him, then the cook in that company, and finally fifteen privates who'd made the kick were heard. I made the cook take them back to the company and feed them another breakfast. After that I made my usual inspection tour over the camp, complimented some, raised Cain with others, and by that time it was the hour for the officers meeting. I have one every day at 11:45 and tell them who had the best company that day and why and who had the worst and why also, and then listen to suggestions and sometimes accept them. . . .
Today at ten-thirty I have to make a speech on citizenship and at 4:30 P.M. pin a decoration on a doctor from Little Rock in the name of the President.
Eddie McKim was out to see me last night after I'd gone to bed. I went to bed at eight-thirty, so he wasn't to blame for that. He left about ten-thirty and

is going home today. I hope my daughter is as good a girl as she should be. She hasn't written her dad yet. Maybe she's too busy practicing. I'm glad she's started again because I do want her to be a pianist.

I wish you were both here. It has been lovely so far as weather is concerned and I'm sure you'd have had a good time. I hope your mother's foot is all right. There are a lot of men in that profession. I'm glad you got a good one. Well here comes the morning woe, so I'll have to postpone until tomorrow. Hope I get a letter.

Your loving Harry

Camp Pike, Ark.

Dear Bess: August 25, 1933

Yesterday was a blank except for the buttons. It looked good to me just to see that handwriting on a box. Even the mail orderly has found out how to approach me with a request. He'll make it when he's handing me your letter.

I pinned some medals on the old doctor from Little Rock yesterday and got my picture in the *Gazette* again. That's the third time. I haven't seen a *Star* for so long I've forgotten what it looks like. I hope the county is running as it should. I've not worried about it a great deal. There was only one mistake made on this trip and that was when you and Margy didn't come down with me. I get awful lonesome in the evening. Even tried to play contract bridge last night and set my partner at stated intervals. Being a major however he was very polite about it and didn't tell me straight out that I knew nothing about it.

I hope I get a letter today. Glad you called Mamma. I guess I'll write her today for the first time since I arrived. Hope my daughter hasn't forgotten how to write. We may have to put her back in the first grade this fall.

Love to you both,
Harry

Camp Pike, Ark.

Dear Bess: Sunday, August 27, 1933

I finally got one letter yesterday afternoon. It helped the day wonderfully. You've no idea how terribly lonesome it is in a camp on a half-holiday. All I could do was to watch a bridge game, be bored by border service stories, or listen to Colonel Sullivan tell about Kansas State Agricultural College R.O.T.C. Being not vitally interested in any of them, all I could do was get out my high-brow detective literature and entertain myself.

I read your letter about six times and then went back and read all I had received. I could have gotten in the car and gone to Little Rock to a show but that would have been no fun. All these officers are strangers to me and none of them want to go anywhere with the camp commander anyway.

While it looks good from the sidelines to have control and get your name in both papers every day and pictures every other day it's not a pleasant position. However it's good experience.

I had a pest of mosquitoes last night for the first time too. They must have read your letter. Don't bother about the Fisher woman. Someday maybe I can afford a man secretary who'll stay on the job. Please don't miss any more days writing. I guess Margaret's forgotten how.

Love to you both,
Harry

Camp Pike, Ark.
Dear Bess: Monday, August 28, 1933

Well the camp is drawing rapidly to a close. I'll probably be starting for home when you get this. I want to be there Wednesday evening if I possibly can. Governor McNutt of Indiana is coming on Thursday morning and I'm responsible for him, so I'll have to meet him. . . .

We got no mail yesterday so of course there was no letter. This will in all probability be your last one. I suppose Margaret has forgotten entirely how to write. That's too bad because I'd expected to make a special trip to Little Rock and now I won't have to.

I hope you are all well and that the weather is fine. It has been hot for the last two days but not seriously that way. Been trying to rain and hasn't succeeded.

Kiss my baby even if she doesn't think of her dad any more.

Lots of love,
Harry

Here Truman visits the artist who was executing the heroic figure of Andrew Jackson destined for the courthouse in Kansas City.

[Hotel Governor Clinton, New York City]
Dear Bess: January 1, 1934

I am starting 1934 right you see by writing you the first letter of the year. I arrived about one o'clock. The Baltimore & Ohio stops in Jersey City and hauls the passengers over on buses. We crossed on a ferry and I wished for you and Margaret and thought of New Orleans. The Hudson is just about as wide as the "old Missip" at its mouth.

I am on the twenty-fifth floor and my window overlooks all southern Manhattan—the Empire State Building is three blocks away and I can see the Chrysler and Manhattan Life Towers too. The sun is shining this morning—I got so sleepy I didn't get your letter done on the first. I went out at six-thirty and walked up Fifth Avenue to Forty-second and then over to Broadway. Went to a picture show and got so sleepy I left. It wasn't any good anyway. All about two men and one girl and then Mary McCormack sang. If she's an opera star our country's in a bad way for talent. I had intended being really very decent and going to the Metropolitan Opera, they were giving *Traviata*, but decided I'd better save my money.

I am on my way to look at Andy and the friezes [see below] and then I'll go back to Washington, leaving here at 2:00 P.M.

I'm not so sure I care as much for this proposed job [federal relief administrator, Mo.] as I thought I was going to. There'll be almost as many rocks heaved at me as there are now. But I'll look into it.

You don't know how I wish you were here. We'd have a time. We'll do it yet before the year is out. Kiss my good little girl and think always of your
Dad

[Willard Hotel, Washington, D.C.]

Dear Bess and Margaret: January 2, 1934
Well here I am back in Washington at 8:30 P.M. After mailing your letter this morning I walked from the Governor Clinton Hotel at Thirty-First and Seventh Avenue to 4 West Tenth Street, where Mr. Keck has his studio and also where he lives. It was a long walk but interesting even if it was cold as it could be, almost. I went over to Broadway and walked down Broadway to Twenty-Third, where the Flatiron Building is and then walked down Fifth Avenue to Tenth. People were rushing this way and that and jaywalking against lights and everything else so that the worst hick town can have nothing on New York— at least not this morning from eight-fifty until nine-forty on two of their busiest streets.

Mr. Keck had four Andrew Jacksons and the castings of the friezes of Law and Justice. We are going to be proud of them I tell you. He says that the Law, which is Moses, will be better than Mohamet and I believe him. We took Andy all apart and put one man on one horse and then tried him on another until there was a combination that will be unbeatable. Mr. Keene and Mr. Wight were both there and we spent a most enjoyable morning after which Mr. Keck took us around on Sixth Avenue to a fine eating place, gave us a real martini, oysters, roast beef, and everything. Then I caught a taxi and my train and here I am back in politics. From the height of the esthetic to the basement of the practical, and I confess I like them both. . . .

Tomorrow I'm to see Senator Clark and Mr. Burr and the rest and really make up my mind on what I'm to do.

I wish you and Margy were here to share this immense room. They are treating me as if they thought I amounted to something at the hotel anyway; even if they will skin me to death on the cost, it makes a difference. When Neal and Lewis come I'll make them take over a share of it anyway. When I get things as I want them you'll always be with me. No matter what comes or goes you're always my sweetheart with the prettiest blue eyes in the world and all that goes with blue eyes. The most of the men I meet and go around with wonder why I have only one sweetheart. I'll tell you why. When I was very young I set a certain young lady up as my ideal and she's still it, and will always be whether she wants to or not, and you know who she was, is, and eternally will be. Now I'm lonesome and thinking of you and writing you instead of going to a show. I got disgusted last night because I didn't have your hand to hold (that's all I go to shows for anyway) and left, so I didn't try any tonight. You'd better put this in the fire and not let your sweet little daughter read it because she might get the impression that her dad is only a sap, and if I can be great to anyone I want to be to her.

Kiss her for me and all the love in the world to you,

Harry

Candidate for the Senate, 1934. *Harry S. Truman Library*

The Truman cavalcade, 1934. *Harry S. Truman Library*

TEN

FRESHMAN SENATOR

Truman was never daunted by what he could not control, and the chicanery surrounding his election to the United States Senate was no exception. He knew that once elected he could pursue his own honest ends. The Pendergast machine was corrupt—but then so was the St. Louis machine, and he preferred the approval of Tom Pendergast to that of the party leaders in St. Louis.

Upon reaching Washington and being sworn in, he welcomed the national proportions of his responsibility. He no longer considered himself a local politician. He represented the citizens of Jackson County, indeed, of all Missouri, and would do what was best for them. He also intended to fulfill the expectations of the Founding Fathers who had drawn up the Constitution of the United States; they believed that two Senators from each state with six-year terms—one-third of the Senate's membership coming up for reelection every two years—would constitute a governing body that could be more effective with national issues than was possible for the House of Representatives.

The business of moving into a cramped Washington apartment, however, was hardly exhilarating, nor was initiation to the supposed comradeship of the Senate. Most Senators ignored Truman, considering him the Pendergast machine's Senator (the Boss in Kansas City seems himself to have said something to the effect that just as industries had their representatives, so some political bosses would have theirs). One of the few Senators who showed any concern for him was Burt Wheeler of Montana, who befriended him and helped him with committee assignments.

Gradually the novelty wore off; Truman recalled the advice of a political friend in Missouri who had told him that at first in the Senate he would wonder how he got there, but after six months would wonder how the others got there. He noticed that only a few Senators, perhaps a dozen, were leaders of the Upper House—those who worked at the job. From the outset he determined to be one of them.

[Washington, D.C.]
Dear Bess: June 17, 1935

Your card was a lifesaver this morning. I have never in my life spent such a lonesome night. I went *"home"* at nine-thirty after I'd talked to you and when I opened the apartment door I thought I heard Margaret say, "Hello Dad"— and I asked, well where is mother, as usual, and then I walked all around to make sure I wasn't dreaming, read the *Congressional Record,* put a sheet on your bed, and turned in. Every time I'd hear that young lady in the next apartment I would be sure my family were coming in. We'll never do it again. . . .

Met with Interstate Commerce Committee a few minutes and told them I had to leave, came down here and locked the door so I could write. I sort of need a phone but I guess I can make out. I've gotten so I can hardly write. You see what lack of practice does. Kiss my baby, tell your mother and mine hello, and say I want to be remembered to all the family.

I miss you terribly,
Harry

Washington, D.C.
Dear Bess: June 18, 1935

I've been wandering around like a lost soul this morning. Letters, letters, letters, all over my desk and everywhere else. Maybe when I go to hell they'll give me some other punishment and I won't have to answer letters to people who want what I can't give them. . . .

Jim Farley was eating at Harvey's and I got him to come over and shake hands with the boys. They said that after meeting both Hopkins and Farley they could go home and highhat everybody in Platte County, including the governor and Henry Dillingham.

The Senators all pretended to miss me and were very cordial to me—so was the Vice President. He appreciated my contribution [a bottle of liquor] so much he wouldn't even *open* it. Took it and locked it up and said he'd save it until he really had the stomach-ache or some other fitting ailment for which there would be an excuse to use it. . . .

I am sending you a check. I hope it will cover things, if not tell me about it. Do you think you can make out with it and three hundred after the first until August? If you can I'll get all insurance and everything paid up next month. If you don't think you can I can put off some of them.

How's Margaret and the baby and everybody else? I wrote Margaret yesterday in the Senate while Huey [Long, of Louisiana] was spouting.

The bell is ringing and I have to run. I'm looking for a letter tomorrow. It's a wrench to be without you. I never missed you so much before when I'd be away temporarily. Kiss my baby.

Lots of love,
Harry

Washington [D.C.]
Dear Bess: June 22, 1935

Your letter came on the second mail so everything is all right today. I did tell Miss Margaret some things she should do both for herself and her mother, and I suspect she is studying them over before she shows you the letter.

I expected to go to bed early last night but didn't get there until 10:00 P.M. because I was fool enough to tell a fellow who holds a job in the Government Printing Office, who is a Missourian and who is the Master of a Lodge, that I'd come out and talk to them. Since I'd run out on him on another occasion I had to go, but didn't stay late.

The Senate had a session today so Huey could make a speech. Bennett and I went to a dinner, or lunch I guess would be better, for Bernarr McFadden, the editor of *Liberty,* and the owner of a lot of other magazines. All the Missouri Congressmen were there. He's quite an interesting old codger. Sixty-seven and still runs foot races and wrestles. Wrote one of those books Myra gave me on eyes. Runs a health hotel in northern New York. He'd been to Birmingham, Alabama, organizing some athletics for underprivileged kids down there. Drives his own plane and drinks nothing but buttermilk. Kind of hard on Bennett and me to attend a dry lunch in this town.

Guess you had a nice lunch. Glad the draft arrived O.K. Hope Margie has a nice party. Nettie came in this morning and said she'd come out every day till she got her job. I offered to pay something today and she said she'd rather have it next week 'cause she'd just spend it.

I've got to go and get ready for Clark's dinner tonight.
                              Love to you by the carload,
                                             Harry

Washington, D.C.
Dear Bess: June 26, 1935

I got two letters this morning but none from Margaret. The two today make up for the loss yesterday. . . .

I am getting sick and tired of going out to dinner. I'd like just once to eat a sandwich and go to bed with a clear head. I wish we could get enough ahead to go into business in some quiet county-seat town and get out of the whirl but I know that will never happen. . . . Kiss my baby and keep writing.
                                    Lots of love,
                                       Harry

[Washington, D.C.]
Dear Bess: June 28, 1935

This is the day sixteen years ago that I made a plunge and took a chance for which I have been a better man. My only regret is that it was not done ten years sooner. I hope Red Sands did his duty today. You really don't deserve a letter or a telegram or any flowers. I only got a *postcard* and an answering telegram.

I am going to punish you by not mailing this until tomorrow morning. I have found time to think of you and write you every day. I wonder if you are now or ever have been sorry you did it on June 28, 1919. You see you have been married to a financial failure and the reason for that is that I have always believed in doing as I'd be done by, and to make money and keep it you must be a pirate or strike an oil well or a gold mine. Had I not been a fool patriot in 1917, I'd had the oil well. And maybe would have turned pirate and been successful. I am hoping to make a reputation as a Senator, though if I live long enough that'll make the money successes look like cheese. But you'll have to put up with a lot if I do it because I won't sell influence and I'm perfectly willing to be cussed if I'm right.

I've never had but one golden-haired, blue-eyed sweetheart and she's still the same blue-eyed, but now maybe silver-haired, sweetheart and just as perfect and as beautiful as I dreamed of when I was ten and twelve and sixteen.

I am at the flat writing this at four-thirty. The Senate recessed at five-thirty yesterday to Monday. I could have made the New York trip but didn't do it because Harrison [Senator Pat Harrison of Mississippi] invited me to a meeting at [Joseph P.] Kennedy's house at seven o'clock this evening. Kennedy runs the Securities Commission and I ought to know him. . . .

Kiss Margie, love to you,
Harry

The new Senator found himself among members of the Upper House whose names he proudly relates to Bess in the letter below (William G. McAdoo and Hiram Johnson of California, Carl Hayden of Arizona, John H. Bankhead of Alabama, David I. Walsh of Massachusetts, Key Pittman of Nevada, Francis R. Duffy of Wisconsin, Tom Connally of Texas, Augustine Lonergan of Connecticut, Theodore Bilbo of Mississippi, Edward R. Burke of Nebraska).

[Washington, D.C.]

Dear Bess: June 29, 1935

This day starts right anyway. Your letter was in the first mail. You tell Heinie [Edgar Hinde, postmaster of Independence] if he doesn't do better, I'll still pull that investigation. I see Julian Friant's boy every day and he keeps me informed. He said yesterday that his dad was much better. Yes, Mr. Ferguson has been to see me and I have been trying to help him. Tom Miller from California is also here trying to get a job. He wants wholesale help—brought his brother along—and both want me to put them right with McAdoo and Johnson, neither one of whom they know. If you don't think that was a diplomatic job you're mistaken. I finally sent them on their way rejoicing without doing anything. You know I never saw Tom Miller but once before in my life and he was so busily engaged in making love to the Swope girl that he didn't see me then. It's too bad sometimes to have such a good memory.

I couldn't keep from calling you last night and I sure wished I was home.

Hope you had a pleasant wedding day without the principal necessity for a wedding, to wit: a husband.

The party last night was a real affair. Harrison, Hayden, Bankhead, Walsh, who'd bust if a pin were stuck into him, Pittman, Duffy, Connally, Lonergan of Connecticut, and one or two others whom I can't remember—Bilbo, Burke, and I were the only new ones there. It is the finest home I've seen. Out west of Washington on the Potomac, a grand big house a half mile from the road in virgin forest with a Brussels carpet lawn of five acres all around it, a swimming pool in the yard, and all the other trimmings. There is a motion picture theater in the sub-basement. It was built by a young Chicago millionaire at a cost of $600,000, then he drank himself to death in two years, and his chorus-girl widow is trying to borrow $40,000 on it and can't. Kennedy has it leased, furniture and all, and it is a grand place. I was complimented to be included in the party, and it did me no harm. . . .

Lots of love to you and Margie,
Harry

Washington, D.C.

Dear Bess: Sunday, June 30, 1935

It is now five o'clock and I have all my goods and chattels in the car in the Senate garage. Nettie came out and cleaned up at three o'clock and I am in transit to a new roost. I am waiting for the manager of the LaFayette Hotel to call me. If he doesn't do it pretty soon I am going on over to the Continental. Yesterday was a very busy day. I dictated as many letters as usual and then took a couple of the boys whom Colonel Hickman had put to work out to dinner, and after I got rid of them I went out to Harry Hawes' house to another dinner and a meeting of the "Hound Dogs." Marvin McIntyre, secretary to the President, was there as was the Minister to Costa Rica, in whose honor the party was given. We played five-cent poker and I won five dollars, the Costa Rican Minister lost ten and he screamed like a Jewish merchant. He is a Jew I think. At least he looks and talks like one.

I slept until 9:00 A.M. and then packed up. Some job. I had to do a lot of squeezing but got it all in after a fashion. The laundry ruined my linen suit— the double-breasted one I got in Baltimore. They put two red stains on the front of it and pinned a note on it saying they had cleaned it twice and couldn't get 'em out. I'd only worn it in the Senate and there were no stains on it when I sent it. I raised the roof on it but I guess it's a loss. . . .

Kiss my baby, love to you,
Harry

Many letters, such as the one below, reveal concern about finances. Truman had gotten free of the haberdashery's debts when Vivian purchased the bank note for $1,000 at sheriff's sale. But in the senatorial election of 1934, Truman had *received almost no help from the Pendergast machine and largely financed himself, once more going into debt.*

Washington [D.C.]
Dear Bess: July 3, 1935
. . . I am glad you're not sorry that you took the plunge sixteen years ago. Just for that I'll have to talk sordid things in this letter. I have a bill from Woolf's for $55.00, one from Jeleff's for $53.20, one from Garfinckel's for $55.85, and the grocery people sent me one for $9.53. If you say these are all right, I'll pay them but I'll wait until I hear from you. I am sending you a draft Friday for $200 and if you need more I'll send more. I'll have to have about $150–$175 for room rent and at least that much for laundry and meals; as nearly as I can figure we ought to be about $150 or $200 to the good at the end of this month, and next month if I get home we can beat it a couple of hundred more and perhaps get enough ahead to get furniture and fixtures for next year. I guess we ought to be happy we have no doctor's bills and all of us are well. If I made everybody I've gotten jobs for since 1927 pay me by the month as Bulger used to, we'd have a nice tidy sum to the leeward every month, but I'm just a d.f. I guess I can't take it that way.

I'd have sent you the draft today but I couldn't get anybody to go uptown for me in time. The darned banks close at 2:00 P.M. you know.

I hope you are cool and happy and having a good time. I'm sorry to talk money and bills and I wouldn't if I were a millionaire.

I walk down to Pennsylvania Avenue and eat breakfast—usually at Childs'. Everything is all right at Drain's. I told you that Leonard said he'd give us an apartment at a special price next year. I leave my car in the Senate garage and ride the bus or cab. Either one is twenty cents.

I have Mrs. Drain's dish on my desk and will send it home tonight by Vic. Please write every day. Your Sunday note came after I'd mailed your letter yesterday. I got a nice one today as you can see.

Kiss baby and lots of love,
Harry

More Senators appear below (Royal S. Copeland of New York, Huey Long of Louisiana, and Henrik Shipstead of Minnesota; James A. Reed was a former Senator from Missouri whom Truman had once supported).

Washington [D.C.]
Dear Bess: July 4, 1935
Well this is the nation's birthday. I was up at six-thirty, had breakfast at seven-thirty, and I'm down at the office now waiting for the picnickers to come. They were to be here at eight but I expect nine or nine-thirty will about hit them. I was extravagant yesterday and bought a swimming suit. Probably won't put it on. But I thought I'd better have it along. I am thinking of going over to

Annapolis tomorrow and sleeping off about twenty-four hours. Senator Lonergan told me that there is a nice cheap, reasonable beach close there. I probably won't go when the expense stares me in the face. The best thing I can do would be to stay here at the office and write a half-dozen speeches on various subjects and be ready for the homecoming.

I am going to prepare one on farming and foreign trade, one on social security, one on the Bank Bill, one on bureaucratic government, and if Mr. Reed gets too smart I'm thinking of telling what I know about him.

I had to sit in the chair all yesterday afternoon and say, "Without objection the amendment is agreed to." The bill was the water transportation regulation one and there were from two to ten amendments on every page—there were seventy-odd pages so you see I had a very pleasant time. Copeland and Huey and Shipstead got into arguments with Wheeler but I had no rulings to make. I am having the record sent to the house, thought maybe you'd like to have some more wastepaper around.

It has been a round of funerals hasn't it? I'm glad you sent Mize a nice remembrance for his mother. How did it happen? and who did it?

You know when you pass fifty all you do is go to funerals of your friends.

Tell Bill Southern he owes me a letter. Is he mad or something? I got a dandy from Heinie yesterday. I'd threatened him with an investigation and he said I'd better have it done before I got home or I'd be a part of the investigated.

Tell Margie I'm still looking for that letter. You can give her a kiss anyhow.

Love to you,
Harry

Washington [D.C.]

Dear Bess: July 5, 1935

Well the letter was in the first mail this morning so it evidently was here yesterday and so I am feeling better even if it is the day after the Fourth.

We had a very nice time. Arrived at Mrs. Robie's place at about eleven o'clock, went swimming, and then had a grand lunch. The outfit all went riding in a big motorboat except Bud and Mrs. Bud, Mrs. Messall, and me and Harry Salisbury. I went to sleep and didn't get up until 5:00 P.M. Bud and his wife went home and the boat riders came back and had a ball game until dark, shot firecrackers, and we came home arriving about nine-thirty. I was in bed by ten and slept like a log. There won't be any session of the Senate until Monday. I wish I'd started home at noon on Tuesday. I could have been in Independence Wednesday evening and started back Saturday. Of course it would have been a very strenuous drive—I could have done it however. They say though that after fifty, things like that ought not to be done. So I didn't do it. . . .

Kiss my baby and lots of love,
Harry

Washington, D.C.
Dear Bess: July 6, 1935

I am paying all the bills but one insurance bill to Tom McGee and he won't mind waiting. I paid Garfinckel and Jelleff and Woolf Bros., so we haven't anything staring us in the face now but the one insurance account at McGee's and my government policy, which I can pay August 1 and still be all right. You're absolutely right about not eating and wearing clothes. I guess if we'd go to one of these camps where they wear no clothes, we might get ahead on the clothes account but it would be worse when we came out because we'd have no old ones to fall back on. . . .

You needn't be uneasy about anybody seeing your letters. They are under lock and key. They belong to me and cannot be published without your permission so don't worry about them. . . .

Kiss the baby and write regularly.

Lots of love,
Harry

[Washington, D.C.]
Dear Bess: July 9, 1935

Two letters came this morning and I was most happy to get them. I am sorry I made a mistake going to the office picnic. It never occurred to me that there would be anything wrong with it. The same people who were there before came and the same things were done. I had a saltwater swim and a good nap and felt fine after it was over. John I guess told his mother that I'd gotten over the blues somewhat I guess. You shouldn't take a piece of idle gossip and try to twist it into something unpleasant. Mrs. Griggs you know likes to give people the worst motives. I am on the point of increasing Johnnie's pay from $120 to $135, but if he's going to become a gossip about me I'll be hanged if I'll do it. Probably my letter on finances made you feel badly. I am sorry if it did. I sent Woolf Bros. a check for $55.25. I guess they'll send it back. I am enclosing you another $100.00 to pay for the auto. I forgot all about it.

I suppose Mrs. Griggs' remark makes you curious about my evenings. Well I've been reading the Bank Bill, the Social Security Bill, Water Carrier Bill, and Freeman's *Lee* at night as well as the *New York Times*. Been to see one show —H. Rider Haggard's *She*. It was very good. I wanted to see Joe Brown in *Alibi Ike* but didn't. I went to dinner with Clark and Sid Stephens Saturday and Mrs. Clark at the Shoreham. Saw Mrs. Cochran and Jack. Got home at ten-thirty even then. I am to have dinner with assistant manager of Pennsylvania Railroad tonight and that's all I have on for this week. So I guess I'll finish Freeman's volume one. You sort of gave me a blue feeling again. I'll be glad when this damned session is over. I think maybe we'd better get a flat and stay here summer and winter.

Kiss my baby and love to you,
Harry

The names of more Senators follow (Lewis B. Schwellenbach of Washington, James E. Murray of Montana, Nathan Bachman of Tennessee, Frederick Van Nuys of Indiana, Richard B. Russell, Jr., William H. Dietrich of Illinois, Robert Reynolds of North Carolina, Matthew Neely of West Virginia, William J. Bulow of South Dakota).

Washington, D.C.

Dear Bess: July 11, 1935

Well McAdoo's party was a very successful and rather dignified affair. There were only five new Senators there. Burke, Schwellenbach, Murray, Bilbo, and the junior senator from Missouri. Hatch, Clark, Bachman, Van Nuys, Russell of Georgia, Dietrich, Lonergan, Bob Reynolds, Neely, Bulow, and some-one else who is a two-year-old was there. Sixteen sat down and it was a fine dinner served upstairs in a grand suite. Everybody got to air his grievance against the administration and everybody had one. Bilbo and I kept still but it was a very interesting sidelight on how the political affairs of the nation are handled by the brain-trusters. Old man Lonergan said he was against everything they are doing but he'd keep on being a Democrat and voting, he supposed, for what he didn't believe. Neely was the bitterest of all and I think probably he had a right to be. His worst enemies were given the best jobs. McAdoo let Clark preside and after about five had talked I slipped around to the host and left, it was then eleven-thirty and I suppose there were at least five more speeches. I am at the office though at 7:00 A.M. as usual.

I sure appreciated your letter. It came on time yesterday afternoon. Carl Gray is a son of the president of the Union Pacific. He was once president of the Missouri Reserve Association and the national one too. I think he is now vice-president of the Great Northern or one of those railroads up there. He was a great friend of Colonel Elliott and claimed to be one of mine. I don't know whether to send him anything or not. I wouldn't send Roper anything.

I have been watching the papers on apartments but have had no chance to look yet. Your suggestion about Margey's bed is O.K. I thought I'd call Mr. Leonard before I leave for home and ask him if he'd rent that fourth-floor two-bedroom apartment in 3011 at a reasonable rate by the year. There have been some nice six-room houses advertised for lease too. But heat and upkeep are terrible and I haven't looked at any of them yet.

I'm sorry to hear of Judge Beeman. He was a good-natured fat man and never was the same after he went broke. It takes a tough citizen to climb down the ladder after being at the top and he couldn't stand it. I'm looking for a letter today. Kiss Margey—she sent me a grand letter.

Love to you,

Harry

Washington, D.C.
Dear Bess: July 12, 1935

Your Tuesday letter came on the last mail yesterday and the Wednesday one came on the first mail today. I took the one home yesterday at three o'clock and read it four or five times. I am sorry I made the telegram so formal but I was trying to make Uncle Sam pay for it. . . .

I'd like very much to build the house and we'll look it over when I get home. But you know a house said to cost $8,500 will cost $10,500 and it is necessary to have a lot clear—and one where we'd want to be will cost $2,500 anyway. So you can see how it piles up. There would be at least $2,000 or $2,500 in furniture too. Maybe I can make a gamble next fall and hit a pot of gold. If I'd played my hunch last fall we'd have had enough to build two houses. My 1920 experience buying a house almost made a coward out of me. . . .

Kiss Margaret for me and keep on writing—lots of love.

Harry

Washington, D.C.
Dear Bess: July 14, 1935

I went to the public health dentist yesterday and had two front teeth filled. That dark one and the one I broke at home. The gold had become loose in the dark one and that's what made it dark. Dr. Marshall took out the gold, ground out the black, and put in a white filling and that tooth is as white as any I have now. It had begun to hurt a little, hence the fixing.

There was no letter when I got back and I had to go to the Appropriations Committee to argue a $240 million deficiency bill. It was noon when I got back to the office. . . .

I took a Baltimore bath and came to the office this A.M. at eight-thirty and there was yesterday's letter. I was sure glad to get it. I sent you some stationery yesterday although the slightly yellow brand you are using is all right. I don't care what stationery you use as long as I get the letter.

Yes Mrs. Griggs is deviling me for a job. I can't get her one because she can't do anything but cook and that's not the sort of job she wants. She'd like one, so John says, where she could draw her pay and not do much work. People are never grateful or satisfied and since I don't expect them to be either I'm never disappointed.

How did the kids' party and show come out? I saw it rated mention in the hometown paper of Thursday. The *Star* had quit coming and I'm not going to send them $7.50 for another six months. The *Post* comes for nothing.

Doc Copeland sent me his book called the *Dr. Copeland's Home Medical Book,* by Royal S. Copeland M.D., a Physician of National Reputation, with the Doc's picture on the cover. There are 582 pages and I'm wondering if he'll bill me for it, remembering of course the experience of the beauty parlor operator at the Shoreham.

I'm going to mail this letter in the post office so you ought to get it on time.

Rust is coming to see me about the 1424 16th Street apartment tomorrow. I'll tell you what he says then. Kiss my baby.

Loads of love and keep writing,
Harry

In an effort to get Bess back to Washington from Independence Truman tried to find a reasonable but attractive apartment—no easy task.

Washington, D.C.
Dear Bess: July 17, 1935
. . . I have been out apartment looking this morning. The one at 1821 Nineteenth was directly across from the school but wouldn't do. They were remodeling an old house—one of the three-story kind—and making an apartment of each floor. No private entrance or anything.

There was one at 1726 Massachusetts that's a dandy but the rent's too much. It had a grand hall, living room and dining room, two bedrooms, two baths, and closets galore, two-car garage and a Missouri nigger for a janitor—graduate of Lincoln University at Jefferson City. They asked $160 per month. I fell out of there in a hurry. Found a rather nice place at 1921 Kalorama Road. It was a northwest corner, fifth-floor apartment—two bedrooms, two baths, living room, small dining room, large hall, $125 per month. No garage. Then I looked at a house at 2218 Cathedral, a block north of Connecticut. It was a house like Pete Allen's. They were painting and papering it from cellar to attic. It had a two-car garage and was just the same size and kind as Pete's house. They wanted $90 per month. I then went down to the Highlands at California and Connecticut. They had a nice two-bedroom apartment on the southeast corner, fourth floor, at $125 —better I think than 1921 Kalorama Road. Then I looked at the Westmoreland, right behind the Highlands on California. They wanted $100 for a two-bedroom apartment on sixth floor, and $79.50 for one on fourth floor that had four rooms. It is an old place but the location and rooms were very nice. You'll notice that all these places are within two or three blocks of the school. I am going to look at 2400 Sixteenth Street and the Jefferson tomorrow and a couple of houses. I bet I find something that'll suit before I quit. Margey owes me a letter. Kiss her anyway.

Love to you,
Harry

Washington, D.C.
Dear Bess: Tuesday, July 23, 1935
Well I wish I hadn't called you. I wanted to see you and Margey so badly after I'd talked to you that I almost played baby. It was a fine thing to listen to you anyway. We'll never do this again. We've got to work out some way to make ends meet and have a place to live in Washington. I'm thinking about moving August 1 because I'm paying twice too much rent. I see places advertised every

day from $40 to $55 that would be just as nice as where I pay that much every two weeks. You need not send the book Nellie brought over. I'm hoping to read it if I ever get a chance. Yes I was at Strickler's house for dinner. Kenne's stayed at the LaFayette. I only saw them the one time.

About that 1424 apartment. I don't think they'd split it but the one way. Dan Nee, of course, would like to be governor but I am doubtful of his making the race. While Pendergast and Clark are friendly now, I'm of the opinion that they won't stay that way if Clark gets a notion he's strong enough to overturn the machine. If he had the governor, he could do it. Pendergast isn't so dumb, but while he has the whole show now he knows he can't keep it forever. Clark, as you know, is a potential candidate for the White House in 1940. He's been trying to be a radical conservative. That, you know, is some job. Pendergast hasn't made up his mind yet who will be governor. He'll announce it sometime soon. If the man is smart and politically minded he can say who Clark's successor will be and can deliver the 1940 delegation at the national convention. Clark is in St. Louis now opening a law office. You know he's just as hard up as we are but his wife doesn't know it. He played utility stocks in Insull's heyday and lost. He told me he had to borrow all he could get to keep out of the courts and that he was still doing it. So he's opening this law office to try and make some money honestly. I think Clark's ethics are of the highest order and I'm sure that's one reason he's busted.

Well you'd better put this in a safe place because it may not work out that way. Don't let any of our job holders work you into any political hole. I know you're too smart to let 'em do it. Your White House press interview showed you're a genius. Just keep it up.

Kiss Margey, love to you,
Harry

[Senate Chamber]

Dear Bess: Wednesday, July 24, 1935

Your Monday letter came while I was out apartment hunting. I got to the office at six-thirty, read all the mail, straightened up my desk. Went to breakfast at eight-thirty, finished dictating to Jane at 9:45, and went out on Sixteenth Street to see three places advertised in the *Post* this morning. Went to 1925 Sixteenth first—it is a block from the Roosevelt, south, in the middle of the block between T and U. The apartment was on the fourth floor. It had a nice living room, small dining room and kitchen, two bedrooms, and two full baths. It was a very nice apartment and they wanted $87.50 for it. It was on the Sixteenth Street side. Then I went out to 2400 Sixteenth Street. They showed me the nicest apartment I've seen. It was on the west side with windows on three sides. A fine large living room, large dining room. Two nice bedrooms and two baths. It was a beauty, No. 312, a lucky number, but they wanted $150 per month without maid service and no furniture. They'll furnish it for $225, so I went away with my head down. Then I went to the Presidential at 1016 Sixteenth Street. It faces east on Sixteenth between K and L. They had a nice apartment with a living room, dining room, kitchen, two bedrooms, and one bath. Plan, about the same as 1925 Sixteenth. They wanted $110. There was another on the seventh floor, the first one was on the fifth, with two bedrooms, living room, and kitchen, no dining room. Bedrooms were very small. Wanted $75 for that and that's all I saw. Will look further tomorrow.

Love to you both,
Harry

Here Truman refers to Senators Gerald P. Nye of North Dakota, Robert M. LaFollette, Jr., of Wisconsin, Carter Glass of Virginia, Alva B. Adams of Colorado, Joseph R. Robinson of Arkansas, Charles L. McNary of Oregon, Frederick Hale, Wallace White, and W. Warren Barbour of New Jersey.

Washington, D.C.
Friday, July 26, 1935

Dear Bess:

... The Senate convenes at eleven o'clock today to consider the Banking Bill. Senator Nye of North Dakota spoke for four hours after he'd introduced Father Coughlin's bill as an amendment. The priest's campaign manager and the president of the American Bankers Association sat side by side in the gallery. Neither of course knew who the other was. Most of us thought Coughlin wrote Nye's speech. Nye is one of the good-looking, egotistical boys who play to the gallery all the time. He's had the limelight on the munitions investigation for six months and he never comes to the Senate except to make a speech or introduce a bill to abolish the army and navy or to get more money for more investigation and more publicity. Several so-called people's friends in the Senate would be in a hell of a fix if there were not some good old work horses here who really cause the Senate to function. I can't pay much on Nye, La Follette, Black of Alabama, and that brand. Wheeler and Bankhead of Alabama are workers. Wheeler isn't as radical as he's painted and I like him. Glass is a worker. So is Adams of Colorado, Harrison, Robinson, and one or two others. Robinson's gone high hat but he's a good worker nevertheless. On the Republican side, McNary, Shipstead, Hale and White, both from Maine, and the ex-prize fighter from New Jersey, Barbour, are the best workers. There isn't a so-called progressive who does anything but talk. Your letter just came. Glad you had a good time at Thelma's. There's rumor that August 15 is the day. I hope it is. Wrote Frank this A.M. about the mill. Kiss Margey.

Love to you,
Harry

Washington, D.C.
Monday, July 29, 1935

Dear Bess:

Well I found a letter when I got back from New York last night and after reading it I had to call you up. I am somewhat disappointed that you don't look with favor on coming back. A sensible survey of the situation though would say you are right. I'm not sensible about it. I couldn't go to sleep until one-thirty thinking about you and home and Missouri in general. So of course I have a headache this morning. I got another letter this morning and one from Margey. That'll cure the headache. I won't look at any more apartments until I see you. I am sure we can get lined up somewhere we'll like and I always think 3016 will be the place, although I haven't talked to Mr. Leonard.

Pendergast was as pleased to see me as if I'd been young Jim. We talked for three hours about everything under the sun. Discarded a couple of prominent candidates for governor—canvassed all the rest and decided on nobody. I am going to get him to talk with Clark and me in about two weeks and I'll bet we can agree on someone. . . .

I am coming home Thursday if everything holds together. Make a speech at Agency—visit Stayton's camp and come back the following Friday. That'll give me time to see Murray, the governor, St Louis, and Springfield and maybe make things tick a little. I'll hate to come back without you. Kiss my baby.

Love to you,
Harry

[Senate Chamber]

Dear Bess: August 9, 1935
You don't know how much I appreciated the letter that came in this morning's mail. I was so devilishly homesick—I could see you standing out there in the yard watching me drive away and I don't think you kissed me good-bye, or you can put it around the other way if you want me on the defensive. Then I didn't call you from Richmond but it was so late when we got there and I didn't write from there either. We had a very strenuous trip what with high-water detours and what not, and I found Harry Salisbury being taken to the hospital as soon as we arrived. They operated on him for appendicitis about an hour after I called you. I was over to see him with Johnnie this morning and he was doing fine. Doctor said he could go home Wednesday. I sent his dad a wire this morning telling him about it and that Harry is getting along all right.

When I come home next time we are going to take a week's vacation and then maybe I can see you more than twice. I like the Continental and probably with a change or two will stay. You don't know how handy it is. Kiss Margey and tell her to write me a letter. I'm getting this off in a hurry.

Love to you,
Harry

[Washington, D.C.]

Dear Bess: August 11, 1935
I am back in Washington at three o'clock. I left New York at ten-thirty this morning after having breakfast with Emmett O'Malley at the Hotel Commo-

dore. We then walked up to the Waldorf and I had a most pleasant visit with T. J. P. He was as pleased to see me as a ten-year-old kid to see his lost pal. I found that the governor had been on my side in everything he talked about and it looks as if everything is going to come out all right. I talked about county affairs too, and he's going to straighten them out along lines I suggested. It is much more pleasant going up there on the train than it is driving and my whole expense was only about five dollars more, so I guess it's worth the difference. . . . Wish I were home. Kiss Margey.

Love to you,
Harry

Washington, D.C.
August 12, 1935

Dear Bess:

I have two letters this morning, one of them airmail. It was most enjoyable to have them. The [Kansas City] *Times* came too without my name on the list. I guess they all make mistakes and I happened to be the victim of this one. I know that Duke Shoop gave the fellow the names as they should be. I think the governor had a grand time. We all had dinner at the Occidental on Friday night, the governor, Caskie Collet, Sam Hargis, Bennett Clark, Duke Shoop, and two more whom I can't remember now. I went back to the office at ten and signed my mail and then went to bed. They came down to my office Saturday at ten and as soon as Bennett arrived we took them to call on the Vice President and Senator Bachman and called up the White House, but the President was out of town so we didn't go up there only officially. We had lunch and then I left at three o'clock for New York. Wrote you from there and as soon as I got back.

I've had a very strenuous morning. The desk looked like a wreck even after I'd given Mildred a hundred letters Saturday and Jane as many today. But I'll catch up by tomorrow night if no more Missourians come to town.

It looks now as if we'll quit very shortly and I ought to be home September 1 sure. I am still at the Continental. I got two more schoolboys jobs since coming back. Messall gets them and I get the credit. I brought another boy from St Louis with me. He went to work this morning. He said that Leo Bird told somebody he came home with a Senator and that person wanted to know what place I played on the Washington ball team. Now beat that. I am sending Margey the funnies from Washington papers of yesterday and a movie picture that looks like her. Please keep up the letters. You don't know how much I appreciate them. I have a letter from Fred Boxley at the Cumberland Hotel in London. He's not feeling very well but is improved over what he was when he left. Didn't say when he'd be back.

Kiss the baby, or Miss Margaret rather.

Love to you both,
Harry

Washington, D.C.
Dear Bess: August 14, 1935

You can always tell whether I'm writing from my office or the Senate by the brand of stationery I use. Yesterday I got a letter and this morning there was one in the first mail this morning. It makes the day brighter and cooler. Yesterday it was ninety-eight, but a big rain came up about six-thirty just as I got into the hotel. It was nice and cool all night. Wouldn't I look fine in a rain-soaked Palm Beach? But I beat it in. Mildred had bad luck yesterday. The good-for-nothing Dryden man went crazy on a bus over at Leesburg, Virginia, and it took all the police of the town to take care of him. Messall and Mildred and a capital policeman went after him, and he's now in the emergency hospital. They say he wasn't drunk but a heat victim. I am skeptical about it. It put Mildred out of commission of course. I'd throw him in the Potomac if I had my way.

I'm glad you went to see Mary on her birthday. She'll appreciate it. I'm hoping to be home in two weeks. Kiss Margey.
Love to you,
Harry

[Senate Chamber]
Dear Bess: August 15, 1935

I was most happy to get the letter. I am glad it's cool and pleasant. We are having a hot wave. Yesterday and today and the day before were scorchers. I guess your hot wave came over here and you received a cool one from Alaska. At least that's the way the weather map looks.

Harry Salisbury was moved to his boarding house yesterday. He seems to be doing fine. I was over to see him last night. We now have another invalid in town and on our hands, one William Dryden. He's made Mildred believe that he's in bad shape and she's all sorry for him and I guess I'll have to help her out with him. I went up to see him this morning and he was tickled to death. He'd made all of them believe he'd had a heatstroke. I said, "Bill, how much hootch did it take to give you this stroke?" And he said he only had one drink he could remember. Of course I won't tell Mildred. Let her think well of him. I like him but he's like all the rest of the alcoholics—undependable. . . .

I wonder if Margey is ever going to write her dad? I'm glad you saw Mamma and Mary and that they were feeling well. I'm looking for letters. Kiss Margey.
Love to you,
Harry

Washington, D.C.
Dear Bess: August 16, 1935

Your letter came in the first mail this morning. I'm sure glad you are having good weather. It's hotter than Tophet here. Some prostrations every day. I think however that prostrations are sometimes laid to heat when they'd happen anyway.

I'd like to go to Santa Fe with Frank and Natalie but we'd better figure out a trip and take it. You know how they do. Right at the last minute something will happen and they won't go. Which way do you want to go? North, West, or South? East is out. We won't go in that direction. How'd you like to go to the Surf Hotel in Chicago for a week and ride up to Milwaukee on a boat? Or go to Duluth, Minnesota, and do the same thing? Or go to Estes Park and stay a week or two? We won't leave our daughter at home. That's final. Maybe you'd prefer Bella Vista or Van Buren or Eureka Springs, Arkansas. Hot Springs isn't bad you know. At least have some preferences by the time I get there, which will be about the twenty-sixth of August and we'll pull right out. You know if I get started at home I can't get away. Hope your cool weather holds. Kiss Margey.

Love to you,
Harry

Truman writes here about the death in a plane crash of humorist and writer Will Rogers.

Washington, D.C.

Dear Bess: Monday, August 19, 1935

. . . It was an awful accident in Alaska and of course we can't see the why. But I'd rather be put out at the top of my career than to come down the ladder and die of remorse. No one has done more to give us common sense than Will Rogers. He's almost a second Mark Twain. The world is better for having produced him. I'm glad his mother didn't believe in birth control.

I am hoping to see you Sunday or Monday and then we'll pull out for somewhere for a couple of weeks. Tell Margey I'm looking for a letter.

Love to you,
Harry

Below Truman refers to Senators Millard Tydings of Maryland and Homer T. Bone of Washington.

[Senate Chamber]

Dear Bess: Friday, August 24[23], 1935

It is now 10:00 P.M. and the Senate is considering the Flood Control Bill and the sarcastic and cynical Senator from Maryland is making a speech against it. Huey and Bone and most everyone are trying to make him ridiculous and without success. Tydings has a most peculiar complex. He's a most selfish and egotistical person. I don't know which is more insincere, Tydings or Huey. I urged Huey to jump him about the ship subsidy, a bill Tydings is for, one of the worst pieces of graft in the history of the country. But Tydings I think was attorney for a banking outfit, interested in starting a ship line from Baltimore to several European ports by having Uncle Sam pay the bill. The government spent some six or seven millions on the project, and Mr. Morgan and Kermit Roosevelt seem to have been the only ones who made a profit. But he's against flood control in the Mississippi Valley. I don't like him. He's not on the level. But he's having a good time and the galleries are laughing. He's even pulverized Huey, which is something even if he is wrong. We'll pass the bill anyway. Tomorrow we get done. I go to New York with Bennett and start home on Sunday afternoon. That ought to put me there Tuesday, as I said this morning.

Hope my daughter is recovering from her accident. I'll forgive her for not writing since she was crippled. Kiss her for me. Hope to see you Tuesday.

Love to you both,

Harry

	[Senate Chamber]
Dear Bess:	Saturday, August 24, 1935

I think I dated your yesterday's letter the twenty-fourth but I was a day ahead if I did. We finished up at 12:15 A.M. yesterday and didn't do as much business as we did in four hours the day before. Old Hiram Johnson is talking on neutrality this morning. He's already spoiled an hour and there's no telling how much longer he'll talk. Everybody is very anxious to quit, so he's not getting much [of a] house.

That was a nice letter from the woman who found the ten. I can't even remember what I was doing with money in a shirt pocket. I'm glad you gave her half of it.

I'm also pleased that Margaret's arm is all right. She evidently isn't able to write yet, because I have no letter from her.

There is only one thing in the way of adjournment in a hurry. The cotton Senators are threatening a filibuster against the deficiency appropriation unless the [Agricultural Adjustment Administration] withdraws its order to lend only nine cents a pound on cotton. Maybe we can get them pacified, at least I hope we can. Joe Robinson, you know, is one of them.

Johnson has quit talking now and Connally and Pittman are having an argument with Gore [Sen. T. P. Gore of Okla.] as a sharpshooter. I've got to get Bennett to New York if I can.

Kiss my baby and I'll see you as soon as the wheels will let me arrive after this show quits.

Love to you,

Harry

	Washington [D.C.]
Dear Bess:	December 4, 1935

I overslept again this morning. It seems that for some reason I'm way behind on sleep. It was 10:00 A.M. before I got started on an apartment hunt again and I found one for $130 per month all furnished and everything. Bud and I went looking again this morning and stopped again at the Sedgwick to see how the unfurnished apartment would look. Vic and I stopped there yesterday and were told we could see it by appointment. We made the appointment for eleven o'clock, in the meantime looking for anything we could see. We looked at one on Biltmore just east of the new bridge on Calvert Street. It had squeaky floors and worn-out rugs, but a Weber grand piano, one old-fashioned bathroom but the rent was $125. We marked it off the list and went on up to the Sedgwick. When we got there the apartment was occupied by H. Comer Howell, son of the famous Clark Howell, editor and owner of the *Atlanta Constitution.* Evidently a remittance man of a great family. He had a fat wife who evidently ran things. The apartment was ideal. Two bedrooms, two baths, nice large living room, *small* dining room, fine kitchen, and all kinds of light and air. Rental $130 month. They were pleased to death for me to have it and I could have kissed them for letting me have it. I'll bet that there isn't another one available like it in the town at twice the price. I sent them a check for $130 as soon as I got back to the office and she called up to know if we wanted her silver too. Scared me to death, I thought she wanted to cancel out on me. They will move out on Christmas Day and we can come in any time after that. If I hadn't come on, we'd never have gotten it. It sure is a load off my mind. . . .

Lots of love to you both,
Harry

Washington, D.C.
December 6, 1935

Dear Bess:

Well I thought sure I'd have a letter today but not a sign of one. Had intended to go to New York last night but didn't because I had a headache and went to bed at seven o'clock. Got up at six this morning and feel fine. I think I've found out what is making me so tired. Those new spectacles don't work. I just wasted about forty dollars on them. I'm going to have my old ones put back in the good frames and let it go at that.

You don't know how I wish you were here. Dreamed about you last night. Thought we were going through a flood together. We got through without disaster. The weather has been fine—sunshine every day. I have been taking a walk every morning and I think soon as I get my glasses fixed I won't have any more tired spells. Send me some of your cards. The Brazilian Embassy is having a reception and I'll send them out. It is next Friday and Saturday. How many are you supposed to leave? Three or four or just one?

Kiss my baby and for goodness sake write or phone or wire or do something.

Love to you both,
Harry

Washington, D.C.
December 7, 1935

Dear Bess:

Well your airmail letter came just after I'd dropped your special down the chute and I'd no more than read the questions about the apartment than Mr.

and Mrs. Howell came in and answered them all. She thought there would be bed linen enough; she'd come downtown to buy some pillowcases. She thought perhaps you'd better bring some tablecloths, said there'd be doilies, napkins, and things like that for breakfast but she wanted to take her tablecloths with her. There is a garage in the basement at five dollars per month and thirty-five cars occupy the space of twenty, so I'd imagine it's about like the one last year. He said the street is packed most of the time. She wanted to leave her silver but when I told her we had ours she said she would store hers. They are moving out December 23 after having all rugs and curtains cleaned. The apartment manager is supposed to clean floors and walls and said she'd do it. I don't know just when I'll leave for home. There are a hundred things to be attended to here and the sob boys find it a little more difficult to reach me here. Stonebreaker took me to a show last night and when we got there it was *Anything Goes*. I didn't tell him I'd seen it. Kiss Margey.

Love to you,
Harry

Washington, D.C.

Dear Bess: December 8, 1935
    Well I've been here *six* days and have *one* letter. None came yesterday and none in this morning's mail. So I guess I'll have to phone collect to see if you are all up and around. You don't know how badly I feel when I don't get a letter. I had a terrific headache yesterday. Went to Baltimore last night and got one excellent boiling out—feel fine this morning. In fact I'd be in excellent spirits if that letter had been here when I came in—nothing but squawks from job hunters in the bundle. I am going to dinner with Bud today, with Johnnie and Harry Tuesday, and with Oscar Wednesday. Oscar came in to see me yesterday afternoon and I judge he is doing well with his job. He looks fine and seems to be as happy as can be. Ask Margaret how many weeks allowance are coming to her and if she has been a good girl. I'm glad to hear of that good report card. It sure will be a wonderful improvement when you all get here. I'm sending the Washington funnies to Margaret. Give her a kiss for me and

Love to you,
Harry

Washington, D.C.

Dear Bess: December 9, 1935
    It sure was pleasant to get to talk to you and I wanted to come home so badly I almost laid the phone down and went to the station. My head however is getting much better and if I can just stay out of reach of the torment, I think it will get entirely all right.
    Had a fine dinner at Bud's, and Johnnie and Harry came out and we had a very pleasant evening playing draw poker at one-tenth of a cent ante. We

needed some of Missouri's funny money to settle up. Leighton Shields called me to go to lunch, but I couldn't go. He is coming in at three o'clock. I'm afraid he's going to be a nuisance.

Went down to see General Craig this morning and had a most pleasant visit with him. He immediately wanted to know how you were and when you were coming to Washington.

Mr. Hinde is too efficient. Here is my Thursday letter returned to me by the Independence post office. I don't know how I'm going to get word to you if this keeps up.

Kiss my baby, love to you both,
Harry

By the end of his first year in the Senate, Truman was beginning to develop an interest in railroad regulation; typically, he began at the beginning, with the basic law, the Interstate Commerce Act.

Washington, D.C.
December 11, 1935

Dear Bess:

Well I am up to date on *all* correspondence, have no appointments except to eat dinner with Oscar, and my head doesn't ache. You've no idea how very pleasant that is. If you and Margey had just come on with me everything would be perfect. I dread the trip home because I know what they'll do to me.

And yet it's a peculiar feeling to have nothing hanging over me. I keep wanting to do something—there's a driving force inside me that makes me get into things. I can't sit still and do nothing. I've read the interstate commerce law in the last two days and will start on the court decisions unless something interferes. I'm going to be better informed on the transportation problem than anyone here, including Eastman, if I can manage it. I'm also studying the banking law.

I wish I'd get a letter every day but they just haven't got lined out yet. The apartment business is all lined out now and I look for nothing to worry us there. We can get Nettie if we want her I'm sure. Kiss Margey and keep writing.

Love to you both,
Harry

Washington, D.C.
December 18, 1935

Dear Bess:

. . . Just called Mrs. Howell and she wants to take her towels and I told her to do it. She's leaving us a toaster, fan, and vacuum cleaner and everything else I think that's necessary. I'm sure you'll like the apartment except the dining room, but the living room can be used if we need more room for guests at meals. In my opinion it's almost as good as the Broadmoor at two hundred dollars and twice as nice as last winter. I wish and wish for financial independence when this time of year comes, but you know about wishes and horses. I guess if I'd been

Margaret Truman, c. 1935. *Historical Pictures Service, Chicago*

money mad we'd be living in California and be afraid to come home. Anyway we can do that even if we can't have what Senators' families are supposed to. Pianos rent for six dollars per month and you pay moving charges. We'll look further however.

Kiss Margey and love to you,
Harry

Washington, D.C.
January 1, 1935 [1936]

Dear Bess:

I am starting the year right and I hope you are. I had a most lonesome night out at the apartment all by myself. Tell Margey there is no radio and she'd better make that bargain with her grandmother. The toaster is all right but I don't think the electric iron is any good. There's a new Hoover vacuum cleaner and other things seem to be all right. Nettie got dinner for me last night and I ate alone in state. There are five big closets and plenty of bedclothes apparently and lots of towels and things. Their dishes aren't anything to brag about, but I think everything is better than last winter. Please look in my right-hand drawer at the top of the chiffonier and put that little shaving brush in your bag. Put in a Gem razor too. It is in a white case. I'll leave it at the office. Also put in that last artillery journal and *Annals* [of the American Academy of Political and Social Science]. There's a little black book about utilities in Missouri I'd like to have too. I think they are all together. Someone has stolen all the tools out of your car and I have to get another set. I can't tell whether it was done at home or on the road. It's a good thing I had no punctures. Here are a couple of wedding announcements and an invitation to Mrs. Garner's dinner. I thought you'd better answer it. Guffeys are having an at-home Sunday. That, I guess, takes cards same as

Mrs. Brazilian Ambassador did. Please hurry and get here but don't take Margey out too soon. I'll send check and franks [franked envelopes] tomorrow. Kiss Margey.

Love to you,
Harry

Washington, D.C.

Dear Bess: January 4, 1935 [1936]
   Well I got a letter this morning and it had been mailed January 2, so I was exactly right. You had not written me at all although I called you Monday when I got here and have written you every day. No wonder I had a headache yesterday. Maybe you were too busy with Miss Margey or maybe you didn't have time or something. I do wish you'd let me hear at least every other day. I ought to call you and talk about seven or ten minutes and reverse the charge.
   I wish you were both here. I am getting cranky and need someone to put me back in a good mood. I accepted the Craig dinner. It had to be a written one. I sent it on one of these sheets, which I guess was out of line. Did the same thing for the Forbes Morgan dinner to the national committee. Hope I haven't made a real social error. You'd better get here and look after these things or I'll have us out in the back yard socially. I'll do my best however. I saw Guffey yesterday and he insisted that I come personally to his reception, and I guess I'll have to go. There are only two names on the card but I saw in the paper where Joe and Mrs. Robinson and two or three others were helping him. I guess, I'll make out some way. I don't even know which corner to turn up so I'll just put 'em in as is.
   I am sure glad Miss Margey is so much better—maybe that will mean a day or so sooner. Nettie comes every morning and cleans up and fixes everything for breakfast. She's gotten dinner for me twice, but I'm going to the Hickman's tonight and Oscar's tomorrow and I suspect I'm going to have to go to the Shields' one day. If people would only let me alone, I could get along. It's like Lucy and Mize—they really do embarrass the mischief out of me. I don't do things for people for a reward, if I did I ought to be rich. I do it because I like to do it, but if they just keep harping on it I get sick of it. I'd almost rather they'd pull a Judge Barr stunt than to be forever thanking me and feeding me. Tell Old Nick he'd better send me some sausage. He told me he thought he'd kill hogs after I left so my wife and child would be sure and get it. Glad Fred got the case. I'll keep track of Nettie's bills.
   Hope you will write regularly from now on.

Love to you both,
Harry

Below Truman refers to Senators Joseph Guffey of Pennsylvania, Sherman Minton of Indiana, Marcus A. Coolidge of Massachusetts, Alben Barkley of Kentucky, and James F. Byrnes of South Carolina.

Washington, D.C.
Dear Bess: January 6, 1936

Well the day and the session started off right—I got a letter this morning. Johnnie brought it up. Said he was sure I wanted it right away. I went out to Oscar's for dinner yesterday and took them back over and showed them the apartment. They thought you might like it. Went on over to Guffey's at five-thirty and had a grand time. Joe Robinson's wife, Mrs. Clark, and one or two others were helping Guffey's three sisters. I found one kindred soul in Minton. His wife hadn't come and he didn't know what to do with himself. He forgot his cards and he was just having a h--- of a time. He said never, never would he come to town again without Mrs. Minton. He and I and old Senator Coolidge and Barkley were the only ones not dressed, as Jimmy Byrnes said, like nigga preachers. Byrnes said here I am at Bennett's suggestion all dressed up like a nigga preacher, and then Bennett wears spats and I don't have any. It was a nice party except that Barkley got sick and they had to send for a doctor and no one knew where to find one. I don't think it was serious. It wasn't what you think, because he hadn't had one. I saw old Doc Copeland give him a pill and that might have done it. I don't know about giving Ann that card because it says not transferable and I'd hate to have the child get the door shut in her face. I'll send you the papers for Tuesday or Wednesday. Hope everybody is well and that I'll see you Saturday. If you leave Thursday, I will.

Love to you both,
Harry

Washington, D.C.
Dear Bess: [January 16, 1936]

Well I haven't been so disappointed since I lost the 1924 election. I don't believe I will be again for a long time. I wanted you to come so badly in the morning. I'd made up my mind that you were in St. Louis this morning and then here came that telegram. I honestly believe that house is infected with cold germs or something.

I'm afraid now that there will be another round and you'll never get here. If you ever arrive, I'll never let you out of my reach again. You won't get any letters Friday or Saturday and maybe this one won't arrive so you'll get it.

I went to the committee meeting yesterday, had lunch with the President and dinner with Forbes Morgan. He has a house out on Massachusetts Avenue next to the Japanese Embassy. It has rooms as big as a town hall. We didn't get enough to eat because half his guests came without saying they would. I was supposed to go to the Supreme Court reception at the White House but I didn't. Bennett and Mrs. Clark and I went to Harvey's and got us a sandwich instead. Then I took them home and went to bed. Got my picture in the Washington *Post* along with Farley and Garner. They took a lot of them at the meeting.

Your badly disappointed dad and sweetheart,
Harry

Senator McAdoo's patronage problems, related below, were the same as Truman's—both men were junior Senators, and the Roosevelt administration ignored them in favor of their senior colleagues. Truman perhaps was unsure of the reason for the President's behavior toward McAdoo, who had been Secretary of the Treasury in the Wilson administration when Franklin D. Roosevelt was Assistant Secretary of the Navy. But the President was giving Missouri patronage mostly to Bennett Clark and seemed to be showing, implicitly, his disdain for the Senator from the Pendergast machine.

                                                                    Washington, D.C.
Dear Bess: June 15, 1936

Well after searching the desk from truck to keelson we found the pass. It was sticking in a little book on the campaign I'd been carrying around and had almost thrown away a time or two. You'll have ball passes enough to last you for the season I hope. Here is a bill from Margie's school. Shall I pay it? I thought you might want a cookbook too.

It is surely lonesome at that apartment without you. Elsie called me and said she was out when I called and was not in bed. They are coming after the picture and lamp tonight. The Senate did nothing today. I had lunch with McAdoo. He's been treated shamefully by the President. He said people had been appointed in California who were his (Mc's) bitterest enemies. We had a very pleasant lunch discussing our troubles. He's a smart old bird and I think would still like to run for President.

I'll get my bonus bonds tonight and will lock them up. Shall we send Miss Margie to school with them or make a payment on a house?

                                              Kiss the *baby*,
                                                    Harry

                                                                    Washington, D.C.
Dear Bess: June 15, 1936

You don't know how much I appreciated the letter this morning. I am going to pack the pillow and the hangers right away. Margie's music is in the baseball game. We should have put it in the back of the car. It would have ridden on top of the grips or the spare tire. Vic [Victor Messall, senatorial secretary] got me twenty-four dollars in rent while I was gone for the apartment. It was all cleaned up so nicely I couldn't tell that anyone had been there. Nothing was missing. Nettie had simply put everything in my drawer and I hadn't found it. The table will be all right at the office and I'll get everything done as it should be, so don't worry. I'm calling Elsie now to come and get the picture. She's not up, at least she didn't answer the phone. Here are your passes to the ball games. When you don't want it let Hunter have it. Leighton Shields just quit talking to me. I'm due at Interstate Commerce. Will write you some more later. Kiss my *baby*.

                                              Love to you,
                                                    Harry

[Washington, D.C.]

Dear Bess: June 17, 1936

Your letter came this morning and I was sure glad to get it. I did not write you yesterday because I couldn't get a chance. It was a hectic day, so we are even. Oscar and Elsie came and got the lamp and picture Monday night. I'm going out to dinner with them tonight. So is Dick Duncan. I sent all the clothes we left to the laundry, have packed up the pillow, all the silk comforts are there and so is everything else. The people who stayed there broke the crystal lamp in Margaret's room and I'll have to spend four or five dollars for another one but at that I'm twenty dollars to the good. Should I recommend Grace Rowe to the Kansas City school board? She wrote me a letter asking for an endorsement. I am rather hesitant about giving any endorsements unless the one endorsed can make good. The board would probably give the job, and then if she didn't make good they'd blame me. If you say she is all right, I'll endorse her. . . . I'm working my head off trying to clean up. Hope you keep on writing. I wrote you a silly letter last night and tore it up.

Kiss the *baby*,
Harry

Washington, D.C.

Dear Bess: June 20, 1936

This day starts right anyway—there was a letter when I came down. I got a lamp, or Bud did rather, at Woodward's for five dollars. I think I told you that it was crystal and not glass. Of course a cheap one couldn't break. Nettie says she thinks the wind blew it off the little table by Margaret's bed. They were using it for a reading lamp. The one on the head of the bed was out. My opinion is that they or Nettie knocked it over. But I'm nineteen dollars ahead anyway. We got the table down here yesterday; so now everything is here but the radio. Shall I leave it here as your mother told me to? Hope you found some clothes you liked, and that it's not too hot. . . .

Kiss Margie, love to you,
Harry

Senator Truman was in Philadelphia to attend the Democratic National Convention.

[The Majestic, Philadelphia, Pa.]

Dear Bess: Monday [June 22, 1936]

Yesterday was a dull day until I arrived here and got Miss Margie's telegram. I had no letter from you, which of course was a great disappointment. But I suppose every man hopes he's a hero to his child and I'm no exception. It was a nice telegram.

Bud and Mr. Helm came up with me in the Plymouth. I had so much baggage I didn't want to come on the train. It took me all morning to pack up and get out of the flat. It was a good thing I had all the grips I did. It was like moving an actor and all his costumes. How would you like for me to just go and get a house and take a chance on ever getting out on it? I'm sick of this two-time move every year and we'd be no worse off. It costs more than we get for the stay in Washington no matter what we do, and that rent if we were smart enough could be an investment. Kiss my sweet child.

Love to you,

Harry

[The Majestic, Philadelphia, Pa.]

Dear Bess: June 22, 1936

. . . It was a pleasure to hear of Margaret going to the Baptist Sunday school. She ought to go to one every Sunday—I mean *a* Sunday school. If a child is instilled with good morals and taught the value of the precepts laid down in Exodus 20 and Matthew 5, 6 and 7, there is not much to worry about in after years. It makes no difference what brand is on the Sunday school. Kiss *my* baby.

Love to you,

Harry

Bennett Clark's drinking, mentioned below, made Truman even more irritated that the President gave Clark the Missouri patronage—for Clark paid little attention to his Senate duties.

[The Majestic, Philadelphia, Pa.]

Dear Bess: June 25, 1936

. . . Myra asked me if Bennett was the only one in the family who took spiritus frumenti. Apparently there must have been cause for the question. Now that's nothing but just plain gossip, and I'm not in the habit of telling it to you or anyone else.

There is only one paper here that is nice to us. All the rest are violently against the administration. They have drawn out the meeting for two days too many. That's to pay Philadelphia back its $250,000 by letting merchants and hotels take wartime toll from us. I guess it's all right but the delegates have a right to growl about it because they had to come. Idle spectators should take their medicine.

Hope to see you *very* soon. Would you mind looking over my army shirts and things and get Mr. Leach to press them in the usual way, with three creases down the back and two in front—cotton ones and wool too? I must be out of reach as nearly as I can until after the primary. I've had at least ten invitations to speak at picnics. Kiss my baby and lots of love to you both. Wish I could see you. No one has taken a drink in my room yet.

Harry

[The Majestic, Philadelphia, Pa.]

Dear Bess: June 26, 1936

Your good letter came yesterday just as I was leaving for New York to see the eye doctor. It made the day perfect, if one can be that way in either New York or Philadelphia. I am glad Natalie is improving. It was too bad you missed Mamma and Mary. I wish they had been home.

The eye man is a real one. He gave me the works without drops and I believe will fix me up. I tremble however to think what it will cost me. I must go back Tuesday for the final and I guess I'd better do it. I can hardly see to read any more and it looks as if he can make me see better anyway. One of the Mills was in having his boy examined and he had three offices and three nurses going, but took time to visit with me. He's Harry Jobes' brother-in-law on his wife's side and looks like Cochran when Cochran was his largest around.

Well you'll get this on the great day and I'll be away again. I think I said last year I'd never do it again, but the devil has a hand in most things. Do you seriously regret that action seventeen years ago when you promised to "love, honor and obey"? I know that you have had a difficult time sometimes, particularly when the income wouldn't and doesn't meet the outgo, and I sometimes wish I'd gone after things like other men in my position would have but I guess I'm still fool enough to like honor more. I hope you believe I'm right.

The only regret I have about today (the twenty-eighth) is that it didn't happen in 1905 instead of 1919. You were, are, and always will be the best, most beautiful, and sweetest *girl* on earth.

Kiss Margie,
Harry

Washington, D.C.

Dear Bess: Sunday, June 28 [1936]

I was so lonesome last night I just had to spend four dollars to call you up. If I'd stayed in Philly, it would have cost me five for a hotel and I'd gotten wet besides. The *New York Times* said this morning that everyone got soaked but they stayed anyway, 105,000 of them, to hear and see the President and Cactus Jack. That's a real tribute. His speech was a masterpiece I think. The convention was like all such gatherings, just one grand yell from start to finish, and in order to find out what went on it was necessary to read the papers or go down to a hotel and listen to the radio. You couldn't tell what was happening by being on the floor. I was there every day and every night except Thursday night. When they nominated Roosevelt I left after an hour. Jim Pendergast got the leg of his pants ripped down the front on a railing during the demonstration. Luckily he had another pair—it was a Ted Marks suit. I went to bed early Friday night, got up at 5:00 A.M. real time, and drove down here. Cleaned up the pressing mail and slept all afternoon, called you up, and then went to bed. I've been cleaning off my desk this morning. Have two wastebaskets full of "important" paper to throw away.

I hope you are enjoying the day. It's just about as hot here as it was in Independence June 28, 1919. I wish I had a gray-checked suit to celebrate in, but I haven't so put on a white one. There is no special prize for seventeen years of married life that I could discover, so you'll have to make out without any. I'd like to be there to take you out to dinner though. Lots of water has gone under the bridge since then. War heroes are no longer that. They are now looked upon as a sort of nuisance and are considered fools to have gone. Clark made the statement that if his pa had been President, there'd have been no war at all. Oh well!

I think my sweetheart is better looking today than ever, if that is possible, and you know it is not fashionable now to think that of the same one. Please kiss Margie and I hope I get that letter tomorrow. It wasn't in the mail this morning.

Love to you and I hope for at least seventeen more.

Harry

Summer camp, as the Senator relates below, was a vacation from Washington—if "having a wonderful time" indeed meant that.

Ft. Riley, Kans.

Dear Bess: July 6, 1936

I called you last night and talked to Fred. He said he'd tried to postpone the call until you got home but I insisted on putting it through. Of course I'm sorry I didn't get to talk to you, but I can't be lucky every time. Anyway the charge was reversed because they wouldn't accept long-distance calls at the camp. I had to pull my sensational prerogative to get it through at all.

I had dinner with Father Tiernan last night and then called on the post commandant. He'd called on me in the afternoon. His name is Mayo and he's an Englishman who was educated at Eton, came to U.S. when he was eighteen, and now commands the post while General Henry is in Germany with the Olympic team. Father Tiernan wants you and Margie to stay with him when you come out a week from Wednesday. He has a beautiful apartment and the nicest middle-aged lady for a housekeeper. If you want to do it, it will help the Padre here on the post and will be perfectly all right.

I'm having a wonderful time. They have given me a private mount and an orderly to take care of it. I couldn't ask for anything better. Henninger is here and they all seem glad to have me with them. You know I like it.

Don't forget to write. I called yesterday and wrote today. Kiss my baby.

Love to you,

Harry

[Washington, D.C.]

Dear Bess: Tuesday, January 4, 1937

Well I've gone and done it. I missed writing you both Sunday and Monday. You should however give me credit for J. K. Vardaman's call, a wire from

Cincinnati, and a phone call on Sunday night. The facts are that I can't find anything and I can't get to my desk. All day yesterday the telephone men were working on it and this morning another phone man is doing it all over. I'm sitting at Bud's desk now waiting for a chance to get to mine. But I sure will have a grand office when I get through. There are two rooms as big as my old private office, both with fireplaces, and two other rooms the size of the girls' room in the old office. There is also a storeroom for books and stationery. The building manager has been exceptionally nice to me. I wish you and Margie were here to help me enjoy it. . . .

I'll not miss any more this weekend. Then I'm going to make you a proposition. Kiss Margie and I hope for a letter.

Love to you,
Harry

Washington, D.C.]

Dear Bess: January 5, 1935 [1937]

Well here is an invitation from Mrs. Roosevelt. You are supposed to be there on January 13. I *want you to be* present. I am going out with Vic tonight to get an apartment at the Kennedy-Warren. If I get it, I'll call you and then come after you.

I just can't stand it without you. If we are poorer than church mice, what difference does it make? There is only one thing on earth that counts with me and that is you and Margie.

Love to you,
Harry

The opening of a new Senate session evidently reminded Truman of his induction into the Upper House two years before; below he notes an incorrect procedure that he would not have recognized two years earlier.

Washington, D.C.

Dear Bess: January 6, 1937

Well I got a letter this morning and things look somewhat brighter. You may get a phone call from me to come at once because I'm about to rent an apartment at the Kennedy-Warren for the season. It has two bedrooms, two baths, a large living room, and good kitchen and half a dining room—with gas and lights furnished—and I'm offering $150 per month for it. If I get it, you had just as well start packing and I'll be after you Sunday. You just don't know how lonesome it is when I think you're not coming at all. I am enclosing you a letter from Mr. Harris which was opened by mistake and one from Margie's school which was opened on purpose.

Hope you get your invitation to lunch with Mrs. President. I thought maybe you'd be here in time to go if I get the apartment.

We opened up yesterday with all the pomp and circumstance that the

Senate can stir up. The only stir was caused when Senator Neely walked down by himself, and the two Florida Senators tried to maneuver for seniority. They swore 'em both in at once, so Florida has no senior Senator.

Love to you both,
Harry

[Washington, D.C.]

Dear Bess: January 7, 1937
   . . . The old sun of a gun who owned that apartment or the lease on it would not let me have it. His wife would, but he only wanted to let it for three months and $200 rent. I am sure she would have let me have it for $150 and six months, in fact she said as much. Whenever I do run into one you are coming if it is April 1. I never was so disappointed because I thought I had it. Even sent you a description of it. I've been spending today cleaning up. They fixed me up a nice sitting room next to my office and even moved in an icebox. It belonged to the nurse across the hall and she put a crepe ribbon around it when they moved it in to me.
   I thought I'd lost your picture but found it very carefully put away in the bottom drawer. Wouldn't that have been a calamity. The note you sent with it to Ft. Sill is in the back of it. ["You didn't expect me in Ft. Sill so soon, did you? I'm depending on this to take you to France and back—all safe and sound. Bess."] Well I'm about to cry, so you kiss Margie.

Harry

Washington, D.C.

Dear Bess: January 8, 1937
   No letter today. I guess it must have been stopped by sleet or cold wave. Your telegram rather unseated me. I was under the impression that if I found a bargain in a place to stay, you would still come. Was talking to Nate Bachman today and he said Mrs. B. called him and told him she had bought a burro and he asked her what she did that for when she had plenty of horses, and she told him that her inclination was to buy a jackass because he'd been away so much. He found out that she was getting it for her grandbaby. Maybe I'm in the jackass class. . . .
   I wish you were here. Kiss Margie.

Love to you,
Harry

Washington, D.C.

Dear Bess: Sunday, January 10, 1937
   Well no letter today. I had one yesterday and none the day before. I'm enclosing a check for Miss Margaret Truman, even if she didn't write or say boo this week to her dad.

Put on my soup and fish last night and went to the naval reserve officers' dinner. We sold Walsh and some Republican Congressmen, Dirksen of Illinois, Moss of Minnesota, Church of Illinois, and Scott Lucas a Democrat of Illinois. It was a rather boresome affair and I got home at ten o'clock and went to bed. Have been over here at the office since nine o'clock getting more straightening up done. Mr. Trimble was in to see me. He is head of F.H.A. in Kansas City. Mr. Henderson just called me and I'm going out there for dinner. They still seem to want me. It is always nice out there. Then I have to go to Guffey's for a lot of hooey and to bed about nine I guess.

I am working on a speech on safety but don't know whether I'll ever deliver it or not. I've about come to the conclusion that nothing will happen to my bill no matter what I do. I've been politicking around among the Senators and Congressmen, distributing a little hootch where it would do the most good, and trying to find out what they think of Bennett Champ Clark for President. Impression is pretty favorable, especially since he is on the wagon again.

I got old Glass to take me off the District Appropriations Subcommittee because I don't care what happens to Washington. It can fall in the Potomac for all I care. I'm going on the Military Subcommittee. I've about decided I'm for war anyway. At least if I had to be away from home, I'd have some men to look after. Kiss Margie and write when you can.

Harry

Washington, D.C.

Dear Bess: January 12, 1937

Well it's all here, the mail I mean, and I guess you were too busy to write me Monday, or Sunday I guess would be the day today's letter should have been written. I have been very busy today going over a tremendous mail and trying to get my judge matter straightened out with Clark. It looks as if we'll get it done tomorrow or next day, probably the day after that. You know how the potential presidential candidate keeps his appointments. One at 10:00 A.M. means about 4:00 P.M. two days afterwards. He's been sober for two whole days though, and we may get it done.

Went to dinner for the Legion National Commander last night and saw a dozen or so Senators and as many Congressmen. Jim Farley was sitting in the lobby at the hotel (the Mayflower) talking to Senator Bailey [J. W. Bailey of North Carolina], who as you know is the most pompous and big-headed senator next to old Walsh of Massachusetts. Maybe I lack dignity. . . .

Write when you can. Kiss Margie and love to you.

Harry

Roosevelt's second inauguration caused Truman some difficulty. As he relates below, he was short of tickets to the ceremonies; Governor Stark had brought a trainload of Missourians expecting tickets.

Washington, D.C.
Dear Bess: January 18, 1937
     Most happy to get your and Margaret's letters on the first mail this morning.
I like your ritzy stationery, except for its size. It does not hold enough. I am being
terribly besieged for tickets to the President's show, and I've just received a list
of Stark's trainload and have been tearing my hair ever since. There won't be half
of them at the show because we can't fit 'em in. Otto Higgins, Powell Grover,
Henry McElroy, Jr., Bill Kitchen, Dick Nacy are all on the train and every
bloomin' one of 'em will want a ticket. Well it's just too bad. They'll have to get
mad I guess. I gave O'Malley and will give Roger two apiece, gave Mrs. Griggs
one and Mrs. Henderson two, gave Mrs. Boone one and Mrs. Swofford one, and
you can see what I have left. You know I had to buy thirty-three dollars worth
of tickets to the Missouri Society affair. Every member of the delegation had to
do that and then they gave us a box. Mrs. Swofford and Vic's and Bud's wives
are going to help me take care of my fifteen colonels at the ball. Now aren't you
sorry you're not here? I wish most sincerely I wasn't. I'm glad you told me what
you sent each of the newlyweds.
     I'd have come home this Saturday if it were not for the ice on the mountains
and the floods in Indiana and Ohio. I'll slip up on you one of these days before
you know it.
                              Kiss Margie, love to you,
                                   Harry

                                                                      [Washington, D.C.]
Dear Bess: January 26, 1937
     Well this day is right. Bud brought me a letter to Wheeler's committee and
I read it while Mr. Whitney—*the* Mr. Whitney, [former] president of the New
York Stock Exchange—was telling what he thought of taking one thousand
shares of Allegheny Corporation at twenty dollars per share when it was selling
at thirty-five dollars when he was passing on its listing on the New York Stock
Exchange. He had a very difficult time. I felt rather sorry for him but he was
wrong. The movies notified me that the pictures of the Missouri people here last
week would be shown for my benefit at Keith's next week, so I can decide for
myself whether to go to Hollywood. Tell Margie that the Vice President sent me
a fine picture of himself for her all autographed to her by him. I'll send it to her.
     Ed McKim left yesterday afternoon after having what he claimed was a
grand visit. I'm glad Roger and all of 'em enjoyed themselves. Joe Clements and
Polly Compton were in to see me yesterday. I took 'em to lunch and I think they
enjoyed it. Burke, who is sitting beside me while I write this, says his daughter
is much better.
     We have been listening to various things in the Senate. The new Louisiana
Senator made a speech on foreign bonds. Guffey made a speech on the courts.
He wants to investigate the writers of the *Nine Old Men.*
                              Kiss Margie and keep writing,
                                   Harry

Pennsylvania train, no. 30 to Washington

Dear Bess: February 1, 1937

It was good to hear your voice last night, but not half as good as really seeing and talking to you—even if my combination of words makes you sick sometimes. I'm a clown and a fool but I've never cared much how words were combined if their meaning happened to be honest and sincere, and that is all words are for. Maybe you don't know it, but I'd rather lose a hand or have an eye pulled out than make you a moment's suffering or hurt—either mentally or physically. I've seen so much difficulty caused by sheer unthoughtfulness that I've tried all my life to be thoughtful and to make every person I come in contact with happier for having seen me. Maybe that's silly too. I don't know. I've never paid any attention to what people here said about me and very little to what they say to me, because most people only mean about half they say.

Well, the sun has been shining all afternoon, although it snowed all fore-noon in St. Louis. The B.&O. canceled their 11:58 train last night and the Pennsylvania 12:30 A.M. train gets to Washington at exactly the same hour as the one that leaves at nine the next morning, so I decided to take the noon train, Spirit of St. Louis, and arrive at 9:25, two hours after the other two. The governor was most cordial, but he is going to do as he pleases—and so would I if I were in his shoes. I really believe he'll make one of Missouri's real ones. Anyway he's not a booze fighter nor is he running after the ladies. So if we don't get jobs for the faithful, maybe the state will profit anyway. He likes pomp and circumstance and maybe that's all there is to any of it. The train is rough.

Kiss Margie, love to you,

Harry

Washington, D.C.

Dear Bess: February 6, 1937

I'm glad you received my train letter. It was a long time getting there. You should have all by now. I'm afraid I was rather maudlin in the train letter. I'd had a great deal of Scotch and soda just before lunch with a gentleman who was very much interested in the Senate. But I meant it anyway. . . .

Hope you are all well and happy. Kiss Margie and keep writing.

Love to you,

Harry

John W. Snyder, with whom Truman visited Gettysburg, was a long-time fellow officer at summer camp; years later he became Secretary of the Treasury in the Truman administration.

Washington, D.C.

Dear Bess: February 7, 1937

Well I've walked up some five or six hundred steps with John Snyder reviewing the battle of Gettysburg, and we had a grand time doing it. When we arrived back in Washington about five o'clock I refused to have dinner with either or both Jake and him, coming on down to the office and looking over the mail, then getting stamps, envelopes and stationery and coming over to the hotel with a certainty in my mind that a special would be in the box. Well it wasn't! I guess there must have been a slip-up somewhere and I'll probably get two tomorrow.

John and Jake agree with me that Marse Robert had insurmountable difficulties at Gettysburg and that the Almighty was on the side of Meade just as he was at Waterloo with Wellington. We read Freeman's description, studied the maps, and by every rule of military maneuver, Lee should have won. Vardaman didn't go with us but we let him in on the discussion. It looks as if John would get Jake's job. He's going to work for a St. Louis bank at some $25,000 per year. So I'll have to tell Mr. Roosevelt he doesn't want on the Federal Reserve Board. I feel like kicking him but I don't blame him. Snyder advises me to study law and finance and get myself a job like it. Maybe I can but I doubt it. I'm too much enamoured of the Sermon on the Mount to be a good banker.

Kiss Margie. I hope I get two tomorrow.

Love and repeat indefinitely,
Harry

Washington, D.C.

Dear Bess: February 10, 1937

I didn't accept the Lucky [Strike] offer. Wouldn't my friends, who know my love for cigarettes, have a grand time wondering how much it takes to buy me. I'm glad you are all well, so am I and I expect to stay that way. I'm going to Oscar and Elsie's for dinner tonight. There has been considerable flu here but it doesn't seem to be the fatal kind. You'll get a small package from Mr. Julius Garfinckel's along about Saturday, your seventy-second birthday or maybe it's your thirty-second—I haven't kept very close count on it. It would make no difference if it were your one hundred and fifty-second—to me you'd still be the prettiest, sweetest, best, and all the other adjectives girl on earth—in heaven or in the waters under the earth. You were not only Juno, Venus, Minerva all in one but perhaps Proserpina too. (You'd better look that one up.)

Anyway I never had but one from the time I was six and a half to date—and maybe that's more foolishness according to modern standards, but I'm crazy enough to stay with it through all eternity.

Kiss Margie, love to you,
Harry

[Senate Chamber]

Dear Bess: February 11, 1937

You should get this February 13 and I hope it will be a happy, sunny day. I almost came home. The sun is shining beautifully here and then I saw in the paper that it is frozen up out there again and I gave up the idea. I could have taken the train but the least I can do it for would be over one hundred dollars and we need those dollars too much. So I sent you a little present. Mrs. Messall advised me on it and I hope you like it.

I played hookey from the Appropriations Committee this morning and went to the War College to hear a lecture on Robert E. Lee by Dr. Freeman. He's the man who wrote the four-volume life of Lee that John Snyder gave me. I think he gave one of the greatest talks I ever heard.

I wish I could talk to you about putting our daughter's picture in the paper. Of course I'm complimented and proud that they should want to, but will it have any undesirable effect upon her? She, I'm sure, will have all her mamma's common sense but I wouldn't like to give her a publicity complex too young. You know what happened to Mary McElroy. If you want to print it, go ahead. Your judgment in the matter is better than mine. Hope the sofa came out all right. Did you ever get my watch? I sure miss it.

Kiss my baby, love to you,
Harry

Truman favored President Roosevelt's proposal to "pack" the Supreme Court by appointing new—and presumably more liberal—justices to balance senior justices who refused to retire. The Court had been striking down New Deal legislation. Typically, however, Roosevelt did not make a frontal attack on the problem, which was the conservatism of the senior justices; instead the President claimed that the Court needed more members to handle the work. In relating his position on one of the warmest political issues of the day, Truman had to be careful not to imply a lack of support for the President. Anything he said was likely to be misconstrued.

Washington, D.C.
Dear Bess: February 12, 1937
. . . I have never changed my mind on the Court and have never made but one statement on it, and that was to the *New York Times* on Tuesday, and they printed it as I sent it and the *Star* copied it word for word. There is no use trying to straighten it out. It would only make it worse. As you know they'd like to make me out a know-nothing but I don't believe they can. Hope you had a nice birthday. Where is Margie's letter? Kiss her anyway.

Love to you,
Harry

Washington, D.C.
Dear Bess: February 13, 1937
Happy birthday! and I hope you have at least fifty more. I wanted to be there so badly to help you celebrate I don't know how to express it. If your new dress doesn't fit you, send it back and we'll get a *larger* one.

I'm glad you went to Mrs. Strickler's luncheon for Mrs. Boxley. I rather think it is better to pay no attention to the childish actions of people anyway.

The more I watch the behavior of my colleague, the more I'm impressed with the necessity of that attitude. He is so thoroughly impressed with his importance and dignity that he is continually offending people and continually being offended. It will be very hard for him at home next time even with all of us for him if some smart campaigner comes out against him. It might wake him up though if someone did. He is against the President on the Court issue, as was to be expected. I honestly believe that this issue will split both the old parties, and I'm of the opinion that this is what F.D.R. wants. He, you know, reads a lot of history and I think would like to be a Monroe, Jackson, and Lincoln all in one—and is probably succeeding. Only history will tell.

Well more good wishes. Kiss Margie.

Love to you,
Harry

Tom Pendergast's legal problems were well-publicized at this time. The disrespectful letters that Senator Truman here tells Bess about were perhaps a result of his association with the Boss.

Washington, D.C.

Dear Bess: Sunday, February 21 [1937]

I waited in vain for a letter today and so I am late getting this one off. The mail gets heavier and heavier. It's worse than the Wheeler-Rayburn Bill. The nasty things that some of my "friends" have said to me rather hurts sometimes. For instance old man Porter, president of the [Kansas City] Power and Light, wrote me the most patronizing letter you ever saw. I burned him to a cinder and mailed it while it was hot. I also let one of my country newspapermen have both barrels, and he came back with the sweetest letter you ever saw. . . .

Kiss Margie, love to you,
Harry

[Washington, D.C.]

Dear Bess: February 25, 1937

Was glad to get your Tuesday letter this morning. Mr. Southern of course is against the President. He always has been. Whenever labor and hours come up he's against labor and for unlimited hours. My father was the same way. They honestly believe that every man ought to have to work from daylight to dark and that the boss ought to have all the profit. My sympathies have been all the other way, and that is the reason for my lack of worldly goods. I just can't cheat in a trade or browbeat a worker. Maybe I'm crazy but so is the Sermon on the Mount if I am. . . .

Please *take care* of yourself.

Love to you, kiss Margie,
Harry

Washington, D.C.
Dear Bess: February 26, 1937

Well no letter today. I sat up and read the debates in the Constitutional Convention of 1787 last night. It was in terrible print and I have a headache today, both from the print and the debates.

I am getting some awfully dirty letters from some of my constituents but I don't care. Some of them are funny and some of 'em need a punch in the nose. But I suppose that is part of the game. When everything is over and done with we'll wonder why we were so wrought up about it. I'm going to vote for the increase regardless of what they say about it. It is my opinion however that it won't reach a vote. Some sort of compromise will be reached I think where some of the Court will retire and we'll vote on an amendment. They have just sent me another carload of books from the Library of Congress. Time I wade through them I'll either know it all or I won't know anything.

Hope I get a letter before the day is over. Here are some things you may be interested in.

Love to you, kiss Margie,
Harry

[Washington, D.C.]
Dear Bess: Thursday, April 1, 1937

The Governor General of Canada just came in and we had to adjourn for ten minutes while we let him make a speech. That isn't often done by the Senate you know. Only members, ex-members, members of the House, and governors of states have the privilege of the floor, so we recessed and let the Canadian governor in. The old Vice President had on his negro preacher coat, but he stuttered over the word excellency when he made the introduction.

Nate Bachman, McAdoo, Chavez, and Stewart McDonald were in his office for a good reason about noon, and Nate asked the Vice President what he was wearing his shadbelly coat for. A shad, you know, is white underneath. He said Mrs. G. laid it out for him and he had to put it on or not wear any and he could not come in his shirt sleeves.

The governor was a real Limey. He made a very good speech, and then we all walked around and shook his hand. Then he left. We're trying to pass the Guffey Bill and I hope it'll be done by night.

No letter today. I'm still looking for it.

Kiss Margey, love to you,
Harry

Dear Bess: [Washington, D.C., Apr. 5, 1937]

Was sure glad to get your two-tone letter—it looked very nice. I thought sure you had run out of ink and then used your heart's blood to let me know how much you loved me and then you told me it was just another brand of ink. I was glad to get the clipping. It has created quite a furor, mostly "roar" upstairs.

I sent Mrs. Luxich a check for $2.27. After adding the light bill to the gas bill and deducting $3.00 that was what was left. I suppose Elsie will embarrass me Wednesday night when I have dinner with them by telling me she expects to add to the population of the country. Well I'll congratulate her. I'm always for the new arrivals. It's one of our principal reasons for being here I think. Some thousand generations from now we may arrive at perfection. . . .

I did forget to put a special on your Friday letter but you ought to have had two today. Frederick M. Smith is here today. Had lunch with him. He is a very brainy man. You'll wonder how he can be and still believe his Book of Mormon, but he is.

Wish we could listen to *Lohengrin* again. Kiss Margey. Love to you and don't miss any more days writing.

Harry

Washington, D.C.

Dear Bess: April 6, 1937

I surely appreciated your wire but I'd already made up my mind not to wear a blue shirt. I went down to Garfinckel's and bought me a new collar and tie, so I ought to be in the right fix. I'd be happy if an earthquake or a fire or something would make it impossible for me to get there, but no such things ever happen when they are badly needed.

I am very sorry I forgot to put that special delivery stamp on the Friday letter. I won't forget again. Had dinner and a most pleasant conversation with Dr. Smith last night. He gave me an exact duplicate of George Washington's penknife, which he had purchased at Alexandria Lodge. I was very pleased with it. I gave him a new penny for it.

Had lunch with Bill Hicks today and he said he'd had a pleasant conversation with you over the phone. I've been having a grand time at my subcommittee meeting. McKellar and Wheeler had a tilt today, as well as the P.O. and the Interstate Commerce Commission. Maybe we'll get the truth after a while.

Kiss Margie and love to you,
Harry

When the pressures of Senate routine and Missouri politics mounted, Truman worried about his health—sleeping, eating—and relates below the first of several trips to an army hospital in Arkansas.

[Park Hotel] Hot Springs, Ark.

Dear Bess: Saturday, September 11, 1937

I arrived at nine-thirty this morning after a seventy-mile drive over a very rough road. You should have been along. It was over a mountain range and the most beautiful scenery. Goes through Ouachita National Forest. So you see I got to Ouachita even if it is spelled in a peculiar manner.

Have a beautiful room at the Park Hotel for $3 a day, tub and shower, a big fan, and everything but a radio, and I can live without that I guess. It would cost me at least $4.50 for the same thing at the Arlington and I believe it's cooler. This is a beautiful day and I wish you were all here. If you and Margie were along, I'd be fixed in good shape.

I didn't know I was so tired. Slept until noon at Tulsa and went to bed at seven and slept until seven at Russellville. I'm not going to visit the hospital until Monday—after some more sleep and then I know they'll find nothing.

Kiss my girl and write me a letter, because if I'm not discovered I'm going to stay a week. Love to you both and remember me to all the family.

Harry

Hot Springs, Ark.

Dear Bess: Wednesday, September 15 [1937]

I thought sure I'd get a letter today but I was doomed to disappointment. It was a very great pleasure to talk to you last night, however, and I hope you do it again tomorrow. Today was my busy day. I got up at six-thirty, had breakfast at seven-thirty, a blood test at eight, throat and nose at nine; eyes at nine-thirty, and a real Hot Springs bath at ten. They really do it scientifically here. Then I had a tooth exam at eleven-thirty. They are going to X-ray tomorrow and give me another eye test. There is a very fine eye man here and he seems to be very much interested in getting me properly fixed. My astigmatic axis has changed again and he says that *may* cause the headaches.

They are really feeding me. I was half starved too I reckon, but I'm eating all they give me now and it's plenty. It surely is a place to rest, and they treat me like a king.

Had another picture show tonight—Lily Pons in *The Girl from Paris.* It was good too. Then Congressman Crosser and three army colonels and myself talked until ten o'clock settling all the country's ills. I'm writing this in bed. Kiss Margie.

Love to you—call me,
Harry

Hot Springs, Ark.

Dear Bess: Monday, September 20, 1937

It sure was a pleasure to get your special yesterday. I have not had a before-breakfast walk since I came here last Monday. They are always doing something to me by seven o'clock, so I don't get a chance. I have to go to the lab for another and more elaborate blood test this morning. I saw all the doctors yesterday and told them I'd have to leave Thursday morning and it was O.K. I am not yet on a diet and it looks as if I won't be. There are only two more tests and then I'll be reported sound in mind and limb and salable on any block.

We took a drive yesterday and didn't get a chance to write you. They organized a penny-ante game on the fourth floor and asked for amateurs. I reported and by nine o'clock, quitting time, I had not only learned how to play but had $1.25 of their funds. Funny how easy it is to learn some things and how hard others. For instance, I've been trying to memorize the preamble to the Constitution and can't. Kiss Margie. Sorry she didn't get to Colorado. Guess I won't see you either until Friday. Love to you. Writing this at 6:30 A.M.

                                                        Harry

                                                        Hot Springs, Ark.
Dear Bess: September 21, 1937
    It was a pleasure indeed to get two letters from you this morning, but it was a disappointment when you didn't come down. Hope the family decide to drive down. I'll be leaving here Thursday A.M. and will be home Friday sometime. My teeth are 100 percent. No extractions necessary; heart all right; and so is every-thing else. Will hear from the complete blood test tomorrow. Dieting is over-board. That was principally the difficulty—starvation. The rest has been just what was needed. The staff here know their business and they have no reason for fooling me. I've about made up my mind to do it once a year. They say I should have twenty-one baths for a full course. I'll get eight and I'll say they are the real thing.
    What has happened to the writing arm of a certain young lady who calls me dad? She didn't even acknowledge my communication enclosing check for a stated amount. Is she sick or just sleeping?
    Hope you can come down. Love to you.
                                                        Sincerely,
                                                        Harry

                                                        [Hotel New Yorker, New York City]
Dear Bess: October 29, 1937
    You'll wonder what I'm doing in New York. Well I had a date to see T. J. Sunday and Colonel Littlejohn, post quartermaster of West Point who was at Hot Springs with me and asked me to come up to the game tomorrow. Virginia Military Institute is to play the army at the Point, so I'm going. Mr. Stark, and Mr. Clark, and cotton, corn, etc. will have to worry along without me. For once I'm doing what I want to and not what I ought to. I got here at seven-thirty, called both T. J. and the colonel, and now I am going to bed and get one good night's sleep.
    You know what made me write instead of wire? Well I turned on the noon radio and the Cities Service hour was going over W.E.A.F. A couple of kids were singing "They'll Never Believe Me" from the *Girl from Utah,* and I sat here and thought of another couple of kids listening to Julia Sanderson and Donald Brian singing that beautiful melody and lovely sentiment, and I wished so badly for the other kid that I had to write her to sort of dry my eyes. I hope you remember. I'll never forget it. And I wish you were here with your second edition and we'd

all go to a show instead of going to bed and I probably would disappoint both T. J. and the colonel.

I needed something to sort of relieve my nerves anyway. It has been a most trying and patience-straining week. I wanted to punch the witnesses rather than question them because they'd robbed and abused a great property and a lot of the "widows and orphans" you hear so much about. I really had to verbally pulverize the ringleader yesterday. New York papers had my picture on the financial page and really gave me a nice write-up. Even Mr. Hearst gave me the best of it. So I'm calming down somewhat.

Kiss Margey and I wish I could kiss you,

Harry

Washington, D.C.

Dear Bess: November 6, 1937

Well the letter came late-mail yesterday. I was glad to get the clipping about the governor and the election board. Rather glad you did not go to Bill Duke's tea if you felt you could get away without driving into a post. Hope you don't get a cold. I haven't had a headache until yesterday, and that wasn't caused by any overwork here but because I'd mixed things up so for the thirteenth. I certainly need a guardian. I had a letter from Vivian about the opening of the water plant in Washington Township, I had promised him I'd come and talk about county planning, etc., so as to give the section a boost. He's worked so hard on it and it may mean that we could get a buyer for that two hundred acres and save the farm, which as you know is my greatest worry because of Mamma. She knows nothing of the extremity to which the mortgage holders have been pressing us for payment. In fact when Vivian and I went to see them last when I was at home they told us point-blank if something wasn't done by December 1 they'd take over. Well I'm afraid it would kill her and I want to keep her alive as long as I can. . . .

I've certainly been raising hell in that committee. They had rumors in New York papers that Wheeler was not behind me. I wired him and he told me he is for me and to let 'em have it, and I have. It's rather a wearing job though.

Kiss Margey, love to you,

Harry

Washington, D.C.

Dear Bess: Sunday, November 7, 1937

Well I'd hoped to be on the road home today but I'm not only here but it looks like I'll be tied here until Thursday night. This so-called committee work is nothing but drudgery and publicity, all so depressing sometimes. I'm not so sure that even after I've aired all the Missouri Pacific dirty linen that anything but another chance to dirty some more will come of it. You can't change human greed for money in a committee. The money hogs control the counting, and there's no use trying to keep 'em from it. All we can do is to make the yoke as easy as possible.

It was nice to talk to you last night, only I wish I'd been there instead of a thousand miles away. Your and Margaret's special came promptly this morning just as I was leaving the hotel for a walk. I'll send Catherine downtown for the hair nets. I wish you and Margey were here. . . . Hope to see you before long.

Love to you,
Harry

Washington, D.C.
November 9, 1937

Dear Bess:

Your Saturday letter came at noon yesterday and I was sure glad to get it when I got back from the hearings. I sure want to go to a picture show or two with you and Margey but this devilish hearing is getting really into a bog. We had Mr. George Whitney and S. Parker Gilbert before us yesterday. Mr. Whitney is very much inclined to feel his position. He came to my office at about a quarter to ten and told me what he was going to do. I simply asked him who the chairman of the committee happened to be and he immediately dismounted and went along like a gentleman. . . .

If I quit this thing now, they'll say that Kemper and the Boss pulled me off, and I'm going to go through with it if I don't get home at all. It is a mess and has created a terrible furor in New York. Guaranty Trust and J. P. Morgan have used every means available to make me quit. I'm going to finish the job or die in the attempt. I sure hate it but you can see where I am.

Kiss Margey, love to you,
Harry

Washington, D.C.
November 20, 1937

Dear Bess:

The mail was all right this morning. *The* letter was there. I'm sure sorry to hear about Dr. Wilson. Hope he can come out of it. I'm glad you sent flowers to Henry Chiles. It is certainly too bad that those boys have to lose a good mother. Whatever you get for Mrs. Gardelli will be all right. You know more about how these things ought to be done than I'll ever learn. I'm glad that Margaret enjoyed her dancing school. I guess the reason boys are so scarce is that boys haven't changed much. A team of horses couldn't have gotten me pulled into one when I was the age of those boys, and I was considered rather below par by most of my associates at that.

Eddie Jacobson came in yesterday and I took him to lunch. We organized a tenth-of-a-cent poker game last night and rolled him of fifty cents and Vic of fifty-four cents. If it hadn't been 10 percent settlement you can see where that decimal point would have been. Everybody had a good time, went home sober at eleven oclock, and Eddie and I are waiting for breakfast at the office now. The lunchroom does not open until eight-thirty.

I'm going to Baltimore today to get my picture made for the movies in the Martin bomber [see postscript] that's going to Russia. They are not going to fly it. Hope you haven't frozen. I see it is 16 out there today.

Kiss Margie, love to you,

Harry

It's a passenger plane not a bomber, the Washington *Post* says.

Washington, D.C.

November 21, 1937

Dear Bess:

Well this is a beautiful, cold Sunday morning. If you and Margey were present, it would be perfect. For some reason which I can't explain I slept until nine-fifteen, although I went to bed at ten. Maybe it was because I was out in the air most of yesterday.

We were supposed to leave here at nine o'clock but for some reason—really a headache from the night before I think—Al Holland didn't show up until ten-thirty. We got to the Glenn Martin plant at noon and the picture men were just on the point of leaving because they were afraid we weren't coming. I went through the factory with the general manager and saw a lot of planes under construction for the Dutch East India Company and the government of the Argentine.

The one we went to see was out in the back yard. Its wing spread is 157 ft., body 91 ft. long, and it's 20 ft. high, has four 1,000-hp. motors, and will go 225 mi. per hour. It can go 5,000 miles on one fill-up and will carry twenty-six people and several thousand pounds of freight and mail. Russia owns it, and it cost them $750,000. It weighs 63,000 pounds. We had a grand time, ended up with lunch at the Belvedere in Baltimore. Got back here at six and called you at seven. Glad I didn't miss you. Here's Mrs. Black's letter. Thought it was an invitation—I opened it. Here's a wedding invitation. I don't know him very well but he was on my campaign committee from Ruby Ganett's office.

Kiss Margey, love to you,

Harry

Washington, D.C.

November 24, 1937

Dear Bess:

I had a nice letter from Margey today and none from her mamma. I waited until nine-fifteen this evening hoping I'd still get one and I thought once I'd go on to bed and not write. I was so lonesome I took a fool notion to go to a picture show—the first one I've been to since we went to the Midland and sat up in the heaven [balcony]. It was Leslie Howard and Bette Davis in *It's Love I'm After* and it is a scream. Well after I'd laughed my blue spell off I just came back to the office and here's your letter.

We've been on the Farm Bill all day—Pope taking up all the time explaining its constitutionality, etc. I presided part of the time and no rows took place. Burke, Minton, Halsey, and several more are all going to the football game Saturday. We're going on the train. Canfil called and said he'd come and go with me. Ten to one he doesn't show up. I gave Vic two of my tickets. I get four now being on the Military Appropriations. Vic asked me out to eat turkey tomorrow —so did Elsie but I'd already promised Vic. She said the boy is doing very well and growing to beat the band. Mrs. Gardelli is still in the anticipation stage.

Found a tailor today who agreed to press my clothes correctly so I guess I can begin to look decent again soon. I took him three suits today. He's an old Dane down here on Pennsylvania Avenue and I believe he'll do a good job. Hope I get two letters tomorrow.

Kiss Margie, love to you,
Harry

Washington, D.C.
November 30, 1937

Dear Bess:

Well I guess you kept your threat and didn't write Sunday. No letter this morning, but I received one from Mamma in her own handwriting thanking me for her birthday letter and telling me how nice the stockings were Margaret gave her. I rented an apartment today from Mrs. Nally. We take it January 1 at $110 per month. It has a nice living room twenty-three feet long, a dining room about ten by twelve, two bedrooms, one bath, and five or six closets. You'll have to pick out your furniture after you arrive. It is a very nice place on the fourth floor. The people who took it September 15 had to leave town. It is as new and clean as if it had never been lived in before. We'll have to get a rug for the living room and maybe for one bedroom, then whatever you think you need to sit on in the living room, the balance of the dining-room furniture, twin beds for one room and a single for the other. I guess we can stay at the hotel while you're buying furniture.

Fred Canfil went home last night. He took me to O'Donnell's Sunday night after we went to the show and ordered a dozen fried oysters. I ordered a half-dozen and when he wasn't looking I put three of mine in his dish. He ate the whole fifteen, a half a head of lettuce, three or four rolls, a bottle of beer, and a cup of coffee. Said it was a pretty fair meal, although he thought he only had a dozen oysters.

Kiss Margey, love to you,
Harry

As District Attorney Milligan in Kansas City investigated the Pendergast machine, the Senator in Washington followed the proceedings with distaste, evident in this letter.

Washington, D.C.
Dear Bess: December 4, 1937

The letter came on the second mail yesterday and I hope it will do the same thing today. The lease for the apartment came this morning and I'm having Vic read the fine print. Then I'll sign and send 'em a check for January.

Was glad to get the *Star's* settlement of the Milligan matter. They seem to have the matter well in hand. But we'll see how it comes out in the end. I expect to be here as long as Mr. Shoop or Mr. Roosevelt, either. I don't know where *Life* got that picture but it wasn't one of the best. They had me in the wrong column. The newsboys in the Senate gallery make those assignments according to their own ideas and prejudices. For instance Drew Pearson called Ellender the "Kingfish's" minnow the other day. It was all uncalled for because Ellender is a good, hard-working, decent, and able Senator. Some mean, nasty remark in a column or an article gets reaction while the truth wouldn't. So there you are. The *Star* and the *Post-Dispatch* are having spasms over Milligan. Well he's a drunkard, libertine, and a grafter but he's helping them now, so he is a great man. But it will work out in the end.

Perry, Vic, Joe O'Brien and I had dinner last night at a Chinese restaurant. It was very good. Vic couldn't eat much. Mrs. Gardelli went to the hospital yesterday.

Kiss Margey, love to you,
Harry

[Carroll Arms Hotel, Washington, D.C.]
Dear Bess: Sunday, December 5, 1937

Your special, enclosing one from Margaret, arrived on time. I was out driving around and didn't get it until noon. I am glad the play went off all right. I was sure it would. Wish I could have seen it.

Today is my father's birthday. He'd be eighty-six if he'd lived. I always wished he'd lived to see me elected to this place. There'd have been no holding him. I'll go and see the furniture men just as soon as I can. But I don't want to make any purchases until you see whether you like them or not. I've always wanted to take part in the furnishing of a house. But my ideas have always run to such extravagant tastes that I'm afraid you wouldn't approve. I'd like to have rugs and carpets from Bokhara and Samarkand, pictures by Frans Hals, Holbein, and Whistler, with maybe a Chandler pastel and a Howard Chandler Christy or two with Hepplewhite dining room, mahogany beds (big enough for two), etc. ad lib. Well it can't be done—so we'll have to do what we can and I want you satisfied. What do you want for Christmas?—a feather bed or a potato peeler? Maybe you'd like a washing machine or just a plain tub and washboard.

Margaret told me you had taken her list away from her and it made her head ache to create another. What does she want?

Love to you both,
Harry

Washington, D.C.
Dear Bess: December 6, 1937
    . . . I had dinner with Jim Nugent last night. He is a very clever person and
I like him but just the same he's a railroad *lobbyist*. He was very careful not to
ask me any very leading questions but I could tell that he is here for the C.M.
& St. Paul [Chicago, Milwaukee, and St. Paul] *because he knew me*. I'll take all
the dinners he has to put out and then do what I think is right. I can see no harm
in talking to anyone—no matter what his background. In fact I think everyone
has a right to be heard if you expect to get all the facts. Of course it is the job
of some people to befog the issue and cover up the facts. I don't put Jim in that
class.
    I'm having dinner with Vic and another old lobbyist tonight—Colonel
Stephenson by name. He's with the Pennsylvania Railroad and a very agreeable
gentleman, but I am sure I know what he wants—but in spite of that I'll have
a very pleasant evening discussing national defense.
    Will try to see some furniture this afternoon if the Senate doesn't work too
late.
                        Kiss Margey, love to you,
                                Harry

Washington, D.C.
Dear Bess: December 7, 1937
    Well I guess you really did miss writing me this time. None came yesterday
even on the late mail. That's the first miss in a long time. I guess maybe you had
a right to miss one since I missed on Wednesday. But I had no chance on that
trip.
    It is cold as real winter this morning and I used it as an excuse to get up
half-hour late and miss my walk. Yesterday was a real day's work. I put the biggest
rail receivership attorneys in the United States through a real grilling and practically told 'em they ought to be tried for unethical practices. I am sure the big
corporations will never want anything to do with me any more. But they sick their
high-hat bar associations on some little ambulance chaser when he's trying to get
bread for his family, and the attorneys for the National City Bank and Kuhn,
Loeb and Co. can fix a federal court, tell receivers and trustees what to do, and
practically shut out all other lawyers from a $700 million bankruptcy—and they
are all right. I told 'em they were no better than the little shysters, and they are
not.
    Here is a letter from Mrs. Garner. I opened it because I thought I might
have to phone her you weren't here. Mr. Shoop is having a cocktail party
tomorrow night and I am invited. What do you think of that? Had a letter from
the governor asking us to stay at the mansion at the first opportunity. Maybe he
thinks that appeals to a country boy.
                        Kiss Margey, love to you,
                                Harry

Washington, D.C.

Dear Bess: December 12, 1937

It was great to get a special and then talk to you too. I am somewhat doubtful about sending that furniture out without your seeing it first, and also I have always wanted to shop for it with my gal as every other person has done from Adam down. But for some reason we've never been able to do what everybody else takes for granted.

Had lunch with the governor yesterday and he seemed to enjoy it very much. He gave an interview to Helm, which if true puts quite a different view on some things. Maybe I can straighten him out yet. If I could only be at home, I know that could be done.

I'm going to a football game this morning between the House pages and the Senate pages at Catholic University stadium. Hope the Senate boys win but I'm afraid they won't.

Old Man Norris came up to me yesterday and said that he thought my rail hearing was the highlight of the special session. I almost went out because he's hardly spoken to me since I've been here. I guess he did it because his colleague had told the New York *Sun* that it was time wasted.

I'm going to make a speech on it in the Senate before we adjourn and let the country and everyone else know just what is the trouble with railroad financing anyway. It probably will catalogue me as a radical but it will be what I think. Wish you were here so we could hold hands on all the sofas and beds in Washington before we buy.

Kiss Marge and love to you,
Harry

Washington, D.C.

Dear Bess: December 13, 1937

. . . It is cold as it can be this morning and snow is the forecast, but if it hits as well as in past forecasts there won't be any. I walked about two miles this morning and never did get warmed up, so you know it was cold.

Justice Brandeis' tea was really a tea. A Mrs. January sat at a little table and made each individual guest a cup and each one sat and drank it and then another came up. She said she was formerly from St. Louis and she seemed to be a very nice person—but I wanted to say whoa January when my cup was full. We always called the mules January. The Justice spent more time with me than any of his other guests and seemed very much interested in what we are doing to the railroad and insurance companies. Both he and Mrs. Brandeis are as nice as they can be. I wish you'd been here to go. It was a rather exclusive and brainy party. I didn't exactly belong but they made me think I did.

Kiss Margey, love to you,
Harry

Washington, D.C.
Dear Bess: December 14, 1937

The mail was right again this morning—the letter was there—also one from Marg and one from John Gledhill, which almost made me cry. He's all broken up over the unexpected death of the girl he was getting ready to marry. Said she had a clot in her heart and couldn't come out of it. I'll have to write him today and I wish I didn't. You remember him. He was in the office with Myra.

Too bad John has been so weighted down with his postal duties. I think he's looking for an excuse to quit and I've an idea he'd be better off, but it would sure be hell on the government. I don't know what I want for Christmas. Some socks and ties are always useful. A fellow from Springfield is sending a turkey. So don't buy one unless you want to bring it back here with you. We've a box of potatoes from Idaho and five pounds of coffee the colonel from West Point sent me— so we can have coffee and potatoes. I don't drink coffee and you won't eat potatoes. We should do fine with that start. I'm glad you had the piano tuned. I'm coming on the train. There's no use having two cars back there when we'll need 'em here. . . .

Kiss Margey, love to you,
Harry

Washington, D.C.
Dear Bess: December 16, 1937

The mail must have slipped off the truck today. It is three o'clock and no letter. We had a night session last night—lasted until eleven o'clock. We may get to a vote before we quit tonight. I hope we do and then we'll sure get recessed before this year ends. We've tentatively agreed to quit December 22 and I'm sure we will. I've really stirred up a hornet's nest in the Railroad Committee. The president of the New York Bar has been down to see about investigating those rich and snooty lawyers who have been helping the bankers to loot the railroads, and the chairman of the House Committee was over to see me about bringing impeachment proceedings against that old Chicago judge about whom I gave out the mean interview. So maybe I've done some good after all.

The other furniture man called me this morning and said he would have an estimate for me tomorrow. I'm going to see what he has to offer and try to make arrangements to get in one day after we arrive. I may put in the bedroom outfit and you and Margey can sleep in the beds and I can sleep on the floor the first night.

Hope the ice melts before we start back.

Kiss Margey, love to you,
Harry

ELEVEN

HARD WORK PAYS OFF

In the second half of his initial term in the Senate, between 1938 and 1940, Truman found himself in the worst political trouble that he would ever have to face, not excepting his uphill fight for the 1948 election. The problem was two-fold. The Pendergast machine collapsed in Kansas City—with indictment and then confession of Boss Tom and his departure for the federal penitentiary at Leavenworth. In addition, Governor Stark wanted a part in national politics and hoped for the vice presidency or a Cabinet post. Failing such offices he was glad to oppose his erstwhile political friend, Senator Truman.

Meanwhile the Senator was coming close to legislative triumph: Congress passed the Truman-Wheeler Transportation Act in the autumn of 1940.

Ft. Riley, Kans.

Dear Bess: July 4, 1938

This is what you might call corresponding under some difficulty. My pen is dry, the wind is blowing a gale, and the flies are about to eat my legs up. I have a tent about twenty yards from the shower and I expect to be in that shower in about half an hour. Arrived at about eight o'clock this morning and have seen everyone. There are some two hundred reservists here and most of them are oldtimers whom I've known for some time. Marvin Casteel of the Highway Patrol is here along with Jo Zach, Snyder, Vaughan, Ed Moore, the postmaster at Clinton, and a lot of others. They have a very pleasant schedule fixed up and I believe we'll have an enjoyable ten days. They are giving me a horse and have agreed to cut out the social affairs, so I guess I'll be all right. Sorry this ink is so blurry but I can't get any more until tomorrow—everything on the post is closed.

Kiss my baby and keep cool.

Love to you,
Harry

Ft. Riley, Kans.

Dear Bess: July 6, 1938

. . . Spent the morning with the outfit on the trainer range. They do a very good job on practice firing. Colonel Peek and I have gotten rid of the tea drinkers and have really made a regiment of it. There are sixty-seven officers here and thirty of them are new R.O.T.C. university graduates and fine young men. They know more about firing than I did on November 11, 1918. So you see they are pretty good.

Kiss Margie and keep writing. I've made some notes on letters you can send to Vic.

Love to you,
Harry

The Park, Hot Springs, Ark.

Dear Bess: Nov. 17, 1938

Hot Springs is all prosperous. Things are all pepped up here. Nearly all the stores on the avenue have new fronts, and some of the others are getting them. The Arlington garage seems to be full of Packards, Chrysler eights, and Cadillacs. They've taken up the car tracks and the town looks fine. They're advertising the alligator and ostrich farms again. So I guess the No'thern Republicans are spending again.

I'm going up to the hospital tomorrow and I hope the damned thing's full. I am sleeping almost day and night and I'm sure I need no hospital treatment. They treated me fine but I made more nuisance contacts than I've made in a long time and I know I'll make a lot more if I go over there. I also made some nice ones too—Littlejohn and the two Smiths were fine. But I also found a lot of would-be pensioners too.

They gave me the best room in the house here after the negro bellboy recognized me going up in the elevator. The clerk didn't know me and I never told him.

Wish you and Skinny were here. We'd have a grand time. Keenan wanted Canfil's place and date of birth. They're going to appoint him. They figure they'll need Harry next session.

Kiss Margie, love to you,
Harry

As a member of the Interstate Commerce Committee, Truman was sometimes able to combine business with pleasure, as the following letter shows in describing an inspection trip of army engineering projects on the Mississippi.

Aboard the *General Newton*

Dear Bess: December 15, 1938

It has been "sho' nuff" lonesome without any letter or telegram or phone call from you and as soon as I get to "N' Oilins" (as these people call it), I'll remedy that situation.

I have been having a fine, educational trip. We drove from Memphis to Rosedale, Mississippi, Tuesday morning where we got aboard the River Commission boat *Control*. It is a sternwheeler with two smokestacks and cabins, deck (I'd call it a front porch), as is the *General Newton*, on which we now are. The *Newton* is a little bit more luxurious than the *Control* and can run a little faster. They are both about forty years old and driven by steam power. First thing I did when I got aboard was to go down and inspect the engine room and power plant, which of course pleased the engineer. We came down the river all afternoon looking at levees and cutoffs and dredges and everything else that requires government money to run—including a couple of generals, numerous colonels, an admiral, and some working soldiers. The river work is under the direction of the army engineers. The admiral has charge of the Coast and Geodetic Survey work and the rest of 'em are all enthusiastic River Control men. . . .

Ross Collins and William Whittington (I want to call him Dick and ask about the cat)—two Congressmen from Mississippi—are along and I find that Ross isn't such a bad boy as the papers make out. He took me on a sight-seeing tour of Natchez yesterday and told me that Natchez would be a fine town if they weren't all living in the past. We saw some of the famous old houses and then got back to the boat. He told me very confidentially that all the riffraff and trash came from Louisiana. Said that his mother always cautioned him to stay away from that state and its people. All this said with a twinkle in his eye and for the benefit of Senator Overton, who of course resented it vigorously—Collins all the time pretending he was speaking facetiously but afterwards assuring me it was all true—that no respectable Mississippian would associate with Louisiana people.

We transferred to the *Newton* Tuesday night while we were tied up and are riding it all the way to the end. Will call you when I arrive.

Love to Margie and you,
Harry

Washington, D.C.
July 5, 1939

Dear Bess:

Well I arrived in good shape. When I put on my clean shirt and the same gray silk suit I had at home, Mildred remarked that I looked fresh as a daisy—and I felt that way. . . .

Went over to Biffle's office after the Senate quit and had a drink with Senators Wagner, Herring, and Ellender. Wagner said some nice things and Herring said he intended to campaign all the Iowa border counties of Missouri. There are a number of letters from all over the state giving the governor a real dressing down. One calls him Dr. Jekyll and Mr. Hyde—for T.J.P. to get elected, and against him to get headlines.

Herring said the President was very emphatic to him in an interview, after the one with Barkley, in wanting me to be reelected, said that Roosevelt thought the governor "an egotistical fool." Wish I could publish that!

I wasn't going to call you but I had to do it. It's hell when you have only one sweetie. But if hell's like that, I want to go there. . . . I'm going to lick that double-crossing, lying governor if I can keep my health. If I do then I can really do something here for Missouri. I know I could if Old Jack [Garner] or Wheeler should happen to be the fair-haired boy.

Tell my baby (big, sweet girl if she likes it better) that her dad wants to hear from her as well as her mamma.

Love to you,
Harry

Washington, D.C.
Dear Bess: July 11, 1939
. . . Mrs. Swanson almost broke up the funeral. Said she didn't want Harry Byrd on the committee. Of course Old Man Glass, as the Virginia senior, was given the right to appoint the Senate committee and naturally he wouldn't leave Byrd out. Old Garner told Barkley to tell her that we were all tired using the Senate Chamber for a funeral home and if she didn't like the way we did things, it would be called off. Well it wasn't called off. I want no state funeral. Please remember that.

Hope you didn't catch cold on that porch sleep on the first cool night. I won't be in St. Louis. Looks like I can't get away at all. We may adjourn now in two weeks after today's neutrality action. Hope so.

Kiss Margey and two for you,
Harry

Washington, D.C.
Dear Bess: July 20, 1939
. . . Have been going to bed at nine o'clock and getting up at six for a whole week now and am feeling fine except that at night I am always mighty tired. More people have been in to see me lately and they all seem to have impossible problems. Mrs. Roby is very anxious to get Bill into the Naval Academy. She called me and told me all about it and I told her the only way Bill could get an appointment was through the competitive exam held for the District. I can't appoint anyone outside Missouri unless he can establish a residence there. She wasn't sure whether she wanted to spend the thousand dollars on the preparation or not. Al Holland is still out of luck too and hunting for a job. He called me at 6:45 this morning and wanted to come down and talk to me about it, and I let him come. I wonder what these people did for a father confessor before I came? It must be something in my face I guess. My own family use me for the same purpose and so do all the political boys. But I never do 'em much good— only with sympathy and maybe that's what they want.

Kiss Margey, love to you,
Harry

Washington, D.C.

Dear Bess: July 24, 1939

Well just to keep the record 100 percent I'm writing this morning in spite of the fact that I won't get a letter and even though it may be lost. Paul Nachtman came in this morning from the B. & O. train and we had breakfast together. He ate a farm hand's breakfast. Said he quit smoking and had gained forty pounds. Maybe that's the reason the present-day gals pay so much tribute to George Washington Hill of the American Tobacco Company. They are trying to keep thin. . . .

Well you had a change of heart, didn't you? The letter came. Millie came running in with it and said she hoped she could keep her job another day. I always threaten to fire 'em all if I don't get a letter. She'll write you about the Pepper Bill. It probably won't pass at this session. We are now trying to adjourn on the second. Barkley wants to get home to vote in the Kentucky primary on the fifth. They are nominating a governor this time. . . .

Kiss Marge, love to you,
Harry

After months of hearings, Truman and Wheeler began the tedious work of getting a bill through Congress.

Washington, D.C.

Dear Bess: July 28, 1939

. . . I succeeded in getting a real rail bill agreed to and on the Senate calendar yesterday. It regulates subsidiaries and holding companies of railroads. It is the real reform bill that Wheeler and I have been working for in the investigation. Have held copious hearings on it as chairman of the subcommittee. Wheeler said I couldn't get it out. The railroads said they couldn't stand it, and no one thought it could be done. I got Lowenthal and Taylor, two of our young attorneys, to get the chief counsels of the Santa Fe, Pennsylvania, New York Central, and Union Pacific into a conference and the bill is on for passage. That's a real job. The *Christian Science Monitor* of July 26 had a grand editorial on the Wheeler-Truman Bill, and by the way that bill, amended out of all semblance to itself, passed the House day before yesterday and they passed it as the Wheeler-Truman Bill. So if we ever can agree on it, it will be our bill. We've got until the next Congress adjourns to do it. So you see I've been working. No letter yet today at 11:00 A.M.

Kiss Margey, love to you,
Harry

Washington, D.C.

Dear Bess: July 31, 1939

Well this Monday has a good beginning. Your Saturday letter was in the first mail when I came over at seven. Am sure glad Dan Deets is back in circulation and that the weather for once is good. Hope it stays that way—but it won't.

Too bad about Lucy's father. When my time comes I want to go out like a light and not create a lot of business for hospitals, nurses, and doctors.

You were anxious about my evenings. I haven't had any this last week as we've worked every night. Maloney wanted me to go to dinner with him and his Mrs. and Bell and Shannon Saturday night at the Congressional Club, but, thank goodness, it was too late to go when we quit. Minton and I went to a picture show, which I told you about. We went to the ball game yesterday on a couple of free tickets he had, and Washington won five to two. They've been constant losers. I went up to the Metropolitan by myself and saw *Man about Town*. It is a very funny show. The nigger steals the screen.

I usually read myself to sleep every night. Have found another book on the Civil War, by Colonel A. H. Burne, an Englishman. He makes a comparison of the leadership of Lee, Grant, and Sherman in the last year of the war. Looks like he's going to rate them in that order. . . .

Kiss Margey, love to you,
Harry

Washington, D.C.

Dear Bess: August 1, 1939
    Well this is August 1 and it looks like adjournment in three or four days, by Saturday anyway. I have an invitation to go to Virginia Beach on Friday with my legionnaire friends at Richmond but I doubt if I can go. Probably if I did, I'd get a case of sunburn that I can as well do without. I'm taking the ham to the kitchen to be baked for adjournment. So you see we are getting close.

It must be lonesome without the kids. You never realize how much you want 'em around until it's too late. You can sympathize with me when you and Margey ran off.

The K.C. *Star*, the *Post-Dispatch*, and the *Star-Times* in St. Louis are giving Mr. Stark dig after dig. It looks as if their hero has feet of clay (or rotten apples). The political situation is going to be something to write history about next year, and if I do win out then watch out. I've made some good friends up here and we'll go to town in accomplishment the next six years. . . .

Kiss Margery, love to you,
Harry

Washington, D.C.

Dear Bess: August 2, 1939
    Was glad to get your letter this morning and I've been running around like a chicken with its head off all day, so I'm late getting the answer off.

The proposed Colorado trip sounds all right to me. I'd like to see Pikes Peak and some of the other things they brag about out there up close, and I'd also like to do it the leisurely way—if that's possible. Also be glad to have your mother along. The car's plenty big enough to haul all you'll need, unless you stay a month, and four people—and do it comfortably. . . .

Have been getting bills through for various lobbyists and trying to get Jimmy Byrnes to let Schwellenbach and La Follette have money to keep on making headlines as well as fronting for Wagner to do the same thing on banking and currency. Funny they pester me—Tydings and Townsend are the other members of the committee. Maybe I've answered it.

Hope to see you soon and be on the way to Colorado.

Kiss Margie, love to you,
Harry

Washington, D.C.

Dear Bess: August 4, 1939

Well this is nigger picnic day. But they don't have 'em like they did in days past. I remember once going to Washington Park with our washwoman to a Fourth of August celebration. I'll never forget it. Had chicken and catfish fried in corn meal and was it good!

The short but sweet *note* of Wednesday just now came. The girls usually bring it right in when the letter comes. They seem to think it makes things easier on them when I get my letter. . . .

I was in the chair yesterday awhile and Johnson of Colorado was making a speech on keeping beer ads off the radio. I wrapped for order and requested that the Senate be quiet so the Senator from Colorado could be heard—and the Senator from Colorado said he didn't want to be heard, he was just making a speech. I had to really call for order then. . . .

Kiss Margey, love to you,
Harry

Washington, D.C.

Dear Bess: August 5, 1939

. . . My ham went over big. We had it today at noon. The Vice President, Barkley, Wheeler, Jim Byrnes, Guffey, Hatch of the famous bill, Minton, Lucas, Herring (without the blond), Swartz, Chavez, La Follette, Burke, Austin, Stewart, Halsey, and Biffle were present. If you'll read the *Record* today, you'll wonder how that outfit could sit down together, but they did and had a grand time. Maybe Johnny Walker, Ballantine, and Mr. Gin had something to do with it, but it was a most pleasant party. And they all expressed a hope that I'd be elected in 1940, and I'm crazy enough to believe they meant it. Anyway, they meant it while the alcoholic gentlemen mentioned above had control.

The Arcade Sunshine Laundry just about ruined my tan suit Ted made for me. I told Reathel and Catherine if you were here, I'd get a new one—and they've gone to work on the laundry. Maybe I will anyway.

Hope to see you in at least seven days. I'm not going to drive home first and I may go to Nashville on the way home to get some Andy Jackson facts for a speech.

Kiss Margey, love to you,

Harry

Washington, D.C.

Dear Bess: August 6, 1939

The special was there when I came down, and this blue Sunday is a lot brighter. Hope you enjoyed your luncheon with Mrs. Moffett and Miss Carr and that you found the skirt you want for Skinny. Hope she hasn't got a cold. Maybe she is making sure of the Colorado trip. I'm glad you let the Andrews woman work on you again. The report sounds very encouraging. Your blood pressure is ten higher than mine. As long as it stays in that neighborhood there is no danger from that quarter.

I'm cleaning house this morning, washed three handkerchiefs and six socks, threw away a couple of bushels of papers, and can see a couple of square feet of the mahogany on the desk. Hope to be able to pull out of here by Wednesday or Thursday. . . .

Kiss Margie. Love to you. Hope to see you soon,

Harry

For a second time, Roosevelt poked fun at Governor Stark; Senator Truman was glad to hear it but wasn't sure the President meant what he said.

Washington, D.C.

Dear Bess: August 9, 1939

. . . Yesterday was some day. Went to see the President about a bill, and he insisted on talking Missouri politics and telling me what a funny governor we have. He didn't say phony, but that's what he meant. Actual quotation: "I do not think your governor is a real liberal. . . . He has no sense of humor. . . . He has a large ego." These statements in a lot of other conversation I can't repeat now. Invited me to ride on his train across Missouri. Said: "Be sure and get on that train, for you can rest assured your governor will *without* any invitation." Then I saw Tommy Corcoran in Guffey's office and he quoted Charlie Hay in almost the very words of the President.

Saw Mr. Clark immediately afterwards. He was cockeyed but very affectionate. Said he was going to announce for me as soon as he got to Missouri and made a survey. It's all too much for one day.

Kiss Margey, love to you,

Harry

Washington, D.C.

Dear Bess: September 20, 1939

It was good to talk with you last night. I unloaded my baggage and got the policeman on the door to help me carry it up. Cochran had left word for me to come to a party for Dickmann, but I was too tired to make it.

Went to bed at ten o'clock after reading the *Star* and the *News*. Bill Helm just called me and told me I'd been selected as the principal speaker at the truckmen's meeting in Chicago and that they'd pay me for coming. If aviation and trucks and rails all are of the same mind, Wheeler's and my bill must be pretty good. Anyway I'll go talk with them. Propaganda is the thing these days. There are at least five thousand cards and letters on the table that came before I did, and this morning's mail is so big it will take all day and maybe tomorrow to distribute it. We got nearly a thousand on the first mail. Father Coughlin and the pacifists are organized. It will have no effect on me.

I heard Hitler's speech over the radio as I came along yesterday and he did himself no good in this country. Dorothy Thompson peels the hide off Mr. Lindbergh in her column this morning and I agree with her. We'll have a historic session. Wish you were here. I'm going to have a lonesome time. Having lunch with Dickmann. Kiss Margey. Hope you called Mamma and told I got here.

Love to you,
Harry

Truman's first reference to World War II, which began on September 1, appears below.

Washington, D.C.

Dear Bess: September 22, 1939

Was very happy to get your letter. Reathel brought it in and said she hoped I wouldn't fire her now. . . .

Danford and I talked the war over. We're both mighty blue over it. Neither of us think that England and France can kick the Germans and Russians. They were beaten in the last war when we got in. If Germany can organize Russia and they make England give up her fleet, look out—we'll have a Nazi, or nasty, world. The President seems to have had a good reaction. Minton says it'll take a month. Everybody else says January 1. I don't know.

Mr. Shoop just can't see how Clark can support anyone but Stark. Well he may do it.

Kiss Margie, love to you,
Harry

Washington, D.C.

Dear Bess: September 23, 1939

. . . I am somewhat depressed by the world situation. It's terrible. The radio says Holland has flooded its lands and that Russia and Germany will go into

Rumania. Then these nutty letters—they'd drive a sane man to drink. Two came to me addressed Cenator and one spelled war with two r's. They are nearly all from St. Louis and nearly all have German names. The Bund is working.

Kiss Margie. I may call you from St. Louis Monday night at eleven o'clock.

Love to you,
Harry

Washington, D.C.
Dear Bess: September 24, 1939

Got another letter yesterday afternoon, dated Thursday, with the Stark clippings. Mr. Southern evidently has forgotten his statement that no governor should run for another office while he's in power. I suppose he could never bring himself to ask the governor to resign while he's running. That of course would be the ethical thing for him to do.

I am most happy you are again back in line. You should not have gotten out seriously. My patronage troubles were the result of the rotten situation in Kansas City and also the jealous disposition of my colleague. While the President is unreliable, the things he's stood for are, in my opinion, best for the country, and jobs should not interfere with general principles. With most people they do. I can't say that they have in the case of Minton and Schwellenbach. We are all in the same boat. . . .

Wonder if Margie has a sore finger or something? I've looked in vain for a letter from her. Kiss her anyway.

Love to you,
Harry

Washington, D.C.
Dear Bess: September 29, 1939

Your Sunday letter was waiting for me when I got in, and I was glad to get it. Glad you got the Sunday letter. We get a delivery on Sunday morning, but it only includes the night's mail so you'd better continue to spend the dime. I'll send the dimes and they are worth the price. I am thinking seriously of going down to Richmond and sleeping over the weekend. I'm way behind you know. Whenever I do that I keep worrying for fear someone from home is sick or something else is wrong so you or some of the rest of the family would want me, and I don't sleep much more than if I stay here and enjoy the interruptions.

Here's a lot of scandal. Betty has left Stewart. Vic told me confidentially, so don't remark on it unless they do to you. And—Mrs. M. bought a house while Vic was in Missouri without consulting him. Said she told him he'd spent $8,700 for rent in seven years and she had the money for a down payment and he'd have talked her out of it if she'd told him. The house is way out Northwest somewhere —Vic didn't know the address. Said he guessed they could always sell it if they had to. And—Oscar got drunk again and they fired him for good. Stewart McDonald called me and said they just could, and would, not take him back again. He not only got drunk but ran his car out in Maryland, wrecked it, and got into jail besides. It's a mess but I don't see any way to help him. Thought you'd better hear from me than someone else.

Kiss Margie, love to you,
Harry

Washington, D.C.
September 30, 1939

Dear Bess:

This is Saturday and Vic is moving into their new house. I went out yesterday with him and looked at it. It is about eleven miles from here—two miles beyond the end of Connecticut Avenue out in Maryland. It is a lovely place—upon a hill overlooking a new resident district. The Gardellis have a house in the same neighborhood. The house fronts east on a lot 125 ft. front by 160 ft. deep, has a south porch screened in and 20 feet square. There are four rooms on the first floor, living room to the left of center hall as you go in, library on the right paneled in natural wood, kitchen at left and end of the hall and directly behind the living room, and opening from it by double lattice doors is the dining room. There is a toilet and shower at the right across from the kitchen. It opens into the library and hall too. Three bedrooms and two bathrooms upstairs. It is a lovely place. It ought to be for $16,000. Vic said the payment would be $100 per month. She must have made a single down payment.

Got the airmail yesterday afternoon. White may be right, you never can tell. Barr and Byam would really make a pair to draw to, what? Hope you got Natalie a coat. Well we are in the midst of a terrific struggle and I hope we answer it for the country's welfare. Going to Richmond today to stay till Monday maybe and try to sleep.

Kiss Margie. Love to you. Don't be downhearted at what they say about me. You know if it's true.

Harry

Washington, D.C.
October 2, 1939

Dear Bess:

. . . Pittman and Borah held forth today. Connally is the hero tomorrow and then Vandenberg. Connally told us to ask him questions if he forgot anything. Burke said he'd not do it for he remembered asking Tom one when Black was up for confirmation. He was going to ask Connally why he'd voted against Hughes for confirmation and was now for Black. But he started his question by saying, "Am I right"—hesitated for effect, and old Tom said, "Well if you are, it is the first time in my recollection." And the rest of Burke's question faded out. Tom said Burke wanted to do him like the negro did a little fish he'd caught. He said the fish just kept jumping around in the negro's hand and finally "the nigger said,

'Hole still little fish. I just wants to gut you.' " Tom said that was all Burke wanted
to do to him. . . .

Kiss Margie, love to you,
Harry

Washington, D.C.

Dear Bess: October 4, 1939
    Your letter came just now and I am glad the special finally got there. I have
to go to old man Logan's funeral—Barkley made a special request. I'm going over
to Caruthersville and make a neutrality speech Sunday, so I'll have lots of letters
when I get back here. Will call you from Memphis and from Caruthersville so
we won't be out of touch. Barkley, Halsey, et al. think I should take advantage
of the free ride to the funeral to help the situation on earth here, so I'm going
to do it.
    Glad you don't feel too badly about Oscar. He's a lovable kid and I'm always
sympathetic to the weak boys. Might have been one myself under certain conditions. But along lines like that I'm rather like my mamma, and she has no
weaknesses except to talk too frankly.
    I'm pleased at the car deal. You will get the radio yet. The Chrysler, I think,
is a better buy. We're learning how to deal at last. There's a hundred dollars we'd
never have had if we'd jumped at the first offer. Whenever you think they've
reached the end of their deal, take the car home and I'll fix it up when I get there.
They told me that any deal I made would be either cash or credit. . . .

Kiss Margie, love to you,
Harry

Kansas City, Mo.

Dear Bess: Saturday, October 7, 1939
    I had a nice rest yesterday and I am in good shape to meet the folks up at
Caruthersville. I'm on the Frisco ready to pull out—have my train ticket and my
plane ticket in my pocket. It is a good thing. I went out walking yesterday
afternoon after taking a nap. I'd bought my tickets in the morning.
    Left my wallet in my blue suit pocket, hanging in the closet—and someone
came in while I was gone out and rifled it. Whoever it was got $33. Had I not
paid for my tickets I guess I'd been out that too. I think the hotel will stand for
it. Only had $4 in my pocket, and that will have to run me until I can get to
Caruthersville. I'm so happy I'd paid out $45 for a plane ticket and $20 for my
railroad ticket in the morning. I'll get the plane cost back when I get to Washington. Even if the hotel doesn't come across, I'm ahead anyway.
    It's the first time it ever happened to me and there have been times when
it would have been two or three hundred dollars. I just didn't take all the things
out of my coat pockets because I expected to wear this suit today. I'd had on my
very dark gray for Logan's funeral. Well anyway it's something. I nearly fell over

when I went to pay the hotel bill and the wallet was empty. It gives you a sinking sort of feeling. Hope to call you Sunday morning.

Love to you, kiss Margie,
Harry

Hotel Majestic, Caruthersville, Mo.
Dear Bess: October 8, 1939

Well I'm in the toe of the boot [the southeast corner of Missouri], and they have really given me a workout. They met the train at Hayti, six miles from here, in force and paraded me over to this hotel. Then took me to lunch and out to the fair. I had to give the prize calf to the winner, hang the horseshoe on the winner of the Legion Derby, and give the winner's owner a silver cup. Then make a speech to twelve thousand people at 8:00 P.M.

This morning I have to go to church. The Baptist preacher is the uplift power in politics down here, and having spent the afternoon with the low-brows and having to do it again, it was thought I should do something to take the taint off. The preacher introduced me to the town when I spoke down here in the 1934 campaign. He is also feeding me at noon. Then I have to go to the fair again, give away some more prizes, and then go to Memphis to dinner tonight and make a cotton speech.

There are four factions in this town, and they are all for me. Something that never happened before. They don't like Stark. He was here Thursday, and fifteen of the leaders had dinner with him. They investigated and found not one of them for him.

I hope to find four letters when I get to the office at eight-thirty tomorrow. Will I?

Kiss Margie, love to you,
Harry

Washington, D.C.
Dear Bess: October 9, 1939

Well I arrived on time. Had a Pullman berth on the plane. It was more comfortable after I became accustomed to the engine noise. I dreamed the plane fell, but it didn't as you can see. There were 20,100 paid admissions to the fair Sunday afternoon, and I shook hands with at least a third of 'em. Gave away another prize and crowned a jittery race horse with a floral horseshoe before a grandstand full of people. My speech went over big apparently. At least a hundred people remarked about it.

The preacher's dinner was a dandy. He preached a good sermon, invited me into the church office, and nearly all the congregation came in to see me. Old Judge McCarthy was along with me and he seemed to have a grand time too. The preacher's two sons and their wives were there for dinner—two grand young men—and Mrs. Foster's mother was also present. One of the boys had a four-year-old daughter who was almost as pretty and cute as our baby used to be at that age. Reverend Foster is the most influential preacher in southeast Missouri and he spent the whole time getting all the facts on Pendergast and Stark. I made lots of hay I'll tell you. But it was hard work. They nearly pulled me to pieces. The Memphis crowd finally rescued me, and we had dinner in the Peabody Hotel at 10:00 P.M. *Raather* stylish hour, what?

There were four lovely letters—three from you, one from Margaret. Nice note of Mary McElroy's. I'll thank the Brazilian. Yes, the laundry came on time. I should have told you. Now I haven't missed a day writing—even on the funeral party I took time out to write. Glad you roofed the barn. Hope Frank didn't take it too hard. I don't know about writing Gates. I'd better wait and talk to him. I'd be pretty mad if someone took up my private affairs with my brother. Hope I didn't leave out answers to any questions.

Love to you, kiss the baby,
Harry

Washington, D.C.

Dear Bess: October 10, 1939

Had an airmail letter yesterday and one this morning. I was glad also to get your wire yesterday. Not possible for me to get there. Glad the candy arrived— I was out buying it when I got robbed. I'm sure one of the bellhops got the money.

Your teeth should be fixed at once. I have my own dentist and he's the best I know, but you don't like him. So you pick the one you think you can trust and *get the job done.* I never did think Berry knew anything, but if you wanted him it was all right. . . .

Harry Hawes called me and said that he'd heard from several sources that the governor is on the toboggan, and he was inclined to believe it. Well if a counterfeit like Mr. Stark can fool the people, they'll deserve what they get. . . .

Much love to you both,
Harry

Washington, D.C.

Dear Bess: October 13, 1939

Your letter came at ten this morning and I am most happy it did. I'll thank the Columbia Pictures man as soon as I can. I'm certainly sorry about Fred's eye. No one appreciates eyes as I do. Mine have been a handicap for fifty years. . . .

I went over to Aberdeen yesterday after all. It was a grand demonstration. I came to the conclusion that anti-air artillery is not enough against a plane attack in force. We must also have plenty of planes for defense as well. That's a real admission from an artilleryman, and that was not the intention of the demonstration either.

Brought Dewey Short back with me and he told me an earful about the Republican estimate of Stark. It is far from high. He also told me that my position had improved exceedingly in the last three months. I'm sure he wouldn't be telling me what I wanted to hear.

I'll go look at that car. I'm satisfied with it if you are. The color is good too. Why don't you get some new curtains if you want them? Hope you and Chris had a nice ride.

Wish I were rich enough to fly home every weekend—we're working this Saturday however.

Love to you both,
Harry

John C. Truman, son of Vivian, planned to marry a Catholic; for the Senator, the inter-faith marriage posed no problem at all, as he tells Bess in the following letter.

Washington, D.C.
October 16, 1939

Dear Bess:

. . . I was much surprised at J. C.'s announcement. It doesn't seem possible. He was a twin and an ordinary pocket handkerchief would cover them both. We must be slowly and gradually leaving the middle-age bracket, what? Was very glad to hear that Mamma and Mary got home safely. I have been uneasy about them ever since I heard it. Mary got her expenses paid to go, and Mamma wanted to go, so go she did. You never can tell what a change of water and diet will do to an eighty-seven-year-old and I was afraid of the road too. My family won't be seriously put out by J. C.'s Catholic in-laws. Mamma's youngest sister and our favorite aunt was a Catholic. In my opinion people's religious beliefs are their own affair, and when I don't agree with 'em I just don't discuss religion. It has caused more wars and feuds than money, and that seems a shame too.

That dumb car salesman ought to have his head examined. You tell him that a Senator has two legal residences. But I suppose we'll have to pay it now.

Kiss Margie, love to you,
Harry

Washington, D.C.
October 18, 1939

Dear Bess:

Was most happy to get your Monday letter enclosing J. C.'s invitation. Well, if he wants to become a Catholic I have no objection, of course. Now don't pass the buck to me on the wedding present—you know more about what is correct than I ever will. I'm very fond of those nephews. You ought to appreciate how I feel toward them by your own feeling for Fred's children. You put the amount into the present that you'd want to put into it for your own nephew. Get 'em something they can use and can't break up.

Here's another one, too, who'll have to have a present. She's a tough egg, but Lester Jordon would cut a throat for me and we'll have to come across with something. Five dollars is enough for this one. This is her second venture. The first one resulted in a cross-eyed son, so cross-eyed it makes your head ache to look at him. Just as bad as the crazy movie actor, Roscoe Ates, or whatever his name is.

Hope you got your hat all right and that the bridge game was a success.

Went to see *Mr. Smith Goes to Washington* last night with Minton. Sat in a box with J. Monroe Johnson and Mrs. Johnson, with Louis Johnson next to us is another box. Jim Farley, old man Norris, Wheeler, Guffey and a lot of other Senators were present. It makes asses out of all Senators who are not crooks. But it also shows up the correspondents in their true drunken light too. And that reminds me that the chief correspondent for the *Post-Dispatch* came by and told me the *P.-D.* had decided to give me a fair break in their news columns for the coming campaign.

May see you Friday night at 8:47 K.C. time at the airport; will call if it happens. Is Margie's hand paralyzed?

Love to you both,
Harry

[Senate Chamber]
October 27, 1939

Dear Bess:

Well we are about to get the bill passed. Mr. Clark had his spasm, and we just skinned him alive. Mr. La Follette had his and got a worse licking. I haven't been to the office since ten-thirty and I guess no letter came. Mildred brought me the letters to sign and didn't bring it, so I guess I'll get two tomorrow.

Ralph Truman came over from Baltimore this morning and we went to see Bennett. Ralph is at Baltimore for the National Guard Association meeting. Clark has recommended him for W.P.A. director to take Murray's place. But I'm of the opinion he won't get the job. As I told you yesterday, I think I have Harry Easley lined up for the job. Looks like everybody got rich in Jackson County but me. I'm glad I can still sleep well even if it is a hardship on you and Margie for me to be so damn poor. Mr. Murray, Mr. McElroy, Mr. Higgins, and even Mr. P. himself probably would pay all the ill-gotten loot they took for my position and clear conscience. What think you?

I disgraced you last night. Minton, Hatch, and I went to the Gaiety. It was a most rotten show, but there were a couple of vaudeville acts that were worth seeing. We met a couple of Congressmen, one from Indiana and one from Ohio, with their wives going in. The ladies seemed to be as embarrassed as we were— and they should have been.

I've had an avalanche of Missourians today who wanted in the gallery. They all got in.

Had lunch with Eddie Cantor, the Vice President, Barkley, and a dozen of the elect today. Eddie's a grandpa and Barkley told a Kentucky story—an old fellow who said he didn't mind being a grandpa but he hated to be married to grandma. Kiss Margie. Get your teeth fixed.

Harry

Washington, D.C.

Dear Bess: October 28, 1939

We finished the job last night in a blaze of personalities by Tom Connally, Burton Wheeler, and our own Bennett Champ. It was light entertainment for the galleries—almost as good as *burlesque*. I am to go to Rochester, New York, Wednesday night for a speech on the R.R. bill at the request of the Rochester Chamber of Commerce and on Friday at New York City. The railroads are sponsoring the meetings I suppose. If I could just get the waterway fellows to take me on now, there could be no accusation of partiality—but they won't. They are against the bill.

I won $1.50 on the number of votes cast against the bill last night. We made up a pot, each putting in $1.00. There were about thirty in it. I guessed twenty-nine, and Minton guessed thirty. We agreed to split if either won. Minton got $5.00 out of the pot and I got half of it, so I didn't lose my dollar.

I'm glad the new bus is doing so well. I put fifteen gallons in the tank to begin with. Hope it is making twenty miles. That will be too good I fear. Hope you and Miss Margie didn't get your heads burned.

It would be most thoughtful, I believe, for you to send the First Lady a corsage. I'm not going to be able to get there, and if you don't want to go don't do it. If I remember correctly when I flew home to introduce her, she didn't even say thank you. You do as you please.

Kiss Margie, love to you,
Harry

The Senator had a reputation in New York for being anti-Wall Street, which indeed he was. Here he seems to have enjoyed his reception by a group of city millionaires.

Washington, D.C.

Dear Bess: November 4, 1939

I arrived back in the capital at seven this morning to find Congress adjourned. I didn't get any pay for those meetings. I'd be in the paid lobbyist class if I took pay to get my bills approved, so I only took railroad fare. . . . We got on the New York Central and went to New York City that night, and at noon I spoke to all the big bankers you read about in the papers. Kuhn Loeb, Morgan-Stanley, Brown Bros. and Harriman, and a lot of others. Some of 'em I'd panned in good fashion before the R.R. Committee. They were most courteous to me however. Last night I had dinner at the University Club with Pierpont Davis and a lot of millionaires. There were thirteen at the table. One had been president of the American Bankers Association last year, and the rest were just like him. They were trying to impress the country boy I guess, but the country banker told me as we went to the train that the sale had been the other way. He was pleased because I'd told them some things that they should know about financial statesmanship and public ethics. They asked for it, and I spoke from the shoulder. Hope you got that hat for Natalie and your furs and *got your teeth fixed*. Hope to see you next week.

Love to you both,
Harry

Washington, D.C.
Monday, November 6, 1939

Dear Bess:

. . . I am to see the President Wednesday if things work out as they should. Then that plane leaves on Thursday at 8:00 A.M. from Bolling Field. I am enclosing you the itinerary. If I go, I'll write or wire you every day from wherever we are. Since Minton and Swartz are going I thought I might be better off making this inspection of national defense than to be there taking it on the chin with the Long trial, Mr. Higgins, and Mr. Murray. At least they can get no interviews from me. We will have to consider a $2 billion defense bill, and maybe I'd know more about it.

Now all the above is an alibi to justify my really wanting to go—and the only qualm of conscience I have, and it is a bad one, is that it is by myself and not with you and the daughter. Maybe you won't feel too badly about it because I've never taken a pleasure trip since I can remember without you. I just think I'll go though. It won't cost a penny and will not add to the government cost. What do you really think?

Love to you,
Harry

FIX YOUR TEETH

The Washington-Youree, Shreveport, La.
Saturday, November 11, 1939

Dear Bess:

. . . It is raining this Armistice Day, just as it was on another one I can remember some twenty-one years ago. It may clear up by one o'clock, when we're scheduled to leave—just as it did at eleven on that other day.

You know it makes some of us who went on that Crusade, and it was one no matter what Nye and my colleague may say, wonder sometimes just what fate really holds in store for civilization. Maybe we need a purge just as the Romans did in the fifth century. But I wish that it didn't have to be done by another Attila or Genseric. I'm trying to get the President to join with the Queen of Holland, the King of Belgium, and the three Scandinavian Kings in a world broadcast on

Moral Rearmament on December 2, and I believe he'll do it. It might bring a sane peace. . . .

Kiss Margie and I can hardly wait to get to Ft. Sill for those letters.

Love to you,
Harry

Aboard Bomber no. 26 Shreveport to Ft. Sill, Okla.

Dear Bess: November 13, 1939

I suppose by this time you've seen by the papers that our plane took fire at Montgomery, but it was on the ground and there was no danger. The sergeant put it out with a little hand fire extinguisher before the post fire department got there. Don't worry about the situation, because the army is taking every precaution. They simply can't afford a serious accident on this trip.

We were royally treated at Shreveport, just as we were at Louisville and Montgomery. On account of foggy weather we are one day late, but they'll make that up on the way to Panama. I am hoping that I'll have all kinds of mail at Ft. Sill. We are due to arrive there in about an hour and a half. We have a most excellent pilot, who told me that these planes we are riding in had to fall apart before they'd fall. I guess he thought I was jittery on account of the Montgomery incident.

We are now flying above the clouds, and it is an experience. I did it once before, on the way from Chicago to Washington by way of Cincinnati and Pittsburgh. That time it was dark and thunderstorms were under us. Now it is only fog.

Hope I have a couple of letters when I land. This one must be mailed at once, so I'll have to seal it now.

Kiss Margie for me, love to you,
Harry

How do your new teeth feel?

Aboard Army Plane no. 26 Brownsville to Veracruz

Dear Bess: November 14, 1939

It sure was grand to find a telegram and letter from you and my baby here. Everything has been going as fine as can be since the fire at Montgomery field. In fact the army has had the jitters ever since, and I suppose it's just as well. We have had extra care in every way possible. They gave us packs at Ft. Sill with a 45., a machete, emergency rations, and a parachute for use over the Central American and Mexican jungles. Hope we won't need 'em. The weather is fine, the wind behind us, and the Gulf is visible on the left, Mexico on the right. Looks just like Texas. . . . Hope I can mail this at Veracruz.

Love to you,
Harry

Army transport, Veracruz to San Salvador
Dear Bess: November 15, 1939

Arrived at Veracruz at noon, were met by the Mexican Army and Navy and the American consul. The consul's name is Cochran and he's from Philadelphia. He'd only been here a week and so couldn't tell us much about the place. They took us to the plaza and turned us loose. Gave us rooms about twenty feet square paved with tile, ceilings twenty feet tall, and bathtubs of 1890. The hotel was constructed about the time Cortes came and is a beautiful building.

We did see the house the Conqueror lived in and the city hall he built in 1526. It is the oldest European building on the American continent. The cathedral is beautiful, but they had an earthquake last year and had to cover it with concrete to keep it from falling down. . . .

Hope you are all well and that I'll have a letter in Panama. Love to you. Kiss the baby. Hope your new teeth are comfortable.

Harry

Aboard the transport, San Salvador
Dear Bess   November 16, 1939

We are all at the airport and have been for an hour waiting for some Congressmen to get here. If they don't come soon, we'll go off and leave them.

This place is as you'd expect it. The most beautiful setting in a valley completely surrounded by mountains. The city has no tall buildings, because of earthquakes—which come about every twenty years. The last bad one was in 1917. There is a beautiful cathedral and has some lovely homes, but the city itself is not beautiful to see—too much poverty, although there are no beggars. Veracruz was full of 'em.

The President gave us a reception yesterday afternoon at five o'clock, and the American minister had one at six-thirty. It was a grand affair. They had the police band and all the trimmings. It was informal dress however.

The American Consulate or whatever you call the place a minister lives in, is magnificent. So was El Presidente's house.

The hotels have lobbies like palaces with tile floors, plants, etc. poinsettias by the hundreds and hibiscus and other red flowers. Gurney says the hedge is hibiscus and some other long word is the other pink flower. We just took off, left one Congressman, and my pen ran out of ink. We are up seven thousand feet now and headed for San José, Costa Rica, where we'll do it all over again tonight and then go to Panama. Had a cable from Vic that Marvin Casteel was made W.P.A. director. Well it could be worse. He voted for me in 1934 when Clark told him not to. They're giving us quinine tablets now every day and my head rings.

Kiss Margie, love to you,
Harry

Truman's knowledge of Latin American politics was limited to impressions, and when he met President Somoza of Nicaragua he failed to see through the dictator's charm. The Somoza family had taken over in the early thirties and would maintain its rule until the late seventies.

Guatemala City
November 22, 1939

Dear Bess:

. . . The President of Nicaragua is a regular fellow. He met us when we landed, gave us a reception at his house—palace would be a better word—had an informal dinner for us at the finest club I've been to, and then saw us off this morning. When I told him that Margie went to school with his daughter he gave me his place card, endorsed to her, and brought the stamp cancellation to the airport this morning.

We went to the races this afternoon where we met the President of Guatemala. He is said to be the best of the Central American Presidents. His name is Ubico and is given credit for eliminating graft in this country—the only one south of the Rio Grande where it has been done. Even Mr. Somoza hasn't tried to eliminate it. . . .

Kiss Margie, love to you,
Harry

The St. Anthony, San Antonio, Tex.
November 25, 1939

Dear Bess:

. . . I am shipping you the souvenirs and my summer clothes. There are three little bottles of that supposed-to-be finest French perfume, which I thought I'd give to you and Margie and Mary. There is another box with four little bottles in it I thought might do for the girls in the office and Mrs. Messall. There is a white sweater for you and a blue scarf for you and two blue sweaters for Margie. There are four little petit-point purses, one for your mother, one for mine, and one each for the Noland girls. There are two filigree silver bracelets, one for you and one for Mary and a little one for Margie. There are rings for all of you. The one with the big round set for perfume I thought maybe you'd like. There's a little bracelet for Marian and a little ring for David.

There are three Guatemala lunch cloths, which I thought maybe you'd want to give to Christie, May, and Natalie, and then if you wanted [illegible]. There are three shirts for the boys at the farm and a ring for Martha Ann. The jackets were so pretty I bought four of them, and you will have to help me to decide what to do with them.

Thought you could give one of the little rugs or runners to J.C. and one to your mother and one to mine and one to Christine.

If you don't like this distribution and you think of a better one or there is anything you want, why just take it. The coats are the only puzzle. I thought maybe you and Margie might want one apiece, and then we could decide what to do with the other two. I hope you'll notice one of 'em is blue. This is a picture of old [Popocatapetl] which I hope you'll have framed and let me claim. There's a box of Yardley soap for you, and the Chinese jewelry you can do what you please with; it was given to me. The watch is for Margie, and the sewing bag was evidently wrapped up by mistake, for I didn't buy it. Maybe the old lady in Guatemala had a stroke of conscience for charging so much and threw it in. I think those rugs and runners are exquisite and you keep as many as you want to. I don't *want to give away* the shoes and summer clothes. I can use 'em next year. Hope you won't think I was too extravagant. The broach is for Aunt Ella, and the extra rings are for the office force if you think it all right.

Love to you,
Harry

[Fairmont Hotel, San Francisco, Calif.]

Dear Bess: December 1, 1939
        . . . I hope Uncle Jim didn't hurt you too badly and I hope you get some good teeth. *Be sure and have all* the bills now unpaid in the Washington office when I get there, so I can pay them.

We had a beautiful ride from the City of Angels, stopping at Moffett Field at the southern end of San Francisco Bay for an inspection and for lunch. We left there at one-thirty and arrived at Hamilton Field at 2:00 P.M. After the usual salute and inspection we witnessed a bombing exhibition by some of our prize bombers. They are supposed to be the best in the world. They can hit the target six out of ten times from twenty thousand feet up. No modern antiaircraft gun, except our new 105, can reach them at that height. I have learned much on this trip that will be good for national defense and for more intelligent voting when I get to that point on defense legislation. We flew over the whole length of the San Francisco Bay—saw Oakland Bridge, Golden Gate Bridge, Alcatraz, the ferries, and everything else you read about in that bay, from the air. It looked just as I thought it would. This, you know, is one of the world's great cities and it is San Francisco—not Iowa, Kansas, Nebraska, and Oklahoma retired farmers, as the city in southern California is. Chavez took us out to dinner at an Italian place. There was too much to eat and I came back to the hotel to write you. The rest went on a slumming expedition. I guess I'm not built right. I don't enjoy 'em—never did, even in Paris, and I was twenty years younger then.

They are after me to make a broadcast on a national hookup tomorrow evening. If I do it, I'll write you.

Kiss the baby, love to you,
Harry

Fairmont Hotel, San Francisco, Calif.

Dear Bess: December 2, 1939
        . . . We had a very busy day today. Inspected the army post of embarkation, Angel Island, a receiving depot for recruits and a discharge depot for those

leaving. They discharged more men there last year than the total number in the army. The embarkation port is called Ft. Mason. Angel Island is Ft. McDowell, and we had to pass Alcatraz to get to it. Then we went to Ft. Funston, where they have the 16-inch guns. They shoot a 1,100-pound projectile twenty-five miles very accurately. This evening Minton, Gurney, Shafer, and I had dinner at the Fisherman's Wharf and then walked through Chinatown. It is very interesting and you could buy yourself poor. I bought so much in Panama and Mexico I didn't buy.

Kiss Margie, love to you,
Harry

Fairmont Hotel, San Francisco, Calif.

Dear Bess: December 3, 1939
Well I guess I'm spoiled. I thought maybe I'd get a letter when I got back to the hotel from Monterey, but of course there was no delivery so I'll probably get it at Ft. Hamilton at noon tomorrow. We had a very strenuous day—drove to Monterey, 120 miles by way of the redwoods, and inspected some forts and drill fields, stopped in Salinas for cocktails and then drove back here arriving at 8:00 P.M. Wish I'd kept a diary on the auto rides. It took longer to drive that 120 miles than it did to go from Veracruz to San Salvador. We had a highway patrolman for an escort too and made good time. . . .

In Mexico City they had four cops meet us at the port and take us to that robber hotel at a rate that made my hair curl. The Mexican driver didn't seem to hear or care a damn for four sirens going wide open and a procession of dignitaries moving through traffic at fifty miles per hour.

In Nicaragua we rode in the Presidente's car with a couple of outriders and a bird on the front seat beside the driver with a tommy gun all cocked and ready to go. The car had bulletproof windows, so that was some comfort. The President of El Salvador had two machine guns on the front porch and two on each side of the entrance to the grand hallway.

I go to Washington State tomorrow and I hope start for Washington City on Thursday.

Kiss Margie, love to you,
Harry

[Washington, D.C.]

Dear Bess: December 9, 1939
. . . After we left you yesterday I remembered that I hadn't said a word about how nice you looked. You always look so good to me that I'm tongue-tied just as I was when I was a little boy hoping to carry your books. They all seemed to understand why I would go to bed every night instead of to the shows and dances after they'd seen why—you and Margie.

We landed in Chicago at 2:20 and unloaded Minton. He was really very sorry to leave, as we were to leave him. Then we went on to Battle Creek, landed there at 4:00 P.M. Central Time, 5:00 P.M. Eastern. It was so near sundown we stayed all night. The Chamber of Commerce put us up at the Post Tavern—built by Post Toasties Post. It has $500,000 worth of paintings hanging in the lobby, coffee shop, and mezzanine floor—and they are really most beautiful to look at. Most of them are scenes from the farm, seascapes, snow pictures, river scenes, and I saw only two naked women and they weren't offensively so. . . .

Kiss Margie, love to you,
Harry

The valedictorian of Truman's high-school class appears here.

Washington, D.C.
Dear Bess: Sunday, December 10, 1939
You don't know how much I appreciated your special, which woke me up this morning. Yesterday is no more of a dream to you than it is to me. You looked so pretty, and your furs and hat and teeth were so nice I could only see the whole ensemble and not any detail. . . .

I went out to Charlie Ross's house to breakfast at 1:00 P.M. today. . . . Charlie had a program of our graduation on May 30, 1901, and he is a sentimentalist just as I am. He got it out and passed it around, and he didn't write that editorial but had to publish it or get fired. And the St. Louis outfit were sore at him because he wouldn't endorse Cochran in 1934. McAtee told me that—not Charlie. Barnet Nober, who writes foreign affairs for the *Post* here, paid me a very high compliment too. He was full of Scotch and said he rated me one of the few men in the Senate—honest of purpose. They, none of them, like Stark or Milligan.

Kiss Margie, love to you,
Harry

Washington, D.C.
Dear Bess: December 12, 1939
It was a much brighter day today. Catherine brought me a letter just before noon and asked if she could stay another day. I'd threatened to fire 'em both if I didn't get one. Can't understand why you haven't had letters from me. I've only missed Saturday and I wired you on that day. Of course the Sunday letter was written about 3:00 A.M. and I may have addressed it wrong. I'd just returned from the Gridiron dinner. But I sent it airmail.

I am glad the teeth fit—no matter what they cost they'll be worth the money. You are the only one who seems to be worried about Taylor's bill. I managed to get it paid today, along with quite a number of others. In spite of my widespread shopping tour I did not spend as much last month as usual and when I get my refund on the hotel bills from the War Department I won't be out so very much for the whole trip. Taken privately it would have cost five thousand dollars. . . .

Hope to see you soon.

Kiss Margie, love to you,
Harry

Washington, D.C.

Dear Bess: December 15, 1939

It was grand to talk with you and Margie. I'm so homesick I'm about to blow up and have been for two months. It is a miserable state of affairs when a man dreads showing up in his home town because all his friends are either in jail or about to go there. But that has been my state of mind ever since the special session. The *Star* and even Willie [Hearst] never fail to emphasize my friendship with people whom they think may be a detriment politically to me. Maybe I'm getting thin-skinned or something. Anyway I've got no business writing you about it.

Vic and I went back and looked at the apartment again at 403 H in Tilden and it is really better than I thought. They've agreed to completely redecorate it and clean the floors although the floors are in good condition. They also agreed to put the refrigerator in good condition and do whatever else was needed to make things shipshape. Mrs. Messall is going by today with Mrs. Gardelli to pick out the paper. I thought she could and would do a better job than I would. She was glad to do it but she hoped you'd be pleased. Said she liked to do things of that sort. The apartment people and Miller, the janitor, seemed very highly pleased that we were coming back. The negro was grinning all the way to the back of his neck when he saw me give a check for the first month's rent. It begins January 1, but we may go in any time we wish.

The girl and Vic are going to move the furniture in as soon as the apartment is ready. Hope to see you Monday at six-thirty on the Missouri Pacific.

Kiss Margie, love to you,
Harry

Aboard army transport KF8

Dear Bess: December 20, 1939

Well here I am some 6,500 feet in the air and as the fellows on the Panama trip would say, it's "Dear Bess" again. We took off just about 7:55 and at ten o'clock we were crossing the Ohio River just west of the Indiana line. That's moving. We also flew over the house of Independence, but I didn't see anyone I could recognize—a mile and a quarter up is rather far away for that.

The colonel seems to know his business and if we run into no bad weather we should be in Miami by one-thirty or two at the rate we're moving. I can't tell whether we're in Kentucky, Tennessee, or Alabama—according to Tom Sawyer's way of reckoning we are still in Illinois, for it's still brown and that's what Illinois used to show on the map. Tennessee's pink and Alabama's yellow.

Part of Missouri was covered with white clouds just as the funny isthmus was in Mexico, and we couldn't see the ground until we came to the Ohio. But it is beautifully clear now and I hope it stays that way until we get to Miami.

I'm the only passenger and seem to be in charge. The colonel asked me if I was ready to take off and has just had the sergeant give me a cup of coffee. We are over Nashville, Tennessee, now, in two hours and forty minutes from K.C.

They are trying to make Atlanta for a connection with the plane from Washington. Looks like we'll do it. If we do, I'll mail this there.

Kiss Margie, love to you,
Harry

Aboard army transport 15, between Florida and Cuba

Dear Bess: December 21, 1939

We were up at 4:00 A.M. today. Drove around for thirty minutes trying to find a place to eat breakfast. Every other street in Miami is one way and it seemed all of 'em went the way we didn't want to. We arrived at the airport at six o'clock —it is fourteen miles from town—and were in the air at six-thirty. When the sun came up it was very beautiful. It looked as if it were below the ocean. That was because we are 3,900 feet up and there is a layer of broken clouds below us. You could see the sun between the clouds and the water, and it looked as if you were seeing through the water. We are going to land in Cuba for gas and oil and then go on to San Juan. The distance from Miami to Puerto Rico is 980 miles in a straight line, but the way we go it is 1,150. They want to keep in sight of land all the way if possible, although we can't see any now.

They make us wear a collar with a bib on it fastened at the waist with a strap. There are two little cords to pull if we get in the water and a cylinder of gas blows it up and makes a life preserver out of it. We hope we won't have to use 'em.

I am hoping to mail this in Cuba along with a card for Margaret. I couldn't get any cards in Miami last night. The Chamber of Commerce fed us and it was too late afterwards and too early this morning. The hotel clerk gave me one which I sent her. Hope to see you Sunday.

Kiss Margie, love to you,
Harry

Hotel Everglades, Miami, Fla.

Dear Bess: December 21, 1939

Well here we are in Florida. It is a most excellent thing for California and Florida that there is a climate to talk about. Ft. Huachuca, Arizona, and old man Garner's Godforsaken Uvalde country really are better places to see and the land is worth something for production—if there were water.

Here water is most plentiful and soil is all they need. It is as flat as a pancake and the principal product seems to be hotels, filling stations, Hebrews, and cabins.

The prices of some of the cabins would make those at the Muehlebach seem extremely reasonable.

We passed over a German boat at Ft. Lauderdale, which had run into port out of reach of a British cruiser, which we could also see. The pilots were very accommodating and flew low over St. Augustine and Daytona Beach, where they race the fast cars. It all looked as rich and Godforsaken as California.

I joined the party at Atlanta and we had lunch there. Thomas, Shafer, and I are the party. No wonder they high-pressured me. Weather's fine and I should be on schedule Sunday.

Kiss Margie, love to you,
Harry

Washington, [D.C.]
June 11, 1940

Dear Bess:

You see I started the "dear" in the wrong place [near the date], being in such a hurry to say it. I also just had a couple of nuts in here, one a job hunter and the other a hillbilly from Barry County who claimed he'd written up the National Defense Aviation Program and that they should give him a job. He was really nutty.

This town and the Senate have about gone nuts entirely on the war. Josh Lee and Pepper have proved conclusively that they are both A-1 demagogues, and Barkley has almost gotten hard-boiled enough to be a leader. I'm afraid it won't last. Vic and the Hebrew are having a hard time to get along. Snyder called me yesterday and told me that there was not much to it but personal jealousy and not to pay too much attention to it. I asked Mary Chiles to head my women's division. Hope she will do it. . . .

Love to you both,
Harry

Washington, D.C.
June 17, 1940

Dear Bess:

It was good to talk with you last night. I was reaching for you all night long —and you weren't there. I didn't tell you or Miss Margie how much I appreciated your help Saturday. Both of you did untold and yeoman service, and the more I think of that day's work, the more pleased I am. The able and distinguished Senator from Washington spent the whole day telling such Senators as would listen that I had a good and glorious meeting, but that I had treated him with marked discourtesy in that he'd ridden 1,070 miles to make his last political speech for me and then had to hunt me up when he arrived. I had to stand some unmerciful kidding on that statement. Barkley has about made up his mind to speak for me in St. Louis.

Mr. Clark took his hair down today (what's left of it) and told me his plans to help me. And they are good plans. Said he expected to spend all his time after

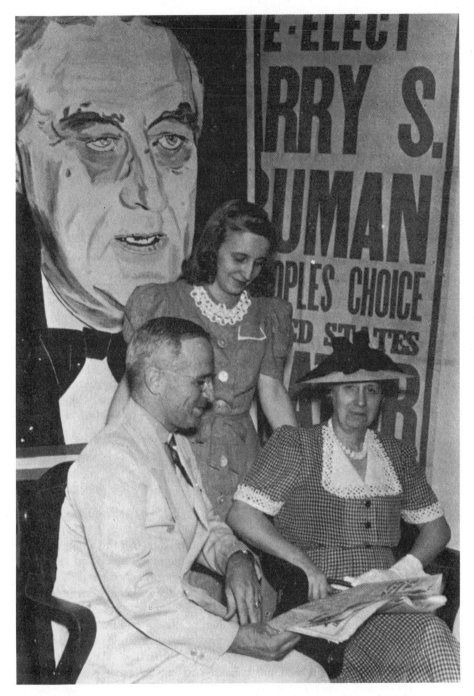

Candidate for reelection, 1940, in front of Roosevelt poster. *Copyright unknown*

the Democratic Convention riding over Missouri lining up the antis and the pro-Germans for me. That's just what he said. Said he wanted me to win as badly as he wanted to in 1932, that he hated Stark and Maurice Milligan equally but that he liked Tuck. That he thought a statement now from him would hurt more than it would help, and he's right on that.

Gillette has a report that will make mincemeat out of the governor. He will release it whenever I say so. I guess I'll ask him to make two reports—a preliminary one and a final one. He says Stark couldn't be seated if he was elected. Uplifters are all alike.

Kiss Margie. Love to you. It's a good thing I came back.

Harry

Campaigning for a second term as Senator meant travel again to many of Missouri's 114 county courthouses.

Hotel Statler, St. Louis, Mo.
Dear Bess: Sunday, 12:15 A.M., July 7, 1940
Well I finally got Mr. Vic set down at headquarters and got a plan together for the coming week. So you'll have it, here it is:

Sat., July 6	7:00 P.M. Columbia
Sun., July 7	8:00 A.M. St. Louis breakfast Union Brewers
Mon., July 8	Van Buren
Tues., July 9	9:00–10:00 A.M. Willow Springs
	2:00 P.M. Thayer
	7:30 P.M. West Plains
Wed., July 10	10:00 A.M. Mountain Grove
	11:00 A.M. Cabool
	12:00 Noon Houston lunch
	2:30 P.M. Salem
	7:30 P.M. Rolla

Stay at Pennant [Hotel]

Thurs., July 11	10:00 A.M. Steelville
	2:30 P.M. Sullivan
	7:30 P.M. Washington

Probably stay all night at Jefferson City

Fri., July 12	2:30 P.M. Fulton
	7:30 P.M. Mexico
Sat., July 13	2:30 P.M. Moberly
	7:30 P.M. Hannibal

Sun., July 14 through Wed., July 17 Chicago

Thurs., July 18	2:30 P.M. Brookfield
	7:30 P.M. Chillicothe
Fri., July 19	10:00 A.M. Trenton
	2:30 P.M. Bethany
	7:30 P.M. Maryville

Sat., July 20   11:00 A.M. Tarkio lunch
                     2:30 P.M. Mound City
                     4:00 P.M. Savannah
                     7:30 P.M. St. Joseph
Sun., July 21   Cameron Father Wogan's picnic

Then I'll come home and fly to Washington Sunday afternoon or at 3:00
A.M. Monday, stay in the capital until Wednesday, and start out again.

If you and Margie want to come to Chicago, meet me in Hannibal Saturday
and we'll catch the Burlington. You can catch me at some of the places on the
list. Will call you whenever I can.

Love to you, kiss Margie,
Harry

Washington, D.C.

Dear Bess: July 23, 1940

I'm thinking August 6 all the time and I wrote Aug. for the month [deleted
above]. Most happy to have the airmail this morning. Every Senator and office
boy seems to be interested in my fight. That's a compliment anyway.

Hope Aunt Ella can make the trip. Do you think that you and Margie ought
to go somewhere for her hay fever? I can furnish you with the necessary funds
if you want to go. Colorado, Minnesota, or wherever you think. You could go to
Brainard, Minnesota and be in reach of the camp up there if I go to it. What
do you say?

I'm awfully glad Margie wants to go to our high school. She's a levelheaded
young lady—like her ma.

Will call you from Sedalia tomorrow night. Taking train to arrive there at
9:30 P.M. Will start out at Salisbury at 10:00 A.M. Thursday, Keytesville at 2:00
P.M., Brunswick 4:00, and Carrollton at 8:00 P.M., Hardin at 9:00 P.M. Next day,
Cuba and Cape Girardeau. Saturday, Sikeston, Malden, and Poplar Bluff. Rest
Sunday and start at Lamar, Nevada, Rich Hill, and Butler Monday. Harrisonville,
Belton, and K.C. Tuesday. Will stay at home Tuesday night April 30, and go to
St. Louis, thirty-first. Barkley is coming to K.C. and St. Louis on thirtieth and
thirty-first. Will stay in St. Louis until Saturday and then come home.

Probably have to go back to St. Louis Sunday, fourth. Home Monday to
stay—I hope.

Kiss Margie—love to you. Hope I won't offend you any more. Guess I'm
getting cranky.

Harry

*For Bess, Washington was no city to come home to, but for Truman—after
six years in the Senate—it had become almost a home. Below he tells of being
welcomed there after victory in the primary.*

Washington, D.C.

Dear Bess: August 9, 1940

It was nice to talk with you last evening. John and I were discussing 'cabbages and Kings and sealing wax and things.' Plenty of sealing wax. Had dinner at the Carroll Arms and I went to bed at nine, slept until seven, and have been answering the phone most ever since.

It certainly is gratifying (to put it mildly) when every employee in the building—elevator boys, policemen, waiters, cooks, negro cleanup women, and all—were interested in what would happen to me. Biffle told me last night over the phone that no race in his stay here had created such universal interest in the Senate. He's having lunch for me today. I guess it will be a dandy. It almost gives me the swell head—but I mustn't get that disease at this late date.

I'll never forget Tuesday night if I live to be a thousand—which I won't. My sweet daughter and my sweetheart were in such misery it was torture to me. I wished then I'd never have made the fight. But it was a good fight: state employees—five or six thousand of them—the police departments of St. Louis, Kansas City, St. Joseph, and every election board in the state where there is one, all the big papers except the *Journal,* and those papers using every lie told on me as the truth. I hope some good fact-finder will make a record of that campaign. It will be history someday.

Anyway we found out who are our friends, and it was worth it for that. Love and lots of it. When do you want to come on here? It's going to be mighty lonesome. Kiss Margie. Tell all the family hello.

Harry

Washington, D.C.

Dear Bess: August 10, 1940

Well I thought maybe I'd get a letter today but Uncle Sam or the transportation system must be out of joint, because none has come as yet. I'm still hoping. Letters of congratulation are still pouring in. I thought it was propaganda on the Burke-Wadsworth Bill, but it wasn't.

You should have been in the Senate yesterday when I slipped in at the back door. Hiram Johnson was making a speech and he had to call for order. Both floor leaders and all the Democrats made a grand rush. Biffle had lunch for twelve of 'em and if you don't think we had a grand time. I thought Wheeler and Jim Byrnes were going to kiss me. Barkley and Pat Harrison were almost as effusive. Schwellenbach, Hatch, Lister Hill, and Tom Stewart, and Harry Swartz almost beat me to death. Dennis Chavez hadn't taken a drink since the Chicago Convention but he said he'd get off the wagon on such an auspicious occasion and he did with a bang. Minton hugged me and I asked him why he didn't do that to Rush Holt and he'd never have to cuss him any more. Well as you can see it was a grand party.

Snyder and I had dinner together again at the Army and Navy Club upon the roof. It turned cold here last night and I had to pull up the bedspread.

Hope the margin is getting better. Remember me to all the family.

Kiss Margie, love to you,

Harry

In 1938 Mrs. Martha Ellen Truman had again renegotiated her farm mortgage, this time by borrowing from the school fund of Jackson County. In the summer of 1940 the county officials foreclosed, and neither the Senator nor his brother, Vivian, had enough money to stop the proceedings. The farm had been in the family for a century. Truman relates this saddening event, a bitter defeat at the very moment of electoral triumph.

Washington, D.C.

Dear Bess: August 13, 1940

Was happy to get your letter of yesterday and the enclosures. I'm enclosing you one. Glad you went to see Mary and Mamma. The damned county court and the lovely sheriff are ordering them to move off the farm. I only hope I can catch old Montgomery, J. C. Nichols, and Roy Roberts where I can take the heart out of 'em. Imagine your mother being forced out of 219 North Delaware. Mine has been calling that farm home since 1868. She helped her father set out those maple trees in the fall of that year.

Under a forced sale with everything against it the farm brought $1,600 more than the original lien. The damned *Star* never mentioned that. They are renting a house in Grandview, and I've advised them to move into it. It's a wrench but I guess we can stand it as we stood a defeat for three hours. That was an awful three hours though, wasn't it? . . .

I am hoping to see you Sunday. Maybe you'll want to come back with me and help find an apartment. How about it?

Kiss Margie, love to you,

Harry

Washington, D.C.

Dear Bess: August 24, 1940

. . . The chiselers are still arriving in droves and they almost pester me to death, but I have to be nice to them. I am enclosing you an announcement of a new baby for which we'll have to get a present of some sort. I sent its papa a letter of congratulation. He is the only real friend politically we have left in Johnson County. Cap Turner is his name (E.S. Turner, Chilhowee, Missouri). . . .

Hope everyone is well and that the weather still stays agreeable.

Kiss Margie, love to you,

Harry

Washington, D.C.

Dear Bess: August 29, 1940

Your Tuesday letter was in the morning mail. There have been so many planes grounded that airmail is all late. I'm really disgusted with that damned Jew and Al Holland. We all make mistakes and they are two of 'em. Vic is a dumb chick and doesn't know anything about organization or cooperation, but I don't think he's trying to do any undermining. He'd not know how. He had a Frank Lee complex on political lugs and I wouldn't be surprised if he is "short" some of the money collected, but I'm of the opinion that the others are equally "short." That happens in every campaign. Al Holland is no good as far as I can see, and as soon as I can cut the smart Hebrew loose, I shall do it. Vic, of course, eventually will have a successor, but I don't want to turn him out of doors. The girls are all right, so don't let that worry you. I could break the necks of those fellows for bothering you—and I may do it. All I want to do is to keep them quiet until after November and then I'll move 'em quick. They all act like a bunch of ten-year-old children. The absurdity of the whole thing makes me want to laugh or cuss a blue streak.

Don't let it worry you. There's nothing to worry about. We passed the Draft Bill last night. Will pass the big Appropriation Bill today and the Transportation Bill then comes up. It'll take a couple of days. Will then take up the Tax Bill.

Love to you, kiss Margie,

Harry

Washington, D.C.

Dear Bess: August 31, 1940

. . . You're going to have to protect me from Mary Chiles. She now wants to be National Committeewoman after I get the boys in the Second District to put her on the committee. Next thing she'll want to be Senator or governor. She's almost as ambitious as Stark. Hope she never sees this. McDaniel showed me a letter she wrote him in which she said the only reason she managed my women's division instead of his was because I'd asked her first. It was written on my stationery too!

Hope you had a nice time with the Shieldses. Still hope I get the letter today.

Love to you, kiss Margie,

Harry

Washington, D.C.

Dear Bess: September 1, 1940

. . . I've never had an experience with an office force just like that one in St. Louis. About four of them were plain nuts. It just goes to show that nearly all the troubles in the world are caused by a lack of balance in the human mind.

One small grain of common sense in Berenstein's head or Vic's would have stopped the whole thing. We ought to have lost with such a setup—but it was all we could get. All my political friends were on the run advising me to get a job, etc., and I had to take the tools at hand. The million pieces of mail sent out from there did do some good. It was finances that caused the trouble. They each wanted to go south with a little money, and I think that happened. You can't stop it in a campaign unless you have the money and pay the bills yourself.

It was nice to talk with you last night. I was afraid you'd think I was on that plane if I didn't call. My reservation was for Friday night and I had to cancel it. I'm going to say in a loud voice, "I told you so," when the Senate meets.

Kiss Margie, love to you,
Harry

Washington, D.C.
September 3, 1940

Dear Bess:

The mail was right this morning—Sunday's letter was in it. . . .

John Snyder and I had dinner together last night and discussed the situation. He is going home Friday. We hope to liquidate Mr. Berenstein and his boys and to get the whole situation worked out before very long.

We tried to go see *Boom Town* but couldn't get in. So we went to the Capitol and they put on that Jack Pot Show where they ask questions and pay for the answers. The ignorance of the American public is something appalling. The simplest questions would require four or five people to answer. The show was no good, so we left before it was over.

Some bird is coming in and I'll have to quit.

Love to you,
Harry

Washington, D.C.
September 4, 1940

Dear Bess:

Yesterday was a banner day. I received *two* letters. . . .

We won't have much session today because of Lundeen's death. Glad you sent the wire. Don't throw Margie's congratulations away. Sixteen years are very short in retrospect. Remember how you cried because you thought I was displeased she wasn't a boy? Well I'm glad she's not and there are nephews enough to continue the name anyway. We have been most lucky in health, happiness, and our daughter. No wealth but we've made a lot of people happy by being able to make recommendations, and we may yet stay out of the old peoples' home— you never can tell. I wouldn't give my friends for all the money in the world, and I'm just a plain, damn fool—as everyone will tell you.

The two boys who kept the books in the St. Louis office came in today. Berenstein tried to keep 'em from coming. They had no dirt to spill. But they are nice Jewish boys. I'm going to help 'em get jobs. They worked for nothing in the campaign.

Mr. Berenstein floats higher and higher. He had intended to be chairman of the state committee and let Al and Budy help him run it. Now he's in touch with Chairman Flynn, and I suppose will want to take his place if he can arrange it.

Snyder is going home to take him down a peg. I wonder how the world ran before we met him. No letter today, but I guess I should be glad for two yesterday.

Kiss the *baby,* love to you,
Harry

Washington, D.C.
Dear Bess: September 12, 1940
Well I arrived on time. Slept well from K.C. to St. Louis. Did the same nearly all day on the B. & O. and went to bed at seven-thirty. I am in much better shape than I was when I left here. . . . will see Snyder tomorrow on financing the fall campaign. Got a nice letter and a check for a hundred dollars from John Griggs. You'll have to move him up a little now, won't you?

I am going to try and see the President Monday or Tuesday and ask him to come to Missouri. He won't, of course, but I will have made the effort and maybe he'll tell me what Lloyd Crow wanted. He told Jim Byrnes that Stark is the biggest bore he ever talked to. Said the same thing he said to me—no sense of humor. He didn't help himself by running from the Jefferson City meeting.

I hope to be able to leave here on the eighteenth and be home on the nineteenth. If I can leave a day earlier, I'll let you know.

We'll go to Marcelline on the nineteenth for the dinner, to Wellston for the High School dedication, to Moberly for the opening on Saturday, home Saturday night, and you and I will go to St. Louis Sunday for the Grand Lodge meeting—after which we'll see what happens.

Kiss Margie, love to you,
Harry

Washington, D.C.
Dear Bess: September 14, 1940
. . . It looks like I'm going to have to agree to the reappointment of Milligan as district attorney to fill out his term. And I guess it is the best politics anyway. Some of my Kansas City friends will be hopping mad about it. And I don't feel so good about it myself. But the Hatch Act has just about put a stop to the political usefulness of all federal employees anyway.

Mr. Clark came down to see me last night after the Senate session, and I couldn't get rid of him. He said he'd like to be back in the army, and then he put on a complete infantry drill in my office. I guess Mrs. Clark is still out of town. Hope to see you about Friday, no, Thursday afternoon, the nineteenth anyway.

Kiss Margie, love to you,
Harry

Washington, D.C.
Dear Bess: Sunday, September 15 [1940]
... Well I had to recommend Milligan. Now I guess Jim will be on his ear.
Rog Sermon sent me a hot letter yesterday, Mary Chiles is mad—if I can just
do something to make the state chairman and McDaniel angry, I'll be batting
100 percent. Vic, Canfil, and Berenstein seem to have cooled off, but I guess that
mess can easily be started again too. I don't care much of a damn what they do
or don't, from here out I'm going to do as I please—and they can like or not as
they choose. I've spent my life pleasing people, doing things for 'em, and putting
myself in embarrassing positions to save the party and the other fellow, now I've
quit. To hell with 'em all. Now I feel better anyway.

I'm going to Bankhead's funeral. Old John and Lister Hill asked me to, and
I was too weak to refuse. True to form, you see. Hope you are feeling fine. The
girls are both working.

Kiss Margie, love to you,
Harry

Washington, D.C.
Dear Bess: Sunday night, September 15, 1940
Well I just struck a dry hole. Called, and you were at a show. Hope it
was a good one and I'm glad you could go. But I've been working all day. Had
both girls and Vic here trying to catch up. We didn't. My desk is a mess, just
killed a cockroach. He walked right out on the arm rest where I'm writing
this as impudently as a sassy nigger. We're still answering personal letters dated
August. . . .

Leighton Shields came to see me Saturday and wanted me to take him to
see the President. I told him I couldn't get an engagement for myself, let alone
a customer. Said he wouldn't take any of my time. I wonder whose he'd take.
I'm not going to see the President any more until February 1, and then he's going
to want to see me. I rather think from here out I'll make him like it.

Hope you had a nice time tonight. Tomorrow I'll be riding to Alabama with
what's left of the late Speaker. Anyway he died in the harness and that's something. . . .

Love to you,
Harry

Hotel Pennsylvania, New York, N.Y.
Dear Bess: September 28, 1940
Well here I am in New York all alone. I went to see the National Democratic Committee to head off the governor and got the job done. They have the
same impression of him that everyone else has. I was expecting to go back to
Washington this afternoon but was so tired I decided to sleep. So I'm not going
back until tomorrow. Can you imagine coming to N.Y. to sleep? It won't cost

me any more to do it here and I was never so tired in my life. It looks as if there was never so much to do and so little time in which to do it. My desk looks like a cyclone had piled up all the unanswered letters in the world, and I don't think I'm ever going to get to the bottom of them.

The Congress will not adjourn. They all seemed extremely happy to see me and that was especially true of the Vice President. He gave me a reception in his office with Burke, Schwellenbach, Chavez, Minton, and Barkley. For some reason they seem to like your old man. The only regret I have is that I didn't just bundle you up and make you come along. I need somebody I can tell my troubles to most awful bad—and it looks as if you are it. Up to now I've tried to keep them from you because I never want to be a cause of worry to you. Kiss my beautiful daughter and wish for one from me yourself. You should be here to get it.

Love to you,
Harry

Washington, D.C.

Dear Bess: Tuesday, October 1, 1940

... I'm glad you went to see Mamma. No matter how much front she puts on she hates to leave the farm, even if it has been nothing but a source of worry and trouble to us for about fifty years.

The place has brought bad luck and financial disaster to everyone connected with it since my grandfather died in 1892. If we'd been smart and sold it right after the World War when I had the stock sale, we could have been no worse off if we'd spent all the money in riotous living. Well it's gone anyway and may the jinks go with it. . . .

I dictated as hard as I could yesterday to all three girls, and the pile on the desk is as high as ever this morning. I'm doing the same today and then tomorrow I'm writing three speeches and then try to start for home. McKittrick has balled up the Social Security and it looks as if I'm going to have to straighten it out. Hope you continue to have good weather. It's cold and damp here. Love to you. Has my baby a sore finger?

Harry

IV

LEADING THE COUNTRY

As THE THIRTIES CAME TO AN END the Junior Senator from Missouri seemed to be mired in local politics, in particular his rivalry with Governor Stark. Economic depression worldwide and the rise of Hitler in Germany were then only secondary concerns for the future president. His preparation for handling issues of this magnitude was gradual—the political skills, knowledge, and reputation developing from his work in the senate. He was especially effective in getting the Transportation Act, 1940, passed. He also pushed through Congress the Civil Aeronautics Act, 1938. Many of the other senators respected him as one of the perhaps dozen prime movers in the Upper House.

Truman was a no-nonsense legislator, willing to meet with his constituents and do for them what he properly could, willing to perform the necessary social duties at luncheons and dinners, unwilling for the most part to go on senatorial junkets—unless he saw a considerable public value in them. But no one observing the graying, serious man from Missouri—getting into his office at seven-thirty each morning, frequently finding time to dine at nothing more elegant than the local Hot Shoppe, taking the bus to a nondescript apartment house—would have thought him a future international leader. His activities seemed as remote from major world affairs as was Missouri.

Truman began his second term in 1941 without the slightest presidential ambition, with only a modest pride that he had shed his Pendergast associations and become Senator in his own right. The next task he set his mind to ended up putting him on the road to national leadership: the establishment of a Senate Special Committee to Investigate the National Defense Program. The work of keeping the committee together, bringing out its reports, pitilessly holding the glass of publicity to defense failures, whether in the U.S. Army or so-called civilian life—and in the latter, both capital and labor—kept him busy.

By 1944 the leadership of the United States and of the alliance against Germany and Japan lay in the hands of the great triumvirs: Roosevelt, Winston Churchill, and Joseph Stalin. The course of the war was becoming certain after establishment in June of a second front in France. But unknown to the American people, and probably even to the British and Soviets, was the declining health of President Roosevelt. When his condition became apparent, in the summer of 1944, the national leaders of the Democratic party—excluding the President himself, who seemingly refused to recognize what might happen to national and international leadership if he were to die—virtually conspired to displace then-Vice President Henry A. Wallace. The party leaders, mostly bosses of large cities and all of them seasoned politicos, considered Wallace a visionary, a man without the slightest political judgment; they talked Roosevelt into running for a fourth term with Truman.

During the hustings that fall, campaigning not merely for himself but also for the ailing President, Truman knew he was actually running for the presidency. Election as Vice President would mean succession, eventually, to the nation's highest office. What he could not calculate, and resolutely refused to consider, was the date that Roosevelt might die. After a vice presidency that lasted only until April 12, 1945, Truman suddenly found himself leading the country.

The Truman presidency lasted almost eight years, until January 1953, and at the outset seemed strange to millions of Americans accustomed to Roosevelt. Once the war ended in Germany, on May 8, and in the Far East, on August 14 (followed by a ceremonial termination aboard the battleship *Missouri* in Tokyo Bay on September 2), criticisms of the new President began to mount. By 1946 there was much talk of a Missouri Compromise, of a "gray little county judge," of a man with only a high-school education filling the shoes of a Groton and Harvard graduate. A parallel was drawn with the presidential succession after World War I, and people recalled another small-town president, Warren G. Harding of Marion, Ohio. The Republican party looked to victory in 1948, whereupon the scrappy Truman fought his way to electoral victory by whistle-stopping across the country.

Victory over the "economic royalists" in Republican ranks and announcement of a Fair Deal early in 1949, akin to the Rooseveltian New Deal, did not mean that liberal domestic programs would pass Congress; for the most part they did not. Nor did it mean that personal triumph would last for another four years. Truman's second administration started like the first, on an upbeat, leading to a downbeat. The president enjoyed a momentary public esteem that was soon overshadowed by the country's fear of communism in government and by the uncertainties of the Korean War.

During both terms, Truman managed a leadership of American foreign relations that in retrospect compels enormous respect. Polls of presidential leadership in subsequent years place Truman close to greatness in the pantheon of American Presidents. Seventy-five leading historians in 1962 placed him in the "near great" category—tying with Polk—just after Lincoln, Washington, Franklin D. Roosevelt, Wilson, and Jefferson, all of whom were "great"; John Adams and Grover Cleveland also placed "near great."

Presidential rankings change with the winds of time and whim. But it is not too much to predict that Truman's standing in years to come may well move up second only to Lincoln—and for a reason that is only now becoming clear.

Attacks on his integrity as well as judgment aside, it is becoming evident that Truman's presence in the White House ensured the turning of American foreign policy from isolationism. Truman sponsored what became known as the Truman Doctrine, of 1947, together with the Marshall Plan for reconstruction of Western Europe, announced that same year, and the North Atlantic Treaty Organization, formed in 1949. These major moves toward a constant U.S. participation in the affairs of Europe were followed by U.S. entrance into the Korean War, which probably prevented the communization of both Japan and South Korea.

TWELVE

THE COMMITTEE

Hardly had Truman taken his seat in the Upper House of the Congress that met in January 1941 when his mail, always large, swelled with letters from constituents writing about malfeasance in contracts let for construction projects at Fort Leonard Wood in Rolla, Missouri. Army quartermaster officers were letting contracts on a cost-plus basis, which encouraged tremendous profiteering, and when the Senator inquired of the army about this matter, officers in the quartermaster corps in Washington virtually told him to mind his own business. Truman knew that whatever was happening in Leonard Wood was happening everywhere else in the country, as the army hastily enlarged its encampments to house and care for hundreds of thousands of draftees. Always suspicious of the regular army's ineptitude, he made a personal reconnaissance by automobile, driving in a great arc down into the South, and back up through Arkansas, Oklahoma, and Missouri. Sure enough, the regulars were up to their old tricks —sanctimoniously claiming to supervise what they were too inept to control. Hundreds of millions of tax dollars were going down the drain.

And it was not merely the inefficiencies of constructing camps. The Missouri Senator had just finished studying the practices of Wall Street bankers and lawyers in regard to railroads; he knew that in the rush of defense contracts for military equipment as well as camp construction the profiteering would be enormous—unless a watchdog committee somewhere within the government, ideally within the Senate, could be immediately and constantly attentive.

The resultant committee, which Truman established in a crafty manner one dull day in the Senate, when hardly any Senators were on the floor, turned out to be perhaps the major accomplishment of the Upper House during the war years. The Missourian who became its chairman sensed immediately that the Roosevelt administration looked upon it with disfavor, for any watchdog committee that became critical would seem to be questioning the conduct of the President of the United States. The formidable leader residing at 1600 Pennsylvania Avenue heartily disliked criticism from anyone, trouble from Congress not the least. He may have instructed Senator James F. Byrnes, who controlled the Appropriations Committee, to award Truman's committee the princely sum of

$15,000 to investigate federal expenditures that already had reached into the tens of billions and would go far higher. Undaunted, Truman chose a very able investigator to head his inquiries: the lawyer Hugh Fulton, who brought together a small group of able assistants. As members of the committee, the Missouri Senator chose his best colleagues, men who would work not only hard but also as a team. They thereupon began investigations of the financing and technical performance of contractors for camp construction and for the manufacture of airplane engines, steel plates—altogether some thirty national programs. Often they found ineptitude, frequently chicanery. After each investigation their method for reform was a unanimous report, made public. The threat of exposure in the public report usually brought miscreants to a change of heart, resulting in renegotiation of too-liberal contracts or correction of faulty manufacturing procedures.

By the year 1944, when the Democratic National Convention assembled in Chicago, the Truman Committee, as it was known, had become widely publicized and much admired. If President Roosevelt had had any initial apprehensions, he now forgot them, appreciating the political care as well as the efficiency with which Truman had conducted the investigations—the way in which the Missourian had sought to solve problems rather than apportion political blame. When someone asked Roosevelt about the Truman Committee in the spring of 1944, his response was immediate. "Oh yes," said the President, "that was this committee, this investigating committee, that I, uh, er, created back in 1941, was it not?"

Beginning in 1940, when Mrs. Martha Ellen Truman was forced to move, together with Mary Jane, into an unfamiliar house in Grandview, her health became ever more uncertain. At the outset she fell downstairs and broke her hip. After recovery she seemed weaker, but her son was happy to see a reassertion of her old cantankerousness, as he tells Bess below.

Washington, D.C.
Dear Bess: March 19, 1941
What do you mean I haven't time to read what you write? I told the gals they'd all be fired tonight if I didn't get a letter. They seemed right glad one came —so was I.

Glad you went to see Mamma. She must be much better, the way she's standing them around. She has a notion she can do just as she did before the fall and she never did like help around the house. Hope it works out all right.

I've been going around in circles today. Saved the Jackson County Court from insolvency—damn 'em. But I have too many friends who'd suffer if I hadn't done it. Mr. Nichols came in and cried on my shoulder again. The *Post-Dispatch* has him scared pink. I thought I could see him skinned alive and like it but I'm not enjoying it at all. Not built right, I guess, to man a chopping block. Also the lovely mayor of St. Louis must have spent five dollars crying on my shoulder over the phone and I helped him. I'm going to run out of coals one of these days and use a knife. I am being besieged by the Tiff Miners in White County for help on an appropriation, and my investigating committee is getting really hot. Feel better about it now. Looks like I'll get something done. We meet tomorrow. It's still colder than any day last winter but will be over tomorrow.

Tell Chris to behave herself. She has too much at stake to take any chances.

Kiss my little girl, love to you,

Harry

Washington, D.C.

Dear Bess: March 23, 1941

Well no letter came from anybody this morning but job hunters and people who want to make appointments with me at Jefferson City. I had hoped there'd be one here this morning. Maybe I'll get one out at the flat. I came out even on bread and butter this morning, so I won't buy any more. I'll use raisin bread until Tuesday, and I guess there's some butter in the icebox. I'm also up to date on milk and buttermilk. Every time I want something to drink, I take buttermilk and I've started to walk again. Walked up to the Mayflower yesterday at noon for lunch with the Stricklers and walked out to Chevy Chase Circle and back this morning before I came down here. . . .

I am enclosing you your new old man. How do you like my new face? Maybe you'll want to try my beauty shop next time. We're afraid he's deserted his wife or killed his mother-in-law or something somewhere else in the paper and that I'm posing for him. Hope for two tomorrow. Hope Christie is home.

Kiss Margie, love to you,

Harry

Washington, D.C.

Dear Bess: June 14, 1941

Well here I am at the apartment, and I have all the lights turned on to keep something or someone from getting me. It is a most lonesome place, but clean as a pin. The suit and laundry were in the hall, and both papers for today were in the package receptacle.

I can't get over thinking about running away without saying good-bye to Fred and your mother. The more I think of it, the worse it gets. And I never thought of it until we were at the crossroad that goes to Marshall and then I had a blue day from then on. We had to stand up for the graduation and listen to Otis make a speech on "Scraps of Paper." The scraps were Magna Carta, the Constitution of the United States, and the Declaration of Independence. The judge has all the tricks of a finished orator but he was funnier than he was good, and I'm not thinking of him as a biased judge either. . . .

Kiss Margie, love to you,

Harry

Washington, D.C.
Dear Bess: June 19, 1941

Today is a good day—the letter came. If it had not I'd probably have had a nervous breakdown—because I had played poker with the counselors of the Investigating Committee until midnight, winning the tremendous sum of $6.50. They were more nearly in my class than those House fellows. Had to go or be a high hat. When I arrived at the office I found 'em waiting. Aluminum pipeline people, my subcommittee on Interstate Commerce, Frank Monroe, two committees on Military Affairs and one on Appropriations. So you see I've had a busy day and I hope I can go to bed early tonight.

But I can't, just got called out of the Senate to see Neal Helm, Orville Zimmerman, and some oilmen. Have to go to dinner with 'em. The Honorable Senator Bailey just told me I am doing a good job on investigations. (Maybe I'm wrong.)

I haven't seen the coat but I'll take another look. Was it cloth or the velvet one? I saw the velvet one but not the cloth one. Sent you the key. Maybe it's still in the trunk. My standing in the Senate and down the street [1600 Pennsylvania Avenue] gets better and better. Hope I make no mistakes. If I weren't working from daylight until dark, I don't know what I'd do. Hope I won't be long here alone.

Kiss Margie, love to you,
Harry

The Eastman Hotel, Hot Springs National Park, Arkansas
Dear Bess: July 27, 1941

Happy day today, twenty-eighth—wish you were here to celebrate it at the Arlington in a suite like the Blackstone's—or maybe the Chicago hotel would be better. I am sorry I didn't stay in New Orleans and buy you a bracelet or something—but I'm saving all my money for three years hence when I'll have to buy you a pair of silver slippers. You know they are expensive.

It was nice to talk with you last night and I'm uneasy about your mother. Don't leave anything undone that you ought to do for her. If you need funds I'll get 'em.

I am going to the hospital this afternoon and will stay until a week from tomorrow anyway. Saw the men in charge this A.M. and they are very fine men. Both here when I was here before, but there is a new commandant. Will try to talk to you tomorrow.

Love to you, kiss Margie for me,
Harry

Army and Navy Hospital, Hot Springs, Ark.
Dear Bess: June 28, 1941

It was a grand telegram and I acted like a sentimental old fool when it came. I moved in at 3:00 P.M. yesterday, and they started in on me at six this morning. I had to swallow a sinker on a rubber tube and it took me two hours to do it and then I had to keep it down two hours and a half after drinking two glasses of water and eating two pieces of toast. They pumped out a sample before the toast and one every half hour afterwards until they had five all told. It was most uncomfortable.

They took my blood pressure. It was only 94. The doc looked at it and took it again. Then said, well you do need rest sure enough. They start on the gall bladder in the morning and then heart, teeth, etc. By Saturday we'll know it all.

Well I wish you were here or I was at home. It's not nice to spend your wedding day in a hospital. . . .

I may not be able to write every day if they work on me too much. But I'll do the best I can.

Love to you and my baby,
Harry

Army and Navy Hospital, Hot Springs, Ark.

Dear Bess: June 30, 1941

Well ten minutes after yesterday's letter left I got two, yours of twenty-eighth; and twenty-third forwarded from Washington. There was one from Mary in the Washington envelope too. Then I got your June 27 letter this morning —so in spite of all the clinics it's a good day. Got all the gall bladder pictures today. Had to take dye yesterday afternoon and no breakfast this A.M. or dinner last night. Then a picture at eleven o'clock and a glass of milk and cream with a couple of raw eggs in it. They let me have lunch, a couple of lamb chops, spinach, mashed potatoes, and a cup of coffee.

Had all my teeth photographed and my heart tested in between times.

The main doctor on this floor came in and told me the stomach pump operation showed a shortage of certain essential acids, which could be easily remedied, and he was sure that would *probably* turn out to be the whole trouble. I have done nothing but sleep almost night and day, and Fred says I look much better than when I came in, in spite of the mauling I've taken. They are giving me everything in the book. Wish you were here to take it too. By all means get the checkup you want. We can stand it better now than ever. For some unaccountable reason we've done better than we ever did on expenses. I guess that Masonic expense account helped on trips. Will let you know all I know. Glad your mother is better and that Mamma's eyes are all right.

Love to you,
Harry

Army and Navy Hospital, Hot Springs, Ark.

Dear Bess: July 1, 1941

I found this high-hat stationery [United States Senate, Washington; at upper left, Harry S. Truman, Missouri] in my bag and thought maybe you'd appreciate hearing from a United States Senator. . . .

I am still on the merry-go-around. Had what they called a metabolism test this morning. They put a clothespin on my nose and stuck a rubber tube attached to an oxygen tank and an electric writing machine into my mouth, and I had to breathe that way for five minutes while the pen made something like that on a piece of paper. Then I went up to another ward and had a tube stuck in the other end for some purpose best known to the doc. Tomorrow more stomach photos and nose and throat. . . .

Those were nice clippings. Hope our mothers continue to improve. Heat is not bad here at all. I have a cool room. Glad Marg is having a nice time. Wish I could have been at T.P. party.

Harry

Army and Navy General Hospital, Hot Springs, Ark.

Dear Bess: July 5, 1941

Well I hope you are having a grand time at Ben's this day. I have the final report, and there is *nothing* the matter but fatigue. The heart is perfect, teeth 100 percent, lungs all clear, intestinal tract is unobstructed and normal, eyes need other glasses—probably the ones I broke of Doctor Key's.

Need rest and relaxation and I'm going to take it along with some pills to balance lack of hydrochloric acid in the stomach caused by fatigue. That's what causes the nausea.

My routine will be breakfast at 7:30, walk one hour, Hot Springs bath 9:30, sunbath 10:30, rest at 11:00, lunch 12:30—nap afterwards, penny ante poker 5:00 to 6:30, then dinner, to bed at 9:00 and do it over. I'll try to be home on Friday afternoon or Saturday morning, see Mamma and Aunt Ella, and then you, and I leave for the capital so I can be there Monday, July 14, before noon. How does that suit? Just had a wire from Harry saying everything O.K. there. I feel better, nearly 100 percent.

Love to you,
Harry

Army and Navy Hospital, Hot Springs, Ark.

Dear Bess: July 7, 1941

Was glad to talk with you yesterday and glad to get a letter too. I am feeling like a new man. Had a letter from Harry Vaughan enclosing me some checks to sign for the committee. I sent him a check for the rent and told him to go out to the apartment and get the mail and put the bills on my desk.

I am walking every morning and taking a sunbath too. I'm as red as an Indian from head to foot and that 140 degree water really makes it hot in the bath.

Went up and had my eyes tested this morning. The major gave me a test Saturday and double checked it today. Said I needed a new prescription and some drops to squirt up my nose—a slight sinus stoppage, which he said would tend to help cause that accommodation spasm I've been having.

A Jewish reserve officer from Little Rock came over in his Cadillac car and

took Fred and me to the lake and a boat ride yesterday. He's a grand person—
a cavalryman whom we've known since the war. Name's Rosenbloom but doesn't
act it at all. We'll see you Saturday.

Kiss Margie, love to you,
Harry

Washington, Ind.

Dear Bess: August 4, 1941

. . . I hope my mamma has continued to improve. When you know her, she
is a grand old woman. She hates her enemies and makes no bones about it. And
she's for her friends, strictly on emotion in both cases. Maybe it's better that way.
I didn't inherit it from her. I do a lot of analyzing of my own reactions before
I blame anyone else, and then I don't blame 'em much. But I do like my friends.

Kiss Margie, lots of love,
Harry

Washington, D.C.

Dear Bess: Friday night, August 15, 1941

It was quite a wrench to see you go away. I watched the train pull out as
I walked up the platform and I felt most decidedly lonesome.

I'm glad the d--- Senate acted according to its usual form and that the
weather conspired with it so I could take you to the train. I am more of a
sentimentalist at fifty-seven than I was at sixteen—and that is a most astronomi-
cal statement.

You know at sixteen I had read *all* the books, including the encyclopedias,
in the Independence Public Library and had been through the Bible twice and
I thought—and *still* think—that you were Esther, Ruth, and Bathsheba, all
combined. And I still believe in Santa Clause, in spite of my friend T.J.P.,
O'Malley, Murray, et al. Guess I'm a real d--- f---. Saw old man Shannon this
morning, and he is a sentimentalist too—but a political one. There is some
difference if you can figure it out. . . .

Be sure and kiss my baby for me. I'm glad she's a beautiful lady too—aren't
you?

Love to you,
Harry

Aboard army transport

Dear Bess: August 16, 1941

We left Bolling Field at 6:25 this morning and had a bucking-bronco ride
to Knoxville. Just enough clouds to make the plane bounce. Got to Knoxville at
9:25 and set our watches back to 8:25. Went up to 7,500 feet from there to
Memphis and had a pleasant, smooth ride. Most everyone took a nap. Had lunch

at Memphis and are now headed for Dallas. Just hit some more clouds. We are one and a half miles above Sulphur Springs, Arkansas, and going 145 miles an hour. Didn't get our fast plane, but we have a good one and two good pilots. It rained for three hours last night but was nice and clear this morning. It has been a beautiful day all the way across. Jim Mead bought *Life*, *Newsweek*, and a *Time* at Memphis, so we have considerable news to read.

Hope to call you from Dallas tonight. We'll stay at the Adolphus Hotel and then head for L.A. (and it stands for the town this time not the physical condition of my fat secretary). Hope you made the train connections all right. They usually make up the lost time. Tell everyone hello and kiss Margie for me.

Love to you,
Harry

The Biltmore Hotel, Los Angeles, Calif.

Dear Bess: Monday, August 18, 1941

It was nice to talk to you last night and also to find a good letter when I got to my presidential suite. The sun is shining out here this A.M. but it isn't uncomfortably hot. I put on my gray suit and expect to be comfortable.

The box was full of phone calls, one from Mrs. Paul, which I shall answer today. A Mr. Pruitt and his wife came up to see me, said he is a son of a man whom I know living at Slater. Said he had two Packard cars and wanted me to use one of them. Thanked him and said no. Then he wanted me to bring all the Senators and come to dinner. I guess I'll be turning 'em down from now on. We went to Mr. Carroll's show last night and it is good but not new. Same old stunts Weber and Fields were doing forty years ago without the mike. We had a good dinner but I suspect it will cost the committee in somebody's expense account.

Here's a clipping from Dallas. Please save it for me. I'm up before breakfast to write this. Kiss my baby.

Love to you,
Harry

Biltmore Hotel, Los Angeles, Calif.

Dear Bess: Thursday, August 21, 1941

Well I spent yesterday at San Diego. The navy sent a big transport plane for us. We left the airport here at 9:00 A.M., arrived at San Diego at 10:00, and Admiral Blakely took us in charge for the usual show around. Looked at marine barracks under construction and had lunch with the recruits. A Missouri boy from St. Louis waited on me, one from New York took care of Mead, and one from Washington, Wallgren.

Looked over the new marine base camp and then got another walk around a plane plant, the Consolidated—said to be the biggest of 'em all. The managers are all such liars you can't tell anything about the facts. Each one says he's having no trouble and everything is rosy but that the other fellow is in one awful fix. By questioning five or six of them separately I've got an inkling of the picture, and it is rather discouraging in some particulars but good in others. We are turning out a very large number of planes and could turn out more if the navy and army boys could make up their minds just what they want.

Labor is a problem. The same brand of racketeer is getting his hand in as he did in the camp construction program. Some of 'em should be in jail. Hold some hearings today and tomorrow, spend Saturday and Sunday in San Francisco, and open in Seattle Monday. I haven't had a chance to see anything or do anything except go to that awful Earl Carroll show. Have about fifty phone calls a day, and all the crackpots in California have tried to see. Will try to call Miss Jessie today. Called Mrs. Shields yesterday and she seemed very pleased about it. She should have been, it cost enough.

Kiss Margie, love to you,
Harry

Olympic Hotel, Seattle, Wash.

Dear Bess: August 24, 1941
. . . We left the grand St. Francis Hotel at 10:00 A.M. today in the general's car, with him telling us all about how to save the country and pointing out the shipyards, etc., on the way to the airport. He's six feet, four inches tall and big all around and, I am told, an efficient officer. But they are all bores when they talk to Senators.

We got on the same navy plane we came up from L.A. in and got up here at four-thirty. Went up to 12,700 feet when we passed Mt. Shasta and it was cold as wintertime. They turned on the heat. It was a beautiful ride and clearer than it was in 1939 when I passed that way before. Flew over Portland and passed Mt. Rainier at about the same distance as we did Mt. Shasta but not so high up.

Mt. Whitney, which we passed going into Los Angeles, is 14,495 feet high, Mt. Rainier 14,408, and Shasta 14,162. The Chamber of Commerce of Tacoma put a ninety-foot tower on top of Rainier and advertised it as the highest peak in continental U.S. The government wouldn't let 'em count it, so California still has the highest mountain.

Work in earnest starts tomorrow. Tuesday Mead and Brewster go to Alaska and I stay here and work.

Kiss Margie, love to you,
Harry

Spokane, Wash.

Dear Bess: August 30, 1941
I am at Lew Schwellenbach's house staying all night after a most pleasant day at the Washington College of Agriculture at Pullman looking over a plant to make magnesium metal from magnesite ore.

Schwellenbach, Wallgren, a Mr. Coleman, chairman of the Democratic committee who drove us over here yesterday, or Thursday, and myself rode in the car together. We discussed everything from the President to Senator Bone and Washington State scenery.

There is a geologist and professor of metalurgy at the Pullman College who showed us how he had made magnesium metal by a new process. Lew said he had talked with this professor when he (Lew) was president of the board of regents of the University of Washington and that the professor had something. I believe he has and I am going to recommend the expenditure of a million dollars of federal money to see what he has. If we can make this ore into metal for as little as 10 cents a pound, and they say we can, that means it can compete with aluminum at 6 cents a pound. The present price of aluminum is 14 cents, and it has been 21 cents. By experiments we've seen at the Northrop plane plant we can make lighter, safer, and faster planes for less money from magnesium than are being made from aluminum, and the housewives can keep their pots and pans. Our shortage will be solved and a cutthroat monopoly broken up. . . .

Lew had a Lieutenant Colonel Murrow come over and tell me about England and the war. He is a brother of the one mentioned in Shirer's *Berlin Diary*. I had a most interesting evening. We talked independent air force—à la General Mitchell, German plan, English plan, or no plan—and tried to work out a solution of our own. We didn't succeed, but I am hoping we can find a solution. . . .

Lew says I am doing something worthwhile and that he is proud to call me friend, and Mrs. S. said he'd not been able to turn a wheel since I wired him I'd stop here. He told me that he had set all his work for next Tuesday so this week would be free for any day I happened along. It's worth six years of hard work and drudgery and a Stark campaign to have made friends like Lew and Shay Minton.

Kiss Margie, love to you,
Harry

The Masons met at Milwaukee, and after the convention Senator Truman went to Chicago for a committee meeting. At the Milwaukee meeting something unexpected and sad happened; Truman writes of it to Bess.

The Stevens, Chicago, Ill.
September 16, 1941

Dear Bess:

. . . Arrived here at eleven o'clock Standard Time, or ten-thirty really, because I caught an eleven o'clock electric car to Milwaukee. They are on daylight saving, so by Chicago time it was twelve o'clock. Got to the beer town at one o'clock Standard Time. It is ninety-five miles and I walked over to the parade. They had all the streets blocked and wouldn't let me into it, so I walked the whole length of it to the hotel where the Missourians were staying. Saw Clem White from St. Joe and several other fellows. They told me about Fred Chambers falling over in Bennett's room. I went over to see Bennett, but he wasn't available. I don't think Fred had been indulging in spiritus frumenti, because he [Fred] was not in the habit of doing it.

Clem White told me he [Fred] had been kidding Bennett about being so long getting ready to go to the Missouri caucus that he sat down in a chair and crossed one foot over his knee and was dead before anyone realized that he was even out. Just shows that we are all past the age of 1917. . . .

Say hello to your mother.

Kiss Margie, love to you,
Harry

[Melbourne Hotel, St. Louis, Mo.]

Dear Bess: September 18, 1941

Vic and young Ed McKim and his red-haired football player friend kept me up until one o'clock yesterday morning, so I overslept and decided I'd start southwest to St. Louis and not go back to Milwaukee. I am very sure I did the proper thing, because I went to bed at nine-thirty last night and feel as if I can dictate my report with a clear head. And by the way, I feel better than I have for a month. Been reading Chicago, Milwaukee, and St. Louis papers and talking to people who are not influenced by that crazy Washington complex, so I've begun to get a straight point of view. The country is usually the place to find out what is right. Anyway I'm in better condition both mentally and physically. There will be quite a strenuous ten days ahead of me, but I'm going to try and get Roy Webb to be doorkeeper and driver for me and if I can I'll come out all right.

I went out and took a walk last night and saw where Sally Rand was at the Fox right around the corner. Went in to see what she looked like. Her bubble dance was very nice and decent but the show was rotten, so I left and finished my walk. Even the news picture was no good. Wish I had my baseball pass. St. Louis plays Boston this afternoon, here. The town and the papers are wild about the race between Brooklyn and the Cards. Brooklyn writers are accusing St. Louis of being everything we thought it was in *our* campaign. But I want St. Louis to win. We can't let a bunch of Kike trolly dodgers slander our biggest town, even if we would have agreed last year.

I'll be happy when my Masonic career ends and I can work altogether on the Senate Committee, go where I please, say what I want to, and maybe do the country some good. Say hello to your mother.

Kiss Margie, love to you,
Harry

Hotel Muehlebach, Kansas City, Mo.

Dear Bess: September 24, 1941

Got two letters today. What a day that made it. I mean I got two yesterday because it is now 12:10 A.M., September 24. I held court all day yesterday (Monday) and saw everybody who had the nerve and the patience to wait. This suite has a dining room with a living room off of it with double doors between, then there is a hallway and a twin-bed room. There are two bathrooms and an extra toilet. I sat in the dining room at the head of the table so everybody in the living room could see me and then I put the customer with his back to the double doors, both open and occasionally while he was telling me his tale of woe I'd smile and nod to someone waiting and you'd be surprised how fast they went through. I must have seen a thousand people counting Friday, yesterday, and today.

Jim Pendergast, Tom Evans, Joe McGee, and Bill Boatright spent two hours with me yesterday—Monday afternoon—*in the bedroom* talking about the city situation. Mr. Gage spent one hour in the same place this morning telling me what he thought. And I spent from 2:30 to 4:30 in the P.O. at Independence today (Tuesday) talking to John Thompson, Les George, young Gabriel and Heinie. Roger is in Washington with Bell. So I have heard every angle of the city, county, and state situation. Mr. Aylward sent an emissary to see me also. My, what a difference from last year this time and what a kick there is in it. They all cuss Clark and wonder what I am going to do for the poor old *"Party."* What should I do?

Joe O'Brien, Fred Canfil, Gene Damon, and Ed McKim have all been helping me. Today at noon I took 'em all over to Rugel's place on the highway north of the Armour-Swift-Burlington bridge and fed 'em. Roy Webb's wife runs it for Rugel. Roy has driven me everywhere.

Had dinner tonight (Tuesday) with Mamma and Mary. Mamma is in fine spirits. She gave Roy a great kick. . . .

You should see Geo. Marquis' biography of your old man for the Grand Lodge *Proceedings.* You'd be like the old lady at the funeral of her husband, you'd have someone check to be sure it is the right corpse. Hello to Mrs. W.

Kiss Margie, love to you,
Harry

Melbourne Hotel, St. Louis, Mo.
Dear Bess: Saturday, September 27, 1941
. . . The dinner was at the Plaza Hotel. There were three hundred tickets sold and they all came. Roy said I made a good speech and so did the Chinese consul general from Chicago, Dr. Chen by name, who is a law graduate of Chicago U., has master's degree from Harvard, and one or two others from various and sundry colleges. He said Japan is whipped. Hope he's right. Said we caused the prolongation of the war by letting Japan have oil and scrap iron. Course he's right.

Drove back to K.C. after the show and had a flat tire. John Welsted, the singer, rode with me and it didn't take long to change the tire. While I was getting Spina to give me a haircut I sent Roy down to our White Rose Station and had a whole new set of tubes put in. Three of those old tubes had been patched and I'd never had 'em off the car. I'm going to have yours looked over when I get back, and Mr. Lon is going to hear from me. . . .

Barney Dickmann took me to lunch just now. Went by to see Bennett on the way to the Key Club, and he was pie-eyed as usual. You know he was supposed to talk the situation over with me at Milwaukee, same condition there, then here. Everybody is off him. You never have heard anyone as roundly cussed even by his henchmen.

Talked to Harry Vaughan a while ago and told him to call you. Have a lunch date with Collet tomorrow.

Have changed the schedule. Will go to Springfield Wednesday afternoon and Caruthersville Saturday and Sunday of next week and then start to Washington.

Lots of love,
Harry

Dear Bess:

Dunn Hotel, Popular Bluff, Mo.
October 3, 1941

Well the Springfield trip was a success. . . . The St. Louis and Springfield papers have treated me with senatorial consideration. It's a lot different from last year. Everybody is off of Clark. His own people cuss him the most. He's in a lot worse shape than I was when Pendergast went to jail. It may change but I doubt it. He won't see anyone, never keeps his appointments, and is constantly plastered when he can be seen. Just think what he's thrown away. In 1936 he was the fair-haired boy. Farley and the President were both boosting him. And he just threw it away. He got the worst booing at the Legion convention in its history, so Bill Kitchen told me. Bill's his friend too.

Well my tour of duty as Grand Master ended up in a blaze of glory anyway. All the opposition had to eat crow and like it. My good friends were the happiest men you ever saw and I felt like it was worth all the effort and time.

Will bring home the papers. Be in Caruthersville tomorrow and Sunday. Will start for Washington Sunday afternoon and drive leisurely and *carefully* home. Will phone you Sunday morning before church this time. Best regards to your mother.

Kiss Margie, love to you,
Harry

Dear Bess:

Hotel Majestic, Caruthersville, Mo.
October 5, 1941

Well again it was nice to talk with you, but you didn't seem to be in the happiest frame of mind. I know I've been gone a long time but I haven't wasted one minute.

The Grand Lodge session still stands out as one highlight in everything I've done. Nearly everything possible came up for me to rule on, and not a single criticism from the smart boys who sit behind the Grand Master and make comments. The Past Grand Masters sit there and find fault if they can. I got seven thousand dollars appropriated for soldier relief, and got the Grand Lodge's business finished in record time, and the new G.M. installed, and the thing closed up by twelve-thirty Wednesday—a real record. Was mobbed worse than the new boss after the close. The custom is "God save the King—the King is dead." (It's the other way around.) Everybody wants to stand in well with the new man but this time it was different. Every mean, old son of a gun who fought me last year and the preceding years was in line to say how well the job had been done—and one or two really cried on my shoulder and said they were sorry. So it was worth all the trouble and worry and work to make 'em like it. And I didn't have to be mean to anybody.

The governor said my address was the best one he'd ever heard, and he's heard twenty-five or thirty of them.

I have gotten a picture of the political setup too that is worth all the time and tales of woe I've listened to. Clark is the most unpopular man in Missouri except Lindbergh. The Democrats are guilty of every mistake in the calendar and conditions for me are reversed. *They* are kowtowing now and asking for help. But I can't see why I should, at this time, take a lot of abuse and go to a lot of trouble to save a wreck that insists on sinking anyway. I'm about in the notion to let it sink and then save the salvage, or the flotsam and jetsam would be a better way to put it. . . .

Clark's bacon won't be cooked for three years anyway, so why worry? Stark is grooming himself to run against him and so is Allen McReynolds. He came to Springfield to see me. Tom Hennings has ambitions too and so has Roy McKittrick. But conditions may be reversed and Clark go in on a landslide. Remember me in January 1940? Odds were all against me, but now it's the other way. Well, you are tired of this. . . .

Kiss Margie. Remember me to your mother and I hope you're not too tired by this time. But I had to get it off my chest and you are the victim.

Love to you,
Harry

Hotel Roanoke, Roanoke, Va.

Dear Bess: Monday, November 10, 1941

It was a very great pleasure to talk to you and my baby tonight. She doesn't like being my baby—she wants to be my young lady, and of course she is. I stopped yesterday at the place where Lee surrendered and I thought of what he must have endured in the days before that act became necessary.

You know a great man can take a defeat and still be great. Lee is one of the few in history who took it and was still great in after life. I think Washington could have done it. Maybe Lincoln could. Alexander couldn't, neither could dozens of others who fill pages of history. We are in the midst of one of the periods of history—and that is what sometimes gives your old man the headache and the pain in the middle. If I could only use the historical background to see what's to be expected—then there'd be no headache. What we do is of vital importance to our daughter's generation and the next one. But as old man Patrick said, "Any schoolboy's afterthought is worth more than the greatest general's forethought." You remember him—he wore a skullcap.

Kiss Margie, love to you,

Harry

Hotel Peabody, Memphis, Tenn.

November 15, 1941

Dear Bess:

It was nice to talk with you and Margie awhile ago. The letter was waiting for me as was one from Mary. She said Mamma was still having a lot of trouble with her eyes but that she could walk around a lot better than ever. I was thinking about her birthday last night and then you mentioned it in your letter. Let the magazine keep on going to her and then get her some trinket or other. She's as appreciative of anything she gets as a kid would be. Your judgment is good as there is.

I went out to the maneuvers and looked over the field pretty thoroughly. Talked with privates, lieutenants, captains, and majors. That's high as I went. I know that if some general got onto me, I'd be free no longer and he'd have insisted on pomp and circumstance and my fun would have ceased right there. My Battery boy had been sent up to some little town in North Carolina a hundred miles from Columbia along with the whole Missouri regiment. If I'd have come down directly from Washington, I'd have seen them and Father Tiernan too but I was too lazy to drive a couple of hundred miles out of my way to see them. I had wanted to go to Charleston too to see the naval setup there but didn't for the same reason. I can understand what happened to Senator Barkley. He's been making all those side journeys—and I think he worries a lot about his responsibilities too. At the Democratic Convention in Chicago I came in an ace of passing out the night the Vice President was nominated. You didn't know it, but I had to hang on to a railing for fifteen minutes until somebody got me a cup of water. Stark would have sworn I was crocked, but he didn't see the performance. I've been rather careful ever since. . . .

Kiss Margie, love to you,

Harry

[Hotel Peabody, Memphis, Tenn.]

November 16, 1941

Dear Bess:

Again it was nice to talk with you. I got up at 7:15 A.M. and went through the usual procedure. Had breakfast in the coffee shop downstairs and they charged me fifty-five cents for tomato juice, a little dab of oatmeal, and milk with toast. I don't mind losing one hundred dollars on a hoss race or in a poker game with friends but I do hate to pay fifty-five cents for a quarter breakfast. Guess I've got a screw loose and that can't be helped.

Neal Helm came to see me and took me, Fulton, and some of his cotton friends down here in Memphis to dinner. He came early to warn me not to do what his friends wanted because he was of the opinion it would be bad politics in Missouri. I'd already decided not to do it but I was pleased that Neal thought of my political interests before he did his own financial ones. The people who are built like that are few and far between. . . .

Kiss Margie, love to you,
Harry

Writing this letter on the morning of a fateful day, Truman dispatched it by mail as he rushed for a small plane that took him to a larger plane by which he returned to Washington. He arrived in time to be present for the historic session of Congress on Monday, December 8, when President Roosevelt asked for war against Japan.

[Pennant Hotel, Columbia, Mo.]
Dear Bess: December 7, 1941
Well it was very good to talk with you this morning. Roy and I went to breakfast immediately afterwards, looked over the hanger across the road, took a walk toward Columbia, and then he left for Springfield. I've had lunch and a nap and have been reading last night's *Star* and *Journal* along with today's *Post-Dispatch* and *Globe Democrat*.

It's funny how things change around in thirteen months. I'm on the front pages of the Kansas City *Star*, St. Louis *Star-Times*, and Kansas City *Journal* for yesterday and am on the front page of the *Post-Dispatch* editorial section for today and mentioned in about three or four other places in the other parts of the paper and the *Globe*.

Had a nice visit with the family and with Mamma and Mary. Went over to see Aunt Ella and Nellie and Ethel. Do you know that they have never been to see Mamma since she was hurt? I don't understand 'em. I've saved their jobs and their location on two specific occasions and I'd do it again, but I think they should at least have shown some personal interest in the old lady I'm most interested in, don't you? Your mother looks fine and so do they all. . . . Hope you and Margie enjoyed the day. Kiss her for me.

Love to you,
Harry

Below appears one of Truman's few hostile comments about President Roosevelt. The Senator appreciated Roosevelt's capacity for national leadership, and favored almost all his measures, but did not fail to see the President's petty side.

Washington, D.C.
Dear Bess: December 21, 1941
Well I found a letter under the door as I came in just now and that makes the day as beautiful as the weather says it is. Glad you called home. It looks now

Harry S. Truman Library

as if I'll get away on Monday evening by National Limited. Be home Tuesday evening in that case. The President is supposed to call me about my committee but I don't suppose he will, and I'll probably have to rush right back for the purpose of seeing him. It must be done or I'd tell him to go to hell. He's so damn afraid that he won't have all the power and glory that he won't let his friends help as it should be done. The more I think of it, the pleasanter and more satisfactory it would seem to be under some old S.O.B. like Lear and just have one job to do and nobody's welfare to think of but a regiment's. There is some difference in being responsible for 1,420 and doing the same job for 130,000,000.

Harry Newman has asked me to dinner this afternoon at five. I'm going home and sleep some and then go. Had a fine time at Baltimore, and those Jews took me in the little poker game.

Kiss Margie, love to you,
Harry

[En route aboard Missouri Pacific R.R. to St. Louis]

Dear Bess: December 28, 1941

I found this [letterhead reads "Grand Lodge of Missouri, Ancient Free and Accepted Masons, Harry S. Truman, Grand Master"] in my briefcase and thought I might as well use it. The date [of the present letter] is the wedding anniversary of my mother and father in 1881. Some time ago, I'd say as we reckon time, but only a snap of the fingers in the universe. . . .

We almost missed the train after waiting for it, didn't we? See that that dumbell orders those seats and then the conductor will be looking for you. I'll make arrangements about your space on the B. & O. if the agent meets me at St. Louis. I hated to leave but my job must be done now sure enough and I wouldn't have had a minute's peace, and neither would the family, if I'd stayed at home. Too much publicity. Somebody said the last *Time* is still calling me the fox-faced little Senator. Maybe I am. As Bulger used to say, it's better to be that than nothing.

Wish you and Margie were along. But I can't have everything I guess. If there are any editorials please cut 'em out. Say hello to everybody and kiss my baby.

Love to you,
Harry

[Senate Chamber]

Dear Bess: December 30, 1941

. . . Senator Doxey from Mississippi was the host today at a luncheon at which the cartoonist of the Washington *Star*, who made those cartoons of me, Fulton Lewis, Jr., and a special writer for the *Post* were present, as were all the real people in the Senate and one or two S.O.B.'s (that stands for Senate Office Building). I sat next to Worth Clark.

Barkley came in late after attending a party for Mr. Litvinoff. He said that the Russian had made a very good common-sense speech—in English—in which he said that their job is to beat Hitler and that they can't get into the Jap unpleasantness until that's done. I still think they are as untrustworthy as Hitler and Al Capone. . . .

Kiss Margie, love to you,
Harry

[Washington, D.C.]

Dear Bess: December 31, 1941

Well here is the last day of the year again. Your pencil letter came after I'd
sent yours yesterday and Reathel just came in and handed me your yesterday one,
so the mail got through. I hated to go off and leave you but you should see my
desk. It is almost as bad as ever and getting worse and Mrs. Dryden has just
informed us we won't see her until the eighth. She evidently doesn't realize that
there's a war on. Everybody is working tomorrow and I'll still forgo answering
about fifty important letters.

We had a blackout last night at 7:45 and I moved your blue chair into the
little hall between the bedrooms, took Margie's radio and *Adventure,* opened the
coat-closet door, and really had a very pleasant fifteen minutes. The radio announced the beginning and the end of the trial. It seemed to work very success-
fully.

John Snyder and his family and I were going down to one of the high-hat
Reynolds Metals official's farms tomorrow at Richmond, but we both decided
we'd better work, so I'm going out to see them this evening instead. Harry and
Mrs. Vaughan will be there too.

I went down to the Hamilton Bank and rented a safety box today in both
of our names. I'll put the savings bonds and insurance policies in it. You'll have
to go down and sign up for it when you get back. Mrs. Goodman is asking us
all to dinner on Friday the ninth and I told them we'd come. Glad you got the
train fixed up the way you want it. Just be on it is all I'm hoping for now. Kiss
Margie. Tell everybody hello.

                                Love to you,
                                Harry

                                              Washington, D.C.

Dear Bess: January 3, 1942

Just seven years ago I was being interviewed, photographed, and sworn in
as the junior United States Senator from Missouri. It has been an interesting and
hectic experience. Railroads, airlines, campaigns, holding company death sen-
tences, Supreme Court reorganization, defense tours, and the investigation—
quite a list. . . .

Paul McNutt called me and told me that the Nurserymen's Association had
called him and asked him to recommend Lloyd Stark for appointment to the
National Garden Committee. He wanted to know if I thought he should. I told
him that the ex-governor is a self-made S.O.B. and I didn't think he's fit for
dogcatcher in a Philippine village. Paul said O.K. he won't be appointed. Guess
I've got a mean disposition. See you Tuesday.

                                Kiss Margie, love to you,
                                Harry

City of San Francisco, Union Pacific train to Coast
Dear Bess: Monday, March 8, 1942

This is quite the nicest train I've ever been on. Harry and I have a stateroom that would make the Mayflower or the Waldorf hard competition. Ed got on at Omaha and was supposed to get in with us but as it was 3:20 A.M. he was considerate and didn't. I found him at 8:00 A.M. four or five cars ahead of us and we had a grand breakfast together, after which we came back to our stateroom and started a 5-10-20 poker game. I ended up with most of the chips—about seven dollars winner. He and Harry have gone off to take a nap, leaving instructions for me to do the same. I am taking the time out to write you a letter. Sent you one from Chicago yesterday. This has been a most satisfactory day for me. No phone calls, no tales of woe, no letters, no committees, no newspapermen— just a chance to study the chances of getting another five or three to make a set of threes. Pat McCarran is on the train and has been very much interested in my proposed investigation of the magnesium plant in his state. They burned up the records yesterday, so I guess there must be something there. Will write you from San Francisco tomorrow.

Kiss my girl, love to you,
Harry

[Washington Duke Hotel, Durham, N.C.]
Dear Bess: April 26, 1942

It was nice to talk with you on Vivian's birthday. He's fifty-six and a grandpap—doesn't seem possible. I always think of him as the younger boy whose propensity for getting into trouble at home and abroad was one of my real growing-up worries. Not bad things but just boy fights and quarrels with people where there was no necessity for it—but he recovered from it and now I'm his pet worry. He is so afraid that someone will throw me a curve now that he gives me a lecture every time I see him.

The hills and orchards looked exceedingly pretty yesterday and Friday as I drove down. Redbud, dogwood, apple blossoms and green leaves on the trees made a very beautiful picture. I'm glad I don't live in a tropical country. Those people never can appreciate the return of the daughter Ceres from Pluto's palace.

I'm going to have one hell of a time resting—but I know I should. I keep thinking of things I should do. The *Star* and the *Post-Dispatch* are trying to take over the Democratic party and I can't stand for that—and now I won't have to. But I'll try to forget it for a week. Love to you both. Kiss Margie.

Much love,
Harry

[Washington Duke Hotel, Durham, N.C.]
Dear Bess: April 27, 1942

Well I'd hoped for a letter from you and I had a poor hunch that my daughter might send her dad a letter. This pen is like the post-office variety. Saw in the paper this morning where they had found an Egyptian pen supposed to be the oldest in the world and the columnist wanted to know if that was where the P.O. got theirs.

I took a drive over to Raleigh this morning. Saw the capitol—from the outside, and then came back by Chapel Hill. It's a pretty place and is on a hill. The road is like the old one to Excelsior Springs—black and crooked.

This resting business is a terrible bore. I listen to the radio until I get sick of it, then I walk all over town, even went to a picture show yesterday afternoon —saw Donald Duck, and Claudette Colbert in *Remember the Day*. So you know I'm losing my grip.

Got my picture in the paper and they still don't know I'm in town! How's that for foolin' 'em? Do hope I get a letter tomorrow.

Kiss my baby, love to you,
Harry

In the spring of 1942 war was going badly for the Allies, in Europe as well as the Far East, as Truman relates here.

[Washington Duke Hotel, Durham, N.C.]
Dear Bess: Thursday, April 30, 1942
Well the day started off all right anyway, even if I didn't do so well sleeping last night—a letter in the first mail.

Got awake and began fighting the war, and running the committee, and finally got started on a mystery story by Mary Roberts Rinehart, and then fought the war some more and by that time most of the night was gone. But I feel all right now. That German peace offensive worries me. If Britain were to run out on us, or if China should suddenly collapse, we'd have all that old isolation fever again and another war in twenty years. We must take this one to its conclusion and *dictate* peace terms from Berlin and Tokyo. Then we'll have Russia and China to settle with afterwards.

I'm sure glad you went to the office. It's much better for you to go there a few days a week and see what goes on. The girls are way above the average, but the only really conscientious one is Reathel. Miss Catherine is a born gossip and nosey—Vic, Frank Lee type—and Millie is flighty as an airplane. Bill's Irish and 100 percent but new and they put it over on him. You don't have to say a word only just drop in and do some signing. It helps all concerned. I have to go out to the public library and get some lowdown on No'th Ca'lina, so I won't get my facts mixed. There's a nice hotel in Chapel Hill and I'll stay there tonight and then start for Virginia. Send your next letter to the Homestead Hotel, Hot Springs, Virginia. Should be there tomorrow night. Hope you liked the speech.

Kiss Margie, love to you,
Harry

[The Homestead, Hot Springs, Va.]
Dear Bess: May 1, 1942

Well this is the second one today, but if I wait until morning it won't go out until tomorrow night and you won't get a Sunday letter, and whether you want it or not you'll get one—besides, I found a nice letter here waiting for me as I had hoped in Roanoke at lunchtime. . . .

When I came into the hotel a whole company of men in all sorts of attire were starting on a mountain walk. I've seen no women yet except a couple of gray-haired dowagers sitting in the lobby scanning the walkers. The lobby is a mile by a half in size. They have horses, golf, tennis, swimming, walking, baths, and so forth ad lib. Never saw such a place—and for some reason they think I'm somebody. (Read *Newsweek* for May 4 and *Fortune* just out.) If they don't stop saying nice things about your old man, he's goin' to be ruint. But, Mommy, I've wanted so badly to make good in the Senate so you and my sweet baby wouldn't be ashamed of me. And also to make two nasty newspapers in Missouri eat *crow* —and they got to do it. His first name is Lloyd. Now you've got to help me more than ever so I won't be a damn fool or a stuffed shirt.

I'm so proud of Margie—she's her mamma over again, only not quite so pretty. If she'd only had your pretty curls, she'd have been perfect. I'm glad she has that Great-Grandma [Mary Jane Holmes] Truman's nose. I can claim that much of her anyway. Give her two kisses and a new five-dollar bill for her dad. If I send her one, she'll say I'm bribing her again for a letter. It was more important to win that place than write her dad.

Love to you,
Harry

[The Homestead, Hot Springs, Va.]
Dear Bess: May 2, 1942

. . . I sent Margaret a couple of thrillers, which I've finished yesterday and what I mean they are. One of 'em has a murder in every chapter. I'm going to sleep some this afternoon and catch up. My plastics people won't arrive until tomorrow. My speech is at ten-fifteen Monday and I ought to be able to make a getaway by noon anyway. Will probably spend the night at Charleston, West Virginia. No. 60 is the closest east-and-west highway to this point. I'll probably cross the Ohio on Tuesday and take no. 52 to Cincinnati, as I may take no. 35 out of Charleston and go to Indianapolis. Will phone you Monday night where I am. Hope you and Margie have a nice weekend. Glad you liked that $20.00 show for $2.50.

Love to you,
Harry

[En route to Washington, D.C.]

Dear Bess: Saturday, June 13, 1942

. . . Had a funny experience a little while ago. There's a woman with a little girl across the aisle. The child's about two and into everything, including my section. Another little, yellow-hair girl about five came out of the drawing room after a fight with her brother and told the woman she is Mrs. Hobby's daughter. The kids came over to my section and she came after them and asked me if I'd heard that Mrs. Hobby's kids are on the train. Then she said, "I just heard up in the diner that Senator Truman of Missouri is on the train." I said, "Is that so?" Then a soldier from Ft. Knox came along and called me by name and I felt like a fool.

Well it's going to be mighty lonesome without you. Hope it won't be too long.

Kiss Margie, love to you,
Harry

Washington, D.C.

Dear Bess: June 16, 1942

Well I'd never have made it today if I hadn't got three letters—two from you and one from Margie. I've been going like a madman since 6:00 A.M. It is now 7:00 P.M. Fixed up the laundry and left it with the office, had breakfast, and came down to a real hectic day. Had callers galore and three committee meetings —Military Affairs, Interstate Commerce, and Appropriations. Got to two of 'em. Nelson and I are going to have it up one side and down the other. He asked me to hold up a report until he could talk to me and then talked to Tom Connally and sent me a nasty letter. Well Tom came to see me and wanted to know what I would do. I told him I'd stand pat on the report. He called Nelson and Nelson is coming down tomorrow, but I'm still standing pat.

Alex Sachs, Berenstein, and forty others were here. Berenstein is mad as a wet hen because I didn't get his Jewish boy friend a commission. I can't say I'm sorry about either contingency.

Mrs. McLean wants us for dinner Sunday and the Gunston folks sent me a check for $50 for the speech. Should I return it or keep it? Also got an expense check for $30 from the Masons. I told 'em $25 and they added $5 for you. Reckon you'll get it? Kiss Margie. I hate to face the apartment without you.

Love to you,
Harry

Normally a placid man to colleagues and subordinates, Truman was managing a hectic schedule and momentarily, as he relates below, let his tiredness show. He regretted it, even though he had good reason to be irritated with Senator Connally and a member of his own staff.

Washington, D.C.

Dear Bess: June 18, 1942

Got a nice, short letter today. Hope you and Helen had a nice time. I can see why Margie likes to see things again and again she likes. I saw *Florodora* six times, *Pinafore* a dozen maybe, *Lohengrin* four or five, *The Girl from Utah*, three, and I could keep on naming them. I'd never get tired of 'em. I've read the Good Book six or seven times maybe and am still behind on the real things in it. Wish I had nothing to do but read Shakespeare, Tennyson, Plutarch, et al. just over and over and over—but I have to listen to a lot of thieves and boobs testify to half facts and lies and then make reports on 'em that cause fights and recrimination.

Had a grand time today. Really made a monkey out of Tom Connally on the floor. He *read* one of our committee reports for the first time *and* he read it *on the floor*. You should read the *Record* of today. Also had a set-to with old McKellar in the Appropriations Committee and made him back up. Guess I'm getting cranky. I came very nearly firing Charlie Clark. He called a press conference of his own and put me in bad with the *New York Times* and several other papers, then failed to bring me the revised report as ordered, and I had to make some corrections from the floor. I was so put out I gave him a regular army call down. Bill got scared and Fulton was stricken dumb. Guess they thought I couldn't get mad. I hated to because I always want to break somebody in two. This one goes out on time.

Kiss Margie, love to you,
Harry

Washington, D.C.

Dear Bess: June 19, 1942

Had your good letter of Thursday today. Wouldn't it be a travesty to send you home to avoid a bombing and get you hit by a bolt of lightning? Glad you and Helen had a nice day. The P-Ks came today. They'll be carefully and selfishly preserved. I'll send Miss Kerr the check as suggested. No refund from Gunston. Here's Margaret's report card, which you can acknowledge. I don't know whether the signer is Mr. Mise or Mrs. and decided it would be something of a *fox pass* [sic] if I address her dear sir.

Suppose you'll read today's *Record* about what happened yesterday. I'm in the black two-inch headlines in the Baltimore *Sun*, *P.-M.* and most eastern papers. The *Herald* had double column, as did the evening *Star*. And the funny part about it all is that Tom Connally and Scott Lucas don't even get honorable mention. It's a funny world. Two years ago now enough mean things couldn't be said about me and now the top stars of the Senate can't put me in the doghouse—and I was fearfully handicapped by Mr. Clark's bungling (my Clark not Bennett).

Hope Margie's package comes O.K. and I guess it will. I wrote the piano people a mean letter and they sent out a new piano today. Haven't seen it but

I hope it is all right. Dave B. went home mad today. I told him the War Department thought his Jewish boy a draft dodger. He'd tried to get John Sullivan and Al Holland to take him on. Now I hope he stays in St. Louis and I hope his boy friend gets drafted. May stay home tomorrow. Everybody advises it. Guess I'm getting cranky.

Kiss Margie, love to you,
Harry

Washington, D.C.
June 20, 1942

Dear Bess:

No letter today and I've threatened to fire the whole office force. Guess the air mail is delayed somewhere—not at Independence. I really put in a day yesterday. Two committee hearings of my committee on transportation. Had lunch with Barkley, Ellender, and O'Mahoney. Ellender was the host. We'd asked him to listen in on the hearing because he's on Naval Affairs and had been along when the committee met in New Orleans. It was an interesting hearing and an interesting lunch. We're going to have a terrific steel shortage—one that will make aluminum look plentiful and for exactly the same reason that aluminum, copper, lead, and zinc are short. W.P.B. strategic metals section is controlled by the men who control the metals. They can't see the necessity for taking the chance of losing that control by an expansion program to *win* the war. But I am going the keep raising hell and hope for the best.

I went uptown today—and *bought* two suitcases. Looked at Woodward's, Palais Royal and at Becker's. They had two lovely ones at Woodward's that I wanted most awful bad. But I saved $24.50 by taking the ones I got at Becker's and they will answer the purpose just as well and are made by the same people. The ones I want were cowhide sole leather, and the ones I got were just belly leather I guess.

Played hookey by leaving at ten o'clock, shopping, going to a picture show —by myself—and having lunch with Tom Veatch at the Willard. Now I'm back signing the mail. Hope the package comes.

Love to you,
Harry

Washington, D.C.
June 21, 1942

Dear Bess:

The day will be all right—the special came just now. I didn't wake up until eight-thirty—isn't that something for me? I was so tired last night I could not go to sleep. Went to bed an hour after I called you and rolled and tossed for a long time and then got up and drank a bottle of Pepsi, wrote a speech on free government, and then at eleven-thirty tried it again. I went right to sleep that time and made it through.

You should read Joe O'Mahoney's speech in Thursday's appendix to the

Record. It was given over a national hookup and it is the sanest defense of Congress yet. Maybe I'm prejudiced. He mentions me as one of the saviors. . . .

Love to you, say hello to the folks,
Harry

Regular officers frequently angered Truman with their pretensions of professionalism, as did General Brehon B. Somervell, who challenged the constitutional rights of Congress. Truman tells Bess about it here.

Washington, D.C.

Dear Bess: June 25, 1942

. . . I spent the afternoon on the military subcommittee of Appropriations, with Somervell and another lieutenant general and a couple of major generals, a brigadier, and a half-dozen colonels and majors. They are asking for $43 billion—and they'll get it without a whimper to waste and riot and create a fascist government if Somervell can manage it. I want to keep the strings on them, just as we do the others, but I'll have no support, but they know I'm there.

It is really an alarming situation. The Congress has given away all its powers of control and then wonders why people hold it in contempt. I want to be specific in the delegation of powers and have them terminate at a specific time.

Since we are in session all the time the appropriations could be made in $10 billion chunks as well as $43 billion.

The piano is same color as the bookcase, a little wider than the other one, and made by Baldwin. It has a good tone and looks all right. Mrs. Ricketts let them in. I locked the back hall door and everything is O.K. . . . Love to you. Kiss Margie. My best to the rest of the family. How's Frank?

Harry

Washington, D.C.

Dear Bess: June 27, 1942

Well I *doubt* if you will remember it but tomorrow is an anniversary of vital importance. Wish I was there to celebrate it. Had expected to be. . . .

Twenty-three years have been extremely short and for me altogether most happy ones. Thanks to the right kind of a life pardner for me we've come out reasonably well. A failure as a farmer, a miner, an oil promoter, and a merchant but finally hit the groove as a public servant—and that due mostly to you and lady luck. The lady's best roll of the dice was June 28, 1919. We have the prettiest and sweetest daughter in the world, a reasonably comfortable living, and the satisfaction of having helped everybody we possibly could, both in the family and out of it. And my sweetheart is the same one I've always had—just as good looking and lovable as when she was sixteen.

Hope the rains quit, it's been coming down in sheets here. Is there anything I can bring from the apartment that you want, now's a good time.

Love to you, lots of absentee hugs,

Harry

Washington, D.C.

Dear Bess: June 28, 1942

Well this is *the day*. Lots of water has gone over the dam. There've been some terrible days and many more nice ones. When my store went flooy and cost my friends and Frank money, when Margie came, don't think I ever spent such a day, although the pains were yours. And to name one more, when we thought Stark had won and when I lost actually for eastern judge. But the wins have far outweighed 'em. June 28, 1919, was the happiest day of my life, for I had been looking forward to it for a lifetime nearly or so it seemed. When a man gets the right kind of a wife, his career is made—and I got just that.

The greatest thing we have is a real young lady who hasn't an equal anywhere. That's all the excuse we need for living and not much else matters.

It was grand to say hello last night. I was so tired I could hardly sit up. Went to bed right away after playing Margie's song record and the Minuet (in G) and Chopin waltzes. It's pretty lonesome around there without you. . . .

Kiss Margie, lots and lots of love and happy returns,

Harry

[En route to Washington, D.C.]

Dear Bess: July 22, 1942

I am twelve hours late getting this off. Intended to write as soon as I got to St. Louis. The B. & O. man met me and put me right on the train. Then the stationmaster came and talked to me about his boy in camp at Ft. Lewis, Washington. The porter gave me a pillow—and I went to sleep. Have slept *all* day. Woke up for lunch but couldn't get into the diner, so had 'em bring me a sandwich and some buttermilk, then didn't wake up again until just now and we are pulling out of Cincinnati! The *Record* is sure good for sleep. Never got more than ten pages read.

I never hated to leave as badly as I did last night. We haven't had a nicer week since June 28, 1919, and I'm not so sure you enjoyed that one very much, because you wanted to come home. Anyway I liked both of 'em very much, even if you did not enjoy the heat on one and being away from mamma on the other.

Have seen no one on the train I know but the dining car conductor and a waiter. By morning I should be going good if I sleep all night as I have all day.

Tell my baby she has a *most* beautiful voice—to keep it *natural* without any

gimcracks, pronounce her words clearly and in *English* so they can be understood
—and she'll be a great singer. Tell everybody hello.

Love to you,
Harry

[Senate Chamber]
Dear Bess: July 23, 1942
Well this day is all right now. Millie gave me a letter just now. I came on
over here after dictating about fifty or sixty, talking to Fulton for an hour, and
doing a lot of other things. . . . I got home at ten-thirty, unpacked my grips,
opened up the flat, and it was not dusty nor hot. Got to bed about twelve, got
up this morning and made up the laundry, and as I had the car to bring my bags
home I took the laundry over to 712 Lamont Street and told 'em to be sure and
finish it all. There were seven shirts, three pair of pajamas, some underwear,
sheets, towels, pillowcases, etc., and I thought I'd better get it done, because if
I leave here again next week I'd be out maybe. Have hearings on Tuesday,
Wednesday, Thursday of next week and have set one for the sixth of August. Do
you think you can get that old coot to finish up those teeth so you can come back
with me Tuesday night? I have an invitation for dinner with the Atwills on
Saturday night and Mrs. McLean on Sunday, so you'd better come on. Hope
you're well and happy.

Kiss my baby, love to you,
Harry

Washington, D.C.
Dear Bess: July 24, 1942
Well here is another day past and gone. I had my plans all made to get a
letter off to you at 8:00 A.M. but things happened in fast and furious style. 'Twas
very nearly as bad as the Federal Building at home. I cleaned up a little last night
and didn't get to bed until eleven-thirty. Listened to old man Hull on the radio
and he made a good speech too but sounded as if he was about to lose his upper
plate every once in a while. Got down here at seven forty-five and went at it.
Hoped for a letter on the first mail but none came, nor did any come on any other
mail. . . .

Kiss Margie, love to you,
Harry

Washington, D.C.
Dear Bess: July 26, 1942
. . . If you have any turnip seed they should be sown today—I forgot to tell
you over the phone. This also is Nellie Noland's birthday. She must be sixty-two
or thereabouts but I guess she won't tell you.

I came on home to get the special but it failed to come through—too much rain I suppose. I've been listening to the newscasters and reading the editorial and columnist comment on the war and it gives me the dumps sure enough. The country would be better off if all the column writers were in jail and all the broadcasters were shot, but I guess we can't do it.

There ought to be a smart government man who could give out facts in a series of one paragraph for each fact and the papers should use that instead of columnist comment. The President told Lister Hill and me that's what he intended to do—but you know the President.

Kiss my daughter, love to you,
Harry

Washington, D.C.

Dear Bess: July 27, 1942

The letter came just as I got back from Bill's dinner. Mrs. Boyle had a good roast beef dinner, and Lou and I enjoyed it. Then she and Lou went to look at a couple of houses in the neighborhood which were for rent furnished. Thinks maybe he'll take one for a couple of months and then let Mrs. H. spend the time looking.

I hope the dental work gets lined out. I have been worried about the condition of those teeth. Please get the whole job done while you are at it.

Just let the shirts and bathrobe stay there. I'll leave here Friday night and get home Saturday night, too late to make a speech, vote Tuesday and start back. I have a steel hearing on Thursday, August 6. Will have Higgins tomorrow, Kaiser and Land Wednesday, and probably Douglas, Martin, and the chairman of the Air Committee of the War Production Board on Thursday. Clean up my desk and the apartment Friday and start for home. The Washington papers are still giving the Congress the dickens and without justification. That psychological sabotage sheet the *Herald* had a nasty editorial by Waldrup yesterday and so did the Washington *Post*. Of course they want an anti-Congress. They'd rather lose the war if that would discredit the President. Eugene Meyer owns the *Post* and the McCormick-Patterson outfit own the Chicago *Tribune*, the New York *Daily News*, and the Washington *Herald*. How they all hate the New Deal.

Kiss Margie, love to you,
Harry

Washington, D.C.

Dear Bess: July 28, 1942

Well this day is a lot better than yesterday—two letters, Sunday's, Monday's. Yes the specs came. And they bother me much. Good to read with but I don't know whether I'm going to make out on the seeing part or not. You know I'm as bad on spectacles as George is on teeth. And I don't suppose I'll ever again get a fit like Ben Key gave me. I was tired Sunday but not now.

I am having dinner with John Snyder tonight and I'll find out about Mrs.

S. and Drucie. They are not here now. Can't tell you anything about the Shields situation except what Breck Long told me. He said positively he was on the boat. I have been drinking tomato juice at home and eating at the Hot Shoppe and Senate lunchrooms. Had dinner at the Continental last night. Will eat somewhere with Snyder tonight and somewhere else with someone else tomorrow night. I did not start the milk or the paper because I'd just have to stop it again Friday. . . .

Glad you saw Mamma and Mary. There will be no month's vacation for me. My hearings start again on August 6, so you see what I get for getting in all the papers. My meals are staying down the last two days.

Love to you,
Harry

Washington, D.C.
August 5, 1942

Dear Bess:

Just twenty-five years ago today I was inducted into the service of the federal government as a first lieutenant of field artillery, N.G. In the opinion of the regular army, N.G. stood for no good. But it turned out differently. I was lucky, got to France, fired some three-inch bullets at the Boche, got home, got my sweetheart, went broke, became a politician, and to some extent am putting a small finger into the next war. What will another twenty-five years bring? You answer, I can't.

It was nice to talk with you this A.M. Had an airmail from Mary after the doctor was there yesterday and things seemed to be in much better shape with Mamma. Hope you called her. I didn't think to remind you to but I'm sure you did. . . .

Hope your mother is still on the mend. She seemed much better Tuesday morning.

It is cool and cloudy here. Been sprinkling rain nearly all day. The girls have been out trying to see the Queen of Holland but have had no luck so far. She's late or lost or something. My desk wasn't piled quite so high as usual. Been dictating all afternoon and will be up to date tomorrow.

Kiss my baby, love to you,
Harry

Washington, D.C.
August 6, 1942

Dear Bess:

Was a rather hectic day. Had the steel hearing and it is a mess. A call came from old man Baruch saying he'd been appointed by the President to go into the rubber situation and that he wanted my help to get the facts. He was very complimentary to my way of doing things and told me he also might make a steel investigation along with mine. The *American* magazine wants to interview me on the situation. I told 'em I'd take it under advisement. The Columbia Broadcasting Company wants me to open a roundtable for them tomorrow on the situation. I may not do it and then again I may. Jimmy Byrnes was over at the Senate today and told me I'd better make the broadcast. I think that's what he came over for, because he said the husband of his only and favorite niece was the man who is putting on the broadcast.

The Queen of Holland was a nice old lady. She made a good speech and was very gracious to all the people around her. She spoke rather brokenly but it was understandable. Maybe you heard her, because all the networks carried it. My steel hearings will continue all through the next week. Hope a solution can be found but I doubt it. We are surely balled up.

Was most happy to hear Mamma is better. I've had a hunch all along she'd get over this attack. Sometime however one will get her.

Kiss Margie, love to you,
Harry

In the following letter Truman refers to a newspaper story that quoted him as urging the chairman of the War Production Board to "take the bull by the horns and cut off a few heads."

Washington, D.C.

Dear Bess: August 7, 1942
No letter today but maybe the plane got grounded. But I'm still hoping—there's one more mail. Made the front page of the *New York Times* this morning —and the Baltimore *Sun,* Washington *Times Herald,* and a lot of others, as well as the last edition of the Washington *Star* last night. And I wasn't intending to make any headlines, they just came out by accident. Some witness made a remark and I took him by telling him what Nelson ought to do. Never thought of the headline. But it did no harm and may do a lot of good.

Had lunch with old man Ickes today and enjoyed it even if he did give me fish and cucumbers. There were some other things too. He's a character. Think he wanted to be sure I wasn't going to shut down the committee. Sent you a wire awhile ago. I'm to make a five-minute speech on the steel situation. Shouldn't have done it, but Jim Byrnes came over and high-pressured me. Old Knox has asked Dave Walsh to investigate me on the nasty remarks I made about his Bureau of Ships. That ought to be good.

Here's a letter for Miss Mary Truman. Guess it's for our charming daughter and not her aunt. Hope for two letters tomorrow.

Kiss my baby, love to you,
Harry

Washington, D.C.

Dear Bess: August 9, 1942
Well it was nice to get the Friday letter and to get to talk with you over the phone. Margie sounded rather sleepy. Hope you are both well and cool. I had to dig out a blanket last night.

Nearly froze the night before, so I just pulled out one of those in the bag hanging on the door and did it feel good! But it will in all probability be hotter than the hubs of the hot place before the week's gone again. Fulton wanted me to go to the farm with him Friday afternoon, but I told him that I had to stay close to a phone and a plane. But if Mamma continues to improve, I can safely go to Maine I suppose. They will make arrangements so I can get a plane in Boston if it is absolutely necessary, so I guess it will be safe.

I seem to have really stirred up the animals here in the steel business. Some of the really tall boys are getting scared. It is funny, sure enough, to have Haskell sending me special letters with his editorials. The world will probably stop going around if that keeps up.

Hope that letter gets to the apartment. I'll be going back out there in a few minutes.

Kiss Margie, love to you,
Harry

Washington, D.C.

Dear Bess: August 9, 1942
. . . Bill Southern had an editorial in his spasm of the sixth in which he said [those] old nuts Montgomery and Yost would be the first time since 1900 that the eastern part of the county controlled the court. Then Chrisman and the Collier scandals were in control, then came Bulger and the Ross-Pryor scandals, and the only clean slate in the whole history of the last fifty years was from 1927 to 1935 when some $50,000,000 were spent on hospitals, courthouses, and roads by eastern Jackson County really. And old Monty wanted me to pay him a commission on the new courthouse elevators, which he didn't earn. Oh well.

Kiss Margie, love to you,
Harry

[The Eastland and The Congress Square, Portland, Me.]

Dear Bess: Sunday, August 16, 1942
Well this is the day of the Lone Jack picnic to celebrate the Battle of Lone Jack, and have I had a picnic. We came up here from New York on the Boston and Maine Railroad by way of the crookedest and roughest track I've ridden over since the Leaky Roof quit running from Kansas City to Springfield. Senator Brewster met us here and we had breakfast over at another hotel where we saw Claude Pepper. He's up here for a Democratic rally tonight for the man opposing Wallace White.

We went to the launching at eleven o'clock and Mr. Pepper came too—uninvited—getting into the front row for pictures, etc. Then they balled up the program and left Kilgore out but Mrs. Kilgore christened one of the ships, so he didn't care. He's one of the nicest men I know anyway. They short-waved us to England. Then we had lunch and launched some more and then put a couple of new destroyers into the bay—went to a clambake and just now got in at 9:10 P.M.

They gave me a whole lobster, half a chicken, a dozen clams, two ears of corn, a hard-boiled egg, a sweet potato half as big as my head, a cup of coffee, and two doughnuts. All, down to the potato, was cooked on hot stones covered with seaweed and covered with canvas, piled up in a big pile. I ate a little of everything to show my hosts I appreciated the hospitality—but it was a *mess*.

I'd hoped for a letter here. Will write you from Dexter tomorrow.

Kiss Margie, love to you,
Harry

Aboard army transport plane, Boston to Washington

Dear Bess: Thursday, August 20, 1942

We had a nice day's rest at Mr. Gannett's camp on Moosehead Lake. He took us a boat ride, showed us all his pet wild animals, and took us a walk in the woods. He has pheasants, quail, and several other wild birds, including turkeys which he raises for the game warden. He also has pet deer, rabbits, and squirrels. It is a beautiful camp on a big island in the lake with all the luxuries of the Waldorf-Astoria. I had two excellent nights' sleep—and gained four pounds.

We left there at seven-thirty this morning and Kilgore, Brewster, and I took a plane at Greenville, at nine o'clock, for Bangor, inspected the air base there, and then flew to Bar Harbor, where we looked over another one and some secret plane catchers. Had lunch at the Pot and Kettle Club, made up of millionaires and ex-presidents of Yale and Harvard.

I left at two o'clock by plane for Boston. It took us two hours and a half on account of a fifty-mile-an-hour headwind. I got off the ground at Boston again at 4:40 P.M. and hope to land in Washington at 6:30 P.M. You'll know I did if you get this. Tomorrow I'm going to inspect Camp Leonard Wood with Under Secretary of War Patterson, weather permitting. We'll leave Washington before breakfast and get back after supper. I am trying to put some backbone into him just as we did Nelson. If it works, it will be worth the trip.

You should have seen the ovation those extra high hats gave your old man today at Bar Harbor. I don't understand it. Hope there's a pile of letters at the office for me. Will write you again tomorrow aboard an army transport.

Kiss Margie, love to you, and hello to all the rest of the family,
Harry

Aboard army transport plane, Rolla to Washington, D.C.

Dear Bess: August 21, 1942

Well we left Washington at seven o'clock this morning and arrived in Rolla at eleven—five hours—inspected the camp after a chicken dinner and at two-thirty the 6th Division passed in review for Mr. Patterson, the Commanding General Ridley, and the Missouri Senator. . . .

We have Bayard Swope, Colonel Ginsburg, Patterson's executive and a smart man, two brigadier generals, and a couple of colonels aboard.

It has been a good day for me. I got in some good licks on War Department policy, both with Swope and Patterson. I believe it will help. I am more surprised every day at the respect with which the special committee is regarded by people in high places. If I can just keep from making any real errors, we are on the way to really help win the war and to make the job more efficient and quicker. That means fewer of our young men killed and a chance for a more honorable settlement. So you must pray for me to go the right way.

Kiss Margie, lots of love to you,
Harry

The article referred to below appeared in the November issue of American; *it was a scorcher. Entitled "We Can Lose the War in Washington," it discussed how "a large proportion of Washington makes its living by unraveling one another's red tape." He complained of "lack of courageous unified leadership and centralized direction at the top."*

Washington, D.C.
Dear Bess: Sunday, August 23, 1942
    . . . I went to the office today at nine o'clock and had an interview with the *American* magazine. There'll be an article in the October issue—by me—on the situation. I wouldn't take any pay for it. Nelson's interviews are the result of what I'm saying. I told Batt what was what and I hope it gets results. If Nelson does as he talks, all will be well. I gave Patterson a dose of the same medicine. And I've sicked Brewster on him too. Maybe we'll win the home front yet.

It's hot as Hades here today. Hope it's cooler there.

Kiss Margie, love to you,
Harry

Washington, D.C.
Dear Bess: August 23, 1942
    I'm going round and round today. Gage called up as did Bill and I've had union plasterers, Drew Pearson, the St. Louis *Star Times*, a major general named Baird, who has been rolled and who is a friend of Fred Canfil's, besides calls from the navy, the undersecretary of war, a Senate session, lunch with Harry Moore and several Senators, and a fight on the Senate floor over votes for soldiers. I took no part in the fight. Mary [Colgan] Romine's lawyer came in and told me all of her troubles. So you see what publicity does to a Senator. . . .

I'm having dinner with John Snyder tonight. He's going to cry on my shoulder too I guess. Hope you are as unhappy without me as I am without you.

Lots of love,
Harry

Washington, D.C.

Dear Bess: August 25, 1942

Just received your Sunday letter. It poured down rain all day Sunday nearly —not all day, but from the middle of the afternoon on. I had one heck of a time getting something to eat that evening. I started out in my raincoat and went down to the Hot Shoppe. It was full to the doors. Came back and got in the car, which I'd by good luck brought home at noon, and drove to Wisconsin and Military Road, same situation; then to Bethesda and it was worse. It was pouring rain all the time. Finally stopped at the chicken place at Connecticut and Nebraska and ate at the counter. So I suppose that's why I didn't get your letter yesterday.

You'll have plenty of time to do your shopping and anything else you want to do, but I'm not coming back here without you and my baby. The country can go to hell if I have to.

That was a nice note from Mrs. Dudley. I'm sure glad I went to see him. Had a letter from Mary saying that Mamma is better than ever. I don't see how she does it.

Our girl Dale Baker announced her engagement to the office force this morning and you never heard so much oh-ing and ah-ing and chattering in your life. She said she was getting the nicest man in the world and I told her that's what she ought to think, but I was of the opinion he'd gotten the best of the bargain.

That'll mean another wedding present. Catherine and Reathel are extremely mysterious about their war jobs but told me this morning it had something to do with antiaircraft. You'll have to cross-examine them.

Love to you,
Harry

Washington, D.C.

Dear Bess: August 26, 1942

Well it was sure good to talk to you last night. I'd gone to sleep in the chair over the papers. Woke up about eleven o'clock and went out to look at the moon. It was a beautiful clear night and the moon was almost completely covered by the earth's shadow. Just one little silver edge was out of it. The covered part was as red as blood and very dim. I guess that means plenty of blood will be spilled and I don't have to be a prophet to say that either. I went out the back way and no one was looking or paying any attention to the moon. I looked out of the front windows and no one was on the street or paying the slightest attention to a most unusual celestial show. It shows what the war does to people. Then I thought you and Margie ought to see it and I also wanted a good excuse to spend three dollars on a call and you got it. I'm sorry you couldn't see the eclipse. But maybe that means no blood spilled in that section. I hope so anyway.

No letter this morning. Now don't you let a shortsighted old man disturb you about your looks and age. You're still the prettiest girl in the world with

Margie a close second. And you are prettiest *naturally*. Don't go Lucy on the hair idea and I don't want an artificial face looking at me. I want it the way I like it and the way it's best looking. . . .

Love to you,
Harry

Washington, D.C.
August 27, 1942

Dear Bess:

. . . I have been going quite a bit today. Got up at six-thirty and went down to the Hot Shoppe for breakfast. Came back and cleaned up the house (more or less). You probably won't notice any particularly clean spot but you should have seen it before I started. Mostly dust and newspapers. I put all the windows down and locked up the closets and Margie's room, so I guess it'll all be there when I get back with my two *young* ladies.

Went to the bank to see about those coupons and put three more savings bonds into the box. The coupons are not due until September 15. The Senate had a session and I attended that and then had a most interesting lunch with General Marshall. Guffey was the host and ten Senators were present. He told us all about the whole situation and it did us all good. Things are not half as black as they are painted and we are winning on all fronts today. Made us all feel better. Will see you Monday.

Much love,
Harry

[The Coronado Hotel, St. Louis, Mo.]
September 26, 1942

Dear Bess:

Arrived exactly on the dot. It was a good thing I had a bedroom, because there were three people from Kansas City on the train who had been pestering Bill and me for the week. One of 'em sat himself at the table with me at lunch —and I had to pay.

There were several other people on the train whom I knew, and if I'd been accessible—well, I'd probably have stayed up all night. So I got off easily I guess.

I am going to call your mamma and my mamma tonight and then call you, and I hope I'll find you all at home. Thought I would run up home tonight but I'm so tired I guess I'd better go to bed. . . .

Love to you both,
Harry

[The Coronado Hotel, St. Louis, Mo.]
Sunday, September 27, 1942

Dear Bess:

Just twenty-five years ago I was trying to fire a barrage, with which I could never catch up. Do you suppose I am doing that again? We'd opened the drive on September 26 at 5:00 A.M. by firing three thousand rounds per Battery up until eight o'clock and then moving toward the front. My Battery went into position behind a hedge on the enemy's side of no man's land and Major Gates, Lieutenant Jordon of my Battery, and I walked across the little creek which had a high-sounding river name and over which all the bridges had been destroyed. We'd no more than gotten on the enemy bank of the creek than a swarm of bees went overhead, at least that's what I thought—but the noise was being made by machine gun bullets. Well we sat down awhile and I sent word back to the Battery to take a shot at the machine gun. We saw that we couldn't move the Batteries up that road, so we went back and turned to the right down no man's land and spent the rest of the afternoon and until 4:00 A.M. the twenty-seventh getting across the creek and into position. At six o'clock I received orders to begin firing at 5:00 A.M. and I never could catch up on digging the trails deep enough to fire so never fired a shot. Moved up some more and fired some more. I was in the saddle and on foot from 5:00 A.M. the twenty-fifth until 10:00 P.M. the twenty-seventh. I expect that would give me a pain now, don't you? Well age is sure coming out on me. I started out to say how nice it was to talk to you awhile ago. Your mother sounded fine and so did mine. . . .

Kiss Margie. Love to you. Glad the young lady got what she wanted.

Harry

A quarter-century before Truman wrote the following letter from a hotel room in Joplin, his mining company had been located just across the state line, in Commerce, Oklahoma. If he had any feelings about what a turn of fortune had brought him back to this area, he did not write about them to Bess.

[Hotel Connor] Joplin, Mo.

Dear Bess: October 23, 1942

. . . The meeting last night was a grand success. Forrest Hanna was there and made a good speech for thirty minutes, and your old man made a poor one as usual for five minutes, they introduced the Cooper brothers, the star ball players from Independence, and sold a lot of bonds. When I looked at the Jefferson City paper this morning I saw that I had been the principal speaker and that Hanna had also spoken! You can't beat a reporter when he's told to find for the plaintiff.

We are doing a lot of good politically and otherwise too. Didn't get the letter but hope to have two at St. Joe.

They are waiting to take me to dinner and then a radio speech. Mrs. Easley is in the hospital waiting for a boy.

Love to you and Margie,

Harry

[Hotel President, Kansas City, Mo.]

Dear Bess: October 25, 1942

I just sent you a letter because I wanted to be sure and get it off. The over-efficient and extremely loyal Mr. Canfil was waiting to be sure I got it in the mail. Whenever he finds out that I want to do something he never stops until it is done if it breaks up a party or smashes the present schedule. He knew I wanted to get a letter off to you every day, so he waited until I did, so he could see it in the mail. *He's a bird.* When we get into a hotel suite he proceeds to examine it from end to end scattering cigarette ashes on the floor, in the wash bowl, the toilet, the bathtub and everywhere else. If a chronic bore comes around, he stands it until he sees I'm worried and then he proceeds to throw him out either by words or with his two hands. But I like the son of a gun, and he'd cut a throat for me. I get exasperated sometimes nevertheless. . . .

Tell Margie her dad had hoped to be surprised somewhere on the road by a letter from his baby.

Love to you,
Harry

[Hotel President, Kansas City, Mo.]

Dear Bess: November 2, 1942

. . . Went to see Mamma at 3:00 P.M. and she was as full of pep as she used to be years ago. She told Fred what she thought of the present Baptist preacher and preachers in general and particular. She insisted that she'd told certain Republicans in town that if they'd turn on the radio at six-fifteen they'd at least hear a white man speak. All Republicans are black to her. She doesn't know what *Eleanor* has done to the Democrats. . . .

Had lunch with Bryce Smith at the Kansas City Club. Saw the *Star* crowd, the McGees, the Jesters, and all the uplifters and "best citizens." Jim Reed was in the lobby and Bryce said, "There's Reed. Don't you want to speak to him?" I said the old so-and-so didn't mean a thing to me and unless I had to I didn't care to notice him. He got on the same elevator with us and some Jew (who evidently was a guest of someone) called attention to the fact that there were two U.S. Senators on the elevator. When we got off he called Reed's attention to the fact that I was on the scene. He said, "Why hello Harry. I didn't see you." I said, "Hello Senator, it was always hard for you to see me." And things passed off very pleasantly. . . .

Love to you both,
Harry

Washington, D.C.

Dear Bess: June 21, 1943

Well the day started right anyway—there was a letter in the first mail. You talk about your hectic days after that—well I'm going to tell you what happened.

First, Mr. Boyle turned up, which is something. He's in the doghouse with me, Mrs. Boyle, and Mrs. Fulton. Can you think of any way he could be in a more unsatisfactory position? You know I'm an easy mark with my family and my help, but when a day of reckoning comes it's bad to be on the receiving end. Ask Vic or an investigator or two I've had to fire. I was so put out with Bill I wouldn't explode on him today because he'd be on the way to Kansas City if I had. But I can't get a substitute right now, so tomorrow he'll get very calmly and coldly bawled out. His trouble is scotch and soda, or just scotch—soda never hurt anybody. . . .

It's been hotter than the hinges of Mr. Pluto's residence, and that's rather warm.

Do you need any money? Have you enough to meet what's necessary? I'll send you some or you can draw a check, but keep me posted if you draw the check because I paid out a quarterly income tax payment for us both and it was a real blow, but we can make it O.K.

Kiss Margie, love to you,
Harry

Washington, D.C.

Dear Bess: June 22, 1943

. . . Mr. Byrnes said he wanted to cooperate with the "Truman Committee" and he wished he had one like it in the House to cooperate with. Went back and heard more labor and social security money trouble and came over to sign my mail at 5:00 P.M. The Cement Association was laying for me as was the K.C. Southern R.R. and Mr. Budd of the famous locomotives. We met him at Baringer's party that Sunday and offered to take him home. He's being renegotiated and he wants to keep $3 million profit instead of one. Wish I had one-tenth of one, don't you? The *Time* and *Life* came in to see me. They are getting up an article for *Life* on your old man. Ain't it awful? *Time, Life, Saturday Even' Post, Click*—what can I do? Here's the letter I wrote for the Strickland boy. Also a classic from our negro phone gal, Candy Citi—it took me two hours to figure it out.

Kiss Margie, love to you,
Harry

[Washington, D.C.]

Dear Bess: June 28, 1943

Well I hope you received my yesterday's special before you left Independence. I asked you some very pertinent questions which I wanted you to be thinking about when Mr. Sands made a certain delivery to you on the train in Kansas City. If that young (middle-aged, really) man did not make that delivery, the devil had better be on his side when I see him.

It was nice to talk with you even if I couldn't reach you tonight. I did the best I could under the circumstances. It fell to my lot to make the fight on National Youth Administration in the Labor-Social Security Bill. The resolution or amendment was introduced by me Saturday and by consent went over until eleven o'clock this morning. My statement on it was about a paragraph. Then Downey made a two-column speech on it. They recessed and Guffey opened the ball today after some nice remarks on Barkley's return by Vandenberg. Kilgore, Mead, Barkley, and Pepper all made speeches for my amendment. Then Byrd, McKellar, and McCarran called us liars and misanthropes in the most polite language with some interruptions by those on my side. To the astonishment of Mr. Byrd, La Follette and Walter George made speeches for our side. Mr. George really took McKellar and Byrd to a cleaning.

Well the vote finally came, as it always does, and Mr. Clark informed me that he hoped I wouldn't be beaten by more than fourteen. Well it added up forty for me, thirty-eight against. He changed his vote and asked for a reconsideration, which he had a right to do, and I asked that Mr. Clark's motion to reconsider be tabled and it was by forty-one to thirty-seven. He acted like a ten-year-old child and gave notice that he'd ask for recommitment to the committee tomorrow. Of course it won't happen and he'll be three times licked by the "junior senator" instead of twice.

There were some nice things happened. Hatch sent me a note that he voted for me, not the amendment, and Scott Lucas made a statement in the *Record* that almost made me sprout wings. You ought to read it. Anyway on one amendment Mr. Byrd, Mr. Clark, Mr. McKellar, and Mr. McCarran were all squelched—a record.

Hope you landed safely. Kiss Margie. Love to you. My best to Fred, Christie, the kids, and your mother.

Harry

[Washington, D.C.]

[Dear Bess:] June 28, 1943

Well it's twenty-four short years. Seems like yesterday to me. These flowers are all I could do from this distance, but each one of 'em is a kiss for a happy year from your old man. Hope there'll [be] twenty-four more and two to spare and then I'll give you a gold band to bind the bargain forever. I also hope we won't ever be so far apart again.

Twenty-four years of happiness.

Love, from Harry

When the Masons held their national convention in Chicago, Senator Truman was on hand. As he mentions in the letter below, his Kansas City supporters had not forgotten how St. Louis brothers had mixed Masonry and politics during the Lodge voting in 1940, when Truman was in line to become Grand Master of the Masons of Missouri.

[Palmer House, Chicago, Ill.]

Dear Bess: July 4, 1943

I'm sorry I got you out of bed but I wanted to talk to you so badly and I wanted to do it before the gang found me. At that we were interrupted (I forgot my dictionary).

I told Margie all about how I got licked yesterday. So you'll have to get her to tell you. I forgot to put in her allowance and had to send her two letters— but that'll make her owe me two or maybe two and a half.

It is a very great relief to get away from that office but it was necessary to bring some work along. Catherine and Reathel have gone on their vacations— to Maine. Now isn't that sompin'. I hope Luretta will be back Tuesday—she's a little help anyway. Of course in a pinch I can draw on the committee help downstairs.

Well the gang are gathering here. It is a fight between Kansas City and St. Louis and it looks as if I may be able to pay some of those St. Louis guys who knifed me in 1940 in the Missouri Grand Lodge. Isn't it funny how chickens come home to some people?

Business Week has a big write-up on the committee. Will send it if I can get one. *Life* is getting out a special issue—ain't it awful? So is *Saturday Evening Post*. Kiss Margie. My best to your mother, Fred, and kids.

Love to you,
Harry

[Palmer House, Chicago, Ill.]

Dear Bess: July 5, 1943

The letter came as I hoped it would this morning. I have been standing in line shaking hands with hundreds of Shriners from New Hampshire to Washington State and from California to Florida. They all look at me as if I were Jumbo in Barnum's Circus. One old guy asked if this was the real Truman or just a state senator being used for show purposes.

It scares me to death the things they say to me and about me to the other people in the Kansas City delegation. I thought I was coming here to have a good time with a bunch of the boys from K.C. whom I know and I've turned out to be their drawing card—but at that I don't believe our man will win. Anyway he says it's some help and I hope it is, because he's a nice fellow. He gave me the honorary degree the other night for the DeMolays. I've learned something anyway. I'll know better than to be the two-headed calf again.

Hope you saw some nice fireworks. I'm going to see Sherman Minton tomorrow. Say hello to everybody.

Kiss Margie, love to you,
Harry

[Washington, D.C.]

Dear Bess: July 12, 1943

Another hectic day and no letter from you to make it lighter. I suppose the airmail is late because it's been raining in spurts since Saturday—some of them pretty heavy spurts. I really think my brother had a good time. He broke down and told me all about each of those four boys and Martha Ann. They are all morally nice kids, but entirely different. Said J. C. [Vivian's son] was doing an especially fine job at the Remington plant and that they had given him quite a hazing because he is a nephew. They've transferred him around three times, giving him what they thought were impossible jobs, and he's made records on all of 'em. He's also broken the record as a papa. Three in three years. But we didn't discuss that. Then we talked of Fred and Martha Ann. It seems that there is a contrary streak in those two which contains all the features of our side and certain of two strains from their mother. Those two have it in their heads that they don't want any reflected glory from a certain uncle and that they won't even ask papa for a boost. Said J. C. and Harry had remonstrated with them on that attitude. I told him that I thought it was admirable but unusual. Some smart aleck in Independence told Martha Ann she wouldn't have a job in the Independence schools if her name were Smith instead of Truman. So she went to Arizona and got a better job where no such name is known. You, of course, remember the antics of the redhead when I had him here.

It seems that Harry is the politician and the diplomat as well as an untiring physical worker. He's Mamma's favorite and that's what she says, but I was always afraid that she might be putting undue stress on the name.

It seems that Gilbert has a very keen mind and none of the characteristics of the other three. That's the way I'd put him down. Anyway they are all pretty good boys and it's a remarkable job in this day and age not to raise a jitterbug or a zoot-suiter.

I had to do a little bragging too and the brother said he was very much impressed with his niece and that he thought she had real character to be as nice and unaffected as she is under the handicap of her dad—then he said, "I guess her mother ought to have credit for that." Well she ought—so what. He told Mr. Guffey a horse trade story that caused the Senator from Pennsylvania to tell me today at lunch that perhaps that farmer brother of mine could tell me how to make some high-up people here behave. The Senator from Pennsylvania took me out into his beautiful back yard (garden in the capital) and *very confidentially* wanted to know what I thought of Henry Wallace. I told him that Henry is the best Secretary of Agriculture we ever did have. He laughed and said that is what he thinks. Then he wanted to know if I would help out the ticket if it became necessary by accepting the nomination for Vice President. I told him in words of one syllable that I would not—that I had only recently become a Senator and that I wanted to work at it for about ten years.

Mr. Kilgore and Mr. Wallgren came in from Louisville, where I'd sent them to look at another Curtiss-Wright plant. It is also a dud and a burden on the government. They've spent $13 million and not a single plane. That's cheap compared to Columbus, where they've spent $103 million for the navy and we still wonder why. I've refused to see the Curtiss-Wright president but may break down and do it.

Colonel Henderson was in also. The army is still kicking him around. So was Harry Jobes. Roy Roberts is in town also. I had a dinner date with Henderson and Harry, and Roy asked me to meet some newspapermen at his room in the same hotel (the Statler). I did and incidentally told him that I knew a couple of crooks and jailbirds who'd be glad to give the *Star* a front-page interview on the Curtiss plant at Cincinnati if he felt that justice should be done them. His face got so red that I was sure he'd have a stroke but he didn't, more's the pity. He simply laughed and said I *had* him right.

I am at home by myself and so lonesome that I'm running off at the pen instead of the head. Hope I'll be 1,070 miles closer to you by next Monday night.

My best to all the family. Kiss my pretty daughter and tell her to kiss her most beautiful mamma for me.

Love to you,
Harry

Washington, D.C.

Dear Bess: July 13, 1943

Well a better day—a letter with my baby's picture in it. It was a swell and a diplomatic statement. The old man himself couldn't have done as well with all his expert advice. I suppose you are glad to have Mrs. Fred Wallace back home. How did she find her mother? I hope she recovered her sight all right.

Well I've had the usual hectic day. Several customers came as usual. I'm being haunted by Leighton Shields and Colonel Henderson and I suppose I deserve it. Had lunch with Forrestal and his assistant and took the old coupe down to get the window fixed so it would go up and down and have the gear shift put into workable condition. It runs like a new one now and I almost hate to sell it. We'll see when we get it home.

Here are the paper's spasms on the federal judges. Have had nothing but nice letters from home about Duncan. Mr. Roberts wants to have breakfast with me tomorrow so I guess he's got some skulduggery up his sleeve. You see also that the St. Joe paper was very nice. I've got to run in order to get the car greased. Looks like I'll get off all right on Thursday afternoon.

Kiss Margie, love to you,
Harry

Washington, D.C.

Dear Bess: July 14, 1943

Well here I am at home once more writing to you. Got a nice letter full of bills which, considering everything, were very conservative and which I am able to pay and have something left in the bank account. Between you and me we have really done a remarkable job of making ends meet and managing to meet insurance payments, etc. We've also saved a little and our baby will get her education. The insurance will keep you when I kick in and perhaps leave a little nest egg for our beautiful singer. I hope so anyway.

I took the old car to the station this morning to be oiled, greased, and filled for the start, which I hope to make tomorrow. Caught a bus and got off at California Avenue to get a streetcar, then remembered I had a breakfast date at the Statler with Mr. Roberts and Mr. Shoop. It was only 7:35, so I walked to the Statler by way of Connecticut Avenue, Dupont Circle, Massachusetts Avenue, and Sixteenth Street and then had to wait on Mr. Roberts to put his shirt on. . . .

My best to the family, love to you, kiss Margie,
Harry

[White Swan Hotel, Uniontown, Penna.]
Dear Bess: July 15, 1943
Well here I am with a good start toward home. I made up the laundry and put it in the car, tried to clean house and gave it up because it wasn't dirty anyway. There is a little dust here and there but unless you look very carefully you don't see it, and you'll clean up anyway, so I gave that up. But I did put clean sheets and pillowcases on, and put the spreads back.

Well, I arrived at the office at seven-thirty, packed my briefcase, cleaned off my desk, and wrote Mamma a letter, then in came Colonel Henderson with the Nebraska maternal granddad of one of his sons' progeny and I took 'em to breakfast.

They left and I started to dictate a bunch of letters and in came your persistent and pestiferous friend from China. Thank God I got him a job in the antitrust division with my friend Tom Clark, who succeeded Arnold, at $5,500 a year. Then he (illegible) me for a job for Jr. and I gave it to him and he wanted me to call the attorney general and be sure he is an assistant attorney general and I did and he is and then I had hysterics and went and got a haircut. Ran into Hatch and Benton and got stuck for speeches on the 29, 30, 31, 1, 2, 3, 4, 5, 6, 7, 8 of August from Des Moines, Omaha, Sioux City, Lincoln, Topeka, Salina, and I don't know where else.

Had a session over the phone with Brewster and one with Fulton, settled all the post office controversies with Mr. Clark—gave him one and got three and got him to agree to Mr. Canfil for U.S. marshal. I also put him and Mr. Bill on the wagon. He won't stay but Bill will. He's a contrite gentleman. I gave him the scare of his lifetime.

Had lunch with Jim Mead, Wallgren, Kilgore, Biffle, and Halsey, and canceled my radio speech they were bound I should make and got in the car at two-thirty. Went by the laundry and left the dirty clothes and then went by home and picked up some more clothes—those I bought at Hot Springs—and my swimming suit and also those two good, light suits Ted made me, hoping I can get him to fix them.

Wallgren wants to take me on a boat trip on Puget Sound. I hope I can do it. I'll call you from somewhere on Sunday morning and let you know when I'll get to Colorado.

Hope everybody is well and *cool* and happy. I had to put on my coat on Negro Mountain [Somerset County, Pennsylvania].

I also approved three reports today, got the *Congressional Record* altered, and changed the *Journal*—without unanimous consent. Looks like I've arrived in the Senate.

Love to you, kiss my pretty baby,
Harry

[Hotel Lincoln, Indianapolis, Ind.]

Dear Bess: July 16, 1943

I've had quite a day. If you can imagine me leaving Uniontown at 7:00 A.M. after having breakfast at six-thirty and driving all day in the hot sunshine—keeping the speed indicator below forty most all the time and never more than forty plus, you can understand why I could hardly write my name on the register when I arrived about six o'clock—really about seven o'clock, because the watch went back an hour at Richmond. It was actually eleven hours driving to make exactly 370 miles. You know I've made 570 in that time.

I still had some of the grand box lunch Mrs. Boyle made for me and I didn't have to stop only at roadside parks to eat. I don't know whether I told you yesterday she sent over a shoebox with six deviled-eggs, a whole fried chicken, six bread-and-butter sandwiches, and some cupcakes sealed up in this Cellophane. I ate chicken, a deviled-egg, and a bread-and-butter sandwich for supper last night in Frostburg. Then I had my usual breakfast in Uniontown—a big tomato juice, Post Toasties (couldn't get oatmeal), toast and milk. Well by ten-thirty this morning I was hungry as a bear. So I stopped at one of Ohio's roadside parks west of St. Clairsville and ate a deviled-egg, a couple of pieces of chicken, and a bread-and-butter sandwich out of Mrs. Boyle's shoebox.

I stopped in St. Clairsville to get the old car tightened up. I had cultivated a rattle underneath that sounded as if I was going to lose the running gear. Fortunately I stopped at the right place and found a fellow who knew the Imhoffs and the Lewises. In fact they all live in the same block. So he tightened up everything for $1.68. He asked me my name when he was making out the bill and almost had heart failure when I told him—that's how the Congressmen came up.

When I registered at the White Swan last night the clerk said he hoped I wouldn't investigate him. The Lincoln clerk said the same thing. Ain't that an awful reputation?

Well I stopped at another Ohio park on the east side of one of those dams west of Springfield and ate the rest of the chicken and deviled-eggs but I still have some cupcakes and bread-and-butter sandwiches left—and I'm hungry now. So I'll have to go buy a meal I guess.

If all goes well, I'll get to St. Louis tomorrow—go and see John Snyder, who is in the hospital having his rupture sewed up, and then go to Jefferson City and stay all night. I'll see Dick Nacy and then go to Kansas City. See all the folks and come to Colorado soon as possible. Kiss Margie. Love to you. My best to your mother, Chris, and the kids.

Harry

[Hotel Evans, Vandalia, Ill.]

Dear Bess: July 17, 1943

Well His Majesty of the lower regions—Mr. Pluto—and I'm not thinking of the famous water, overtook me here today. I stripped the gears in the old coupe. And what I mean I stripped 'em right. It had been rather contrary about shifting from low to reverse to high right along, but I thought maybe things would hold out until home grounds were in sight. I stopped in Knightstown for a Coke and had some trouble yesterday—was too close to the curb on a slant and I'd had trouble in Washington in front of the' most important office building in the United States.

Well today I drove up to old man Evans' hotel and before I could stop on the perpendicular I hit the curb on a very slight angle. I couldn't budge the gearshift and finally ran up on the curb, as I did in Washington, and got shifted to reverse and backed out into the street with much help and comment by Sunday bystanders. When I changed from reverse, for some reason, she gave a sudden click and refused to go forward or back—wouldn't even go sideways. So a good-hearted citizen pushed me to the good garage and they took out the transmission. There she was, stripped, after I'd waited some three hours to see what was the matter. They could only phone St. Louis for gears. We postponed that and I called Mr. Canfil—and wonder of wonders, got him. He'll be here in the morning and we'll load all the bushel or so of parts into the car and tow it home where Mr. Deets can make me a new car. You know it has never been right since that nut busted it in the parking station. Talked to Bill and he gave me good advice too. Old man Evans was almost too happy for words that I had to stay overnight. Will call you tomorrow. Kiss Margie. My best to all the family.

Love to you,
Harry

[Hotel President, Kansas City, Mo.]

Dear Bess: July 21, 1943

It's probably July 22 because I know it is very late. Canfil and I were supposed to be on the way to Denver today but the garage man at Vandalia called me (he sent me a wire and I called him) and told me the car was fixed and ready to come home. So—instead of going to Colorado today Mr. Canfil and I got up early and went to Vandalia, Illinois, a distance of 322 miles. We left here at 6:50 this morning and arrived in the Illinois town at 2:45—strictly within the speed regulations. . . . The old thing made more than eighteen miles per gallon all the way out and that garage man, also, is a real one. My bill was only $31.95 and I thought it would be three times that. . . .

Kiss Margie. *Love to you.* Hope to see you Friday night.

Harry

Washington, D.C.

Dear Bess: July 26, 1943

. . . Well Bill's finally gotten straightened out. I went over there on Thursday and had dinner with him and a couple of his friends. We played a little poker and Bill got tight. He called me the next morning and said he had to go after Mrs. Boyle and the girls, who were up at Fulton's farm. Well about noon Saturday Mrs. Boyle called up just frantic to know where Bill was. Well he and his drunken friend from Kansas City got lost and stayed all night at a roadside camp and we all thought he was in jail. Mrs. Boyle was so mad she threatened to take the girls and go to Kansas City. Bill came sneaking in here Monday and he's just now got back so I talk to him decently. I guess he's like every one of the rest of us—the continual pounding gets on his nerves. . . . Hope you are all packed and I wish I were too.

Lots of love,
Harry

Des Moines, Iowa

Dear Bess: July 29, 1943

I hope that you and Margie and Christie and the kids got home safely from the station and I hope that everyone was convinced I had a good time and didn't want to leave. . . . I had the dumps for most of the evening remembering what you said about my being a Senator (wish I'd stayed a clodhopper). I'm in for a real go-around up here and am afraid I'm going to like it. I also called on the Vice President. She was in and glad to see me; he wasn't—had gone somewhere to speak.

Kiss Margie, love to you,
Harry

Truman never forgot a supporter who had been with him when times were rough, as in the case of Con Mann, below, who had helped him almost twenty years before.

Chicago, Ill.

Dear Bess: August 15, 1943

. . . Went to dinner with Con Mann and his wife and two nephews and their wives at the Palmer House. It was the same show that was here when the Shrine party took place.

Con is an old, old man. He can hardly walk and he just sits and looks at you and once in a while makes a remark. He was always for me, however. He sent me $150 in that eastern judge campaign when I was beaten and he gave Canfil $500 in that first senatorial and also the second one—and he wasn't asked to do it. This is the third time he's asked me to address this convention, so I thought I'd better do it before he dies. My best to your mother. Kiss my baby.

Lots of love to you,
Harry

[Hotel Last Frontier, Las Vegas, Nev.]

Dear Bess: August 18, 1943

Here I am in "Babylon," one of the last frontier towns. Reno's the other one. This place is a grand one to stay. It has air-conditioned rooms and everything you ever read about in frontier days. There's roulette, blackjack, one-armed bandits (slot machines), and a scientific dice table. I am up on top of all of them because I let 'em alone, but I had a kick out of watching people play. There's something about gambling that gets into men and women. T.J.P. [Thomas J. Pendergast] couldn't hold himself when ponies were at the stake ready to go. My Swede Senator just can't resist roulette and the dice table. If I'd gone along with him, my financial position would have been much improved. But I don't want to get that complex. I like to play poker for reasonable stakes and if I were rich I'd break a roulette bank once in a while, but since I'm not I can't afford to take chances—because when you can't afford to lose you can't afford to win ethically. Wish I had no ethics. But the world would be a terrible place in which to live if nobody had a code of morals. . . .

My best to your mother. Hope my baby is happy.

Love to you,
Harry

[The Arlington Hotel, Hot Springs, Ark.]

Dear Bess: September 7, 1943

Went to the hospital this morning and had a visit with General Gold-thwaite. He took me to the nose expert, who poked around in the upper reaches of my head, through the nose and made me shed about a half pint of tears. He said there was some inflammation, ordered me to the X-ray room, where they took four pictures of my head. I'm to go back in the morning and find out if I have a clogged brain pan. From what the nice-looking young captain said, there won't be much to do except probably put drops up my nose. He put some stuff up in my head on cotton and left it awhile, and things feel and look better even now. . . .

Love,
Harry

[Hotel President, Kansas City, Mo.]

My dear Sweetie: October 2, 1943

It was so nice to talk with you awhile ago, and I wanted to talk to you the whole time but felt that your mother would be most anxious to talk to her children and Margie would be almost passing out to talk to her aunts and uncles that I just couldn't bring myself to monopolize the telephone.

They were all extremely happy to talk to all of you. Frank thought it was an expensive proceeding but I noticed he had water in his eyes when he finished talking to his mother—so it was worth it.

My mother has really had an upset. She was pale as a ghost today when I went out there and I found she'd had a chill yesterday, although the furnace was on and so was the gas grate. She's aged considerably in the last year—more than in the previous ten—and I suppose the end must come even after ninety years, but I don't want it to. She's one of the leftovers of the feudist-pioneer days— the days that created the things for which we fight today. She's no diplomat as your daughter is, she's no purist in speech as you are, but she has something the country needed fifty years ago and which is gone now, but I have hopes that maybe the purge we're going through will bring back. I'm opposed to backward views, however, except as examples. We looked back in 1920 and that's what's the matter today. Lot's wife looked back, and see what happened to her. At that, she was a jewel compared to old Lot. He was as bad and no account as they make them—but they didn't tell us that at Sunday school. I found it out by reading the record—which I still do. . . .

Kiss Margie, love to you,
Harry

Shenandoah, Iowa

Dear Bess: October 3, 1943

Hope you noticed I've learned how to spell this town. I left Kansas City at about eleven o'clock and arrived at four-thirty. That's well within the speed limit, and I got twenty-two miles to the gallon. Here are those A tickets. I'm sending you five. That's twenty gallons, or is it fifteen?

I feel like a heel staying away so long, but if I can sneak in that rest, it'll get me by the winter, and I believe I ought to have this tooth photographed by the Hot Springs staff. I'm almost sure it ought to come out, but I'm like you, I don't want to do it.

Mamma looks so pallid and she can hardly see anything—but she won't admit it. I fear very much that another of those pass-outs may be her last. But I hope not. . . .

My best to everybody, love to you,
Harry

[Warwick Village, Jefferson City, Mo.]

Dear Bess: October 6, 1943

. . . I am so glad your mother can be there with you and I hope you two had a good trip down in town. You draw a check for what you need. I didn't buy any bonds last month so we have at least a thousand dollars in the bank. We'll buy double this month when I get back. Also we can begin buying regularly again when your check starts. If we can manage three or five hundred-dollar bonds every month until the end of the term, we won't starve until I can get a job if we are beaten in 1946. If I were up now, there'd be no opposition—but you never can tell.

Your letter made me feel 100 percent better. It was much more cheerful. I am prouder of my baby every day. I think that groaning about school is a pose and if she enjoys it we should give her some argument on it now and then.

Hope to get your reaction to the speech today. Kiss Margie for me. She owes me a letter. My best to your mother.

Love to you,
Harry

Robert Hannegan, mentioned below, had been collector of internal revenue for St. Louis and was being appointed head of the internal revenue bureau in Washington. A question arose over his successor in St. Louis.

[The Park, Hot Springs, Ark.]

Dear Bess: October 11, 1943

. . . Mr. Hannegan had a reception for Clark after it was over and all the politicos from St. Louis and out state were there. *Clark stayed sober.* Jim Pendergast, Jim Aylward, and Barney Dickmann were present, as were Mike Kinney, Jim Finnegan, John Sullivan, Tony Sestric, and a *negro* or two. Neal and the southerners weren't happy over that and neither was Mrs. Hannegan. But there were only two of them and they behaved better than some of the Irish.

I believe that we have helped the political situation and improved Clark's position. My Jefferson City speech seems to have rung the bell with the Democrats and a lot of Republicans. Clark and I tentatively agreed on Hannegan's successor. It will be either ex-Congressman Sullivan or Finnegan. I'm a little on the side of Finnegan because he was for me in 1934 and that sort are rare birds in St. Louis. He has been a star football player, municipal judge, and prosecuting attorney in St. Louis. But he has Clark's weakness, although he's been on the wagon for more than a year. You know John Sullivan, of course, and he'd probably be the best bet. But the *Post-Dispatch* couldn't have as serious a hemorrhage over him as over Finnegan. I'm hoping that someday that paper will pass out in the midst of one of its Democratic spasms. . . . My best to your mother.

Lots of love to you,
Harry

[The Park, Hot Springs, Ark.]
Dear Bess: October 12, 1943
    I was sure I'd find a letter here last night but I didn't and none this morning.
I've been to the hospital and the news is rather good. They photographed the
tooth again and all those around it and gave me the same diagnosis that the man
in Washington did and I didn't tell 'em about him.
    This Lieutenant Colonel Selby here at this place is one of the nation's best
dental surgeons. He ran an iron rod up the side of my face, did a lot of grinding,
and casually announced that he was sure he'd save the bridge and the tooth. I
have to go back tomorrow for more torture.
    Old General Goldthwaite is in bed himself for a rear-end operation. I went
in to see him and told him I'd come up to gloat. He laughed and then screwed
up his face with pain. It's impossible to laugh, cough, sneeze, or move without
pain when you have that operation.
    I've got a fine corner room with all the conveniences, and if the sun comes
out I hope to take a sunbath. Kiss Margie. My best to your mother.
                                    Lots of love to you,
                                        Harry

[Hotel Jayhawk, Topeka, Kans.]
Dear Bess: February 22, 1944
    Here we are at the Kansas capital. They tell me it was the biggest meeting
since Woodrow Wilson was here when he was governor of New Jersey. The place
was crowded to the utmost capacity and they were standing around the wall and
in the hall leading to the elevator. It was the roof garden of this hotel and the
same place I spoke last summer on [illegible]. They all seemed to be satisfied with
what I said. It was broadcast over Senator Capper's radio station and he wouldn't
let them pay for it because it was my speech. For all his shortcomings—and you
know they are the sort I abhor—he does things that touch the heart. . . .
                    My best to your mother, loads of love to you,
                                        Harry

[Olympic Hotel, Seattle, Wash.]
Dear Bess: [Mar. 28, 1944]
    Well it was sure grand to talk to you yesterday. I'm so far away I don't feel
so well about it. Miss you and my baby and your mother. Specially miss that
evening ceremony of taking the medicine with you. Hope someday you and I can
just sit around and enjoy a perpetual honeymoon without worrying about bread
and butter and public opinion. Guess I'm just a damned, sentimental old fool.
I've always had you on a pedestal and despite the fact that you try to climb down
sometimes, and I don't blame you for trying, I'm not going to let you. From
Sunday school days, to grade school days, to First World War days, to the Senate,
to World War II you are just the same to me—the nicest, prettiest girl in the
world. Most of my associates think there's something wrong with me because I

believe in that oath I took in a certain little Episcopal Church in Independence, Missouri, *about* twenty-five years ago. But I don't care what they think. . . .

My best to your mother. Kiss my pretty girl and lots of love to you.

Harry

Hotel President, Kansas City

Dear Bess: July 13, 1944

. . . Just gave Mr. Roberts a tough interview saying I didn't want the Vice Presidency. Also told the West Virginia and Oklahoma delegations to go for Barkley. Also told Downey I didn't want the California delegation. Mr. Roberts says I have it in the bag if I don't say no—and I've said it as tough as I can.

Sent you a little piece of change last night by special delivery. Hope you have it by now. . . .

Don't know any more gossip or scandal so I'll quit for this time. Start for Chicago tomorrow, arrive Saturday. Will be at Stevens Saturday night, Morrison Sunday. Kiss my baby. My best to Mother and family.

Lots of love to you,
Harry

After the nomination, Truman had to decide if he could remain chairman of his committee. A vice presidential campaign in 1944 would be especially strenuous because of President Roosevelt's incapacity. Would Truman have enough time to wear both hats? A sense of party loyalty made his choice clear, but the decision was an emotional one nonetheless.

Washington, D.C.

Dear Bess: August 4, 1944

How do you like my fancy stationery [no letterhead]? Looked the place over for some Senate sheets and there were none. Yesterday was a hectic day. The train was late. Fulton met me at Martinsburg, West Virginia, and we talked over every angle of the committee and came to the decision that for the best interests of all concerned I'd better quit. I had made my mind up on that when the nomination was forced on me. I have never in my life wanted to sit down and really blubber like I did when I told 'em I was quitting. I didn't do it—but they did. Connally, Mead, Kilgore, Brewster, Benton, Ferguson were there—so were Fulton, Halley, and one or two others of the staff. . . .

Loads of love,
Harry

Washington, D.C.

Dear Bess: Monday, August 14, 1944

It was nice to talk to you yesterday. I'd been mopping the floors and was I hot. Will run the sweeper and dust everything before I leave. I didn't get a great deal of dust off the floors and there isn't much on the furniture.

The Truman family at the Chicago convention, 1944. *Harry S. Truman Library*

Margaret reading congratulatory telegrams. *Chicago* Sun

Senator Truman. *Chicago* Tribune

Vice-presidential candidate and Bess in the Connecticut Avenue apartment. Clock at right shows it was an early (or late) breakfast. *UPI*

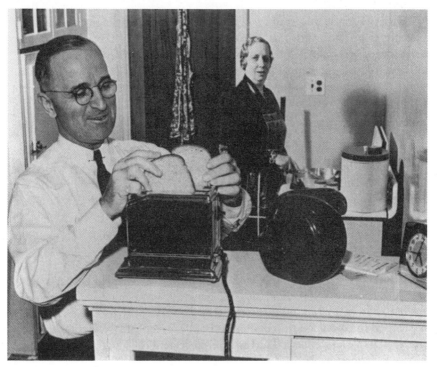

It was a good thing I shut off the phone. There were a dozen calls, but they answered them promptly downstairs and I didn't hear them. Slept all afternoon, got up at six instead of five, and the Hot Shoppe was packed, so I came on down to the office and ate at the Carroll Arms. Chicken dinner costs $1.75 there and $1.10 at the Hot Shoppe. It was good though and I then came into the office and found that the girls had been working, so I signed a lot more letters, read all the accumulated mail, and got home at nine o'clock, read some more Sunday papers, and went to bed at ten-thirty.

Had a letter from Abie Burkhart. His boy was killed in action June 22 in the assault on one of those South Pacific islands. It was a pitiful letter, because he was all wrapped up in that boy. I've been scared for Ed McKim's boy, but Ed doesn't seem to be as uneasy as I am. He's on Guam. . . .

Kiss Margie, love to you,
Harry

Washington, D.C.

Dear Bess: August 18, 1944

Was glad to talk with you last night even if it was on a sad subject. Brings the war close to home when boys you know are its victims. Abie's and Eddie's boys were the kind you hope to see grow up. I'm very much afraid they represent a class who have the country's welfare at heart and who are getting killed for it. We'll have the culls and shirks left to father the next generation. Perhaps that's the reason we hardly make any progress in human relationships over the thousands of years. The real Roman citizens were killed off in the Punic Wars, so Rome turned to conquered countries for citizens. Spain, Venice, Prussia, England have all gone the same way. Wonder if we should too. It will take us several hundred years to feel it, so I guess there's no use for a prospective Vice President to worry about it—is there? . . .

Kiss Margie, lots of love,
Harry

At the White House luncheon mentioned here, Truman again sensed the Roosevelt charm, as well as the Roosevelt guile. Later that afternoon he saw Hannegan, who had become chairman of the Democratic national committee, and Edwin W. Pauley, its treasurer.

Washington, D.C.

Dear Bess: August 18, 1944

I succeeded in getting Mr. Canfil out of town this morning. He had a grand time while he was here. Made all the girls, including the new one, very angry—and then fed 'em sundaes and soft drinks until they were not as angry as they wanted to be. He tried to horn in on the committee, but it was too late. Nevertheless he did some good while he was here. The Justice Department called me and told me that he had done more as U.S. marshal for the good of the service than any other marshal they had. For a wonder he'd read all their regulations and told 'em (as he always does) in words of one syllable, with expletives, where said regulations conflicted. He'd cleaned out all the jails in his bailiwick where there had been prisoners unlawfully held, and he had been instrumental in preventing the sentencing of ignorant draft dodgers where they were willing to join up and serve. So in spite of his blustering his heart is in the right place. He makes me madder than I can express it sometimes, but if I wanted the Federal Building moved in spite of opposition I'd have him undertake it. And he'd do the job or bust a hamstring. But he's gone home and is bringing the Central American suitcase to trade you for a loan of the Hunter Allen-Marino Phelps Gladstone bag. Let him have it.

As you know he's given me the reveille clock, a grand, wool blanket, and some other things, so if he keeps the bag, I'll still be in his debt and I can't forget 1940.

Wish you'd been here for the White House luncheon today. I went down to the Mayflower and had a meeting with Hannegan, Pauley, and Paul Porter. Got there at 11:00 A.M. At twelve-thirty I started to walk over to the White House, which is only four and a half blocks. Met Louis Johnson in front of Harvey's and talked to him about five minutes. Arrived at the front gate of the White House on time and was told to go to the office. I was first supposed to be there at one o'clock but they called and said the President wanted to see me fifteen minutes before one. I was there at 12:45, but old man Hull was with him and one o'clock would have fitted in with me. Hull was trying to get the British and Russian envoys to the coming conference in to see the President tomorrow afternoon. But—the Russians were delayed at Nome and the President finally said that if all of 'em, Russian, British, et al., were not at his office by nine-fifteen Saturday evening, they need not come because he was leaving for Hyde Park at ten-fifteen and they'd have to wait until he came back.

I went in at about five to one and you'd have thought I was the long lost brother or the returned Prodigal. I told him how I appreciated his putting the finger on me for Vice President and we talked about the campaign, reconversion, China, postwar employment, the George and Kilgore Bills.

Then lunch was announced and we went out into the back yard of the White House under an oak tree planted by old Andy Jackson, and the movie men and then the flashlight boys went to work. He finally got hungry and ran 'em out. Then his daughter, Mrs. Boettiger, acted as hostess and expressed a lot of regret that you were not there. I told the President that you were in Missouri attending to my business there, and he said that was O.K. He gave me a lot of hooey about what I could do to help the campaign and said he thought I ought to go home for an official notification and then go to Detroit for a labor speech and make no more engagements until we had had another conference. So that's what I'm going to do. Hope to get things in shape here so I can start home Sunday evening. Maybe I can do it tomorrow evening. If that happens, I'll be at home Sunday at six o'clock.

I went back to the Mayflower and had a conference with Bob Hannegan and Pauley. Bob's to see the President tomorrow. I've got to wait and see what's done by those two. Pauley told me that *all* my expenses of whatever nature would be paid by the national committee and that he wanted me to take Hugh Fulton and Matt Connelly wherever I went and not to hesitate on the cost! I guess I've really arrived. Mr. Porter came to my press conference in the office at 4:00 P.M.

and I heard him tell Bob and Pauley that I needed no guardian because all the press boys liked me and that no one in his recollection handled them better. He didn't know I heard him.

Well this is strung out too much. But the President told me that Mrs. R. was a very timid woman and wouldn't go to political meetings or make any speeches when he first ran for governor of N.Y. Then he said, "Now she talks all the time." What am I to think?

Kiss Margie, lots and lots of love to you,
Harry

Aboard the Milwaukee to Spokane, Wash.

Dear Bess: October 20, 1944

Well I suppose you'll be off me for life but I have had the most strenuous two days in all my campaigning history. At Los Angeles there was not a minute from my arrival until I left that wasn't taken up except an hour or two on Sunday. I managed to call and get in a letter or two there. They drove me to Bakersfield after the most enthusiastic meeting I'd had—110 miles to catch my car, which had left L.A. at 5:00 P.M. We arrived in San Francisco at 8:00 A.M., got off at Berkeley, and drove in over the long Bay Bridge. Had a tough press conference soon as it was possible and then reception after reception, just as in Los Angeles, Congressional, legislative, C.I.O.-A.F. of L., Longshoremen, etc. The San Francisco luncheon was a success. The afternoon was just the same as the morning, except I got in a call. Took the train at 7:00 P.M. and went to bed. Thought I'd have all the next day to catch up and write letters. But I had to make a speech at Klamath Falls, Oregon, at 7:30 A.M. A delegation got on there and then it was town after town. At Eugene there were one thousand on the platform and I shook hands with all of 'em after a speech. After that it was town after town, and a delegation from each town to ride a piece of the way. Got to Portland an hour late, which was a break. They had lined up a radio speech at this station and a handshaking until the dinner. Too late for that, but by the time I had put on a clean shirt, it was time for the meeting at seven-thirty. It was a fine banquet at the biggest hotel and they forced me to shake hands with everybody there, six hundred, and the state chairman stood on one side of me and pawed me over while he introduced 'em. Wrote a hundred autographs and went to the hotel where the delegations began. Wallgren got in about ten and we talked until midnight and then went to bed. Got up at six and started on yesterday. Left Portland in Mon's car and the newsmen in another at 8:15; Vancouver, Washington, 10:00; Kelso, 11:30; Chehalis radio broadcast 12, Centralia lunch. At all these places, an open-air meeting, speech, handshake. Went to Olympia for a big meeting on the capitol steps, at least two thousand out. Got away without the handshake because we were fifteen minutes late. Tacoma next. Spoke in a square, right in the center of town, to at least twenty-five hundred. Dodged the handshake except for those who could greet me and made Seattle at five-thirty. Washed my face and started in again, made a radio speech at seven-fifteen to the country with Paulette Goddard—she was in L.A.—drank a glass of milk and went to the biggest meeting of all. There were ten thousand in the same hall where

Harry, Margaret, and Bess at a whistle stop. *Copyright unknown*

Dewey spoke to five thousand, and were they enthusiastic. They applauded so much that my radio time ran out before I was half through the speech. Hudson and a pretty star from Hollywood followed me, but I could not stay. Mrs. Wallgren was there and seemed so pleased to see me. She wanted to be remembered to you. Got on the train at 9:00 P.M. and fell into bed. Am up this 5:00 A.M. to meet Lew Schwellenbach.

Hope Lew will mail this for me. As far as I know the schedule, it had been changed only by adding towns. We stop in Butte tonight and then Minneapolis and St. Paul. I don't know whether Milwaukee is still in or not. Peoria is. We'll arrive at the Marquette Hotel at noon the twenty-fifth I believe. Then after the speech on the twenty-sixth go to Akron, Ohio and from there to Massachusetts somewhere. Then Providence, Rhode Island, and New York October 31. Then Pittsburgh or Charleston, West Virginia, and then Independence. I thought I'd pick you and Margaret up at Washington on the way as soon as I know definitely what's what and we'll take this car to K.C. with us and release it there. We'll stay at the Muehlebach and not open the house until after election. I don't want to start back until the twelfth if that won't keep Margie too long. Had a nice visit with G. Walter. He's turned Democrat. Said he couldn't stand Dewey and that he believed me.

Kiss Margie, lots and lots of love,
Harry

Truman never belonged to the Ku Klux Klan, although William Randolph Hearst easily picked up an old canard that he had. Back in the twenties, when entering politics, the Senator had given ten dollars to a Klan organizer, but the organizer gave the money back when Truman refused to promise that he would, if elected to the Jackson County court, fire Catholic employees.

New York Central, Chicago to Cleveland

Dear Bess: October 27, 1944

   . . . Mr. Hearst has been having a grand time accusing me of being a Ku Kluxer. Hugh says we have him for a million-dollar libel suit. Be nice to tour South America at his expense, wouldn't it? I speak in Toledo, Cleveland, and Akron today. Albany, N.Y., at ten tomorrow and then Massachusetts. Sure will be glad to see you and my baby. Counting the days.

Love,
Harry

Mary, Mamma, and Vivian in 1944. Kansas City Star

THIRTEEN

SIXTEEN HUNDRED
PENNSYLVANIA AVENUE

In the first year and a half of Truman's presidency, from April 1945 until the end of the year 1946, the new President's principal responsibility was ending the war—with military victory over first the Germans in Europe, then the Japanese in Asia. Thereafter he had still to end the war—through negotiating or forcing an acceptable arrangement for world peace with the country's new antagonist, the Soviet Union.

President Truman discovered during the years 1945–1946 that even though he was chief executive of the most powerful nation in the world, a country that in early summer of 1945 possessed the number one army, navy, and air force, he could not have his way in the business of world peace. In the Soviet Union he had an opponent that seemed to have its own purposes in Europe and Asia, and to possess a leadership bent on turning peace into antagonism, perhaps even war, against the United States.

Understanding of the impossibility of ending the war in anything more than a formal way came slowly to the Truman administration, its leader not the least. In the past a great war would always be followed by a great peace, not by a slow winding down of hostilities. Certainly the tortuous maneuver by one of the major victors toward another, as after V-E and V-J Days, 1945, was unprecedented. The neither-peace-nor-war nature of the ending of World War II also grated against Truman's very modus operandi in public affairs, local, national, or international. He liked to snap things off, get them over with—but by resolution of difficulties through equitable adjustment. He had always worked this way. In July 1945 he went to the Potsdam Conference expecting a peace conference. At the outset of the meetings in Berlin he ,thought he could work with Stalin, who seemed eminently reasonable, perhaps more so than the "windy" Prime Minister of Great Britain. But then as the meetings wore on and what had appeared simple became ever more complicated, it was evident that the Soviets desired no real end to the hostilities plaguing Europe and the world since 1939; the President's optimism lessened. He left the German capital feeling that even his "ace in the hole," the atomic bomb, might not do much more than end the war in the Far East—it would not resolve the troubles in Europe. The months passed, and arguments continued. By the close of the year 1946 he was not yet certain what he would do about Russian hostility, but he intended to bring peace if he could.

Meanwhile the domestic front, as people had come to describe American domestic politics during the war years, saw economic upheaval. By the end of 1946 it resulted in a return of a Republican Congress—what became in Truman's mind the worst Congress in a century, a do-nothing, vindictive body of men in the House and Senate that was worse than the group that had impeached President Andrew Johnson after the Civil War. Johnson's Congress at least was forthright, its purposes clear. The Eightieth Congress was, however, composed of men who, Truman believed, had learned nothing beyond the wisdom of the year 1890. It was too benighted, he thought, to understand its own purposes and was thereby the more dangerous, nationally and internationally.

[The White House]
Dear Bess: June 6, 1945

Well I'm getting better organized now. My office force soon will be shaken down and so will my Cabinet when I've gotten State straightened out. War and Navy I shall let alone until the Japanese are out of the picture.

It won't be long until I can sit back and study the whole picture and tell 'em what is to be done in each department. When things come to that stage there'll be no more to this job than there was to running Jackson County and not any more worry.

Foreign relations, national finances, reconversion, and a postwar military policy will be the big headaches—and they can all be solved if the Congress decides to help me do a bang-up job, and I believe they will do that. . . .

President Truman. *Harry S. Truman Library*

Well I'm facing another tall day as usual. But I like 'em that way. I'm never half so worn out when I have too much to do as I am when there is too little. Trouble is I'm working the help to death.

Tell my baby I was glad to talk to her last night as well as to her mamma.

Lots of love,
Harry

At a United Nations Conference in San Francisco the Russians were being difficult, but the President took heart, he tells Bess, when Stalin overruled the Soviet delegation.

[The White House]

Dear Bess: June 7, 1945

I didn't get to phone you last night. I lost the phone number you gave me by putting it where I could find it. Whenever I do that with an important paper or memo it is as effectually lost as if it had never existed. But I wrote you a letter —and I haven't received one. You can't claim to be "busier" than I am either.

Yesterday was a hectic day. Had both good news and bad. Stalin agreed to our interpretation of the veto at San Francisco and a reconsideration of the Polish question, but we lost the election in Montana and the Republicans are jubilant over it.

Davies came to see me again and told me some more about Winnie. Had a session with Hannegan. He thinks Biddle, one of your right-side-of-the-tracks boys who acts as if he came from the other side, would make a good Librarian of Congress. I doubt if Congress would think so. But it has possibilities as appeasement for the crackpots.

The Colonel and Mrs. Boettiger came to tell me goodbye at four o'clock. They brought the boy along and he was as lively as he could be. Took a look in his room to see if any toys were overlooked. I had a nice visit with them. She is a charming person and certainly has brains. . . .

Lots of love,
Harry

[The White House]

Dear Bess: June 12, 1945

Just two months ago today, I was a reasonably happy and contented Vice President. Maybe you can remember that far back too. But things have changed so much it hardly seems real.

I sit here in this old house and work on foreign affairs, read reports, and work on speeches—all the while listening to the ghosts walk up and down the hallway and even right in here in the study. The floors pop and the drapes move back and forth—I can just imagine old Andy and Teddy having an argument over Franklin. Or James Buchanan and Franklin Pierce deciding which was the more useless to the country. And when Millard Fillmore and Chester Arthur join in for place and show the din is almost unbearable. But I still get some work done. . . .

Write me when you can—I hope every day.

Lots of love,

Harry

[The White House]

Dear Bess: June 19, 1945

Well it looks as if I'm off to Wallgren's at last. That is providing the weather is all right. I'll go to Olympia and rest a few days and then go to San Francisco on June 25 instead of 22, speak on June 26, and come directly to Independence. Landing about 1:00 P.M., twenty-seventh. Stay there until Saturday, thirtieth, and come on back here so I can send the treaty to Congress on the second of July. The Russians have caused the delay. But I'm not going to wait any longer.

Hope everything is going well with you. The letter came yesterday afternoon all right. It was promptly given to me—unopened—so you see I do have some good help. Is Margie solvent? Hope you are too. Give everybody my best.

Lots of love.

Harry

P.S. Eisenhower's party was a grand success. I pinned a medal on him in the afternoon. He is a nice fellow and a good man. He's done a whale of a job. They are running him for President, which is O.K. with me. I'd turn it over to him now if I could.

The President prepared to attend the Big Three Conference at Yalta in the Crimea; he tells Bess it will be a circus.

[The White House]

Dear Bess: July 3, 1945

It was nice to talk with you a little while ago. I am in the President's study and have been here since dinner (fried chicken, carrots, French fried potatoes, asparagus, rolls, and peaches and cream) reading, reading, reading and signing until I'm sick of seeing that sprawling signature. I have a briefcase full of "agenda" and minutes of Yalta, Teheran, Casablanca, Quebec, San Francisco and numerous notes by Byrnes, Hopkins, Davies. Hopkins is sick and can't go. So I'll have to depend on Leahy and Byrnes. I hate to go—but I hated to go to San Francisco—I didn't want the thing I received at Chicago—so I guess it makes no difference what I want, I'm elected to do a job. Here's hoping I can do it.

You should have seen the Senate yesterday. They were all there and they gave me such a reception as you hear about but never see. I could hardly get 'em shut off. And it was the same after it was over. Don't believe there'll be but two votes against it, Hiram Johnson and Curley Brooks. Bertie'll vote Brooks, and old Johnson is too old and contrary to admit he's been wrong for twenty-seven years.

I really had a good time after the speech. Went back in Biffle's office and held a reception. Every Senator came in but California's Johnson. We fought the ten years I was there all over again.

Prettyman and I are trying to get all the clothing we need together. I have to take my negro preacher coat and striped pants, tails, tux, winter clothes and spring ones, high hat, soft hat, and derby. It'll be a circus sure enough. But we will get it done I hope.

We leave at 7:00 P.M. Friday for Norfolk where we board a cruiser. Will phone you Friday before I leave. Wish you and Margie were going. We'd call on the Kings of Norway and Denmark and maybe Georgie too. Hope I don't have to but am afraid I will.

Hope Miss Margaret had a good time tonight. Give my best to the family.

Lots of love,
Harry

[En route to Norfolk, Va.]

Dear Bess: July 6, 1945

I'm on the train, bound for Norfolk, to take the boat ("ship" is navy) for Antwerp. I am blue as indigo about going. You didn't seem at all happy when we talked. I'm sorry if I've done something to make you unhappy. All I've ever tried to do is make you pleased with me and the world. I'm very much afraid I've failed miserably. But there is not much I can do now to remedy the situation.

Tonight I sat in the front row with Vaughan, Vardaman, Snyder, and others and listened to a most beautiful band concert by the Air Corps Band—a million-dollar organization. They were most pleased to play for *me!* Why I can't understand.

Now I'm on the way to the high executioner. Maybe I'll save my head. Let's hope so. George VI R.I. sent *me* a personal letter today by Hailfax. Not much impressed. Save it for Margie's scrapbook.

Love to you,
Harry

[Aboard U.S.S. *Augusta*]

Dear Bess: July 12, 1945

This has been a most restful and satisfactory trip. Haven't been sick a minute! We left Norfolk Sunday, July 7, at seven o'clock and spent a pleasant sunny day. Went to church at ten-thirty with the ship's captain, officers, and men. It was a nice, short service such as we attended at Bethesda. Sat around and talked to Secretary Byrnes and Admiral Leahy most of the morning. Took a nap in the afternoon and discussed some important business with Charlie Ross and the newsmen. Went to a dull picture show in the evening and to bed at 11:00 P.M. Monday inspected the ship from bridge to engine room. Gave the boys a treat I suppose. They saw the President and he saw them. Found a boy aboard named Lawrence Truman from Owensboro, Kentucky. He's the great-grandson of my grandfather's brother and a very nice kid. He has eyes just like Margaret's.

Been in the navy four and a half years.

On Tuesday we had firing practice. They fired the eight-inch, five-inch, and forty-millimeter guns. Nice entertainment for an artilleryman. Up to the time we were ready to shoot we'd had the sea to ourselves, but when it was time to fire two merchantmen and an airplane hove into sight.

The forties are antiaircraft and are most interesting. They fire like a machine gun and have a range up to a mile or so. We have a couple of planes on board and they expect to launch them today. They are launched by a catapult and loaded with a crane.

I sure dread this trip, worse than anything I've had to face. But it has to be done. Lord Halifax brought me a longhand letter from George VI asking me to visit him and the Queen at Buckingham Palace. I thanked him and told him I would if I could. Think I'll come home as *fast* as I can when it's over though. If you and Margie were along, we'd stop.

> Love to you, a lot of it, kiss my baby,
> Harry

In Potsdam the President stayed in a house owned by a book publisher. The Russians ordered the man to move out and carted his furniture and books to a nearby woods—to be buried in shell holes. They furnished the house from other confiscated mansions. Truman, we see here, obviously misunderstood the circumstances.

Berlin
Dear Bess: July 16, 1945

We arrived in Berlin yesterday afternoon about three o'clock. Were received with all the honors possible. The Russian, British and our own ambassadors and ministers met us at the airport. I reviewed the troops drawn up as a guard of honor and then we were taken to a house in Potsdam, where I am told the head of the movie colony lived before the Russians came in. He is not available for interview now. Most of us believe that he is somewhere between here and Siberia on probably *special duty*.

The Prime Minister came to see me this morning. He brought his daughter and Mrs. Eden, and we had a very pleasant conference. I am expecting to see the marshal from Russia either this afternoon or tomorrow, and then business starts.

This house is on a beautiful location—overlooks a lake—and I have all the comforts of home and get as much waiting on as I get at the White House, which I am sure is too much.

Tell Margaret she still owes me a letter.

You send your letters to the White House with instructions that they be forwarded on to me and I will get them almost as promptly as if you sent them to me in Washington.

> Lots of love,
> Harry

  Berlin

Dear Bess: July 18, 1945

I've only had one letter from you since I left home. I look carefully through every pouch that comes—but so far not much luck. I had to dictate you one yesterday in order to get it off in the pouch. I told you about Churchill's call and Stalin's calling and staying to lunch.

The first session was yesterday in one of the Kaiser's palaces. I have a private suite in it that is really palatial. The conference room is about forty by sixty and we sit at a large round table—fifteen of us. I have four and they each have four, then behind me are seven or eight more helpers. Stalin moved to make me the presiding officer as soon as we sat down and Churchill agreed.

It makes presiding over the Senate seem tame. The boys say I gave them an earful. I hope so. Admiral Leahy said he'd never seen an abler job and Byrnes and my fellows seemed to be walking on air. I was so scared I didn't know whether things were going according to Hoyle or not. Anyway a start has been made and I've gotten what I came for—Stalin goes to war August 15 with no strings on it. He wanted a Chinese settlement [treaty with China giving territorial and other concessions to the USSR]—and it is practically made—in a better form than I expected. Soong did better than I asked him. I'll say that we'll end the war a year sooner now, and think of the kids who won't be killed! That is the important thing.

I told a three-star general as I got off the boat at Antwerp that I'd like to see my nephew Harry if it wouldn't upset things or detach him from his outfit. They found him on the *Queen Elizabeth* at Glasgow, Scotland, just ready to sail. They gave him the choice of sailing or coming to see his uncle. He is here—a sergeant and the nicest-looking soldier you can imagine. He was as pleased as could be to see me—and am I proud of him! I gave him a pass to Berlin signed by Stalin and me. He'll stay a few days and then I'll have him flown back to his outfit. He says it's the finest section (he's chief of it) in the army—the right spirit sure enough.

Wish you and Margie were here. But it is a forlorn place and would only make you sad.

Please write and tell the young lady her dad can still read.

                                     Lots of love,
                                     Harry

The letter below relates Stalin's promise to go to war against Japan on August 15. That the President worked to get such a statement from the Russian ruler shows that he believed Soviet entry necessary for a quick end to the Pacific War. Truman did not think American force alone, conventional or nuclear (the United States had exploded a plutonium test device at Alamogordo, New Mexico, on July 16), could defeat the Japanese.

Berlin
Dear Bess: July 20, 1945
It was an experience to talk to you from my desk here in Berlin night before last. It sure made me homesick. This is a hell of a place—ruined, dirty, smelly, forlorn people, bedraggled, hangdog look about them. You never saw as completely ruined a city. But they did it. I am most comfortably fixed and the palace where we meet is one of two intact palaces left standing. . . .

We had a tough meeting yesterday. I reared up on my hind legs and told 'em where to get off and they got off. I have to make it perfectly plain to them at least once a day that so far as this President is concerned Santa Claus is dead and that my first interest is U.S.A., then I want the Jap War won and I want 'em both in it. Then I want peace—world peace and will do what can be done by us to get it. But certainly am not going to set up another [illegible] here in Europe, pay reparations, feed the world, and get nothing for it but a nose thumbing. They are beginning to awake to the fact that I mean business.

It was my turn to feed 'em at a formal dinner last night. Had Churchill on my right, Stalin on my left. We toasted the British King, the Soviet President, the U.S. President, the two honor guests, the foreign ministers, one at a time, etc. etc. ad lib. Stalin felt so friendly that he toasted the pianist when he played a Tskowsky (you spell it) piece especially for him. The old man loves music. He told me he'd import the greatest Russian pianist for me tomorrow. Our boy was good. His name is List and he played Chopin, Von Weber, Schubert, and all of them.

The ambassadors and Jim Byrnes said the party was a success. Anyway they left in a happy frame of mind. I gave each of them a fine clock, specially made for them, and a set of that good, navy luggage. Well I'm hoping to get done in a week. I'm sick of the whole business—but we'll bring home the bacon.

Kiss Margie, lots and lots of love,
Harry

Berlin
Dear Bess: July 22, 1945
The letter came last night while I was at Joe's dinner. Was I glad to get it! No your taste in hats is *not* screwy. If you ever cultivate the same sort of yen for crazy hats that the two you gave those Paris ones to, have, I'll refuse to go to church with you. I'd say that is a dire threat. Your hats suit me and theirs do not.

I can't get Chanel Nº5. Padre says there is none to be had—not even on the black market. His home station is in Paris. But I managed to get some other kind for six dollars an ounce at the American P.X. They said it is equal to Nº5 and sells for thirty-five dollars an ounce at home. So if you don't like it, a profit can be made on it. I bought you a Belgian lace luncheon set—the prettiest thing you ever saw. I'm not going to tell you what *it* cost—you'd probably have a receiver appointed for me and officially take over the strong box. But I came out a few dollars to the good in the game of chance on the boat, so it's invested in a luxury for you. . . .

But I seem to have Joe and Winnie talking to themselves and both are being exceedingly careful with me. Uncle Joe gave his dinner last night. There were at least twenty-five toasts—so much getting up and down that there was practically no time to eat or drink either—a very good thing. Being the super-duper guest I pulled out at eleven o'clock after a lovely piano and violin concert by a dirty-faced quartet. The two men play the piano, the two women the violin. I never heard any better ones. Chopin, Tschaikowsky, Liszt; Hungarian Rhapsody, Russian, Ukrainian, and Polish folk dances—it was real music. Since I'd had America's No. 1 pianist to play for Uncle Joe at my dinner he had to go me one better. I had one [pianist] and one violinist—and he had two of each.

He talked to me confidentially at the dinner and I believe things will be all right in most instances. Some things we won't and can't agree on—but I have already what I came for. Hope I can break it off in a few days.

The weather is perfect and I feel fine. The boys say there's never been a conference as well presided over. The Senate gave me some good experience.

Lots and lots of love, kiss the baby,
Harry

Berlin

Dear Bess: July 25, 1945

We have been going at it hammer and tongs in the last few days and it looks as if we may finish up Sunday. I hope so at any rate. I told them yesterday that I intend to head for Washington at the earliest possible moment and that when we came to an impasse I would leave.

We have accomplished a very great deal in spite of all the talk. Set up a council of ministers to negotiate peace with Italy, Rumania, Bulgaria, Hungary, Finland, and Austria. We have discussed a free waterway program for Europe, making the Black Sea straits, the Danube, the Rhine, and the Kiel Canal free to everyone. We have a setup for the government of Germany and we hope we are in sight of agreement on reparations.

So you see we have not wasted time. There are some things we can't agree to. Russia and Poland have gobbled up a big hunk of Germany and want Britain and us to agree. I have flatly refused. We have unalterably opposed the recognition of police governments in the Germany Axis countries. I told Stalin that until we had free access to those countries and our nationals had their property rights restored, so far as we were concerned there'd never be recognition. He seems to like it when I hit him with a hammer.

I see Drew Pearson has been taking an interest in Vietta. If that so-and-so ever says anything to your or Margaret's detriment I shall give him a little Western direct action that he'll long remember. I don't care what he says about me but I can get hotter than a depot stove when he mentions my family.

Kiss Margie, lots of love,
Harry

Berlin

Dear Bess: July 29, 1945

It made me terribly homesick when I talked with you yesterday morning. It seemed as if you were just around the corner, if six thousand miles can be just around the corner. I spent the day after the call trying to think up reasons why I should bust up the conference and go home.

Byrnes and I conferred all day on this and that and the other thing and finally got things down to the point of final agreement on Lend-Lease with the British, French, and South American countries, and for the Big Three, reparations and the Western boundary of Poland. If we can get a reasonably sound approach to those two things, we can wind this brawl up by Tuesday and we'll head for home immediately. Stalin and Molotov are coming to see me at eleven o'clock this morning and I am going to try to straighten it out.

I like Stalin. He is straightforward. Knows what he wants and will compromise when he can't get it. His foreign minister isn't so forthright.

The British returned last night. They came and called on me at nine-thirty. Attlee is an Oxford man and talks like the much overrated Mr. Eden and Bevin is an English John L. Lewis. Can you imagine John L. being my Secretary of State? Well we shall see what we shall see. I believe after reading all the minutes, we have obtained all we came for and that there will be a good report to the country. Just the two things to settle but they are the hardest of course.

The Senate vote was great and will have a very fine effect over here. Pray for me and keep your fingers crossed too. If I come out of this one whole there'll be nothing to worry over until the end of the Jap War.

Kiss Margie, lots of love to you,

Harry

Berlin

Dear Bess: July 31, 1945

It was surely good to talk with you this morning at 7:00 A.M. It is hard to think that it is 11:00 P.M. yesterday where you are. The connection was not so good this morning on account of the storms over the Atlantic.

We have been going great guns the last day or two and while the conference was at a standstill because of Uncle Joe's indisposition, the able Mr. Byrnes, Molotov, and Attlee and Bevin all worked and accomplished a great deal. I rather think Mr. Stalin is stallin' because he is not so happy over the English elections. He doesn't know it but I have an ace in the hole and another one showing—so unless he has threes or two pair (and I know he has not) we are sitting all right.

The whole difficulty is reparations. Of course the Russians are naturally looters and they have been thoroughly looted by the Germans over and over again and you can hardly blame them for their attitude. The thing I have to watch is to keep our skirts clean and make no commitments.

The Poles are the other headache. They have moved into East Prussia and to the Oder in Prussia, and unless we are willing to go to war again they can stay and they will stay with Bolsheviki backing—so you see in comes old man reparations again and a completely German-looted Poland. . . .

I'll sure be glad to see you and the White House and be where I can at least go to bed without being watched.

Kiss my baby, lots and lots of love,

Harry

I've got to lunch with the Limey King when I get to Plymouth.

Henry L. Stimson, whom Truman praises in the letter below, began his career of public service as district attorney in New York City in 1906; he was Secretary of War in 1911, when Truman was a corporal in the Missouri national guard. Stimson's last Cabinet meeting discussed the international sharing of nuclear secrets, albeit after suitable safeguards—a far cry from the military concerns of 1911.

[The White House]
Dear Bess: September 22, 1945
. . . Pinned a medal on Stimson yesterday. If anyone in the government was entitled to one it is that good man. He wept a little as did Wainwright when he received his. We then had a stormy Cabinet meeting discussing the atomic bomb. Lasted two hours and every phase of national and international politics was discussed. It was very helpful. I must send a message down on it soon.

The funny part of the meeting was that those on the right of me were "Left" and the others on the left were "Right." Stimson, Acheson, Interior (Fortas for Ickes), Schwellenbach, Wallace, Hannegan, McNutt were arguing for free interchange of scientific knowledge, while Vinson, Clark, Forrestal, Anderson, Crowley were for secrecy. Anyway I'll have to make a decision and the "Ayes" will have it even if I'm the only Aye. It is probably the most momentous one I'll make.

Love to you and Margie, hello to everybody. I'm off for Jefferson Island.

Harry

[The White House]
Dear Bess: December 28, 1945
Well I'm here in the White House, the great white sepulcher of ambitions and reputations. I feel like a last year's bird's nest which is on its second year. Not very often I admit I am not in shape. I think maybe that exasperates you, too, as a lot of other things I do and pretend to do exasperate you. But it isn't intended for that purpose.

When you told me I might as well have stayed in Washington so far as you were concerned I gave up, cussed [Senator] Vandenberg, told the Secretary of Agriculture to give all the damned cotton away for all I cared, and then smiled over the phone at Henry Wallace and I'm afraid hurt Admiral Leahy's feelings by not asking him to go on the boat [the President's yacht, the U.S.S. *Williamsburg*]. At least Matt [Connelly] said I did and I called the old admiral up and asked him to go. . . .

You can never appreciate what it means to come home as I did the other evening after doing at least one hundred things I didn't want to do and have the only person in the world whose approval and good opinion I value look at me like I'm something the cat dragged in and tell me I've come in at last because I couldn't find any reason to stay away. I wonder why we are made so that what we really think and feel we cover up?

This head of mine should have been bigger and better proportioned. There ought to have been more brain and a larger bump of ego or something to give me an idea that there can be a No. 1 man in the world. I didn't want to be. But, in spite of opinions to the contrary, *Life* and *Time* say I am.

If that is the case, you, Margie, and everyone else who may have any influence on my actions must give me help and assistance; because no one ever needed help and assistance as I do now. If I can get the use of the best brains in the country and a little bit of help from those I have on a pedestal at home, the job will be done. If I can't, no harm will be done because the country will know that Shoop, the *Post-Dispatch*, Hearst, Cissy, and Patterson were right.

Kiss my baby and I love you in season and out,
Harry

[The White House]

Dear Bess: June 10, 1946

Well I just returned from my morning walk. Looked in to see if you were up. You were apparently because the bed was all made up. Well I miss you terribly —no one here to see whether my tie's on straight or whether my hair needs cutting, whether the dinner's good, bad, or indifferent. So far the eats have been all right. Had a nice meal yesterday at noon. Jim and Frances Pendergast were my guests. We ate at twelve because Jim wanted to catch a one-fifteen plane. I think he enjoyed sleeping in Lincoln's bed very much.

We finally got our elevator. I charged John Snyder with wanting a headline. He denied having anything to do with it. Said some smart aleck in the D.C. office had simply asked for an elevator for a public building and then vicariously turned it down.

Looks like His Majesty of Siam chose to go to hell rather than come to see us. I can't tell by the papers whether he shot himself or was assassinated. The pictures show him a very personable young man. Well anyway I don't have to worry about that state dinner.

Spent yesterday afternoon and evening working on veto message. Had Rosenman and Clifford doing spade work and then Allen, Snyder, Ross, and Steelman punch holes in the documents and I made the decisions.

Hope things are all right with you. Remember you are very much missed here. The *New York Times* Magazine has a lovely article on you. Did send it.

Lots of love,
Harry

[The White House]

Dear Bess: June 11, 1946

Just back from a nice walk. It is a beautifully cool morning and I feel fine. Still a little hoarse but that will wear off.

Spent yesterday and Saturday and Sunday composing a veto to the Case Bill. It is a very good document but will create a lot of vilification for me I'm sure. I'm used to it by now. Had Ross, Matt, Allen, Snyder, Clifford, Hassett, and Steelman over to dinner last night after the final draft and we had a very pleasant time. Played a little five-cent poker and settled the affairs of the world generally.

Snyder was unanimously approved by the Finance Committee—a great slap at Pearson, the Sop Sisters [Stewart and Joseph Alsop], and Miss Fleeson.

It sure is a lucky thing I did not make Jackson Chief Justice. He has surely gone haywire. You never can tell how men will react. He was so dead sure he would be Chief that he had to take it out on somebody. And did he skin Black! It is terrible for public confidence in the courts. Goes to show that when you have an organization of dissenters it won't work. They all want to be Holmeses and Brandeises and you can't run the Court that way nor can you run the country unless a majority can work together.

Wish all of you were back. I'm going on a round of pleasure this week to keep from being lonesome. Olson and Johnson tomorrow night and the Hard Rock Club on Thursday.

Kiss my baby and tell her I hope her right hand isn't sore or paralyzed.

Lots of love,
Harry

[The White House]

Dear Bess: June 13, 1946

Your letters of June 10 and 11 arrived on time. You can address them as you like—but none of my family letters are opened by anyone but me. They never were. Margie's, May's, and Mary's letters are never opened and I don't think but one of yours ever was and that was before we were properly organized.

Senator Bankhead died yesterday afternoon. Mr. Pearson should feel happy. He caused the death of the old Senator. So he's just as much a murderer as if he'd shot or poisoned him. . . .

They are fixing the hole in the hallway and I have to walk under a scaffold when I go out the study door. I'll look for a letter.

Lots of love,
Harry

Administration of price controls bothered the President, as he tells Bess. Rationing had ended in 1945, and Truman hoped to contain prices long enough to allow the economy a return to peacetime production without inflation.

[The White House]

Dear Bess: June 14, 1946

. . . Office of Price Administration is a mess, brought on principally by the pinheads who have administered it. It seems the late President had a positive genius for picking inefficient administrators. His Court appointments are some-what disgraceful too. I've about come to the conclusion that he wanted to do everything himself and get all the acclaim for successful accomplishment and then have a dumb cluck to take the blame for what failed.

Went to a Hard Rock Club party at the Statler last night and had a good time. Lost twenty-six dollars, a quarter at a time, between 9:00 P.M. and midnight, but enjoyed the evening.

Hope everything is well with you. Kiss the baby for me.

Lots of love,
Harry

[The White House]

Dear Bess: June 15, 1946

Rose handed me your letter yesterday and I was glad to hear from you. Hope you were able to get dressed before you went to town!

The maritime strike was settled at the last moment. I wonder what comes next. Appointed John Steelman to succeed John Snyder as O.W.M.R. [Office of War Management and Reconversion] head. Pat McCarran found a way to hold up Vinson's appointment. Some day I'll have an opportunity to level him off. Probably won't do it but it should be done.

Jim Byrnes and I have finally corralled old Baruch I think. The stuffed shirt will have something more to do than sit on a park bench and pass out impossible advice. There never was a greater egotist unless it was Franklin D.

Gave some more Medals of Honor to five kids yesterday who performed unbelievable feats to win them. I always fill up when I read those citations. . . . Tell everybody hello.

Kiss the baby and lots of love to you,
Harry

[The White House]

Dear Bess: June 18, 1946

. . . I was so tired last night I went to bed at nine o'clock and slept straight through. Looks like the more sleep I get the more I want. Had a rather strenuous day—a lot of customers like Chavez, Dean Acheson, Barkley, Rayburn, McKellar to start with, Paul Porter and the chairman of the House conferees on O.P.A., Paul Brown.

Doesn't look as if we'll get a decent price control bill and I'll have to start another fight. This time directly with Congress. There never was one like it. Even old Andy Johnson's wasn't quite so nutty even if they did try to impeach him.

They were frankly mean and admitted it. This one puts on a long face and plays hypocrite. Well we'll see. I still have some tricks up my sleeve.

Hope you are having a pleasant time. Wish the time would come when we could have a vacation together. Do you suppose it ever will? Tell everybody hello.

Lots of love to you,
Harry

[The White House]
June 19, 1946

Dear Bess:

. . . That washing machine seems to be doing overtime duty. Hope it holds up. I am glad you agreed to the fence. The souvenir hunters would probably carry everything off without it. Hope you had a good time with Mrs. Duncan.

As to that Washington State trip, Mon sent me a letter inviting me and it evidently was leaked out there before it was mailed. I am not counting on anything but trouble and work right here.

Things have eased up somewhat but not enough to justify a vacation for me. Since I'm not accustomed to vacations it won't matter much.

Closing up this hole in the third floor is some job. That floor is solid concrete nearly a foot thick and steel enforced. It'll probably take another week to finish it.

Everybody in town is going to the big fight today. Of course I can't go. I can't even go to the television show here. To tell you the truth it is no disappointment to me. I wouldn't go if I could. I don't like that yellow nig and I wouldn't like to see him knock out a fool white Irishman. . . .

Lots of love,
Harry

[The White House]
June 20, 1946

Dear Bess:

. . . Mr. Keck, the sculptor, was with me most of yesterday making a bust for the Senate. He has done an excellent job, so the spectators say. He is making it in clay and then he uses a hammer and chisel on a block of marble. Told me had made a heroic piece for the Huey Long memorial in Louisiana. Mr. Neild got him that job. He is now making a statue of Al Smith called The Sidewalks of New York. He said Smith had approved the model before he died. Said all three of his boys are grown up now and that two of them had been in the service. They were all in knee britches when I was in New York on the Andrew Jackson statue. . . . Say hello to everybody.

Lots of love,
Harry

[The White House]

Dear Bess: June 21, 1946

A letter came yesterday. Made the day brighter. I'm glad the car incident has turned out all right from our side. I'm sorry for the fellow who had his neck broken though. It seems that the photographs showed things exactly as Mr. Nicholson reported. . . .

Everybody was confirmed yesterday by the Senate. Looks now like they may wind up by July 20. I had thought maybe of going to Alaska but I don't know. We'll talk it over. Alaska trips have been fatal to Presidents and humorists.

Charlie Ross was almost redheaded yesterday he was so mad at Eddie Locket of *Time.* The Hard Rock Club gave me a party in return for several I've given them, and Eddie reported it. They expelled him from the club but that doesn't undo the devilment.

Time, Hearst, and the Sop Sisters and Pearson love to belittle me and this was only another opportunity—but it was pretty dirty. Say hello to everyone.

Lots of love,
Harry

[The White House]

Dear Bess: June 22, 1946

The longest days are here—now they go down and down to winter and darkness. Wish they'd stay this long and this cool all the time. It has been exceptionally pleasant. I suppose it is saving up a heat wave to greet you when you come in.

I have fixed up a grand ceremony for Mr. Vinson. Going to do it on the south portico with all the trimming—band, Supreme Court, Ambassadors, Cabinet, Congress, and the Common People. If that doesn't recreate some respect for the Court, I know of nothing else to do. Anyway very few in my position have the chance to make a Chief Justice. . . .

Lots of love,
Harry

[The White House]

Dear Bess: St. John's Day, June 24, 1946

. . . Had breakfast all alone at 9:00 A.M. Sat around and read the papers awhile and then took a good walk—a mile and a quarter over to a haunted house on the reservation. It has fifteen rooms and is vacant. A man is said to have murdered his wife because she had other men around while he was visiting another woman! Anyway he's in the pen and has been for eighteen years.

Came back to the pool—walked mind you, and had a swim and a sunbath. Then a further study of probabilities. We had dinner at 5:00 P.M. and I arrived back at White House at eight-thirty and went to bed. Slept like a log. How would you like to spend a vacation at Shang-ri-la? If you get home in time we could spend the long Fourth of July weekend there. I've signed a bill giving it to all the government employees, so why not the top employee take one too? I could be available on the phone and still get some rest and sleep and if you wanted someone for the weekend there is plenty of room. . . .

Kiss the baby, lots of love,
Harry

After becoming President, Truman soon learned how inquisitive the press could get. He didn't like it.

[The White House]

Dear Bess: August 7, 1946

Where is my ten dollars? You just can't believe in your old man's luck and judgment can you? Well I am afraid I can't either sometimes—especially the *judgment*. Anyway the stuffed shirt, Mr. Slaughter, was unseated in exactly the same way he was seated, statesman or not. The beautiful part of it is that Mr. Roberts is very much put out.

At the same time I was telling off Mr. Porter, Charlie Ross was telling the drunken Mr. Roberts the same thing!

Porter was outside Sermon's store with his notebook out jotting down items for publication and I suggested to Roger that he invite him in. Then I proceeded to tell Mr. Porter that I had gotten out of bed at five-thirty, brushed my teeth, shaved, and attended to certain unmentionable personal matters, put on my underclothes, my shirt, tie, pants, and coat. Had then eaten an egg on toast, after drinking some tomato juice, and wound up with a glass of skimmed milk. Then he was informed that neither I nor my family were appreciative of the spying tactics he had used. I told him I knew of his sitting across the street with a spy-glass, that he had followed me to John Hutchison's house, and that he and his boss Roy Roberts were only trying to get something nasty on me and that it was not appreciated. He said he was only obeying orders. That was what I wanted him to say. Mr. Shoop told Charlie that Mr. Roberts felt very badly about my attitude, which made me very happy. . . .

Kiss Margie, lots of love,
Harry

[The White House]

Dear Bess: August 9, 1946

Two letters today! Made it very bright and happy. You know that there is no busier person than your old man—but he's never too busy or too rushed to let his lady love, the only one he ever had, hear from him *every* day no matter what portends. It hurts just a tiny bit when he finds that trips uptown, time to dress etc. interfere with letters from his lady love. But complaints never got anyone anywhere—so "as the fates decide." . . .

Thanks for the ten. If you need it I'll send it back. Glad Dr. Greene went to see Mamma. She is on the way out. It can't be helped; but I wish it could. She's a trial to Mary, and that can't be helped either. Wish you could be more patient with both. But I can't ask too much I guess. . . .

Lots of love to you,
Harry

[The White House]
Dear Bess: August 10, 1946
    . . . I still have a number of bills staring me in the face. Byrnes called me from Paris this morning asking me not to veto a State Department reorganization bill, which I'd told Clark Clifford I was sure is a striped-pants boys' bill to sidetrack the Secretary of State. Jimmy told me it wasn't but I'm still not sure.
    I have another one under consideration, which restores civil and military rights to a captain in the quartermaster department. He was court-martialed in 1926 in Panama for some seven or eight charges under the ninety-third and ninety-sixth articles of war. Dick Duncan is interested because the fellow's from St. Joe and he put the bill through the House and I put it through the Senate on two occasions, and Roosevelt vetoed it both times.
    When I read the record I'm not so sure Roosevelt wasn't right! Ain't it awful what a difference it makes where you sit! I gave the whole thing to Clifford and told him to give me a coldblooded report on it.
    I have another one which is a pain in the neck. Hayden, my good friend, and King want it signed. Anderson wants it disapproved and it looks like Anderson is right. It sure is hell to be President.
    I am leaving here—I hope Friday next—for a two-weeks cruise up the east coast to Maine—no stops anywhere. Will tell you more about it when I know more. Tell everybody hello.

Lots of love to you,
Harry

[The White House]
Dear Bess: August 12, 1946
    Well it is another day. But another dollar. It was another $40 from your letter. Wish your mother wouldn't insist on assuming these bills. She should sit back and let us do the worrying as she didn't in days gone by. I'd like her to feel she hasn't a financial worry in the world as long as I have a job and I want my mother to feel the same way. Don't tell her, but I'll invest her payment of the grocery bill in the game of chance, which I anticipate on the *Williamsburg* beginning Friday. You know I'm almost like a kid—I can hardly wait to start. We are leaving at 2:00 P.M. Friday, will go down the Potomac and up the Chesapeake Bay to the Maryland-Delaware Canal, into Delaware Bay and up the Jersey coast to Sandy Hook, into Long Island Sound to Block Island Sound to Nantucket Sound. We'll *probably* stop at Newport for water and then go to

Portsmouth, New Hampshire, for supplies and then along the Maine coast to the Bay of Fundy and back the same way. Do you know that this will be my first vacation since the interrupted one in Colorado where the pictures of my hanging out washing were taken?

I'm most happy you went out to Vivian's party. I have a terrible time with my immediate family about which you, of course, know not a thing. But that visit will help a lot. Glad Dr. Greene thinks Mamma is improving.

Called you anyhow on Sunday and you were at Vivian's—but I called. Will call you Thursday evening and tell you the final plans.

Kiss my baby. Should I send you money? You can draw a check.

Lots of love,
Harry

[The White House]
Dear Bess: August 14, 1946

Well I've spent the day signing and refusing to sign bills. Interviewed the finance minister of Saudi Arabia—a real old Biblical Arab with chin whiskers, a white gown, gold braid, and everything. He is the most powerful man in the Arabian Government next to the old King. We had a most pleasant visit discussing his application for a $10 million loan from the Export-Import Bank, guaranteed by the Arabian-American Oil Company. He told me he wanted to build a railroad across the Arabian desert from the Red Sea to the Persian Gulf and that their government wanted to restore some ancient dams for impounding water for irrigation. I told him he should send for a Moses to strike rocks in various places with his staff and he'd have plenty of water. The old man came right back and said modern science and the United States could take the place of a Moses!

Yesterday I signed an Indian bill with a lot of dressed-up Indians in the picture. One of them gave me a scalping knife and told me to use it on the Republicans.

I am going out to Bob Hannegan's for dinner tonight to meet some "liberal" politicians. Hope Pepper's not present. Suppose you saw his announcement that he and Henry or just he would be a candidate for President in 1948. The old *Herald Tribune,* N.Y., said "Pepper throws two hats in the ring—both his own."

Tomorrow morning I am taking the photographers for a walk. They will know they've been somewhere. We leave at 6:30 A.M.

Tomorrow night I call Mrs. Truman—hope she's home! Kiss my baby. Love to you, lots of it, and tell everybody hello.

Harry

[The White House]
Dear Bess: August 16, 1946

. . . There was no special implication in my remark about the family except that I have a time getting them all to get along. The reason I was so glad you went out to Vivian's was because that is the first all-out get-together in forty years. Ralph and his half brothers never visit each other, the Nolands and the Colgans hardly ever speak to each other, and they've all been at outs with Mamma and Mary. So you see what I meant. Now you mustn't begin putting hidden meanings on my remarks too. Every newsman does that and I fool 'em because I always mean what I say.

Wish you and Margie were going along on the trip. I am enclosing you a schedule. I shall invest your ten dollars if a game of chance should ever develop. One probably will. It's cold here this morning and raining although I got in my walk. Kiss my daughter for me.

Lots of love to you,
Harry

[U.S.S. *Williamsburg*]

Dear Bess: August 18, 1946

It has been a very pleasant cruise. We left Washington in a pouring rain but ran out of it in the night. The weather Saturday was beautiful and today it has been perfect.

We went through a canal between Chesapeake Bay and the Delaware River yesterday about noon and then went swimming at five o'clock in Delaware Bay.

Headed straight out to sea, headed for the east end of Long Island. We are now entering Narragansett Bay in Rhode Island and it is beautiful, water blue and clear as can be, sky a deeper blue, the shore line purple and green with white houses now and then—makes a very lovely picture. We shall land in a few minutes after which we'll go home with Captain Foskett for dinner.

The guests have been congenial and the game of chance has been profitable to me. Your ten has increased tenfold with interest! . . .

Lots of love to you,
Harry

[U.S.S. *Williamsburg*]

Dear Bess: August 19, 1946

Your two letters of 15 and 16 caught up with me here at Quonset. They surely looked good when they came. Glad Sue had no trouble. Of course I'd like to be grandpa and except for having to call you gramma it would be very nice.

But if the child wants to sing, let her try it. She has a lovely voice, but I hope the prima donnas—one in particular—do not spoil her. Think maybe she is past the spoiling stage by now anyway. . . .

I am enclosing a Boston *Globe* article about Miss Truman. It is datelined Independence and is Associated Press—the White House press service is not responsible. It is a nice article.

Kiss my baby and remember me to everybody else.

Lots of love to you.
Harry

[U.S.S. *Williamsburg*]

Dear Bess: Thursday, August 22, 1946

Well you didn't expect to hear from me in mid-Atlantic but here I am in the most beautiful of harbors. I couldn't write you at sea because the yacht would stand first on one end and then the other. Then it would roll over about forty-five degrees and back the other way. I lost my breakfast, my lunch (of the day before), and ate nothing until yesterday morning when I got well and didn't miss a meal after that. Have had a sunbath every day including Tuesday, the day of the rough sea.

But I'm so glad I made the change. I was running into political storms all over Massachusetts, New Hampshire, and Maine. John Sullivan, Undersecretary of the Navy, wanted me at his house, Bob Hannegan wanted me to ask Joe Kennedy, whom I dislike, on board, and the Maine Democrats heard I might be at Bath and Casco Bay and they insisted I let them stage a party and informed me that I mustn't see Brewster, whom I didn't expect to see—so, I just ditched 'em all and I'm so glad now, seasick and all.

We are anchored in the bay and have absolute privacy. I can swim every day, sleep, and go walking without disturbance.

The Governor General paid his call and I have to return it and that's all. The weather is what you dream about. I'm riding in Governor General's landau behind two white horses to call on him. He was in command at Plymouth and lent me his barge when I called on King George.

While Truman sought refuge from the public eye aboard the *Williamsburg*, Bess found her privacy at 219 North Delaware. *Harry S. Truman Library*

Wish you and Margie were here. We'll do it again someday with our own party. My best to everybody.

Kiss Margie, lots of love to you,
Harry

The U.S.S. Williamsburg *was a small yacht without enough ballast and depth to take a storm easily, as the President relates below.*

[U.S.S. *Williamsburg*] off the Virginia Capes

Dear Bess: September 2, 1946

We are coming into Hampton Roads this morning in most beautiful weather, after a stormy voyage. We left Bermuda Friday morning with lovely sunshine and a smooth sea. By dinnertime it was raining and blowing and the *Williamsburg* was doing gyrations unheard of in the experience of the seadogs aboard. I had managed beautifully until dinner time, but from then on it was every man for himself, and I went to bed and stayed there most of yesterday and until 5:00 A.M. this morning.

But it did me a world of good, my weight is down to 170. I have a beautiful coat of tan and feel ready for the fray no matter what it is. About four-thirty Saturday morning we hit the worst of the storm. The furniture was taking headers in every direction and it was necessary to stay in bed to keep your legs on. Nothing was broken in my quarters except a full bottle of Listerine, which knocked open one of those little cupboards at the side of the mirror in the bathroom. It fell in the wash bowl luckily and ran down the drain. No broken glass on the floor. Everything else survived all right. But the place looked like a cyclone had hit it. Papers, books, chairs, clothing, yours, Margaret's, and Mamma's pictures mixed up with *Time, Life, Newsweek, Reader's Digest, Collier's, Saturday Evening Post,* luggage, and pillows. Looked as if it never would be in shape again. But it is and you'd never know it happened. Have had a grand rest. Wish you and Margie had been along except in the rough sea.

Maybe we can take a Caribbean cruise this winter. Remember me to everybody and lots and lots of love. Sure miss you and the baby.

Harry

[The White House]

Dear Bess: September 3, 1946

. . . Rose and Reathel and Luretta, Bill Simmons, old Jackson, Wade, Taylor and Ferguson, the policemen, all beamed at me like I was the returned prodigal. They act as if they like me. Crim, [illegible], and West showed me various improvements made while I was gone. The new chandeliers are beautiful, my rug has been cleaned, and they've enclosed my bathtub with plate glass. They are cleaning and scrubbing Margie's room and they've polished up your mother's, Lincoln's, the Rose, and yours. When the elevator's finished it'll be a new house—when we get floors and a heating system. Then probably the roof will fall in. I'm in favor of making it a museum and giving the Presidente a rent allowance and then we could go back to 4701 or somewhere else. . . .

Lots of love to you,
Harry

[The White House]

Dear Bess: September 6, 1946
. . . The newsmen's party went off without a hitch. The dining room looked fine, the meal was excellent, and the private news pictures were funny. Vaughan had taken several hundred feet of color film and the navy man had taken some regular movies not fit for publication. Nothing that anyone couldn't see but not the thing to publish. For instance he got one of Hannegan in white shorts scratching a part of his anatomy not usually touched in public and one of Snyder in a bathing suit going head over heels in a medicine-ball game. . . .

Give my best to everybody and lots of love to you,
Harry

[The White House]

Dear Bess: September 9, 1946
. . . I slept well but hot, and some mosquitoes bit my hands and face. Night before last I went to bed at nine o'clock after shutting all my doors. At four o'clock I was awakened by three distinct knocks on my bedroom door. I jumped up and put on my bathrobe, opened the door, and no one there. Went out and looked up and down the hall, looked into your room and Margie's. Still no one. Went back to bed after locking the doors and there were footsteps in your room whose door I'd left open. Jumped and looked and no one there! The damned place is haunted sure as shootin'. Secret service said not even a watchman was up here at that hour.

You and Margie had better come back and protect me before some of these ghosts carry me off. Vivian called last night. He's at the Statler and will have breakfast with me this morning. Hope everybody is well.

Lots and lots of love,
Harry

[The White House]

Dear Bess: September 10, 1946
. . . The Blue Room is torn up now. They have been washing windows, cleaning Venetian blinds, cleaning the chairs, and scrubbing the floor. There is no carpet in the State Dining Room and the third floor looks like an attic. I go up there for sunbaths on the days I can get them in. I told old Mayes yesterday when I started up there that a few more days would make me as brown as he

is. He said, "You'd better not get that brown, they won't let you stay in a first-class hotel." . . .

This seaman's strike is the most of all the headaches. I'm in the middle no matter what happens. But I'll have to take it. Pearson and Winchell are lying again. Some day I'll have to shoot 'em both.

Lots of love,
Harry

[The White House]
Dear Bess: September 12, 1946
. . . Tomorrow is Pershing's birthday. Just twenty-eight years ago today I was following up the drive on Saint-Mihiel. Spent the night awake and with the horses harnessed. It was rather nerve wracking.

Monty came to see me yesterday. We were having pictures taken out on the lawn and he wanted to know when it was built. I told him in 1792 and that in 1814 the British burned it down, and from then on it had to be painted white. He said that they ought to pay for it or else we should burn Whitehall.

Hope everybody is well and that there'll be no more delay in my letters. Vivian went home last night. I guess Canfil will go today. I am going out to Clifford's to dinner today. Forrestal, Frank Walker, Allen, and one or two will be there.

Kiss my baby and lots of love to you,
Harry

[The White House]
Dear Bess: September 13, 1946
I failed to answer your question about your car. It seems to me that if you can get a good price for it you may as well sell it and buy a bond, and then when we leave the great white jail a new car can be bought. The new cars won't have the bugs out of them for two or three years anyway. Be sure though that no regulations or price ceilings are in any way infringed, no matter how good you may think the friendship of the person you sell to may be. The temptation to take a crack at the first family for pay is almost irresistible and so far we've escaped any factual misdemeanor and I'd like to finish with that reputation. Save the number. . . . Say hello to everybody.

Lots of love,
Harry

Secretary of Commerce Wallace—he had accepted the Cabinet post after Truman became Vice President—seems to have been ill at ease as an assistant to the man he had opposed at the Chicago convention. In the letter below the President relates the beginning of his efforts to avoid taking Wallace's resignation. Wallace had made a speech in Madison Square Garden that placed him publicly in opposition to Secretary of State Byrnes, who was trying to deal with the Russians in Paris.

[The White House]

Dear Bess: September 15, 1946

Well it is a beautiful Sunday morning and I slept until six-thirty after going to bed at two. I was intending to go up to the mountain Friday but it turned so cold I was sure it would be uncomfortable and then between maritime strikes, Henry Wallace's fiasco, and a vicious effort to cause an open break between Hannegan and Snyder by Pearson I thought here was the best place for me. This place gets more and more uncomfortable. It seems that no one can be trusted any more to deal squarely with facts as they are. Wallace now seems to have his eye on 1948. Hannegan is acting like a ten-year-old child and of course Byrnes has the pouts. Jim Mead came to see me about the New York campaign and then shot off his mouth as he went out the front door. The Jews and crackpots seem to be ready to go for Dewey. If they do, Jim's beaten and so he has to grasp at straws. There is no solution for the Jewish problem and I fear the crackpots would turn the country over to Stalin if they had half a chance.

LaGuardia came in and said he'd seen Stalin and he looked well. He went out the front door and said he'd support Lehman but not Mead. I suppose it will be this way until the election and then in all probability get worse. So I'll have to stand it. I've been through the toughest time in our history and I guess I can stand some more.

We had a nice dinner last night and then a right good game of chance. It is a most agreeable crowd and I think they all enjoyed it. I did and it was a relief from the headlines. Hope you're having a nice time and that your weather is as good as it is here.

Kiss my baby and lots of love to you,

Harry

[The White House]

Dear Bess: September 17, 1946

Received your letter of Friday yesterday. Hope you had a nice visit with Paul Rider and Mrs. Bostian. Don't understand the loss of the napkin. You don't suppose our very close friends are becoming souvenir hunters, do you? I am sorry to hear of Mrs. Gregg's death. But when you get our age that's about all you hear —is the passing of people you've known all your life and waiting for your own.

Would like to see the goods the President of Lebanon's wife sent.

The returned representative of U.S. to Rumania brought you a cloth and napkins handwoven by the native people. It is cotton but very beautiful. General Ike brought me one of these Mexican Indian blankets from the President of Mexico with my picture woven in it. Except for the picture it is a beautiful thing. . . .

Lots of love,

Harry

[The White House]

Dear Bess: September 19, 1946

Yours of Tuesday came last night. That was a good picture of Margaret in the clipping enclosed. Glad you are getting packed up.

Henry came to see me last night and stayed from three-thirty to six. He finally agreed to make no more speeches until Byrnes comes home. I don't think I ever spent a more miserable week since Chicago.

I simply had to tell Henry that he could make no more speeches on foreign affairs. He didn't want to quit the Cabinet because I told him he had the right to do as he pleased outside the Cabinet. He finally agreed to stop talking. This affair of Wallace is one of the worst messes I've ever been tangled up in and I hope another one doesn't come up again soon but it undoubtedly will.

The crackpots are up in arms and we'll probably lose the Congress and New York and then we'll have a time sure enough. But it can't be helped. I hope we can manage to get over the next two years without too much trouble. The world picture is none too bright. Looks like Marshall will fail in China. I'm not sure that with Henry muzzled, Byrnes will bring home the bacon. We're staring another round of strikes in the face. The army and navy are at each other's throats again and my Cabinet family just keep bickering all the time. So it goes and I have to keep a straight face and grin about it. But you'll say, well you brought it on yourself and so I have no consolation whatever.

I don't suppose I deserve any! Well anyway it's only five days to Tuesday. Tell everybody hello.

Lots of love,
Harry

[The White House]

Dear Bess: September 20, 1946

I was in communication with Byrnes yesterday and assured him that the ground would not be cut from under him. I shall make a statement on it this morning at a press conference.

I have written a letter to Henry asking for his resignation. After our long talk of day before yesterday he evidently held a session of his help and every word of our two-hour conversation was quoted in the [Washington] *Daily News*. I told Henry in the confidential letter that I could never talk frankly to him again, therefore it was best he resign. I also told him that I didn't believe he could work on a team, particularly a team as important as the President's Cabinet. I expressed the opinion that he would undoubtedly be happier out of the Cabinet than in it.

I marked the letter personal and confidential. We'll see whether he'll give that out or not.

We agreed on exactly what he would say to the press. He said just what he agreed to and then answered questions which completely nullified his agreed statement. Then when I saw the news piece I hit the ceiling.

So now I'm sure I've run the crackpots out of the Democratic Party and I feel better over it. Henry told me during our conversation that as President I couldn't play a square game. That I shouldn't let my right hand know what my left did, that anything was justified so long as we stayed in power. In other words the end justifies the means.

I believe he's a real Commy and a dangerous man. If I can't play square I won't play. It's four days!

Lots of love,
Harry

[The White House]
September 21, 1946

Dear Bess:

Well I fired Wallace but not by the letter I'd written. I called him and told him he ought to get out. He was so nice about it I almost backed up. I just don't understand the man and he doesn't either. Now that's some statement. I am enclosing you two clippings from the *News*. One by Tom Stokes on Wallace, which I think may be correct, and an editorial—over which I almost shed tears. I did sit down and write John O'Rourke a note (he's the editor of the *News*) telling him that now he could call me crazy, crook, or incompetent and I'd never fall out with him.

The reaction to firing Henry is terrific. The stock market went up twenty points! I've had an avalanche of telegrams from Maine to California agreeing with the action. I've also had some from New York, Detroit, and California calling me a traitor to F. D. R. and a warmonger. But I think I'm right. Charlie Ross told me I'd shown I'd rather be right than President and I told him I'd rather be anything than President, and Clifford said, *"Please* don't say that."

Anyway it's done and I feel like Mon Wallgren's Swede. This Swede owned a fine retail business and was doing fine, but according to Mon he became somewhat intimate with a lady named Gina Olson. Gina came to his store one day and told Ole (Mon's Swede) that she thought she was due to produce a child but that she wasn't sure. She told him that she was going to see the local doctor and find out for sure. Well Ole walked the floor, kicked and cussed himself for a fool and wished he'd behaved. Gina came back shortly and told Ole that the Doc could not see her until the next day. So they decided to take a walk and discuss the situation. The walk led them to the town reservoir. Gina said to Ole with Mon's Swede accent, "You know if what I believe is true is confirmed by the doctor tomorrow, I shall come up here and jump into that reservoir." Ole threw his arms around her and said, "Oh Gina, you don't know what a load you take off my mind!" Also in Mon's Swedish dialect.

Well Henry's demise makes me feel like Ole did—but not for the same reason, thank God. That reminds me, I had a telegram from Steve Early which said, "Thank God. Steve." Just three days.

Lots of love,
Harry

Dear Bess: Monday, November 18, 1946

This place is what I hoped it would be and what I was certain it would not be. I am in a house built on the southern plan, with "galleries" all around upstairs and down. It is the house of the commandant of the submarine base. They have no commandant at present, so I'm not "ranking" anyone out of his house. . . .

I'm seeing no outsiders. I don't give a damn how put out they get. I'm doing as I damn please for the next two years and to hell with all them. . . .

The only regret I have is that you are not here. If you and Margie were with me, I'd be sure we were back in Biloxi. You know, I guess I'm a damn fool, but I'm happier when I can see you—even when you give me hell I'd rather have you around than not.

Lots of love,
Harry

[The White House]
Dear Bess: Friday, December 20, 1946

Well I was glad to hear from you last night. I'd only been home thirty minutes. We had a nice dinner party at the Navy Secretary's house. I had a visit with his wife and his son Pete. Jim Byrnes came in for one drink and stayed for dinner! You can't beat that. He told stories on F. D. R., Hull, and the campaign of 1932. We had a grand time but the game of chance was delayed a full hour as a result. And I was right. I took 'em to town so am solvent for Christmas if I'm as lucky tomorrow night.

It is snowing steadily this morning and if it keeps up we'll surely have a white Christmas. When I went walking yesterday morning the old moon and two morning stars, Jupiter and Mars, were almost in line. I told Anderson that when those stars and the old moon came into line we'd have a snowstorm—so here it is.

We'll probably get a new moon tomorrow and then good flying weather for the trip home.

Tell my nice daughter to keep on being nice. Remember me to everybody.

Lots of love,
Harry

[The White House]
Dear Bess: Saturday, December 21, 1946

Had letters from you and Margie yesterday afternoon. Was glad to get them. I was never so lonesome when you all left. But I've been as busy as usual. Put my military training program into effect by starting off a new committee to make a complete survey of the situation. The Sabotage Press is not pleased with the committee. So it must be a good one. Anyway they had a very successful kick-off meeting and I hope eventually we'll get some action.

Saw the Greek Prime Minister with Byrnes. Almost had to throw him out of the office. Even Byrnes, as great a conversational pig as he is, was out-talked and after a half hour I began ushering him to the door—he was still going at top speed and finally had to have the door shut in his face.

You'd better be listening to my world-wide Christmas broadcast because I'm going to make a most important announcement. Wish I could come home sooner but I can't. There is just too much to do. . . .

Take care of yourself and I'll see you Christmas Day before dinner. Spank Margie for me, *lightly.*

Lots of love,
Harry

[The White House]

Dear Bess: Sunday, December 22, 1946

I am in your office writing this. I told Margie (your pen's no good) in the note I just finished to her that "Conscientious" objectors were marching up and down in front of the White House with prison stripes on and carrying signs on which, I suppose for I haven't been able to read them, they ask for the release of their comrades in jail. Well damn few of them are honest. If the country from Revolutionary times on had had only conscientious objectors where would we be? In the late total war we would be under the heel of Japan or Hitler. Neither prospect is pleasant to contemplate.

The only one of 'em I ever came in contact with, whom I thought to be on the level, was the little skinny pharmacist's mate to whom I gave the Congressional Medal of Honor out in the back yard of the White House. He'd carried wounded man after wounded man to safety from under fire at the front and finally was shot himself and still kept working on the other wounded. He said he thought he could serve the Lord acceptably under fire if he himself didn't try to kill anybody. He did his heroic job on Okinawa.

Was sure glad to talk to you just now. And I am just as sorry as you are that I can't be there Tuesday. But as I told you, I'm giving the world a real Christmas message by saying we're declaring the end of hostilities.

I'll bring Maggie her coat and jewels. Hope you'll be able to hear my message. Tell everybody hello.

Lots and lots of love,
Harry

[The White House]

Dear Bess: December 31, 1946

Well I'm making progress. The Attorney General, Secretary of the Treasury, John Steelman, Clifford, and Jim Webb of the Budget, met in my office at three-thirty yesterday and today I declare the end of hostilities. All are agreed!

Now that is something. Wish it could have been done Christmas Eve, but it had to soak in I guess. The Attorney General has been working on it since last January and Richmond Keech, who was also present, has been on it for more than six months. . . .

I am spending tonight on the yacht and expect to have a good time. Tell Margie I haven't heard from her.

Lots of love,
Harry

FOURTEEN

CHANGES FOR THE FUTURE

Paramount for the United States in 1947, President Truman believed, was the reevaluation of the injunctions of presidents Washington and Jefferson. He wanted the United States to assume the burden of international affairs on a full-time, responsible basis—no longer could the country hope to intervene, as Washington had said in his Farewell Address of 1796, only during extraordinary "combinations and collisions" of the powers of Europe. Jefferson, too, had warned against "foreign entanglements," a phrase that had become equally outmoded. The national interest of the United States now demanded, Truman believed, exertion in international matters as never before, to guard against a power such as the Soviet Union acquiring enough strength to overwhelm American defenses—to end American liberties.

Announcing a policy of this sort to a country that had just won massive wars in Europe and Asia was an awkward task, even more so because Congress was dominated by the opposition party. The Democrats were divided into three parts, left, middle, and right, with the left led by the followers of Henry Wallace, the right by those of Governor Strom Thurmond of South Carolina, and the center highly uncertain of Truman's own leadership. The party, it turned out, was so fragile a construct that in 1948 it wavered uncertainly in favor of General Dwight D. Eisenhower, who was then so obscure a politician that no one, not even Ike himself, knew his party allegiance. Without much of a political base, and appealing to a tired people, Truman nonetheless went ahead. That he succeeded, and brilliantly—with the Truman Doctrine of March 12, 1947, the Marshall Plan announced early in June of the same year, and the North Atlantic Treaty in April, 1949—was a measure of his triumph.

Asia was another matter, and the Korean War exposed so many confusions that countless Americans, perhaps even a majority, came to believe America's Far Eastern policy under Democratic management had been fraught with error. Here Truman rightly saw the complete lack of alternatives in China, short of a massive military intervention (which even the Republican rightwingers admitted was politically impossible). In Japan he went along with MacArthur's policies, which were those of the State Department, until his American proconsul defied the

President during the Korean War; whereupon Truman transported him back to the United States to what became a well-earned oblivion. Until the Eisenhower administration, however, Americans continued to believe that Truman somehow —in a way they quite understandably could not describe, since he had not erred in the first place—had chosen wrong over right in Asia.

When Truman left office in 1953, he had achieved his goal of changing the country's foreign policy.

                                                      Key West

Dear Bess: March 15, 1947

I am getting some much needed rest and already feel and look much better, so they all say. Have been going to bed at eleven o'clock and getting up at seven or eight, so you see I'm really doing some sleeping. My throat seems to be clearing up.

I hope Margie is all right. I never wanted anything to be successful so much in my whole life except her birth.

I'm sure she can do it. If you want me to come home and sit by you, I'll do it. But if you think you can stand it without me, I'll take some more sun. Sam Rosenman and Stuart Symington came in yesterday and we put them to bed on the ship. They leave today. Will call you tomorrow.

                    Lots of love,
                    Harry

                              [The White House]

Dear Bess: June 30, 1947

Well I am up as usual with the chickens and the cows. The weather is soggy and foggy—but I am going to take a walk just the same—but not a very long one.

The ghosts walked and walked last night. I left all the doors open. That gave me a chance to hear all the pops and creaks in your room, the hall, and Margie's and your mother's room. But it didn't keep me awake. The good sergeant came at nine o'clock and gave me a good rubbing down. I went to sleep as soon as he finished and didn't wake up until five-fifteen.

You should be approaching the great city of Cincinnati. I always think of the *Prince of Pilsen* when that city is mentioned. You and I saw or heard it together, as we did a lot of other shows, which at the time I could not afford. *The Girl from Utah* left the greatest impression on me because of the song "They'll Never Believe Me." You'd just said you'd take a chance on me. Wasn't it a terrible chance? Never did I think I'd get you into all the trouble you're in now. Well you didn't have to take the chance did you?

                    Lots of love,
                    Harry

[The White House]
Dear Bess: July 3, 1947
       . . . The new plane is here but I won't see it until Sunday. You should see
the new luggage Hank brought me from some outfit in Los Angeles. It is
aluminum, waterproof when closed, and will float if the plane should fall in the
ocean. I'm sure that you'll take one piece and Margie the other—and so I'll still
have to use sinkable baggage.
       Had a nice note from little Bess Wells—said she was billed to speak on the
White House at Dearborn! I am enclosing you a letter from Rt. Hon. W. L.
Mackenzie King—unopened. Coolidge would have opened it. . . .
                                        Lots of love,
                                        Harry

       After Secretary of State Marshall announced what became known as the
Marshall Plan, representatives of the countries of Western Europe met in Paris
to devise a program; Truman hence remarks to Bess how careful he has to be with
his forthcoming speech at Charlottesville—so that he will not disturb the negotia-
tions.

                                                              [Near Charlottesville, Va.]
Dear Bess: July 4, 1947
       . . . After a real merry-go-round at the office I had lunch with Admiral Leahy
and John Snyder on the porch at one-fifteen and we left at two-fifteen for this
beautiful spot. Arrived at about six Washington time—five here. They are on
standard time. I've never been at a more comfortable and lovely place. Stanley
and Mrs. Woodward met us at the front door and took us to the back terrace,
where *after* the "One More Club" had taken some pictures we had a real mint
julep—Kentucky-style—frost and everything. Had a grand dinner and then in-
dulged in a small game of chance—lost three dollars and a half. Admiral Leahy
was the big winner, something over forty dollars. He's a tough player as you'd
imagine. I'm up as usual this morning before anybody else and have walked over
the place. It is beautiful from every angle. I am going to have a grand weekend
soon as I get past the damned speech. I have to be careful after the Paris blowup,
but I'd like very much to explode on the Bolshies—but Marshall hopes I won't.
So, of course, I won't. . . .
                                        Lots of love,
                                        Harry

                                                              [Near Charlottesville, Va.]
Dear Bess: July 5, 1947
       Mrs. Woodward handed me your letter at the front door when we returned
after attending Admiral Halsey's cocktail party at the University of Virginia.
They have made him head of their fund-raising campaign.
       I had a grand and responsive audience, and the gang all expressed the

opinion that the objective was attained in the delivery of the message. I hope that is true. I want world peace more than ever I wanted anything in my life, except what I obtained June 28, 1919.

Colgate Darden told me that three Presidents had visited Charlottesville within his recollection and none had received the welcome and turnout the fourth one did.

He's president of the University. Ed Stettinius, Harry Byrd, Howard Smith, and Robertson—the other Virginia senator—all made the same remark to me.

After the speech we went to the home of Monroe at 4:00 P.M. It is a beautiful place. Should be publicly owned. The owner showed me around it. He has restored it and has obtained much of Monroe's furniture. Jefferson built the house for Monroe while Monroe was in Paris.

Right after the speech we had a "stand up and hold your plate and ice-tea glass" luncheon at the university. Mrs. Astor came up to me, said she liked what I am doing but she feared I was becoming too much like a Yankee. I told her I couldn't possibly be as nearly Yankee as she'd aped the British and she almost had a stroke. But the Virginians all were of my opinion. Admiral Leahy told her he believed she'd turn Commie [which] also added to the gay mood of the occasion. She is just an old smart aleck who thinks she had a reputation to keep up. Apparently she's not very popular around here.

Clark Clifford is going back to Washington this morning and I am getting him to mail this for me.

Hope your Lotawana picnic was the success you anticipated. I'm sure it was. Your weather isn't any better than ours. Hope it holds out in both places. Can't see why you'd hold out on me for a letter. If you knew how badly I needed to receive them, you would not count them on me. This job gets worse every day. Look what old Knutson and his Demorepublicans are trying to do to me now. But I'm going to lick 'em or go down fighting.

Lots of love,
Harry

[The White House]
Dear Bess: July 6, 1947
. . . Had a letter from Vivian in which he was very much disturbed over an article written by Pegler on the ballot situation in Kansas City. It is a most libelous article but I can't take notice of it. Vivian goes so far as to say he would not countenance it even against a Republican President! Neither would I, but I'd only advertise a sewer rat if I noticed it. . . .

Lots of love,
Harry

[The White House]

Dear Bess: July 7, 1947

Just finished our telephone conversation—and I am sure you'll agree that Margie should have no future handicap by having her music teacher say she had to go on charity to get a career. You know the lies that have been told about me and my business disasters. They never tell that all bills were paid and that my partner paid his part when he could.

We can't take a chance—so see that she's paid—no matter what the future holds for the teacher. . . .

Lots of love from your harassed old man,
Harry

[The White House]

Dear Bess: July 9, 1947

No letter today, but because of two yesterday I suppose I should not complain.

Had a couple yesterday. But—it was a hell of a day. Had a long meeting with the secretaries at nine o'clock, Admiral Leahy 9:45 to 10:10, Steelman and Jacob S. Potofsky at 10:15. Potofsky is Sidney Hillman's successor and he wanted to reassure me that the Political Action Committee is 100 percent for me. Adolf Berle, Jr., came in yesterday to assure me that the New York Liberal party is 100 percent for me. "Ain't that funny." Neither of 'em is for anybody but themselves and their own special interests.

Had to listen to Burt Wheeler for one whole hour tell me all about South America. He went down there on a special mission ($10,000 fee and expenses) but he knows all about Brazil, Uruguay, Argentina and Chile. Another funny one. Senators and ex-Senators go to S.A., Germany, Japan, China, spend two or three days and know all about the countries and know all the answers. Guess I'm dumb.

The foreign minister of Peru came in and gave me a beautiful silver tray. It's more beautiful than the one you took home.

Then I had to receive forty-two Democratic national committeemen and women from Texas, Oklahoma, Arkansas, Louisiana, Mississippi, Tennessee, Kentucky, and West Virginia.

Had a good time with them and told them a lot, as they did me.

Then to top off the morning had to listen to Mrs. Ogden Reid for twenty minutes. She didn't take a long breath! . . .

Lots of love,
Harry

[The White House]

Dear Bess: July 10, 1947

. . . Bill Hassett is still on the mend. So is Rose's niece. I cut a half-dozen buds out of the rose garden and had the rose men fix 'em up real fancy and sent them to her. She told Rose to tell me she'd press 'em and keep them. . . .

The damned Republicans and the Demopublicans are sending another tax bill tomorrow. Hope I can get sustained. It will be a veto record if I can.

Had a grand session with Marshall today. He's one fine man.

Hope all goes well and that everybody is well. Ask Margie if I should send her Sol Bloom's pen!

                                        Lots of love,
                                        Harry

                                                        [The White House]
Dear Bess: July 12, 1947
No letter yet today, but I haven't given up hope. I was up at five-thirty and at the desk at six. Listened to all the news broadcasts and came to the conclusion that the tax veto will "probably" stand up. Even the sabotage sheet was not sure. And at noon the Scripps-Howard *News* has this big black headline, "Hill Likely to Sustain Tax Veto," and they are 100 percent against me. Several Southern Senators have called to say they'd vote to sustain. Maybank, Dick Russell, and Olin Johnson to be specific. That is a big hole in Mr. Demopublican Byrd's lineup. And do you know he had the monumental gall to insert himself beside me at Charlottesville for a picture! Even Pepper is no worse—and he's got religion. Said he'd join no third party in '48—Henry Wallace or anyone else! Can't understand it.

Went to work as usual today. No appointments—thank God. Sent for Pete Brandt of the terrible *Post-Dispatch* and gave him an outline of what flood control really is in the whole Mississippi Valley. Rather took him off his feet because he knew only St. Louis.

Barkley just called me and said we can lick 'em. I can't hardly believe it. Wouldn't that be sumpin'? . . .

                                        Lots of love,
                                        Harry

                                                        [The White House]
Dear Bess: July 26, 1947
This is turnip day and Nellie Noland's birthday. I sent her a telegram—did not refer to turnip day. My old baldheaded uncle, Harrison Young, told me that July 26 was the day to sow turnips—sow them "wet or dry, twenty-sixth of July." In 1901 he went to the seed and hardware store in Belton and stated to the proprietor, Old Man Mosely, a North Carolinian, that he wanted six bushels of turnip seed—enough to sow the whole county to turnips. Mr. Mosely asked him what he expected to do with so much seed. My old uncle told him that it was his understanding that turnips are 90 percent water. Nineteen hundred one was the terribly dry year. Therefore if the whole farm were planted to turnips maybe the drought would be broken.

You and I graduated that year from high school and I spent quite some time on the farm, then Tasker Taylor was drowned in the Mo. River, just above the Independence pumping station, and I became a timekeeper for L. J. Smith's railroad construction outfit. That experience was very useful to me when those R.R. hearings were going on.

You see age is creeping up on me. Mamma is ninety-four and a half because she never lived in the past. I'll never be ninety-four and a half but I'm not going to live in yesterday either.

Dr. Graham went out today and is to call me tonight. So, I may run in on you Sunday. But I should clean up these bills before I leave. Hope all the family are in good health. Give my "baby" a kiss.

Lots and lots of love,
Harry

[The White House]
September 22, 1947

Dear Bess:

. . . Am having a Cabinet luncheon after a session with Marshall at twelve-thirty. The world seems to be topsy-turvy, but when you read the history after the Napoleonic Wars and the first World War they are no worse, only cover more territory.

I can't see why it was necessary for me to inherit all difficulties and tribulations of the world—but I have them on hand and must work them out some way —I hope for the welfare of all concerned.

Russia has at last shown her hand and it contains the cards Marshall and I thought it would.

All we can do is go ahead working for peace—and keep our powder dry. . . .

Lots of love,
Harry

[The White House]
September 23, 1947

Dear Bess:

. . . Marshall and Lovett were in yesterday morning and went over the European situation from soup to nuts with me. It's pretty bad but not quite as bad as I thought it would be. If it works out as planned it will cost us about 16 billions over a four-year period. I canceled 42 billions in appropriations for the last half of 1945, so if we can buy peace and quiet for about two-fifths of half a year's war cost it will be cheap at the price. But I don't know what squirrelheads like Taber, Herter, Bridges, and Byrd will think of it. All of 'em are living in 1890 when a billion-dollar Congress beat the Republicans in 1892. That was for the two years too.

This amount of 16 *billion* is just the amount of the national debt when Franklin took over. He ran it up to 40 odd and then the war came along and it is 257 but we can't understand those figures anyway.

The sixteen countries seem to have done an honest job at Paris. Our difficulty is corn crop shortage, price inflation, and the concerting of South and Central American countries to help us. But it is not so bad as two wars three and seven thousand miles away. And that's what it was April 12, 1945.

It's a most beautiful day and cold. It was forty-two degrees this morning. But sunshine gives a better outlook and I need that. Have some very grave decisions to make between now and Saturday. Hope you are having a nice time. Kiss my girl.

Lots of love,
Harry

[The White House]

Dear Bess: September 27, 1947

Received your Thursday letter yesterday afternoon, also one from Mary and one from Vivian—but none from daughter Margaret.

I am sure glad the Secret Service is doing a better job. I was worried about that situation. Edgar Hoover would give his right eye to take over and all Congressmen and Senators are afraid of him. I'm not and he knows it. If I can prevent, there'll be no NKVD [Soviet Secret Police] or Gestapo in this country. Edgar Hoover's organization would make a good start toward a citizen spy system. Not for me. . . .

Lots of love,
Harry

At the very time the American government was seeking to build economic foundations in Western Europe, Marshal Tito of Yugoslavia created tension, as Truman wrote Bess, by threatening to attack weak Italy. Greece and Turkey were just as weak, and Truman had already offered them support against the Russians.

[The White House]

Dear Bess: September 30, 1947

Yesterday was one of the most hectic of days, as I told you. I'm not sure what has been my worst day. But here is a situation fraught with terrible consequences. Suppose, for instance, that Italy should fold up and that Tito then would march into the Po Valley. All the Mediterranean coast of France then is open to Russian occupation and the iron curtain comes to Bordeaux, Calais, Antwerp, and The Hague. We withdraw from Greece and Turkey and *prepare for war*. It just must not happen. But here I am confronted with a violently opposition Congress whose committees with few exceptions are living in 1890; it is not representative of the country's thinking at all. But I've a job and it must be done —win, lose, or draw.

Sent letters to Taber, Bridges, Vandenberg, and Eaton requesting them to call their committees together as soon as possible. Had my food committee together and will make a radio speech Sunday. To feed France and Italy this winter will cost 580 million, the Marshall Plan 16.5 billion. But you know in October and November 1945 I canceled 63 billion in appropriations—55 billion at one crack. Our war cost that year was set at 105 billion. The 16.5 is for a four-year period and is for *peace*. A Russian war would cost us 400 billion and untold lives, mostly civilian. So I must do what I can. I shouldn't write you this stuff but you should know what I've been facing since Potsdam.

Bill Helm's book is a great disappointment. It is a buildup of Bill and not a biography of me. Too bad. The Potomac has a bad effect on all of 'em.

Hope you have a nice time, a good party at the Muehlebach. I'm sure you will. I haven't resumed my walks yet but will in a day or two. Too much to read. General Bradley made a report to me today on his European trip and he remarked on my having had to make more momentous decisions than nearly any other President. He's right, and I hope most of 'em have been right. . . .

Tell the baby I'll write her soon. Hope Frank doesn't get another boil.

Lots of love,
Harry

[The White House]
Dear Bess: October 2, 1947
. . . Sunday I'm to state the case. It will be at ten-thirty E.S.T., or nine-thirty C.S.T. We've gone back to God's time, thank Him. The silliest thing I know of is daylight saving time. Why don't they get up with me? . . .

I've had the usual day. The British ambassador brought in Admiral Tenney, who was with Roosevelt in the Red Sea when he met Ibn Saud. He said F.D.R. was in a heck of a fix for a smoke. And he couldn't smoke or drink in the presence of the old Arab King. He said that when luncheon was served Ibn and F.D.R. each had to go down to the "dining saloon" (as he called it) in an elevator. The King of Arabia went first. When F.D.R. went down he stopped the elevator halfway and smoked three cigarettes so he could stand the lunch.

Then I had Bidault and Bonnet. They tried to give me the rush act. It didn't work. But they left me apparently in a happy frame of mind.

Had Myron Taylor in too. Looks as if he and I may get the morals of the world on our side. We are talking to the Archbishop of Canterbury, the bishop at the head of the Lutheran Church, the Metropolitan of the Greek Church at Istanbul, and the Pope. I may send him to see the top Buddhist and the Grand Lama of Tibet. If I can mobilize the people who believe in a moral world against the Bolshevik materialists, who believe as Henry Wallace does—"that the end justifies the means"—we can win this fight.

Treaties, agreements, or a moral code mean nothing to Communists. So we've got to organize the people who do believe in honor and the Golden Rule to win the world back to peace and Christianity.

Ain't it Hell!

Lots of love,
Harry

To help Western Europe until the Marshall Plan appropriations passed Congress, Truman proposed interim economic aid, but in order to ship food abroad, it had to be conserved in America.

The White House
Dear Bess: October 3, 1947
. . . I'm going on the radio Sunday night at ten-thirty with Harriman, Anderson, Marshall, and Luckman to tell the country what I think the people should do to help meet the situation we are facing. I'll talk to you Sunday morning and we'll decide what to do about the dinners. We'd better announce them, I think, and then cancel if we decide that's the thing to do.

You are right about what I'm facing. But I've got to meet it with all I have. It may not be enough but if the Almighty didn't make my brain container big as it should be, I'll have to use what he gave me. Congress will get its share of the responsibility but I can't and won't shirk mine.

I'm hoping to sleep over Saturday and Sunday so as to be in good shape Sunday night.

Pinned a medal on the Chief Justice today—a surprise performance, and he wept. Mrs. Vinson was very highly pleased and wanted me to say to you, she missed you. . . .

Lots of love,
Harry

[The White House]
Dear Bess: October 7, 1947
. . . I've been having a time with my throat and tongue again. I am talking in whispers part of the time but we managed on Sunday night to get by in good shape. In fact everyone said I sounded fine.

We are putting it over too. The Catholics are all mad because we asked for Tuesday for meatless day instead of Friday. The turkey growers are up in arms because three holidays come on Thursday. But I suppose we can eat turkey on those days.

I believe it would be a good thing to call off the White House dinners and just have receptions. You'd better be the one to announce it I think. I'll be mighty glad when you all get back here. . . .

[no signature]

[The White House]

Dear Bess: October 10, 1947

. . . Another hectic week drawing to a close—and what I mean hectic. Wonder what the next one will bring forth. I'd hoped to be able to hop a plane tomorrow and fly home but I can't leave now, much to my regret. I'm staying in the White House over the weekend. Harry Vaughan has gone to San Francisco to meet the first returned dead soldier, sailor, and marine. They wanted me to go to New York when it happens up there but I'm not. It seems sort of ghoulish and besides I don't believe in returning them. Mrs. Patton did the right thing when she left the general in the cemetery with his men. But I have to send a representative. . . .

Lots of love,
Harry

James F. Byrnes had resigned in January, 1947; soon after, his book appeared
—Speaking Frankly.

[The White House]

Dear Bess: October 13, 1947

It was good to talk to you yesterday and to get your Friday letter. I spent most of the day reading reports and Jim Byrnes' book.

No one was in the Senate, on the Supreme Court, or in the executive branch while Mr. Byrnes was engaged in running those sections of the government. The story is accurate though on the facts. Roosevelt and I only play minor roles, however, such as approving things put up to us by Mr. Byrnes.

You know there is an old saying, "Oh! that mine enemy would write a book." Well I wish my so-called friends would quit trying to write one.

Between Morgenthau, Ickes, Hopkins, and Byrnes the history of the last ten years will be as completely fogged as if Pearson and John O'Donnell with the collaboration of Bertie McCormick and Willie Hearst had written it. Maybe that's a good thing. . . .

Lots of love,
Harry

Key West

Dear Bess: February 28, 1948

Was glad to get your letter in the pouch yesterday. They always bring it to me first. Hope the weather has cleared up and that you and Margie and your mother are all in good health. . . .

Well everyone here is cultivating a wonderful tan. Mine is coming along fine. I keep my face shaded because it received its whole quota in Puerto Rico and the Virgins.

Have been resting very well, but the work comes along just the same. I've been reading and signing messages, executive orders, statements, letters etc. at the usual rate. . . .

Dr. Graham set us a shining example of what not to do yesterday. He and Clifford had an argument as to whether they could run a mile in eight minutes. So they laid out a course along the sand on the beach and timed each other for 440 yards. Graham did it in seventy-six seconds and Clifford in eighty-six and then they each almost passed out, particularly the Doc. Well I gave 'em hell and they promised not to do a fool stunt like that again.

Admiral Leahy says the same sun shines at the house as at the beach so he stays at the house and writes on his memoirs. I hope he'll stick to that writing job because it needs to be done. Will call you tomorrow around noon if all goes well.

Lots and lots of love,
Harry

The White House
Dear Bess: June 28, 1948

Twenty-nine years! It seems like twenty-nine days.

Detroit, Port Huron, a farm sale, the Blackstone Hotel, a shirt store, County Judge, a defeat, Margie, Automobile Club membership drive, Presiding Judge, Senator, V.P., now!

You still are on the pedestal where I placed you that day in Sunday school 1890. What an old fool I am.

H.S.T.

The President prepared for his nomination at the Philadelphia Convention; he reports to Bess the Democrats' disorganization.

[The White House]
Dear Bess: July 9, 1948

I've been trying to write you ever since arrival here but just now succeeded in getting it done. I've had only one walk, that yesterday morning for twenty minutes and no swim at all. . . .

Went over the platform again at 4:00 P.M., came back to the House at seven, had a big dinner, and went to bed at eight-thirty. Never been as tired and groggy in my life. Think the sun had some effect after all.

Yesterday was the most hectic. Matt kept running in people to talk to me —people I didn't want to see. These birds around me have all turned politicians and precinct captains—and they know nothing about it.

Finished the outline for the platform and sent it to Philly. Settled the railroad strike and had Fred Vinson to dinner. He stayed until 11:30 P.M. talking about everything.

I still don't know what our program is. Biffle called and said he had a suite for you and Margie at the Drake. Evidently they expect you to come to the convention Tuesday or Wednesday. I don't know which. I'm supposed to go up there Wednesday or Thursday. Maybe I can tell you what we are supposed to do Sunday on the phone. I don't know now. It's worse than Chicago if that's possible. I wish I'd stayed on the farm and never gone to war in the first place!

Well take care of yourself. Kiss the daughter and tell everyone hello. Hope your mother is all right.

Lots of love,
Harry

The convention was hardly over—with Truman nominated, and Senator Alben Barkley chosen as his running mate—when the Berlin Blockade again created trouble. It had begun just before the convention, and Truman announced an airlift of supplies to the Western sectors of the German capital. American military leaders threatened the President's diplomacy by recalling General Lucius D. Clay, just when Truman was trying to negotiate. Meanwhile Israel had declared its independence, on May 14, and the Middle East was in turmoil. The President tells Bess he has been too busy to write.

[The White House]
July 23, 1948

Dear Bess:

I have been trying to get a letter off every day—hoping every day I'd get one—both the try and the *hope* in vain. Have had a hectic week. My muttonhead Secretary of the Army ordered Clay home from Germany and stirred up a terrific how-dy-do for no good reason. Marshall and I had decided it was not necessary for him to come and so told Forrestal—but you know how smart that Defense setup thinks it is.

To cap it all off, Forrestal comes in with all his help and reads me a letter suggesting I order all atomic bombs turned over to the army. Now wouldn't that be a nice peace gesture?

Marshall and I have had to do a lot of the proper sort of talking to offset these two blunders, but I think we are on top of the situation.

It looks as if the Russkies are going to come in without a fight. If they do and we get the Israelites settled down, things will be in such shape in foreign affairs that we can go to work in earnest on that bunch of "Hypercits" known as Republicans.

They sure are in a stew and mad as wet hens. If I can make them madder, maybe they'll do the job the old gods used to put on the Greeks and Romans. . . . My best to everybody. Kiss my baby, lots of love to you,

Harry

[U.S.S. *Williamsburg*]
September 11, 1948

Dear Bess:

I accompanied Margie to the train yesterday at noon. We arrived at the station just about two minutes ahead of leaving time for the train. They drove us into the east entrance but we walked from the fence to the train. Margie thought that was showing discrimination.

We made it to the car and she plastered my left cheek with lipstick as she went aboard and very carefully wiped it off with her glove! Had a wire from her about 5:00 P.M. signed "Skinny." I'd been stewing around about not hearing from her and Captain Dennison started to call Mrs. Stewart, and they told him at the White House that this telegram signed "Skinny" was there. He very timidly asked me if that by any chance could be Margie. Went back to the White House and saw a lot of customers and finally arrived aboard here at one-thirty when I was due at twelve-thirty. It rained and rained but I won a bet that the sun would shine all day today, and it has and is. I'm out on the "back porch" of my deck in a swimming suit taking more burning. We've had a very satisfactory conference on the western speeches. . . .

My finance meeting Thursday was a grand success. Margie "stole the show." We're off to win I think.

Lots of love,
Harry

Elected President in his own right, and with the Berlin Blockade at an end, Truman had time to think of the Walrus and the Carpenter and Cabbages and Kings.

[Blair House, Washington, D.C.]
June 6, 1949

Dear Bess:

Old Mayes was nearer right than he thought when he was ribbing me about weeping tonight instead of working. I did read documents, clean out the safe,

Ratifying the Japanese Peace Treaty, 1952. Photoworld

and put your Rio jewelry away, and then I sat here and thought about the Walrus and the Carpenter and cabbages and kings. I wonder if you will be able to get a carpenter who'll join hands with a plumber and do what you want done. You know that there is a loudspeaking man whose nickname is "Walrus." He might help with strawberries instead of the oysters in the original piece. . . .

We have a speech to write for Little Rock. I guess Peace, Home and Mother, Morals and Dogma will have to be the subject. Albert Pike, who wrote the book on Morals and Dogma, lived in Little Rock. He was a major general in the Confederate Army and there is a monument to him at Indiana Avenue and Fourth Street here—but it's made of sandstone and unrecognizable. But he's a good subject in the Great State of Arkansas. Hope you get in safely.

Lots of love from your very lonesome Oldman,

Harry

[Blair House, Washington, D.C.]

Dear Bess: May, or is it June, 7, 1949

I'm sitting here with a "long time" record on playing almost as loud as Margie plays it. I'm waiting, of course, for a call from a certain beautiful lady who has "gone west." I may wait in vain but I hope not.

Joe Davies came to see me about 6:00 P.M. I insisted on coming to the Blair House. He wants me to go up to northern New York to his summer home in the Adirondacks. Says Fred Vinson and certain other big shots will be there. Williams, the president of the Milwaukee R.R. whom I once grilled for his life in the railroad hearings, and Crawford, president of the Pullman Company whom I made let loose of his car factory! Wouldn't that be a pleasant party?

Talked to Miss Skinny a few minutes ago and she is fine. Been working all day she said. I read her a letter I'd received from a little town west of Asheville in No'th Ca'lina where she makes her first appearance. The husband of the lady promoter was inviting us down to the concert. Maggie says we're not wanted there! She didn't give me a chance to tell her I wouldn't be there—she just told me we couldn't.

As usual I've had some day. The Budget Director, Old Man Doughton, a commission to see that blacks, yellows, reds, and whites get the same treatment in the armed services, the Acting Secretary of State, the Secretary of Defense etc. ad lib. And finally Ambassador Joseph Davies, Esq.

Hope you arrived safely and found all in good health. Had lunch with John Pye for our No. 2 Doctor Harris. He's leaving for Johns Hopkins for a specialist position. Saw Doc Graham and he said your mother is better than she's been in two years. Hope that keeps up.

Say hello to Frank, George, Natalie, and May. Call Mary if you can catch her.

Lots of love,

Harry

[Blair House, Washington, D.C.]

Dear Bess: June 29, 1949

Well, the first day has gone by thirty years ago! I need no commiseration, only congratulations.

Thirty years ago I hoped to make you a happy wife and a happy mother. Did I? I don't know. All I can say [is] I've tried. There is no one in the world anyway who can look down on you or your daughter. That means much to me, but I've never cared for social position or rank for myself except to see that those dear to me were not made to suffer for my shortcomings.

I've told Ethel on many occasions that ancestors, as such, do not appeal to me except for good physique and an honorable name. We can never tell what is in store for us. I'm very sure that if you'd been able to see into the future on May 8, 1919, when we had our final argument, you'd have very definitely turned your back on what was coming.

Business failure, with extra responsibility coming, political defeat at the same time. Almost starvation in Washington those first ten years and then hell and repeat from 1944 to date. But I wouldn't change it, and I hope you wouldn't.

Margie is one in ten million, there's none to compare with her mother. I had a good mother and so have you and a good sister. My brother is himself but in the end "right." Yours are the same sort, so—what have we had but the best of luck and a most happy thirty years. Hope we can have thirty more equally as happy without so much responsibility.

Wish you were here for the river trip Saturday, Sunday, and Monday. But we can't have everything. We never have.

Remember the Blackstone, the first visit, not the last, Port Huron, Detroit Statler, and the trip home? Maybe in 1953 we will be able to take that trip over again.

Hope you have a good weekend—I'm going to try as best I can to have one —it would be so much better if you were here. Lots and lots of love to you. Glad you liked the "doodads."

                                        Harry

[Blair House, Washington, D.C.]

Dear Bess: July 2, 1949

It was good to talk to you last night. I'm glad your mother is feeling better, and I hope Vietta comes out of it. You don't suppose the old negro is suffering from an attack of Potomac fever do you? Anyway whatever it is, we must look after her. I'll always be grateful for her attentions to Margie, no matter what she does.

I bought some bonds in our mutual names and will put them in the safety box next week. If we have good luck over the next period, we'll have enough to retire and live comfortably for the next thirty years and leave Margie a nice, fat nest egg. Never thought it would happen, but you never can tell what the "three old ladies" have in store for you.

Margie and I are leaving shortly for the yacht. Drucie and Jane are going along, and tomorrow a few highbinders will join me, and we'll study probabilities. This afternoon, tonight and tomorrow morning I am working on the economic message and a budget speech, which I hope to deliver about next Friday evening over four networks. It will be a dinger and will take the Byrd-Republican crowd to town in words of one syllable. . . .

Lots of love,
Harry

Key West

Dear Bess: March 26, 1950

I've just found that a special pouch is going up tonight, so I thought I'd get a note off to you. I am going to church in a few minutes and then to the beach. We'll have lunch at two o'clock and then I'll spend the afternoon with Jim Webb, who will arrive at one-thirty. They are doing all they can to ruin Dean and the foreign policy. The paper says this morning that the "great" Styles Bridges has joined the pack. Well we'll take them to town as we did before.

Admiral Leahy sent me a specially bound copy of his book with a most wonderful inscription in it. I wish you would call him and inquire about his health just before you come down. He is very much disappointed because he couldn't come.

I talked to Margie last night immediately after you did. Said she is fine but tired. I'll be happy when you both arrive. . . .

Take care of yourself and I'll call you directly.

Lots of love,
Harry

[Blair House, Washington, D.C.]

Dear Bess: June 2, 1950

I sent you a note yesterday and hoped for one from you today. It hasn't come yet, but it is only five-twenty E.D.T. Today, as usual, has been a busy one. Had my usual walk, swim and beating from the sergeant. Dr. Graham gave me a going over yesterday and decided it was not necessary to repeat today. I am in good shape physically and hope to stay that way for at least another two years, six months, and twenty days. Then the millennium.

Had a Cabinet meeting at ten—a most satisfactory one. At 10:45 we adjourned, and I asked them all into my office so I could present Barkley his gold medal. The presentation was a complete surprise to him as he did not know it was finished. His wife and her daughter and his two daughters were there, as were some Senators and House members and the Cabinet. Mrs. Nellie Ross gave me the medal, and I presented it to him. He made a nice short thank-you speech and ended by saying he didn't know why he received it. Then I called on the Chief Justice to tell him why. Fred made a lovely little speech, all the guests shook hands with the Vice President, and the ceremony ended. It is the first time Congress has voted a Vice President a gold medal. . . .

Lots of love,
Harry

[Blair House, Washington, D.C.]
Dear Bess: June 3, 1950
    Well I've had the usual big day. Blevins Davis came in yesterday at Fred's request and unloaded some of his troubles about a European tour of the Met. Ballet. I turned it over to Bill Hassett and Jim Webb and hope it works out.
    You should have seen Blevins high-hat George Jessel, who was in to see me about a National Theater. I told him that Blevins had talked to me about it, and maybe they could join hands. Matt got them together, and Blevins treated George just as you'd expect Madam Tetrazzini to treat Sis Hopkins. But they finally agreed on an approach which may work. . . .
    It was nice to talk to you. Margie's washing her hair, and I'm writing you. She's agreed to breakfast at nine-thirty in the morning. Believe it or not. Take care of yourself.

Lots of love,
Harry

[Blair House, Washington, D.C.]
Dear Bess: June 7, 1950
    I was surely glad to get your letter yesterday. You are right about the University of Missouri being late in every particular. They have always taken their cue from old Joe Pulitzer and Bill Nelson's successors. Both made their money and their reputations on character assassination just as did Hearst and the McCormicks.
    But I have other fish to fry. One of them is Donnell, and this trip is to kindle the fire. I had always said that I'd never accept a degree from my home state university because of their attitude, but for various and sundry reasons I'm doing it.
    Charlie [Ross] urged it, and the president and half the faculty came and *begged* me to do it, and since it is timed right to help Allison I accepted.
    Looks like we won a victory in Iowa. This morning's paper said that Dr. Graham in North Carolina would have a run-off. They blame the Supreme Court decision on segregation for it. There always has to be a reason of some sort.
    That was a nice note from the mayor. Hope he is doing a good job. If he is, it shows that no man is indispensable. I'm sure that is true. Old man Baruch received a degree from Washington University in St. Louis and, of all things, made a McCarthy speech. He had been to see every member of the Cabinet trying to get a front door entrance to the White House. He'll never get it. He

and old Jones may stand in the snow as far as I'm concerned from now on. I had the pleasure of telling off a lot of "fat cats" last night. Matt said it was a superb job. I hope so.

I'm hoping to see you before too long.

Lots of love,
Harry

[Blair House, Washington, D.C.]
Dear Bess: June 11, 1950
Here it is Sunday and the most beautiful day I've seen here this year. I didn't get up until seven! Been working on the pile of papers that had accumulated while I was away and reading all the New York, Baltimore, and Washington newspapers since Friday.

For a wonder, there's not a mean remark in them—even the Sops, Pearson and old Mark Sullivan are friendly. Then the *Post-Dispatch* and the *Globe-Democrat* had friendly editorials. I am sure I'm slipping.

The St. Louis meeting was a most successful one. The Battery breakfast was short, dignified and to the point. There were seventy-five of them there.

We marched from Seventeenth and Olive to the old courthouse—about a mile and a half. It was hot but no one fell out. The governor, the mayor, Louis Johnson, and all my fat and thin aides had to march also. I reviewed the parade for an hour and then looked over the river front park plans, went over the speech and then went to the platform about two blocks away. The mayor, Stuart Symington, and the French ambassador made excellent speeches, and then I came on.

I've never had such profuse statements and congratulations. Four of our Congressmen were on the platform, Sullivan, Karst, Karsten and Carnahan, the Archbishop of St. Louis, Dr. Reader, Past Grand Master of Missouri and present secretary of the Grand Lodge and a Baptist preacher, the governor, Forrest Donnell, and 35th Division bigwigs.

When high Catholics, low Baptists, and cross-purpose politicians of both parties seem to be in accord—it must be right. I hope it is. The speech at Columbia and the one in St. Louis make a complete résumé of the foreign policy of the United States. No one can misunderstand it or garble it. Acheson will make six speeches in the next month, and I am sure there will be no misunderstanding our position. It has taken five years to get to this point. I am hoping two more will wind it up.

Think—Byrnes, Baruch, Marshall, Molotov, Vishinsky, Attlee, Bevin, Mackenzie King, Churchill—and now Dean Acheson, Schuman, St. Laurent, and Stalin.

Byrnes, Molotov, Vishinsky, and Bevin have been anything but constructive.

The others have brought us to this point. I hope all of us who are left may take us to the right conclusion. It's an awful responsibility. That's what I was thinking when I looked down on those two thousand young people in the rain on Friday.

Lots of love. I miss you—but you *must* take care of your mother.

Harry

While spending a quiet few days in Independence, Truman was roused on Saturday night, June 24, by Secretary of State Acheson, who reported a North Korean attack on the territory of South Korea. Next day, Sunday, the President flew back to Washington for a series of hectic conferences in Blair House, his temporary residence during reconstruction of the White House (he had moved out after the 1948 election, and the entire mansion was rebuilt; he did not move back until 1952).

[Blair House, Washington, D.C.]

Dear Bess: June 26, 1950

We had a grand trip back after we were in the air. Colonel Williams was fooling around waiting for Landry to show up. Landry had gone to some golf course, after asking me if it would be all right for him to play Sunday afternoon. But he should have left the name of the club where he intended to play at the hotel. Evidently he arrived at the airport shortly after we were in the air and reported to us about the time we were over St. Louis that he was fifteen minutes behind us. I told the communications officer to tell him to go back to Kansas City, get in touch with General Vaughan and Ted Marks and bring them in tomorrow.

This morning I called him and told him to call Margie and see if she would like to come back with him. He can wait until Wednesday if she wants to wait.

The crowd at the Washington Airport was made up of the Secretaries of State and Defense and Army, Navy, and Air.

Had them all to dinner at eight and the dinner was good and well served. Fred and Rufus ate up in the parlor on the second floor of the Lee House. We put them over there because those two rooms are air-conditioned, and the others in the Blair House were very hot.

My conference was a most successful one, and there is a chance that things may work out without the necessity of mobilization. Haven't been so badly upset since Greece and Turkey fell into our lap. Let's hope for the best.

Hope your mother is better. She seemed to me to be better Sunday at noon than she was the day before.

I've canceled my sailing trip. Don't want to be too far away. The reason I suggested General Landry call Margie, I am afraid of the R.R. strike.

Lots and lots of love and many happy returns for the thirty-first year of your ordeal with me. It's been *all* pleasure for me.

Harry

One of the administrative casualties of Korea was Secretary of Defense Louis Johnson, and Truman relates below his preparation to ask the secretary for his resignation.

[Blair House, Washington, D.C.]

Dear Bess: September 7, 1950

You are one up on me for letters. That is not customary. I'm glad it happened. The editorial from Roy Roberts' *Star* was very good. I had not seen it and had no other copies. I don't know what's happening—*Life*, dated September 11, has a most favorable editorial on the same subject. Maybe I'm on the wrong track.

Tomorrow I have to break the bad news to Louis Johnson. I think I have a way to do it that will not be too hard on him. General Marshall came to see me yesterday. I told him what I had in mind. He said, "Mr. President, you have only to tell me what you want, and I'll do it. But I want you to think about the fact that my appointment may reflect upon you and your administration. They are still charging me with the downfall of Chiang's government in China. I want to help, not to hurt you." Can you think of anyone else saying that? I can't, and he's of the *great*.

Harriman went to Leesburg and had lunch with him today, and they talked it out. Wonder of wonders, Mrs. Marshall is for it! He could not possibly hurt me.

I'm hoping that I can get Louis Johnson to say publicly that he thinks because of the attacks on him I should ask General Marshall to take over. He can make himself a hero if he'll do that. If he doesn't, I shall simply fire him as I did Wallace and Morgenthau.

As usual I'm having hell and high water every day. But I seem to thrive on it, and Dr. Graham can't find a thing wrong except my propensity to gain pounds when I eat what I want. We were to have a complete checkup beginning Friday afternoon, but because of the Saturday night speech we put it off until Sunday. It requires some strenuous preparations—purgative, enema, etc., ad lib. So the postponement. . . .

Had Mrs. Roosevelt and a U.N. promotion committee in today. She was ecstatic over my world broadcast. Senator Austin also came in. He was highly pleased over a phone call I'd made complimenting him on his set-to with Malik. I have a most interesting cable from Admiral Kirk on his meeting with Vishinsky, who wanted to hand the ambassador a note protesting the shooting down of the Russian plane west of Korea. We advised the admiral to tell Vishinsky to take it up with the U.N. He protested vehemently—but we did not accept the note. The Russian embassy here sent a copy to the Secretary of State who sent it back.

Mon Wallgren came in at this point to talk to me about gas for New England. It is a complicated proposition. Tobin, McCormack and the Massachusetts governor on one side; the Rhode Island Senators, McMahon, Benton et al. on the other. I told Mon to get all the facts, as we did on our committee, make the decision, and I'd back him.

Send me another *note*, and I'll return a longer and more complicated communication.

Lots and lots of love,
Harry

[Blair House, Washington, D.C.]
Dear Bess: June 9, 1951
      Your voice sounded as if you were very tired last night. Please get some rest.
That's what you are at home for. I am sorry Frank is under the weather. Hope
he comes out of it.
      If you want Dr. Graham, he can be there in three hours. You should take
no chances with your mother. We have a doctor to keep us healthy and that is
what he is assigned to do. So don't hesitate if he's needed.
      Here is the latest on Margie. I didn't find it in any of the papers back here.
Will call you at noon today—ten your time—and at 2:00 P.M. tomorrow—noon
your time if we can get Margie.
      Please take care of yourself. I don't think you fully understand that I can
face the world and all its troubles if you and Margie are all right. I don't think
I can do it if you are not.
                                          Lots of love,
                                          Harry

[Blair House, Washington, D.C.]
Dear Bess: June 25, 1951
      It was grand to have you and Margaret on the telephone yesterday. She is
still going at a grand pace for our public relations in Europe, and I think she is
also having a good time.
      After I talked to you, I went for a drive. Picked up the Vinsons and drove
to Leesburg. General and Mrs. Marshall and Mr. Baruch and Mr. Baruch's
secretary and nurse were there. The old man has had an operation on his face.
General Marshall thought it was cancer. So do I—it looked like it. The old man
wept and said he hoped our misunderstanding would be something in the past
and not happen again. Of course I agreed to it. He left shortly after the Chief,
Mrs. Vinson, and I arrived.
      We had a most pleasant afternoon and a good supper with the Marshalls.
Fred and the general told a lot of good stories about their careers and experiences.
It was most interesting.
      Mrs. Marshall's son was there, offered to take me for a swim in one of the
neighbors' pools. I didn't go. He had a date for supper somewhere else, and when
he left, he said "Goodbye, colonel," to General Marshall. The general said all the
family called him colonel—that he said seemed to be his first name to them.
      I'm leaving for Tennessee shortly to speak at the dedication of an air
research center, named for General Arnold. I'm going to tear the Russians and
the Republicans apart—call a spade just what it is and tell Malik if Russia wants
peace, peace is available and has been since 1945. This is the anniversary of the
flight from Independence a year ago that has been quite a day in history. All the
papers except the sabotage sheets gave me the best of it yesterday.
      This week contains another very important—most important—anniversary.
Thursday will be thirty-two years. What a thirty-two years! I've never been

anything but happy for that anniversary. Maybe I haven't given you all you're entitled to, but I've done my best, and I'm still in love with the prettiest girl in the world.

Hope all are well. We'll talk to Margie in Rome next Sunday.

Lots of love,

Harry

With the Korean War stabilized in 1951—after the Chinese had attacked and were driven back to the thirty-eighth parallel—the President prepares to address a conference that was drawing up a Japanese peace treaty in San Francisco.

[Blair House, Washington, D.C.]

Dear Bess: September 1, 1951

I have been resisting an impulse to call you, to call Margaret, to call Vivian, to call Mary Jane.

Went to the fiftieth anniversary celebration of the American League at the ball park this afternoon. Joe Short, Charlie Murphy, Dave Stowe, Admiral Dennison, General Landry with a dozen or so secret service, police, F.B.I., and others saw that I arrived at the game and departed safely. The Chief Justice and his younger son James sat with me in the front row in our box. Fred knew all the old players and all the new ones, and he saw to it that I did a land office business autographing baseballs for them. Old Griff sat on my left and told me what the various players on the Washington team should have done and didn't do. Nick was sitting in the aisle on the other side of Griff and pulling for the home team to beat the Yanks because that would put Boston Red Sox closer to the top. Washington lost 5 to 0. Old Clark said Washington lost because you were not present. I agreed with him.

Charlie Murphy was here a while ago and gave me some papers for use in San Francisco. I've been working on the bond drive speech for Monday evening and my Jap peace speech for Tuesday, an "off the cuff" speech for the Democratic luncheon in Frisco on Tuesday and a dedication speech for the reserve armory in K.C. on Thursday and one for the Tirey Ford Post on Wednesday or Friday. Wish I could come home like anybody else and do as I please.

You should see the Shah's rug. It is beautiful, twelve by sixteen. Never saw a prettier one. The Harrimans brought a grand evening bag. I'll bring it with me.

You ought to see the scimitar old Ibn Saud sent to me. It is 350 years old, belonged to his great-great-great-grandfather. It is in a solid gold sheath incrusted with pearls and rubies. He told Doc it was his most prized possession, and he sent it to me because my doctor had saved his life! Doc performed an operation on his esophagus. Took out a tumor that was slowly choking him to death. He wouldn't let Doc have a helper because he didn't want anyone to know what was the matter with him. So Doc gave him a local and pulled it out. Luckily it wasn't malignant. Then the specialists Doc took with him gave the old man a complete going over and left him sound and in good health.

At 219 North Delaware, summer 1953. *Bradley Smith*

Hope you and Margie are having a nice evening—not as lonely and home-sick as mine. I have your groceries all assembled. If we stop for gas in K.C. on the way out, I'll unload them and send them to you.

Lots of love from your all-time "sweetie."

Harry

After leaving Washington for retirement in Independence the "demon letter writer," as Margaret later described him, wrote little more to Bess—or at least little survived.

[Independence, Mo.]

Dear Bess: February 13, 1957

Here is a non-forgetter. I am sorry it is not something tangible and worth-while. It was my intention to obtain something in the U.S. Capital of Israel but I had no opportunity—particularly after your injunction before I left. Now you are as old as I am but as young and as beautiful as sixty years ago.

You're the nicest sweetheart a man could have.

Harry

Returning to Washington, November 5, 1953. *Harry S. Truman Library*

[June 28, 1957. Envelope addressed
"To: Mrs. Harry S. Truman. From: H. S. T. No. 38."]

June 28, 1920 One happy year.
June 28, 1921 Going very well.
June 28, 1922 Broke and in a bad way.
June 28, 1923 Eastern Judge. Eating.
June 28, 1924 Daughter 4 mo. old.
June 28, 1925 Out of a job.
June 28, 1926 Still out of a job.
June 28, 1927 Presiding Judge— eating again.
June 28, 1928 All going well. Piano. Al Smith.
June 28, 1929 Panic, in October.
June 28, 1930 Depression. Still going.
June 28, 1931 Six-year-old daughter.
June 28, 1932 Roads finished.
June 28, 1933 Employment Director.
June 28, 1934 Buildings finished. Ran for the Senate.
June 28, 1935 U.S. Senator. Gunston.
June 28, 1936 Resolutions Philadelphia. Roosevelt reelected.
June 28, 1937 Grand time in Washington.
June 28, 1938 Very happy time. Margie 14.
June 28, 1939 Named legislation.
June 28, 1940 Senate fight coming.
June 28, 1941 Special Senate Committee. Margie wants to sing.

June 28, 1942 Also a happy time.
June 28, 1943 Lots of work.
June 28, 1944 Talk of V.P. Bad business.
June 28, 1945 V.P. & President. War End.
June 28, 1946 Margie graduate & singer. 80th Congress.
June 28, 1947 Marshall Plan & Greece & Turkey. A grand time 28th Anniversary.
June 28, 1948 A terrible campaign. Happy day.
June 28, 1949 President again. Another happy day.
June 28, 1950 Korea—a terrible time.
June 28, 1951 Key West—a very happy day.
June 28, 1952 All happy. Finish, Jan. 20, 1953.
June 28, 1953 Back home. Lots of *Roses*.
June 28, 1954 A happy 35th.
June 28, 1955 All cut up but still happy.
June 28, 1956 A great day—more elation.
June 28, 1957 Well here we are again, as Harry Jobes would say.

Only 37 to go for the diamond jubilee!

H. S. T.

Here are some ones & some fives. If it is not enough for a proper show, there will be more coming.

Your no account partner, who loves you more than ever!

[The Mayflower, Washington, D.C.]

Dear Bess: January 7, 1959

You'll never know how badly you are missed. Yesterday evening I went out to the Acheson's for dinner. The Woodwards and Florence Mahoney were there. I had a chance to talk to Dean before the others came, and Dean, Stanley, and I had a session after dinner.

As you know, we are up against it for a winning candidate in 1960. After much discussion we came to the conclusion that, at the present time, Stuart Symington is the best bet.

Dean said, and it's true, that we have a dozen good second-place men but no real honest to goodness first-place man. I've had a session with some of the new Senators and expect, today, to have lunch with Hart of Michigan, Hartke of Indiana, Jennings Randolph, and Alaska's two.

Sam Rayburn says he's anxious to see me. I've talked to Lyndon Johnson but things are nowhere near settlement for a proper course. Maybe they never will be and then God help the country.

I've almost become a pessimist! Again I wish, with everything I've got, that you were here.

We are facing the most serious situation since 1859.

Hope all's well with you. I've had two walks yesterday and this morning all by myself. How good that is!

All the love in the world,

Harry

EPILOGUE: LATER YEARS

EPILOGUE: LATER YEARS

FTER HARRY AND BESS TRUMAN left the White House, in January 1953, they took the train back to Independence, Missouri, where the former President often joked that he was naught but a "retired farmer" and one of the three characters that Missouri had ever produced, "along with Mark Twain and Jesse James." Although the office of President was behind him, his sense of humor and his determination to be a responsible citizen were not. If there was anything that he could do to help the Democratic party—a speech or a newspaper article or a book—he was going to do it.

The President, as he was known, out of respect for the great office he had held, managed a careful routine in Independence. He got up early, as usual, and took a walk around the streets he had known decades earlier. Then it was his custom to drive to Kansas City, where for a few years he maintained a suite of offices in the Federal Court Building. Beginning in 1957 he took an office in the Harry S. Truman Library. There he would work from 6:30 A.M., or at the latest 7:00 A.M., until time for lunch and then, after more work, dinner. Only a gall bladder attack, which put him in the hospital for an operation and a recovery that took several weeks, interrupted the schedule. In 1955 Doubleday published volume one of his memoirs, *Year of Decisions*, which dealt only with his initial year in the presidency. The next year the same company published volume two, *Years of Trial and Hope*, which covered his subsequent years in the White House. At the same time he was writing his memoirs, the President raised money for the Truman Library by speechmaking. The building opened in the summer of 1957. The President hoped that it and the attendant museum would attract not only curious visitors but also serious students and scholars who would use his papers and the presidential reference books to write accounts of the nation's first government office.

The President began the sixties by taping 141 interviews concerning the Federal Constitution and the presidency down to the present day. The tapes also include Truman's views of his predecessors and his Republican successor, Eisenhower. They display his well-known jaundiced view of people who could not make up their minds once their duty had become clear. The tapes perhaps over-

With Margaret and Clifton Daniel and family, Bermuda, 1961. *Harry S. Truman Library*

whelmed his assistants, who did nothing with them; the tapes remain on the library shelves. Hoping to make the American people aware of the presidency through pictures, he next turned to television interviews, relating the events of his own administration and the duties of American Presidents generally. The television interviews, like the tapes, did not seem to interest people of his time.

The President sensed that he was out of touch with affairs of not merely the fifties, a Republican era, but also the sixties, during which two Democratic Presidents who had been junior members of Congress during his presidential administration were in control of national destinies. With Kennedy he managed a considerable closeness, after an initially chilly response to Kennedy's decision to run for office; in the summer of 1961, Harry and Bess Truman went to Washington and visited the White House, their first time back. Relations with Johnson likewise were good, at times even close. But Truman was a nineteenth-century man trying to communicate with politicians of the twentieth century, and it was an awkward business.

At the end of the sixties another Republican came to the White House, the

Fiftieth wedding anniversary, 1969. *Ken White*

man Truman had detested personally more than any other national figure with whom he had come in contact. This was the man who in 1952 called Truman a traitor, so the old President firmly believed—the man whom Truman used to call "squirrelhead"—not merely privately but also on one public occasion. By 1969 Harry Truman sensed that his removal from national politics was almost complete.

The President meanwhile had slowed down, following a fall in the upstairs bathroom in 1964, when he had stubbed his toe on a raised floorboard, struck his head, and injured himself badly. He never fully recovered from this accident, even though he managed several public appearances thereafter. It effectively ended his speechmaking, and his activities at the Truman Library. His morning walks were no longer the 120 paces to the minute that he had learned in World War I. The reading in his book-lined study at 219 North Delaware continued, night after night. Passers-by saw the hawklike outline of his face as he looked down at a book in his gnarled hands. He preferred reading about great men or great events in his country's past. Sometimes he read whodunits, apparently to please Bess, who was engrossed by them.

Eventually the President became feeble and rarely left the house. In early December 1972 he at last went to the hospital, where he died the day after Christmas 1972: eighty-eight years old.

The doughty Bess lived on and intended to reach the age of one hundred. She lived in the house alone, watched by secret servicemen across the street, protected by the iron gate and fence put up in 1945, and assisted by house helpers who came in daily. The time came when she could no longer stay alone, and more helpers arrived. In the autumn of 1982, at the age of ninety-seven, Bess died, nearly a decade after her Harry.

LIST OF LETTERS

INDEX

LIST OF LETTERS

SOMETIMES TRUMAN DID NOT DATE HIS LETTERS. In such cases, an estimated date appears below in brackets. Wherever possible, this date is derived from information in the letters themselves. Otherwise, the date reflects the postmark. Complications arise when the postmark is illegible or when the envelopes may have been stored with the wrong letters. The staff at the Harry S. Truman Library has established an approximate chronological sequence. Except in a handful of cases I have followed their order. The vast majority of letters were released in March 1983. Twelve others, however, had been in the files for many years; they are marked below with asterisks. The dates set in italic type indicate letters omitted from *Dear Bess*.

1910: December 31.
1911: January 10, 26; February 7, 16; March *12, 15*, [*19*]; April 1, 12, 17, 24, 27; May 3, 9, 17, 23, 32 [sic]; June 10, 16, 22; July [1], 10, 12, 17, 29; August 14, 27; September 2, 5, 15, 16, 26; October 1, 7, 16, 22, 27; November 1, 14, 22, 28; December 14, 21.
1912: January 3, 12, 25, 30; February 13, 19, 27; March 4, 12, [18], 23; April 1, 8, 29; May [6], [8], 12, [20], 30; June [*10*], [18], [24]; July 1, 8, [17], [22], 30; August 6, [12], [25]; September [5], 9, 17, 23, [30]; October [7], [14], [21], [29]; November [6], [11], [*19*], [26]; December [2], [10], [17], [31].
1913: January [6], [21]; February [4], [10], [18], [24]; March [4], [10], [12], 26; April [2], [7], [postmark illegible], [23], [28]; May [12], [19], [23], [26]; June [2], [10], [30]; July [7], [14], [21], [29], [postmark illegible]; August [5], [postmark illegible], [22]; September [2], [*16*], [17], [30], [postmark illegible]; October [6], [22], [29]; November [4], 6, [10], [18], [19], [25], [29]; December [2], [9], [15], [22], [30].
1914: January [6], [12], [20], [26]; February [3], [17], [20], [24]; March [*10*], [*16*], [20], [24], [*31*]; April [7], [postmark illegible], [18], [postmark illegible]; May [4], [12], 26; June [*postmark illegible*], [postmark illegible] [*postmark illegible*]; July [postmark illegible], [*postmark illegible*], [28]; August [postmark illegible], [18], 31; September [8], [17], [28]; November [postmark illegible], [postmark illegible]; December [1], [29].

1915: January [26]; [postmark illegible]; April [28]; November [4].
1916: January [no postmark]; February 4, [16], [postmark illegible], [19]; March [5], 15, [18], [postmark illegible], [postmark illegible], 23, [postmark illegible]; April [2], [9], [16], [24], 27; May [19], 23, 26,; June 3, 10, 24, [29]; July [12], 25, 28, 30; August 4, 5, 19 [22], 26, 29; September 7; November 16.
1917: January *12*, 23; February [9]; May [9], [27]; July [14]; September 27, [29], 30; October [1], [3], [5], 5, [*postmark illegible*], [9], [11], [15], [*17*], [18], [*19*], [21], [23], [25], [26], [28]; November [2], [3], 7 telegram, [8], [11], [*15*], [17], [*21*], [24], [24]; December [*1*], [9], [14], 15 telegram, [*16*], 22 telegram, [24], 24 telegram, [26].
1918: January [10], *14 telegram, 14 telegram*, [*15*], [*18*], [*25*], 27; February [1], *3 telegram*, [3], [7], [11], 13 telegram, [16], [23], [26]; March [3], [5], [8], [10], [*13*], [*16*], [17], 19 telegram, [20], [21], [24], 24 telegram, [26], [27], *28 telegram*, [28]; April [no date], 14, 17, 23, [*no date*] *cable*, 28; May 5, 5, [*12*], 19, [26], [*30*]; June 2, 8, 14, *19*, 27, *30*; July *4*, 7, 14, 22, 31; August *4, 13, 17*; September 1, 8, 15; October 6, 8, 11, *19 telegram, 20*, 30; November 1, 2, 5, 10, 11, 15, *20*, *23*, 29; December 3, 8, 14, 19, [*undated*] *cable*, 26, 31.
1919: January 3, 7, 11, 12, 19, 21, 26, 27; February 1, *6*, 18, 23, *25*; March *1*, *15*, *24*; April *12 cable, 20 telegram*, 21 telegram, 24, *25 telegram*, 30 telegram; May 31 telegram.

INDEX

ABOUT THE EDITOR

Robert H. Ferrell is one of the leading scholars of the American presidency and is the author of numerous books, including *The Dying President: Franklin D. Roosevelt, 1944–1945, The Strange Deaths of President Harding, Ill-Advised: Presidential Health and Public Trust, Harry S. Truman: A Life,* and *Choosing Truman: The Democratic Convention of 1944.* Ferrell is Distinguished Professor of History Emeritus at Indiana University in Bloomington.

Courtesy of Indiana University Media and Teaching. M Simons/Photographer